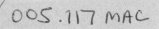
Requirements Analysis and System Design

REQUIREMENTS ANALYSIS AND SYSTEM DESIGN

second edition

LESZEK A. MACIASZEK

PEARSON
Addison
Wesley

Harlow, England • London • New York • Boston • San Francisco • Toronto • Sydney • Singapore • Hong Kong
Tokyo • Seoul • Taipei • New Delhi • Cape Town • Madrid • Mexico City • Amsterdam • Munich • Paris • Milan

Pearson Education Limited

Edinburgh Gate

Harlow

Essex CM20 2JE

England

and Associated Companies throughout the world

Visit us on the World Wide Web at:

www.pearsoned.co.uk

First published 2001
Second edition published 2005

ISBN 0 321 20464 6

British Library Cataloguing-in-Publication Data
A catalogue record for this book is available from the British Library

Library of Congress Cataloging-in-Publication Data
Maciaszek, Leszek.
    Requirements analysis and systems design/Leszek A, Maciaszek.—2nd ed.
        p.   cm.
    Includes bibliographical references and index.
    ISBN 0-321-20464-6
    1. System design.   2. UML (Computer science)   3. Object-oriented programming
(Computer science)   I. Title.

QA76.9.S88M34 2004
005.1'17—dc22

                                                    2004050230

10 9 8 7 6 5 4 3 2 1
10 09 08 07 06 05

Typeset in 10/12 pt Time by 35
Printed by Ashford Colour Press Ltd, Gosport

The publisher's policy is to use paper manufactured from sustainable forests.

MOTTO

The best way to be boring is to leave nothing out

– Voltaire

DEDICATION

For Bożena

Brief contents

Contents

Contents for case studies

- AE – advertising expenditure
- CM – contact management
- TL – time logging
- TM – telemarketing
- UE – university enrolment
- VS – video store

AE

CM

TL

TM

Preface

Outline of the book

The development of an **information system** (**IS**) – from its inception to the deployment to stakeholders – comprises three iterative and incremental phases: analysis, design, and implementation. This book describes the methods and techniques used in the **analysis** and **design** phases. The implementation issues, including code examples, are addressed only to the extent to which they need to be considered in the design phase. Testing and change management are addressed in a separate chapter at the end of the book.

The text concentrates on **object-oriented software development**. The *Unified Modeling Language* (*UML*) is used to capture modeling artifacts. Emphasis is placed on the development by elaboration where the same modeling language (UML) is used throughout the development lifecycle. Analysts, designers, and programmers "speak" the same language, although they perhaps use the dialects (profiles) of the language fitting their individual needs.

The early applications of object technology targeted graphical user interfaces (GUIs) and focused on the speed of developing new systems and the speed of program execution. In this book, I emphasize the application of object technology in **enterprise information systems** (**EIS**) development. The challenge is the large volume of data, complex data structures, shared access to information by many concurrent users, transaction processing, changing requirements, etc. The main advantage of object technology for EIS development is in facilitating *system supportability* (understandability, maintenance, and scalability).

Developing enterprise information systems is synonymous with doing **analysis and design "in the large."** No EIS project can succeed without following strict *development processes* and without understanding the underlying *software architectures*. The development is large-scale, object-oriented, iterative and incremental. The system deployment involves some kind of client/server solution, where the clients provide the user interface and the servers manage a database and possibly also application logic. Client and server run in separate processes and communicate via object messaging.

The book proposes a detailed approach to the analysis and design of enterprise information systems with UML. It identifies ways to:

■ harness the complexity of large system models;

■ improve software architectures;

■ facilitate software readability, maintainability, and scalability;

- promote layered structuring of objects;
- handle component integration; and
- improve modeling of collaboration for use cases, etc.

Distinguishing features

This book has a number of features that, when combined, create a unique offering. The *"teach-by-example" approach* is the cornerstone of the text. The main discussion is based on six case studies and a tutorial-style review and reinforcement chapter. The *case studies* are drawn from six application domains, each with its own unique features and educational benefits. The domains are *university enrolment*, *video store*, *contact management*, *telemarketing*, *advertising expenditure*, and *time logging*. The *tutorial* refers to an *online shopping* application for purchasing a computer over the Internet.

To facilitate self-education, the case studies and the tutorial are formulated using the *question-and-answer* and *exercise-and-solution* principles. The practical material is further extended and diversified through questions and exercises formulated at the ends of chapters. Selected questions/exercises are provided with answers/solutions. A separate "guided tour" (contents for case studies) at the beginning of the book provides links to pages with questions and answers and exercises and solutions grouped by the case studies. This section can serve as an alternative table of contents for examples scattered in the text.

The book discusses principles, methods, and techniques of good analysis and good design. Special attention is paid to the *design phase*. Design is not treated as a straight-forward transformation from analysis. The book acknowledges the difficulties and intricacies of large-scale object-oriented client/server system development. In many ways, the book takes a fresh look at "design-in-the-large," at iterative and incremental development of large systems, and at the capabilities and limitations of tools and methods in large software production.

A unique character of the book comes from a balanced blend of practical explanation and theoretical insight. A major premise is to avoid unnecessary over-complication, but without the loss of rigor. The book *"speaks" from experience*. Topics that are not relevant to industry or that are only of specialized research interest have been excluded.

The book is on the *"cutting edge" of information technology*. It uses the standard in visual system modeling – UML. It addresses the developments in web and database technologies. In this context, the Internet-driven shift from "thick clients" (i.e. large desktop computers) back to server-based computing is acknowledged. The analysis and design principles discussed in the text apply equally well to conventional client/server solutions and to modern component-based distributed applications.

Software development is not amenable to "black–white," "true–false," "zero–one" solutions. Good software solutions come from good business analysts and system designers/programmers, not from blindly applied algorithms. A policy of the book is *to warn* the reader about *potential* difficulties that the advocated approach cannot entirely resolve. In consequence, it is hoped that readers will apply their acquired knowledge with care and will not assume unrealistic expectations of the ease with which the approach can be applied (and thereby, possibly, fail more dramatically).

In summary, the distinguishing features of the book are:

- The book relates the theories to reality – in the form of practical problems and limitations, which will have to be addressed when applying the approach "in the field."

- The book gives special attention to the design phase. Design is *not* treated as a straightforward transformation from analysis, and the difficulties and intricacies of large-scale client/server system development are acknowledged.

- A wealth of non-trivial examples and questions/exercises with some answers/solutions are included in the book, and all remaining answers/solutions are included in the supplementary materials available to instructors from the book's website. The instructor's manual is not an afterthought – it has been written concurrently with the text and is meticulous.

Intended readership

In tune with the growing demand for university courses to be more relevant to industry practice, this textbook is aimed at students and practitioners alike. This has been a difficult task but, it is hoped, it has been successfully achieved. To ensure a *lasting educational benefit*, the implementation aspects of software development are discussed in non-vendor-specific terms (although commercial CASE tools have been used in illustrations and solutions).

The book is aimed at **computer science and information systems curricula**. As it contains both "high-level" system modeling topics and "low-level" user interface and database design issues, the book should be attractive to courses in *systems analysis*, *systems design*, *software engineering*, *databases*, and *object technology*, and to *software project* courses that require students to develop a system following the development lifecycle: from requirements determination to the user interface and the database implementation. The book is designed for a one-semester course, but it can potentially be used over two one-semester courses – one on requirements analysis and the other on system design.

For the **practitioner's audience**, the presented theories are related to realities. Most problem statements, examples, and exercises are drawn from the consulting practice of the author. We have adopted a policy of warning the reader of potential difficulties or limitations with advocated approaches. The following categories of practitioner are likely to benefit most from the book: business and system analysts, designers, programmers, system architects, project leaders and managers, reviewers, testers, technical writers, and industry trainers.

Organization of the book

The book provides comprehensive coverage of object-oriented analysis and design of enterprise information systems. The material is presented in an order consistent with modern development processes. The book consists of **ten chapters**. The coverage is more or less equally balanced between the analysis and design topics.

Readers with varying amounts of background knowledge should be able to accommodate the text. Some chapters contain special *"crash course" sections* to get readers with less technical background up to speed. The main sections in this category are "Fundamentals of object technology" in Chapter 3 and "Relational database model" in Chapter 8.

The last chapter of the book is dedicated to *review and reinforcement* of the entire material. Having such a chapter at the end of the book should meet the expectations of many university courses. After all, the review and reinforcement principle is the cornerstone of any lasting education.

Summary of changes in the second edition

Although the first edition of RASD had a very good reception and resulted in translations of the book into several languages, there is always scope for improvement, particularly in technology-influenced areas like systems development. The main changes (hopefully improvements) in RASD 2e are:

■ Elimination of the subtitle "Developing Information Systems with UML." Contemporary systems development implies modeling in UML. There is no need any more to assert to the reader that the book uses UML.

■ Answers to odd-numbered questions and solutions to selected exercises have been added at the end of chapters. This makes the book more useful for self-education. The remaining answers and solutions are available to instructors on the book's website, together with a wealth of other teaching material.

■ "Guided Tutorial", previously in Chapters 2 and 6, has been extracted into a separate chapter. Moreover, the tutorial has been relocated to Chapter 10 and extensively revamped and extended to serve as a review and reinforcement chapter entitled "Tutorial-style Review and Reinforcement."

■ Chapters 2 and 3 have been swapped. This is because the requirements analysis (now in Chapter 2) does not need a prior knowledge of objects and object modeling (now in Chapter 3).

■ The title of Chapter 3 has been changed to "Objects and Object Modeling" to reflect the change from the explanation of objects in general and by a guided tutorial to the explanation of objects via UML and by examples.

■ Chapter 4 ("Requirements Specification") has been enriched by an explanation of the overriding importance of the system's architectural framework to the supportability of the developed system. Accordingly, the chapter has introduced an architectural framework subsequently enforced in the discussion in the following chapters.

■ The content of Chapter 6 has been changed, mostly as a result of the relocation of the material from/to other chapters. The tutorial has been moved to Chapter 10. Some program design topics have been obtained from Chapter 9. The discussion on system architecture has been significantly extended. Consequently, the new title of the chapter is "System Architecture and Program Design."

- Chapter 7 ("User Interface Design") has been modified and enriched in several ways. The benefits of the Java Swing library have been used to explain some UI design principles. The window navigation models based previously on the UML activity diagrams have been replaced by a new UML profile – the user experience (UX) storyboards.

- Chapter 8, now titled "Persistence and Database Design," has been extended with discussion about designing of persistent objects, including the patterns for managing persistency within the adopted architectural framework. Previous detailed discussion about object and object-relational databases has been dropped (because of the continuing dominance of the relational databases in enterprise information systems and because of the difficulty of the material). The saved space has been filled with database topics moved from the previous Chapter 9, such as transaction management.

- After the material from the previous Chapter 9 has been moved to the earlier chapters, the previous Chapter 10 has become the new Chapter 9. This chapter too has been extended. In particular, a section on test-driven development has been added.

Supplementary materials

A comprehensive package of supplementary material is provided on the ***companion website***. Most of the web documents are freely available to readers, but some material is password-protected for the benefit of instructors who have adopted the textbook in their teaching. The home page for the book is simultaneously maintained at:

```
http://www.booksites.net/maciaszek
http://www.comp.mq.edu.au/books/rasd2ed
```

The web package includes:

1. ***instructor's resources*** with:
   - *lecture slides* in Microsoft PowerPoint;
   - *answers and solutions* manual containing annotated answers and solutions to all review and exercise questions from the end of each chapter;
   - *assignments and projects* – ready-to-use assignments and projects for students, complete with model answers and solutions;
   - *examination testbank* – ready-to-use examples of examination questions with answers/solutions.
2. ***students' resources*** with:
   - printable *lecture slides* in Acrobat Read format;
   - *model files* for Rational Rose (.mdl), Magic Draw (xml.zip), and PowerDesigner (.pdm) solutions to the case studies, the tutorial, and all other modeling examples in the textbook.
3. ***Errata & Addendum*** document dedicated to corrections of errors and omissions in the book.

For further information

Your comments, corrections, suggestions for improvements, contributions, etc. are very much appreciated. Please direct any correspondence to:

Leszek A. Maciaszek
Department of Computing
Macquarie University
Sydney, NSW 2109
Australia
email: `leszek@ics.mq.edu.au`
website: `www.comp.mq.edu.au/~leszek/`
phone: +61 2 98509519
facsimile: +61 2 98509551
courier: North Ryde, Herring Road, Bld. E6A, Room 319

Acknowledgements

The writing of this book would be impossible without interactions with friends, colleagues, students, industry gurus, and all the other people who, consciously or not, have shaped my knowledge in the subject area. I am truly indebted to all of them. An attempt to list all their names would be injudicious and impractical – please accept a blanket "thank you."

My appreciation goes to lecturers and students at universities and practitioners around the world who cared to provide feedback and point out deficiencies in the first edition of this book. Their feedback is gratefully acknowledged in this second edition.

If I were to mention one name without whom this project would have never happened, this would be Keith Mansfield of Pearson Education in London. He had a vision for the first edition of this book as well as for my later book entitled "Practical Software Engineering." He was then a constant source of encouragement and support in the production of this second edition. Thank you, Keith.

Guided tour

Chapter openings set the scene for more detailed discussion

Case study **examples** provide problem statements to consider

The book is based on six **case studies** to illustrate the concepts in a real-life application. The **problem statements** introduce these

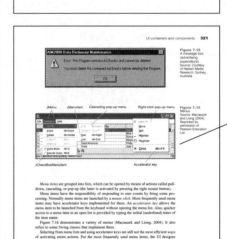

Numerous **annotated screenshots** to draw out key points

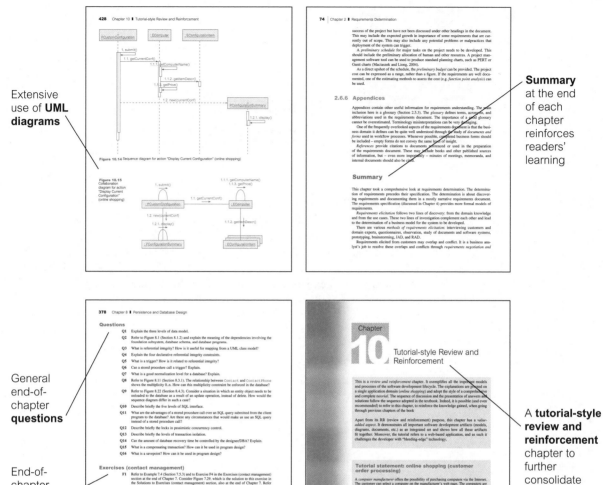

Extensive use of **UML diagrams**

Summary at the end of each chapter reinforces readers' learning

General end-of-chapter **questions**

End-of-chapter **exercises** specific to each case study

A **tutorial-style review and reinforcement** chapter to further consolidate learning

Publisher's acknowledgements

We are grateful to the following for permission to reproduce copyright material:

International Business Machines Corporation for Figures 1.4, 9.5, 9.6 and 9.7 from Rational Suite Tutorial 2002, copyright 2002 by International Business Machines Corporation; Nielsen Media Research Australia for Figures 5.25, 6.21, 6.25, 7.1, 7.2, 7.3, 7.5, 7.6, 7.7, 7.8, 7.9, 7.11, 7.12, 7.13, 7.14, 7.15, 7.20, 7.21, 7.26, 7.27, 7.28, 9.9, 9.10, 9.11, 9.12, 9.13, 9.14 and 9.15; Pearson Education Limited for Figures 4.21, 6.2, 7.16, 7.17, 7.18, 9.3 and 9.4; and Sony UK for Figures 10.12 and 10.13.

Chapter

The Software Process

The intention of this chapter is to describe – at an overview level – a number of strategic issues in the software development process. Since the topic is treated at an overview level and some issues are contentious, the reader does not have to agree with the author to benefit from the rest of the book (and possibly re-evaluate his/her opinion when reaching the end of the text).

The educational value of this chapter is in introducing the reader to processes and approaches that underlie modern software development. The reader may already be familiar with many of the ideas and topics discussed in this chapter from experience, everyday use of computers or from reading related literature. Such a reader may choose to skim this chapter and proceed to Chapter 2.

1.1 The nature of software development

The literature on information systems (IS) management is full of examples of failed projects, exceeded deadlines and budgets, faulty solutions, unmaintainable systems, etc. The Standish groups's seminal research into the success and failure of IS projects reported that only one out of three software projects complete on time and on budget (Standish, 2003). Even when successfully delivered to the users, many systems are plagued by reliability, performance, security, maintainability, and other problems.

To understand the reasons behind these problems, we first need to understand the nature of software development. In a now classic paper, Brooks (1987) identified the essence and accidents of software engineering. The *essence* of software engineering is embodied in the difficulties inherent in the software itself. These difficulties can only be acknowledged – they are not amenable to breakthroughs or "silver bullets." According to Brooks, the essence of software engineering is a consequence of the inherent software complexity, conformity, changeability, and invisibility.

The "essential difficulties" of software define software development invariants. The invariants state that software is a product of a creative act of development – a craft or an art in the sense of that activity performed by an artisan rather than a fine artist. In a typical state of affairs, software is not a result of a repetitive act of manufacturing.

Once the invariants of software development are understood, one should address the *accidents* of software engineering – the difficulties due to software production practices, which are amenable to human intervention. We group various "accidental difficulties" into three categories:

1. stakeholders;
2. process; and
3. modeling language and tools.

1.1.1 The software development invariants

There are some essential properties of software that are not susceptible to human intervention. These properties remain invariant in all software projects. They need to be acknowledged in the projects. The task of software development is to ensure that the invariants do not get out of control and do not exert any undue negative impact on the project.

Software is inherently *complex*. In contemporary systems, the complexity is the function of the mere size of the software (such as expressed in lines of written code) and the function of interdependencies between the components of which the software product is composed.

The complexity of software varies with the nature of application domains to which the software is applied. It turns out that application domains that are computationally intensive typically lead to less complex systems than domains that are data-intensive. Data-intensive applications include *enterprise information systems*, which are the main subject of this book. Such systems process huge volumes of data and business rules, frequently inconsistent or ambiguous. Building software that is able to accommodate all business data, rules, and special cases is inherently (invariantly) difficult.

The difficulty is increased by three other essential properties reported by Brooks: *conformity*, *changeability*, and *invisibility*. Application software must conform to a particular hardware/software platform on which it is built and must conform and integrate with existing information systems. Because business processes and requirements are in a constant state of flux, application software must be built to accommodate change. And although application software produces visible output, the code responsible for the output is frequently buried deeply in "invisible" programming statements, binary library code, and surrounding system software.

Software is *developed* rather than *manufactured* (Pressman, 2001). Of course, one cannot deny that advances in software engineering introduce more certainty into development practices, but the success of a software project cannot be guaranteed. This can be contrasted with traditional branches of engineering, such as civil or mechanical engineering. In traditional engineering, the products (artifacts) are designed with mathematical precision and then manufactured (frequently in multiple quantities) using machinery and production lines.

The software product, once developed, can be duplicated (manufactured) at minimal cost, but in the case of enterprise information systems the duplication is never needed. Each system is unique and is developed for a specific enterprise. The difficulty is in the development, not in the manufacturing. Accordingly, the entire cost of software production is in its development.

To ease the development effort and cost, the software industry offers partial solutions in the form of reusable software components, which can be taken advantage of in the development process. The challenge is in putting together little pieces of the solution into a coherent enterprise system that meets the needs of complex business processes.

Software practices encourage the development of systems from customizable software frameworks or packages – *commercial off-the-shelf* (COTS) solutions or *enterprise resource planning* (ERP) systems. However, a software framework can only deliver a routine accounting, manufacturing, or human resources system. These routine solutions must be adapted to particular business processes that an enterprise wants and needs to conduct. These business processes must be defined, and a model for the system must be developed. The emphasis is changed from "developing from scratch" to "developing by customizing the software framework," but the very nature of the development process is still the same in both cases.

Conceptual constructs (models) for a final solution, so that they satisfy the specific needs of an organization, have to be created for any system. Once created, the software framework's functionality is customized to correspond to the conceptual constructs. Programming tasks may be different, but requirements analysis and system design activities are similar to those in development from scratch. After all, a conceptual construct (model) is the same under many possible representations (implementations).

Equally importantly, it is unlikely that an organization can find a software framework to automate its *core business* activities. A core business activity of a telephone company is telephony, not human resources or accounting. Accordingly, the software in support of core business activities has less opportunity to rely on software components or frameworks. Moreover, the software in support of supporting business activities (such as accounting) must include targeted and unique solutions to deliver a competitive advantage to an organization. As noticed by Szyperski (1998, p.5): "Standard packages create a level playing field and the competition has to come from other areas."

In every case, the development process should take advantage of *component technology* (Allen and Frost, 1998; Szyperski, 1998). A component is an executable unit of software with well-defined functionality (services) and communication protocols (interfaces) to other components. Components can be configured to satisfy application requirements. Some most influential component technologies include web services, *Common Object Request Broker Architecture* (CORBA) from Object Management Group (OMG), *Distributed Component Object Model* (DCOM) from Microsoft, and *Enterprise JavaBeans* (EJB) from Sun.

Packages, components, and similar techniques do not change the essence of software production. In particular, the principles and tasks of requirements analysis and system design remain invariant. A final software product can be assembled from standard and custom-made components, but the "assembly" process is still an art. As Pressman (2001) observes, we do not even have software "spare parts" to replace broken components in systems "on the road."

1.1.2 The software development "accidents"

The software development invariants define the essence and create the greatest challenges in software production. It is critically important that the "accidents" of software development do not add to the complexity and to the potential lack of supportability of the software product. *Supportability* is defined by a set of three system features: software understandability, maintainability, and scalability (extensibility).

The accidents of software development can be attributed mostly to the fact that an information system is a social system. Its success or failure depends on people, their acceptance and support for the system, the processes used in the development, management practices, the use of software modeling techniques, etc.

1.1.2.1 Stakeholders

Stakeholders are people who have a stake in a software project. Any person affected by the system or who has influence on system development is a stakeholder. There are two main groups of stakeholders:

1. customers (users and system owners); and
2. developers (analysts, designers, programmers, etc.).

In ordinary communication, the term "user" is routinely used to mean "customer." Notwithstanding this fact, the term "customer" better reflects the desired meaning. First, the customer is the person who pays for the development and is responsible for making decisions. Second, even if the customer is not always right, the customer's requirements cannot be arbitrarily changed or rejected by developers – any conflicting, unfeasible or illegal requirements must be renegotiated with customers.

Information systems are *social systems*. They are developed by people (developers) for people (customers). The success of a software project is determined by social factors – technology is secondary. There are many examples of technically inferior systems that work and benefit customers. The inverse is not true. A system with no benefit (perceived or real) to the customer will be abandoned no matter how technically brilliant.

In a typical situation, the main causes of software failure can be traced to the stakeholder factor. At the *customer* end, projects fail because (e.g. Pfleeger, 1998):

- Customer needs are misunderstood or not fully captured.
- Customer requirements change too frequently.
- Customers are not prepared to commit sufficient resources to the project.
- Customers do not want to cooperate with developers.
- Customers have unrealistic expectations.
- The system is no longer of benefit to customers.

Projects also fail because the *developers* may not be up to the task. With the escalation in software complexity, there is a growing recognition that the skills and knowledge of developers are critical. Good developers can deliver an acceptable solution. Great developers can deliver a superior solution quicker and cheaper. As the famous one-liner from Fred Brooks says: "Great designs come from great designers" (Brooks, 1987, p.13).

The excellence and commitment of developers is the factor that contributes most to software quality and productivity. To ensure that a software product is successfully delivered to a customer, and, more importantly, to reap productivity benefits from it, a software organization must employ proper management practices with regard to developers (Brooks, 1987; Yourdon, 1994):

- hire the best developers;
- provide ongoing training and education to existing developers;
- encourage exchange of information and interaction between developers so that they stimulate each other;
- motivate developers by removing obstacles and channeling their efforts into productive work;
- offer an exciting working environment (this tends to be much more important to people than an occasional salary increase);
- align personal goals with organizational strategies and objectives;
- emphasize teamwork.

Process   1.1.2.2

A software *process* defines the activities and organizational procedures used in software production and maintenance. The process aims at managing and improving collaboration in the development and maintenance team so that a quality product is delivered to the customers and so that it is properly supported afterwards. A process model:

- states an order for carrying out activities;
- specifies what development artifacts are to be delivered and when;
- assigns activities and artifacts to developers;
- offers criteria for monitoring a project's progress, for measuring the outcomes, and for planning future projects.

Unlike modeling and programming languages, software processes are not susceptible to standardization. Each organization has to develop its own process model or customize it from a generic process template, such as the template known as the *Rational Unified Process* (RUP) (Kruchten, 2003). A software process is an important part of the organization's overall business process and determines the organization's unique character and competitive position in the marketplace.

The process adopted by an organization must be aligned with its development culture, social dynamics, developers' knowledge and skills, managerial practices, customers' expectations, project sizes, and even kinds of application domain. Because all these factors are subject to change, an organization may need to diversify its process model and create variants of it for each software project. For example, depending on the developers' familiarity with the modeling methods and tools, special training courses may need to be included in the process.

Project size has probably the greatest influence on the process. In a small project (of ten or so developers), a formal process may not be needed at all. Such a small team is likely to communicate and respond to changes informally. In larger projects, an informal communication network will not suffice and a well-defined process for controlled development is necessary.

1.1.2.2.1 *Iterative and incremental process*

Modern software development processes are invariably *iterative* and *incremental*. System models are refined and transformed through analysis, design, and implementation phases: details are added in successive *iterations*, changes and improvements are introduced as needed, and *incremental releases* of software modules maintain user satisfaction and provide important feedback to modules still under development.

There are various variants of the iterative and incremental process. The variants of special significance include (Maciaszek and Liong, 2004):

- the spiral model;
- the Rational Unified Process (RUP);
- model-driven architecture (MDA);
- the agile development process.

The spiral model, defined by Boehm (1988), serves as a reference point for the more recent models, including the three models listed above. RUP is a relatively flexible process that offers a support environment (called the RUP platform) to guide developers with various document templates, explanations of concepts, development ideas, etc. MDA is based on the idea of executable specifications – generating the software from models and components. Agile development proposes a framework in which people and team collaboration are considered more important than planning, documentation, and other formalities.

As the RUP states: "An iterative process is one that involves managing a stream of executable releases. An incremental process is one that involves the continuous integration of the system's architecture to produce these releases, with each new release embodying incremental improvements over the other" (Booch *et al.*, 1999, p.33).

The success of an iterative and incremental process is predicated on early identification of the *system's architectural modules*. The modules should be of similar size, be highly cohesive and have minimal overlaps (coupling). The order in which the modules are to be implemented is also important. Some modules may not be able to be *released* if they depend for information or computation on other modules yet to be developed. Unless iterative and incremental development is planned and controlled, the process can degenerate into "*ad hoc* hacking" with no control over the project's real progress.

1.1.2.2.2 *Capability maturity model*

A major challenge for every organization engaged in software production is to improve its development process. Naturally enough, to introduce process improvements, the organization has to know what the problems are with its current process. *The capability maturity model* (CMM) is a popular method for process assessment and improvement (CMM, 1995).

CMM has been specified by the Software Engineering Institute (SEI) at Carnegie Mellon University in Pittsburgh, USA. Originally used by the US Department of Defense

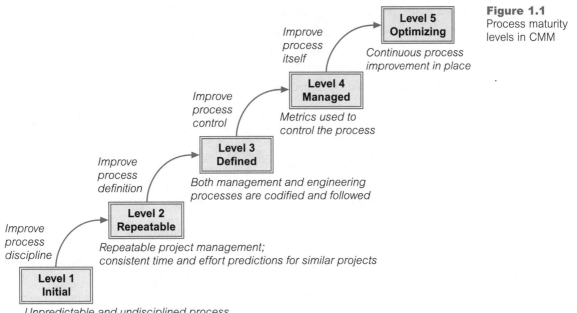

Figure 1.1
Process maturity
levels in CMM

to assess the IT capabilities of organizations bidding for defense contracts, it is now widely used by the IT industry in America and elsewhere.

CMM is essentially a *questionnaire* that an IT organization fills in. The questionnaire is followed by a verification and attestation process, which assigns the organization to one of the five CMM levels. The higher the level, the better the process maturity in the organization. Figure 1.1 defines the levels, gives a short description of the main features of each level, and indicates the main areas of process improvement necessary for the organization to achieve a higher level.

Arthur (1992) calls the levels of maturity "the stairway to software excellence." The five steps on the stairway are chaos, project management, methods and tools, measurement, and continuous quality improvement. Experience has shown that it takes several years to progress one level up the maturity scale. Most organizations are at level 1, some at level 2; very few are known to be at level 5. The following few questions show the difficulty of the task. An organization that wants to be at CMM level 2 must provide positive answers to all these questions (and more) (Pfleeger, 1998):

- Does the software quality assurance function have a management reporting channel separate from the software development project management?
- Is there a software configuration control function for each project that involves software development?
- Is a formal process used in the management review of each software development prior to making contractual commitments?
- Is a formal procedure used to produce software development schedules?

- Are formal procedures applied to estimating software development cost?
- Are statistics on software code and test errors gathered?
- Does senior management have a mechanism for the regular review of the status of software development projects?
- Is a mechanism used for controlling changes to the software requirements?

1.1.2.2.3 *The ISO 9000 family of quality standards*

There are other process improvement models besides CMM. Of particular interest are the ISO 9000 family of quality standards, developed by the International Organization for Standardization. The ISO standards apply to the *quality* management and the *process* to produce a quality product. The standards are generic – they apply to any industry and all types of business, including software development.

The main premise of the ISO 9000 family of standards is that if the process is right then the process outcome (product or service) will also be right. "The objective of quality management is to produce quality products by building quality into the products rather than testing quality into the products" (Schmauch, 1994, p.1).

As per our earlier discussion about the process, the ISO standards do not enforce or specify processes. The standards provide models of *what* must be accomplished, not *how* activities must be performed. An organization requesting an ISO certification (also called registration) must say what it does, do what it says, and demonstrate what it has done (*ibid.*).

A litmus test for an ISO-certified organization is that it should be able to make a quality product or provide a quality service even if its entire workforce were to be replaced. To this aim, the organization has to *document and record* all its formal activities. Written procedures must be defined for each activity, including what to do when things go wrong or customers complain.

As with CMM, ISO certification can only be granted after an *on-site audit* by an ISO registrar. These audits are then repeated at regular intervals. Organizations are impelled into the scheme through competitive forces stipulated by customers demanding that the suppliers of products and services be certified. Many countries have adopted ISO 9000 as national standards. The adoption is particularly strong in Europe.

1.1.2.3 Modeling language and tools

Stakeholders and processes are two elements in the triangle for success. The third element consists of a modeling language and tools. Modeling artifacts have to be communicated (language) and documented (tools). Developers need a *language* to build visual and other models and discuss them with customers and fellow developers. The language should allow the construction of models at varying levels of abstraction to present proposed solutions at different levels of detail. The language should have a strong *visual* component as per the popular saying that "a picture is worth a thousand words." It should also have strong *declarative semantics*, i.e. it should allow capturing "procedural" meaning in "declarative" sentences. We should be able to communicate by saying "what" needs to be done rather than "how" to go about doing it.

Developers also need a *tool* for computer-assisted software engineering (CASE). A CASE tool enables the storage and retrieval of models in a central repository and graphical and textual manipulation of models on a computer screen. Ideally, a repository should provide for a shareable multi-user (i.e. multi-developer) access to models. Typical functions of a *CASE repository* are to:

- coordinate access to models;
- facilitate collaboration between developers;
- store multiple versions of models;
- identify differences between versions;
- allow sharing of the same concepts in different models;
- check the consistency and integrity of models;
- generate project reports and documents;
- generate data structures and programming code (forward engineering);
- generate models from existing implementation (reverse engineering).

Note that a CASE-generated program is just a code skeleton – computational algorithms need to be coded by programmers in the usual way.

Unified modeling language

1.1.2.3.1

"The Unified Modeling Language (UML) is a general-purpose visual modeling language that is used to specify, visualize, construct, and document the artifacts of a software system" (Rumbaugh *et al.*, 1999, p.3). The Rational Software Corporation, currently part of IBM, developed UML, which unifies the best features of earlier methods and notations. In 1997, the Object Management Group (OMG) approved UML as a standard modeling language. Since then, UML has been further developed and has been widely adopted by the IT industry.

UML is independent of any software development process, although Rational later proposed a matching process called *Rational Unified Process* (Kruchten, 2003). A process that adopts UML must support an *object-oriented approach* to software production. UML is not appropriate for old-style structured approaches that result in systems implemented with procedural programming languages, such as COBOL.

UML is also independent of implementation technologies (as long as they are object-oriented). This makes UML somewhat deficient in supporting the detailed design phase of the development lifecycle. By the same token, however, this makes UML resilient to specificities and frequent changes in implementation platforms.

The UML language constructs allow modeling of the static structure and dynamic behavior of a system. A system is modeled as a set of collaborating *objects* (software modules) that react to external events to perform tasks of benefit to customers (users). Particular models emphasize some aspects of the system and ignore aspects that are stressed in other models. Together, a set of integrated models provides a complete description for the system.

UML models can be categorized into three groups:

1. *state models* (which describe the static data structures);
2. *behavior models* (which describe object collaborations); and
3. *state change models* (which describe the allowed states for the system over time).

UML also contains a limited number of *architectural constructs* that allow the system to be modularized for iterative and incremental development. However, UML does not advocate any particular *architectural framework* that designed systems can or should conform to. Such a framework would specify a desired layered structure of system components and principles of component communications.

1.1.2.3.2   *CASE and process improvement*

Process improvement is much more than the introduction of new methods and techniques. In fact, the introduction of new methods and techniques to an organization at a low level of process maturity can bring more harm than good.

An example in point is the CASE technology. An *integrated* CASE tool can allow multiple developers to collaborate and share design information in order to produce new design artifacts. Such a CASE tool imposes certain processes that the development team has to obey to take advantage of this technology. However, if the development team has not been capable so far of improving its processes, it is extremely unlikely that it will assimilate the process dictated by the CASE tool. As a result, the potential productivity and quality gains offered by the new technology will not materialize.

This observation is not to say that CASE technology is a "risky business." It is only risky when used to drive the entire development process and the development team is not ready to embrace the process. However, the same CASE methods and techniques would always bring personal productivity and quality improvements to individual developers who use the technology on their own local workstations. Modeling software artifacts with pencil and paper may make sense in a classroom situation, but never on real projects.

1.2   System planning

Information system projects have to be planned for. They have to be identified, classified, ranked and selected for initial development, for improvement, or perhaps for elimination. The question is: which IS technologies and applications will return the most value to the business? Ideally, the decision should be based on a clearly defined *business strategy* and on careful and methodical planning (Maciaszek, 1990; Bennett *et al.*, 2002; Hoffer *et al.*, 2002).

Business strategy can be determined through various processes known as *strategic planning*, *business modeling*, *business process re-engineering*, *strategic alignment*, *information resource management*, or similar. All these approaches undertake to study fundamental business processes in an organization in order to determine a long-term vision for the business and then to prioritize business issues that can be resolved by the use of information technology.

This said, there are many organizations, in particular many small organizations, with no clear business strategy. Such organizations are likely to decide on information systems development by simply identifying the current most pressing business problems that need to be addressed. When external environment or internal business conditions change, the existing information systems will have to be modified or even replaced. Such a *modus operandi* allows small organizations to refocus quickly on their current situation, take advantage of new opportunities, and rebuff new threats.

Large organizations cannot afford constant changes of business direction. In reality, they frequently dictate directions for other organizations in the same line of business. To some degree, they can mold the environment to their *current* needs. However, large organizations have to look carefully into the *future*. They have to use a planning-based approach to identifying development projects. These are typically large projects that take a long time to complete. They are too cumbersome to be changed or replaced easily. They need to accommodate or even target future opportunities and threats.

System planning can be carried out in a number of different ways. A traditional approach is nicknamed *SWOT – strengths, weaknesses, opportunities, threats*. Another popular strategy is based on *VCM – value chain model*. More modern variations for developing a business strategy are known as *BPR – business process re-engineering*. The information needs of an organization can also be assessed by using blueprints for *information system architecture* (ISA). Such blueprints can be obtained by analogy from descriptive frameworks that have proved successful in disciplines other than IT – for example, in the construction industry.

All system planning approaches have an important common denominator: they are concerned with *effectiveness* (doing the right thing) rather than *efficiency* (doing things right). Efficiently solving the wrong problem does not do much good!

The SWOT approach   1.2.1

The SWOT (strengths, weaknesses, opportunities, threats) approach allows the identification, classification, ranking, and selection of IS development projects in a manner that is aligned with an organization's strengths, weaknesses, opportunities, and threats. This is a top-down approach that starts with the determination of an organization's mission. The *mission statement* captures the unique character of an organization and specifies its vision of where it wants to be in the future. In a good mission statement, emphasis is placed on customer needs rather than on the products or services that an organization delivers.

The mission statement, and a business strategy developed from it, take into consideration the *internal company strengths and weaknesses* in the areas of management, production, human resources, finance, marketing, research and development, etc. These strengths and weaknesses must be recognized, agreed upon, and prioritized. A successful organization has a good realization of a current set of strengths and weaknesses that guide the development of its business strategy.

Examples of *strengths* include:

- ownership of brand names and patents;
- good reputation among customers and suppliers;

- exclusive access to resources or technology;
- cost advantage due to production volume, proprietary know-how, exclusive rights or partnerships.

Frequently, a *weakness* is the absence of a potential strength. Examples of weaknesses include:

- unreliable cash flow;
- inferior skills base of the staff and reliance on some key staff members;
- poor location of the business.

The identification of internal company strengths and weaknesses is a necessary, but not sufficient, condition for successful business planning. An organization does not function in a vacuum – it depends on external economic, social, political, and technological factors. An organization has to know of *external opportunities* to be taken advantage of and *external threats* to be avoided. These are factors that an organization cannot control, but knowledge of them is essential in determining the organization's objectives and goals.

Examples of *opportunities* include:

- new less restrictive regulations, removal of trade barriers;
- a strategic alliance, a joint venture, or a merger;
- the Internet as a new market;
- the collapse of a competitor and the resulting opening of the market.

Any changes to the environment with a potential negative impact are threats. Examples of *threats* include:

- potential for a price war with competitors;
- technology changes extending beyond the capability of assimilating them;
- new tax barriers on the product or service.

Organizations pursue one or very few *objectives* at any given time. Objectives are normally long-term (three to five years) or even "timeless." Typical examples of objectives are to improve customer satisfaction, to introduce new services, to address competitive threats, or to increase control over suppliers. Each strategic objective must be associated with specific *goals*, usually expressed as annual targets. For example, the objective "to improve customer satisfaction" can be supported by the goal of fulfilling customer orders more quickly – within two weeks, say.

Objectives and goals require management *strategies* and specific *policies* for the implementation of these strategies. Such managerial instruments would adjust organizational structures, allocate resources and determine development projects, including information systems.

Figure 1.2 shows the relationships and derivation rules between concepts involved in SWOT analysis. The SWOT matrix defines the position of an organization in the marketplace and matches the organization's capabilities to the competitive environment in which it operates.

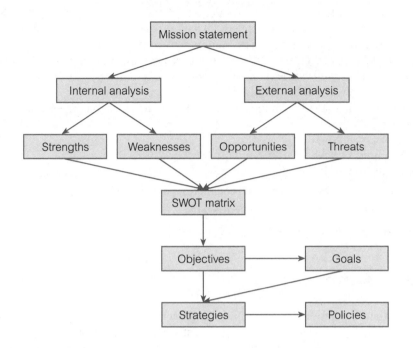

Figure 1.2
SWOT framework

The VCM approach

1.2.2

The VCM (value chain model) assesses competitive advantage by analyzing the full chain of activities in an organization – from raw materials to final products sold and shipped to customers. In the value chain approach, the product or service is the medium that transfers *value* to customers. The chain metaphor reinforces the point that a single weak link will cause the whole chain to break. The model serves the purpose of understanding which value chain configurations will yield the greatest competitive advantage. The IS development projects can then target those segments, operations, distribution channels, marketing approaches, etc. that give the most competitive advantage.

In the original VCM approach (Porter, 1985), organizational functions are categorized into *primary activities* and *support activities*. The primary activities create or add value to a final product. They are divided into five successive stages: (1) inbound logistics (receiving inputs to the product or service); (2) operations (using inputs to create the product or service); (3) outbound logistics (distributing the product or service to buyers); (4) sales and marketing (inducing buyers to purchase the product or service); and (5) services (to maintain or enhance the value of the product or service). These stages receive proper IS support, which includes, for example, (1) warehousing systems, (2) computer manufacturing systems, (3) shipment and scheduling systems, (4) ordering and invoicing systems, and (5) equipment maintenance systems.

The support activities do not add value, at least directly. They are still essential, but they do not enrich the product. The support activities include (1) administration and infrastructure, (2) human resource management, (3) research and development, and – quite understandably – (4) IS development.

While VCM is a useful tool for strategic planning and determination of IS development projects, the reverse is also true. The omnipresent computerization facilitates business changes, and this in turn creates efficiencies, cost reductions, and competitive advantages. In other words, *IT can transform an organization's value chains*. A self-reinforcing loop between IT and VCM can be established.

Porter and Millar (1985) identified five steps that an organization can take to exploit IT opportunities:

1. Assess the information intensity of products and processes.
2. Assess the role of IT in industry structure.
3. Identify and rank ways in which IT could create a competitive advantage.
4. Consider how IT could create new businesses.
5. Develop a plan to take advantage of IT.

1.2.3 The BPR approach

The BPR (business process re-engineering) approach to system planning is based on the premise that today's organizations must reinvent themselves and abandon the functional decomposition, hierarchical structures, and operational principles that they are now using.

The concept was introduced by Hammer (1990) and Davenport and Short (1990). It immediately generated interest as well as controversy. An extended description of BPR can be found in the books by the originators (Davenport, 1993; Hammer and Champy, 1993a).

Most contemporary organizations are structured into *vertical units* that focus on functions, products, or regions. These structures and work styles can be traced back to the eighteenth century and to Adam Smith's principle of the division of labor and the consequent fragmentation of work. No one employee or department is responsible for a *business process*, which is defined as "a collection of activities that takes one or more kinds of input and creates an output that is of value to the customer" (Hammer and Champy, 1993a).

BPR challenges Smith's industrial principles of the division of labor, hierarchical control, and economies of scale. In today's world, organizations must be able to adapt quickly to market changes, new technologies, competitive factors, customer demands, etc.

Rigid organizational structures in which business processes have to cut across many departments are obsolete. Organizations must focus on business processes rather than individual tasks, jobs, people, or departmental functions. These processes cut *horizontally* across the business and end at points of contact with customers. "The most visible difference between a process enterprise and a traditional organization is the existence of process owners" (Hammer and Stanton, 1999).

The main objective of BPR is to radically redesign business processes in an organization (hence, BPR is sometimes known as a *process redesign*). Business processes have to be identified, streamlined, and improved. The processes are documented in *workflow diagrams* and subjected to a *workflow analysis*. Workflows capture the flow of events, documents, and information in a business process and can be used to calculate the time, resources, and costs needed for these activities.

Davenport and Short (1990) recommend a five-step approach to BPR:

1. Determine the business vision and process objectives (the business vision derives from the mission statement; the objectives concentrate on cost and time reductions, quality improvements, staff empowerment, knowledge acquisition, etc.).
2. Determine the processes to be re-engineered.
3. Understand and measure the existing processes (in order to avoid past mistakes and establish the baseline for process redesign and improvement).
4. Identify information technology (IT) levers and how they can influence the process redesign and improvement.
5. Design and build a "prototype" of the new process (the "prototype" is a workflow system that is the subject of iterative and incremental development).

The major hurdle in implementing BPR in organizations lies in the need to embed a horizontal process in a traditional vertical management structure. A serious BPR initiative requires changing the organization around the development teams as the primary organizational units. These teams are responsible for one or more end-to-end business processes.

Sometimes a radical change is unacceptable. The traditional structures cannot be changed overnight. A radical push can meet with defiance, and the potential benefits of BPR can be compromised. Under such circumstances, an organization can still benefit from modeling of business processes and attempting just to improve them, rather than re-engineer. The term "Business process improvement" (BPI) is used to characterize an improvement initiative (Allen and Frost, 1998).

Once business processes are defined, the process owners require IT support to improve the efficiency of these processes further. The resulting IS development projects concentrate on implementing the identified workflows. The combination of the *effectiveness* of BPR and the *efficiency* of IT can give dramatic improvements in all contemporary measures of an organization's performance, such as quality, service, speed, cost, price, competitive advantage, and flexibility.

The ISA approach 1.2.4

Unlike the approaches already described, ISA (information systems architecture) is a bottom-up approach that offers a *neutral architectural framework* for IS solutions that can suit a variety of business strategies. As such, the ISA approach does not include a system planning methodology. It simply offers a framework that leverages most business strategies.

The ISA approach was introduced in a paper by Zachman (1987) and later extended by Sowa and Zachman (1992). An insignificantly modified version of the original paper has been published (Zachman 1999).

The ISA framework is represented as a table of thirty cells organized into five rows (labeled 1 through 5) and six columns (labeled A through F). The rows represent the different *perspectives* used in the construction of a complex engineering product such as an information system. These perspectives are those of five major "players in the game," the five IS participants:

1. planner (determines the scope of the system);
2. owner (defines an enterprise conceptual model);
3. designer (specifies a system physical model);
4. builder (provides detailed technological solutions);
5. subcontractor (delivers system components).

The six columns represent the six different *descriptions* or *architectural models* that each of the participants engages with. Like perspectives, the descriptions are quite different from each other but at the same time they are intrinsically related to one another. The descriptions provide answers to six questions that each participant is concerned with:

A. *What* is the thing made of? (i.e. data, in the case of IS).
B. *How* does the thing function? (i.e. business processes).
C. *Where* is the thing located? (i.e. location of processing components).
D. *Who* works with the thing? (i.e. the users).
E. *When* does the thing occur? (i.e. the scheduling of events and states).
F. *Why* is the thing taking place? (i.e. the motivation of the enterprise).

The combination of perspectives and descriptions in thirty cells provides a powerful taxonomy that establishes a complete architecture for an IS development. The vertical perspectives may differ in detail but, more importantly, they differ in essence and they employ different modeling representations. Different models emphasize the different viewpoints of the participants. Likewise, the horizontal descriptions are prepared for different reasons. Each answers one of the six questions.

The most attractive feature of the ISA approach comes from providing a framework that is likely to be flexible enough to accommodate future changes in business conditions and resources. This is because an ISA solution is not derived from any particular business strategy. It is just a framework for a complete description of an IS system. The framework draws from experiences of more established disciplines – some with a thousand or so years of history (such as classical architecture).

1.3 Systems for three management levels

Associated with system planning is the recognition that an organization has three management levels:

1. strategic
2. tactical
3. operational.

The three levels are characterized by a unique focus of decision making, by a distinct set of required IS applications, and by the specific support required from IT. It is the task of system planning to define a blend of IS applications and IT solutions that is most effective for an organization at a particular point in time. Table 1.1 defines the issues involved in

Table 1.1 IS and IT support for different levels of decision making

Level of decision making	Focus of decision making	Typical IS applications	Typical IT solutions	Pivotal concept
Strategic (executive and senior management levels)	Strategies in support of organizational long-term objectives	Market and sales analysis, Product planning, Performance evaluation	Data mining, Knowledge management	**Knowledge**
Tactical (line management level)	Policies in support of short-term goals and resource allocation	Budget analysis, Salary forecasting, Inventory scheduling, Customer service	Data warehouse, Analytical processing, Spreadsheets	**Information**
Operational (operative management level)	Day-to-day staff activities and production support	Payroll, Invoicing, Purchasing, Accounting	Database, Transactional processing, Application generators	**Data**

matching decision-making levels to IS applications and IT solutions (cf. Jordan and Machesky, 1990; Robson, 1994; Benson and Standing, 2002).

The IS applications and IT solutions that offer the greatest returns to an organization are those at the *strategic level*. However, these are also solutions that are the most difficult to implement – they use "bleeding-edge" technology and demand very skillful and specialized design. After all, these are the systems that can give an organization a competitive edge in the marketplace.

At the other end of the spectrum, systems in support of the *operational management level* are quite routine, use conventional database technology, and are frequently customized from prepackaged solutions. These systems are unlikely to provide a competitive edge, but without them the organization is not able to function properly.

Every modern organization has a full suite of operational-level systems, but only the best-managed organizations have an integrated set of strategic-level IS applications. The main technology for storing and retrieving data for high-level strategic and tactical decision making is known as a *data warehouse* (Kimball, 1996).

The last column in Table 1.1 associates three pivotal IS concepts (data, information, and knowledge) with systems at the three levels of decision making. The definitions of the pivotal concepts are:

■ *Data* – raw facts representing values, quantities, concepts, and events pertaining to business activities.

■ *Information* – value-added facts; data that have been processed and summarized to produce value-added facts revealing new features and trends.

■ *Knowledge* – understanding of information, obtained by experience or study, and resulting in the ability to do things effectively and efficiently; knowledge can be in a person's mind (*tacit knowledge*) or documented in some structured form.

As an example, a telephone number is a piece of *data*. Grouping telephone numbers by geographical areas or by customer rating of their owners results in *information*. Understanding how to use this information in telemarketing to entice people to buy products is *knowledge*. And, as jokingly noted by Benson and Standing (2002), deciding not to phone someone in the middle of the night is *wisdom*. More seriously, wisdom is sometimes considered to be the ultimate pivotal IS concept. It is then defined as the ability to use the knowledge to make good judgments and decisions.

1.4 The software development lifecycle

Software development follows a lifecycle. The term is so popular that it is frequently written as one word – *lifecycle*. The lifecycle is an orderly set of activities conducted and managed for each development project. The processes and methods are the machinery for a lifecycle implementation. The lifecycle identifies:

- the applied modeling approach;
- the exact phases along which the software product is transformed, from initial inception to phasing it out; and
- the method (methodology) and associated development process.

The typical lifecycle begins with a business *analysis* of the current situation and of the proposed solution. The analysis models are subjected to more detailed *design*. The design is followed by programming (*implementation*). The implemented parts of the system are *integrated* and *deployed* to customers. At this point, the system becomes *operational* (it supports daily business operations). For successful operation, the system undergoes *maintenance* tasks.

This book concentrates on analysis and design, and it touches on implementation. Risking some simplification, business analysis is about what to do, system design is how to do it using the available technology, and implementation is doing it (in the sense that a tangible software product is delivered).

1.4.1 The development approach

The "software revolution" has introduced some significant changes to the way software products work. In particular, software has become much more *interactive*. The tasks and behavior of programs dynamically adapt to the user's requests.

Looking back, the *procedural* logic of a COBOL-like program of the past was inflexible and not very responsive to unexpected events. Once started, the program executed to completion in a more or less deterministic fashion. Occasionally, the program would request input information from the user and would then follow a different execution path. In general, however, interaction with the user was limited and the number of different execution paths fixed. The program was in control, not the user.

With the advent of modern graphical user interfaces (GUIs), the approach to computing has changed dramatically. GUI programs are *event-driven* and execute in a random and unpredictable fashion dictated by user-generated events from a keyboard, mouse, or other input device.

In a GUI environment, the user is (largely) in control of program execution, not vice versa. Behind every event, there is a software *object* that knows how to service that event in the current state of the program's execution. Once the service is accomplished, control returns to the user.

This different style of program–user interaction necessitates a different approach to software development. Conventional software has been well served by the so-called *structured approach*. Modern GUI systems require object programming, and the *object approach* is the best way to design such systems.

The structured approach   1.4.1.1

The *structured approach* to systems development is called also functional, procedural, and imperative. This approach was popularized (and *de facto* standardized) in the 1980s. From a system modeling perspective, the structured approach is based on two techniques: DFD (data flow diagrams) for process modeling, and ERD (entity relationship diagrams) for data modeling.

The structured approach is *process-centric* and uses DFDs as a driving development force. In this approach, the system is broken down to manageable units in the activity called *functional decomposition*. The system is hierarchically divided into business processes linked by data flows.

Over years, the structured approach evolved slightly from process-centered to become more data-centered. This has been the direct result of the popularity of the relational database model. The importance of DFDs in structured development has faded a bit in favor of the ERD data-centric technique.

The combination of DFDs and ERDs delivers relatively complete analysis models that capture all the system's functions and data at a desirable level of abstraction, which does not depend on the software/hardware considerations. The analysis model is transformed later into a design model, expressed typically in relational database terms. The implementation phase can then follow.

The structured approach to analysis and design is characterized by a number of features, some of which are not well aligned with modern software engineering:

- The approach tends to be *sequential and transformational* rather than iterative and incremental (i.e. the approach does not facilitate a seamless development process through iterative refinement and incremental software delivery).

- The approach tends to deliver inflexible solutions that satisfy the set of identified business functions but that can be hard to scale up and extend in the future.

- The approach assumes development from scratch, and it does not support the reuse of pre-existing components.

The transformational nature of the approach introduces a considerable risk of misinterpreting original user requirements down the development track. This risk is exacerbated by the progressive need to trade off the relatively declarative semantics of analysis models for procedural solutions in design models and implementation code (this is because the analysis models are semantically richer than the underlying design and implementation models).

1.4.1.2 The object-oriented approach

The *object-oriented approach* to systems development breaks a system down into components of various granularity, with classes of objects at the bottom of this decomposition. Classes are linked by various relationships and communicate by sending messages that invoke operations on objects.

Although object-oriented programming languages (Simula) existed as early as the beginning of the 1970s, the object-oriented approach to system development was popularized only in the 1990s. Later on, the Object Management Group approved a series of UML (Unified Modeling Language) standards in support of the approach.

Compared with the structured approach, the object-oriented approach is more *data-centric* – it evolves around class models. In the analysis phase, classes do not need to have operations defined – only attributes. The growing significance of *use cases* in UML shifts the emphasis slightly from data to processes.

There is a perception that developers use object approaches because of technical advantages of the object paradigm, such as abstraction, encapsulation, reuse, inheritance, message passing, and polymorphism. These technical properties can lead to greater reusability of code and data, shorter development times, increased programmer productivity, improved software quality, and greater understandability. While attractive, these advantages of object technology do not always materialize in practice. Nevertheless, we do use objects today and will be using them tomorrow. The reasons have to do with the new style of *event-driven* programming supported by modern GUIs.

Other reasons for the popularity of the object approach have to do with addressing the needs of newly *emerging applications* and with the preferred ways to fight *application backlogs*. Two of the most important new categories of application that demand object technology are *workgroup computing* and *multimedia systems*. The idea of stopping the application backlog from growing, via the concept known as *object wrapping*, has proved to be both attractive and workable.

The object approach to systems development follows the *iterative and incremental* process. A single model (and a single design document) is "elaborated" through analysis, design, and implementation phases – details are added in successive iterations, changes and refinements are introduced as needed, and incremental releases of selected modules maintain user satisfaction and provide additional feedback to other modules.

Development by elaboration is possible because all development models (analysis, design, and implementation) are semantically rich and based on the same "language" – the underlying vocabulary is essentially the same (classes, attributes, methods, inheritance, polymorphism, etc.). However, note that whenever the implementation is based on a relational database, there is still a need for a complex transformation (because the underlying semantics of the relational model is quite poor by comparison and is orthogonal to object technology).

The object approach alleviates the most important shortcomings of the structured approach, but it does introduce a few new problems:

- The analysis phase is conducted on an even higher level of abstraction and – if the implementation server solution assumes a relational database – the *semantic gap* between the concept and its implementation can be significant. Although the analysis and design can be conducted in an iterative and incremental fashion, eventually the development reaches the implementation stage, which requires transformation to a relational database. If the implementation platform is an object or object-relational database, then the transformation from design is much easier.

- *Project management* is more difficult. Managers measure development progress by clearly defined work breakdown structures, deliverables, and milestones. In object development through "elaboration" there are no clear boundaries between phases, and project documentation evolves continuously. An attractive solution to this difficulty lies in dividing the project into small modules and managing the progress by frequent executable releases of these modules (some of these releases can be internal, others delivered).

- Object solutions are significantly more complex than old-style structured systems. The *complexity* results mostly from the need for extensive inter-object and inter-component communication. The situation can be aggravated by bad architectural design, such as the design that permits unrestricted networks of intercommunication objects. Systems built in this way are difficult to maintain and evolve.

The difficulties with the object approach do not change the fact that "the future isn't what it used to be," in Arthur C. Clarke's words. There is no going back to the procedural style of programming reminiscent of batch COBOL applications. All stakeholders in IS development projects are aware of the Internet, e-commerce, computer games, and other interactive applications.

New software applications are much more complex to build, and the structured approach is inadequate for the task. The object-oriented approach is currently the only popular and practical method to harness the development of new highly interactive event-driven software.

Lifecycle phases

1.4.2

There are some well-defined chronological sequences of action in software production. At a coarse level of granularity, the lifecycle includes five *phases*:

1. business analysis
2. system design
3. implementation
4. integration and deployment
5. operation and maintenance.

The *business analysis* phase concentrates on system requirements. Requirements are determined and specified (modeled). Function and data models for the system are developed and integrated. Non-functional requirements and other system constraints are also captured.

LIB

The *system design* phase divides into two major sub-phases: architectural and detailed design. In particular, the client/server program design that integrates user interface and database objects is explained. Various design issues that influence a system's understandability, maintainability, and scalability are raised and documented.

The *implementation* phase consists of the activity of coding client application programs and server databases. Incremental and iterative implementation processes are emphasized. *Round-trip engineering* between design models and the implementation of client applications and server databases is essential to successful product delivery.

It is impracticable today for software to be developed in one big chunk in a single iteration of analysis, design, and implementation. The software is developed in smaller modules (components), which need to be assembled as well as integrated with modules already operational before they are deployed to customers for production use. This is called the *integration and deployment* phase.

The *operation and maintenance* phase begins at the point when the pre-existing business solution or system is phased out and the new system takes over day-to-day operations. Perhaps paradoxically, operation also signifies the beginning of system maintenance, which includes any corrections and extensions to software. To a large degree, maintenance is not a reflection on the quality of delivered software. It is rather a sign of the times and of the fact that the business environment is in a constant state of flux, demanding regular changes to software.

1.4.2.1 Business analysis

Business analysis (or *requirements analysis*) is the activity of determining and specifying customer requirements. The requirements determination and specification are distinct activities and are sometimes conducted by different people. Accordingly, a distinction is sometimes made between a business analyst and a system analyst. The former determines requirements, the latter specifies (or models) them.

Business analysis, even when conducted in the context of a small application domain, takes a careful look at the enterprise's business processes. In this sense, business analysis is linked to *business process re-engineering* (BPR Section 1.2.3). The aim of BPR is to propose new ways of conducting business and gaining a competitive advantage. These "new ways" are freed from the luggage of existing solutions, including existing information systems.

As a result of BPR initiatives and as a result of a normal course of adding engineering rigor to system development, business analysis increasingly becomes an act of *requirements engineering*. Indeed, requirements engineering is a software development discipline of growing importance, a discipline that links smoothly to the whole field of software engineering (Maciaszek and Liong, 2004).

1.4.2.1.1 Requirements determination

Kotonya and Sommerville (1998) define a *requirement* as "a statement of a system service or constraint." A *service statement* describes how the system should behave with regard to an individual user or with regard to the whole user community. In the latter case, a service statement really defines a *business rule* that must be obeyed at all times (e.g. "fortnightly salaries are paid on Wednesdays"). A service statement may also be some computation that the system must carry out (e.g. "calculate salesperson commission based on sales in the last fortnight using a particular formula").

A *constraint statement* expresses a restriction on the system's behavior or on the system's development. An example of the former may be the security constraint: "only direct managers can see the salary information of their staff." An example for the latter may be: "we must use Sybase development tools." Notice that sometimes the distinction between a constraint statement on the system's behavior and a business rule service statement is blurred. This is not a problem as long as all requirements are identified and duplications eliminated.

The task of the requirements determination phase is to determine, analyze, and negotiate requirements with customers. The phase involves various techniques for gathering information from customers. It is a concept exploration through structured and unstructured interviews of users, questionnaires, study of documents and forms, video recordings, etc. An ultimate technique of the requirements phase is *rapid prototyping* of the solution so that difficult requirements can be clarified and misunderstandings avoided.

Requirements analysis includes negotiations between developers and customers. This step is necessary to eliminate contradicting and overlapping requirements, and also to conform to the project budget and deadline.

The product of the requirements phase is a *requirements document*. This is mostly a narrative text document with some informal diagrams and tables. No formal models are included, except perhaps a few easy and popular notations that can be easily grasped by customers and that can facilitate developer–customer communication.

Requirements specification *1.4.2.1.2*

The requirements specification phase begins when the developers start modeling the requirements using a particular method (such as UML). A CASE tool is used to enter, analyze, and document the models. As a result, the requirements document is enriched with graphical models and CASE-generated reports. In essence, a *specifications document* (the *specs* in the jargon) replaces the requirements document.

The two most important specification techniques in object-oriented analysis are class diagrams and use-case diagrams. These are techniques for data and function specifications. A typical specification document will also describe other requirements, such as performance, "look and feel," usability, maintainability, security, and political and legal requirements.

Specification models can and will overlap. They allow the proposed solution to be viewed from many different angles so that specific aspects of the solution are emphasized and analyzed. Consistency and completeness of requirements are also carefully checked.

Ideally, the specification models should be independent of the hardware/software platform on which the system is to be deployed. *Hardware/software considerations* impose heavy restrictions on the vocabulary (and therefore expressiveness) of the modeling language. Moreover, the vocabulary may be difficult for customers to understand, thus inhibiting developer–customer communication.

This said, some of the constraint statements would, in fact, be imposing hardware/ software considerations on developers. Moreover, the customers themselves may be expressing their requirements in relation to a particular hardware/software technology, or even demanding a particular technology. The lesson is avoid hardware/software considerations, if you can.

1.4.2.2 System design

The definition of *system design* is broader than the definition of *software design*, although undoubtedly software design takes center stage. System design includes the description of a structure of the system and the detailed design of internals of system components. Accordingly, system design is sometimes separated into architectural design and detailed design.

Design continues from analysis. While this observation is certainly true, architectural design can be seen as a relatively self-governing activity aimed at using good and proven design practices to achieve architectural excellence. By contrast, detailed design flows directly from analysis models.

The specification document from the analysis phase is like a *contract* between developers and customers for delivery of the software product. It lists all the requirements that the software product must satisfy. Specifications are handed over to system/software architects, designers and engineers to develop lower-level models of a system's architecture and its internal workings. Design is done in terms of the software/hardware platform on which the system is to be implemented.

1.4.2.2.1 Architectural design

The description of the system in terms of its modules (components) is called *architectural design*. The architectural design includes decisions about the solution strategies for the client and server aspects of the system. The architectural design is also concerned with the selection of a solution strategy and with the modularization of the system. The *solution strategy* needs to resolve client (user interface) and server (database) issues as well as any *middleware* needed to "glue" client and server processes. The decision on basic building blocks (components) is relatively independent of a solution strategy, but the detailed design of components must conform to a selected client/server solution.

Client/server models are frequently extended to provide a *three-tier architecture*, where application logic constitutes a separate layer. The middle tier is a logical tier and as such may or may not be supported by separate hardware. Application logic is a process that can run on either the client or the server, i.e. it can be compiled into the client or server process and implemented as dynamic link library (DLL), application programming interface (API), remote procedure calls (RPC), etc.

The quality of architectural design is tremendously important to the long-lasting success of the system. A good architectural design produces *supportable systems*, i.e. systems that are understandable, maintainable, and scalable (extensible). Without these qualities, the inherent complexity of a software solution escapes control. It is, therefore, crucial that architectural design delivers supportable system structure and that this structure is adhered to during programming and carefully maintained after system delivery.

Detailed design *1.4.2.2.2*

The description of the internal workings of each software component is called *detailed design*. It develops detailed algorithms and data structures for each component. The components are eventually deployed on client, server, or middleware processes of the underlying implementation platform. Accordingly, the algorithms and data structures are tailored to constraints (both reinforcing and obstructive) of the underlying implementation platform.

The detailed design of the *client* (user interface) needs to conform to the GUI design guidelines provided by the creator of a particular GUI interface (Windows, Motif, Macintosh). Such guidelines are normally provided online as part of the electronic GUI documentation (e.g. Windows, 2000).

A major principle for an object-oriented GUI design is that the *user is in control*, not the program. The program reacts to randomly generated user events and provides the necessary software services. Other GUI design principles are a consequence of this fact. (Of course, "the user is in control" principle should not be taken literally – the program would still validate the user's privileges and might disallow certain user actions.)

The detailed design of the *server* defines objects on a database server – most likely a relational (or possibly object-relational) server. Some of these objects are data containers (tables, views, etc.). Other objects are procedural (stored procedures, triggers, etc.).

The detailed design for the *middleware* layer is concerned with the application logic and the business rules. This layer provides a separation and mapping between the user interface and the database aspects of the solution. This separation is crucial for ease of independent evolution of the application software handling the user interface and the database software handling access to data sources.

Implementation 1.4.2.3

Implementation of an information system involves *installation* of purchased software and *coding* of custom-written software. It also involves other important activities, such as loading of test and production databases, testing, user training, and hardware issues.

A typical organization of an implementation team distinguishes two groups of programmers: one responsible for client programming and the other in charge of server database programming. Client programs implement windows and application logic (even if application logic is deployed on a separate application server, there are always aspects of the application logic that have to reside on the client). Client programs also initiate business transactions, which result in activation of server database programs (stored procedures). The responsibility for database consistency and for transactional correctness lies with server programs.

In a true spirit of iterative and incremental development, the detailed design of *user interfaces* is prone to implementation changes. Application programmers may opt for a different appearance of implemented windows to conform to the vendor's GUI principles, to facilitate programming, or to improve the user's productivity.

Similarly, server *database* implementation may force changes to design documents. Unforeseen database problems, difficulties with programming of stored procedures and triggers, concurrency issues, integration with client processes, and performance tuning are just a few reasons why the design may need to be modified.

1.4.2.4 Integration and deployment

Incremental development implies *incremental integration and deployment* of software modules (subsystems). The task is not trivial. For large systems, module integration can take more time and effort than any one of the earlier lifecycle phases, including implementation. As Aristotle observed: "The whole is more than the sum of the parts."

Module integration must be carefully planned from the very beginning of the software lifecycle. Software units that are to be implemented individually must be identified in the early stages of system analysis. They need to be readdressed in detail during architectural design. The sequence of implementation must allow for the smoothest possible incremental integration.

The main difficulty with incremental integration is in intertwined circular dependencies between the modules. In a well-designed system, circular *coupling* of modules is minimized or even eliminated altogether. The fact that two modules depend on each other and neither can function in isolation does not have to involve circular dependencies.

What can we do if we need to deliver one module before the other is ready? The answer lies in writing special code to temporarily "fill the gaps" so that all modules can be integrated. Programming routines to simulate the activity of the missing module are called *stubs*.

Object-oriented systems must be designed for integration and deployment. Each module should be as independent as possible. Dependencies between modules should be identified and minimized in the analysis and design phases. Ideally, each module should constitute a single thread of processing that executes as a response to a particular customer need. The use of stubs as replacement operations should be avoided when possible. If not properly designed, the integration phase will result in chaos and will put at risk the entire development project.

1.4.2.5 Operation and maintenance

Operation and maintenance follows a successful handover to a customer of each incremental software module and eventually of the entire software product. Maintenance is not only an inherent part of the software lifecycle – it accounts for most of it as far as IT personnel time and effort is concerned. Schach (2002) estimates that 67 percent of lifecycle time is spent on software maintenance.

Operation signifies *changeover* from the existing business solution, whether in software or not. Changeover is usually a gradual process. If it is possible, the old and new systems should run in parallel for a while to allow a fallback if the new system does not stand up to the task.

Maintenance consists of three distinct stages (Maciaszek, 1990; Ghezzi *et al.*, 2003):

1. housekeeping
2. adaptive maintenance
3. perfective maintenance.

Housekeeping relates to the routine maintenance tasks necessary to keep the system accessible to users and operational. *Adaptive maintenance* involves monitoring and auditing of the system's operations, adjusting its functionality to satisfy the changing environment, and adapting it to meet performance and throughput demands. *Perfective maintenance* refers to redesigning and modifying the system to accommodate new or substantially changed requirements.

Eventually, the continuing maintenance of a software system becomes unsustainable and the system has to be phased out. *Phasing out* would normally happen due to reasons that have little to do with the *usefulness* of the software. The software is probably still useful, but it has become unmaintainable. Schach (2002) lists four reasons why the software may have to be phased out:

1. Proposed changes go beyond the immediate capability of perfective maintenance.
2. The system is out of maintainers' control, and the effects of changes cannot be predicted.
3. There is a lack of documentation to base future software extensions on.
4. The implementation hardware/software platform has to be replaced, and no migration path is available.

Activities spanning the lifecycle 1.4.3

Some experts and authors also include project *planning* and *testing* as two lifecycle phases. However, these two important activities are *not* really separate lifecycle phases, because they span the whole lifecycle.

A software project management plan is drawn up early in the process, significantly enriched after the specification phase, and evolving through the rest of the lifecycle. Similarly, testing is most intensive after implementation, but it also applies to software artifacts produced in every other phase.

Project progress is tracked to the project plan. Tracking of project progress links to another activity that spans the lifecycle – the activity of collecting project *metrics*, i.e. measuring the development processes and their outcomes.

Project planning 1.4.3.1

A familiar maxim says that if you can't plan it, you can't do it. Planning spans the software project lifecycle. It begins once the *system planning* activities determine the business strategy for the organization and the software projects are identified. *Project planning* is the activity of estimating the project's deliverables, costs, time, risks, milestones, and resource requirements. It also includes the selection of development methods, processes, tools, standards, and team organization.

Project planning is a moving target. It is not something you do once and never change. Within the framework of a few *fixed constraints*, project plans evolve with the lifecycle.

Typical constraints are *time* and *money* – each project has a clear deadline and a tight budget. One of the first tasks in project planning is to assess whether the project is feasible under the time, budget, and other constraints. If it is feasible then the constraints are documented and can only be changed in the course of a formal approval process.

Project feasibility is assessed with several factors in mind (Whitten and Bentley, 1998; Hoffer *et al.*, 2002):

- *Operational feasibility* readdresses the issues originally undertaken in *system planning* when the project was identified; it is the study of how the proposed system will affect organizational structures, procedures, and people.

- *Economic feasibility* assesses the costs and benefits of the project (also known as cost–benefit analysis).

- *Technical feasibility* assesses the practicality of the proposed technical solution and the availability of technical skills, expertise, and resources.

- *Schedule feasibility* assesses the reasonability of the project timetable.

Not all constraints are known or could be evaluated at the time of project initiation. Additional constraints will be discovered during the requirements phase and will undergo feasibility studies. These will include legal, contractual, political, and security constraints.

Subject to feasibility assessment, a *project plan* will be constructed and will constitute the guidance for project and process management. The issues addressed in the project plan include (Whitten and Bentley, 1998):

- project scope;
- project tasks;
- directing and controlling the project;
- quality management;
- metrics and measurement;
- project scheduling;
- allocation of resources (people, material, tools);
- people management.

1.4.3.2 Metrics

Measuring development time and effort and taking other *metrics* of project artifacts is an important part of *project and process management*. Although an important part, it is frequently neglected in organizations at low levels of process maturity. The price is high. Without measuring the past, the organization is not able to plan accurately for the future.

Metrics are usually discussed in the context of *software quality* and *complexity* – they apply to the quality and complexity of the *software product* (Henderson-Sellers, 1996; Pressman, 2001). Metrics are used to measure such quality factors as correctness, reliability, efficiency, integrity, usability, maintainability, flexibility, and testability. For example, software reliability can be evaluated by measuring the frequency and severity of failures, and in the meantime, between failures, the accuracy of output results, the ability to recover from failure, etc.

An equally important application of metrics is measuring the development models (*development products*) at different phases of the lifecycle. Metrics are then used to assess the effectiveness of the *process* and to improve the quality of work at various lifecycle phases.

Typical metrics that apply to the *software process* and can be taken at various lifecycle phases are (Schach, 2002):

- Requirements volatility (percentage of requirements that changed by the time the requirements phase had finished). This may reflect on the difficulty of obtaining requirements from the customers.

- Requirements volatility after the requirements phase. This may point to a poor-quality requirements document.

- Prediction of "hot spots" and "bottlenecks" in the system (frequency at which users attempt to execute different functions in the prototype of the software product).

- The size of the specification document generated by the CASE tool, and other more detailed metrics from the CASE repository, such as the number of classes in a class model. If taken on a few past projects with known cost and time to completion, these metrics provide an ideal planning "database" to predict time and effort on future projects.

- Record of fault statistics, when they were introduced to the product and when they were discovered and rectified. This may reflect on the thoroughness of quality assurance, review processes, and testing activities.

- Average number of tests before a test unit is considered acceptable for integration and release to customers. This may reflect on the programmers' debugging procedures.

Testing 1.4.3.3

Like project planning or metrics taking, *testing* is an activity that spans the software life-cycle. It is not just a separate phase after the implementation. It is much too late to start testing after the software product is implemented. The escalating cost of fixing faults introduced in earlier lifecycle phases is likely to be exorbitant (Schach, 2002).

Testing activities should be carefully planned. At the start, *test cases* have to be identified. Test cases (or test plans) define the test steps to be undertaken in an attempt to "break" the software. Test cases should be defined for each functional module (*use case*) described in the requirements document. Relating test cases to use cases establishes a *traceability* path between tests and user requirements. To be testable, a software artifact must be traceable.

Naturally enough, every developer tests products of their work. However, original developers are blindfolded by the work they have done to produce the software artifact in the first place. To be most effective, a third party should conduct testing methodically. The task can be assigned to the software quality assurance (SQA) group in the organization. This group should include some of the best developers in the organization. Their job is to test, not to develop. The SQA group (not the original developers) is then charged with responsibility for product quality.

The more testing is done in the early development phases, the better the payoff. Requirements, specifications, and any documents (including program source code) can be tested in *formal reviews* (so-called *walkthroughs* and *inspections*). Formal reviews are carefully prepared meetings that target a particular part of the documentation or system. An appointed reviewer studies a document beforehand and raises various questions. The meeting decides if a question is in fact a fault, but there is no attempt to offer an immediate solution to the problem. The original developer will address the fault later. Provided that the meetings are friendly and finger pointing is avoided, the "team synergy" will lead to early detection and correction of many faults.

Once software prototypes and first versions of the software product are made available, *execution-based testing* can be undertaken. There are two kinds of execution-based testing:

1. testing to specs (black-box testing);
2. testing to code (white-box or glass-box testing).

Testing to specs treats the program itself as a black box about which nothing is known except that it takes some input and produces some output. The program is given some input, and the resulting output is analyzed for the presence of errors. Testing to specs is particularly useful for discovering incorrect or missing requirements.

Testing to code "looks through" the program logic to derive the input needed to *exercise* various execution paths in the program. Testing to code complements testing to specs – the two tests tend to discover different categories of error.

Incremental development involves not only incremental integration of software modules but also *incremental* or *regression testing*. Regression testing is the re-execution of the previous test cases on the same *baseline data set* after a previously released software module has been incrementally extended. The assumption is that the old functionality should remain the same and should not have been broken by an extension.

Regression testing can be well supported by *capture–playback tools* that allow the user's interactions with the program to be captured and played back without further user intervention. The main difficulty with regression testing is enforcement of the baseline data set. Incremental development does not just extend the procedural program logic, it also extends (and modifies) underlying data structures. An extended software product may force changes to the baseline data set, thus ruling out sensible comparison of results.

1.4.4 Development models

Development model is about the "how" of software production. The notion of *development model*, sometimes called the *lifecycle model* (Maciaszek and Liong, 2004), has a generic connotation. A project team can adopt the generic model and by doing so choose a particular way of organizing the development. In this sense, the notion of the development model is a description for a development process (Section 1.1.2.2). This section elaborates on development models that have not been standardized and are not used for organizational accreditation; i.e. this section does not discuss the CMM (Section 1.1.2.2.2) and the ISO 9000 (Section 1.1.2.3) standards.

That said, the specific way of doing things, i.e. the development *process*, is always unique for each organization. The process is the consequence of social, cultural, organizational, environmental, and similar aspects of development. The process will also differ from project to project according to its size, application domain, required software tools, etc.

Modern development processes are *iterative and incremental*. Software is produced in many iterations, such that each iteration delivers an incremental (improved) version of the product. Iterations and increments apply to the same scope of the system. This means that a new increment does not add a new functional unit (such as a new subsystem) to the previous increment. An increment improves existing functionality, usability, performance, and other qualities of the system while not changing the system's scope.

Various representative lifecycle models exist for iterative and incremental development. Models of significant popularity include (Maciaszek and Liong, 2004):

■ the spiral model;
■ the IBM Rational Unified Process (RUP);
■ model-driven architecture; and
■ agile software development.

The spiral model

1.4.4.1

The *spiral model* (Boehm, 1988) is a *de facto* reference model for all iterative and incremental development processes. The model was proposed at a time when the structured development approach (Section 1.4.1.1) still dominated, but – being really a meta-model – it is equally well applicable to the object-oriented approach (Section 1.4.1.2). The model places the software engineering activities within the wider context of system planning, risk analysis, and customer evaluation. These four activities are visualized graphically as quadrants, which together create spiral loops on a Cartesian diagram (Figure 1.3).

According to the spiral model, system development begins with *planning* activities. Planning involves project feasibility studies and initial requirements gathering. It also builds project schedules and defines the budget components.

Next, the project enters the *risk analysis* quadrant, in which the impact of risks on the project is assessed. *Risks* are any potential adverse circumstances and uncertainties facing

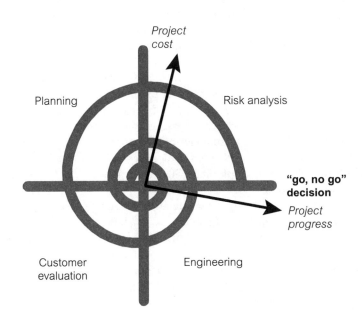

Figure 1.3
The spiral model

the development. Risk analysis assesses expected project outcomes and the acceptable level of tolerance on risk against the probabilities of achieving these outcomes. Risk analysis is responsible for a "go, no go" decision to move to the engineering quadrant. The decision is purely risk-driven and is looking into the future (and must not be motivated by the project costs committed so far).

The *engineering* quadrant addresses down-to-earth development efforts. Project progress is measured in this quadrant. Engineering includes all sorts of system modeling, programming, integration, and deployment.

Before the project enters the next iteration, it is subjected to *customer evaluation*. This is a formal process to obtain customer feedback. The evaluation is conducted against known requirements that the system should satisfy, but any other feedback from customers is also addressed on entry to the next planning quadrant.

1.4.4.2   IBM Rational Unified Process

The IBM Rational Unified Process ® (RUP ®) is defined as a software development process platform (RUP, 2003). The platform provides a development support environment consisting of guiding and learning documents, good practice templates, web-based facilitation techniques, etc. RUP organizes projects in two-dimensional terms. The horizontal dimension represents the successive *phases* of each project iteration. RUP proposes four phases: inception, elaboration, construction, and transition. The vertical dimension represents software development *disciplines*, namely business modeling, requirements, analysis and design, implementation, testing, deployment, and the supporting activities of configuration and change management, project management, and environment. The disciplines represent the project's focus areas or workflows.

The division into phases and disciplines has its merits, but it is fair to say that it causes as many problems as it solves. Its aim is to show the imposition of the horizontal dynamic dimension on the vertical static dimension. Dynamic dimensions represent a project's progress in terms of iterations and milestones. The progress is measured with regard to the static dimension's focus areas and with regard to issues such as activities and artifacts.

In practice, the distinction between the horizontal and vertical dimensions is not always clear. Questions like "what is the difference between construction and implementation or between transition and deployment?" are frequently asked. In order not to add to the confusion, Figure 1.4 shows the vertical RUP disciplines organized in a cycle of activities. The horizontal phases are not shown, but they apply (albeit with varying strength) to each discipline. For example, the inception phase dominates in business modeling, but it does not exist at all in deployment. On the other hand, the transition phase is very involved during deployment, but not in business modeling.

Like the spiral model, RUP emphasizes iterative development and the importance of early and continuous risk analysis. Frequent executable releases underpin the nature of RUP. RUP assumes that the process configuration is customized to the project. The customization means that RUP process components can be selected specifically for the organization, for the task, for the whole team, and even for individual team members. RUP has a universal applicability, but it provides specific guidance for teams that use IBM Rational software development tools.

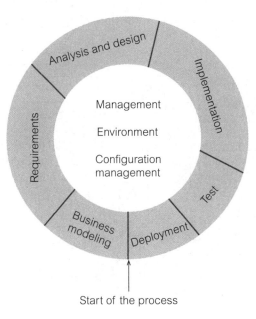

Start of the process

Figure 1.4 IBM Rational Unified Process
Source: Reprinted by permission from Rational Suite Tutorial 2002, copyright 2002 International Busines Machines Corporation

Model-driven architecture

1.4.4.3

Model-driven architecture (MDA) (MDA, 2003; Kleppe *et al*., 2003) is an old idea whose time has (possibly) come. The idea dates back to the programming concept of formal specifications and transformation models (Ghezzi *et al*., 2003). MDA is a framework for executable modeling and generation of programs from specifications.

MDA uses various Object Management Group (OMG) standards to completely specify platform-independent and platform-specific models for a system. The standards that enable such specifications include:

- Unified Modeling Language (UML) for modeling tasks;
- Meta-Object Facility (MOF) for using a standard meta-model repository so that derived specifications can work together;
- XML Meta-Data Interchange (XMI) for mapping UML to XML for interchange purposes;
- Common Warehouse Meta-model (CWM) for mapping of MDA to database schemas and permitting flexible data mining.

MDA aims at deriving platform-independent models, which include complete specifications of the system's state and behavior. This allows the separation of business applications from the technology changes. In the next step, MDA provides tools and techniques to produce platform-specific models for realization in environments such as J2EE, .NET or Web Services.

Figure 1.5 shows how MDA concepts link to the three main development phases of analysis, design, and implementation. PSM and code bridges are interoperability facilities to permit the system under development to span multiple platforms.

Figure 1.5
Model-driven
architecture

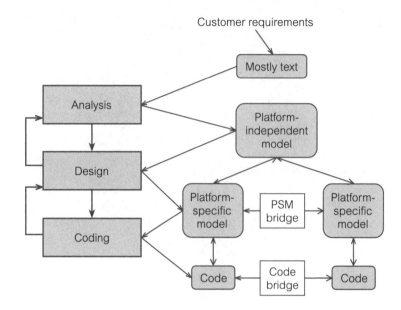

As a natural consequence of executable modeling, MDA also reaches in the direction of component technology. Components are defined in platform-independent models and then implemented in platform-specific ways. OMG uses MDA to create transformable models and reusable components to offer standard solutions for vertical industries, such as telecommunications or hospitals.

1.4.4.4 Agile software development

Agile software development is a more recent contribution to iterative and incremental development models. The concept has been popularized by the Agile Alliance, a non-profit organization committed to agility in software production (Agile, 2003). Agile development embraces change as an inherent aspect of software production, proposes "lightweight" methods to accommodate changing requirements, and gives programming center stage in system development.

In the "Manifesto for Agile Software Development", the Agile Alliance formulated the key points of agility in software production:

■ individuals and interactions over processes and tools;

■ working software over comprehensive documentation;

■ customer collaboration over contract negotiation;

■ responding to changeover following a plan.

Agile development is an iterative and incremental approach with a zest to replace formalities with frequent delivery of executable programs to customers. This zest is made clear in terminology: names of typical lifecycle phases of analysis, design, implementation, and deployment give way to new terms of user stories, acceptance tests, refactoring, test-driven development, and continuous integration (Figure 1.6). A closer look reveals that the

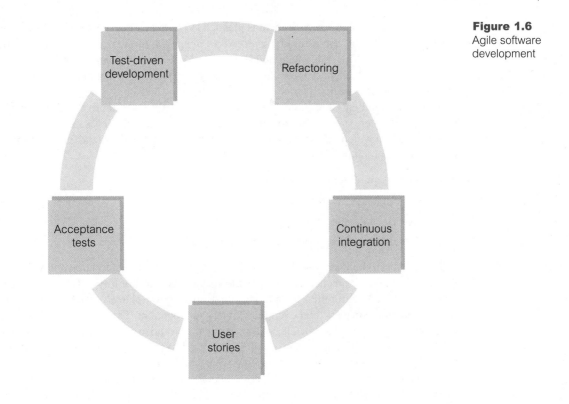

Figure 1.6
Agile software
development

change in terminology does not change the fact that agile development blends nicely with more established iterative and incremental processes.

User stories in agile development correspond to requirements analysis in other models. The stories list and describe the users' views on the features that the system under development should support. The stories are used to plan the development iterations in terms of time and money.

Agile development replaces design-level modeling and implementation with a cycle of acceptance tests, refactoring, and test-driven development. *Acceptance tests* are specifications of programs that an application program under development must pass to satisfy user requirements. As a consequence, implementation is test-driven. Programs are written to pass acceptance tests. This process is called *test-driven development*.

Test-driven development is conducted by pairs of programmers. All programming is done by two programmers using a single workstation to allow discussion, exchange of ideas, and immediate verification of concepts with another person. *Pair programming*, as it is called, also introduces the benefits of *collective ownership*, so that no one person owns the code and there is always a second person who understands the code already written.

Agile development is strong on *refactoring*, which is the activity of improving the code by restructuring (re-architecting) it without changing its behavior. Refactoring assumes that the initial architecture is sound and flexible. It also assumes programming according to good practices and established design and implementation patterns.

Each iteration in agile development is planned to complete in a *short cycle* of about two weeks duration. Short cycles imply *continuous integration* of the new code with the code that already exists. The code integrated at the end of two weeks is a *minor delivery* for customer evaluation. A major delivery for production use is normally planned after three short cycles, i.e. after six weeks.

Agile development contributes some important practices to iterative and incremental development. There are various specific variants and practices that either fall into the category of agile development or can be combined with agile development. The best-known representatives include:

- extreme programming (XP) (Beck, 1999; Extreme, 2003);
- aspect-oriented software development (Aspect, 2003);
- feature-driven development (Feature, 2003);
- lean development (Poppendieck and Poppendieck, 2003).

There have been doubts about the scalability of agile development to large and very large projects. Agile development seems more suited to smaller teams of fifty or fewer developers, highly integrated, committed to outcomes and low-key on plans, formalities, accountability to project managers, and even the delivery to a contract. This kind of approach is at odds with developing large-scale mission-critical enterprise information systems. Such developments are normally done according to the formal and documented practices of CMM and ISO 9000 standards (Sections 1.1.2.2.2 and 1.1.2.2.3).

A recent trend has been to align, adopt, and adapt individual agile development practices to CMM and ISO 9000 organizations. This tendency applies in particular to the design-implementation cycle, where practices such as pair programming and refactoring are applicable. Associated with it is the usefulness of the test-driven development for *intentional programming* – the ability and opportunity to specify the intent of the program in the acceptance test before starting to code the program.

1.5 Problem statements for case studies

Apart from the tutorial in the appendix, this book uses six case studies to exemplify software development concepts and modeling activities. The presentation style of the tutorial and the case studies is similar – the questions are defined and then the solutions are given. This allows the reader to attempt a solution and then compare it with the solution offered. The case studies are:

- university enrolment (UE)
- video store (VS)
- contact management (CM)
- telemarketing (TM)
- advertising expenditure (AE)
- time logging (TL).

University enrolment   1.5.1

University enrolment is a classic textbook example (cf. Quatrani, 2000; Stevens and Pooley, 2000) and is a surprisingly complex application domain with a rich set of business rules that change relatively frequently, yet historical information has to be carefully maintained with relation to business rules in force at different times.

No two universities are the same. Each has its own interesting peculiarities that can be used in case studies to emphasize particular aspects of system analysis and design. The emphasis in our case study is on the intricacies of state modeling with regard to handling the time dimension (temporal information) and capturing business rules in data structures.

Problem statement 1: university enrolment

A medium-sized university offers a number of undergraduate and postgraduate degrees to full-time and part-time students. The educational structure of the university consists of divisions. Divisions contain several departments. While a single division administers each degree, the degree may include courses from other divisions. In fact, the university prides itself on the freedom of choice given to students in selecting courses towards their degrees.

The flexibility of course selection puts strains on the university enrolment system. Individually tailored programs of study must not contradict the rules governing the degree, such as the structure of prerequisite courses required so that the student can qualify for the degree's compulsory courses. A student's choice of courses may be restricted by timetable clashes, maximum class sizes, etc.

The flexibility of education offered by the university has been the main reason behind the steady growth in student numbers. However, to maintain its traditional strength, the current enrolment system – still partly manual – has to be replaced by a new software solution. The preliminary search for an off-the-shelf software package has not been successful. The university enrolment system is sufficiently unique to warrant in-house development.

The system is required to assist in pre-enrolment activities and to handle the enrolment procedures. The pre-enrolment activities must include mail-outs of last semester's examination grades to students together with any enrolment instructions. During enrolment sessions, the system must accept the students' proposed programs of study and validate them for prerequisites, timetable clashes, class sizes, special approvals, etc. Resolution of some of the problems may require consultation with academic advisers or academics in charge of course offerings.

Video store   1.5.2

The second case study is a routine business application typical of small businesses. It is the application to support the operation of a small video store. The video store keeps in stock a wide-ranging disk and tape library of entertainment material. The main operation of the store is rental services.

A typical computer system to support a small video store would be customized from off-the-shelf software or customized from some other proprietary solution. The system would be set on one of the popular database management systems available for a small-business computer.

Although with the database software underneath, the system may be deployed initially on a single machine, GUI development is likely to be done with a simple fourth-generation language (4GL) with screen painting, code generation capability, and a connection to a simple database.

A distinguishing aspect of the video store as a case study is the extensive chain of activities – from ordering of entertainment material through stock management to the accounting associated with rentals and sales to customers. In a way, it is a small-scale *value chain* operation (Section 1.2.2).

Problem statement 2: video store

A new video store intends to offer rentals (and sales) of entertainment material to the wider public. The store management is determined to launch its operations with the support of a computer system. The management has sourced a number of small-business software packages that might be suitable for customization and further development. To assist with the package selection, the store has hired a business analyst whose job is to determine and specify the requirements.

The video store will keep a stock of video tapes, and CDs (games and music), and DVDs. The inventory has already been ordered from one supplier, but more suppliers will be approached in future orders. All video tapes and disks will be bar-coded so that a scanning machine integrated with the system can support the rentals and returns. Customer membership cards will also be bar-coded.

Existing customers will be able to place reservations on entertainment material to be collected at a specific date. The system must have a flexible search engine to answer customer enquiries, including enquiries about material that the video store does not stock (but may order on request).

1.5.3 Contact management

Contact management is a "hot" application domain. Frequently known by the abbreviation CRM (contact or customer relationship management), contact management is an important component of enterprise resource planning (ERP) systems. ERP systems automate *back office* transaction processing applications. Three typical components of an ERP system are accounting, manufacturing, and human resources. CRM belongs to the human resources component.

ERP systems are very large customizable solutions. Some people refer to them as mega-packages. Naturally enough, a CRM component of an ERP solution can be very complex. The case study addresses only a small portion of the CRM problem area.

Contact management applications are characterized by interesting GUI solutions through which the employees of customer relations, or a similarly named department, can schedule their activities with regard to customers. In essence, the contact management system's GUI acts as a diary to record customer-related tasks and events and to keep track of their progress.

The diary has to be database-driven to allow dynamic scheduling and monitoring of tasks and events across many employees. Like most human resource systems, contact management applications require a sophisticated authorization scheme to control access to sensitive information.

Problem statement 3: contact management

A market research company has an established customer base of organizations that buy market analysis reports. Some larger customers have also purchased specialized reporting software from the company. These customers are then provided with raw and pre-aggregated information for their own report generation.

The company is constantly on the search for new customers, even if the new customers may be interested only in one-off, narrowly targeted market reports. Since prospective customers are not quite customers yet, the company prefers to call them contacts – hence, *contact* management system (contacts are prospective, actual, and past customers).

A new contact management system is to be developed internally and be available to all employees in the company, but with varying levels of access. Employees of the Customer Services Department will take ownership of the system. The system will permit flexible scheduling and rescheduling of contact-related activities so that employees can collaborate successfully to win new customers and foster existing relationships.

Telemarketing   1.5.4

Many organizations market their products and services by telemarketing, i.e. by directly contacting customers over the telephone. A telemarketing system needs to support an elaborated process of scheduling the phone calls to telemarketers, facilitating the conversation, and recording conversation outcomes.

Special aspects of a telemarketing system are heavy reliance on the database capability to actively schedule and dynamically reschedule phone calls while supporting concurrent conversations. Another interesting aspect is the capability to dial the scheduled phone numbers automatically.

Problem statement 4: telemarketing

A charitable society sells lottery tickets to raise funds. The fundraising is done in *campaigns* to support currently important charitable causes. The society keeps a list of past contributors (*supporters*). For each new campaign, a subset of these supporters is preselected for telemarketing and/or direct mail contact.

The society uses some innovative schemes to gain new supporters. These schemes include special *bonus campaigns* to reward supporters for bulk buying, for attracting new contributors, etc. The society does not randomly target potential supporters by using telephone directories or similar means.

To support its work, the society decided to contract out the development of a new telemarketing application. The new system is required to support up to fifty telemarketers working simultaneously. The system must be able to schedule the phone calls according to pre-specified priorities and other known constraints.

The system is required to dial up the scheduled phone calls. Unsuccessful connections must be rescheduled and tried again later. Telephone callbacks to supporters must also be arranged. The conversation outcomes, including ticket orders and any changes to supporter records, ought to be maintained.

Advertising expenditure   1.5.5

In the age of globalization and geographical separation of buyers and sellers, selling a product or service is not possible without spending large sums of money on advertising.

Not surprisingly, companies are profoundly interested in knowing how their advertising budgets have been used and how their advertising expenditure (and targets) compare with the expenditure (and targets) of their competitors. Such information can be bought from market research companies, which collect and analyze advertising data.

A special feature of the advertising expenditure domain is a necessary close processing alignment between collecting and storing advertising data in a transactional database and adding the latest data collections to a data warehouse. The data warehouse is then used for the analysis of collected information to produce and sell requested advertising expenditure reports.

Problem statement 5: advertising expenditure

A market research organization collects data on advertising from various media outlets: television and radio stations, newspapers, and magazines, as well as cinema, outdoor and Internet advertisers. The collected data can be analyzed in various ways to measure the advertising expenditure of companies advertising their products. The organization needs to develop an AE application.

The AE system will provide two areas of reporting to the clients of the market research organization. A client may request a report that the advertisements they paid for appeared as they were supposed to (this is called campaign monitoring). A client can also request a report outlining their competitive advertising position in their specific industry (this is called expenditure reporting). The expenditure reports capture the expenditure achieved by an advertiser or an advertised product by various criteria (time, geographical regions, media, etc.).

The expenditure reporting is the core business of the organization. In fact, any AE client (not just an advertising client) can purchase expenditure reports – in the form of custom-designed reporting software or as hard copies. The AE's customer base comprises individual advertisers, advertising agencies, media companies, and media buying consultancies, as well as sales and marketing executives, media planners, and buyers.

The AE has contractual arrangements with many media outlets to receive from them regularly electronic log files with information pertaining to the advertising content of these outlets. The log information is transferred to the AE database and is then subjected to careful verification – partly automatic and partly manual. The task of verification is to confirm that all captured advertisement details are valid and logical in the context of the surrounding information. The manual entry (monitoring) of advertisements for which there are no electronic logs remains a major part of the AE operation.

Once entered and verified, the advertisements undergo valorization – the process of assigning an expenditure estimate to an advertisement.

1.5.6 Time logging

There is a difference between application software and system software. The difference has to do with the fact that system software is a tool marketed and sold in large quantities to the public at large. Examples are word processors, spreadsheets, and database management systems. Increasingly, many such tools provide a generic solution to a well-defined application domain. Time logging is such a tool. Companies can buy a time logging tool to serve as a time and billing application that keeps track of time spent by employees on various projects and tasks.

A special feature of the time logging domain is that it produces a software tool. As such, the tool has to be attractive to buyers, very reliable in use, and designed for future production of new versions. This imposes special requirements with regard to the GUI aspect of the product, with regard to the necessary rigorous testing, and with regard to a scalable architecture of the software.

Problem statement 6: time logging

A software production company is given the task of developing a time logging tool for public sale to organizations in need of time control software for their employees. The company hopes that the TL tool will be in position to compete with the market leader – the tool called Time Logger from Responsive Software (Responsive, 2003).

The scope of the TL project is delineated by the functionality offered by the Time Logger tool. Responsive Software's website (*ibid.*) contains a detailed description of Time Logger's functions. Similar functions need to be present in the TL tool. The following points list the main functions.

The TL tool will allow employees to enter time records, i.e. time spent working on various projects and tasks and time without any work done (pauses, lunches, holidays, etc.). The time can be entered by directly (manually) recording the start and end times or by using the stopwatch facility. The stopwatch facility links to the computer clock and allows the employee to use start/stop command buttons to say when an activity started and ended.

The TL tool will allow clients for whom the work is performed to be identified. Related functions are to bill the clients, produce invoices, and keep track of payments. Work expenses can be calculated using hourly rates and/or a fixed expense component. Some activities recorded in the TL tool will not be billable to clients.

The TL tool will allow the production of customized time reports with various reporting details suppressed or added, as required by the employee.

The TL tool will allow easy changes to time records already entered. It will also provide various sorting, searching, and filtering capabilities.

Summary

This chapter looked at strategic issues of the software development process. For some readers the content of this chapter may have amounted to little more than "motherhood" statements. For readers with some experience in software development, the chapter could have delivered additional cerebral ammunition. For all readers, the intent of the chapter is to serve (not necessarily gently) as an introduction to the much more comprehensive discussions to come.

The *nature* of software development is that of a *craft* or even *art*. An outcome of a software project cannot be ascertained completely at its start. The main *accidental difficulty* in software development relates to *stakeholders* – a software product must give a tangible benefit to stakeholders; it will fail otherwise. The triangle for success includes, in addition to the stakeholders' factor, a sound *process* and the support of a *modeling language and tools*.

Software development is concerned with delivering *efficient* software products. *System planning* precedes software development and determines which products can be most *effective* to the organization. There are various ways in which system planning can be conducted. Four popular approaches were discussed: SWOT, VCM, BPR, and ISA.

Information systems are constructed for three levels of management: operational, tactical, and strategic. Systems that support the *strategic* level of decision making offer the greatest effectiveness. These are also systems that create the greatest challenges to software developers.

In the past, software products were *procedural* – a programmed procedure executed its task more or less sequentially and predictably and then terminated. The *structured development approach* has been successfully used to produce such systems.

Modern software products are *object-oriented* – a program consists of programming objects that execute randomly and unpredictably, and the program does not terminate unless closed by the user. The objects "hang around" waiting for user-generated events to start a computation; they may request services of other objects to complete the task and then become idle again but remain alert – just in case a user generates another event. Modern GUI-based client/server IS applications are object-oriented, and the *object-oriented development approach* is best equipped for production of such applications. The rest of the book concentrates on the object-oriented approach.

Software development follows a *lifecycle*. The main lifecycle phases are analysis, design, implementation, integration and deployment, and operation and maintenance. Some important activities span all lifecycle phases. They include project planning, metrics, and testing.

This book concentrates on two phases of the lifecycle: *analysis* and *design*. Other phases include implementation, integration, and maintenance. Software development comprises a range of other important activities, such as project planning, collection of metrics, testing, and change management. We do not consider any of those to be a separate phase, because they occur repeatedly throughout the lifecycle.

Modern development processes are *iterative and incremental*. The predecessor and reference model for all iterative and incremental processes is the spiral model. This observation also includes the CMM and ISO 9000 standards used for organization accreditation purposes. Other important and popular models include IBM Rational Unified Process (RUP), model-driven architecture (MDA), and agile software development.

Finally, the chapter defined the problem statements for six *case studies* used in successive chapters (alongside the guided tutorial placed in the appendix) to exemplify and explain any non-trivial modeling concepts and techniques. The case studies relate to the university enrolment, video store, contact management, telemarketing, advertising expenditure, and time logging application domains.

Questions

Q1 Based on your experiences with software products, how would you interpret Fred Brooks's observation that the *essence of software engineering* is determined by inherent software complexity, conformity, changeability, and invisibility? How would you explain these four factors? How is software engineering different from traditional engineering, such as civil or mechanical engineering?

Q2 This chapter defines the notion of a *component* as an executable unit of software with well-defined functionality (services) and communication protocols (interfaces) to other components. How is this notion of component linked to the concepts of package, subsystem, and module?

Q3 This chapter argues that *software production is an art or craft*. This observation can be supplemented with the quotation that "Art is a collaboration between God and the artist, and the less the artist does, the better" (André Gide). What lesson, if any, is this quotation providing to software developers? Do you agree with it?

Q4 Recall the definition of a *stakeholder*. Is a software vendor or a technical support person a stakeholder? Explain.

Q5 Which *CMM level of maturity* is needed for an organization to be able to respond successfully to a crisis situation? Explain.

Q6 When explaining the SWOT approach to system planning, the book states that in a good mission statement emphasis is placed on customer needs rather than on the products or services that an organization delivers. Explain and exemplify how targeting the products or services in the *mission statement* can defeat the *effectiveness* objective of system planning.

Q7 Explain the observation that the ISA approach is a convenient framework for the "divide and conquer" method in the realization of large and complex systems.

Q8 Explain how a BPR *business process* relates to the notion of *workflow*.

Q9 What are the three *management levels*? Consider a banking application that monitors the usage patterns of a credit card by its holder in order to block the card automatically when the bank suspects misuse (theft, fraud, etc.). Which management level is addressed by such an application? Give reasons.

Q10 What are the main modeling techniques in the structured development approach?

Q11 What are the main reasons for the shift from the structured to object-oriented development approach?

Q12 An object-oriented system should be *designed for integration*. What does this mean?

Q13 System planning and software metrics are inherently correlated. Explain why this is so.

Q14 Explain the relationship between traceability and testing.

Q15 How does RUP relate to the spiral model?

Q16 Explain how MDA uses and integrates the four OMG standards – UML, MOF, XMI, and CWM. Search the Internet for the latest information on these standards.

Q17 Briefly explain the following three agile development approaches – extreme programming (XP), aspect-oriented software development, and feature-driven development. Compare the second and the third approach with XP from the generic viewpoint of emphasis placed on the phases of the analysis–design–implementation cycle. Search the Internet for information on these approaches.

Answers to odd-numbered questions

Q1 – answer

The Brooks paper (Brooks, 1987) is really concerned with the identification of *reasons for failures of software projects*. Some reasons for failures are a consequence of "essential difficulties" and are therefore invariant. Other reasons – "accidental difficulties" – can be controlled, managed, and perhaps restrained.

The four essential difficulties are (1) complexity, (2) conformity, (3) changeability, and (4) invisibility. The first difficulty – *complexity* – is the most intractable. Many software problems derive from it and from its exponential growth with software size (where "size" can be determined by the number of possible states of the program and the number of communication paths between software objects). Any scaling-up of software always faces a combinatorial explosion in software complexity. "Development in the large" is very different to "development in the small." The difficulty is inherent. It can be constrained only by applying good design practices based on "divide and conquer" approaches and hierarchical layering of software modules (Maciaszek and Liong, 2004).

As opposed to natural systems (such as are studied in biology or physics), the complexity of software is aggravated by three other essential difficulties: conformity, changeability, and invisibility. Software systems have to *conform* to a human-made, messy, and random environment. Being part of this human environment, a new software system must conform to already established "interfaces", no matter how unreasonable they may be.

Software is a model of reality set in a human-made environment. As the environment changes, (so far) successful software is subject to pressures for *change*. The change demands frequently go beyond what is feasible or practical.

Finally, software is an intangible object. It cannot be pinpointed in space. If software is *invisible*, then it cannot be readily *visualizable*. The problem is not in a lack of graphical modeling representations for the software (this book is mostly about such representations!). The point is that no *single* graphical model can fully represent the structure and behavior of software. Developers have to work with a large number of graphical abstractions, superimposed one upon another, to represent a software system – a truly difficult task, in particular if the models are incapable of dividing the solution space into hierarchical layers.

The difference between software and traditional engineering can be established from Brooks's observation that the above four *difficulties* are an essential property of software, but only accidental properties in traditional engineering.

Any attempt to describe software to abstract away its complexity, conformity, changeability, or invisibility frequently also abstracts away the software essence. A software engineer is in the unenviable position of often not being able to ignore (abstract away) some aspects of the problem, because all of them constitute an intertwined essence of the solution. Sooner rather than later, all ignored properties must be reinstated in successive models and the models have to be conveniently linked for complete interpretation. The lesson is clear – *a great software developer is first and foremost a great abstractionist.*

Q3 – answer

This question is related to question 1 above. If we acknowledge essential difficulties in software engineering, then we have no choice but to try to harness these difficulties by delivering *simple solutions*.

"Simple" does not mean "simplistic." Simple, in this context, means "just right" for the users and "easy enough" for developers – not too creative, not too ambitious, without unnecessary bells and whistles. The analysis of completed software projects consistently shows that users are distracted only by unnecessary and complex features. Indeed, some projects fail precisely as a result of such unnecessary complications.

Perhaps the most important advice that a novice developer can get is contained in the *KISS (keep it simple, stupid)* acronym. There is also an equally unflattering version of Murphy's law: *"Build a system that even a fool can use, and only a fool will use it."*

Q5 – answer

An organization would need to be at least at *level 3* of CMM maturity to respond successfully to a crisis situation. An organization at *level 1* relies on key individuals for process management. The process itself is not documented. Even if the development is guided by some established procedures, there is no understanding of how these procedures should change to react to a crisis.

An organization at *level 2* has an intuitive process derived from past experiences. A crisis situation introduces an unfamiliar aspect to the process and is likely to cause the process to break down. If the organization is able to learn from the crisis, then the improvements to its process can make it more resilient in the face of future adversities.

An organization at *level 3* of process maturity has the processes codified and followed for all projects. When faced with a crisis, the organization will not panic and will continue to use the defined process. This "steady as it goes" principle can restore orderliness and calm to the project management, which may be sufficient to overcome the crisis. However, if the crisis is of large proportions, then *level 3* may also be insufficient ("steady as it goes" may turn out to be "steady as it sinks").

Q7 – answer
ISA provides a framework within which manageable system development units can be addressed with various *perspectives* and *descriptions*. With ISA, the development resources can be allocated to the individual *cells* (intersections of perspectives and descriptions), thus facilitating development process and control. The related benefits of ISA include:

- improved communication between stakeholders;
- identification of tools that best support various development cells;
- identification of areas of development strengths and weaknesses;
- integration and placement of development methods and tools in relation to one another;
- providing the basis for risk assessment.

Q9 – answer
The three levels of management are (1) strategic, (2) tactical, and (3) operational. An IS application at the lowest level of decision making (i.e. the operational level) processes business data into *information*. An IS application at the highest level processes business data into *knowledge*. The upward movement through the levels of decision making coincides with the desire to turn information into knowledge. Having knowledge gives an organization a competitive advantage.

The banking application for credit card monitoring belongs to at least the tactical management level. It involves *analytical* rather than *transactional* processing. It analyses credit card transactions against such issues as:

- typical card usage patterns by the card owner;
- probability of fraud based on the location (e.g. country) where the card has been used;
- if the card has been used to withdraw money (for which a PIN has to be entered);
- if the owner has been checking the account over the Internet or by phone (for which a user ID and password have to be entered);
- any past problems with the card;
- if the owner can be reached by phone (before the card is blocked by the bank, an attempt to contact the owner by phone must be made).

Q11 – answer
The object-oriented technology is not "a new kid on the block." In fact, it dates back to the language called Simula developed in the late 1960s. The center stage that object technology takes today is due to a number of factors. The most important factor relates to the advances in hardware, in particular GUIs (graphical user interfaces), which have *enabled* the widespread application of object solutions. Modern GUIs demand *event-driven programming*, which is best served by object technology.

The shift to object-oriented development is also driven by the needs of *new applications* that can be implemented on modern hardware/software platforms. Two main categories of such applications are *workgroup computing* and *multimedia systems*.

Object-oriented technology is also essential for addressing the ever-growing *application backlog* of large systems that are difficult to maintain and even more difficult to re-engineer into modern solutions. *Object wrapping* is a promising approach to fight the application backlog.

Q13 – answer
Gathering the *metrics* of software process and software product is relatively meaningless the first time it is done in an IT organization. The metrics start being useful when they are linked on project completion to such issues as project duration and expended budget. Once such correlation between software metrics and *planning targets* is known for one project, the next project can be planned better.

Metrics from a current project can be compared with what happened on the previous project. If the metrics are comparable with those obtained before, then the system planning can assume that the planning constraints (time, money, etc.) will be comparable as well. This is particularly true if the development team is unchanged, the processes are similar, the application is in the same domain area (e.g. the domain of accounting applications), and the customer base is analogous.

If the metrics are taken consistently on many projects, then the benefits to system planning are even greater. More metrics means more planning precision and the possibility of finding useful past metrics for planning of untypical projects and for modifying plans due to changed circumstances.

Q15 – answer
RUP is a commercial development framework, while the spiral model is a rather theoretical concept. Risking some discord, RUP can be seen as an implementation of the spiral model. Because RUP is a customizable framework, it can be tailored to define a process in which each iteration follows the spiral of planning–risk analysis–engineering–customer evaluation.

As a customized process framework, RUP specifies activities and methods that unify developers and customers. RUP also offers patterns, workflows, templates of documents, project dashboards, and development guidance. The spiral model does not address project management issues and does not propose any specific development practices.

To adhere to the spiral model, a particular RUP process must consider the main concerns of the spiral model in each iteration. These concerns include cyclic changes to schedules and budget, adjustments based on user objectives and constraints, risk identification and resolution, a readiness to kill the project purely on the basis of risk analysis, and engineering activities resulting in prototypes and artifacts that can be immediately evaluated by customers.

Q17 – answer
Extreme programming (XP) is the original, most popular, and most comprehensive of agile development methods. Although it has "programming" in its name, it is really an approach to a software development lifecycle.

XP embraces object technology and embodies some of the best practices of object-oriented development. The practices include development to user stories by on-site customers, test-driven development, pair programming, streamlining of code and improving the design through refactoring, and time-boxed small releases of code to customers. These practices are integrated in a well-defined process.

Aspect-oriented software development is an architecture-centric framework. It emphasizes modularization of software according to so called crosscutting concerns. The concerns can be of various granularity and can be functional or non-functional. Examples of concerns are system security, required concurrency level, and object caching strategy. The argument is that development by concerns (or aspects) delivers scalable solutions with stable architecture resistant to refactoring.

The concerns are programmed separately and factored out of the application code. Because existing programming languages lack the facilities for factoring out the aspect code and rejoining it to the main application code, aspect programming demands special tools (such as AspectJ) to separate application logic and crosscutting concerns. In AspectJ, a rejoining point is any well-defined instant in the execution of the program. This can be an entry or return from a method or an object construction.

Compared with XP, aspect development is merely a programming technique, albeit with an influence on architectural design. As such, aspect programming can be used as an alternative to the frequent refactoring advocated in XP.

Feature-driven development consists of five processes: (1) development of an overall business object model; (2) construction of a features list; (3) planning by feature; (4) designing by feature; and (5) building by feature. Process 1 is done by domain experts and produces a high-level class diagram. Process 2 delivers functional decomposition reminiscent of data flow diagrams. The decomposition is done by subject areas, business activities, and business activity step. Features at the bottom of functional decomposition should not demand more than two weeks of work. Such features are broken down into discrete milestones. The remaining three processes create a plan–design–build cycle. Features are prioritized, designed one feature at a time, and built using extensive unit testing.

Compared with XP, feature-driven development covers similar parts of the lifecycle, i.e. analysis–design–implementation. However, XP iterations lean more on implementation, whereas feature-driven development follows a more classic lifecycle that depends on analysis/design prior to any programming.

Chapter

2

Requirements Determination

Requirements determination is about social, communication, and managerial skills. This is the least technical phase of system development but, if not done thoroughly, the consequences are more serious than in other phases. The downstream costs of not capturing, omitting or misinterpreting customer requirements may prove unsustainable later in the process.

This chapter introduces a broad spectrum of issues in requirements determination. The first part of the chapter distinguishes between functional and non-functional requirements and explains the methods of requirements elicitation, negotiation, and validation, as well as the principles of requirements management.

The second part of the chapter introduces basic graphical modeling techniques for describing a business model relevant to an organization and to a targeted application domain. The structure of a requirements document is also discussed.

2.1 Functional and non-functional requirements

System planning (Section 1.2) defines strategic directions for an organization. Among these strategic decisions is the selection of information systems to be developed. *Requirements determination* is the first phase in the system development lifecycle. The purpose of requirements determination is to provide a narrative definition of functional and other requirements that the stakeholders expect to be satisfied in the implemented and deployed system.

As noted in Section 1.4.2.1.1, requirements define the expected services of the system (*service statements*) and constraints that the system must obey (*constraint statements*). The service statements constitute the system's *functional requirements*. Functional requirements can be grouped into those that describe the scope of the system, the necessary business functions, and the required data structures.

The constraint statements can be classified according to different categories of restriction imposed on the system, such as the required system's "look and feel," performance, and security. The constraint statements constitute the system's *non-functional requirements*. Non-functional requirements are also known as *supplementary requirements*.

Functional requirements need to be obtained from customers (users and system owners). This is a *requirements elicitation* activity conducted by a business (or system) analyst. There are many techniques that can be employed, starting from traditional interviews of customers and culminating (if necessary) in building a software prototype through which to discover more requirements.

The collected functional requirements must be subjected to careful analysis to eliminate duplications and contradictions. This invariably leads to *requirements reviews and renegotiations* with the customers. The agreed-upon set of functional requirements is modeled using graphical notations and further defined in text.

Non-functional requirements are not behavioral in nature. They are constraints on the development and implementation of the system. The level of adherence to these constraints determines software quality. Non-functional requirements can be divided into requirements that relate to (Lethbridge and Laganiere, 2001; Ghezzi *et al.*, 2003; Maciaszek and Liong, 2004):

- usability
- reusability
- reliability
- performance
- efficiency
- supportability
- other constraints.

Usability defines the ease of use of the system. A system is more usable when it is easier to use. Usability is determined by such issues as documentation and help facilities, the training necessary for efficient and effective use, the aesthetics and consistency of the user interface, error handling, etc. Usability is a bit in the eye of the beholder. What is usable for an expert user may be unusable for a novice, and vice versa.

Reusability defines the ease of reuse of previously implemented software components in new system developments. "Software component" is understood here loosely to mean any part of implemented software or even an idea (pattern) that can be reused. Reuse applies to interfaces, classes, packages, frameworks, etc. Reusability is a reflection on the maturity of software development teams and on software engineering as an industrial field.

Reliability relates to the frequency and the seriousness of system failures and how gracefully the system can recover from failures. Reliability is determined by the demanded availability of the system during its operational hours, acceptable mean time between failures, accuracy of produced results, etc. A reliable system is a dependable system – the user can depend on it.

Performance is defined by expectations regarding the response time of the system, transactions throughput, resource consumption, possible number of concurrent users, etc. Performance demands may differ for different business functions, for pick workloads (pick times), for different users.

Efficiency relates to the cost and time of achieving software outcomes and objectives, including the expected level of performance. Efficiency relates to the cost of hardware, software, people, and other resources. A more efficient system uses less resources to perform the same tasks.

Supportability is a set of three constraints: understandability, maintainability, and scalability. Supportability is the ease with which the system can be understood, corrected, perfected, and extended. Supportability is determined by the clarity and simplicity of the architectural design and the faithfulness of the implementation to the design.

The notion of *other constraints* defines all other non-functional requirements for a system. Issues that belong in this category include policy decisions about project infrastructure, legal issues that may affect the project, demanded level of software portability, system inter-operability requirements, and timeliness of product delivery.

Once acceptable to customers, the requirements are defined, classified, numbered, and prioritized in the *requirements document*. This document is structured according to a *template* chosen in the organization for documenting requirements.

Although the requirements document is largely a narrative document, a high-level diagrammatic *business model* is likely to be included. The business model will normally consist of a *system scope model*, a *business use case model* and a *business class model*.

Customer requirements are a moving target. To handle volatile requirements, we need to be able to manage change. *Requirements management* includes activities such as estimating the impact of the change on other requirements and on the rest of the system.

Requirements elicitation

2.2

A *business analyst* discovers the system requirements through consultation, which involves *customers* and *experts* in the problem domain. In some cases, the business analyst has sufficient domain experience, and the help of a domain expert may not be required. A `Business Analyst` is then a kind of `Domain Expert`, as modeled with a generalization relationship in Figure 2.1. (The figure uses the notation of the UML use-case model, which is explained in detail in Chapter 3. Here, the use-case notation is used only for its convenience.)

Requirements elicited from domain experts constitute the domain knowledge. They capture widely acknowledged time-independent business rules and processes applicable to typical organizations and systems. Requirements elicited from customers are expressed in use-case scenarios. They go beyond the basic domain knowledge and capture the unique character of the organization – the way the business is done here and now or how it should be done.

The task of a business analyst is to combine the two sets of requirements into a business model. As shown in Figure 2.1 by means of aggregation relationships (signified with a diamond on the lines), the `Business Model` contains a `Business Class Model` and `Business Use Case Model`.

The `Business Class Model` is a high-level class diagram. A class is an abstraction that describes a set of objects with common attributes, operations, relationships, and semantic constraints. A class model identifies and relates together *business objects* – the fundamental classes in the business domain.

The `Business Use Case Model` is a high-level use-case diagram that identifies major functional building blocks in the system. The model represents business use cases, relationships between them and how business actors interact with them.

Figure 2.1
Influences during
requirements
determination

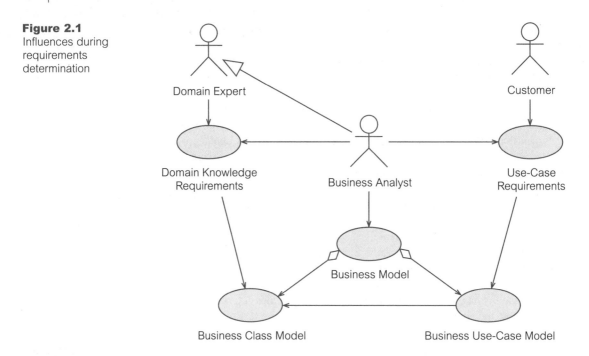

In general, domain classes (business objects) do not have to be derived from or result from use cases (cf. Rumbaugh, 1994). In practice, however, a `Business Class Model` should be validated against the `Business Use Case Model`. The validation is likely to lead to some adjustments or extensions in the `Business Class Model`.

Following Hoffer *et al.* (2002), this book distinguishes between traditional and modern methods of fact finding and information gathering.

2.2.1 Traditional methods of requirements elicitation

Traditional methods of requirements elicitation include interviews, questionnaires, observation, and study of business documents. These are simple and cost-effective methods. The effectiveness of traditional methods is inversely proportional to the degree of *risk* of the project. High risk implies that the system is difficult to implement – even the high-level requirements are not quite clear. In such projects traditional methods are unlikely to suffice.

2.2.1.1 Interviewing customers and domain experts

Interviews are a primary technique of fact finding and information gathering. Most interviews are conducted with customers. Interviews with customers elicit mostly "use-case" requirements (Figure 2.1). Domain experts can also be interviewed if the business analyst does not have sufficient domain knowledge. Interviews with domain experts are frequently a simple knowledge transfer process – a learning exercise for the business analyst.

Interviews with customers are more complex (Sommerville and Sawyer, 1997; Kotonya and Sommerville, 1998). Customers may have only a vague picture of their requirements. They may be unwilling to cooperate or be unable to express their requirements in understandable terms. They may also demand requirements that exceed the project budget or that are not implementable. Finally, it is likely that the requirements of different customers may be in conflict.

There are two basic kinds of interview: structured (formal) and unstructured (informal). A *structured interview* is prepared in advance and has a clear agenda, and many questions are predetermined. Some questions may be *open-ended* (for which possible responses cannot be anticipated); others may be *closed-ended* (with the answer to be picked from a range of provided answers).

Structured interviews need to be supplemented with *unstructured interviews*. Unstructured interviews are more like informal meetings, with no predetermined questions or anticipated objectives. The purpose of an unstructured interview is to encourage the customer to speak his/her mind and in the process lead to requirements that the business analyst would not have expected and would not, therefore, ask questions about.

Both structured and unstructured interviews must provide some starting point and context for discussion. This may be a short written document or email sent to the interviewee prior to the meeting explaining the interviewer's objective or posing some questions.

Three kinds of question should, in general, be avoided (cf. Whitten and Bentley, 1998):

1. *opinionated questions*, in which the interviewer expresses (directly or indirectly) his/her opinion on the issue ("do we have to do things the way we do them?");

2. *biased questions*, similar to opinionated, except that the interviewer's opinion is clearly biased ("you are not going to do this, are you?");

3. *imposing questions*, which assume the answer in the question ("you do things this way, don't you?").

Lethbridge and Laganiere (2001) point to the following categories of question that ought to be asked during an interview:

- Questions about *specific details* for any issue raised during interview. Ask about the five w's: what, who, when, where, and why.

- Questions about *vision for the future*. Interviewees are likely to be blissfully unaware of various system constraints and may be coming up with very innovative, yet unimplementable, ideas.

- Questions about *alternative ideas*. These may be equally well questions to an interviewee and suggestions from the interviewer asking for opinions.

- Questions about a *minimally acceptable solution* to the problem. Good usable systems are simple systems. Finding out what is the minimally acceptable solution is therefore essential for determining a workable scope of the system.

- Questions about *other sources of information*. These questions can discover important documents and other knowledge sources hitherto unknown to the interviewer.

- Questions *soliciting diagrams*. Simple graphical models drawn by an interviewee to explain business processes may prove invaluable for understanding the requirements.

There are many factors to a successful interview, but perhaps the most important are the interviewer's *communication and interpersonal* skills. While the interviewer asks questions and maintains control, it is equally important to listen carefully and be patient so that the interviewee is at ease. To ascertain correct understanding, the interviewer should seek confirmation by paraphrasing the interviewee's statements back to him/her.

To maintain good interpersonal rapport and to obtain additional feedback, a memorandum summarizing the interview should be sent to the interviewee within a day or two, along with a request for comments.

2.2.1.2 Questionnaires

Questionnaires are an efficient way of gathering information from many customers. Questionnaires are normally used in addition to interviews, not in lieu of them. An exception may be a low-risk project with well-understood objectives. In such a project, the passive nature and lesser depth of a questionnaire may suffice.

In general, questionnaires are less productive than interviews, because no clarification can be sought to the questions or to possible responses. Questionnaires are passive – this is both an advantage and a disadvantage. It is an advantage because the respondent has time to consider the responses and can remain anonymous. It is a disadvantage because the respondent does not have an easy opportunity to clarify the questions.

A questionnaire should be designed for ease of question answering. In particular, open-ended questions should be avoided – most questions should be closed-ended. *Closed-ended questions* can take three forms (Whitten and Bentley, 1998):

1. *Multiple-choice questions*, where the respondent must pick one or more answers from the set of answers provided. An additional commentary from the respondent may also be allowed.
2. *Rating questions*, where the respondent has to express his/her opinion about a statement. Possible ratings can be strongly agree, agree, neutral, disagree, strongly agree, and don't know.
3. *Ranking questions*, where the answers provided should be ranked with sequential numbers, percentage values, or similar ordering means.

A well-designed, easy-to-answer questionnaire will encourage respondents to return the completed document promptly. However, when evaluating the questionnaire results, the business analyst should consider possible distortions due to the fact that people who did not respond would have been likely to provide different responses (cf. Hoffer *et al.*, 2002).

2.2.1.3 Observation

There are situations where the business analyst finds it difficult to obtain complete information through interviews and questionnaires. The customer may be unable to convey the information effectively or may have only fragmentary knowledge of a complete business process. In such cases, *observation* may be an effective fact-finding technique. After all, the best way to learn how to tie a tie is by observing the process.

Observation can take three forms:

1. *Passive observation*, where the business analyst observes business activities without interruption or direct involvement. In some cases, video cameras may be used for even less intrusive observation.

2. *Active observation*, where the business analyst participates in the activities and effectively becomes part of the team.

3. *Explanatory observation*, where the user explains his/her activities to the observer while doing the job.

To be representative, observations should be carried out for a prolonged period of time, at different time intervals, and at different workloads (pick times).

The main difficulty with observation is that people tend to behave differently when they are watched. In particular, they tend to work according to formal rules and procedures. This distorts the reality by hiding any work shortcuts – positive or negative. We ought to remember that "work to rule" is an effective form of industrial action.

Study of documents and software systems   2.2.1.4

The *study of documents and software systems* is an invaluable technique for finding both use-case requirements and domain knowledge requirements. The technique is always used, although it may target only the selective aspects of the system.

Use-case requirements are discovered through studies of existing organization documents and system forms/reports (if a computerized solution for the current system exists, as is typically the case in large organizations). One of the most valuable insights into use-case requirements is the record (if one exists) of defects and change requests for an existing system.

Organization documents to study include business forms (completed, if possible), work procedures, job descriptions, policy manuals, business plans, organizational charts, inter-office correspondence, minutes of meetings, accounting records, external correspondence, and customer complaints.

System forms and reports to study include computer screens and reports, together with the associated documentation – system operating manuals, user documentation, technical documentation, and system analysis and design models.

Domain knowledge requirements are discovered by researching business domain journals and reference books. The studies of proprietary software packages, such as enterprise resource planning systems (ERPs), can also provide a wealth of domain knowledge. Hence, visits to libraries and software vendors are a part of the requirements elicitation process (although the Internet allows many such "visits" to be accomplished without leaving the office).

Modern methods of requirements elicitation   **2.2.2**

Modern methods of requirements elicitation include the use of software prototypes, brainstorming, joint application development (JAD), and rapid application development (RAD).

They offer better insights into the requirements, but at a higher cost and effort. However, the long-term payoff may be very rewarding.

Modern methods are typically employed when the *risk* of the project is high. The factors for high project risks are many. They include unclear objectives, undocumented procedures, unstable requirements, eroded user expertise, inexperienced developers, and insufficient user commitment.

2.2.2.1 Prototyping

Prototyping is the most frequently used method of modern requirements elicitation. Software prototypes are constructed to visualize the system, or just part of it, to customers in order to obtain their feedback. A *prototype* is a demonstration system – a "quick and dirty" working model of the solution that presents a graphical user interface (GUI) and simulates the system behavior for various user events. The information content of GUI screens is hard-coded in the prototype program rather than obtained dynamically from the database.

The complexity (and the growing customer expectations) of modern GUIs makes prototyping an indispensable element in software development. The feasibility and usefulness of the system can be estimated through prototypes well before real implementation is undertaken.

In general, a system prototype is a very effective way of eliciting requirements difficult to obtain from customers by other means. This is frequently the case with systems that are to deliver new business functionality. This is also the case with conflicting requirements or when communication problems exist between customers and developers.

There are two kinds of prototype (cf. Kotonya and Sommerville, 1998):

1. The *"throw-away" prototype*, which is to be discarded when the requirements elicitation is completed. The "throw-away" prototype targets the requirements determination phase of the lifecycle. It typically concentrates on the least understood requirements.

2. The *evolutionary prototype*, which is retained after requirements elicitation and used to produce the final product. The evolutionary prototype targets the speed of product delivery. It typically concentrates on well-understood requirements so that the first version of the product can be delivered quickly (although with incomplete functionality).

An additional argument in favor of the "throw-away" prototype is that it avoids the risk of retaining "quick and dirty" or otherwise inefficient solutions in the final product. However, the power and flexibility of contemporary software production tools have weakened that argument. There is no reason why in a well-managed project inefficient prototype solutions cannot be eradicated.

2.2.2.2 Brainstorming

Brainstorming is a conference technique to form new ideas or to find a solution to a specific problem by putting aside judgment, social inhibitions, and rules (Brainstorming, 2003). In general, brainstorming is not for problem analysis or for decision making. It is for generating new ideas and possible solutions. The analysis and decision making is done afterwards and does not involve brainstorming techniques.

Brainstorming applies to requirements elicitation because of the difficulty of reaching consensus among stakeholders on what the concrete requirements are. Moreover, stakeholders tend to have a narrow view of requirements – a view that corresponds to what they are most familiar with.

Brainstorming requires a person who will lead and moderate the session – the facilitator. Prior to the meeting, the facilitator should define the problem/opportunity area for which ideas will be generated. This is known as *probortunity statement* (ibid). The term "probortunity" is the merging of the words "problem" and "opportunity" (this merging also removes the negative connotation of the word "problem").

The probortunity statement defines a scope for brainstorming and takes forms such as question, challenge, concern, difficulty, mystery, or puzzle. In the case of requirements elicitation, the probortunity statement is likely to consist of *trigger questions*.

Lethbridge and Laganiere (2001) give the following examples of trigger questions in a brainstorming session targeting requirements elicitation:

- What features should be supported by the system?
- What are the input data and what are the outputs of the system?
- What classes are needed in the business or domain object model?
- What questions should be raised in interviews or in questionnaires?
- What issues still need to be considered?
- What are the main risks in the project?
- What trigger questions should be asked during this or future brainstorming sessions?

The brainstorming session should be restricted to twelve–twenty people sitting in a circle. A large round table is best for the purpose. The idea is that the facilitator is just "one of the crowd" and all participants feel equal. The session inventory should include notepads, pens, large flipcharts behind each two–three participants, and a projector to present the probortunity statement and trigger questions.

During the session, participants think of answers to trigger questions and either shout them for writing down or write them down on sheets of paper, one idea per sheet. The latter approach is normally preferred, because it does not intimidate people. The answers may then be passed in a circular way to the next person on the left. This serves the purpose of stimulating people to generate even more ideas.

This process lasts until no new ideas are forthcoming or after a fixed period of time (e.g. 15 minutes) passes (Lethbridge and Laganiere, 2001). At this point, participants are asked to read the ideas on the sheets in front of them, likely from other participants (this ensures anonymity). The ideas are written down on a flipchart. A brief discussion may follow.

In the last stage of the meeting, the group takes votes to prioritize the ideas. This can be done by assigning a certain number of votes to each participant. A good technique is to distribute a fixed number of small sticky PostIt notes to each participant and let the participants stick the notes next to the ideas on the flipchart. The counts of notes next to the ideas is the final vote.

2.2.2.3   Joint application development

Joint application development (JAD) is a brainstorming-like technique. It is what the name implies – a joint application development in one or more workshops that bring together all stakeholders (customers and developers) (Wood and Silver, 1995). JAD is included here in modern methods of requirements elicitation, although the technique has a long history. It was introduced (by IBM) in the late 1970s.

There are many JAD brands, and there are many consulting firms that offer the service of organizing and running a JAD session. A JAD meeting can take a few hours, a few days or even a couple of weeks. The number of participants should not exceed 25 to 30. The meeting's participants are (cf. Whitten and Bentley, 1998; Hoffer *et al.*, 2002):

- *Leader* – the person who conducts and moderates the meeting. This person has excellent communication skills, is not a stakeholder in the project (apart from being a JAD leader), and has a good knowledge of the business domain (but not necessarily good software development knowledge).

- *Scribe* – the person who records the JAD session on computer. This person should have touch-typing skills and should possess strong knowledge of software development. The scribe can use CASE tools to document the session and to develop initial solution models.

- *Customers* (*users and managers*) – these are the main participants, who communicate and discuss requirements, take decisions, approve project objectives, etc.

- *Developers* – business analysts and other members of the development team. They listen rather than speak – they are at the meeting to find facts and gather information, not to dominate the process.

JAD capitalizes on group dynamics. "Group synergy" is likely to produce better solutions to problems. Groups increase productivity, learn faster, make more educated judgments, eliminate more errors, take riskier decisions (this may be a negative though!), focus participants' attention on the most important issues, integrate people, etc.

When conducted according to the rules, JAD sessions tend to deliver surprisingly good outcomes. But be warned, 'Ford Motor Co. in the 1950s experienced a marketing disaster with the Edsel – a car designed by a committee' (Wood and Silver, 1995, pp.176).

2.2.2.4   Rapid application development

Rapid application development (RAD) is more than a requirements elicitation method. It is an approach to software development as a whole (Hoffer *et al.*, 2002). As the name suggests, RAD aims at delivering system solutions fast. Technical excellence is secondary to the speed of delivery.

According to Wood and Silver (1995), RAD combines five techniques:

1. Evolutionary prototyping (Section 2.2.2.1).

2. CASE tools with code generation and round-trip engineering between the design models and the code.

3. Specialists with advanced tools (SWAT) – the RAD development team. The best analysts, designers, and programmers that the organization can get. The team works under a strict time regime and is co-located with the users.

4. Interactive JAD – a JAD session (Section 2.2.2.3) during which the scribe is replaced by the SWAT team with CASE tools.

5. Timeboxing – a project management method that imposes a fixed time period (timebox) on the SWAT team to complete the project. The method forbids "scope creep"; if the project is running late, the scope of the solution is trimmed down to allow the project to complete on time.

The RAD approach may be an attractive proposition for many projects, in particular smaller projects that are not in the organization's core business area and that do not, therefore, set the agenda for other development projects. Fast solutions are unlikely to be optimal or sustainable for core business areas. Problems associated with RAD include:

- inconsistent GUI designs;
- specialized rather than generic solutions to facilitate software reuse;
- deficient documentation;
- software that is difficult to maintain and scale up.

Requirements negotiation and validation 2.3

Requirements elicited from customers may overlap or conflict. Some requirements may be ambiguous or unrealistic. Other requirements may remain undiscovered. For these reasons, requirements need to be negotiated and validated before they find their way into the requirements document.

In reality, *requirements negotiation and validation* are done in parallel with *requirements elicitation*. As requirements are elicited, they are subjected to a certain degree of scrutiny. This is naturally so with all modern techniques of requirements elicitation that involve so-called *group dynamics*. Nevertheless, once the elicited requirements are put together, they still need to undergo careful negotiation and validation.

Requirements negotiation and validation cannot be dissociated from the process of writing up a requirements document. *Requirements negotiation* is typically based on a draft of the document. The requirements listed in the document draft are negotiated and modified, if necessary. Spurious requirements are removed. Newly discovered requirements are added.

Requirements validation requires a more complete version of the requirements document, with all requirements clearly identified and classified. Stakeholders read the document and conduct formal review meetings. *Reviews* are frequently structured into so-called *walkthroughs* or *inspections*. Reviews are a form of *testing*.

Out-of-scope requirements 2.3.1

The choice of IT projects and, therefore, the systems to be implemented (and the broad scope of them) are determined during the *system planning* activities (Section 1.2). However, the detailed interdependencies between the systems can only be uncovered during the *requirements analysis* phase. It is the task of requirements analysis to determine the *system boundary* (*system scope*) so that "scope creep" can be addressed early in the process.

To be able to decide if any particular requirement is within or outside the system scope, a reference model, against which to take such a decision, is needed. Historically, such a reference model has been provided by a *context diagram* – the top-level diagram of the popular structured modeling technique called data flow diagrams (DFD). Although DFDs have been superseded in UML by the use-case diagrams, the context diagram is still a superior method of establishing the system boundary.

However, there may be other reasons why a requirement can be classified as being outside the scope (cf. Sommerville and Sawyer, 1997). For example, a requirement may be too difficult to implement in the computerized system and should be left to a human process, or the requirement may have a low priority and be excluded from the first version of the system. A requirement may also be implemented in the hardware or other external device and be beyond the control of the software system.

2.3.2 Requirements dependency matrix

Assuming that all requirements are clearly identified and numbered (Section 2.4.1), a *requirements dependency matrix* (or *interaction matrix*) can be constructed (cf. Sommerville and Sawyer, 1997; Kotonya and Sommerville, 1998). The matrix lists requirement identifiers in sorted order in the row and column headings, as shown in Table 2.1.

The upper right part of the matrix (above and including the diagonal) is not used. The remaining cells indicate whether or not any two requirements overlap, are in conflict, or are independent (empty cells).

Conflicting requirements should be discussed with customers and reformulated where possible to alleviate conflicts (and a record of the conflict, visible to subsequent development, should be kept). *Overlapping requirements* should also be restated to eliminate overlaps.

The requirements dependency matrix is a simple but effective technique for finding conflicts and overlaps when the number of requirements is relatively small. When this is not the case, then the technique may still be used if requirements are grouped into categories and then compared separately in each category.

Table 2.1 Requirements dependency matrix

Requirement	R1	R2	R3	R4
R1				
R2	Conflict			
R3				
R4		Overlap	Overlap	

Requirements risks and priorities   2.3.3

Once conflicts and overlaps in requirements have been resolved and a revised set of requirements is produced, they need to undergo risk analysis and prioritization. *Risk analysis* identifies requirements that are likely to cause development difficulties. *Prioritization* is needed to allow easy rescoping of the project when faced with delays.

The *feasibility* of the project is contingent on the amount of risk that the project carries. *Risk* is a threat to the project plan (budget, time, resource allocation, etc.). By identifying risks, the project manager can attempt to control them. Requirements may be "risky" due to a variety of factors. Typical risk categories are (cf. Sommerville and Sawyer, 1997):

- *technical risk* – when a requirement is technically difficult to implement;
- *performance risk* – when a requirement, when implemented, can adversely affect the response time of the system;
- *security risk* – when a requirement, when implemented, can expose the system to security breaches;
- *database integrity risk* – when a requirement cannot easily be validated and can cause data inconsistency;
- *development process risk* – when a requirement calls for the use of unconventional development methods unfamiliar to developers (e.g. formal specification methods);
- *political risk* – when a requirement may prove difficult to fulfill for internal political reasons;
- *legal risk* – when a requirement may fall foul of current laws or anticipated changes to the law;
- *volatility risk* – when a requirement is likely to keep changing or evolving during the development process.

Ideally, requirements *priorities* are obtained from individual customers first in a requirements elicitation process. They are then negotiated in meetings and modified again when the risk factors are attached to them.

To eliminate ambiguity and to facilitate priority assignment, the number of priority classifications should be small. Three to five different priorities are usual. They can be named "high," "medium," "low," "not sure." An alternative list might be "essential," "useful," "hardly matters," "to be decided."

Requirements management   2.4

Requirements have to be managed. *Requirements management* is really a part of an overall project management. It is concerned with three main issues:

1. Identifying, classifying, organizing, and documenting the requirements.
2. Requirements changes (i.e. with processes that set out how inevitable changes to requirements are proposed, negotiated, validated, and documented).

3. Requirements traceability (i.e. with processes that maintain dependency relationships between requirements and other system artifacts as well as between the requirements themselves).

2.4.1 Requirements identification and classification

Requirements are described in *natural language statements*, such as:

- "The system shall schedule the next phone call to a customer upon the telemarketer's request."

- "The system shall automatically dial the scheduled phone number and simultaneously display on the telemarketer's screen customer information, including phone number, customer number, and customer name."

- "Upon successful connection, the system shall display an introductory text that the telemarketer should communicate to the customer to establish conversation."

A typical system would consist of hundreds or thousands of requirements statements like those above. To manage such large numbers of requirements properly, they have to be numbered with some *identification scheme*. The scheme may include a *classification* of requirements into more manageable groups.

There are several techniques for identifying and classifying requirements (Kotonya and Sommerville, 1998):

- *Unique identifier* – usually a sequential number assigned manually or generated by a CASE tool's database (i.e. the database (or *repository*) where the CASE tool stores the analysis and design artifacts).

- *Sequential number within document hierarchy* – assigned with consideration to the requirement's position within the requirements document (e.g. the seventh requirement in the third section of the second chapter would be numbered 2.3.7).

- *Sequential number within requirements category* – assigned in addition to a mnemonic name that identifies the category of the requirement (where the categories of requirements can be function requirement, data requirement, performance requirement, security requirement, etc.).

Each identification method has its pros and cons. The most flexible and least error-prone is the *database-generated unique identifier*. Databases have a built-in capability to generate unique identifiers for every new record of data under a concurrent multi-user access to data.

Some databases can additionally support the maintenance of multiple versions of the same record (by extending the unique identifier value with the version number). Finally, databases can maintain *referential integrity* links between the modeling artifacts, including requirements, and can therefore provide necessary support for requirements change management and traceability.

Requirements hierarchies   2.4.2

Requirements can be hierarchically structured in *parent–child relationships*. A parent requirement is composed of child requirements. A child requirement is effectively a sub-requirement of the parent requirement.

Hierarchical relationships introduce an additional level of requirements classification. This may or may not be reflected directly in identification numbers (by using dot notation). Hence, the requirement numbered 4.9 would be the ninth child of the parent identified by number four.

The following is a set of hierarchical requirements:

1. "The system shall schedule the next phone call to a customer upon the telemarketer's request."
   1.1 "The system shall activate `Next Call` pushbutton upon entry to `Telemarketing Control` form or when the previous call has terminated."
   1.2 "The system shall remove the call from the top of the queue of scheduled calls and make it the current call."
   1.3 etc.

Hierarchies of requirements allow requirements to be defined that are at different *levels of abstraction*. This is consistent with the overall modeling principle of systematically adding details to models when moving to the lower level of abstraction. As a result, high-level models can be constructed for parent requirements, and lower-level models can be linked to child requirements.

Change management   2.4.3

Requirements change. A requirement may change, be removed, or a new requirement may be added, at any phase of the development lifecycle. Change is not a kick in the teeth, but unmanaged change is.

The more advanced the development, the more costly the change is. In fact, the *downstream cost* of putting the project back on track after change will always grow and will frequently grow exponentially. Changing a requirement just created and not linked to other requirements is a straightforward editing exercise. Changing the same requirement after it has been implemented in software may be prohibitively costly.

A change may be linked to a human error but is frequently caused by internal policy changes or external factors, such as competitive forces, global markets, or technology advances. Whatever the reason, strong management policies are needed to document *change requests*, to assess a *change impact*, and to effect the changes.

Because changes to requirements are costly, a formal *business case* must be made for each change request. A valid change, not dealt with previously, is assessed for technical feasibility, the impact on the rest of the project, and the cost. Once approved, the change is incorporated into relevant models and implemented in software.

Change management involves tracking large amounts of interlinked information over long periods of time. Without tool support, change management is doomed. Ideally, the requirements changes should be stored and tracked by a *software configuration management tool* used by developers to handle versions of models and programs across the development lifecycle. A good CASE tool should either have its own configuration management capability or be linked to a stand-alone configuration management tool.

2.4.4 Requirements traceability

Requirements traceability is just a part, albeit a critically important part, of *change management*. Requirements traceability is about maintaining traceability relationships to track changes from/to a requirement throughout the development lifecycle.

Consider the requirement: "The system shall schedule the next phone call to a customer upon the telemarketer's request." This requirement could then be modeled in a sequence diagram, activated from the GUI by an action button labeled "Next Call" and programmed in a database trigger. If a traceability relationship exists between all these elements, a change to any element will make the relationship open again to discussion – the trace becomes *suspect* (to use one tool's parlance).

A traceability relationship can cut across many models in successive lifecycle phases. Only adjacent traceability links can be directly modified. For example, if an element A is traced to an element B, and B traced to C, then change at either endpoint of the relationship will need to be done in two steps: by modifying link A–B, then B–C. (Chapter 9 explains traceability and change management in detail.)

2.5 Requirements business model

The *requirements determination* phase captures requirements and defines them (predominantly) in natural language statements. A formal modeling of requirements using UML is conducted afterwards in the *requirements specification* phase. Nevertheless, a high-level visual representation of gathered requirements – called *requirements business modeling* – is routinely undertaken during requirements determination.

As a minimum, high-level visual models are needed to determine the system scope, to identify principal use cases, and to establish the most essential business classes. Figure 2.2 shows the dependencies between these three models of the requirements determination phase and the models of the remaining lifecycle phases.

The leading role of use-case diagrams in the lifecycle is indicated in Figure 2.2 by recognizing that the test cases, user documentation, and project plans are all derived from the use-case models. Apart from that, use-case diagrams and class models are used concurrently and drive each other in successive development iterations. The design and implementation are also intertwined and can feed back to the requirements specification models.

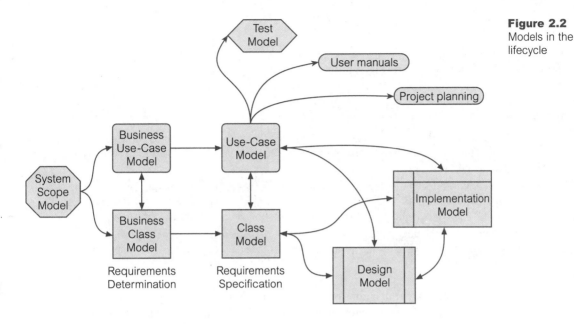

Figure 2.2
Models in the lifecycle

System scope model

2.5.1

Perhaps the main concern in system development is *scope creep* due to ever changing requirements. While some changes to requirements are unavoidable, we have to ensure that the requested changes do not go beyond the accepted scope of the project.

The question is: "How do we define the scope of the system?" Answering this question is not straightforward, because any system is only a part of a larger environment – a part of a set of systems that together constitute that environment. The systems collaborate by exchanging information and by invoking services of each other. Hence, the above question could be interpreted as: "Should we implement the requirements or is the requested functionality a responsibility of another system?"

To be able to answer the scope questions, we need to know the *context* in which our system operates. We need to know the *external entities* – other systems, organizations, people, machines, etc. that expect some services from us or provide services to us. In business systems, those services translate to information – to *data flows*.

The system scope, therefore, can be determined through identification of external entities and input/output data flows between the external entities and our system. Our system obtains the input information and does necessary *processing* to produce the output information. Any requirement that cannot be supported by the system's internal processing is outside the scope.

UML does not provide a good visual model to define the scope of the system. Therefore, the old-fashioned *context diagram* of DFDs (Section 2.5.5.1) is frequently used for the task. Figure 2.3 shows the context diagram for the telemarketing application.

2.5.1.1 Example for system scope modeling

Example 2.1 (telemarketing)

Consider the problem statement for telemarketing (Section 1.5.4) and construct a context diagram for it. Additionally, consider the following observations:

- Campaigns are planned on recommendations from the society's trustees, who decide on worthy and timely charitable causes. The campaigns have to be approved by local government. The design and planning of campaigns is supported by a separate `Campaign Database` application system.

- There is also a separate `Supporter Database` that stores and maintains information about all supporters, past and present. This database is used to select supporters to be contacted in a particular campaign. The selected *segment* of supporters is made available to telemarketing activities for the campaign.

- Orders from supporters for lottery tickets are recorded during telemarketing for perusal by the `Order Processing` system. An order-processing system maintains the status of orders in the supporter database.

A possible context diagram for this example is shown in Figure 2.3. The "bubble" in the center of the diagram represents the system. The rectangles around it designate external entities. The arrows depict data flows. The detailed information content of data flows is not visible on the diagram – the content of data flows is defined separately and stored in the CASE tool's repository.

The `Telemarketing` system obtains information about the current campaign from the external entity `Campaign Database`. This information includes the number and prices of tickets, lottery winning prizes, and the campaign duration.

Similarly, `Telemarketing` obtains supporter details from `Supporter Database`. During a telemarketing call, new information about a supporter may emerge (for instance, that the supporter intends to change their phone number). `Supporter Database` needs to be updated accordingly – hence, the data flow `Supporter Details` is bidirectional.

The main activity is between `Telemarketing` and `Supporter`. The data flow `Conversation` contains information that is exchanged during the telephone conversation.

Figure 2.3
System scope model – context diagram (telemarketing)

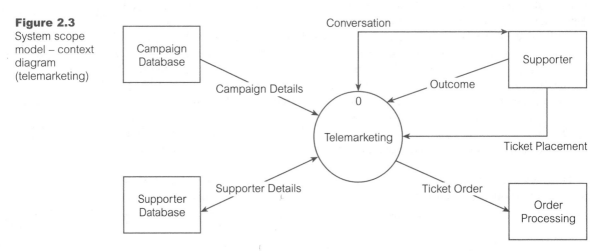

A supporter's reply to the telemarketer's offer to buy lottery tickets is transferred along the data flow `Outcome`. A separate data flow called `Ticket Placement` is used to record details about tickets ordered by a supporter.

Further processing of ticket orders is outside the scope of the system. The data flow `Ticket Order` is forwarded to the external entity `Order Processing`. It can be assumed that after orders are entered, other external entities can handle payments from supporters, ticket mail-outs, prize draws, etc. These are not of concern as long as the current status of orders, payments, etc. is available to the system from the external entities `Campaign Database` and `Supporter Database`.

Business use-case model   2.5.2

A *business use-case model* (Kruchten, 2003) is a use-case model at a high level of abstraction. A business use-case model identifies high-level business processes – *business use cases*. A business use-case can define a process in a way that is abstracted completely from its realization. A *business process* is then dissociated from an *information system process*, and the whole model represents the business point of view and emphasizes social activities (not necessarily supported by computerized system solutions).

In practice, however, business use-case models are constructed for business processes to be supported by the information system under development. In such cases, a business process is conceived as a kind of information system process. A business use-case then corresponds to what is sometimes called a *system feature*. (System features are identified in a *vision document*. If a vision document is present, then it may be used as a replacement for the business use-case model.)

The focus of a business use-case diagram is the *architecture* of business processes. The diagram provides a bird's eye view of desired business and system behavior. The narrative description for each *business use case* is brief, business-oriented, and focused on the main flow of activities. A business use-case model is not adequate for communicating to *developers* exactly what the system should do.

Business use cases are turned into *use cases* in the requirements specification phase. It is in that phase that the detailed use cases are identified, the narrative descriptions are extended to include sub-processes and alternative processes, some GUI screens are mocked up, and the relationships between use cases are established.

Business actors in a business use-case diagram can sometimes represent *external entities* of the context diagram. Such actors are also known as *secondary actors*. They are passive with regard to use cases. To communicate with a use case they need to engage a *primary actor*, central to the system and able to actively communicate with a use case. Primary business actors instigate use cases by sending *events* to them.

Use cases are event-driven. The communication lines between actors and use cases are not data flows. The communication lines represent the flow of events from actors and the flow of responses from use cases. In UML, the *communication relationships* between actors and use cases are expressed as arrowed lines and may be named (stereotyped) as «communicate».

Business use cases can be linked by various relationships. The relationship of significance in business use-case models is an *association relationship*. An association is represented by a line with or without arrowheads on one or both ends of the line. An association with an arrowhead is a *client–supplier* relationship. A client knows something about its supplier. This also means that a client depends in some way on its supplier. UML relationships, other than associations, are not normally encouraged between business use cases.

There is an interesting dichotomy with regard to actors. Many actors must be seen as both external and internal to the system. They are *external* because they interact with the system from the outside. They are *internal* because the system may maintain information about the actors so that it can knowingly interact with the "external" actors. The system specification must describe, as a model, the system and its environment. The environment contains actors. The system may itself keep information about the actors. Hence, the specification holds two models related to actors – a model of the actor and a model of what the system records about the actor.

2.5.2.1 Example for business use-case modeling

Example 2.2 (telemarketing)

Consider the problem statement and the context diagram for telemarketing (Sections 1.5.4 and 2.5.1.1) and construct a business use-case diagram.

A possible business use-case diagram is presented in Figure 2.4. There are two business actors: `Telemarketer` and `Supporter`. `Telemarketer` is a primary actor. `Supporter` is a secondary actor.

`Telemarketer` asks the system for the phone call to a supporter to be scheduled and dialed up. Upon successful connection, `Supporter` is involved as a secondary actor. The

Figure 2.4
Business use-case model (telemarketing)

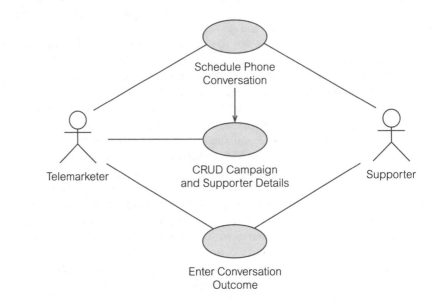

Schedule Phone
Conversation

CRUD Campaign
and Supporter Details

Telemarketer

Supporter

Enter Conversation
Outcome

business use case `Schedule Phone Conversation` (which includes here the establishment of the connection) becomes a piece of visible functionality of value to both actors.

During the telephone conversation, `Telemarketer` may need to access and modify campaign and supporter details. This functionality is captured in the business use case `CRUD Campaign and Supporter Details`. (CRUD is a popular acronym that stands for the four main operations on data: create, read, update, delete.)

There is a client–server association relationship between `Schedule Phone Conversation` and `CRUD Campaign and Supporter Details`. Another way of looking at this relationship is that `Phone Conversation` depends on `CRUD Campaign and Supporter Details`.

Finally, the business use case `Enter Conversation Outcome` serves the purpose of entering the successful or unsuccessful results of the telemarketing action. This use case delivers an identifiable value to both actors.

The omission of other relationships between use cases is arbitrary. In general, all relationships between use cases can be suppressed to avoid cluttering and overcrowding the diagram. Use cases tend to have some sort of communication with most other use cases, and the inclusion of all relationships defeats the purpose of modeling as an abstraction mechanism.

Business glossary

One of the inconspicuous but important aspects of software development is the clarity of business and system terminology. Without such clarity, communication between project stakeholders lacks precision and can result in solving the wrong problem. To improve communication and to avoid misunderstandings, a *glossary* of terms and definitions must be created and shared among stakeholders.

In practice, some glossary of terms is likely to exist in the enterprise, possibly from development of related systems. If it does not exist, building the glossary should start in the requirements determination phase. If the glossary exists, it needs to be reviewed and extended.

The glossary can be written in table format. The table should provide the terms and definitions, sorted by terms and with possible links to closely related terms.

Example for business glossary

Example 2.3 (telemarketing)

Consider the problem statement and the context diagram for telemarketing (Sections 1.5.4 and 2.5.1.1) and construct a business glossary.

Table 2.2 presents an initial glossary of business terms for telemarketing. Words written in italics in the Definition column are references to terms defined elsewhere in the glossary.

Table 2.2 Business glossary (telemarketing)

Term	definition
bonus campaign	A special series of activities, conducted within a *campaign*, to additionally entice *supporters* to buy the campaign *tickets*. Typical examples are giving free tickets for bulk or early buying or for attracting new supporters. A particular kind of bonus campaign can be used in many campaigns.
campaign	A government-approved and carefully planned series of activities that are intended to achieve a *lottery* objective.
draw	An act of randomly choosing a particular *lottery ticket* as a winning ticket.
lottery	A fund raising game of chance, organized by the charity in order to make money, in which people (*supporters*) buy numbered *tickets* to have a chance of winning a *prize* if their number is chosen in a *draw*.
placement	Acquisition of one or more *lottery tickets* by a *supporter* during *telemarketing*. The placement is paid for by a supporter with a credit card.
prize	A reward to a *supporter* who bought a *lottery ticket* that wins in the *draw*.
segment	A group of *supporters*, from the supporters database, who become targets of a particular *campaign* in its *telemarketing* activities.
supporter	A person or organization that exists in the charity database as a previous or potential buyer of *lottery tickets*.
ticket	A *lottery* ticket with a determined money value, identifying a *campaign* and uniquely numbered within all campaign tickets.
ticket order	A confirmed *placement* for tickets, with an allocated order number, and treated as a customer order by the Order Processing Department.
telemarketer	An employee conducting *telemarketing*.
telemarketing	The activity of advertising and possibly selling *lottery tickets* by telephone.

2.5.4 Business class model

A *business class model* is a UML *class model*. Just as with the business use-case model, the business class model is a higher level of abstraction than more concrete class models. A business class model identifies the main categories of business objects in the system.

Business objects have persistent presence in an enterprise database. They have to be contrasted with instances of other software classes, such as the classes handling the user interface or responsible for program logic.

Business classes are normally presented as business data structures, with operations (services) on data suppressed. Even more, a business class model is frequently not explicit about the attribute structure of classes – class names and a brief description are sometimes sufficient.

Business classes can be linked in the model by three UML relationships: association, generalization, and aggregation. Association and aggregation express semantic relationships between instances of classes (i.e. objects). Generalization is a relationship between classes (i.e. types of objects).

Association represents the knowledge that objects of one class have with regard to objects of another class (or with regard to different objects of the same class). The knowledge is about semantic links from an object to one or more other objects. Existence of the links enables navigation between objects (a program can navigate to linked objects).

Associations have the important properties of multiplicity and participation. *Multiplicity* defines the number of possible instances of a class that can be linked to a single instance of another class. Multiplicity is defined on both ends of an association line between classes and can be 0, 1, or n (where "n" means that many objects can be linked).

To show a possibility that some objects in an association may have zero linked objects, the multiplicity may be represented by a pair of values, namely 0..1 or 0..n. The value 0 in the pair indicates that the *participation* of an object in an association to other objects is optional (the object may or may not have association links).

Aggregation is a semantically stronger kind of association; for example, an instance of one class "has" instances of another class. It is said that a superset class "has" a subset class or that a subset class "is a part of" the superset class. For example, Book "has" Chapter.

Generalization is a relationship of classes, such that a class "can be" another class. It is said that a superclass "can be" a subclass or that a subclass "is a kind of" the superclass. For example, Employee "can be" Manager.

Interestingly enough, it is frequently the case that the *business actors* of a business use-case model are represented as *business classes* in the business class model. This is consistent with the observation that actors are frequently both external and internal to the system (Section 2.5.2).

Example for business class modeling   2.5.4.1

> ### Example 2.4 (telemarketing)
>
> Consider the problem statement, the context diagram, the business use-case diagram and the business glossary for Telemarketing (Sections 1.5.4, 2.5.1.1, 2.5.2.1, and 2.5.3.1) and construct a business class diagram. The following hints may be of assistance:
>
> - The emphasis in the system is on call scheduling. The call scheduling itself is a procedural computation, i.e. the solution to it is algorithmic and computational. Nevertheless, the scheduled call queues and the outcomes of calls must be stored in some data structure.
> - As discussed above, information about actors may need to be stored in classes.

A first-cut business class model is shown in Figure 2.5. The diagram contains six classes; two of them (Supporter and Telemarketer) are derived from the actors of the business use-case model. The call-scheduling algorithm obtains a phone number and other

Figure 2.5
Business class
model
(telemarketing)

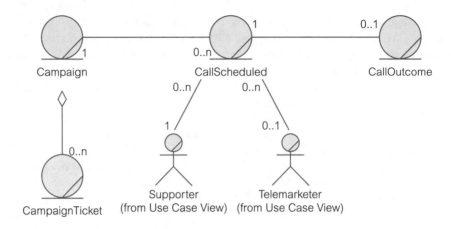

information from the class `Supporter` and schedules the call to one of the currently available `Telemarketers`. The algorithm will ultimately be implemented in the system's database in the form of a *stored procedure*.

The class `CallScheduled` contains the current queue of calls, including those that are currently active. Call outcomes, such as ticket placement, are recorded in `CallOutcome` as well as propagated to other affected classes, such as `CampaignTicket` or `Supporter`.

The class `Campaign` contains `CampaignTickets` and can have many `CallScheduled`. Similarly, `Supporter` and `Telemarketer` may have many `CallScheduled`. The association between `CallScheduled` and `CallOutcome` is one to one.

2.6 Requirements document

The *requirements document* is a tangible outcome of the requirements determination phase. Most organizations produce a requirements document according to a predefined template. The *template* defines the structure (table of contents) and the style of the document.

The main body of a requirements document consists of requirements statements. As discussed in Section 2.1, the requirements need to be grouped into *functional requirements* (service statements) and *non-functional requirements* (constraint statements). Although this can be confusing, functional requirements can be further classified into *function requirements* and *data requirements*. (In the literature, the term "functional requirements" is used interchangeably in the broad or narrow sense. When used in the narrow sense, the term corresponds to function requirements.)

Apart from the requirements *per se*, the requirements document has to address *project issues*. Normally, the project issues are discussed at the beginning of the document and again at the end of the document. In the introductory part of the document, the project's business context is discussed, including the project's purpose, stakeholders, and main constraints. Towards the end of the document, all other project issues are raised, including schedule, budget, risks, and documentation.

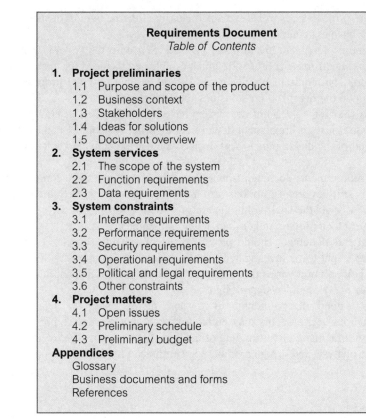

Figure 2.6
The requirements document – table of contents

Document templates

2.6.1

Templates for requirements documents are available from textbooks, standards organizations (IEEE, ANSI, etc.), web pages of consulting firms, vendors of software engineering tools, etc. Over time, each organization develops its own standard that fits its organizational practices, culture, expected readership, types of system, etc.

A requirements document template defines the structure of the document and gives detailed guidelines about what to write in each section of the document. The guidelines may include the content matters, motivation, examples, and additional considerations (cf. Robertson and Robertson, 2003).

Figure 2.6 shows a typical table of contents for a requirements document. The explanations for the content are discussed in the following sections.

Project preliminaries

2.6.2

The project preliminaries part of the document predominantly targets managers and decision makers, who are unlikely to study the whole document in detail. The *purpose and scope* of the project needs to be explained clearly at the beginning of the document, followed by the business context.

The requirements document has to make a *business case* for the system. In particular, any *system planning* efforts (Section 1.2), which established the need for the system, have to be referred to. The requirements document should explain how the proposed system would contribute to the organization's business objectives and goals.

Stakeholders (Section 1.1.2.1) of the system have to be identified. It is important that the *customer* is not just an impersonal department or office – people's names should be listed. At the end of the day, a person will decide whether the delivered software product is acceptable.

Although a requirements document should be as far away from the technical solutions as possible, it is still important to brainstorm *ideas for the solution* early in the development lifecycle. Any off-the-shelf solutions are of special interest. It always makes good business sense to buy a product rather than develop it from scratch.

The requirements document should provide a list of existing software packages and components that ought to be investigated further as potential solutions. Note that taking up an off-the-shelf solution varies the development processes but does not dispense with the requirements analysis and system design!

Finally, it is a good idea to include an *overview* of the rest *of the document* in the project preliminaries section. This may entice a busy reader to study other parts of the document and will facilitate understanding of the document content. The overview should also explain the analysis and design methodology embraced by the developers.

2.6.3 System services

The main part of the requirements document is dedicated to the definition of *system services* (Section 2.1). This part is likely to account for more than half of the entire document. This is also just about the only part of the document that may contain high-level models for the solution – *requirements business models* (Section 2.5). Note, however, that the glossary is moved to the appendix section.

The *scope of the system* can be modeled with a *context diagram* (Section 2.5.1). In explaining the context diagram, the boundaries for the proposed project must be clearly defined. Without this definition, the project will not be able to stand up to the demands of scope creep.

Functional requirements can be modeled with a *business use-case diagram* (Section 2.5.2). However, the diagram will provide only a high-level embracement for the detailed, listing of functional requirements. As discussed in Section 2.4, each requirement has to be identified, classified, and defined.

Data requirements can be modeled with a *business class diagram* (Section 2.5.4). As with function requirements, the business class diagram is not a complete definition of business data structures. Each business class needs to be explained further. The attribute content of classes ought to be described. Identifying attributes of classes must be determined. Otherwise, it is not possible to explain associations properly.

System constraints 2.6.4

System services define *what* the system must accomplish. *System constraints* (Section 2.1) describe *how* the system is constrained when accomplishing its services. System constraints may be set with regard to:

- interface requirements
- performance requirements
- security requirements
- operational requirements
- political and legal requirements, etc.

Interface requirements define how the product interfaces with the users. In the requirements document, we only define the "look and feel" of the GUI. The initial design (screen painting) of the GUI will be conducted during *requirements specification* and later during *system design*.

Depending on the application domain, *performance requirements* can become quite central to the success of the project. In a narrow sense, they specify the speed (the system's *response times*) at which various tasks have to be accomplished. In a broader sense, performance requirements include other constraints – related to the system's reliability, availability, throughput, etc.

Security requirements describe users' access privileges to the information under the system's control. Users can be given restricted access to data and/or restricted rights to execute certain operations on data.

Operational requirements determine the hardware/software environment, if known, in which the system will operate. These requirements may make an impact on other aspects of the project, such as user training and system maintenance.

Political requirements and *legal requirements* are frequently assumed rather than explicitly stated in the requirements document. This can be a very costly mistake. Unless these requirements are brought out in to the open, the product may be difficult or impossible to deploy for political or legal reasons.

Other categories of *constraint* are also possible. For example, some systems may place extra demands on the ease of the system's use (*usability requirements*) or on the ease of system maintenance (*maintainability requirements*).

The importance of watertight definitions for system constraints cannot be overstated. There are numerous examples of failed projects due to omitted or misinterpreted system constraints. The issue is as sensitive with regard to customers as it is with regard to developers. Unscrupulous or desperate developers can play the system constraints card to their advantage in an effort to evade their responsibilities.

Project matters 2.6.5

The final part of the requirements document addresses other project matters. An important section in this part is called *Open Issues*. In here, we specify any issues that can affect the success of the project but have not been discussed under other headings in the document. This may include the expected growth in importance of some requirements that are currently out of scope. This may also include any potential problems or malpractices that deployment of the system can trigger.

A *preliminary schedule* for major tasks on the project needs to be developed. This should include the preliminary allocation of human and other resources. A project management software tool can be used to produce standard planning charts, such as PERT or Gantt charts (Maciaszek and Liong, 2004).

As a direct upshot of the schedule, the *preliminary budget* can be provided. The project cost can be expressed as a range, rather than a figure. If the requirements are well documented, one of the estimating methods to assess the cost (e.g. *function point analysis*) can be used.

2.6.6 Appendices

Appendices contain other useful information for requirements understanding. The main inclusion here is a glossary (Section 2.5.3). The *glossary* defines terms, acronyms, and abbreviations used in the requirements document. The importance of a good glossary cannot be overestimated. Terminology misinterpretations can be very damaging.

One of the frequently overlooked aspects of the requirements document is that the business domain it defines can be quite well understood through the study of *documents and forms* used in workflow processes. Whenever possible, completed business forms should be included – empty forms do not convey the same level of insight.

References provide citations to documents referenced or used in the preparation of the requirements document. These may include books and other published sources of information, but – even more importantly – minutes of meetings, memoranda, and internal documents should also be cited.

Summary

This chapter took a comprehensive look at requirements determination. The determination of requirements precedes their specification. The determination is about discovering requirements and documenting them in a mostly narrative requirements document. The requirements specification (discussed in Chapter 4) provides more formal models of requirements.

Requirements elicitation follows two lines of discovery: from the domain knowledge and from the use cases. These two lines of investigation complement each other and lead to the determination of a business model for the system to be developed.

There are various *methods of requirements elicitation*: interviewing customers and domain experts, questionnaires, observation, study of documents and software systems, prototyping, brainstorming, JAD, and RAD.

Requirements elicited from customers may overlap and conflict. It is a business analyst's job to resolve these overlaps and conflicts through *requirements negotiation and validation*. To do this job properly, the business analyst ought to construct a *requirements dependency matrix* and to assign *risks* and *priorities* to the requirements.

Large projects *manage* large volumes of requirements. It is essential in such projects that the requirement statements be *identified and classified*. *Requirements hierarchies* can then be defined. These steps ensure proper *requirements traceability* in the next project stages as well as proper handling of *change requests*.

Even though the requirements determination does not include formal system modeling, a basic *requirements business model* may be constructed. The business model can result in three generic diagrams: the context diagram, the business use-case diagram, and the business class diagram. It also initiates definitions of terms in the glossary.

A document that results from the requirements determination – the *requirements document* – begins with a high-level description of the *project preliminaries* (mostly for the benefit of the managerial readership). The main parts of the document describe *system services* (functional requirements) and *system constraints* (non-functional requirements). The final part handles other project matters, including the *schedule* and the *budget* details.

Questions

Q1 Search the Internet and/or other sources of information to decipher Hewlett-Packard's FURPS acronym. Briefly describe the meaning of the acronym letters. Discuss how the FURPS model can be related to functional and non-functional requirements?

Q2 Search the Internet and/or other sources of information to learn about McCall's software quality model. Briefly describe the model and show how can it be helpful in requirements determination?

Q3 Requirements elicitation aims at reconciling domain knowledge requirements and use-case requirements. Explain the difference between these two kinds of requirement. Should one of them take precedence over the other in the requirements determination process? Give reasons.

Q4 During interviews, it is recommended that questions that are opinionated, biased, or imposing be avoided. Can you think about the situations where such questions may be necessary for the benefit of the project?

Q5 What is the difference between a survey and a questionnaire in requirements determination and similar tasks?

Q6 What steps would you take to prepare and conduct observation as a requirements determination technique? What practical guidelines would you apply?

Q7 What is prototyping? How is it useful for requirements determination?

Q8 What are the advantages of brainstorming and JAD in comparison with other requirements determination methods?

Q9 What is scope creep? How can it be addressed during requirements determination?

Q10 What are the typical characteristics and capabilities of requirements management tools? Search the Internet for the answer.

Q11 Why should requirements be numbered?

Q12 How are actors in a business use-case diagram different from external entities in a context diagram?

Exercises (advertising expenditure)

E1   *Advertising expenditure* – refer to the problem statement in Section 1.5.5. Draw a context diagram for the AE system. Explain the model.

E2   *Advertising expenditure* – refer to the problem statement in Section 1.5.5. Draw a business use-case diagram for the AE system. Explain the model.

E3   *Advertising expenditure* – refer to the problem statement in Section 1.5.5. Develop a business glossary.

E4   *Advertising expenditure* – refer to the problem statement in Section 1.5.5. Draw a business class diagram for the AE system. Explain the model.

Exercises (time logging)

F1   *Time logging* – refer to the problem statement in Section 1.5.6. Draw a high-level use-case diagram for the TL software tool. Explain the model.

F2   *Time logging* – refer to the problem statement in Section 1.5.6. Develop a glossary of terms for the TL project.

F3   *Time logging* – refer to the problem statement in Section 1.5.6. Draw a high-level class diagram for the TL software tool. Explain the model.

Answers to odd-numbered questions

Q1 – answer

Hewlett-Packard's FURPS is a model for assessing software quality (Grady, 1992). The acronym identifies a set of five quality factors: functionality, usability, reliability, performance, and supportability:

■ *Functionality* defines the feature set and capabilities of the software system. The definition includes a list of delivered functions and the security aspects of the system.

■ *Usability* considers human perception of the ease of use of the system. It includes such issues as system esthetics, consistency, documentation, help facilities, and the training required for effective and efficient use of the system.

■ *Reliability* measures the frequency and severity of system failures, the accuracy of produced output, the mean time to failure, the ability to recover from failure, and the overall predictability of the system.

■ *Performance* evaluates the response time of the system (on average and at pick times), transaction throughput, resource consumption, efficiency under varying workloads, etc.

■ *Supportability* defines how easy it is to support the system. It combines a number of related properties such as software understandability, maintainability (adaptability to change, serviceability), scalability (extendibility), testability, configurability, ease of installation, and ease of localizing problems.

The FURPS model normally applies to assessing quality in a delivered software product. However, the five quality factors can serve as a handy classification for user requirements to be delivered in the system under development. In such a classification, the FURPS functionality component relates to *functional requirements*, and the remaining four factors define *non-functional requirements*.

The one-to-four proportion between functional and non-functional requirements is by no means a reflection on the relative importance of these two categories of requirement. In system development, the effort and cost expended on functional requirements (i.e. system services) frequently outweighs the effort and cost of ensuring non-functional requirements (i.e. system constraints).

Q3 – answer

The *domain knowledge requirements* are obtained from the generic understanding of the application domain. This includes the domain expert's (or the analyst's) experience in the domain, published work about the domain, any widely disseminated practices and regulations, and solutions employed in off-the-shelf systems.

The *use-case requirements* are obtained from the studies of the specific business practices and processes. They capture the ways in which business is done in a particular organization. While some use-case requirements will align with the domain knowledge requirements, others will not (because they reflect the specific ways that the things are done in that organization).

Normally, both kinds of requirement are collected more or less in parallel. It is possible that the initial investigations will focus on the domain knowledge requirements, but eventually all these requirements must be validated with customers. In other words, the domain knowledge requirements are either incorporated in to a use case (and become use-case requirements) or they are discarded.

The process of validating *domain knowledge requirements* is frequently centered on the revisions to the business class model (and – in later stages – to the class model). This is shown in Figure 2.1 by means of a dependency relationship from business use-case model to business class model.

Although not shown in Figure 2.1, the feedback from business class model (and therefore domain knowledge requirements) to business use-case model (and therefore use-case requirements) is also possible. If such feedback happens, it may signify that "the customer is not always right" – the customer is prepared to reassess a use-case requirement to make it correspond to a generic domain knowledge requirement.

Later in the analysis and design process, the use-case requirements take center stage. All development models and artifacts are driven by and validated against the use-case requirements.

Q5 – answer

Both a survey and a questionnaire for requirements determination are questionnaires. The main difference is that a *survey* seeks public verification of some facts, whereas a *questionnaire* (in requirements determination and similar tasks) is a fact-finding device.

Surveys and questionnaires bring about different kinds of inaccuracies and respondents' bias. Survey results can be distorted because of the inability of the respondent to answer a question or by deliberate "coloring" of facts. Questionnaire results can suffer from similar deficiencies, but the distortions can be aggravated by questions asking for an opinion or subjective assessment. Adding to the trouble are questions asking for answers using scaling values.

Q7 – answer

Prototyping is a quick modeling and implementation of the system. A *prototype* is an inefficient, low-quality solution with many implementation compromises. The main purpose of a prototype is to give users an idea about the "look and feel" of the actual system.

The prototype is evaluated by the users and is used to validate and refine requirements for the system to be developed. The prototype provides dynamic visual displays and simulates interaction with a human user. This facilitates the user's understanding of requirements supported by the software and allows appraisal of software behavior.

Provided that proper customer resources are committed to the evaluation of the prototype and the required changes to the requirements are made in a timely fashion, the prototype is one of the most powerful techniques for requirements determination.

Q9 – answer

Scope creep is the growth of customer expectations as the project progresses and the associated demand for new requirements to be implemented in the system. The new requirements are normally not accounted for in the schedule and budget.

A good technique to counteract scope creep is to document all *requests for change* and address them in the context of the system scope model in the requirements document. A high-level scope model is frequently modeled in the context diagram for the system. More detailed requirements are captured in use-case diagrams.

Any demand for new requirements should be modeled in the context diagram and/or use-case diagrams, and the dynamics of changing project parameters should be explained to the customers. The parameters should include the impact on the project schedule and cost.

Scope creep is due not only to changing business conditions but also to shortcomings in the work done during the requirements determination phase. Employing modern methods of requirements elicitation, such as prototyping, can diminish the risk of scope creep.

Finally, developing the system in short iterations with frequent deliveries reduces the need for requirements changes within iterations. Changes between iterations are less troublesome.

Q11 – answer

The system is constructed to satisfy customer requirements. In all but trivial systems, the requirements are defined on several levels, with a higher-level requirement consisting of a number of more specific lower-level requirements. The total number of requirements can easily reach thousands.

To ensure that all customer requirements will be implemented in the system, they need to be *structured and numbered* to start with. Only then can the implementation of requirements be systematically checked and managed.

The project and change management are dependent on the precise *identification* of all requirements. Requirements are allocated to developers and other resources, the project plans are structured in relation to groupings of requirements, defects are traced back to the numbered requirements, etc.

Solutions to exercises (AE)

Note that Maciaszek and Liong (2004) offers additional discussion and solutions for the AE domain.

E1 – solution

The *context diagram*, as shown in Figure 2.7, is a high-level model that identifies the scope of the AE system. There are two external entities: `Media Outlet` and `AE Client`. Media outlets supply advertising data to AE. AE clients receive campaign monitoring reports and expenditure reports from AE.

The transformation of advertising data into reports is the internal function of AE. The advertisement verification, manual entry, and other individual AE functions will acquire and supply data, but these are considered internal data flows within the AE "bubble." For example, the supply of newspapers, magazines, video reels, etc. for manual entry is treated as internal to the system (at least for the time being).

Figure 2.7
Context diagram
(advertising
expenditure)

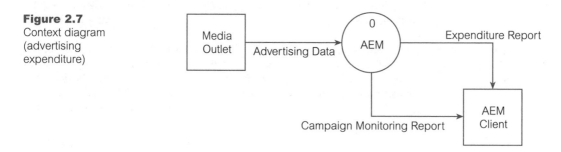

E2 – solution

The business use cases in Figure 2.8 have been organized from top to bottom to signify the sequence of doing the business functions. They constitute the main functional modules of the AE system.

The business use-case model divides the AE system into four business uses cases connected by unidirectional associations. The sequence of associations signifies the main AE business workflow – from data collection to verification, valorization, and reporting.

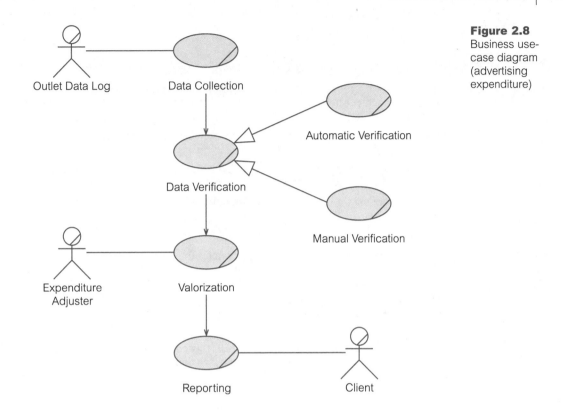

Figure 2.8
Business use-case diagram (advertising expenditure)

Data Collection communicates with Outlet Data Log to obtain advertising log information (this is normally done by electronic transfer). The process of data collection includes matching received advertisement details with the advertisements previously recorded in the AE database. The matching process is not distinguished in the model as a separate use case.

Data Verification confirms that the advertisement details obtained are valid and logical in the context of surrounding information (other advertisements, programs, etc.). Once entered and verified, the advertisements undergo Valorization. This is the process of assigning expenditure estimates to advertisements.

Reporting produces customized reports to clients who buy or subscribe to the reports. Reports can be distributed in various forms, such as e-mail, CDs, or paper.

E3 – solution
The glossary is presented in Table 2.3.

E4 – solution
Six business classes are recognized (Figure 2.9). AdvertisementInstance embodies individual occurrences of an advertisement. Advertisement is a unique piece of creativity that may be broadcast, screened, or published any number of times. AdvertisementProduct captures the product that is the aim of the advertisement.

There are also three organizational classes. Outlet stores information about media companies. Advertiser is an organization that uses the media to advertise a product. Agency is an organization that handles advertising planning and media buying on behalf of an advertiser.

The diagram also shows the principal relationships between business classes. The relationship between Agency and Advertiser is an aggregation. Other relationships are associations.

Table 2.3 Business glossary (advertising expenditure)

Term	definition
advertisement (ad)	A unique piece of creative work that may be broadcast, screened, published, or otherwise exposed any number of times. Each ad exposure by a media outlet is known in the AE system as an *ad instance*.
ad instance	A particular occurrence of an *ad*, i.e. each incidence of an ad broadcast, screening, or publication.
adlink	An association between an *ad*, the *product* it advertises, the *advertiser* who pays for the exposure of the ad, and the *agency* responsible for booking of that exposure.
advertiser	A company that uses an *outlet* to expose an *advertisement* in order to promote a *product*.
agency	An organization that handles the advertising planning and media buying for an *advertiser*. The goal of an *agency* is to optimize advertising expenditure.
category	A name in a hierarchical classification of products. There are an unlimited number of levels in the hierarchy (i.e. category, subcategories, down to products). *Products* may only be categorized at the lowest level of the category hierarchy.
organization	A business entity that AE deals with. There are different types of organization, including *advertisers*, *agencies* and *outlets*. An organization may be one, many, or none of these types.
outlet	An organization that exposes an *advertisement*. This could be a television or radio station, a publication, or a company advertising in cinemas and outdoors.
product	A merchandise or service that may be advertised. Products may be categorized (i.e. a product can belong to a *category* of products).

Figure 2.9
Business class
diagram
(advertising
expenditure)

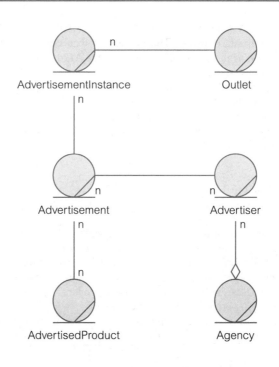

Chapter

3

Objects and Object Modeling

Virtually all modern software systems are object-oriented and are developed using object-oriented modeling. The omnipresence of objects in information systems places knowledge demands on virtually all stakeholders of software projects – not just developers but also customers (users and system owners). To be able to communicate effectively, all stakeholders must have a common understanding of the object technology and the object modeling language. For customers, the knowledge of objects must be just sufficient to understand the main concepts and modeling constructs. For developers, the knowledge must be in-depth and at the level where it can be applied to build models and implement the software.

The main difficulty in learning *object technology* relates to the absence of an obvious starting point and the lack of a clear path of investigation. There is not a top-down or bottom-up learning approach that we know of. By necessity, the approach has to be a sort of "middle-out." No matter how much we advance the learning process, we always seem to be in the middle of that learning (as new issues keep emerging). The first major test of a successful learning process is passed when the reader understands the in-depth meaning of the fact that in an object-oriented system "everything is an object."

The concepts of object technology are best explained using visual representations of the Unified Modeling Language (UML) – the standard object-oriented *modeling language* of today (OMG, 2004). The strength of UML is in providing the whole set of integrated modeling techniques that allow multiple models to be built representing complementary views of the system. Accordingly, this chapter uses UML in two ways – to represent all fundamental concepts of object technology and to explain models and modeling that can be done by means of UML.

3.1 Fundamentals of object technology

A good way to explain object orientation in information systems is to provide an analogy with real-life concrete objects. The world around us consists of *objects* in some observable *states* (determined by current values of the objects' attributes) and exhibiting some *behavior* (determined by operations (functions) performed by these objects). Each object is uniquely *identified* among other objects.

For example, a coffee mug on my desk is in a `filled` *state* because it is shaped to hold liquids and there is still coffee in it. When there is no more coffee in it, the state of the mug can be defined as `empty`. If it falls on the floor and breaks, it will be in a `broken` state.

My coffee mug is passive – it does not have *behavior* of its own. However, the same cannot be said of my dog or a eucalyptus tree outside my window. My dog barks, the tree grows, etc. So, some real-life objects do have behavior.

All real-life objects also have *identity* – a fixed property by which we distinguish one object from another. If I had two coffee mugs on my desk from the same mug set, I could say that the two mugs are *equal* but *not identical*. They are equal because they have the same state – the same values for all their attributes (so, they are the same size and shape, are black, and are empty). However, in object-oriented parlance they are not identical, because there are two of them and I have a choice of which one to use.

Real-life objects that possess the three properties (state, behavior, identity) build up *natural behavioral systems*. Natural systems are by far the most *complex systems* that we know. No computer system has come close to the inherent complexity of an animal or a plant.

Despite their complexity, natural systems tend to work very well – they exhibit interesting behavior, can adjust to external and internal changes, can evolve over time, etc. The lesson is obvious. Perhaps we should construct *artificial systems* by emulating the structure and behavior of natural systems (cf. Maciaszek *et al.*, 1996b).

Artificial systems are models of reality. A coffee mug on my computer screen is as much a model of the real "thing" as is a dog or a eucalyptus tree on my screen. A coffee mug can, therefore, be modeled with behavioral properties. It can, for example, fall on the floor if knocked over. The "fall" action can be modeled as a behavioral *operation* of the mug. Another consequential operation of the mug may be to "break" when hitting the floor. Most, if not all, objects in a computer system "come alive" – they have behavior.

3.1.1 Instance object

An object is an *instance* of a "thing." It may be one of the many instances of the same "thing." My mug is an instance in the set of possible mugs.

A generic description of a "thing" is called a *class*. Hence, an object is an instance of a class. However, as discussed later in this chapter, a class itself may also need to be instantiated – it may be an object. For this reason, we need to distinguish between an *instance object* and a *class object*.

For brevity, an instance object is frequently called an *object* or an *instance*. It is confusing to call it an "object instance." Likewise, it is confusing to use the term "object class." Yes, a class is a template for objects with the same attributes and operations, but a class itself can be instantiated as an object (and it would be strange to call such a creation an "object class object").

An object-oriented system consists of collaborating objects. Everything in an object-oriented system is an object, be it an object of an instance (*instance object*) or an object of a class (*class object*).

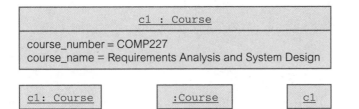

Figure 3.1
An instance object

Object notation

3.1.1.1

The UML notation for an object is a rectangle with two compartments. The upper compartment contains the name of an object and the name of a class to which the object belongs. The syntax is:

```
objectname: classname
```

The lower compartment contains the list of attribute names and values. The types of attributes can also be shown. The syntax is:

```
attributename: [type] = value
```

Figure 3.1 demonstrates four different ways in which an object can be shown graphically. The example shows a `Course` object named `c1`. The object has two attributes. The types of the attributes are not shown – they have been specified in the definition of the class. The attribute value compartment may be suppressed if not required to represent a particular modeling situation. Similarly, the object name may be omitted when representing an anonymous object of the given class. Finally, the class of the object may be suppressed. The presence or absence of the colon indicates whether the given label represents a class or an object.

It is important to note that the object notation does not provide a "compartment" for listing the *operations* that an instance object can execute. This is because the operations are identical for all instance objects, and it would be redundant to store them repeatedly in each instance object. Operations may be stored in a *class object*, or they may be associated with instance objects by other means (implemented in the underlying object-oriented system software).

As an aside, there are some less popular programming languages, such as Self, that allow operations to be attached to objects (not just classes) at run time. These languages are known as *prototypical* or *delegation-based* languages. For such situations, UML allows a third compartment containing operations as a language-specific extension (UML, 2003).

How do objects collaborate?

3.1.1.2

The number of objects of a particular class can be very large. This is true in particular for *business objects* representing business concepts (known as *entity classes*, such as `Invoice` or `Employee`). It is impractical and infeasible to visualize many objects on a diagram.

Objects are normally drawn only to exemplify a system at a point in time or to exemplify how they *collaborate* over time to do certain tasks. For example, to order products a *collaboration* may need to be established between a `Stock` object and a `Purchase` object.

Figure 3.2
Object
collaboration

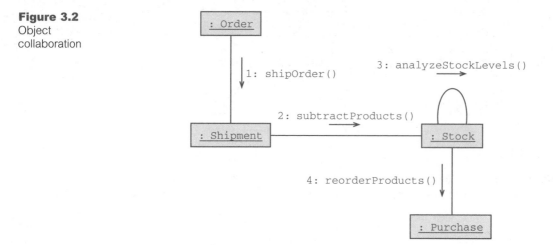

To be precise, objects on collaboration diagrams are so-called *roles*, not objects – they describe many possible objects. Graphically, the roles are presented using the notation of anonymous objects.

System tasks are performed by sets of objects that invoke *operations* (behavior) on each other. We say that they exchange *messages*. The messages call operations on objects that can result in the change of objects' states and can invoke other operations.

Figure 3.2 shows the flow of messages between four objects. The parentheses after the message names indicate that a message can take parameters (like in a traditional programming call to a function). The object `Order` requests the object `Shipment` to "ship itself" (to this aim, `Order` passes itself to `Shipment` as an actual parameter to `shipOrder()`). `Shipment` asks `Stock` in a `getProducts()` message to provide the appropriate quantity of products. At this point, `Stock` analyzes its inventory levels for products to be shipped by performing `analyzeStockLevels()`. If the stock requires replenishment, `Stock` requests `Purchase` to reorder more products in a `reorder()` message.

Although the object collaboration model in Figure 3.2 is shown as a sequence of numbered messages, in general the flow of messages does not impose a strict temporal order on the activation of objects. For example, `analyzeStockLevels()` can be activated independently of `shipOrder()` and `getProducts()`, not in a way related to shipments. For these reasons, the numbering of messages is frequently not used in object collaboration models.

3.1.1.3 Identity and object communication

The question is how an object knows the *identity* of another object to which it wants to send a message. How does an `Order` object know the `Shipment` object so that the message `shipOrder()` reaches its destination?

The answer is that each object is given an *object identifier* (OID) when it is created. The OID is the *handle* on that object – a unique number that remains with the object for its entire life. If an object X wants to send a message to an object Y, then X has somehow to know the OID of Y. There are two practical solutions to establishing OID *links* between objects. These solutions involve:

- persistent OID links; and
- transient OID links.

The distinction between these two kinds of link has to do with the longevity of objects. Some objects live only as long as the program executes – they are created by the program and destroyed during the program execution or when the program finishes its execution. These are *transient objects*. Other objects outlive the execution of the program – they are stored in the persistent disk storage when the program finishes and are available for the next execution of the program. These are *persistent objects*.

Persistent link

3.1.1.3.1

A *persistent link* is an object reference (or a set of object references) in one object in persistent storage that links that object to another object in persistent storage (or to the set of other objects). Hence, to persistently link a `Course` object to its `Teacher` object, the object `Course` must contain a link attribute, the value of which is the OID of the object `Teacher`. The link is persistent because the OID is physically stored in the object `Course`, as shown in Figure 3.3.

The OID of object `c1` is marked here as `CCC888`. The object contains a link attribute named `teacher`. The type of this attribute is `identity`. Its value is the OID of a `Teacher` object, shown here as `TTT999`. The OID is a logical address of the object. This can be implemented as the computer identification number plus the time in milliseconds when the object was instantiated. The programming language environment is able to convert the logical address to the physical disk address where the object `Teacher` is *persistently* stored.

Once the objects `Course` and `Teacher` are transferred to the program's memory, the value of the `teacher` attribute will be *swizzled* to a memory pointer, thus establishing a memory-level collaboration between the objects. (Swizzling is not the UML term – it is used in object databases where the transfers of objects between persistent storage and transient memory are frequent.)

Figure 3.3 illustrates how persistent links are represented in objects. In UML modeling, the links between objects can be drawn as in Figure 3.4. The links are represented as *instances of an association* between the objects `Course` and `Teacher`.

Normally, collaboration links on business objects allow for *navigation* in both directions. Each `Course` object is linked to its `Teacher` object, and a `Teacher` object can navigate to `Course` objects. It is possible, though not frequent in the case of business objects, to allow for navigation in only one direction.

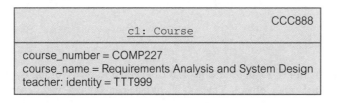

Figure 3.3
The representation of a persistent link

Figure 3.4
Persistent links
in a UML object
model

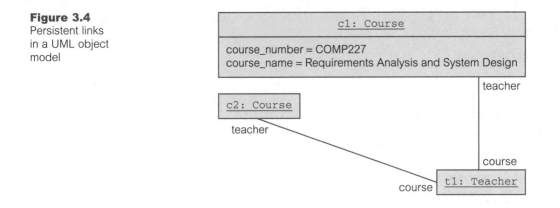

3.1.1.3.2   Transient link

What if no persistent link is defined between `Course` and `Teacher`, and there is still a need to send a message from object `t1` to object `c1` to invoke the operation `getCourseName()`? The application program must have other means to find out the identity of object `c1` and create a *transient link* from object `t1` to object `c1` (Riel, 1996).

Fortunately, a programmer has many techniques that can lead to initialization of the variable `crs_ref` with an OID of memory-resident object `c1`. To start with, it is possible that earlier in the program a link between objects `c1` and `t1` has been established and `crs_ref` still holds the correct OID. For example, the program has executed a search operation on the teacher's `t1` availability and on the timetable for courses and has determined that teacher `t1` should teach course `c1`.

An alternative possibility is that the program has access to a persistently stored table that maps course numbers to teacher names. It can then search on `Course` objects to find all courses taught by teacher `t1` and request the user to determine the course that the message `getCourseName` is to be sent to.

It is also possible that the very task of a program is to create courses and teachers before storing them in a database. There is no persistent link between teachers and courses, but the user enters the information so that each course clearly identifies a teacher in charge. The program can then store the transient links in the program's variables (such as `crs_ref`), and these variables can be used later (during the same program execution) to send messages between `Teacher` and `Course` objects.

In short, there are quite a few ways to establish transient links between objects that are not persistently linked by associations between relevant classes. *Transient links* are program variables that contain OID values of objects that are currently in the program's memory. The mapping (*swizzling*) between the transient and persistent OIDs should be the responsibility of the underlying programming environment, such as an object database system.

3.1.1.3.3   Message passing

Once an object is linked to another object, it can send a message along the link to request a *service* from the other object. That is, an object can invoke an *operation* on another object by sending a *message* to it. In a typical scenario, to point to an object, the sender will use a program's variable containing a link value (OID value) of that object. For example, a *message* sent by an object `Teacher` to find the name of an object `Course` could look like:

```
crs_ref.getCourseName(out crs_name)
```

In the example, the specific object of class `Course` that will execute `getCourseName` is pointed to by the current value of the link variable `crs_ref`. The output (`out`) argument `crs_name` is a variable to be initialized with the value returned by the operation `getCourseName` implemented in the class `Course`.

The example assumes that the programming language distinguishes between input (`in`), output (`out`), and input/output (`inout`) arguments. Popular object-oriented languages, such as Java, do not make such distinctions. In Java, message arguments of primitive data types (such as `crs_name` in the example) are passed to operations by value. "Pass by value" means that these are effectively input arguments – the operation cannot change the value passed. The change is not possible because the operation acts on a copy of the argument.

In the case of message arguments of non-primitive data types (i.e. arguments that are references to user-defined objects), "pass by value" means that the operation receives the reference to the argument, not its value. Because there is only one reference (not two copies of it), the operation can use it to access and possibly modify the attribute values within the passed object. This in effect eliminates the need for explicit input/output arguments.

Finally, the need for explicit output arguments is substituted in Java by a return type of an operation invoked by a message call. The return type may be primitive or non-primitive. An operation can return the maximum of one return value or no value at all (i.e. a return type of `void`). When multiple values need to be returned, the programmer has an option of defining a non-primitive aggregate object type that can contain all the values to be returned.

Class

3.1.2

A *class* is the descriptor for a set of objects with the same attributes and operations. It serves as a *template* for object creation. Each object created from the template contains the attribute *values* that conform to attribute *types* defined in the class. Each object can invoke operations defined in its class.

Graphically, a class is represented as a rectangle with three compartments separated by horizontal lines, as shown in Figure 3.5. The top compartment holds the class name. The middle compartment declares all attributes for the class. The bottom compartment contains definitions of operations.

Attribute

3.1.2.1

An attribute is the *type–value* pair. Classes define *attribute types*. Objects contain *attribute values*. Figure 3.6 illustrates two classes with attribute names and attribute types defined.

Figure 3.5
Class
compartments

Figure 3.6
Attributes

Figure 3.7
Role names that
designate classes
(analysis model)

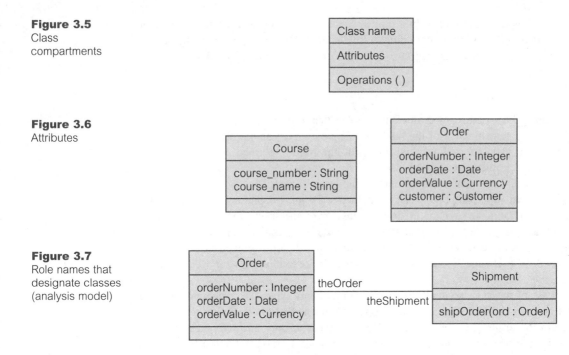

Two different attribute-naming conventions are shown. The attribute names in `Course` use the notation popularized by the database community. The programming language community prefers the convention shown in `Order`.

An attribute type can be a built-in *primitive type*, or it can be a user-defined *non-primitive type*. A primitive type is the type directly understood and supported by an underlying object-oriented software environment. All attribute types in Figure 3.6, except `customer`, designate primitive types. The type of `customer` is a *class* (non-primitive type). However, note that in UML analysis models, non-primitive attribute types are not visualized within the attributes compartment (this is discussed next).

3.1.2.1.1 *Attribute type that designates a class*

An attribute type can also designate a class. In a particular object of the class, such an attribute contains an object identifier (OID) value pointing to an object of another class. In UML analysis models, attributes with class-based types (rather than primitive types) are not listed in the middle class compartment. Instead, the *associations* between classes represent them. Figure 3.7 shows such an association between two classes.

The two names on the association line (`theShipment` and `theOrder`) represent so-called role names. A *role name* identifies the meaning for the association end and is used to *navigate* to an object of the other class in the association.

In the implemented system, the role name (on the opposite end of the association) becomes a class attribute whose type is the class pointed to by the role name. This means that an attribute represents an association with another class. Figure 3.8 shows two classes from Figure 3.7 as eventually implemented.

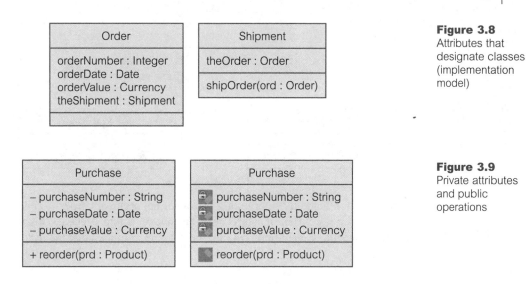

Figure 3.8
Attributes that
designate classes
(implementation
model)

Figure 3.9
Private attributes
and public
operations

Attribute visibility

As explained in Section 3.1.1.2, objects collaborate by sending messages to each other. A message invokes a class operation. The operation services the calling object's request by accessing attribute values in its own object and, if necessary, by sending messages to other objects. For this scenario to be possible, the operations must be *visible* to the outside objects (messages must see the operations). Such operations are said to have *public visibility*.

In a well-designed and implemented object-oriented system, most operations are *public* but most attributes are *private*. Attribute values are hidden from other classes. Objects of one class can only request the services (operations) published in the public interface of another class. They not allowed to manipulate other objects' attributes directly.

It is said that operations *encapsulate* attributes. However, note that the encapsulation applies to classes. One object cannot hide (encapsulate) anything from another object of the same class. Visibility is normally designated by a plus or minus symbol:

+   for public visibility
−   for private visibility

These symbols are replaced in some CASE tools by graphical icons. Figure 3.9 demonstrates two graphical representations to signify attribute visibility. The graphical icon of a lock designates private visibility.

Operation

An object contains data (attributes) and algorithms (operations) to act on these data. An operation is declared in a class. A procedure that implements the operation is called a *method*. The operation (or the method, to be precise) is invoked by a message sent to it. The name of the message and the name of the operation are the same. The operation can contain a list of formal arguments (parameters) that can be set to specific values by means of actual arguments in the message call. The operation can return a value to the calling object.

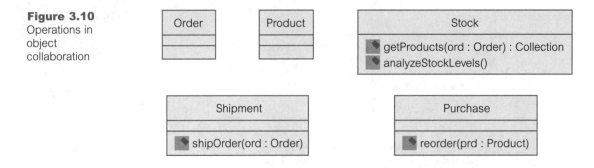

Figure 3.10
Operations in object collaboration

The operation name together with a list of formal argument types is called the *signature* of an operation. The signature must be unique within a class. This means that a class may have many operations with the same name, provided that the lists of parameter types vary.

3.1.2.2.1 *Operations in object collaboration*

An object-oriented program executes by reacting to random events from the user. The events come from the keyboard, mouse clicks, menu items, action buttons, and other input devices. A user-generated *event* converts to a *message* sent to an *object*. To accomplish a task, many objects may need to collaborate. Objects collaborate by invoking *operations* in other objects (Section 3.1.1.2).

Figure 3.10 shows operations in classes necessary to support the object collaboration demonstrated in Figure 3.2. Each message in Figure 3.2 requires an operation in the class designated by the message's destination.

The classes `Order` and `Product` (the latter not shown in Figure 3.2) do not have any operations in this simple example. The `Order` is initiated by the `Order` object when it requests that a `Shipment` object ship it. As a result of the shipment, the stock may need to be replenished with new products.

The `getProducts()` operation demonstrates the return type of `Collection`. This is the collection (set, list, or something similar) of products returned by `Stock` to `Shipment`. The `Collection` type is provided by the programming language. The Java collection comes from the library `java.util.Collection`.

3.1.2.2.2 *Operation visibility and scope*

The visibility of an operation defines whether the operation is visible to objects of classes other than a class that defines the operation. If it is visible then its visibility is *public*. It is *private*, otherwise. The icons in front of operation names in Figure 3.10 denote the visibility that is public.

Most operations in an object-oriented system would have public visibility. For an object to provide a service to the outside world, the "service" operation must be visible. However, most objects will also have a number of internal housekeeping operations. These will be given private visibility. They are accessible only to objects of a class in which they have been defined.

Operation visibility needs to be distinguished from *operation scope*. The operation may be invoked on an *instance object* (Section 3.1.1), or it may be invoked on a *class object* (Section 3.1.2.3). In the former case, the operation is said to have *instance scope*, in the latter case *class scope*. For example, the operation to find an employee's age has instance scope, but the operation to calculate the average age of all employees has class scope.

Class object 3.1.2.3

In Section 3.1.1, the distinction was made between *instance objects* and *class objects*. A *class object* is an object with class-scope attributes and/or class-scope operations. The class scope implies here a global attribute or operation that can be accessed/called on the class itself, not necessarily on an instance object. However, note that in practice, most programming languages do not implement the concept of a class object by instantiating such an object. They instead provide a syntax capability to refer to the class name in order to access a class-scope attribute or call a class-scope operation.

The most common *class-scope attributes* are attributes that hold default values or aggregate values (such as sums, counts, and averages). The most common *class-scope operations* are operations to create and destroy instance objects and operations that calculate aggregate values.

Figure 3.11 shows the class `Student` with two class-scope attributes (underlined) and a class-scope operation (identified by the stereotype `<<static>>`). Note that the attribute `numberOfStudents` is private, but the attribute `maxCoursesPerSemester` is public. Every student has the same allowed maximum number of courses per semester. The operation to calculate the average age of students has class scope because it needs to access the

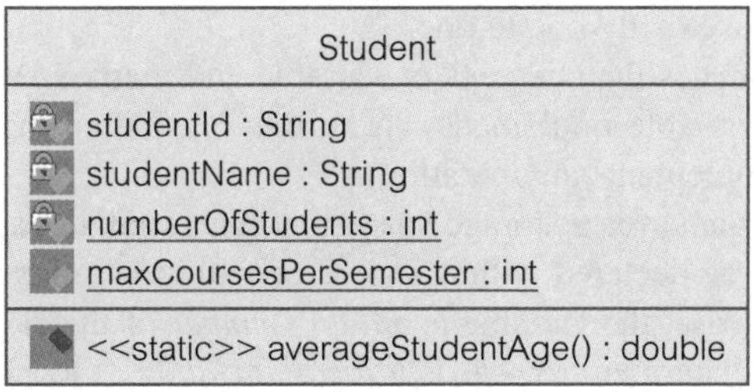

Student

🔒 studentId : String
🔒 studentName : String
🔒 numberOfStudents : int
   maxCoursesPerSemester : int

🔷 <<static>> averageStudentAge() : double

Figure 3.11
Java class with class-scope attributes and operations

```
public class Student
{
    private String studentId; //accessible via Student's operations
    private String studentName; //accessible via Student's operations
    private static int numberOfStudents;
    //accessible only to Student's static methods, such as averageStudentAge()
    public static int maxCoursesPerSemester;
    //accessible via Student:: maxCoursesPerSemester

    public static double averageStudentAge()
    { implementation code here }
    //callable by referring to the class name - Student::averageStudentAge()
    //callable also with an object of the calss - std.averageStudentAge()
}
```

individual ages of students (in `Student` instance objects), sum them and divide the sum by the total number of students kept in `numberOfStudents`.

Figure 3.11 also shows Java code corresponding to the graphical model. Java uses the keyword `static` to distinguish between instance and class properties. In effect, Java defines two kinds of object (instance and class objects) in one class definition (Lee and Tepfenhart, 2002).

The two instance attributes (`studentId` and `studentName`) result in their own copies (storage space) in each instance of the class. Because these two attributes have `private` visibility, they are accessible only to operations defined in `Student` class.

Class-scope (`static`) attributes are stored as single copies (occupy single storage space). In the case of a private static attribute (`numberOfStudents`), this single storage space is shared with all instances of `Student` and is accessible to `Student`'s static operations. In the case of a public static attribute (`maxCoursePerSemester`), the single storage space is shared with all instances of all classes and is accessible with the class name, i.e. `Student::numberOfStudents`.

Class-scope (`static`) operations are callable, if `public`, from any instance of any class. They can be called by referring to the class name (`Student::averageStudentAge()`) or with an object of the class (e.g. `std.averageStudentAge()`).

3.1.3 Variables, methods, and constructors

The discussion so far has used, as far as possible, the generic terminology present in UML analysis models. However, to explain object implementation principles, there is a need to use the terminology present in UML design models and in programming languages such as Java. Frequently, the analysis and design terminology is the same, but sometimes the terminology differs and the mapping between corresponding analysis and design/implementation terms is not exactly one to one.

This section introduces the concepts of variable and method. Variable maps from the notion of attribute (variable implements an attribute). Method maps from the notion of operation (method implements an operation).

A *variable* is the name for a storage space that may contain values for a specific data type. A variable can be declared within a class or within an operation (method body) of the class. In the first case, the variable is a *data member* of the class. In the second case, the variable is not a data member – it is a *local variable*. A local variable is valid only within the scope of the method (i.e. as long as the method executes).

Data members can have instance scope (*instance variables*) or class scope (*class variables*) (Section 3.1.2.3). There are two categories of instance variable – those that implement *attributes* and those that implement *associations*. The former are variables with a primitive data type (they store attribute values). The latter are variables with a non-primitive data type (they store references to objects and, therefore, they implement associations).

It is important to understand that variables storing references to objects are *not* objects (Lethbridge and Laganiere, 2001). During a single program execution, the same variable can refer to different objects and the same objects can be referred to by different variables. A variable can also contain a `null` value, which means that it does not refer to any object at all.

Data members (instance and class variables) can be initialized to any *non-constant* or *constant* value/object. A constant variable cannot change its value after the value has been assigned to it. Constants cannot be defined for local variables. In Java, constants are defined with the `final` keyword.

Instance variables that implement attributes can be initialized at the time they are defined within a class. Instance variables that implement associations are normally initialized programmatically, frequently in the constructor, which initializes objects of the class concerned.

A *method* is the implementation of an operation (a service) that belongs to a class (Lee and Tepfenhart, 2002). A method has a name and a *signature* – the list of formal arguments (parameters). Two methods with the same name but different signatures are considered different. Such methods are known as *overloaded* methods.

A method may *return* (to the calling object) a single value of some primitive or non-primitive type. Formally, all methods must have a return type, but the type may be `void`. The method name, its signature, and its return type are together known as the method *prototype*.

A *constructor* is a special method (the purists would argue that it is not a method at all) that serves the purpose of instantiating objects of the class. Each class must have at least one constructor, but it can have more than one (i.e. constructors can be overloaded). A constructor name is the same as the name of the class for which it is declared. Constructors do not have return types. In Java, a constructor is called with the `new` keyword, e.g.

```
Student std22 = new Student();
```

The constructor `Student()` in the example is the so-called default constructor, generated automatically by Java if omitted in the class definition. The default constructor creates an object with default values assigned for all class variables. In Java, the default values are `0` for numbers, `'0'` for characters, `false` for Booleans, and `null` for objects.

Association   3.1.4

An *association* is one kind of relationship between classes. Other kinds of relationship include generalization, aggregation, and dependency.

An association relationship provides a linkage between objects of given classes. Objects needing to communicate with each other can use the linkage. If possible, messages between objects should always be sent along association relationships. This has an important documentary advantage – the static compile-time structures (i.e. associations) document all possible dynamic message passing that is allowed at run time.

Figure 3.12 shows the association named `OrdShip` between classes `Order` and `Shipment`. The association allows for an `Order` object to be shipped (to be linked to) more than one `Shipment` object (indicated by the association multiplicity of n). A `Shipment` object can also carry (be linked to) more than one `Order` object.

In the simplest case of one-to-one association between an `Order` object and a `Shipment` object, the processing scenario could be as follows. An `Order` object needs to get shipped. To this aim, it instantiates a new `Shipment` object by invoking one of `Shipment`'s constructors. As a result of instantiation, `Order` obtains the reference to the new `Shipment` object.

Figure 3.12
Association

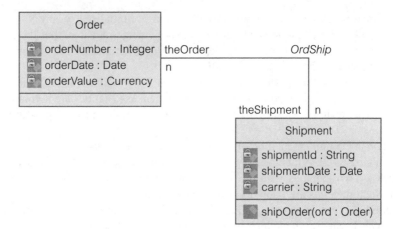

Knowing this, `Order` can send the `shipOrder()` message to `Shipment`, passing itself to `Shipment` in the actual argument of `ShipOrder()`. This way, `Shipment` obtains the reference to `Order`. The only remaining action to establish the association is to assign the `Shipment` reference to the variable `theShipment` and, conversely, the `Order` reference to the variable `theOrder`.

Typically, associations on entity classes (business objects), as in Figure 3.12, are bidirectional. However, unidirectional associations may be sufficient in associations on other categories of classes, such as between classes representing a GUI window, programming logic, or user events.

3.1.4.1   Association degree

Association degree defines the number of classes connected by the association. The most frequent association is of *degree 2*. This is called a *binary association*. The association in Figure 3.12 is binary. Association can also be defined on a single class. This is called a *unary* (or *singular*) *association* (Maciaszek, 1990). The unary association establishes links between objects of a single class.

Figure 3.13 is a typical example of a unary association. It captures the hierarchical structure of employment. An `Employee` object is `managedBy` one other `Employee` object or by nobody (i.e. an employee who is, say, the chief executive officer (CEO) is not managed by anybody). An `Employee` object may be the `managerOf` many employees, unless the employee is at the bottom of the employment ladder and is not managing anybody. Associations of degree 3 (*ternary associations*) are also possible but are not recommended (Maciaszek, 1990).

3.1.4.2   Association multiplicity

Association multiplicity defines how many objects may be represented by a *role name*. The multiplicity states how many objects of a target class (pointed to by the role name) can be associated with a single object of the source class.

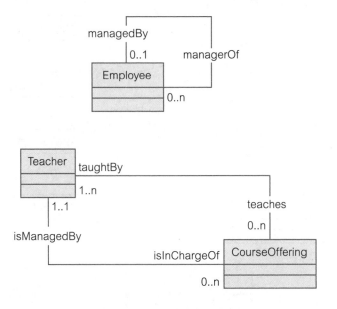

Figure 3.13
Unary association

Figure 3.14
Association
multiplicity

Multiplicity is shown as a range of integers $i1..i2$. The integer $i1$ defines the minimum number of connected objects and $i2$ the maximum number (the maximum number can be shown as n if the precise maximum integer value is not known or is not fixed). The minimum number does not have to be specified if such information is not essential in the model at the level of abstraction applied (as in Figure 3.12).

The most frequent multiplicities are:

```
0..1
0..n
1..1
1..n
n
```

Figure 3.14 demonstrates two associations on the classes `Teacher` and `CourseOffering`. One association captures the assignment of teachers to current course offerings. The other determines which teacher is in charge of an offering. A teacher can teach many offerings or none (e.g. if a teacher is on leave). One or more teachers teach a course offering. One of these teachers is in charge of the offering. In general, a teacher can be in charge of many course offerings or none. One and only one teacher manages a course offering.

Association multiplicity in UML is an imprecise term. The "zero" and "one" minimum multiplicity can be seen as a distinct semantic notion of *membership* or *participation* (Maciaszek, 1990). The "zero" minimum multiplicity signifies an *optional membership* of an object in the association. The "one" multiplicity signifies a *mandatory membership*. For example, a `CourseOffering` object must be managed by a `Teacher` object.

The membership property has some interesting semantics of its own. For example, a particular mandatory membership may additionally imply that the membership is *fixed*, i.e. once an object is linked to a target object in the association it cannot be reconnected to another target object in the same association.

Figure 3.15
Links and extents

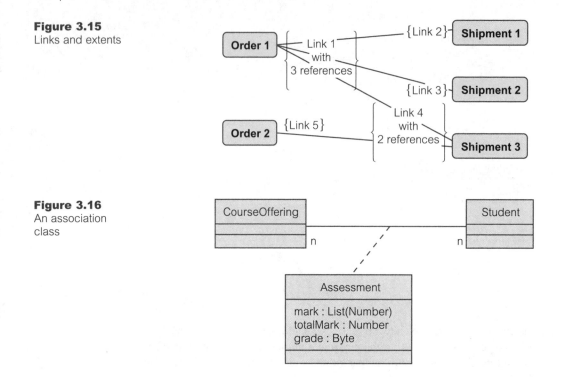

Figure 3.16
An association
class

3.1.4.3 Association link and extent

An association *link* is an instance of the association. It is a *tuple* of references to objects. The tuple can be, for example, a *set* of references or a *list* (ordered set) of references. In general, the tuple can contain one reference only. The link also represents the *role name*, as discussed earlier. The *extent* is a set of links.

Figure 3.15 is a particular instantiation of the association OrdShip in Figure 3.12. There are five links in Figure 3.15. Hence the extent of the association is five. The understanding of association links and extents is important to overall comprehension of the association concept, but the links and extents are not meant to be modeled or otherwise apparent.

3.1.4.4 Association class

Sometimes an association has attributes (and/or operations) of its own. Such an association must be modeled as a class (because attributes can only be defined in a class). Each object of an *association class* has attribute values and links to the objects of associated classes. Because an association class is a class, it can be associated with other classes in the model in the normal way.

Figure 3.16 shows the association class Assessment. An object of the class Assessment stores the list of marks, the total mark, and the grade obtained by a Student in a ClassOffering.

The type of the attribute `mark` is `List(Number)`. This is a so-called *parameterized type*. `Number` is the parameter of the class `List`, where `List` defines an ordered set of values. The attribute `mark` contains the list of all marks that a student obtained in a class offering. That is, if the student "Fred" takes the course offering "COMP227," there will eventually be a list (an ordered set) of marks for him on that course offering. That list of marks will be stored in an `Assessment` object that represents the association between "Fred" and "COMP227."

Aggregation and composition 3.1.5

An *aggregation* is a whole−part relationship between a class representing an assembly of components (*superset class*) and the classes representing the components (*subset classes*). A superset class contains a subset class (or classes). The containment property can be strong (*aggregation by value*) or weak (*aggregation by reference*). In UML, the aggregation by value is called *composition*, and the aggregation by reference is simply called *aggregation*.

From the system modeling perspective, aggregation is a special kind of association with additional semantics. In particular, aggregation is transitive and asymmetric. *Transitivity* means that if class A contains class B and class B contains class C, then A contains C. *Asymmetry* means that if A contains B, then B cannot contain A.

Composition has an additional property of *existence dependency*. An object of a subset class cannot exist without being linked to an object of the superset class. This implies that if a superset object is deleted (destroyed), then its subset objects must also be deleted.

The *composition* is signified by the *filled diamond* "adornment" on the end of the association line connected to the superset class. *Aggregation* that is not composition is marked with a *hollow diamond*. However, note that the hollow diamond can also be used if the modeler does not want to make the decision whether the aggregation is a composition or not.

Figure 3.17 shows a composition on the left and a normal aggregation on the right. Any `Book` object is a composition of `Chapter` objects, and any `Chapter` is a composition of `Section` objects. A `Chapter` object does not have an independent life; it exists only within the `Book` object. The same cannot be said about `BeerBottle` objects. The `BeerBottle` objects can exist outside of their container – a `Crate` object.

Aggregation and composition (as well as the associated notion of *delegation* introduced in Section 3.1.5.3) are very useful concepts in object technology. However, it is unfortunate that commercial programming languages give relatively little support to these concepts. In many languages, aggregation and composition are implemented not differently from the implementation of association, i.e. by means of *buried references* (Lee and Tepfenhart, 2002) (Section 3.1.5.1). Java provides an alternative implementation by means of *inner classes* (Section 3.1.5.2).

Buried reference 3.1.5.1

A *buried reference* implements an aggregation by means of a variable with private visibility that references the subset object. This is not different to the implementation of an

Figure 3.17
Composition and
aggregation

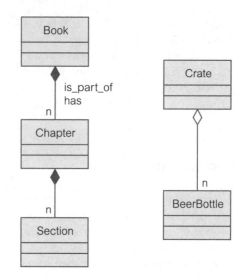

association by means of a private reference. Such implementation does not support any other semantics of aggregation. Hence, for example, to ensure that the deletion of a super-set object also deletes its subset objects, the programmer has to implement such deletions in the application code.

Figure 3.18 is an example illustrating buried references. Book is modeled as the composition of many Chapter objects and one TableOfContents object. Consequently, the Book class has two buried references: private variables theChapter and theTableOfContents. Having these references private hides the identities of the book's chapters and its table of content from other classes. However, this is of little benefit, because the visibility of classes cannot be private with regard to other classes. In the example, Chapter and TableOfContents have *package* visibility (package visibility is implied by the absence of the keyword "public" in front of these classes' names). The package visibility makes the classes visible to all classes in the same package (in Java, every class must be assigned to one and only one package).

The presence of backward references from Chapter and TableOfContents to Book is also the result of imperfect implementation of aggregation/composition. Subset objects must somehow know their owner.

Figure 3.18 illustrates how the superset object can demonstrate to the outside world that it is the owner of subset objects. This is shown in the implementation of the search() operation. The service to search for some string in the book is available in the Book class. The requester can send the search() message to a Book object. The Book object can then forward this request to its Chapter objects by invoking the search() method on these objects. In effect, the requester relies exclusively on the Book object to get the search results back.

3.1.5.2   Inner class

In Java, it is possible to define a class as an internal member of another class. The member class can have class scope, i.e. be declared as static. It is then called a *nested*

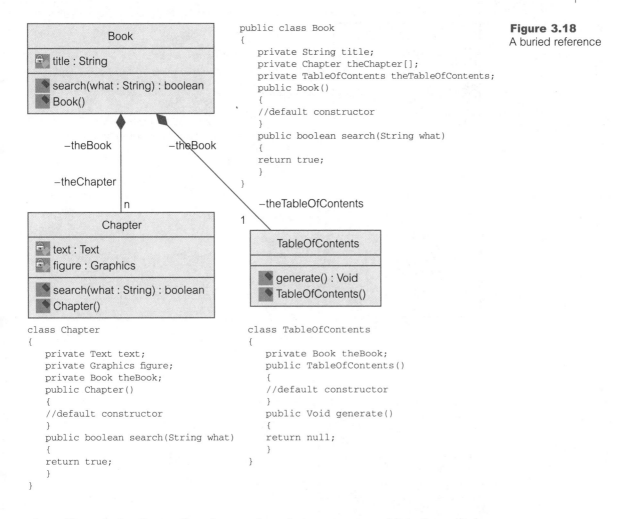

Figure 3.18
A buried reference

```
public class Book
{
    private String title;
    private Chapter theChapter[];
    private TableOfContents theTableOfContents;
    public Book()
    {
    //default constructor
    }
    public boolean search(String what)
    {
    return true;
    }
}
```

```
class Chapter
{
    private Text text;
    private Graphics figure;
    private Book theBook;
    public Chapter()
    {
    //default constructor
    }
    public boolean search(String what)
    {
    return true;
    }
}
```

```
class TableOfContents
{
    private Book theBook;
    public TableOfContents()
    {
    //default constructor
    }
    public Void generate()
    {
    return null;
    }
}
```

class. Alternatively, the member class can have instance scope, and it is then called an *inner class* (Eckel, 2003). It turns out that the inner class could be used as the best Java-supported implementation of aggregation/composition.

An inner class reflects the relationship between the superset instance and its inner subset instances. The superset instance has natural control over its subset objects because it owns them. In the opposite direction, the subset instances have direct access to all members of the superset object, including the private members.

Figure 3.19 shows how essentially the same model as in Figure 3.18 can be implemented with inner classes. In typical situations, an outer class obtains a reference to an inner class by either instantiating the inner object within its own constructor or by having a method that instantiates the inner object. The example uses the former approach. The `Book()` constructor instantiates `TableOfContents` and `Chapter` objects from its constructor (but it could construct them from other private methods to achieve the same level of encapsulation). `Book` redirects all queries to its content to appropriate `TableOfContents` or `Chapter` objects.

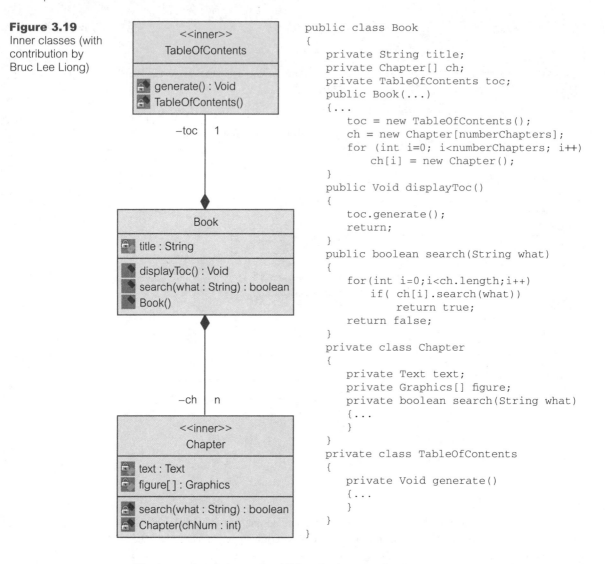

Figure 3.19
Inner classes (with contribution by Bruc Lee Liong)

```
public class Book
{
    private String title;
    private Chapter[] ch;
    private TableOfContents toc;
    public Book(...)
    {...
        toc = new TableOfContents();
        ch = new Chapter[numberChapters];
        for (int i=0; i<numberChapters; i++)
            ch[i] = new Chapter();
    }
    public Void displayToc()
    {
        toc.generate();
        return;
    }
    public boolean search(String what)
    {
        for(int i=0;i<ch.length;i++)
            if( ch[i].search(what))
                return true;
        return false;
    }
    private class Chapter
    {
        private Text text;
        private Graphics[] figure;
        private boolean search(String what)
        {...
        }
    }
    private class TableOfContents
    {
        private Void generate()
        {...
        }
    }
}
```

The inner classes have an additional advantage in the implementation of aggregation/composition – they can be made *private* (whereas the normal classes can have only public or package visibility). Private inner classes can be accessed only from the outer class. This completely hides the implementation of inner classes from all but the outer class, and it reduces dependencies due to changes in this implementation. In Figure 3.19, `TableOfContents` and `Chapter` are known only to `Book` and not to other classes in the system.

Other important benefits of using inner classes are related to the notions of *interface* and *inheritance*. Both these notions are discussed later in this chapter. To those already initiated in these concepts, suffice it to say that an inner class can implement an interface as well as extend (inherit from) a class (Eckel, 2003). The first technique can further reduce dependencies of the program's classes on the inner class, even if the inner class is public.

Everything that is made available to the program's classes are references to one or more interfaces that the inner class invisibly implements. The second technique in effect allows *multiple implementation inheritance*, even though Java is a single-inheritance language. The multiple inheritance comes from the fact that the outer class and its inner classes can inherit independently from other classes.

Delegation 3.1.5.3

Associated with aggregation/composition is the powerful technique of *delegation*. Delegation is a good replacement for inheritance as the code reuse technique (Gamma *et al.*, 1995). Although delegation can be used between any classes, it is at its best when applied to classes related by aggregation/composition.

The idea of delegation is as the name suggests. If an object receives a request to perform one of its services and is unable to deliver the service, it can delegate the work to one of its component objects. Delegating the work to another object does not relieve the original recipient of the message from responsibility for the service. The work is delegated, not the responsibility.

Figure 3.19 gives an example of delegation involving an inner class. The delegation can happen on the search() method. The Book class has search() in its public interface, thus promising this service to the outside world. When Book receives a request to perform search(), it delegates the work to its Chapter objects. Chapter performs the work, Book gets the glory. The requester of the service does not even have a choice of directing the message to Chapter, because Chapter has private visibility.

Technically, the scenario in Figure 3.19 is known as *forwarding* the message, not *delegating*. Delegation is a more complex form of forwarding such that an object delegating the service is passing along a reference to itself (Gamma *et al.*, 1995). However, in the case of inner classes there is no need to pass a reference of the delegating object, because inner objects have direct access to all members of the outer class (by means of language-implemented hidden references).

Figure 3.19 does not illustrate the *code reuse* aspect of delegation and the related benefit of improved *supportability* of programs relying on delegation. The benefits of reusability and supportability require the combining of delegation with interfaces and/or abstract classes (both concepts are discussed later).

The idea is that changes to objects that do the work (to which the work was delegated) do not affect the program as long as the work is done. As an example, assume that Chapter and Section objects have the same type, i.e. they inherit from the same superclass (ideally abstract class) or implement the same interface. It will then be possible to replace at run time the Chapter instances by Section instances in doing the search() operation. This replacement will not be noticed by the client object that requested the search() service.

Generalization and inheritance 3.1.6

A *generalization* relationship is a kind-of relationship between a more generic class (*superclass* or *parent*) and a more specialized kind of that class (*subclass* or *child*). The

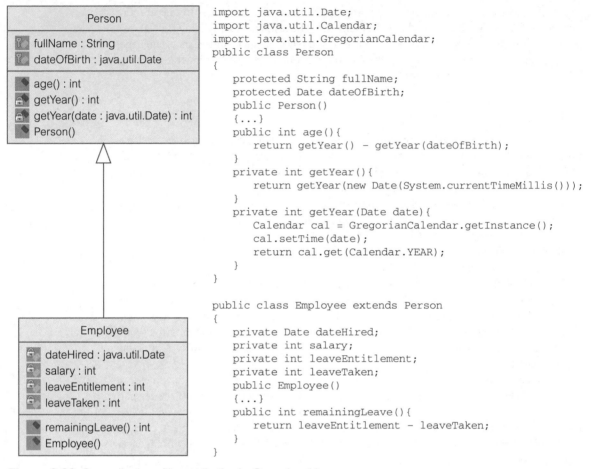

```java
import java.util.Date;
import java.util.Calendar;
import java.util.GregorianCalendar;
public class Person
{
    protected String fullName;
    protected Date dateOfBirth;
    public Person()
    {...}
    public int age(){
        return getYear() - getYear(dateOfBirth);
    }
    private int getYear(){
        return getYear(new Date(System.currentTimeMillis()));
    }
    private int getYear(Date date){
        Calendar cal = GregorianCalendar.getInstance();
        cal.setTime(date);
        return cal.get(Calendar.YEAR);
    }
}

public class Employee extends Person
{
    private Date dateHired;
    private int salary;
    private int leaveEntitlement;
    private int leaveTaken;
    public Employee()
    {...}
    public int remainingLeave(){
        return leaveEntitlement - leaveTaken;
    }
}
```

Figure 3.20 Generalization with contribution by Bruce Lee Liong

subclass is a kind of superclass. An object of the subclass can be used where the superclass is allowed. Generalization makes it unnecessary to restate already defined properties. The attributes and operations already defined for a superclass may be *reused* in a subclass. A subclass is said to *inherit* the attributes and methods of its parent class. Generalization facilitates incremental specification, exploitation of common properties between classes, and better localization of changes.

A generalization is drawn as a hollow triangle on the relationship end connected to the parent class. In Figure 3.20, Person is the superclass and Employee is the subclass. The class Employee inherits all attributes and operations of the class Person (but the private members of Person are not accessible to the Employee objects). The inherited properties are not visibly shown in the subclass box – the generalization relationship forces the inheritance into the background.

Note that inheritance applies to classes, not to objects. It applies to types, not to values. The class Employee inherits the definitions of attributes fullName and dateOfBirth. This is by virtue of the fact that an instance of Employee is also an instance of Person.

Hence, the constructor `Employee()` can set the values for `fullName` and `dateOfBirth` and for the remaining four data members.

But here is a twist. The two attributes in `Person` have private visibility. This implies that the class `Employee` cannot access the `fullName` and `dateOfBirth` values in a `Person` object. This is logical. Somebody named "Joe Guy" is either an employee and a person or he is just a person. If Joe is an employee (and a person), he has his own values for `fullName` and `dateOfBirth` (as well as for `dateHired`, etc.). If Joe is just a person (and not an employee), he again has values for `fullName` and `dateOfBirth` (but not for `dateHired`, etc.).

Although an instance of `Employee` has no right to access attribute values in an instance of `Person`, it can call the `Person`'s `age()` method without referring to the `Person` class name. The inherited `age()` method will access the `dateOfBirth` value of an object on which it is called (i.e. the `Employee` object). Other classes in the program can also call the `age()` method (because of its public visibility), but any such call must either refer to the `Person` class name (`Person::age()`) or call it with a `Person` instance (`person.age()`).

The two private operations in `Person` (two `getYear()` methods) are used internally by the `age()` method to compute the current age of a `Person` object. Java support for manipulating date values is a bit awkward. Java provides several libraries to do the job (as per the `import` statements in Figure 3.20). The first method, `getYear()`, returns the current year. The second parameterized method, `getYear(Date date)`, returns the year for some date in the past.

Polymorphism

3.1.6.1

A method inherited by a subclass is frequently used as inherited in that subclass (i.e. without modification). The operation `age()` works identically for the objects of classes `Person` and `Employee`. However, there are times when an operation needs to be *overridden* (modified) in a subclass to correspond to semantic variations of the subclass.

For example, `Employee.remainingLeave()` is computed by subtracting `leaveTaken` from `leaveEntitlement` (Figure 3.20). However, the employee who is a manager gains a yearly `leaveSupplement`. If we now add the class `Manager` to the generalization hierarchy (as shown in Figure 3.21), the operation `Manager.remainingLeave()` would override the operation `Employee.remainingLeave()`. This is indicated in Figure 3.21 by duplicating the operation name in the `Manager` subclass.

The operation `remainingLeave()` has been *overridden*. There are two implementations (two *methods*) of the operation. We can now send the message `remainingLeave()` to an `Employee` object or to a `Manager` object and we will get a different method executed. We may not even know or care which object is targeted: `Employee` or `Manager` – the proper method will execute.

The operation `remainingLeave()` is *polymorphic*. There are two implementations (methods) for this operation. Both methods have the same name and identical *signatures* – the number and types of parameters (in this case, the parameter list is empty).

Polymorphism and inheritance go hand in hand. Polymorphism without inheritance is of limited use. *Inheritance* permits incremental description of a subclass by reusing and then extending the superclass descriptions. The operation `Manager.remainingLeave()`

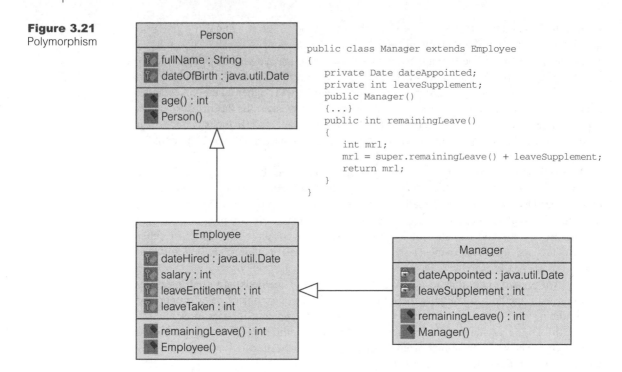

Figure 3.21
Polymorphism

```
public class Manager extends Employee
{
    private Date dateAppointed;
    private int leaveSupplement;
    public Manager()
    {...}
    public int remainingLeave()
    {
        int mrl;
        mrl = super.remainingLeave() + leaveSupplement;
        return mrl;
    }
}
```

is probably implemented by invoking the functionality of `Employee.remainingLeave()` and then by adding `leaveSupplement` to the value returned from `Employee.remainingLeave()`.

3.1.6.2 Overriding versus overloading

Overriding must not be confused with overloading. *Overriding* is the mechanism to achieve polymorphic operations. Overriden methods have identical names and signatures and are placed in different classes of the same inheritance hierarchy. The decision of which method is invoked is taken dynamically at run time. The decision is based on the class of the object to which the variable (from which the method is called) points to and not on the type of the variable (Lee and Tepfenhart, 2002).

If the variable points to a subclass object in the inheritance tree, and the overridden method exists for that subclass, then this overridden method will be invoked. However, if the method is not declared in the subclass, the programming environment will search up the inheritance tree to find the method in a superclass of the subclass. The search will continue up to the base class if the method has not been overridden in any subclasses. If this is the case, the method of the base class will be invoked.

Overloading refers to a situation when multiple methods with the same name are declared in the same class. The methods have the same names, but they have different signatures and possibly also different return types. Unlike overriding, which is a run-time phenomenon, overloading can be resolved at compile time.

Figure 3.20 illustrates overloading in the private methods `getYear()` and `getYear(Date date)`. The former returns the current calendar year. The latter returns the calendar year of some concrete date passed to it as parameter. The program decides statically which method to call. In fact, both methods are called by the public `age()` method declared within the same class (the `Person` class).

Multiple inheritance

3.1.6.3

In some languages, such as C++, a subclass can inherit from more than one superclass. This is called multiple implementation inheritance. *Multiple inheritance* can lead to inheritance conflicts, which have to be explicitly resolved by the programmer.

In Figure 3.22, the class `Tutor` inherits from the classes `Teacher` and `PostgraduateStudent`. `Teacher` in turn inherits from `Person` and so does `PostgraduateStudent` (via `Student`). As a result, `Tutor` would inherit twice the attributes and operations of `Person` unless the programmer instructs the programming environment to inherit only once by using either the left or right inheritance path (or unless the programming environment enforces some default behavior, acceptable to the programmer, that eradicates the duplicated inheritance).

Note that Java does not permit multiple implementation inheritance. Java provides alternative mechanisms, in particular interfaces (including multiple interface inheritance)

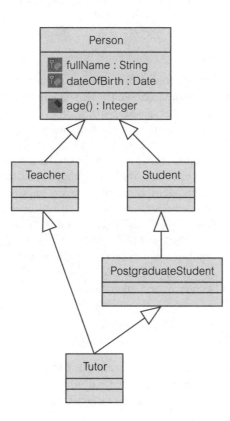

Figure 3.22
Multiple
inheritance

and inner classes, to implement the class structures and behavior corresponding to the model in Figure 3.22.

3.1.6.4 Multiple classification

In most current object-oriented programming environments, an object can belong to only one class. This is a troublesome restriction because in reality objects can belong to multiple classes.

Multiple classification is different from multiple inheritance. In multiple classification an object is simultaneously the instance of two or more classes. In multiple inheritance a class may have many superclasses, but an object is created as an instance of only one of these classes. The "knowledge" of other classes is only available to the object via inheritance.

In the multiple inheritance example in Figure 3.22, each `Person` object (such as `Mary` or `Peter`) belongs to a single class (the most *specific* class that applies to it). If `Mary` is a `PostgraduateStudent`, but not a `Tutor`, then `Mary`'s class is `PostgraduateStudent`.

The problem arises if `Person` is specialized in a few orthogonal hierarchies. For example, a `Person` can be an `Employee` or `Student`, `Male` or `Female`, `Child` or `Adult`, etc. Without multiple classification, we would need to define classes for each legal combination between the orthogonal hierarchies to have, for example, a class for a `Person` object who is a child female student (i.e. the class that could be called `ChildFemaleStudent`) (Fowler, 2004).

3.1.6.5. Dynamic classification

In most current object-oriented programming environments, an object cannot change its class after it has been instantiated (created). This is another troublesome restriction, because in reality objects do change classes dynamically.

Dynamic classification is a direct consequence of multiple classification. An object not only belongs to multiple classes but can also gain or lose classes over its lifetime. Under the dynamic classification scheme, a `Person` object can be just an employee one day and a manager (and employee) another day. Without dynamic classification, business changes such as the promotion of employees are hard (or even impossible) to implement. The implementation problem arises because definitions of object identifiers (OIDs) include the identification of the class to which an object belongs. Dynamic classification would necessitate changes of OIDs, which would defeat the very idea of OIDs (Section 3.1.1.3).

The lack of support for multiple and dynamic classification in programming languages translates to a similar lack of support in UML modeling. Consequently, no graphical models are shown here to enhance the explanation.

3.1.7 Abstract class

Abstract class is an important modeling concept that follows on from the notion of inheritance. An abstract class is a parent class that will not have direct instance objects. Only subclasses of the abstract parent class can be instantiated.

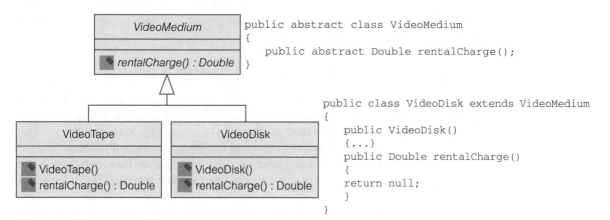

Figure 3.23 An abstract class

In a typical scenario, a class is abstract because at least one of its operations is abstract. An *abstract operation* has its name and signature defined in the abstract parent class, but the implementation of the operation (the method) is deferred to *concrete* child classes.

An abstract class cannot instantiate objects, because it has at least one abstract operation. If it was allowed for an abstract class to create an object, then a message to that object's abstract operation would cause a run-time error (because there would not be an implementation for the abstract operation in the class of that object).

A class can be abstract only if it is a superclass that is completely partitioned into subclasses. The partitioning is complete if the subclasses contain all possible objects that can be instantiated in the inheritance hierarchy. There are no "stray" objects (Page-Jones, 2000). The class `Person` in Figure 3.22 is not abstract because we may want to instantiate objects of `Person` that are not teachers or students. It is also possible that we may want to add more subclasses of `Person` in the future (such as `AdminEmployee`).

Figure 3.23 shows the abstract class `VideoMedium` (in UML, the name of the abstract class is shown in italics). The class contains the abstract operation `rentalCharge()`. Understandably, rental charges are calculated differently for video tapes and for video disks. There will be two different implementations of `rentalCharge()` – in classes `VideoTape` and `VideoDisk`.

Abstract classes do not have instances, but they are very useful in modeling. They create a high-level modeling "vocabulary" without which the modeling language would be deficient.

Interface   3.1.8

The idea of abstract classes is brought to complete fruition in Java interfaces. An *interface* is a definition of a semantic type with attributes (constants only) and operations but without actual declarations of operations (i.e. without implementation). The actual declarations are provided by one or more classes that undertake to implement the interface.

A program can use an interface variable in lieu of a class variable, thus separating the client class from the actual supplier of the implemented method. The client object can determine the value of the interface variable and invoke an appropriate method on the supplier object as determined at run time.

3.1.8.1 Interface versus abstract class

Abstract classes are a powerful mechanism, but they are not helpful in resolving multiple inheritance problems and they are not free from other undesired side effects of implementation inheritance, to be discussed exhaustively later in the book. One such side effect is the *fragile base class* problem – any change in the implementation of the base class has a largely unpredictable effect on the subclasses that inherit from that base class. Since an abstract class can have some methods fully or partially implemented, it can become a fragile base class.

Figure 3.24 demonstrates how an abstract class is of no help in resolving a modeling situation that seems to ask for multiple inheritance. Assuming that the video store (Section 1.5.2) rents not just the movies but also the video playing equipment, the modeler may be tempted to inherit from `VideoMedium`. However, under Java's single-inheritance mechanism, such inheritance will not be allowed. This is because `VideoPlayer` already inherits from `VideoEquipment`, and `VideoMedium` is a class (albeit abstract).

The notion of an *interface* comes to the rescue and provides other advantages in the process (Lee and Tepfenhart, 2002; Maciaszek and Liong, 2004). Like an abstract class, an interface defines a set of attributes and operations, but no objects of it can be instantiated. Unlike an abstract class, an interface does not implement (even partially) any of its methods.

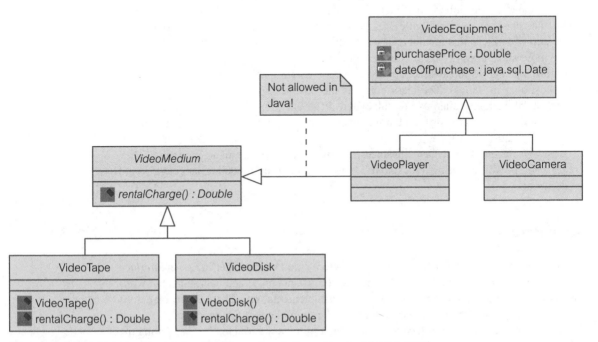

Figure 3.24 Multiple implementation inheritance is not allowed in Java (video store)

The total lack of implementation in an interface seems to be similar to the notion of a *pure abstract class*, available in C++. But even here there is a difference. In the case of a pure abstract class, the only classes that want to implement the pure methods must be sub-classes of that pure abstract class. In the case of an interface, any class in the system can implement the interface. Moreover, the class can implement any number of interfaces.

Implementing an interface 3.1.8.2

Figure 3.25 shows a video store model in which the abstract class of Figure 3.24 is replaced by the VideoMedium interface. Graphically, the interface is recognized by the circle in the name compartment (this is one of few possible UML visualizations). All methods of an interface are implicitly public and abstract, so there is no need to use these keywords in the method's prototype.

Although not shown in Figure 3.25, a Java interface can also include constant declarations (i.e. attributes that are public, static, and final). This is a restriction. A more powerful mechanism should allow declaration in the interface of any attribute typed as another interface or class. This would in effect allow the declaration of associations between interfaces and between an interface and classes. Such a mechanism is not yet supported by Java, but it is alrady envisaged for introduction in the forthcoming UML standards.

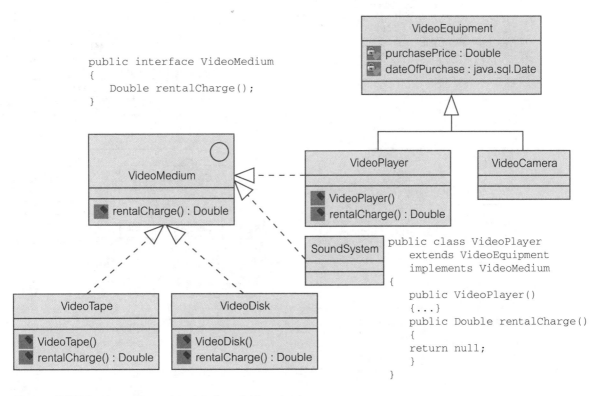

Figure 3.25 Implementing a Java interface (video store)

Also not shown in Figure 3.25, an interface can inherit from another interface (i.e. it can extend another interface). Figure 3.26 illustrates how a class (`VideoPlayer`) can extend a class (`VideoEquiment`) and at the same time implement one or more interfaces (`VideoMedium`).

3.1.8.3. Using an interface

The power of interfaces does not come only from providing a handy resolution to multiple implementation inheritance. Even more importantly, an interface defines a *reference type* that allows separation of client objects from the implementation changes in the supplier objects.

An interface name can be referred to anywhere in the program where the client needs to refer to the class that implements this interface. As a result, the implementation of the

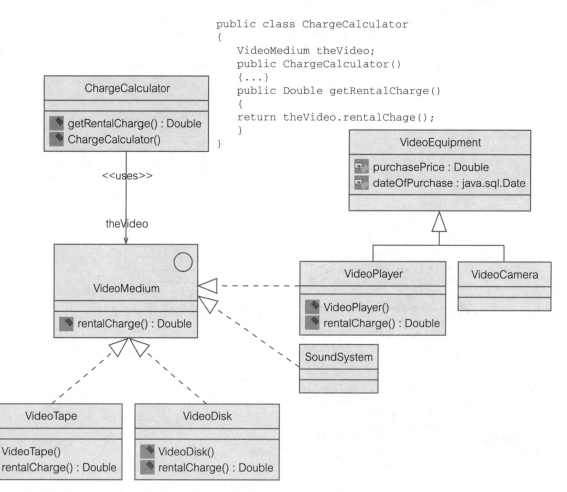

Figure 3.26 Using an interface to eliminate a dependency on the supplier (video store)

interface can change and the client class can work as before and may not even notice the change. This feature of interfaces greatly facilitates the *supportability* of the system.

As an aside, Figure 3.26 also illustrates the use of unidirectional association. The «uses» association is unidirectional from `ChargeCalculator` to `VideoMedium` (this is indicated graphically by the arrow). A `ChargeCalculator` object "knows" of `VideoMedium` object (in the `theVideo` variable), but the model does not maintain the reverse link from `VideoMedium` to `ChargeCalculator`.

Fundamentals of object modeling

This section presents the fundamentals of visual object modeling by demonstrating various UML diagrams and by explaining how they fit together. Each UML diagram emphasizes a particular *view* of the system. To understand the system in its entirety, multiple UML diagrams, representing different views, have to be developed and integrated.

At the most generic level, the UML standard distinguishes three kinds of model – each with its own set of diagrams and related constructs:

1. The *state model* represents the *static view* of the system – it models data requirements and identifies operations that act on these data. The state model represents data structures and their relationships. Operations are added to the state model once they are defined in the behavioral model. The main visualization technique for state modeling is the class diagram.

2. The *behavior model* represents the *operational view* of the system – it models function requirements. The behavior model represents business transactions, operations, and algorithms on data. There are several visualization techniques for behavior modeling – use-case diagram, sequence diagram, collaboration diagram, and activity diagram.

3. The *state change model* represents the *dynamic view* of the system – it models object evolution over time, as permitted by business rules. The state change model represents possible changes to object states (where the *state* is defined by the current values of an object's attributes and relationships with other objects). The main visualization technique for state change modeling is the statechart diagram.

Use-case modeling

The *use-case model* is the main UML representative and the focal point of behavior modeling. In fact, the importance of use cases goes even further. Use cases drive the entire software development lifecycle, from requirements analysis to testing and maintenance. They are the focal point and the reference for most development activities (see Figure 2.2).

System behavior is what a system does when responding to external events. In UML, the outwardly visible and testable system behavior is captured in use cases. A *use case* performs a business function that is *outwardly visible* to an actor and that can be separately *testable* later in the development process. An *actor* represents whoever or whatever (person, machine, etc.) interacts with a use case. The actor interacts with the use case in expectation of receiving a useful result.

A use-case diagram is a visual representation of actors and use cases together with any additional definitions and specifications. A use-case diagram is not just a diagram but also a fully documented model of the system's intended behavior. The same understanding applies to other UML diagrams. Unless stated otherwise, the notion of a *UML diagram* is synonymous with that of a *UML model*.

It is worthwhile emphasizing again the point made in Section 2.5.2 that a use-case model can be viewed as a generic technique for describing all business processes, not just information system processes. When used in such a capacity, a use-case model would include all social business processes and would then identify which of these processes should be automated (and become information system processes). However, despite the attractiveness of this proposition, this is not typical practice in system modeling. Normally only automated processes are captured.

3.2.1.1 Actors

Actors and use cases are determined from the analysis of function requirements. Function requirements are materialized in use cases. Use cases satisfy function requirements by providing a result of value to an actor. It is immaterial whether the business analyst chooses to identify actors first and then use cases, or the other way around.

An actor is a *role* that somebody or something external to the system plays with regard to a use case. An actor is not a particular instance of somebody or something, so somebody named "Joe" is not an actor. "Joe" can play the role of customer and be represented in the use-case model by the actor `Customer`. In general, `Customer` does not even have to be a person. It could be an organization.

A typical graphical image for an actor is a "stick person" (Figure 3.27). In general, an actor can be shown as a *class* rectangular symbol. Like a normal class, an actor can have attributes and operations (events that it sends or receives). Figure 3.27 demonstrates three graphical representations for actors.

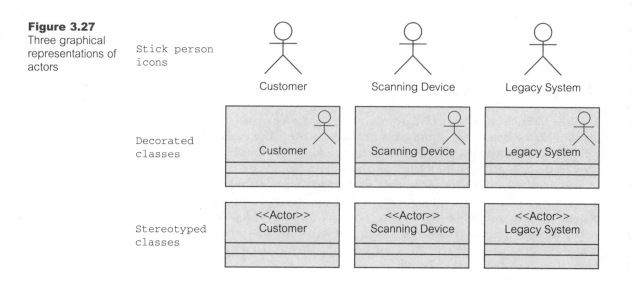

Figure 3.27
Three graphical representations of actors

Use cases 3.2.1.2

A *use case* represents a complete unit of functionality of value to an actor. A use case is a sequence of events of interest to an actor. The actor may either stimulate the use case or the use case can communicate something to the actor.

An actor that does not communicate with a use case is meaningless, but the converse is not necessarily true (i.e. a use case that does not communicate with an actor may be allowed in some situations). There may be some use cases that generalize or specialize main use cases and do not interact directly with actors. They are used internally in the use-case model and assist the main use cases in providing results to actors. This said, purists may disallow modeling in which a use case does not communicate with an actor.

Use cases can be derived from the identification of tasks of the actor. The question to ask is: "What are the actor's responsibilities towards the system and expectations from the system?" Use cases can also be determined from direct analysis of functional requirements. In many instances, a *functional requirement* maps directly to a *use case*.

Table 3.1 shows how selected function requirements for the video store system can be used to identify actors and use cases. Two actors are involved in all four requirements, but clearly the level of actors' involvement varies from requirement to requirement. The `Scanning Device` is not selected as an actor – it is considered internal to the system.

The use cases can be named using the system's or the actors' viewpoint. Table 3.1 leans towards the system's viewpoint: hence, for example, `Accept Payment`, not `Make Payment`.

Naming use cases from the internal system's perspective is not always a recommended practice. It is easy to argue that they should be named from the external actor's perspective.

Table 3.1 Assignment of requirements to actors and use cases (video store)

Req #	Requirement	Actors	Use case(s)
1	Before a video can be rented out, the system confirms the customer's identity and standing by swiping over scanner his/her video store membership card.	Customer, Employee	Scan Membership Card
2	A video tape or disk can be swiped over a scanner to obtain its description and price (fee) as part of the customer's enquiry or rental request.	Customer, Employee	Scan Video Medium
3	Customer pays the nominal fee before the video can be rented out. Payment may be in cash or by debit/credit card.	Customer, Employee	Accept Payment Charge Payment to Card
4	The system verifies all conditions for renting out the video, acknowledges that the transaction can go ahead, and prints the receipt for the customer.	Employee, Customer	Print Receipt

Figure 3.28
Use cases
(video store)

Scan Membership Card

Scan Video Medium

Accept Payment

Charge Payment to Card

Print Receipt

However, the latter approach makes it difficult to connect use cases and models/artifacts developed later in the lifecycle smoothly, because these models/artifacts take a strong system orientation.

Figure 3.28 illustrates the use cases identified in Table 3.1. A use case is drawn in UML as an ellipse with the name inside the ellipse or below it.

3.2.1.3 Use-case diagrams

The use-case diagram assigns use cases to actors. It also allows the user to establish relationships between use cases, if any. These relationships are discussed in Chapter 4. The use-case diagram is the principal visualization technique for a behavioral model of the system. The diagram elements (use cases and actors) need to be described further to provide a complete *use-case model* (see next section).

Figure 3.29 incorporates the use cases of Figure 3.28 into a diagram with actors. The model shows that only the `Employee` actor engages directly with use cases. `Customer` is the secondary actor, depending on `Employee` to achieve most of the goals, hence the dependency relationship between `Customer` and `Employee`. The direct communication between `Customer` and `Charge Payment to Card` signifies the need for the `Customer` to enter their PIN and confirm the payment on the card-scanning device.

In general, use-case diagrams allow a few kinds of relationship between modeling elements. These relationships are discussed in Chapter 4. The «extend» relationship in Figure 3.29 signifies that the functionality of `Accept Payment` may sometimes be extended (supported) by the use case `Charge Payment to Card`.

The relative placement of actors and use cases on the diagram is arbitrary and is left to the "visual sense" of the modeler.

3.2.1.4 Documenting use cases

Each use case has to be described in a *flow of events* document. This textual document defines what the system has to do when the actor activates a use case. The structure of a *use-case document* can vary, but a typical description would contain (cf. Quatrani, 2000):

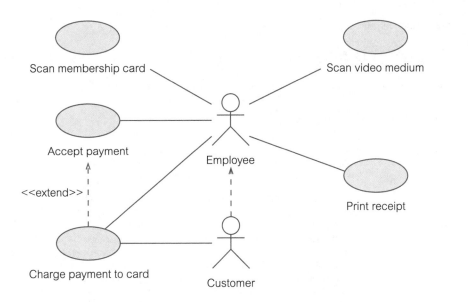

Figure 3.29
A use-case
diagram
(video store)

- a brief description;
- the actors involved;
- the preconditions necessary for the use case to start;
- a detailed description of the flow of events, including:
  - the main flow of events, which can be broken down to show:
    - subflows of events (subflows can be further divided into smaller subflows to improve document readability);
  - alternative flows to define exceptional situations;
- postconditions, which define the state of the system after the use case ends.

The use-case document evolves with the development progress. In the early stage of requirements determination, only a brief description is written. Other parts of the document are written gradually and iteratively. A complete document emerges at the end of the requirements specification phase. At that stage, the prototypes of GUI screens can be added to the document. Later on, the use-case document will be used to produce the user documentation for the implemented system.

Table 3.2 is an example of the narrative specification for the use case `Accept Payment` from Figure 3.29. The specification includes the specification for `Charge Payment to Card`, which extends `Accept Payment`. The tabular form is not the usual way of documenting use cases. Use case documents can consist of many pages (ten or so on average), and a normal document structure, complete with a table of contents, would be the norm.

Activity modeling

3.2.2

The *activity model* can graphically represent the flow of events of a use case. Activity models fill a gap between a high-level representation of system behavior in *use-case models*

Table 3.2 Narrative specification for use case (video store)

Use case	Accept Payment
Brief description	This use case allows an `Employee` to accept payment from `Customer` for a video rental. The payment may be made in cash or by debit/credit card.
Actors	`Employee` (primary), `Customer` (secondary).
Preconditions	`Customer` expresses readiness to rent the video, he/she possesses a valid membership card, and the video is available for rental.
Main flow	The use case begins when the `Customer` decides to pay for the video rental and offers cash or debit/credit card payment. The `Employee` requests the system to display the rental charge together with basic customer and video details. If the `Customer` offers cash payment, the `Employee` handles the cash, confirms to the system that the payment has been received, and asks the system to record the payment as made. If the `Customer` offers debit/credit card payment, the `Employee` swipes the card, requests the `Customer` to type the card's PIN, select debit or credit account, and transmit the payment. Once the payment has been confirmed electronically by the card provider, the system records the payment as made. The use case ends.
Alternative flows	The `Customer` does not have sufficient cash and does not offer card payment. The `Employee` asks the system to verify the `Customer`'s rating (derived from the customer's history of payments). The `Employee` decides whether to rent out the video with no or with partial payment. Depending on the decision, the `Employee` cancels the transaction (and the use case terminates) or proceeds with partial payment (and the use case continues). The `Customer`'s card does not swipe properly through the scanner. After three unsuccessful attempts, the `Employee` enters the card number manually. The use case continues.
Postconditions	If the use case was successful, the payment is recorded in the system's database. Otherwise, the system's state is unchanged.

and much lower-level representation of behavior in *interaction models* (sequence and collaboration diagrams).

The activity diagram shows the steps of a computation. Each step is a *state* of doing something. For that reason, the execution steps for an *activity* are called *action states*. The diagram depicts which steps are executed in sequence and which can be executed concurrently. The flow of control from one action state to the next is called a *transition* (or a *flow*).

If a use-case document has been completed, then activities and action states can be discovered from the description of the *main and alternative flows*. However, activity models can have other uses in system development apart from providing detailed specifications for use cases (Fowler, 2004). They can be used to understand a business process at a high level of abstraction before any use cases are produced. Alternatively, they can be used at a much

Table 3.3 Finding actions in main and alternative flows (video store)

No.	Use case statement	Action state
1	The Employee requests the system to display the rental charge together with basic customer and video details.	Display transaction details
2	If the Customer offers cash payment, the Employee handles the cash, confirms to the system that the payment has been received, and asks the system to record the payment as made.	Key in cash amount; Confirm transaction
3	If the Customer offers debit/credit card payment, the Employee swipes the card and then requests the Customer to type the card's PIN, select debit or credit account, and transmit the payment. Once the payment has been confirmed electronically by the card provider, the system records the payment as made.	Swipe the card; Accept card number; Select card account; Confirm transaction
4	The Customer does not have sufficient cash and does not offer card payment. The Employee asks the system to verify the Customer's rating (which accounts for the customer's history of payments). The Employee decides whether to rent out the video with no or with partial payment. Depending on the decision, the Employee cancels the transaction (and the use case terminates) or proceeds with partial payment (and the use case continues).	Verify customer rating; Refuse transaction; Allow rent with no payment; Allow rent with partial payment
5	The Customer's card does not swipe properly through the scanner. After three unsuccessful attempts, the Employee enters the card number manually.	Enter card number manually

lower level of abstraction to design complex sequential algorithms or to design concurrency in multi-threaded applications.

Actions

3.2.2.1

If the activity modeling is used to visualize the sequencing of actions in a use case, then action states can be established from the use-case document. Table 3.3 lists the statements in the main and alternative flows of the use-case document and identifies action states.

An action state is represented in UML by a rounded rectangle. The activities identified in Table 3.3 are drawn in Figure 3.30.

Activity diagrams

3.2.2.2

An *activity diagram* shows transitions between actions. Unless an activity diagram represents a continuous loop, the diagram will have an initial action state and one or more final action states. A solid filled circle represents the *initial state*. The *final state* is shown using a "bull's eye" symbol.

Transitions can *branch* and *merge*. This creates *alternative* computation *threads*. A diamond box shows the branch condition. The exit from a branch condition is controlled

Figure 3.30
The actions for
a use case
(video store)

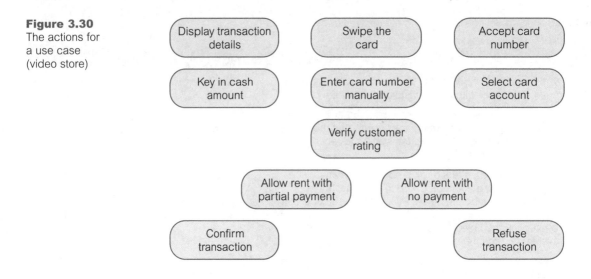

by an event (such as Yes, No) or by a guard condition (such as [green light], [good rating]).

Transitions can also *fork* and *rejoin*. This creates *concurrent* (parallel) computation *threads*. The fork/join of transitions is represented by a bar line. An activity diagram without concurrent processes resembles a conventional *flowchart* (there is no example of concurrent behavior in this section).

To draw the diagram for the video store example, the actions identified in Figure 3.30 have to be connected by transition lines, as demonstrated in Figure 3.31. Display transaction details is the initial action state. The *recursive transition* on this state recognizes the fact that the display is continuously refreshed until the next transition fires.

When in the state Display Transaction Details, the customer can offer cash or card payment, which leads to the execution of one of two possible computation threads. Several actions to manage a card payment are combined in Figure 3.31 in an encompassing action called Handle card payment. This kind of "nesting" of actions is convenient when a transition is possible from any of the nested actions. If this is the case, the transition can be drawn from the encompassing action, as shown for the transition to the branch condition called Payment problems?

Testing of the condition Payment problems? may come from problems with card payment as well as being due to insufficient cash. If there are no payment issues, then the rental transaction is confirmed and the processing terminates on the final state. Otherwise, the customer rating is verified. Depending on the rating, the rent transaction is declined (if [bad] rating), allowed with partial payment (if [good] rating), or allowed with no payment (if [excellent] rating).

3.2.3 Class modeling

Class modeling integrates and embodies all other modeling activities. Also known as *state modeling*, class models define the static structures that capture the internal state of the

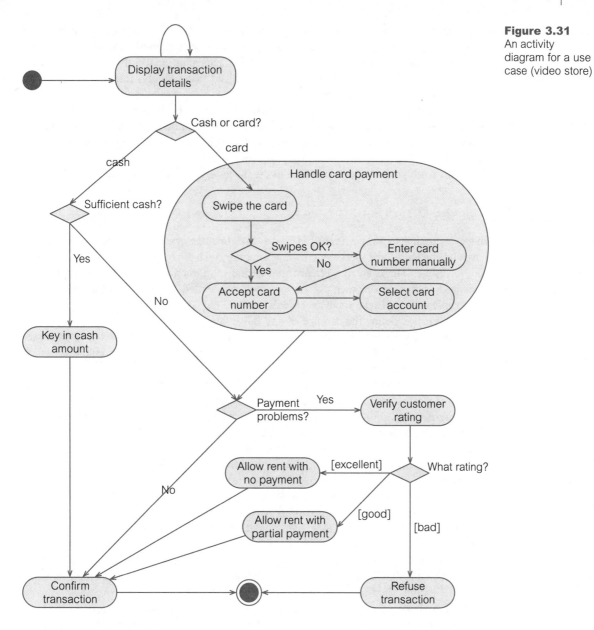

Figure 3.31
An activity
diagram for a use
case (video store)

system. Class models identify classes and their attributes, including relationships. These are static structures. However, class models also define the operations necessary to fulfill the dynamic behavioral requirements of the system specified in use cases. When implemented in a programming language, classes represent both the static structure and the dynamic behavior of the application.

Accordingly, class models are constructed by referring to all the fundamental object technology concepts discussed in Section 3.1. Understanding these concepts is a necessary but not sufficient condition for working with class models. It is a necessary condition for reading (understanding) class models, but it is not a sufficient condition for writing (developing) class models. Developing class models demands additional skills, which have to do with proper use of abstraction and with the ability to (iteratively) integrate a variety of inputs into a single coherent solution.

The outcome of class modeling is a class diagram and related textual documentation. In this chapter, class modeling is discussed after use-case modeling, but in practice these two activities are typically conducted in parallel. The two models feed off each other by providing auxiliary but complementary information. Use cases facilitate class discovery and, conversely, class models can lead to the discovery of overlooked use cases.

3.2.3.1 Classes

In the discussion so far, we have used classes to define *business objects*. Our class examples have all been long-lived (persistent) business entities, such as `Order`, `Shipment`, `Customer`, `Student`, etc. These are the classes that define the *database model* for an application domain. For that reason, such classes are frequently called *entity classes* (model classes). They represent persistent database objects.

Entity classes define the essence of any information system. Requirements analysis is interested predominantly in entity classes. However, for the system to function, other classes are needed as well. The system needs classes that define GUI objects (such as screen forms) – called the *presentation* (*boundary, view*) *classes*. The system also needs classes that control the program's logic and process user events – the *control classes*. Other categories of classes are needed as well, such as the classes responsible for communication with external data sources – sometimes called *foundation classes*. Finally, the responsibility for managing entity objects in the memory cache in order to satisfy business transactions is given to yet another category of classes – *mediator classes*.

Depending on a particular modeling approach, classes other than entity classes may or may not be addressed in any detail in requirements analysis. The same thinking may apply to the definition of operations in early class models. Initial modeling of non-entity classes and the definition of operations may be postponed to the interaction modeling stage (Section 3.2.4), and more detailed modeling may be postponed to the system design phase.

Following the approach taken in finding actors and use cases (see Table 3.1), we can construct a table that assists in finding classes from the analysis of functional requirements. Table 3.4 assigns the functional requirements to the entity classes.

Finding classes is an iterative task, and the initial list of candidate classes is likely to change. Answering a few questions may help to determine whether a concept in the requirements is a candidate class. The questions are:

- Is the concept a container for data?
- Does it have separate attributes that will take on different values?
- Would it have many instance objects?
- Is it in the scope of the application domain?

The list of classes in Table 3.4 still raises many questions. For example:

Table 3.4 Assignment of requirements to entity classes (video store)

Req #	Requirement	Entity class
1	Before a video can be rented out, the system confirms the customer's identity and standing by swiping his/her video store membership card over a scanner.	`Video, Customer, MembershipCard`
2	A video tape or disk can be swiped over the scanner to obtain its description and price (fee) as part of a customer's enquiry or rental request.	`VideoTape, VideoDisk, Customer, Rental`
3	The customer must pay the nominal fee before the video can be rented out. The payment may be in cash or by debit/credit card.	`Customer, Video, Rental, Payment`
4	The system verifies all conditions for renting out the video, acknowledges that the transaction can go ahead, and prints the receipt for the customer.	`Rental, Receipt`

■ What's the difference between `Video` and `VideoTape/VideoDisk`? Is `Video` just a generic term for `VideoTape/VideoDisk`? If so, don't we need a class to describe the video `Movie` or other content of the video medium? Perhaps a class called `Movie` is required?

■ Is the meaning of `Rental` in requirements 2, 3, and 4 the same? Is it all about rental transaction?

■ Perhaps `MembershipCard` is part of `Customer`?

■ Is there a need to distinguish separate classes for `CashPayment` and `CardPayment`?

■ Although a video store employee, as an actor, is not explicitly mentioned in the requirements in Table 3.4, it is clear that the system must have knowledge about which employees were involved in rental transactions. Clearly, there is a need for the class `Employee`.

Answering these and similar questions is not easy and requires an in-depth knowledge of application requirements. Figure 3.32 includes all classes identified in Table 3.4 as well as those raised in the above discussion. Note that the classes `Customer` and `Employee` have already appeared as *actors* in the use-case diagram – hence the annotation "from use case view." This duality of actors as external entities interacting with the system and as internal entities about which the system must have some knowledge is quite common in system modeling.

Attributes

3.2.3.2

The structure of a class is defined by its *attributes* (Section 3.1.2.1). The analyst must have some appreciation of the attribute structure when initially declaring a class. In practice, the main attributes are usually allocated to a class immediately after the class has been added to the model.

Figure 3.32
Classes (video
store)

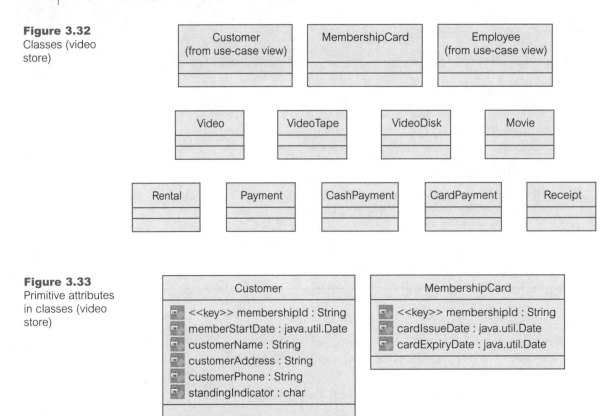

Figure 3.33
Primitive attributes
in classes (video
store)

Attributes are discovered from user requirements and from domain knowledge. Initially, the modeler concentrates on defining *identifying attributes* for each class – one or more attributes in a class that have unique values across all instances of the class. Such attributes are frequently referred to as class *keys*. Ideally, a key should consist of one attribute. In some cases, a set of attributes constitutes a key.

Once identifying attributes are known, the modeler should define the main *descriptive attributes* for each class. These are attributes that describe the main informational content of the class. There is no need, as yet, to start defining *non-primitive types* for attributes (Section 3.1.2.1). Most attributes that look like they require non-primitive types can be typed as strings of characters. The strings can be converted to non-primitive types in later modeling stages.

Figure 3.33 shows two video store classes with primitive attributes. Both classes have identical keys (`membershipId`). This confirms the question, raised in Section 3.2.3.1, that `MembershipCard` is some kind of part of `Customer`. This issue will definitely come back in later modeling stages.

Some attributes in Figure 3.33 are typed as `java.util.Date`. This is a `Date` data type provided by a Java library, and although it is a non-primitive data type, it is not *user-defined* (and, therefore, not contradicting the assumption that only primitive types are used).

In fact, from the Java viewpoint, the `String` data type is also not a primitive type. Some attributes, such as `customerAddress`, are likely to be given a user-defined non-primitive type later on (i.e. some kind of `Address` class will need to be created). For now, such attributes are typed as `String`.

The attribute `standingIndicator` is typed as `char`. This attribute captures the standing (rating) assigned to each customer based on his/her past history of payments, timely return of videos, etc. The rating can range from, say, "A" to "E," where "A" can mean an excellent rating and "E" the worst rating given to the customer (customer about to be excluded from membership).

Admittedly and understandably, there are a significant number of arbitrary decisions in defining attributes in Figure 3.33. For example, the presence of `memberStartDate` in `Customer`, instead of `MembershipCard`, can be questioned. Similarly, the omission of `customerName` and `customerAddress` on `MembershipCard` can raise a few eyebrows.

Associations   3.2.3.3

Associations between classes establish pathways for easy object collaboration (Section 3.1.4). In the implemented system, the associations will be represented with attribute types that designate associated classes (Section 3.1.2.1.1). In the analysis model, the association lines represent associations.

Figure 3.34 demonstrates two associations between three video store classes – `Customer`, `Rental`, and `Payment`. Both associations are of the same one-to-many multiplicity

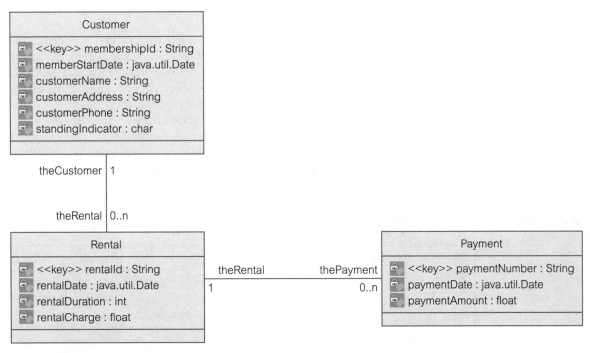

Figure 3.34 Associations (video store)

(Section 3.1.4.2). The role names for the associations are shown. In the implemented system, the role names will be converted to attributes that designate classes (Section 3.1.2.1.1).

`Customer` can be associated with many video `Rental` transactions. Each `Rental` applies to a single `Customer`. There is no indication in the model if more than one video can be rented in a single transaction. Even if this is allowed, all videos have to be rented for the same period of time (as only one value of `rentalDuration` is possible).

It is possible to pay for a `Rental` in more than one `Payment`. This implies that the `paymentAmount` does not have to be paid in full and can be smaller than `rentalCharge`. It is also possible to rent a video without immediate payment (a `Rental` object may be associated with zero `Payment` objects). This is allowed by an alternative flow in the use-case specification (see Table 3.2).

The model in Figure 3.34 does not include an explicit association between `Payment` and `Customer`. From the semantic point of view, such an association is not necessary. The customer for a payment can be identified by "navigating" through the rental transaction. This is possible because each `Payment` object is associated with a single `Rental` object, and each `Rental` object is associated with a single `Customer`. However, it is likely that an association between `Payment` and `Customer` will be added to the model during the design stage (this may be motivated by the considerations related to processing efficiency).

3.2.3.4 Aggregations

Aggregation and composition are stronger forms of association with ownership semantics (Section 3.1.5). In a typical commercial programming environment, aggregations and compositions are likely to be implemented like associations – with attribute types that designate associated classes (Section 2.1.2.1.1).

Figure 3.35 illustrates an aggregation relationship on classes `Customer` and `MembershipCard`. `Customer` contains zero or one `MembershipCard`. The system allows information to be stored about potential customers, i.e. people who do not yet have membership cards. Such a potential `Customer` does not contain any `MembershipCard`, and its `memberStartDate` is set to a null value (meaning that the value does not exist).

The white diamond on the aggregation line does not necessarily mean that the aggregation is by reference (Section 3.1.5). It can also mean that the modeler has not yet decided about the implementation of the aggregation. If the presented diagram is an analysis model, then the implementation of the aggregation is undecided. If it is a design model, then the white diamond indeed means aggregation by reference.

Figure 3.35
Aggregation
(video store)

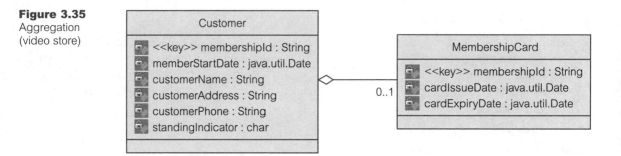

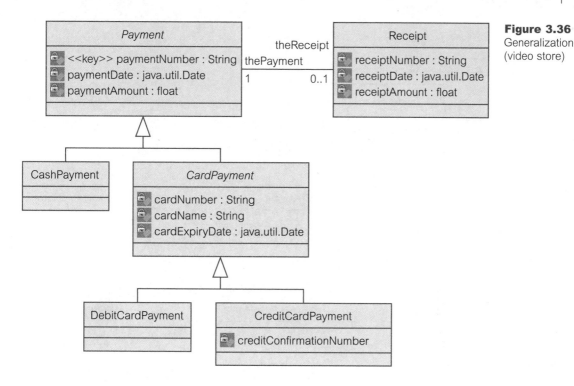

Figure 3.36
Generalization
(video store)

Generalizations

3.2.3.5

Generalization (Section 3.1.6) is a powerful software reuse technique that also greatly simplifies the semantics and graphical presentation of models. The simplification is achieved in two diverse manners, depending on modeling circumstances.

By the fact that a subclass type is also the superclass type, it is possible to draw an association from any class in the model to the superclass and assume that in reality any object in the generalization hierarchy can be linked in that association. On the other hand, it is possible to draw an association to a more specific class lower in the generalization hierarchy to capture the fact that only objects of that specific subclass can be linked in the association.

Figure 3.36 is an example of a generalization hierarchy rooted at the `Payment` class. Because only two kinds of payment are allowed in the video store (cash and card payment), the `Payment` class has become an abstract class (Section 3.1.7). `Receipt` is associated with `Payment`. In reality, objects of concrete subclasses of `Payment` will be linked to `Receipt` objects.

The diagram in Figure 3.36 has introduced two new classes to the video store model. The new classes are `DebitCardPayment` and `CreditCardPayment`, which are subclasses of `CardPayment`. As a result, `CardPayment` has become an abstract class.

Class diagrams

3.2.3.6

The class diagram is the heart and soul of an object-oriented system. The video store examples so far have demonstrated the *static modeling* ability of the class model. The

Figure 3.37
A class diagram
(video store)

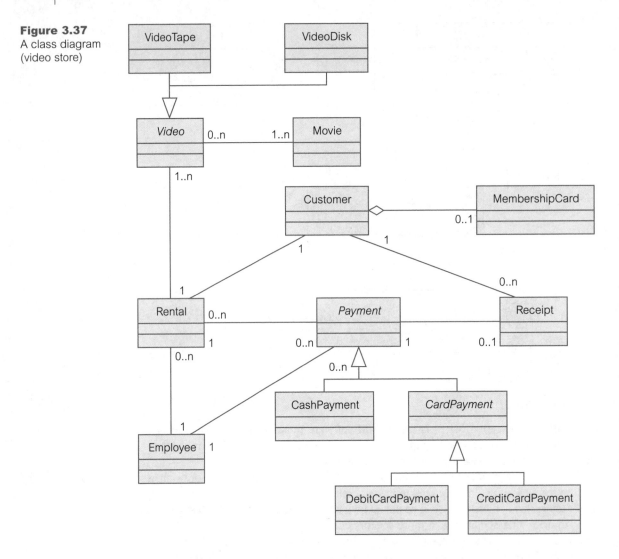

classes contained some attributes, but no operations. The operations belong more to the design than analysis realm. When operations are eventually included in classes, the class model implicitly defines system *behavior*.

Figure 3.37 illustrates the class diagram for video store. The model demonstrates only classes identified in previous examples. Other potential classes, such as `Sale`, `CD`, or `TVProgram`, are not shown. Apart from `Payment` and `CardPayment`, `Video` turns out to be an abstract class. All other classes are concrete.

A careful analysis of the multiplicities of associations in Figure 3.37 reveals that the `Rental` class refers to current rentals only. Each rented video is associated with one and only one rental transaction. Past rentals of the same video are not remembered in the `Rental` class.

A `Video` (i.e. video disk or tape) contains one or more `Movie`. A movie can be available on zero, one, or more video tapes or disks.

Each rental transaction is associated with an `Employee` responsible for it. Similarly, each payment is linked to an employee. The `Customer` information for payment can be obtained by navigating from payment to customer via rental transaction or via receipt.

Interaction modeling

3.2.4

Interaction modeling captures the interactions between objects needed to execute a use case or part of it. Interaction models are used in more advanced stages of requirements analysis, when a basic class model is known, so that the references to objects are backed by the class model.

The above observation underpins the main distinction between activity modeling (see Section 3.2.2) and interaction modeling. *Activity modeling* is frequently done at a higher level of abstraction – it shows the sequencing of events without assigning the events to objects. *Interaction modeling* shows the sequencing of events (messages) between collaborating objects.

Both activity and interaction modeling represent the realization of use cases. Activity diagrams, being more abstract, frequently capture the behavior of an entire use case. Interaction diagrams, being more detailed, tend to model portions of a use case. Sometimes an interaction diagram models a single activity of the activity diagram.

There are two kinds of interaction diagram *sequence diagrams* and *collaboration diagrams*. They can be used interchangeably and, indeed, many CASE tools provide automatic conversion from one model to the other. The difference is in emphasis. Sequence models concentrate on time sequences, and collaboration models emphasize object relationships (cf. Rumbaugh *et al.*, 1999).

Sequence diagrams

3.2.4.1

An *interaction* is a set of *messages* in some behavior that are exchanged between *objects* across *links* (persistent or transient links (Section 3.1.1.3)). The sequence diagram is a two-dimensional graph. Objects are shown along the horizontal dimension. Sequencing of messages is shown top to bottom on the vertical dimension. Each vertical line is called the object's *lifeline*. A method activated on a lifeline is called the *activation*.

Figure 3.38 shows a simple sequence diagram representing the sequence of messages necessary to fulfill the activity "Verify customer" of the activity diagram in Figure 3.31. The diagram engages *objects* of four classes: `Employee`, `RentalWindow`, `CustomerVerifier`, and `Customer`. `Employee` is an actor, `RentalWindow` is a presentation class, `CustomerVerifier` is a control class, and `Customer` is an entity class (Section 3.2.3.1). Object *lifelines* are shown as vertical dotted lines. *Activations* are shown as narrow rectangles on the lifelines.

Processing begins when an `Employee` requests `RentalWindow` to `checkRating()`. When the message is received, `RentalWindow` displays information about the rental transaction being conducted for that particular customer. This means that the `RentalWindow` object holds the relevant `Customer` object. Accordingly, `RentalWindow` passes the `Customer` object in the `verifyRating()` message to `CustomerVerifier`.

`CustomerVerifier` is a control object responsible for the program's logic and for managing the memory cache of entity objects. Because the current rental transaction relates to

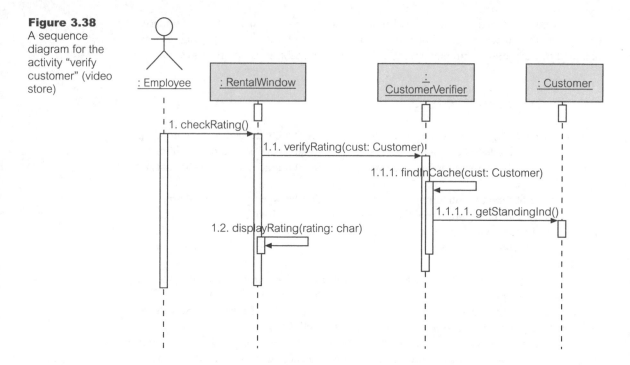

Figure 3.38
A sequence diagram for the activity "verify customer" (video store)

a particular `Customer` object processed by `RentalWindow`, it can be assumed that the `Customer` object resides in the memory cache (i.e. it does not have to be retrieved from the database). Consequently, `CustomerVerifier` sends a *self-message* (i.e. the message to its own method) to find the OID of `Customer`. This is done by the `findInCache()` message.

Once the handle (i.e. the OID) on the `Customer` object is known to `CustomerVerifier`, it requests `Customer` – in the `getStandingInd()` message – to reveal its rating. Objects returned to the original caller by the invoked methods are not explicitly shown in sequence diagrams. A *return* from a message call is implicit at the end of the object activation (i.e. when the flow of control is returned to the caller). Therefore, the value of the `Customer`'s `standingIndicator` attribute is implicitly returned to `RentalWindow`. At this point, `RentalWindow` sends a self-message to `displayRating()` for the employee's consideration.

Figure 3.38 uses hierarchical numbering of messages to show activation dependencies between messages and the corresponding methods. Note that a message to self within an activation results in a new activation. There are other important modeling facilities in sequence diagrams, which are discussed later in the book. Below is a quick recap of the main features of sequence diagrams.

An arrow represents a *message* from a calling object (*sender*) to an operation (method) in the called object (*target*). As a minimum, the message is named. *Actual arguments* of the message and other control information can also be included. The actual arguments correspond to the *formal arguments* in the method of the target object.

The actual argument can be an *input argument* (from the sender to the target) or an *output argument* (from the target back to the sender). The input argument may be identified by the keyword `in` (if there is no keyword then the input argument is assumed). The output argument is identified with the keyword `out`. The `inout` arguments are also possible, but they are rare in object-oriented solutions.

As mentioned, showing the *return* of control from the target to the sender object is not necessary. The message arrow to the target object implies automatic return of control to the sender. The target knows the OID of the sender.

A message can be sent to a *collection* of objects (a collection could be a set, list, array of objects, etc.). This frequently happens when a calling object is linked to multiple receiver objects (because the multiplicity of the association is one to many or many to many). An *iteration marker* – an asterisk in front of the message label – indicates iterating over a collection.

Collaboration diagrams

3.2.4.2

A collaboration diagram is an alternative representation of a sequence diagram. There is a difference in emphasis though. There are no lifelines and activities in collaboration diagrams. Both are implicit in the messages shown as arrows. As in sequence diagrams, the hierarchical numbering of messages may help in understanding the model, but the numbering does not necessarily document the sequence of method invocations. Indeed, some models are more truthful if no numbering is used.

Figure 3.39 is a collaboration diagram corresponding to the sequence diagram in Figure 3.38. CASE tools are able to convert any sequence diagram to a collaboration diagram automatically (and vice versa).

In general, collaboration diagrams tend to be more useful graphically when representing models involving many objects. Also, and unlike sequence diagrams, the solid lines between objects may (and should) indicate the need for associations between classes of

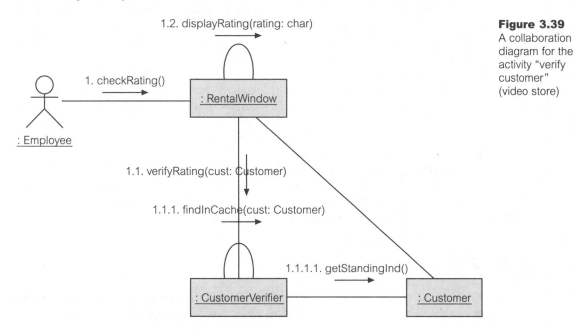

Figure 3.39
A collaboration diagram for the activity "verify customer" (video store)

these objects. Building such associations legitimates the fact that the objects of these classes communicate.

3.2.4.3 Class methods

Examining the interactions can lead to the discovery of methods (operations) in classes. The dependency between interactions and operations is straightforward. Each message invokes a method on the called object. The operation has the same name as the message.

The one-to-one mapping between *messages* in interaction models and *methods* in implemented classes is helpful only to the point to which the interaction model constitutes a detailed technical design – something neither possible nor desirable in the analysis phase. Additional methods will be defined during detailed design and during implementation.

As an aside, note that similar one-to-one mapping exists between *messages* and *associations*, in particular for messages sent between *persistent* (*entity*) objects. Such messages should be supported by persistent links (Section 3.1.1.3.1). Similar thinking should apply to transient in-memory objects, which includes entity objects loaded in memory (Section 3.1.1.3.2). Therefore, the presence of a message in a sequence diagram stipulates the need for an association in the class diagram.

Figure 3.40 illustrates how interactions can be used to add operations to classes. The messages received by objects in the sequence diagram translate to methods (operations) in the classes representing these objects. The class diagram also reveals the return types and visibility of methods. These two characteristics of methods are not apparent in sequence diagrams.

`RentalWindow` receives the request to `checkRating()` and delegates this request to `CustomerVerifier`'s `verifyRating()`. Because `RentalWindow` holds the handle on the `Customer` object that it is currently processing (displays), it passes this object in the argument of `verifyRating()`. The delegation itself uses the association link to `CustomerVerifier`. The association is conducted via the role `theCustVerifier`, which will be implemented as a private attribute in `RentalWindow` (the private visibility is indicated by the minus sign in front of the role name).

The `verifyRating()` method utilizes the private method `findInCache()` to ascertain that the `Customer` object is in memory and to set the `theCust` attribute to reference this `Customer` object (if the attribute has not been previously set). Consequently, `CustomerVerifier` asks `Customer` to `getStandingInd()` by reading its attribute `standingIndicator`. The `char` value of this attribute is returned all the way to `RentalWindow`'s `checkRating()`.

To display `customer`'s rating in the GUI window under the control of `RentalWindow`, `checkRating()` sends a message to `displayRating()`, passing the rating value along. The `displayRating()` method has private visibility because it is called within `RentalWindow` by a self-message.

3.2.5 **Statechart modeling**

An *interaction model* provides a detailed specification for a use case, a part of it, or for one or more activities. A *statechart model* specifies dynamic changes in a class. It describes

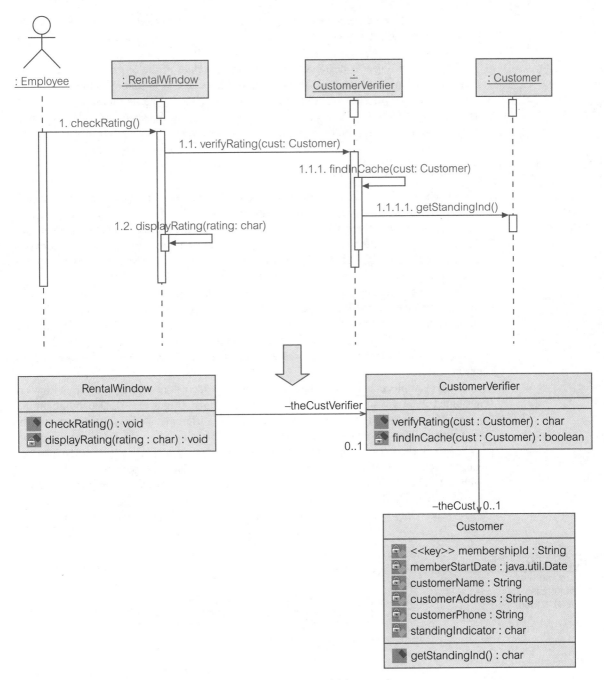

Figure 3.40 Using interactions to add operations to classes (video store)

various states in which objects of the class can be. These dynamic changes describe the behavior of an object across all use cases that involve the class from which the object is instantiated.

A *state* of an object is designated by the current values of the object's attributes (both primitive attributes and attributes that designate other classes). A statechart model captures the life history of the class. An object is one and the same during its lifetime – its identity never changes (Section 3.1.1.3). However, the state of an object changes. A statechart diagram is a bipartite graph of *states* and *transitions* caused by *events*.

3.2.5.1 States and transitions

Objects change the values of their attributes, but not all such changes cause *state transitions*. Consider a `BankAccount` object and an associated business rule that the bank fees on an account are waived when the account's `balance` exceeds $100,000. We can say that `BankAccount` then enters a `privileged` state. It is in a `normal` state otherwise. The account's `balance` changes after each withdrawal/deposit transaction, but the *state* changes only when the balance goes above or below $100,000.

The above example captures the essence of state modeling. State models are constructed for classes that have interesting state changes, not any state changes. What is "interesting," or not, is a business modeling decision. A statechart diagram is a model of business rules. The *business rules* are invariable over some periods of time. They are relatively independent of particular use cases. In fact, use cases must also conform to business rules.

As an example, consider the class `Rental` in the video store case study. `Rental` has an attribute (`thePayment`) that associates it with `Payment` (Figure 3.34). Depending on the nature of this association, a `Rental` object can be in different states as far as the payments for hiring a video are concerned.

Figure 3.41 is a statechart model for the class `Rental`. The states are depicted as rounded rectangles. Events are shown as arrows. The initial state (pointed to by the arrow with blue circle) of `Rental` is `Unpaid`. There are two possible transitions out of the `Unpaid` state. On the `partial payment` event, the `Rental` object goes into the `Partly Paid` state. Only one `partial payment` is allowed according to the model. The `final`

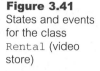

Figure 3.41
States and events
for the class
`Rental` (video
store)

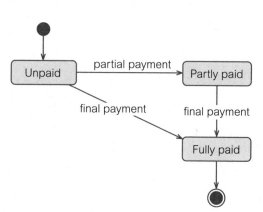

payment event, when in an Unpaid or Partly Paid state, fires a transition to the Fully Paid state. This is the final state (indicated by a blue circle with another circle around it).

Statechart diagrams

A statechart diagram is normally attached to a class, but in general it can be attached to other modeling concepts, e.g. a use case. When attached to a class, the diagram determines how objects of that class react to events. More precisely, it determines – for each object state – what *action* the object will perform when it receives an event. The same object may perform a different action for the same event, depending on the object's state. The action's execution will typically cause a state change.

The complete description of a *transition* consists of three parts:

```
event(parameters) [guard] / action
```

Each part is optional. It is possible to omit all of them if the transition line by itself is self-explanatory. The event is a quick occurrence that affects the object. It can have parameters, e.g. mouse button clicked (right_button). The event can be guarded by a condition, e.g. mouse button clicked (right_button) [inside the window]. Only when the condition evaluates to "true" does the event fire and affect the object.

The distinction between an event and a guard is not always obvious. The distinction is that an *event* "happens" and may even be saved before the object is ready to handle it. At the point of handling the event, the *guard* condition is evaluated to determine if a transition should fire.

An *action* is a short atomic computation that executes when the transition fires. An action can also be associated with a state. In general, an action is an object's response to a detected event. The states can additionally contain longer computations, called *activities*.

States can be composed of other states – *nested states*. The *composite state* is abstract – it is simply a generic label for all nested states. A transition taken out of a composite state's boundary means that it can fire from any of the nested states. This improves the clarity and expressiveness of the diagram. A transition out of a composite state's boundary can also be fired from a nested state.

Consider again the class Rental in the video store case study and think about all states in which Rental can be (not just with regard to payments, as in Figure 3.41, but with regard to all attributes in Rental). Figure 3.42 illustrates a state diagram for the class Rental. The diagram is purposely drawn to take advantage of a variety of state modeling features.

The state model in Figure 3.42 enters the state Transaction Started once the *guard condition* "customer validated and video scanned" is true. The transition to the next state (Rental Charge Determined) requires the firing of the *action* "calculate fees." On the *event* "customer wants to proceed" the Rental object enters the Unpaid state.

The Unpaid state is one of two nested states within the composite state Not Fully Paid. The other nested state is Partly Paid. The Partly Paid state accepts the *transition to self* with the event "partial payment." This allows multiple partial payments before the transaction is paid in full.

In the Unpaid state, when the guard condition "cust rating unsatisfactory" is evaluated to true, a transition is fired into the state Transaction Refused. This is one of two possible final states.

Figure 3.42
State diagram for
the class `Rental`
(video store)

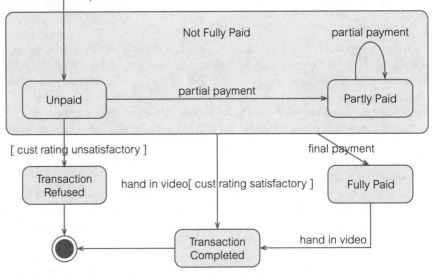

The second final state is `Transaction Completed`. This state is achievable in two ways. First, and preferably, the event "final payment" from the state `Not Fully Paid` results in the state `Fully Paid`. When in this state, the event "hand in video" places the `Rental` object in the state `Transaction Completed`. The second possibility for achieving the state `Transaction Completed` is by the transition from the state `Not Fully Paid`, which is fired by the event "hand in video" under the condition "cust rating satisfactory."

3.2.6 Implementation models

UML provides tools for architectural/structural modeling of physical implementation of the system. The two main tools are component diagrams and deployment diagrams (Alhir, 2003; Maciaszek and Liong, 2004).

"A *component* represents a modular, deployable, and replaceable part of a system that encapsulates implementation and exposes a set of interfaces" (UML, 2003, pp.3–174). The *component diagram* is concerned with modeling the structure and dependencies of components in the implemented systems.

"A *node* is a physical object that represents a processing resource, generally having at least a memory and often processing capability as well. Nodes include computing devices but also human resources or mechanical processing resources" (*ibid.*, pp.3–173). The *deployment diagram* is concerned with modeling the structure and dependencies of nodes that define the implementation environment of the system.

Implementation models are in the physical modeling realm, but they must be defined with due consideration to the logical structure of the system. The main logical building block is the *class*, and the main logical structural model is the class diagram. Other logical structuring concepts are the notions of *subsystem* and *package*.

Subsystems and packages   3.2.6.1

The old Latin dictum *divida et impera* (divide and conquer or divide and rule) recommends that a position of power can be achieved by isolating adversaries and working towards causing disagreements between them. In problem solving, this dictum is frequently used in a slightly different meaning. It requires that a large problem be divided into smaller problems so that, once the solution to the smaller problem is found, a larger problem can be addressed.

The *divida et impera* principle leads to hierarchical modularization of the problem space. In system development, it results in the division of the system into subsystems and packages. The division has to be planned carefully to reduce dependencies in the hierarchy of subsystems and packages.

The notion of *subsystem* specializes (inherits from) the concept of component (Ferm, 2003). A subsystem encapsulates some part of intended system behavior. The services that a subsystem provides are the result of the services provided by its internal parts, i.e. classes. This also means that a subsystem is not instantiable (Selic, 2003).

The services of the subsystem can and should be defined using *interfaces* (Section 3.1.8). The benefits of encapsulating behavior and providing services through interfaces are many and include insulation from change, replaceable implementation of services, extendibility, and reusability.

Subsystems can be structured in architectural layers such that dependencies between layers are acyclic and minimized. Within each layer, subsystems can be nested. This means that a subsystem can contain other subsystems.

A *package* is a grouping of modeling elements under an assigned name. Like a subsystem, the services that a package provides are the result of the services provided by its internal parts, i.e. classes. Unlike a subsystem, the package does not reveal its behavior by exposing interfaces. As noted by Ferm (2003, p.2): "The difference between a subsystem and a package is that, for a package, a client asks *some element inside the package* to fulfill a behavior; for a subsystem, a client asks *the subsystem itself* to fulfill the behavior."

Like a subsystem, a package may contain other packages. Unlike a subsystem, a package can be directly mapped to a programming language construct, e.g. a Java package or a .NET namespace. Like a subsystem, a package owns its members. A member (class, interface) can belong to only one direct subsystem or package.

Figure 3.43
A subsystem and
package

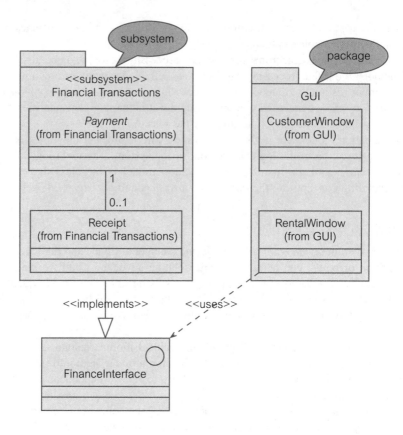

All in all, a subsystem is a richer concept that embodies both the structural aspects of packages and the behavioral aspects of classes. The behavior is provided through one or more interfaces. The client requests the subsystem's services through these interfaces.

As Figure 3.43 illustrates, in UML the graphical difference between a subsystem and a package is only through the use of the stereotype «subsystem». A subsystem is a package stereotyped as «subsystem».

The fact that a subsystem encapsulates its behavior is represented by providing interfaces. The interface FinanceInterface is implemented by the subsystem Financial Transactions and is used by the class RentalWindow in the package GUI.

In general, to minimize system dependencies, interfaces should be placed outside the subsystems that implement them (Maciaszek and Liong, 2004). Although not shown in Figure 3.43, placing all or most interfaces in a package that exclusively holds interfaces is allowed. Alternatively, if GUI classes in Figure 3.43 were the only classes using FinanceInterface, then the interface could be located in the GUI package.

3.2.6.2 Component diagrams

Although a subsystem can be viewed as a specialization of the concept of a component, UML uses a separate graphical element to visualize components. The visualization is

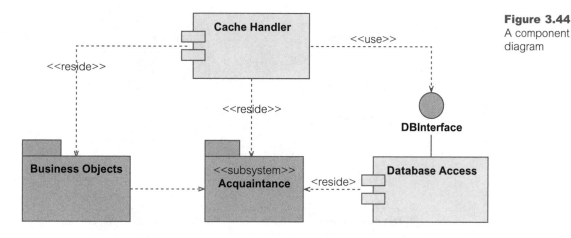

Figure 3.44
A component
diagram

different from the stereotyped package (as in Figure 3.43, which shows a subsystem). A *component* is visualized as a rectangular box with two smaller rectangles. The rectangles provide the interface analogy (as the component implements its public interface).

Figure 3.44 is an example of a component diagram. The example shows two components: `Cache Handler` and `Database Access`. `Cache Handler` uses the interface `DBInterface` implemented by `Database Access`.

A component may be linked with a «`reside`» dependency to other implementation-time modeling elements. Possible elements are class, package, subsystem, or other component. The meaning of the dependency is that the *client* component depends on the *supplier* element and that the supplier element resides in the component (admittedly, the direction of the arrow is somewhat counterintuitive as far as "what resides in what" is concerned). The same modeling element may reside in more than one component (Alhir, 2003), as shown for the subsystem `Acquaintance`. (Later in the book it will be revealed that the `Acquaintance` subsystem contains only interfaces and not any classes.)

In Figure 3.44, the package `Business Objects` and the subsystem `Acquaintance` reside in `Cache  Handler`. To put it another way, `Cache Handler` depends on `Business  Objects` and `Acquaintance`. Additionally, `Business Objects` depends on `Acquaintance`.

Deployment diagrams

3.2.6.3

A *deployment diagram* defines the deployment of components and other run-time processing elements on computer nodes (Alhir, 2003). The node can be any server (e.g. a printer, email, application, web, or database server) or any other computing or even human resource available to components and other processing elements.

Nodes are denoted as three-dimensional boxes. A «`deploy`» dependency from a client component to a supplier node defines the deployment. Figure 3.45 shows that `Cache Handler` is deployed on `Application Server`, and `Database Access` (together with its `DBInterface`) on `Database Server`.

Figure 3.45
A deployment
diagram

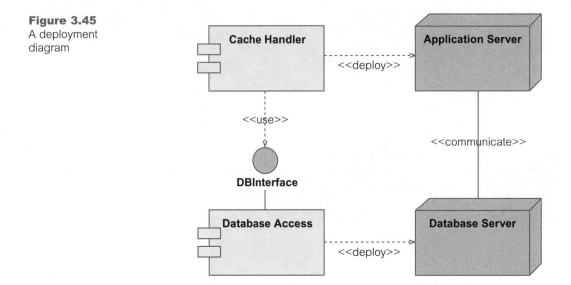

Summary

This chapter has covered quite a lot of ground. It explained the fundamental terminology and concepts of object technology. It also introduced all major UML models and diagrams and illustrated them using a single case study – video store. For a novice to the topic, the task must have been daunting. The rewards will come in the following chapters.

An object system consists of collaborating *instance objects*. Each object has a state, behavior, and identity. The concept of identity may well be the most critical for proper understanding of object systems – it is also the most difficult to appreciate for people with some luggage of experience in conventional computer applications. Navigation along *links* is the *modus operandi* of object technology – something that a reader educated in relational database technology may have difficulty digesting.

A *class* is the template for object creation. It defines the *attributes* that an object can contain and the *operations* that an object can invoke. Attributes can have primitive types or can designate other classes. The attributes that designate other classes declare the *associations*. The association is one kind of relationship between classes. Other kinds are *aggregation* and *generalization*.

A class may have attributes or operations that apply to the class itself, not to any one of its instance objects. Such attributes and operations require the notion of a *class object*. Attributes and operations defined in classes during system analysis are referred to during system design/implementation as *variables* and *methods*, respectively.

A complete method prototype includes the method name, its *signature* (the list of formal arguments), and its return type. A *constructor* is a special method that serves the purpose of instantiating objects of the class.

An *association* relationship provides a linkage between objects of given classes. Association *degree* defines the number of classes connected by the association. Association *multiplicity* defines how many objects may be represented by a *role name*. An association *link* is an instance of the association. An association that has attributes (and/or operations) of its own is modeled as an *association class*.

An *aggregation* is a whole–part relationship between a class representing an assembly of components (*superset class*) and the classes representing the components (*subset classes*). In UML, aggregation by value is called *composition*, and aggregation by reference is simply called *aggregation*. Aggregation/composition is frequently implemented by means of *buried references*. Java provides an alternative implementation by means of *inner classes*. Associated with aggregation/composition is the powerful technique of *delegation*.

A *generalization* relationship is a kind-of relationship between a more generic class (*superclass* or *parent*) and a more specialized kind of that class (*subclass* or *child*). Generalization provides the basis for *polymorphism* and *inheritance*. *Overriding* is the mechanism for achieving polymorphic operations. Commercial programming environments can support *multiple inheritance*, but they do not normally support *multiple* or *dynamic classification*.

Related to inheritance are the notions of abstract class and interface. An *abstract class* is a class that may have partial implementations (some operations may be declared), but which cannot be instantiated. An *interface* is a definition of a semantic type with attributes (constants only) and operations but without any implementation. A class that inherits the interface must provide the implementation.

The UML standard distinguishes three kinds of model: state, behavior, and state-change models. The *use-case model* is the main UML representative and the focal point of behavior modeling. The model defines use cases, actors, and relationships between these modeling elements. Each use case is specified in a text document.

The *activity model* can graphically represent the flow of events in a use case. Activity models fill a gap between a high-level representation of system behavior in *use-case models* and much lower-level representation of behavior in *interaction models* (sequence and collaboration diagrams).

Class modeling integrates and embodies all other modeling activities. Class models identify classes and their attributes, including relationships. Classes belong to various architectural layers. Typical groups of classes are presentation, control, entity, mediator, and foundation classes.

Interaction modeling captures the interactions between objects needed to execute a use case or part of it. There are two kinds of interaction diagram: *sequence diagrams* and *collaboration diagrams*. Sequence models concentrate on time sequences, and collaboration models emphasize object relationships. There is one-to-one mapping between *messages* in interaction models and *methods* in implemented classes.

A *statechart model* specifies dynamic changes in a class. It describes various states in which objects of the class can be. These dynamic changes describe the behavior of an object across all use cases that involve the class from which the object is instantiated. A statechart diagram is a bipartite graph of *states* and *transitions* caused by *events*.

UML provides *component diagrams* and *deployment diagrams* as two tools for architectural/structural modeling of physical implementation of the system. The notions of subsystem and package are related architectural design concepts referred to in implementation models.

Questions

Q1   Why do we need to distinguish between an instance object and a class object?

Q2   What is an object identifier? How can it be implemented?

Q3   What is the distinction between a transient object and a persistent object?

Q4   What are a transient link and a persistent link? How are they used during program execution?

Q5   What do we mean when we say that an attribute type designates a class? Give an example.

Q6   Why are most attributes private and most operations public in a good object model?

Q7   What is the difference between operation visibility and scope?

Q8   What is the difference between "public static" and "private static" members as far as their accessibility is concerned? Give an example.

Q9   In what modeling situations must an association class be used? Give an example.

Q10   "Buried reference" and "inner class" are two mechanisms for implementing aggregation/composition. Do these mechanisms provide sufficient and complete implementation of the semantics assumed in aggregation/composition? Explain.

Q11   Explain the observation that in a typical object programming environment inheritance applies to classes, not to objects.

Q12   What is the connection between overriding and polymorphism?

Q13   How is multiple classification different from multiple inheritance?

Q14   What are the modeling benefits of an abstract class versus the modeling benefits of an interface? Explain by exemplification.

Q15   Explain the main characteristics and complementary properties of a state model, behavior model, and state-change model.

Q16   Can an actor have attributes and operations? Explain.

Q17   Explain the role and place of activity diagrams in system modeling.

Q18   What are entity classes? What other categories of class need to be distinguished in class modeling? Explain.

Q19   What is an actual argument, and what is a formal argument?

Q20   What is the difference between an action and an activity in statechart diagrams? Exemplify.

Q21   Explain why subsystems implement interfaces and packages do not. What would be the consequences for implementation models if the subsystems they refer to did not implement interfaces?

Exercises

E1   Refer to Figure 3.2 (Section 3.1.1.2). Consider the following changes to the logic of object collaboration for shipping products and replenishing stock.

      Shipment and replenishment are separate processing threads. When `Order` creates a new `Shipment` object and requests its shipment, `Shipment` obtains `Product` objects as in

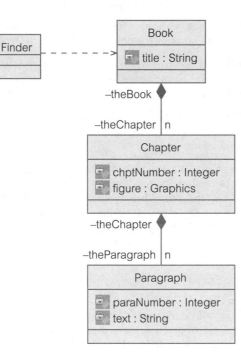

Figure 3.46
Aggregation for
the class Book

Figure 3.2. However, instead of `Stock` managing changes to product quantities, `Shipment` uses its handle on `Product` objects and requests `Product` to `getProdQuantity()` directly.

In this scenario, `Product` knows its quantity and when it has to be reordered. Consequently, when replenishment is needed, a new `Purchase` object is created to provide the `reorder()` service.

Modify the diagram in Figure 3.2 to capture the above changes. There is no need to show messages that instantiate `Shipment` and `Purchase` objects, because the topic of object creation has not been sufficiently explained yet.

E2 Refer to Figure 3.2 and to Figure 3.48 (i.e. the solution to Exercise E1). Define the return types for all messages in both diagrams. Explain how the return values are used in successive calls.

E3 Refer to Figure 3.14 (Section 3.1.4.2). Suppose that a course offering includes lectures and tutorials and that it is possible that one teacher is in charge of the lecturing portion of the course offering and another teacher is in charge of the tutorials.

Modify the diagram in Figure 3.14 to capture the above fact.

E4 Refer to Figure 3.16 (Section 3.1.4.4). Provide an alternative model that does not use an association class and that does not use a ternary association (which is not recommended in this book). Describe semantic differences, if any, between the model in Figure 3.16 and your new model.

E5 Refer to Figure 3.46, in which `Book` contains `Chapter` objects and each `Chapter` contains `Paragraph` objects. The text of the book is stored in `Paragraph` objects. The `Finder` class is a control class. It depends on the `Book` class (this is indicated by an arrowed dotted line). Consider that `Finder` needs to display to screen all `chptNumber` and `paraNumber` that contain a particular search string within `text`.

Add operations to classes that are needed for such processing. Draw an object collaboration diagram and explain how the processing is done, including return types of operations.

E6 Refer to Figure 3.46 and to the solution to Exercise E5 in Figure 3.50.

Extend the class diagram by adding operations to classes that are needed for such processing. Provide pseudo-code or Java code for classes `Finder`, `Book`, and `Chapter`.

E7 Refer to Figure 3.22 (Section 3.1.6.3).

Extend the example by adding attributes to the classes `Teacher`, `Student`, `PostgraduateStudent`, and `Tutor`.

E8 Refer to Figures 3.24 (Section 3.1.8.1) and 3.25 (Section 3.1.8.2).

Extend Figures 3.24 and 3.25 to consider that `VideoMedium` is one kind of `EntertainmentMedium`, the other being `SoundMedium` (such as CDs). Of course, `VideoMedium` is also `SoundMedium`. A similar classification applies to equipment (housing media).

Exercises (video store)

F1 The use-case diagram in Figure 3.29 (Section 3.2.1.3) does not make it explicit that the model is about renting videos (it talks only about scanning cards and video devices, accepting payments, and printing receipts). In practice, a use case will be required that a rental transaction is conducted and is eventually recorded in the video store database. Moreover, the use-case diagram does not check the age eligibility of customers (customers must be over 18 years old to be eligible to rent movies rated R or X).

Extend the use-case diagram to include the above considerations. Also, take into account that the process of renting a video starts after scanning of the customer's card and of video devices takes place and that it is possible (1) to rent a video without payment (in some special cases), (2) age eligibility is checked if the customer is not 18 years old and movies are rated R or X, and (3) to rent a video with or without receipt (depending on customer's request).

F2 Refer to the solution to Exercise F1 (Figure 3.52) and to the activity diagram in Figure 3.31 (Section 3.2.2.2).

Develop a complementary activity diagram for the use case `Rent Video` and the subordinate use cases that extend `Rent Video` (there is no need to repeat the specifications for `Accept Payment`, already developed in Figure 3.31).

F3 Refer to Figure 3.34 (Section 3.2.3.3). Assume that not every `Payment` is linked to `Rental`. Some videos are for sale, and `Payment` may be related to the `Sale` class. Also assume that a single payment can pay for more than one rental. How do these changes impact on the model? Modify and extend the model.

F4 Refer to Figure 3.31 (Section 3.2.2.2). Draw a sequence diagram for the activity `Handle card payment`.

F5 Refer to the class diagram Figure 3.37 (Section 3.2.3.6) and consider the class `Video`. Apart from the information that can be obtained from the class model, consider that the video store sells videos, previously available for rent, once the movie activity threshold reaches certain level (such as when videos with that movie have not been rented out for a week). Also consider that videos are checked regularly to see if they are still operational and may be written off if damaged.

Develop a statechart diagram for the class `Video`.

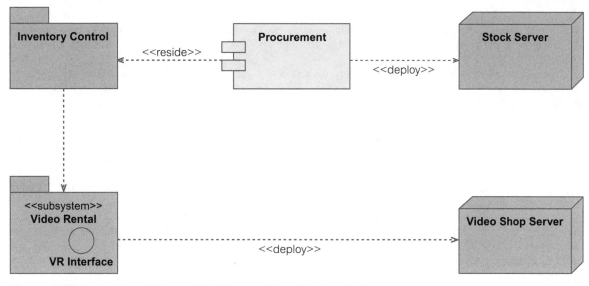

Figure 3.47 An implementation model with some dependencies missing

F6 Refer to the discussion on implementation models in Section 3.2.6, and in particular to the ways in which various dependency relationships are used in component and deployment diagrams. Consider the implementation model in Figure 3.47 with some dependency relationships missing.

Note that the placement of VR Interface inside the Video Rental subsystem box means that Video Rental provides (implements) this interface. An unlabeled arrow from Inventory Control to Video Rental is a generic dependency (Inventory Control depends on Video Rental).

Correct the diagram in Figure 3.47 to show all dependencies.

Answers to odd-numbered questions

Q1 – answer

Most processing in an object system is accomplished by the collaboration of instance objects. *Instance objects* send messages to other instance objects to activate their methods. Hence, a Student instance object can send a message to an Instructor instance object to request consultation. There may be many Instructor objects, but the Student instance is interested in talking to a specific Instructor instance.

At times, however, a message needs to be sent to a group of instance objects. For example, a Student may need to get the list of all Instructor instance objects before deciding on the instance from which the consultation will be requested. An Instructor *class object* is the only object that knows about its Instructor instance objects. The Student instance object should therefore send the message to the Instructor class object to obtain the list of Instructor instance objects.

In general, a class object contains services (methods) that implement efficient access to all instance objects of that class. Such services are essential in order to obtain the current list of instance objects and to perform statistical calculations on instance objects (such as sums, counts, averages). Equally importantly, a class object is responsible for the *creation* of new instance objects.

Q3 – answer

A *transient object* is created and destroyed within a single execution of the program. A *persistent object* outlives the execution of the program. A persistent object is stored in a persistent storage, typically in a database held on a magnetic disk.

A persistent object is read to program memory for processing and may be returned to persistent storage before the program terminates. Of course, the program may choose to destroy a persistent object, thus removing it from the database.

Q5 – answer

An attribute of a class can take values of a built-in type or a user-defined type. The set of *built-in types* supported by an object programming environment is known as *a priori*. The built-in types can be *atomic* (such as int or boolean) or *structured* (such as Date or Time).

A *user-defined type* designates a new *object type* required by the application. That type can be used to implement a *class* so that *objects* of that class can be instantiated.

An *attribute* can be assigned a user-defined object type. A value of such an attribute is an OID to an object of that user-defined type. An attribute is linked to an object of another (or the same) class. We say that the attribute type designates a (user-defined) class. An example is an attribute called theCust in the class called Invoice. The type of that attribute may be a class called Customer.

Q7 – answer

Operation visibility declares the ability of an outside object to reference the operation. Visibility can be public, private, package (the default visibility in Java), or protected (related to the notion of inheritance).

The *operation scope* declares whether the owner of the operation is an instance object (*object scope*) or a class object (*class scope*). Constructor operations, which instantiate new objects, necessarily have class scope. Class scope implies centralized global information about instance objects and should be carefully controlled, in particular in a distributed object system.

Q9 – answer

An *association class* must be used when the association itself has properties (attributes and/or operations). This frequently occurs with many-to-many associations, and sometimes with one-to-one associations. An association class with one-to-many association is unusual.

A many-to-many association between classes Employee and Skill may demand an association class if we want to store such information as dateSkillAcquired. The one-to-one association between Husband and Wife may result in an association class to store marriageDate and marriagePlace.

Q11 – answer

In a typical object programming environment, *inheritance* is an incremental definition of a class. It is a mechanism by which more specific classes incorporate definitional elements (attributes and operations) defined by more general classes. As such, inheritance applies to *types* (classes), not to objects.

Objects are instantiated after inherited elements have been added to the class definition. The values of inherited elements are instantiated in the same way as the values of non-inherited elements.

In general, it is possible to imagine that inheritance can be extended to allow the *inheritance of values* (i.e. *inheritance of objects*). Value inheritance may be useful for setting default values of attributes.

For example, a Sedan object inheriting from a Car object may inherit the default number of wheels (four), the default transmission (automatic), etc. These values may be modified (overridden), if necessary. Some knowledge base tools support inheritance of values.

Q13 – answer

Multiple classification is a program execution regime in which an object is an instance of (and it, therefore, directly belongs to) more than one class. *Multiple inheritance* is a semantic variation of generalization in which a class can have more than one parent class (and it, therefore, inherits from all parent classes).

Multiple classification is not supported by popular object programming languages. This creates problems whenever an object can play multiple roles, such as a `Person` who is a `Woman` and a `Student`. Without multiple classification, we may have to use multiple inheritance to create a specialized class `FemaleStudent`.

Defining classes for each legal combination of parent classes is not necessarily a desirable option, in particular if the objects are likely to change roles over time. Multiple classification can be combined with *dynamic classification* to allow objects to change classes during run time.

Q15 – answer

The *state model* describes the static structure of a system: classes, their internal structure, and their relationships to each other. The *behavior model* describes the actions of the objects in a system in support of business functions: class methods and object collaborations. The *state-change model* describes the dynamic changes in object states over their lifetimes.

The three models offer different but complementary viewpoints, frequently on the same modeling elements. The state view shows the kinds of element that exist in a system. The behavior view ensures that the elements are capable of executing the required system functionality. However, a good state model should be able to gracefully accommodate, new or extended system functionality. The state-change view defines the framework for object evolution and the constraints on objects states that both the behavior and state model must conform to.

Q17 – answer

In older versions of UML, *activity diagrams* were considered a special case of a *state machine* and could even be used in lieu of statechart diagrams. To this aim, activity diagrams were extending the statechart notation and distinguished between *object states* (as in statecharts) and *activity states* (not modeled directly in statecharts). In the current UML, activity diagrams define only behavior by using the control and data flow model reminiscent of Petri nets (Ghezzi *et al.*, 2003).

Unlike most other UML modeling techniques, the role and place of activity diagrams in the system development process is not clear-cut. The semantics of activity diagrams makes them usable at various levels of abstraction and in different phases of the lifecycle. They can be used in early analysis to depict the overall behavior of the system. They can be used to model the behavior of a use case or any part of it. They can also be used in design to give a flowchart-like specification of a specific method or even individual algorithms contained in a method.

All in all, activity diagrams can be seen as "gap fillers" in the system model. They are used as a complementary technique to provide graphical visualization for a flow of events, data, and processes within various other modeling elements.

Q19 – answer

Objects communicate by sending a message from one object to call a method (operation) in another (or the same) object. A message signature includes a list of *actual arguments*. The method being invoked includes in its signature a corresponding list of *formal arguments*. In UML, the actual arguments of a message are called simply *arguments*, but the formal arguments of a method are called *parameters*.

Q21 – answer

A *package* is just a grouping of modeling elements, and it is not concerned with how these modeling elements will be used by the clients. To address such a concern, a special version of a package is provided in UML and is called a *subsystem*.

Graphically, a subsystem is a package stereotyped as «`subsystem`». Semantically, a subsystem hides its modeling elements and reveals only its service to clients. The clients must request the subsystem's services through its provided interfaces.

Modeling access to subsystems via provided interfaces has important benefits for implementation models. If interfaces were not available for subsystems, other components would become dependent on the implementation of classes within subsystems. Such dependencies would create difficulties for the overall system's supportability (understandability, maintainability, and scalability)

Solutions to odd-numbered exercises

E1 – solution

Figure 3.48 is the modified object collaboration. The two threads are numbered separately as 1 and 2. The shipment thread has two dependent messages, numbered hierarchically as 1.1 and 1.2.

Apart from the lack of explanation of how `Shipment` and `Purchase` objects are created, there are a few other details that remain unexplained. For example, the model does not explain how `getProdQuantity()` iterates over possibly many `Product` objects or what exactly makes `Product` send the `reorder()` messages.

E3 – solution

In the modified class diagram (Figure 3.49), two new classes are identified (`Lecture` and `Tutorial`) as subset classes of `CourseOffering`. The subset classes have their own associations to `Teacher`.

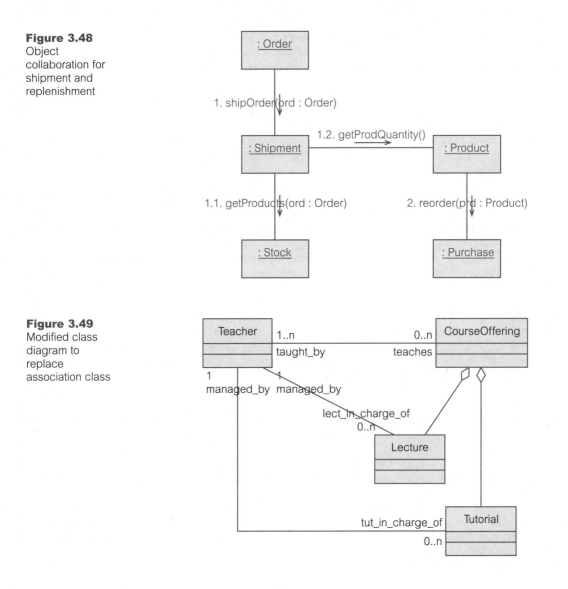

Figure 3.48
Object collaboration for shipment and replenishment

Figure 3.49
Modified class diagram to replace association class

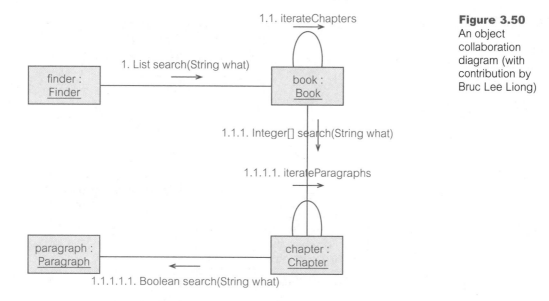

Figure 3.50
An object
collaboration
diagram (with
contribution by
Bruc Lee Liong)

Because a `Teacher` can be in charge of both lectures and tutorials, the roles have different names: `lect_in_charge_of` and `tut_in_charge_of`. This is essential because two attributes will be needed in the implemented classes to capture these two roles (and the role names can then be used as attribute names).

E5 – solution

For explanatory reasons, the solution in Figure 3.50 shows return types, although they are not normally presented in collaboration diagrams. The messages `iterateChapters` and `iterateParagraphs` are just high-level descriptions of the requirement that `Book` has to iterate over many chapters and that `Chapter` needs to iterate over many paragraphs. The details of such loop-based operations are not explained. Because `iterateChapters` and `iterateParagraphs` are just abstractions, rather than messages to methods, there are no parentheses after their names, which would signify a list of arguments.

`Finder` invokes the `search()` operation on `Book`. It eventually returns a `List` of chapter numbers and paragraph numbers containing the string value passed in the argument `what`. Before `Book` can return anything, it iterates over its `Chapter` objects to search for the string value.

However, the text of the book is contained in `Paragraph` objects. Accordingly, `Chapter` iterates over its `Paragraph` objects, and it invokes the `search()` operation on each object. This operation returns just true/false, but for each true outcome, `Chapter` constructs an array of paragraph numbers. This array is returned to `Book`. `Book` can now build a list of chapter numbers and paragraph numbers, and return it to `Finder`.

E7 – solution

Different (and arbitrary) solutions are possible. Figure 3.51 is an example. Note that the example is not Java-based, as Java does not support multiple inheritance.

The attributes `teaching_expertise` and `research_expertise` in `Teacher` are known as *parameterized types*. Both `Set` and `String` are classes. Hence, `String` is a parameter of `Set`. The values of these two attributes are sets of strings.

Figure 3.51
Multiple
inheritance

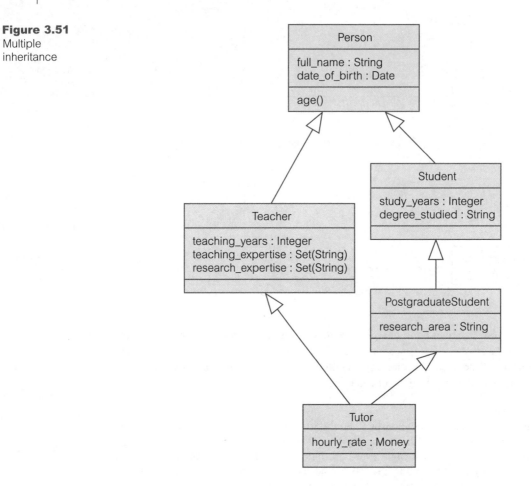

Solutions to odd-numbered exercises (video store)

F1 – solution

Figure 3.52 presents an extended use-case diagram. `Rent Video` is extended by `Print Receipt`, `Check Age Eligibility`, and `Accept Payment`. There are no direct relationships made to the two `Scan...` use cases. The model assumes that `Rent Video` has the information from scanning when the rental transaction is started.

F3 – solution

Figure 3.53 illustrates that the introduction of the `Sale` class leads to new associations, but the "tricky" issue is elsewhere. There is a need in the new model to introduce an association between `Customer` and `Payment`. A payment can be made for more than one rental, and it is possible (as this is not forbidden) that these rentals can be related to different customers. Consequently, without a `Payment–Customer` association it may not be possible to identify a customer of the payment.

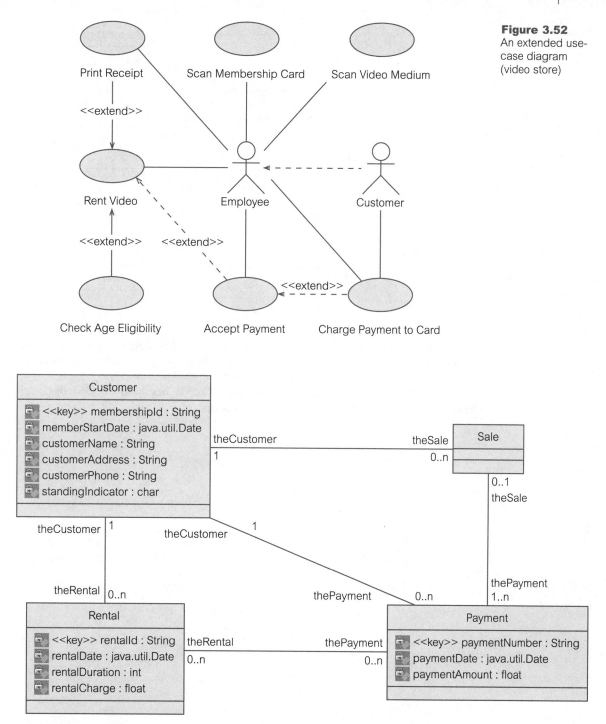

Figure 3.52
An extended use-case diagram (video store)

Figure 3.53 A modified and extended class model

Figure 3.54
A statechart
diagram for the
class `Video`

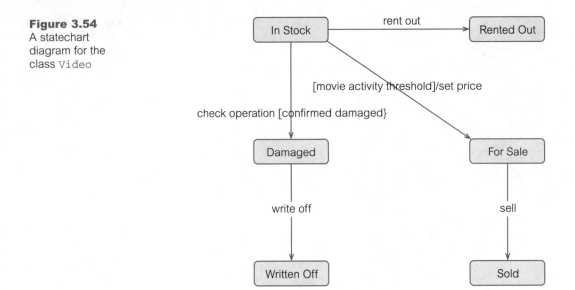

F5 – solution

Figure 3.54 is a statechart model for the class `Video`. Note the use of event followed by a guard condition on transition to the state `Damaged`. Note also the use of a guard followed by an action on transition to state `For Sale`. All other transitions are marked with events.

The model does not identify a start or end state. It has been decided that such identifications are not essential for modeling purposes.

Chapter

4

Requirements Specification

The requirements need to be specified in graphical and other formal models. Many models are necessary to specify the system completely. As introduced in Chapter 3, UML offers a plethora of integrated modeling techniques to assist a system analyst in this job. The process is iterative and incremental. The use of CASE tools is essential for successful modeling.

The requirements specification produces three categories of model: state models, behavior models, and state-change models. Each category offers modeling techniques to work with. This chapter reinforces explanations from Chapter 3 and exemplifies all major UML modeling techniques.

Requirements specification is concerned with rigorous *modeling* of customer requirements defined during requirements determination. The emphasis is on the desired services of the system (*functional requirements*). The system constraints (*non-functional requirements*) are frequently not developed further in the specification phase, although they can be modified as a result of a normal *iteration* cycle.

The requirements specification takes the narrative customer requirements as input and constructs specification models as output. The models (Section 3.2) provide a formal definition for various aspects (views) of the system.

An outcome of the specification phase is an extended ("elaborated") *requirements document* (Section 2.6). The new document is frequently called a *specifications document* (or "specs" in the jargon). The structure of the original document is not changed, but the content is significantly extended. Eventually, the specifications document replaces the requirements document for the purposes of design and implementation (in practice, the extended document is likely to be still called a *requirements document*).

This chapter begins with a discussion of architectural prerogatives. Without a firm architectural framework, there is no hope of developing a supportable system. All modeling must conform to the adopted architecture.

The chapter discusses state modeling before behavior modeling. This does not mean that in practice modeling is conducted in this order. Many models are developed in parallel and feed off each other. This is particularly true of the two principal models: the class model and the use-case model.

4.1 Architectural prerogatives

Before the work on any detailed system specifications can even begin, the software development team must adopt architectural patterns and principles to be obeyed by all developers (Maciaszek and Liong, 2004). This is critically important. Without a clear architectural vision for the system, the analysis phase will invariably deliver specifications for an unsupportable system (if it delivers anything at all!).

The underlying and overwhelming objective of all software modeling must be the minimization of *object dependencies*. To achieve this, the developers cannot allow for indiscriminate object communication, resulting in a messy and incomprehensible network of intercommunicating objects. The complexity of such a (unsupportable) system would increase exponentially with the growth of the model and with the addition of each new object. This cannot be tolerated and must be stopped before it starts making the damage. A clear *architectural model*, with hierarchical layers of objects and restrictions in object intercommunication, must be adopted early in the lifecycle.

4.1.1 Architectural framework

Maciaszek and Liong (2004) advocate the architectural model called *PCMEF*. This acronym stands for the five hierarchical layers of classes: presentation, control, mediator, entity, and foundation. The layers can be modeled as subsystems (Section 3.2.6.1). The PCMEF architecture follows recognized trends in architectural design. For example, it aligns very well with the Core J2EE Tiers (Alur *et al.*, 2003).

Figure 4.1 shows the PCMEF subsystems and dependencies between them. The dotted arrowed lines are dependency relationships. All dependencies are unidirectional. Hence, `presentation` depends on `control`, but not vice versa.

Dependencies align with object communication links. The fact that `presentation` depends on `control` implies a client/server communication. The `presentation` subsystem (client) uses the services of the `control` subsystem (server). A unidirectional dependency does not mean that objects cannot communicate in the other direction. They can. However, such communication must be done using dependency minimization techniques, such as using communication via interfaces or using publisher/subscriber protocols.

The PCMEF architecture, when adopted for a development project, forces the developers to assign each class in the system to one of the five subsystems. This automatically improves the design, because each class contributes to a predefined purpose of the subsystem. The class becomes more *cohesive* and dedicated to a single task.

Coupling between classes, to deliver complete services to clients, is allowed only along the dependency relationships. This may require the use of longer communication paths, but it eliminates networks of intercommunicating objects. Together, the architecture provides for an optimal mix of object cohesion and coupling that satisfies all requirements of the system.

4.1.2 Subsystems

The *presentation* subsystem lies on the boundary with the application clients, i.e. with all computing or human *nodes* (Section 3.2.6.3) that require services of the system under

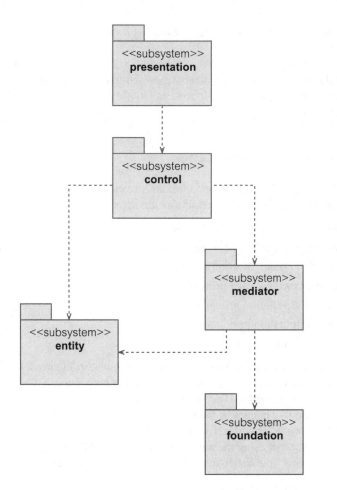

Figure 4.1
The PCMEF
architectural
framework

development. This subsystem consists of classes that handle the graphical user interface (GUI) and assist in human–computer interactions.

The *control* subsystem contains classes capable of understanding what program logic needs to be executed to satisfy a client's request for a service. These requests come from the presentation subsystem. Usually, the processing logic will search for information in entity objects, if these objects reside in the program's memory cache. If they do not reside there, then the control subsystem asks the mediator layer to bring these objects to memory from the database.

The *entity* subsystem manages business objects currently in memory. Unlike in other subsystems, many entity classes are *container classes* – they contain multiple instances of the class. Additionally, containers are linked. Each instance can be associated with many objects of other classes.

The *mediator* subsystem has the responsibility for knowing what is happening on the intersection between the application program and the database. It mediates between the entity and foundation subsystems to ensure that control gets access to business objects. The mediator manages the memory cache and synchronizes the states of business objects between memory and the database (this means that it is also responsible for handling business transactions).

The *foundation* subsystem contains classes that know how to talk to the database. In a typical situation this is a relational database, which understands only SQL. Accordingly, the foundation classes produce SQL to read and modify the database. This layer assists the mediator in business transactions.

4.1.3 Architectural principles

The complete PCMEF framework defines seven fundamental design principles (Maciaszek and Liong, 2004). The principles are named:

1. DDP – downward dependency principle;
2. UNP – upward notification principle;
3. NCP – neighbor communication principle;
4. APP – acquaintance package principle;
5. EAP – explicit association principle;
6. CEP – cycle elimination principle;
7. CNP – class-naming principle.

The *DDP principle* is visualized in dependencies allowed in Figure 4.1. Higher PCMEF layers depend on lower layers. This has an important consequence that lower layers should be designed to be more *stable*. The stability is required so that the dependent clients are not unduly affected by changes to the subsystem.

The *UNP principle* provides for upward communication, which minimizes object dependencies. Instead of using message passing, objects in lower layers rely on interfaces and event processing (publisher/subscriber protocols) to communicate with objects in higher layers.

The *NCP principle* states that objects can communicate across layers only by using direct neighbors. Any communication to non-neighboring subsystems is done in a chain of message passing through intermediate subsystems. In some cases, other dependency-minimizing techniques may be used. One of these techniques uses the APP principle, discussed next.

According to the *APP principle*, a separate layer of interfaces may be defined specifically to support more complex object communication under strict supportability guidelines. The layer is a subsystem of interfaces only. Other objects in the system can use these interfaces and pass them in arguments to method calls, instead of concrete objects. These interfaces are implemented, as required, by classes in PCMEF subsystems. As a result, classes in non-neighboring subsystems can communicate without knowing the concrete suppliers of services (and, therefore, without creating dependencies on concrete classes).

The *EAP principle* attempts to legitimize the run-time object communication in compile-time data structures. According to this principle, if a client class requires services of a supplier class then an association relationship from client to supplier should be established in the class model. The associations make the class dependencies visible in static compile-time structures.

The *CEP principle* undertakes to counteract cyclic calls, and the resulting cyclic dependencies, between classes and other structures (methods, packages, subsystems). Cycles are unavoidable in the sense that messages may need to be exchanged back and forth between a group of classes. However, the dependencies that such cycles create can and should be neutralized using techniques such as the introduction of extra classes to reduce a network of calls to a hierarchy (Maciaszek and Liong, 2004). A purposeful use of interfaces is another cycle elimination technique.

The *CNP principle* seems trivial in comparison with other principles, but its practical significance cannot be overestimated. The principle states that the name of each class and each interface in the system should identify the subsystem/package layer to which it belongs. This can be easily achieved by ensuring that each class begins with a single letter identifying the PCMEF layer (i.e. P, C, etc.). For example, `EVideo` means that the class is in the entity subsystem. Because it is customary for interfaces to begin with the letter I, the second letter in the name may refer to the PCMEF subsystem. For example, `IMVideo` means that the interface is in the mediator subsystem.

State specifications

4.2

The *state* of an object is determined by the values of its attributes and associations. For example, a state of a `BankAccount` object may be "overdrawn" when the value of the attribute `balance` is negative. Since object states are determined from the data structures, the models of data structures are called *state specifications*.

State specifications provide a *static view* of the system (hence, state modeling is sometimes called static modeling). The main task here is to define *classes* in an application domain, and their *attributes* and *relationships* with other classes. *Operations* of classes are normally omitted at first. They will be derived from the models of *behavior specifications*.

In a typical situation, *entity classes* (business objects) are identified first (Section 4.1.2). These are the classes that define the application domain and have *persistent* presence in the database for the system. Classes that service system events (*control classes*) and classes that represent the GUI (*presentation classes*) are not established until the behavioral characteristics of the system are known. Similarly, other categories of classes, such as *foundation* and *mediator classes*, are defined later.

Modeling classes

4.2.1

The class model is the cornerstone of object-oriented system development. Classes set the foundation upon which the state and the behavior of the system are observable. Unfortunately, classes are chronically difficult to find, and the properties of classes are not always obvious. For the same non-trivial application domain, no two analysts will come up with an identical set of classes and their properties. Although the class models may be different, the eventual outcome and user satisfaction may be equally good (or equally bad).

Class modeling is not a deterministic process. There is no recipe for how to find and define good classes. The process is highly *iterative* and *incremental*. Paramount to successful class design is the analyst's

- knowledge of class modeling;
- understanding of the application domain;
- experience with similar and successful designs;
- ability to think forward and predict the consequences; and
- willingness to revise the model to eliminate imperfections.

The last point is related to the use of CASE tools. Large-scale application of CASE technology may hinder the system development in immature organizations (Section 1.1.2.2.2). However, the use of CASE tools for *personal productivity* is always warranted.

4.2.1.1 Discovering classes

No two analysts will come up with identical class models for the same application domain, and no two analysts will use the same thinking processes when discovering the classes. The literature is full of suggested approaches to *class discovery*. Analysts may even follow one of these approaches initially, but the successive iterations will almost certainly involve unconventional and rather arbitrary mechanisms.

Bahrami (1999) goes over the main points of the four most popular approaches for identifying classes:

1. noun phrase approach;
2. common class patterns approach;
3. use-case driven approach;
4. CRC (class–responsibility–collaborators) approach.

Bahrami (1999) attributes each approach to published work, but only the last approach has an indisputable origin. Next, the four approaches are summarized and examples are given for the use of a *mixed approach*.

4.2.1.1.1 Noun phrase approach

The *noun phrase* approach advises that an analyst should read the statements in the requirements document looking for noun phrases. Every noun is considered a *candidate class*. The list of the candidate classes is then divided into three groups:

1. relevant classes;
2. fuzzy classes;
3. irrelevant classes.

Irrelevant classes are those that are outside the problem domain. The analyst cannot formulate a statement of purpose for them. Experienced practitioners are unlikely to include irrelevant classes in the original list of candidate classes. In this way, the formal step of identifying and eliminating irrelevant classes is avoided.

Relevant classes are those that manifestly belong to the problem domain. The nouns representing the names of these classes appear frequently in the requirements document. Additionally, the analyst can confirm the significance and purpose of these classes from general knowledge of the application domain and from the investigation of similar systems, textbooks, documents, and proprietary software packages.

Fuzzy classes are those that the analyst cannot confidently and unanimously classify as relevant. They provide the greatest challenge. The analyst needs to analyze them further and to either include them in the list of relevant classes or exclude them as irrelevant. The eventual classification of these classes into one or the other group will make a difference between a good class model and a bad one.

The noun phrase approach assumes that the requirements document is complete and correct. In reality, this is rarely true. Even if this were the case, a tedious search through large volumes of text might not necessarily lead to a comprehensive and accurate outcome.

Common class patterns approach   *4.2.1.1.2*

The *common class patterns* approach derives candidate classes from the generic classification theory of objects. *Classification theory* is a part of science concerned with partitioning the world of objects into useful groups so that it is possible reason about them better.

Bahrami (1999) lists the following groups (patterns) for finding candidate classes:

- *Concept* class—a concept is a notion that a large community of people share and agree on. Without concepts people are not able to communicate effectively, or even communicate to any satisfactory degree. For example, `Reservation` is a concept class in an airline reservation system.

- *Events* class—an event is something that does not take time relative to our time scale. For example, `Arrival` is an event class in an airline reservation system.

- *Organization* class—organization is any kind of purposeful grouping or collection of things. For example, `TravelAgency` is a class in an airline reservation system.

- *People* class—"people" is understood here as a role that a person plays in the system, rather than as a physical person. For example, `Passenger` is a class in an airline reservation system.

- *Places* class—places are physical locations relevant to the information system. `TravelOffice` is such a class in an airline reservation system.

Rumbaugh *et al.* (1999) propose a different classification scheme:

- *physical* class (e.g. `Airplane`);
- *business* class (e.g. `Reservation`);
- *logical* class (e.g. `FlightTimetable`);
- *application* class (e.g. `ReservationTransaction`);
- *computer* class (e.g. `Index`);
- *behavioral* class (e.g. `ReservationCancellation`).

The common class patterns approach provides useful guidance, but it does not offer a systematic process whereby a reliable and complete set of classes can be discovered. This approach may be used successfully to determine the initial set of classes or to verify whether some classes (derived by other means) should be there or perhaps must not be there. However, the common class patterns approach is too loosely bound to specific user requirements to offer a comprehensive solution.

A particular danger associated with the common class patterns approach relates to the possibilities for misinterpretation of class names. For example, what does an `Arrival` mean? Does it mean arrival on the runway (landing time), arrival at the terminal (disembarkation time), arrival at baggage reclaim (luggage clearance time), etc.? Similarly, the word `Reservation` in the context of a Native American environment has an entirely separate meaning to the one understood here.

4.2.1.1.3 Use-case driven approach

The *use-case driven* approach is emphasized by IBM Rational Unified Process (Section 1.4.4.2). The graphical model of use cases is supplemented with narrative descriptions and with activity and interaction models (Section 3.2). These additional descriptions and models define the steps (and objects) needed for each use case to occur. From this information, we can generalize to discover candidate classes.

The use-case driven approach has a bottom-up flavor. Once the use cases are known and the *interaction models* of the system are at least partly defined, the objects used in these diagrams lead to the discovery of classes.

In reality, the use-case driven approach bears some similarity to the noun phrase approach. The common ground lies in the fact that the use cases specify the requirements. Both approaches study the statements in the requirements document to discover candidate classes. Whether these statements are narrative or graphical is secondary. In any case, at the analysis stage in the lifecycle, most use cases will only be described in text, with no interaction diagrams.

The use-case driven approach suffers from similar deficiencies to the noun phrase approach. Being a bottom-up approach, it relies for its accuracy on the completeness and correctness of the use-case models. Partial use-case models result in incomplete class models. Moreover, the class models correspond to specific functionality and do not necessarily reflect all the important concepts of the addressed business domain. For all means and purposes, this leads to a *function-driven* approach (some proponents of object-oriented methods prefer to call it *problem-driven*).

4.2.1.1.4 CRC approach

The *CRC* (class–responsibility–collaborators) approach is more than a technique for class discovery – it is an attractive way of interpreting, understanding, and teaching about objects. Rebecca Wirfs-Brock and her colleagues (Wirfs-Brock and Wilkerson, 1989; Wirfs-Brock *et al.*, 1990) have popularized the CRC approach.

The CRC approach involves brainstorming sessions, made easy by the use of specially prepared cards. The cards have three compartments: the *class name* is written in the upper compartment; the class *responsibilities* are listed in the left compartment; and the *collaborators* are listed in the right compartment. Responsibilities are the services (operations) that the class is prepared to perform on behalf of other classes. Many responsibilities to be fulfilled require the collaboration (services) of other classes. Such classes are listed as collaborators.

The CRC approach is an animated process during which the developers "play cards" – they fill cards with class names and assign responsibilities and collaborators while "executing" a processing scenario (e.g. a use-case scenario). When services are needed and the existing classes do not contain them, a new class can be created. The new class is assigned appropriate responsibilities and collaborators. If a class becomes "too busy," it is divided into a number of smaller classes.

The CRC approach identifies classes from the analysis of messages passing between objects to fulfill the processing tasks. The emphasis is placed on the uniform distribution of intelligence in the system, and some classes may be derived from the technical design need, rather than discovered as "business objects" as such. In this sense, CRC may be more suitable for the verification of classes already discovered by other methods. CRC is also useful for the determination of class properties (as implied by the class responsibilities and collaborators).

Mixed approach

4.2.1.1.5

In practice, the process of class discovery is likely to be guided by different approaches at different times. Frequently, the elements of all four approaches explained above are involved. The analysts' overall knowledge, experience, and intuition are also contributing factors. The process is neither top-down nor bottom-up; it is middle-out. Such a process of class discovery can be called the *mixed approach*.

One possible scenario is as follows. The initial set of classes may be discovered from the generic knowledge and experience of analysts. The common class patterns approach can provide additional guidance. Other classes may be added from the analysis of high-level descriptions of the problem domain using the noun phrase approach. If use-case diagrams are available, then the use-case driven approach can be used to add new and verify existing classes. Finally, the CRC approach will allow brainstorming the list of classes discovered so far.

Guidelines for discovering classes

4.2.1.1.6

The following is an imperfect list of *guidelines* or rules of thumb that analysts should follow when selecting candidate classes. The guidelines apply to the discovery of *entity classes* (Section 4.2.1.1).

- Each class must have a clear *statement of purpose* in the system.

- Each class is a template description for a *set of objects*. *Singleton* classes – for which we can only imagine a single object – are very unlikely among "business objects." Such classes usually constitute a "common knowledge" to the application and will be hard-coded in the application programs. As an example, if the system is designed for a single organization, the existence of the `Organization` class is not warranted.

- Each entity class must house a *set of attributes*. It is a good idea to determine identifying attribute(s) (*keys*) to assist in reasoning about the class cardinality (i.e. an expected number of objects of that class in the database). However, remember that in general a class does not need to have a user-defined key. *Object identifiers* (OIDs) identify objects of classes (Section 3.1.1.3).

∎ Each class should be distinguished from an *attribute*. Whether a concept is a class or attribute depends on the application domain. `Color` of a car is normally perceived as an attribute of the class `Car`. However, in a paint factory `Color` is definitely a class with its own attributes (brightness, saturation, transparency, etc.).

∎ A class houses a *set of operations*. However, at this stage, the identification of operations can be ignored. The operations in the *interface* of the class (the services that the class provides in the system) are implied from the statement of purpose (ref. the first point above).

4.2.1.1.7   Examples for class discovery

Example 4.1 (university enrolment)

Consider the following requirements for the university enrolment system and identify the candidate classes:

1. Each university degree has a number of compulsory courses and a number of elective courses.
2. Each course is at a given level and has a credit-point value.
3. A course can be a part of any number of degrees.
4. Each degree specifies a minimum total credit points value required for degree completion (e.g. BIT (bachelor of information technology) requires 68 credit points, including compulsory courses).
5. Students may combine course offerings into programs of study suited to their individual needs and leading to the degree in which a student is enrolled.

Let us analyze the requirements in order to discover candidate classes. In statement 1, the relevant classes are `Degree` and `Course`. These two classes conform to the five guidelines in Section 4.2.1.1.6. It is uncertain if the class `Course` should be specialized into classes `CompulsoryCourse` and `ElectiveCourse`. A course is compulsory or elective with respect to the degree. However, it is possible that the distinction between compulsory and elective courses can be captured by an association or even by an attribute of a class. Hence, `CompulsoryCourse` and `ElectiveCourse` are considered, at this stage, as fuzzy classes.

Statement 2 identifies only attributes of the class `Course`, namely `courseLevel` and `creditPointValue`. The third statement characterizes an association between classes `Course` and `Degree`. The fourth statement introduces `minTotalCreditPoints` as an attribute of class `Degree`.

Statement 5 can lead to the discovery of three more classes: `Student`, `CourseOffering`, and `StudyProgram`. The first two are undoubtedly relevant classes, but `StudyProgram` may yet turn out to be an association between `Student` and `CourseOffering`. For that reason, `StudyProgram` is classified as a fuzzy class. This discussion is reflected in Table 4.1.

Table 4.1 Candidate classes (university enrolment)

Relevant classes	Fuzzy classes
Course	CompulsoryCourse
Degree	ElectiveCourse
Student	StudyProgram
CourseOffering	

Example 4.2 (video store)

Consider the following requirements for the video store system and identify the candidate classes:

1. The video store keeps an extensive library of current and popular movie titles in stock. A particular movie may be held on video tapes or disks.
2. A movie can be rented for a particular rental duration (expressed in days), with a rental charge for that period.
3. The video store must be able to answer immediately any enquiries about a movie's stock availability. The current condition of each tape and disk must be known and recorded, together with generic information about the percentage of video tapes and disks in excellent renting condition.

Statement 1 has a few nouns, but only some of them can be turned into candidate classes. The video store is not a class, because the whole system is about it (there would be only one object of that class in the database). Similarly, the notions of stock and library are too generic to be considered classes, at least at this stage. The relevant classes seem to be MovieTitle, VideoTape, and VideoDisk.

Statement 2 says that each movie title has rental rates associated with it. However, it is not clear what is understood by "movie" – movie title or movie medium (tape or disk)? We will need to clarify this requirement with the customers. In the meantime, we may want to declare RentalRates to be a fuzzy class, rather than to store information about rental period and rental charge in the movie title or movie medium class.

Statement 3 states a need for storing information about the current condition of each tape and disk. However, attributes such as videoCondition or percentExcellent Condition can be generically declared in a higher-level abstract class (let us call it VideoMedium) and inherited by the concrete subclasses (such as VideoTape). This discussion is reflected in Table 4.2.

Table 4.2 Candidate classes (video store)

Relevant classes	Fuzzy classes
MovieTitle	RentalRates
VideoMedium	
VideoTape	
VideoDisk	

Example 4.3 (contact management)

Consider the following requirements for the contact management system and identify the candidate classes:

1. The system supports the function of "keeping in touch" with all current and prospective customers so as to be responsive to their needs and to win new contracts for products and services offered by the organization.

2. The system stores the names, phone numbers, postal and courier addresses, etc. of organizations and contact persons in these organizations.

3. The system allows employees to schedule tasks and events that need to be carried out with regard to relevant contact persons. Employees schedule the tasks and events for other employees or for themselves.

4. A task is a group of events that take place to achieve a result. The result may be to convert a prospective customer to a customer, to organize product delivery, or to solve a customer's problem. Typical types of event are phone call, visit, sending a fax, and arranging for training.

Statement 1 contains the notions of customer, contract, and product. Our generic knowledge and experience tells us that these are typical classes. However, contract and product are not concepts within the scope of the contact management system and should be refuted.

`Customer` is a relevant class, but we may prefer to call it `Contact` on the understanding that not all contacts are current customers. The distinction between a current and prospective customer may or may not warrant the introduction of classes `Current Customer` and `ProspectiveCustomer`. As we are not sure, we will declare these two classes as fuzzy.

Statement 2 sheds new light on the discussion above. We need to distinguish between a contact organization and a contact person. `Customer` does not seem to be a good name for the class. After all, `Customer` implies only a current customer, and the name can embody both organization and contact person. Our new proposal is to name the classes `Organization`, `Contact` (meaning a contact person), `CurrentOrg` (i.e. an organization that is our current customer); and `ProspectiveOrg` (i.e. an organization that is our prospective customer).

In statement 2, a few attributes of classes are mentioned. However, postal and courier addresses are composite attributes and they apply to two classes: `Organization` and `Contact`. As such, `PostalAddress` and `CourierAddress` are legitimate fuzzy classes.

Statement 3 introduces three relevant classes: `Employee`, `Task`, and `Event`. The statement explains the scheduling activity. Statement 4 further clarifies the meaning and relationships between the classes, but it does not implicate any new classes. Table 4.3 shows the candidate classes for contact management.

4.2.1.2 Specifying classes

Once the list of candidate classes is known, they should be specified further by placing them on a class diagram and by defining the class properties. Some properties can be entered and displayed inside graphical icons representing classes in class diagrams. Many other properties in the class specification have only textual representation. CASE tools provide easy editing capabilities to enter or modify such information through dialog windows with tabbed pages, or similar techniques.

Table 4.3 Candidate classes (contact management)

Relevant classes	Fuzzy classes
Organization	CurrentOrg
Contact	ProspectiveOrg
Employee	PostalAddress
Task	CourierAddress
Event	

This section discusses class specification at a relatively high level of abstraction. The emphasis is placed on proper class naming and on assignment of attributes to classes. Identification of class operations is not considered and more advanced modeling capabilities of UML are not used – they are discussed in Chapter 5 and later.

Naming classes

4.2.1.2.1

Each class has to be given a *name*. In some CASE tools a *code* for the class, possibly different from the name, may also be assigned. The code would conform to the naming conventions demanded by a target programming language or database system. The code, not the name, is used for the generation of software code from the design models.

It is recommended practice to enforce a uniform convention for class names. The PCMEF convention (Section 4.1.3) is that a class name begins with a capital letter signifying the architectural layer (subsystem/package) to which the class belongs. The proper name of the class, following the letter identifying the layer, also begins with a capital letter. For compound names, the first letter of each word is capitalized (rather than separated by an underscore or hyphen). This is only a recommended convention, but it has a reasonable following among developers.

The name of the class should be a singular noun (e.g. `Course`) or an adjective and a singular noun (e.g. `CompulsoryCourse`) whenever possible. It is clear that a class is a template for many objects, and using plural nouns would not add any new information. At times, a singular noun does not capture the true intention of the class. In such situations, using plural nouns is acceptable (e.g. `RentalConditions` in Example 4.2).

A class name should be meaningful. It should capture the true nature of the class. It should be drawn from the users' vocabulary (not from the developers' jargon).

It is better to use a longer name than to make the name too cryptic. Names longer than thirty characters are unwieldy (and some programming environments may not accept them, if the CASE tool is working with class names instead of class codes). Longer descriptions are also possible, in addition to class names and codes.

Discovering and specifying class attributes

4.2.1.2.2

The graphical icon representing a class consists of three compartments (class name, attributes, operations) (Section 3.1.2). The specification of class attributes belongs to *state specifications* and is discussed here. The specification of class operations is discussed later in this chapter under the heading of *behavior specifications* (Section 4.3).

Attributes are discovered in parallel with the discovery of classes. Identification of attributes is a side effect of class determination. This does not mean that attribute discovery is a straightforward activity. On the contrary, it is a demanding and highly iterative process.

In the initial specification models, we define only the attributes that are essential to an understanding of the *states* (Section 3.2.5) in which objects of that class can be. Other attributes may be temporarily ignored (but the analyst must make sure that the existence of the ignored information is not lost by failure to record it in the future). It is unlikely that all class attributes will be mentioned in the requirements document, but it is important not to include the attributes that are not implied by requirements. More attributes can be added in subsequent iterations.

Our recommended convention for *attribute names* is to use small letters but capitalize the first letters of successive words in a compound name (e.g. `streetName`). An alternative approach is to separate words by an underscore (e.g. `street_name`).

4.2.1.2.3   Examples for class specifications

Example 4.4 (university enrolment)

Refer to Example 4.1 and consider the following additional requirements from the requirements document:

1. A student's choice of courses may be restricted by timetable clashes and by limitations on the number of students who can be enrolled in the current course offering.
2. A student's proposed program of study is entered in the online enrolment system. The system checks the program's consistency and reports any problems. The problems need to be resolved with the help of an academic adviser. The final program of study is subject to academic approval by the delegate of the head of division and is then forwarded to the registrar.

Statement 1 mentions timetable clashes, but we are not sure how to model this issue. It is possible that we are talking here about a use case that procedurally determines timetable clashes. The second part of the same statement can be modeled by adding the `enrolmentQuota` attribute to class `ECourseOffering`. It is also clear now that `ECourseOffering` should have attributes `year` and `semester`.

Statement 2 reinforces the need for the `EStudyProgram` class. We can see that `EStudyProgram` combines a number of course offerings currently on offer. Therefore, `EStudyProgram` should also have attributes `year` and `semester`.

The closer analysis of fuzzy classes `CompulsoryCourse` and `ElectiveCourse` (Table 4.1) leads to the observation that a course is compulsory or elective *with relation to* the degree. The same course may be compulsory with relation to one degree, elective with regard to another degree, and it may not be allowed towards some other degrees. If so, `CompulsoryCourse` and `ElectiveCourse` are not classes in their own rights. (Note that we are not entering here into the realm of modeling with generalization (Section 3.1.6).)

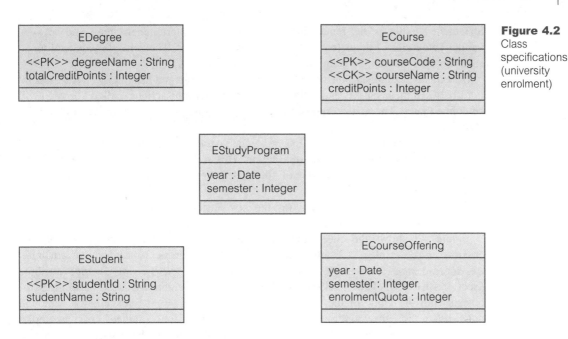

Figure 4.2
Class specifications (university enrolment)

Figure 4.2 represents a class model conforming to the discussion so far. Additionally, we used *stereotypes* <<PK>> and <<CK>> to mean a primary key and a candidate key, respectively. These are unique identifiers of objects in the classes concerned. Data types for attributes have been specified as well. Data types conform to Java.

The classes `EStudyProgram` and `ECourseOffering` do not have identifying attributes. They will be added to these classes when the *associations* (Section 3.1.4) between classes are discovered.

Example 4.5 (video store)

Consider the combined requirements listed in Example 4.2 and the following additional requirements:

1. The rental charge for entertainment items (such as movie) differs depending on the item category and on the entertainment medium containing the item. In general, an entertainment medium can be a video medium or just a sound medium. A video medium can be a VCR tape, DVD or game CD. A music CD is a sound medium, but some music CDs are available in video formats, such as VCD or DVD-A.

2. The system stores information about employees and identifies the employee responsible for each rental transaction performed on behalf of a customer.

3. A separate transaction is generated for renting for different durations. Items on each rental transaction can relate to more than one medium (as long as all items are rented for the same duration). A medium can contain movies, TV programs, games, or music.

4. The employees of the video store tend to remember the codes of the most popular movies. They frequently use a movie code, instead of movie title, to identify the movie. This is a useful practice, because the same movie title may have more than one release by different directors.

Statement 1 explains that rental charges vary between entertainment items and between various categories of items (e.g. `EMovie`, `EGame`, `EMusic`). They also vary depending on entertainment medium housing the item (e.g. `EVCRTape`, `EDVD`, `ECD`).

Statement 2 establishes the need for classes `EEmployee` and `ECustomer`. The associations between these classes and a class managing rental transactions (called `Rental`) will be defined later. The main responsibilities of the `ERental` class are defined in the third statement.

The main responsibilities of the `ERental` class are defined in statement 3. Many rented items can be processed in a single transaction. This statement also explains that an entertainment medium can contain one of four categories of item: movies, TV programs, games, or music.

Statement 4 adds `movie_code` (as the key attribute) and `director` to the class `EMovie`. Other attributes are as discussed in Example 4.2.

Figure 4.3 shows the class model for the video store application as per the discussion in Examples 4.2 and 4.5. `EMovie.isInStock` is a *derived* attribute. `EVideoMedium.percentExcellentCondition` is a *class-scope* (*static*) attribute (Section 3.1.2.3). This attribute will contain the percentage of `EVideoMedium` objects with the value of the attribute `videoCondition = "E"` (excellent). Although not shown in the diagram, a class-scope operation (named, for example, `computePercentageExcellentCondition`) would need to be associated with that attribute to compute its current value on demand.

Example 4.6 (contact management)

Refer to Example 4.3 and consider the following additional information:

1. A customer is considered current if a contract with that customer exists for delivery of our products or services. However, contract management is outside the scope of our system.
2. The system allows the production of various reports on our contacts based on postal and courier addresses (e.g. find all customers by post code).
3. The date and time of task creation is recorded. The "money value" expected from the task completion might also be stored.
4. Events for the employee will be displayed on the employee's screen in calendar-like pages (one day per page). The priority of each event (low, medium, or high) is distinguished visually on the screen.
5. Not all events have a "due time" associated with them – some are "untimed" (they can be performed at any time during the day for which they were scheduled).
6. The creation time of an event cannot be changed, but the due time can.
7. On an event's completion, the completion date and time are recorded.
8. The system also stores identifications of employees who created tasks and events, who are scheduled to do the event ("due employee"), and who completed the event.

Analysis of statement 1 tells us that the notion of the current customer is derived from the association between `EOrganization` (as a customer) and `Contract`. The association may be quite dynamic. Hence, the classes `CurrentOrg` and `ProspectiveOrg` are not

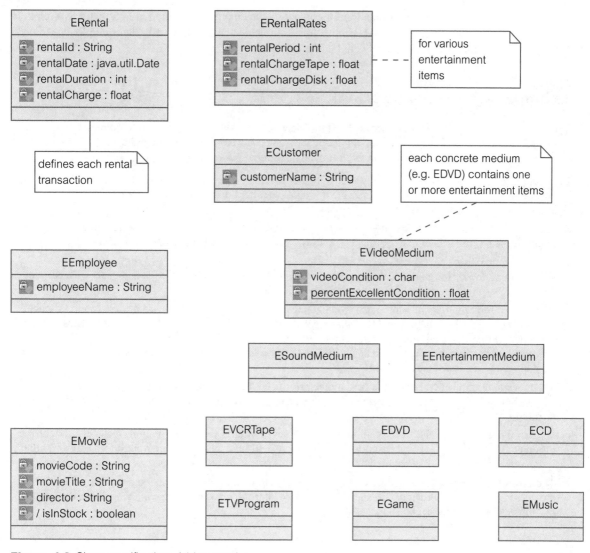

Figure 4.3 Class specifications (video store)

viable. Moreover, our system is not involved in contract management and is not responsible for the maintenance of class Contract. The best we can do is to model the solution by a derived attribute Organization.isCurrent to be modified as necessary by the contract management subsystem.

Statement 2 provides the reason for having two address classes: EPostalAddress and ECourierAddress.

The remaining statements provide additional information about the attribute content of the classes. There are also some hints about association relationships and integrity constraints (to be discussed later).

The class specification for contact management is presented in Figure 4.4. No relationships are modeled yet. Hence, for example, statement 8, which relates employees to tasks and events, is not reflected in the model.

Example 4.7 (telemarketing)

Refer to Section 1.5.4 (problem statement 4) and to Section 2.5, which presented the requirements business model for the telemarketing application. In particular, consider the business class diagram in Figure 2.5 (Section 2.5.4.1). Take into consideration the following additional information:

1. A campaign has a title that is generally used for referring to it. It has also a unique code for internal reference. Each campaign runs over a fixed period of time. Soon after the campaign is closed, the prizes are drawn and the holders of winning tickets are advised.

2. All tickets are numbered. The numbers are unique across all tickets in a campaign. The total number of tickets in a campaign, the number of tickets sold so far, and the current status of each ticket are known (e.g. available, ordered, paid for, prize winner).

3. To determine the performance of the society's telemarketers, the duration of calls and successful call outcomes (i.e. resulting in ordered tickets) are recorded.

4. Extensive information about supporters is maintained. Apart from normal contact details (address, phone number, etc.), this information includes historical details such as the first and most recent dates when a supporter had participated in a campaign along with the number of campaigns in which they participated. Any known supporter's preferences and constraints (such as unwelcome times to call or the usual credit card used in ticket purchases) are also kept.

5. The processing of telemarketing calls needs to be prioritized. Calls that are unanswered or where an answering machine was found need to be rescheduled to try again later. It is important to have alternative times when attempting repeat calls.

6. We can try calling over and over again until a call attempt limit is reached. The limit may be different for different call types. For example, a normal "solicitation" call may have a different limit to a call to remind a supporter of an outstanding payment.

7. The possible outcomes of calls are categorized to facilitate data entry by telemarketers. Typical outcomes are success (i.e. tickets ordered), no success, call back later, no answer, engaged, answering machine, fax machine, wrong number, and disconnected.

From statement 1 we can derive a few attributes in the class `ECampaign`. `ECampaign` contains `campaignCode` (**primary key**), `campaignTitle`, `dateStart`, and `dateClosed`. The last sentence in statement 1 refers to campaign prizes. A closer look should convince us that `EPrize` is a class on its own – it is drawn, it has a winner, and it must have other properties not explicitly stated, such as description, value, and ranking within other campaigns' prizes.

We add `EPrize` to the class model together with the attributes `prizeDescr`, `prizeValue`, and `prizeRanking`. We observe that the date on which prizes are drawn is the same for all prizes in the campaign. We add the attribute `dateDrawn` to the class `ECampaign`. A winner of the prize is a supporter. We can capture this fact later in an association between `EPrize` and `ESupporter`.

Statement 2 says that each ticket has a number, but the number is not unique across all tickets (it is only unique within a campaign). We add the attribute `ticketNumber`,

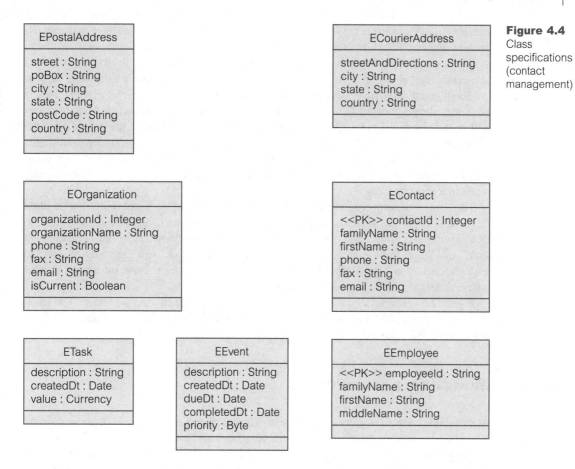

Figure 4.4
Class
specifications
(contact
management)

but we do not make it a primary key within `ECampaignTicket`. Two other attributes in `ECampaignTicket` are `ticketValue` and `ticketStatus`. The total number of tickets and the number of tickets sold are attributes of `ECampaign` (`numTickets` and `numTicketsSold`).

Statement 3 uncovers a few challenging issues. What data structures do we need to compute telemarketers' performance? To start with, we need to come up with some measures by which the performance can be expressed. One possibility is that we compute an average number of calls per hour and an average number of successful calls per hour. We can then calculate a performance indicator by dividing successful calls by the number of calls. We add the attributes `averagePerHour` and `successPerHour` to the class `ETelemarketer`.

To calculate telemarketers' performance indicators, we need to store the duration of each call. The placeholder for this information is the class `ECallOutcome`. We add the attributes `startTime` and `endTime` to that class. We assume that each call outcome will be linked to a telemarketer by an association.

Statement 4 results in attributes to be included in the class `ESupporter`. The attributes are `supporterId` (primary key), `supporterName`, `phoneNumber`, `mailingAddress`, `dateFirst`, `dateLast`, `campaignCount`, `preferredHours`, and `creditCard-Attributes`. Some of these attributes (`mailingAddress`, `preferredHours`) are complex enough to expect that they will have to be converted to classes later in the development process. We store them as attributes for now.

Statement 5 refers to the class `ECallScheduled`. We add to it the attributes `phoneNumber`, `priority`, and `attemptNumber`. We are not quite sure how to support the requirement that successive calls should be made at different times of day. This is obviously the responsibility of the scheduling algorithm, but a support in data structures will be necessary. Fortunately, some light on this issue is provided in the next statement.

Statement 6 results in a new class, `ECallType`. The class contains attributes `typeDescr`, `callAttemptLimit`, and also `alternativeHours`. The latter is a complex data structure, similar to `preferredHours` in `ESupporter`, and it will eventually result in a separate class.

The last statement categorizes call outcomes. This is a direct hint that a class `EOutcomeType` is needed. Possible outcome types can be stored in attribute `outcomeTypeDescr`. It is not clear what other attributes can be included in `EOutcomeType`, but we are convinced that they will emerge with the study of detailed requirements. One such attribute could be `followUpAction` to hold information about a typical next step for each outcome type.

Figure 4.5 demonstrates a class model that concludes the discussion above. The associations already established in the business class model (Figure 2.5) are retained. No new associations have been added.

4.2.2 Modeling associations

Associations connect objects in the system. They facilitate collaboration between objects. Without associations, the objects can still be related and can collaborate at run time, but this requires computational means. For example, an object can acquire an identity of another object in the process of the program passing objects in messages. Alternatively, two objects may share the same attributes and the program can search for the same attribute values in two objects (this is akin to referential integrity in relational databases).

Associations are the most essential kind of relationship in the model, in particular in the model of persistent "business objects." Associations support the execution of use cases and, therefore, they tie together the state and behavior specifications.

The PCMEF framework reasserts the importance of explicit associations in the program in the EAP principle (Section 4.1.3). The principle demands that if two objects communicate at run time, then a compile-time association between these objects should exist.

4.2.2.1 Discovering associations

Finding the main associations is a side effect of discovering classes. When defining classes, the analyst takes a decision about the class attributes, and some of these attributes are associations to other classes. Attributes can have primitive data types or they can be typed as other classes, thus establishing relationships to other classes. In essence, any attribute with a *non-primitive data type* should be modeled as an association (or aggregation) to a class representing that data type.

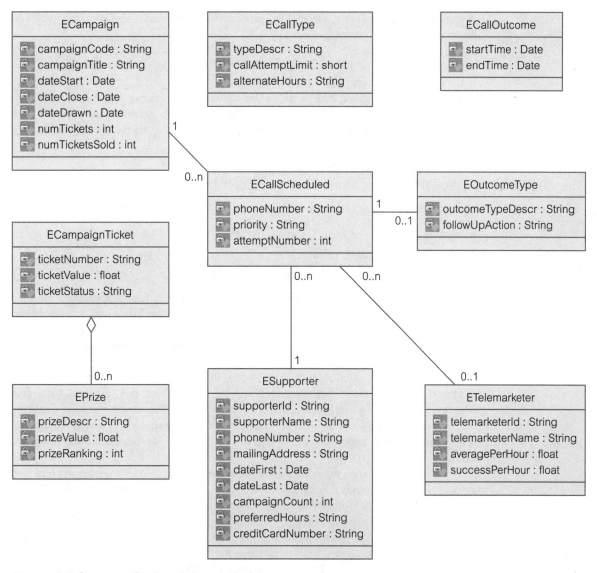

Figure 4.5 Class specifications (telemarketing)

Doing the "dry run" of use cases can discover the remaining associations. Collaboration paths between the classes, necessary for a use-case execution, are determined. Associations should normally support these collaboration paths.

Although associations are used for message passing, there is a difference between a *cycle of associations* and a *cycle of messages*. Association cycles, such as the simplest possible cycle in Figure 3.14 (Section 3.1.4.2), are frequent and perfectly acceptable. Message cycles, such as two or more objects exchanging messages back and forth in a circular manner, are troublesome because they introduce difficult to manage run-time dependencies. Accordingly, the PCMEF framework recommends that message cycles be eliminated (the CEP principle – Section 4.1.3).

Occasionally, a *cycle of associations* does not have to commute (be closed) to fully express the underlying semantics (Maciaszek, 1990). That is, at least one of the associations in the cycle can be *derived*. Figure 3.34 (Section 3.2.3.3) contains a relevant example. A derived association is redundant in the semantic sense and should be eliminated (a good semantic model should be non-redundant). It is possible, and indeed likely, that many derived associations will nevertheless be included in the design model (e.g. for efficiency reasons).

4.2.2.2 Specifying associations

The specification of associations involves:

- naming them
- naming the association roles
- determining the association multiplicity (Section 3.1.4.2).

The rules for giving *names for associations* should loosely follow the convention for naming classes. However, the PCMEF's CNP principle for prefixing names with a letter identifying the architectural layer (Section 4.1.3) does not apply to association names. This is because association names do not have representations in the implemented system. They serve only a modeling purpose.

By contrast, association roles are represented in the implemented system by attributes in classes linked by the association (Section 3.1.2.1.1). Accordingly, the rules for giving *names for association roles* should follow the convention for attribute names – starting with lower case letters and capitalizing the first letter of any successive words building up multi-word names (Section 4.2.1.2.2). It is customary to begin role names with the word the (e.g. `theOrderLine`).

If only one association connects two classes, the specification of association name and association roles between these classes is optional. A CASE tool would distinguish each association internally through system-provided identification names.

Role names can be used to explain more complicated associations, in particular *self-associations* (*recursive* associations that relate objects of the same class). If provided, role names should be chosen with the understanding that in the design models they will become attributes in classes on the opposite end of an association.

The *multiplicities* should be specified for both ends (roles) of an association. If unclear, the lower and upper multiplicity bounds can be omitted at this stage.

4.2.2.3 Example for association specifications

Example 4.8 (contact management)

Refer to Examples 4.3 and 4.6. Use the requirements given in these examples to discover and specify associations on classes in the contact management system.

The association model for contact management is presented in Figure 4.6. To demonstrate the flexibility of association modeling, the use of association names and role names is unsystematic. The figure also contains the code for the class `ETask`. The code has been generated automatically by the CASE tool used (Rational Rose). Note that if role names are provided on the graphical model, then they are used by the code generator. Otherwise, the CASE tool generates the role names, as shown by the presence of the instance variable `theEEvent` in the generated code even though the role name for the association to `EEvent` is not provided in the model.

The multiplicity of all associations between `EPostalAddress` and `ECourierAddress` on the one hand and `EOrganization` and `EContact` on the other is "one." However, exclusive OR constraints are set on the two pairs of associations. In UML, "an *xor-constraint* indicates a situation in which only one of several potential associations may be instantiated at one time for any single instance" (UML, 2003, pp.3–69). An xor-constraint is shown as a dashed line named `{Xor}` connecting two or more associations (the curly brackets in UML signify a constraint condition imposed on the model). Let us explain using the association between `EOrganization` and `EPostalAddress`.

On "one" end of the association, an `EOrganization` object is connected to a maximum of one `EPostalAddress` object, but only if the postal address of the organization is known. On the opposite end of the association, a particular `EPostalAddress` object relates to an `EOrganization` object *or* to an `EContact` object.

The multiplicity of the role `theContact`, between `ETask` and `EContact`, is unspecified. The requirements have not explained whether a task must be directly linked to a contact. If so, we are still not sure if it can be linked to more than one contact.

Finally, there are three associations between `EEvent` and `EEmployee`. These associations determine which employee created an event, which is due to perform it, and which will eventually complete it. At the time of event creation, the employee who is going to complete that event is unknown (so the multiplicity on the employee end of association `completed` is "zero or one").

Modeling aggregation and composition relationships

4.2.3

Aggregation, and its stronger form – *composition*–carries the "whole–part" semantics between a composite (superset) class and a component (subset) class (Section 3.1.5). In UML, aggregation is treated as a constrained form of association. This is a gross underestimation of the modeling significance of aggregation. Suffice to say that aggregation, along with generalization, is the most important technique for reusing functionality in object-oriented systems.

The modeling power of UML would be greatly facilitated if the language supported the four possible semantics for aggregation (Maciaszek *et al.*, 1996b):

1. "ExclusiveOwns" aggregation
2. "Owns" aggregation
3. "Has" aggregation
4. "Member" aggregation.

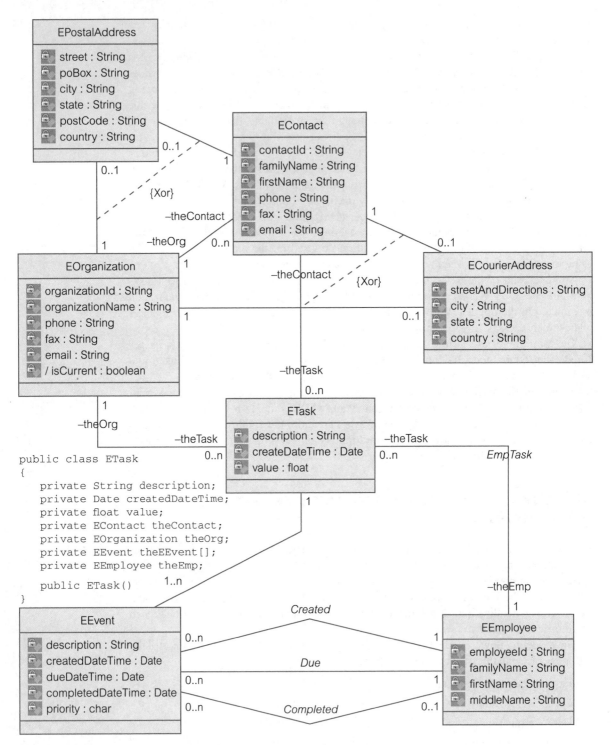

Figure 4.6 Association specifications (contact management)

The *ExclusiveOwns* aggregation states that:

- component classes are *existence-dependent* on their composite class (hence, deleting a composite object propagates down so that the related component objects are also deleted);
- aggregation is *transitive* (if object $C1$ is part of $B1$, and $B1$ is part of $A1$, then $C1$ is part of $A1$);
- aggregation is *asymmetric* (*irreflexive*) (if $B1$ is part of $A1$, then $A1$ is not part of $B1$);
- aggregation is *fixed* (if $B1$ is part of $A1$, then it can never be part of Ai ($i \neq 1$)).

The *Owns* aggregation supports the first three properties of an *ExclusiveOwns* aggregation, that is:

- existence-dependency
- transitivity
- asymmetry.

The *Has* aggregation is semantically weaker than the *Owns* aggregation. This aggregation supports:

- transitivity
- asymmetry.

The *Member* aggregation has the property of purposeful grouping of independent objects – a grouping that does not make assumptions with regard to existence-dependency, transitivity, asymmetry or the fixed property. It is an abstraction whereby a collection of component members is considered as a higher-level composite object. A component object in a Member aggregation can at the same time belong to more than one composite object (hence, the *multiplicity* of a Member aggregation can be *many to many*).

Although *aggregation* has been recognized as a fundamental modeling concept for at least as long as *generalization* (Smith and Smith, 1977), it has only been given marginal attention in object-oriented analysis and design (with the exception of "perfect match" application domains, such as multimedia systems). Fortunately, this trend may be reversed in the future because of the contributions and insights from the methodologists working on *design patterns*. This is evident, for example, in the treatment of aggregation (composition) in the seminal book by Gamma *et al.* (1995).

Discovering aggregations and compositions 4.2.3.1

Aggregations are discovered in parallel with the discovery of associations. If an association exhibits one or more of the four semantic properties discussed above, then it can be modeled as an aggregation. The litmus test is to use phrases "*has*" and "*is part of*" when explaining the relationship. In the top-down explanation, the phrase is "has" (e.g. Book "has" Chapter). In the bottom-up interpretation, the phrase is "is part of" (e.g. Chapter "is part of" Book). If the relationship is read aloud with these phrases and the sentence does not make sense in English, then the relationship is *not* an aggregation.

From a structural point of view, aggregation frequently relates together a large number of classes whereas an association is quite meaningless beyond the binary degree (ref.

Section 3.1.4.1). When we need to relate more than two classes together, a *Member* aggregation may be an excellent modeling proposition. However, note that UML permits *n-ary associations* between three or more classes. Such associations are not recommended in this book.

4.2.3.2 Specifying aggregations and compositions

UML provides only limited support for aggregation. A strong form of aggregation in UML is called *composition*. In composition, the composite object may physically contain the part objects (the "by value" semantics). A part object can belong to only one composite object. The UML *composition* corresponds (more or less) to our *ExclusiveOwns* and *Owns* aggregations.

A weak form of aggregation in UML is simply called *aggregation*. It has the "by reference" semantics – the composite object does not physically contain the part objects. The same part object can have many aggregation or association links in the model. Loosely speaking, the UML *aggregation* corresponds to our *Has* and *Member* aggregations.

The *solid diamond* in UML represents a composition. The *hollow diamond* is used to define an aggregation. The rest of the aggregation specification is consistent with the association notation.

4.2.3.3 Example for aggregation and composition specifications

Example 4.9 (university enrolment)

Refer to Examples 4.1 and 4.4. Consider the following additional requirements:

1. The student's academic record should be available on demand. The record should include information about the grades obtained by the student in each course that the student enrolled in (and has not withdrawn without penalty, i.e. within the first three weeks from the beginning of the semester).

2. Each course has one academic in charge of a course, but additional academics may also teach in it. There may be a different academic in charge of a course each semester, and there may be different academics for each course each semester.

Figure 4.7 demonstrates a class model that emphasizes aggregation relationships. EStudent "has" EAcademicRecord is a UML composition ("by value" semantics). Each EAcademicRecord object is physically embedded in one EStudent object. Despite the existence of the association Takes, EAcademicRecord includes attribute courseCode. This is necessary because the association Takes will be implemented by the variable takesCrsoff in EStudent typed as a *collection*, e.g. Set[ECourseOffering]. The attribute takesCrsoff is independent of the information in the embedded EAcademicRecord object, although it ultimately links EStudent to ECourse.

ECourse "has" ECourseOffering is a UML aggregation ("by reference" semantics). Each ECourseOffering object is logically contained in only one ECourse object. ECourseOffering can also participate in other aggregations and/or associations (e.g. with EStudent and EAcademicInCharge).

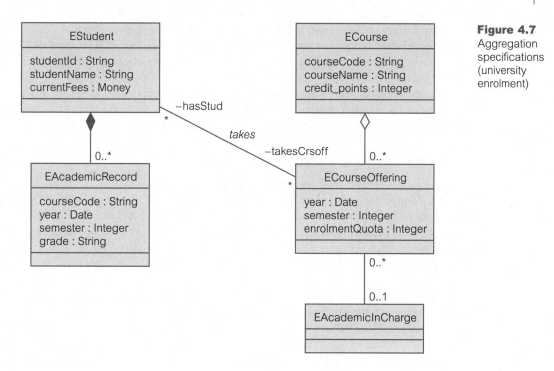

Figure 4.7
Aggregation
specifications
(university
enrolment)

Modeling generalization relationships 4.2.4

Common *features* (attributes and operations) of one or more classes can be abstracted into a more generic class. This is known as *generalization* (Section 3.1.6). The generalization relationship connects a generic class (*superclass*) with more specific classes (*subclasses*). Generalization permits *inheritance* (*reuse*) of the superclass features by the subclasses. In a conventional object-oriented system, inheritance applies to classes, not to objects (types are inherited, not values).

Apart from *inheritance*, generalization has two objectives (Rumbaugh *et al.*, 1999):

1. substitutability
2. polymorphism.

Under the *substitutability* principle, a subclass object is a legal value for a superclass variable. For example, if a variable is declared to hold `Fruit` objects, then an `Apple` object is a legal value.

Under the *polymorphism* principle (Section 3.1.6.1), the same operation can have different implementations in different classes. A calling object can invoke an operation without knowing or caring which implementation of the operation will execute. The called object knows to what class it belongs and executes its own implementation.

Polymorphism works best when it is used hand in hand with inheritance. It is frequent that a polymorphic operation in the superclass is defined but no implementation is provided. That is, an operation is given a *signature* (the name and the list of formal arguments), but an implementation must be provided in each subclass. Such an *operation* is *abstract*.

Abstract operation should not be confused with *abstract class* (Section 3.1.7). The latter is a class that does not have any direct instance objects (but its subclasses may have instance objects). There may be no instances of `Vegetable`. The only direct instances are the objects of classes `Potato`, `Carrot`, etc.

In reality, a class with an abstract operation is abstract. A concrete class, such as `Apple`, cannot have abstract operations. While abstract operations are captured in *behavior specifications*, abstract classes are the domain of *state specifications*.

4.2.4.1 Discovering generalizations

An analyst observes many superclasses/subclasses when the initial list of classes is determined. Many other generalizations are detected when defining associations. Different associations (even from the same class) may need to be connected to a class at a different level of generalization/specialization. For example, class `Course` may be associated with a `Student` (`Student` *takes* `Course`), and it may be connected to a `TeachingAssistant` (`TeachingAssistant` *teaches* `Course`). Further analysis can show that `Teaching Assistant` is a subclass of `Student`.

The litmus test for generalization is in using the phrases *"can be"* and *"is a kind of"* when explaining the relationship. In the top-down explanation, the phrase is "can be" (e.g. `Student` "can be" a `TeachingAssistant`). In the bottom-up interpretation, the phrase is "is a kind of " (e.g. `TeachingAssistant` "is a kind of " `Student`). Note that if a `TeachingAssistant` is also a kind of `Teacher`, then we have established *multiple inheritance* (Section 3.1.6.3).

4.2.4.2 Specifying generalizations

A generalization relationship between classes shows that one class shares the structure and behavior defined in one or more other classes. Generalization is represented in UML by a solid line with an *arrowhead* pointing to the superclass.

A complete specification of generalization includes a number of powerful options. For example, one can further define a generalization relationship by specifying its *access*, identifying whether the class grants *rights* to another class, or deciding what to do in a *multiple inheritance* situation. These issues are discussed in Section 5.2.

4.2.4.3 Example for generalization specifications

Example 4.10 (video store)

Refer to Examples 4.2 and 4.5. The classes identified in Figure 4.3 (Example 4.5) imply a generalization hierarchy rooted at the class `EEntertainmentMedium`. They also imply a parallel generalization hierarchy rooted at a class that can be named `EEntertainmentItem` or `EEntertainmentItemCategory`.

Our task is to extend the model in Figure 4.3 to include generalization relationships and to establish the basic association relationship between the two generalization hierarchies. To capture some state differences between classes in the generalization hierarchy originating from the class `EEntertainmentMedium`, assume that the storage capacity of an `EDVD` allows multiple versions of the same movie to be held, each in a different language or with different endings. There is no need to decipher the peculiarities of game and music CDs in the model.

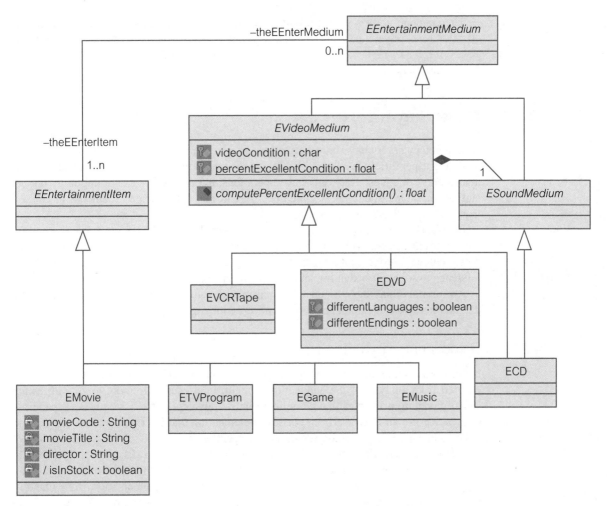

Figure 4.8 Generalization specifications (video store)

Figure 4.8 is a modified class model for video store that emphasizes generalization. The generalization hierarchy states that `EEntertainmentMedium` "can be" `EVideoMedium` or `ESoundMedium`. `EVideoMedium` "has an" `ESoundMedium`. `EVideoMedium` "can be" `EVCRTape`, `EDVD`, or `ECD`. `ECD` is a "kind of" `ESoundMedium`, but in some cases `ECD` is also a "kind of" `ESoundMedium`. Further intricacies of `ECD`, such as classification into game and music CDs or distinguishing between `VCD` and `DVD-A` formats, are not considered. The second generalization hierarchy states that `EEntertainmentItem` "can be" `EMovie`, `ETVProgram`, `EGame`, or `EMusic`. `EEntertainmentMedium`, `EEntertainmentItem`, `EVideoMedium`, and `ESoundMedium` are *abstract classes* (shown by italicizing their names). Abstract classes do not instantiate objects (Section 3.1.7). `EVideoMedium` objects are instantiated by the *concrete classes* `EVCRTape`, `EDVD`, and `ECD`. The *abstract operation* `computerPercentExcellentCondition()` must be declared (implemented) within these concrete classes.

The concrete classes inherit all attributes from their superclass. Hence, for example, all `EVCRTape` objects have an instance variable `videoCondition` and a class variable `percentExcellentCondition`, and they are associated with an `EEntertainmentItem` object via instance variable `theEEnterItem`.

4.2.5 Modeling interfaces

Although they do not have implementation, *interfaces* provide some of the most powerful modeling capabilities (Section 3.1.8). Interfaces do not have attributes (except constants), associations, or states. They only have operations, but all operations are implicitly public and abstract. Operations are declared (i.e. turned into implemented methods) in classes that implement these interfaces.

Interfaces do not have associations to classes, but they may be targets of one-way associations from classes. This happens when an attribute that implements an association is typed with an interface, rather than with a class. The value of any such attribute will be a reference to some class that implements the interface.

An interface may have a generalization relationship to another interface. This means that an interface can extend another interface by inheriting its operations.

4.2.5.1 Discovering interfaces

Unlike other modeling elements discussed so far in this chapter, interfaces are not discovered from analysis of the application domain. Interfaces have more to do with using sound modeling principles that determine robust and supportable systems. By separating classes that use an interface from classes implementing that interface, interfaces result in systems that are easier to understand, maintain, and evolve.

Interfaces are fundamental for enforcing architectural frameworks, such as the PCMEF framework (Section 4.1). They can be used to break cyclic dependencies in the system, to implement publish/subscribe event schemes, to hide the implementation from unauthorized clients, etc. In a typical situation, an interface reveals only a limited portion of the behavior of an actual class.

4.2.5.2 Specifying interfaces

Interfaces represent classes and, therefore, they may be shown using a typical class rectangle stereotyped with the keyword «`interface`». An alternative symbol that replaces the stereotype keyword with a small circle in the upper right corner of the rectangle is also allowed (this was the notation used in Section 3.1.8). It is also possible to display an interface as a small circle with the name of the interface below the circle.

A class that uses (requires) the interface can be indicated by a dashed arrow pointing to the interface. For clarity, the arrow can be stereotyped with the keyword «`use`». The class may use (require) only selected operations from the complete list of operations supplied by the interface.

A class that implements (realizes) the interface is indicated by a dashed line with a triangular end. This notation is similar to the generalization symbol, except that the line is dashed. For clarity, the line can be stereotyped with the keyword «implement». The class must implement (provide) all operations supplied by the interface.

Example for interface specifications   4.2.5.3

Example 4.11 (contact management)

Refer to Examples 4.3, 4.6, and 4.8. Consider in particular the classes EContact and EEmployee in Figure 4.6. These two classes have some attributes in common (firstName, familyName). The operations that provide access to these attributes can be extracted into a single interface.

Let us assume that there is a need to display information about overdue events to the screen. The relevant presentation-layer class has the responsibility for displaying a list of overdue events together with names of contacts and employees, as well as with the additional contact details (phone and email) to contacts.

Our task is to propose a model such that the presentation class uses one or more interfaces implemented by EEmployee and EContact to support part of the "display overdue events" functionality.

Figure 4.9 contains two interfaces in two different graphical representations. The interface IAPerson is implemented by EEmployee. The interface IAContactInfo is implemented by EContact. Because IAContactInfo inherits from IAPerson, EContact also implements operations of IAPerson.

POverdueEvents is a presentation class. The model shows three operations in POverdueEvents. The operation displayEmployee() accepts IAPerson as an

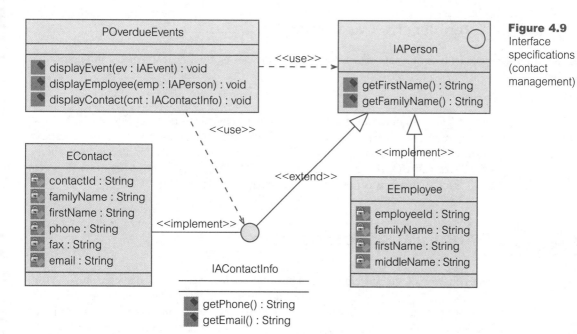

Figure 4.9
Interface specifications (contact management)

argument and is, therefore, able to perform `getFirstName()` and `getFamilyName()` methods on a given `EEmployee` object.

Similarly, the operation `displayContact()` obtains an `IAContactInfo` object. It can then call the methods supplied by `IAContactInfo` and implemented in `EContact`. There are four such methods: `getPhone()`, `getEmail()`, `getFirstName()`, and `getFamilyName()`.

4.2.6 Modeling objects

Modeling is concerned with definitions of systems. A model is not an executable system and, therefore, it does not show instance objects. In any case, the number of objects in any non-trivial system is very large, and representing them graphically is impossible. Nevertheless, when modeling classes, we frequently imagine objects and discuss difficult scenarios using examples of objects.

4.2.6.1 Specifying objects

UML provides a graphical representation for an *object* (Section 3.1.1.1). We can draw object diagrams to illustrate data structures, including relationships between classes. Object models can be used to illustrate how object states change over time and to examine how objects can collaborate during an execution of the system.

4.2.6.2 Example for object specifications

Example 4.12 (university enrolment)

Our task in this example is to show a few objects representing the classes from the class model in Figure 4.7 (Example 4.9).

Figure 4.10 is an object diagram corresponding to the class model in Figure 4.7. It shows that a `Student` object (Don Donaldson) physically contains two `AcademicRecord` objects (for courses COMP224 and COMP326). Don is currently enrolled in two courses: COMP225 and COMP325. One offering of COMP325 was given in semester 2 in year 2000. Rick Richards was the academic in charge of that offering.

4.3 Behavior specifications

The behavior of the system, as it appears to an outside user, is depicted in *use cases* (Section 3.2.1). Use-case models can be developed at different levels of abstraction. They can apply to the system as a whole in order to specify the main functional units in the application under development. They can also be used to capture the behavior of a UML *package*, a part of the package or even a *class* within the package.

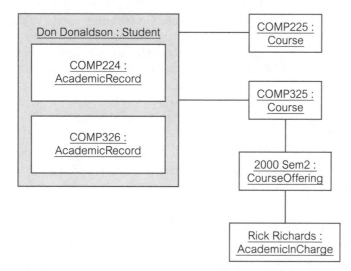

Figure 4.10
An object diagram
(university
enrolment)

During *analysis*, use cases capture the system requirements by focusing on *what* the system does or should do. During *design*, use-case views can be used to specify the behavior of the system as it is to be implemented.

The behavior entailed by a use case requires that computations be performed and that objects interact to execute a use case. *Computations* can be modeled with activity diagrams. *Interactions* of objects can be specified with sequence diagrams or collaboration diagrams.

Behavior specifications provide an *operational view* of the system. The main task here is to define *use cases* in the application domain and to determine which *classes* are involved in the execution of these use cases. We identify class *operations* and the *message passing* between objects. Although object interactions trigger changes to object states, in behavior specifications we define an *operational view on a frozen state* of the system. Changes in object states are explicitly depicted in *state-change specifications*.

Use-case models should be developed iteratively and concurrently with class models. The classes determined in state specifications will be elaborated further and the most important operations identified. However, note that state specifications define mostly *entity classes* ("business objects"). As behavior modeling proceeds, other layers of classes (Section 4.1.1) will be revealed.

Modeling use cases

4.3.1

Use-case modeling is tightly integrated with requirements determination (Chapter 2). Textual requirements in the requirements document need to be traced down to use cases in the specifications document. If use cases drive the rest of the development process, then the process is *function-driven* (Section 4.2.1.1.3).

Like class modeling, use-case modeling is inherently *iterative* and *incremental*. The initial use-case diagram can be determined from the top-level requirements. This could be a *business use-case model* (Section 2.5.2). Further refinements should be driven by more detailed requirements. If user requirements change during the development lifecycle, those changes are made first in the requirements document and then in the use-case model. Changes to use cases are then traced down to the other models (Rational, 2000; Hoffer *et al.*, 2002).

4.3.1.1 Discovering use cases

When discovering use cases, the analyst must ensure that they adhere to the essential features of the use-case concept. A use case represents (Hoffer *et al.*, 1999; Rumbaugh *et al.*, 1999; Quatrani, 2000; Kruchten, 2003):

- a *complete* piece of functionality (including the *main flow* of logic, any variations on it (*subflows*), and any exceptional conditions (*alternative flows*));
- a piece of *externally visible* functionality (not an internal function);
- an *orthogonal* piece of functionality (use cases can share objects during execution, but the execution of each use case is independent of the others);
- a piece of functionality *initiated by an actor* (but once initiated, the use case can interact with other actors) – however, it is possible for an actor to be only on the receiving end of a use case initiated (perhaps indirectly) by another actor;
- a piece of functionality that delivers an identifiable *value to an actor* (and that value is achieved in a single use case).

Use cases are discovered from the analysis of:

- requirements identified in the requirements document;
- actors and their purpose in the system.

Requirements management issues were discussed in Section 2.4. We recall that requirements are typed. For the discovery of use cases, we are interested only in *functional requirements*.

Use cases can be determined from the analysis of tasks performed by actors. Jacobson (1992) suggests asking a range of questions about actors. Answers to these questions can result in the identification of use cases. The questions are:

- What are the main tasks performed by each actor?
- Will an actor access or modify information in the system?
- Will an actor inform the system about any changes in other systems?
- Should an actor be informed about unexpected changes in the system?

In analysis, use cases address identifiable needs of actors. In some way, these are *actor use cases*. Since use cases determine major functional building blocks for a system, there is also a need to identify *system use cases*. System use cases extract commonality from actor use cases and allow generic solutions applicable (via inheritance) to a range of actor use cases to be developed. The "actor" of the system use case is the designer/programmer, not the user. System use cases are identified in the design phase.

Specifying use cases 4.3.1.2

Use-case specification includes graphical presentation of actors, use cases, and four kinds of relationship:

1. association
2. include
3. extend
4. generalization.

The *association* relationship establishes the communication path between an actor and a use case. The *include* and *extend* relationships are stereotyped by the words «include» and «extend». The *generalization* relationship allows a specialized use case to change any aspect of the base use case.

The «include» relationship allows the common behavior in the included use case to be factored out. The «extend» relationship provides a controlled form of extending the behavior of a use case by activating another use case at specific extension points. The «include» relationship differs from the «extend» relationship in that the "included" use case is necessary for the completion of the "activating" use case.

In practice, projects can easily get into trouble by putting too much effort into discovering relationships between use cases and determining which relationships apply for specific pairs of use cases. In addition, high-level use cases tend to be so intertwined that relationship links can dominate and obscure the diagram, shifting the emphasis from proper identification of use cases to relationships between use cases.

Example for use-case specifications 4.3.1.3

Example 4.13 (university enrolment)

Refer to the problem statement for the university enrolment system in Section 1.5.1 and to the requirements defined in Examples 4.1 and 4.4 in Section 4.2.1. Our task is to determine use cases from the analysis of functional requirements.

Figure 4.11 shows a high-level use-case diagram for university enrolment. The model contains four actors and four use cases. Each use case is initiated by an actor and is a complete, externally visible, and orthogonal piece of functionality. All actors, except Student, are *initiating* actors. Student obtains examination results and enrolment instructions before the program of study for the next semester (term) can be entered and validated.

The use case Provide Examination Results *may* «extend» the use case Provide Enrolment Instructions. The former does not always extend the latter use case. For example, for new students, the examination results are not known. This is why we modeled the relationship with the «extend» stereotype, not «include».

The «include» relationship has been established from the use case Enter Program of Study to the use case Validate Program of Study. The «include» relationship

Figure 4.11
A use-case
diagram
(university
enrolment)

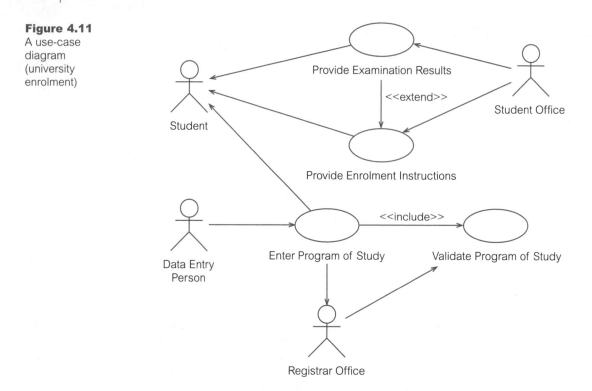

signifies that the former use case always includes the latter. Whenever the program of study is entered, it is validated for timetable clashes, special approvals, etc.

Example 4.14 (contact management)

Refer to the problem statement for the contact management system in Section 1.5.3 and to the requirements defined in Examples 4.3 and 4.6 in Section 4.2.1. Our task is to determine use cases from the analysis of functional requirements.

There are three actors and five use cases in the use case diagram for Contact Management (Figure 4.12). An interesting aspect of the model is that actors are related by generalization relationships. `Customer Services Manager` "is a kind of" `Customer Services Employee` who in turn "is a kind of" `Employee`. The generalization hierarchy improves the expressiveness of the diagram. Any event performed by an `Employee` can also be performed by `Customer Services Employee` or `Customer Services Manager`. Consequently, `Customer Services Manager` is implicitly associated with (and can initiate) every use case in the model.

The use case `Create Task` includes `Schedule Event` because of the requirement that the task cannot be created without scheduling the first event. The «extend» relationships signify the fact that the completion of an event can trigger changes to the organization or contact details.

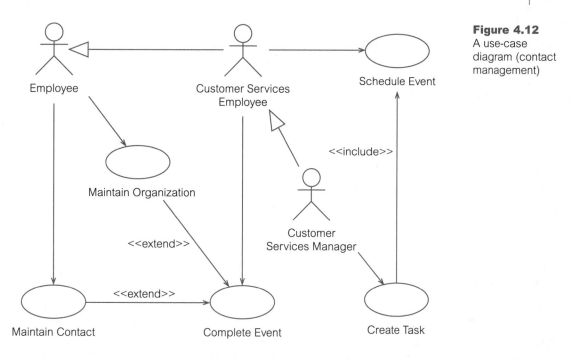

Figure 4.12
A use-case
diagram (contact
management)

Example 4.15 (video store)

Refer to the problem statement for the video store system in Section 1.5.2 and to the requirements defined in Examples 4.2 and 4.5 in Section 4.2.1. Our task is to determine use cases from the analysis of functional requirements. For one of the use cases, write narrative specifications with the following headings: summary, actors, preconditions, description, exceptions, and postconditions.

There are six use cases and only two actors in the use-case diagram for video store (Figure 4.13). Secondary actors, such as `Customer` or `Supplier`, are not shown. These actors do not initiate any use cases. The actor `Employee` initiates all use cases. The relationship between actors `Scanning Device` and `Employee` is a *dependency*, stereotyped by the analyst with the phrase «depends on».

Table 4.4 illustrates that the graphical representation of use cases is but one aspect of the complete use-case model. Each use case in the diagram has to be documented further in the CASE tool repository. In particular, a narrative description is necessary. Table 4.4 uses one popular structure for the narrative specification of use cases (Section 3.2.1.4).

Example 4.16 (telemarketing)

Refer to the problem statement for the telemarketing system in Section 1.5.4 and to the requirements defined in Examples 2.1–2.4 and Example 4.7. Our task is to determine use cases from the analysis of functional requirements.

Figure 4.13
A use-case
diagram
(video store)

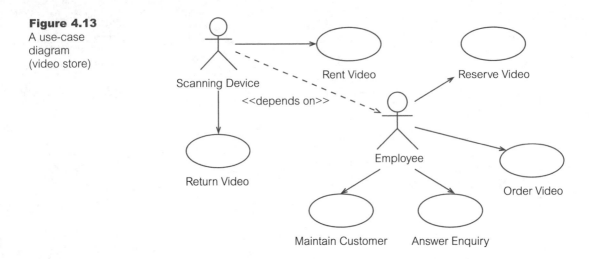

Table 4.4 Narrative specification for use case "Rent Video" (video store)

Use case	Rent Video
Brief description	A customer wishes to rent a video tape or disk that is picked from the store's shelves or that has been previously reserved by the customer. Provided that the customer has a non-delinquent account, the video is rented out once payment has been received. If the video is not returned in a timely fashion, an overdue notice is mailed to the customer.
Actors	Employee, Scanning device.
Preconditions	Video tape or disk is available to be hired. Customer has a membership card. Scanner devices work correctly. Employee at the front desk knows how to use the system.
Main flow	A customer may ask an employee about video availability (including a reserved video) or may pick a tape or disk from the shelves. The video and the membership card are scanned and any delinquent or overdue details are brought up for the employee to query the customer about. If the customer does not have a delinquent rating, then he/she can hire up to a maximum of eight videos. However, if the rating of the customer is "unreliable," then a deposit of one rental period for each tape or disk is requested. Once the amount payable has been received, the stock is updated and the tapes and disks are handed to the customer together with the rental receipt. The customer pays by cash, credit card or electronic transfer. Each rental record stores (under the customer's account) the check-out and due-in dates together with the identification of the employee. A separate rental record is created for each video hired. The use case will generate an overdue notice to the customer if the video has not been returned within two days of the due date, and a second notice after another two days (and at that time the customer is noted as "delinquent").
Alternative flows	A customer does not have a membership card. In this case, the "Maintain Customer" use case may be activated to issue a new card. An attempt to rent too many videos. No videos can be rented because of the customer's delinquent rating. The video medium or membership card cannot be scanned because of damage to it. The electronic transfer or credit card payment is refused.
Postconditions	Videos are rented out and the database is updated accordingly.

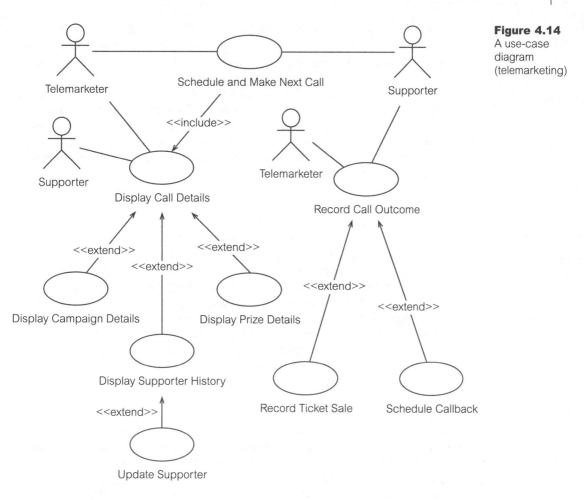

Figure 4.14
A use-case
diagram
(telemarketing)

The solution in Figure 4.14 consists of a number of use cases. The actors communicate directly with three use cases: `Schedule and Make Next Call`, `Record Call Outcome`, and `Display Call Details`. The latter can in turn be extended to `Display Campaign Details`, `Display Supporter History`, and `Display Prize Details`. The use case `Update Supporter` extends `Display Supporter History`. `Record Ticket Order` and `Schedule Callback` can extend `Record Call Outcome`. It is assumed that the actors can communicate indirectly with the extension use cases, but no explicit communication links are drawn to those use cases.

Modeling activities

4.3.2

Like traditional *flowcharts* and *structure charts* popularized in the structured methods for procedural program design, activity diagrams represent the flow of logic in object-oriented programs (albeit at a high level of abstraction). They have the possibility of representing a *concurrent control*, in addition to any *sequential controls*.

Activity models are used extensively in the *design*. However, they also provide a great technique for expressing computations or workflows at the level of abstraction applied in the *analysis*. Activity graphs can be used to show varying levels of detail of a computation.

Activity models can be particularly useful for defining the flow of *actions* in the execution of a use case. Actions are performed by objects (as operations), but activity diagrams do not explicitly visualize the *objects* that perform the actions. Consequently, an activity graph can be constructed even if the class model is not developed or is underdeveloped. Eventually, each activity will be defined by one or more operations in one or more collaborating classes. The detailed design for such collaboration is likely to be modeled in an interaction diagram (Section 3.2.4).

4.3.2.1 Discovering actions

Each use case can be modeled by one or more activity graphs. An event from an actor that initiates a use case is the same event that triggers the execution of the activity graph. The execution proceeds from one *action state* to the next. An action state completes when its computation is completed. External event-based interruptions, which would cause the action state to complete, are allowed only in exceptional situations. If they are expected to be frequent, then a statechart diagram should be used instead.

Actions are best discovered from the analysis of sentences in the *narrative specifications* of use cases (Table 4.4). Any phrases with verbs are candidate actions. The description of alternative flows introduces decisions (branches) or forks for concurrent threads.

4.3.2.2 Specifying actions

Once the activity states are discovered, the specification of actions is a relatively straightforward process of connecting them by *transition lines*. Concurrent threads are initiated (*forked*) and *rejoined* with *synchronization bars*. Alternative threads are created (*branched*) and *merged* with *decision diamonds*.

External events are not normally expected on activity graphs. However, the graphical techniques exist if external events must be included. Similarly, the graphical notation exists for object flow states to represent an object that is an input or output of an action.

4.3.2.3 Example for activity specifications

Example 4.17 (video store)

Refer to Example 4.15 and in particular to the narrative specification for use case "Rent Video" (Table 4.4). Our task is to design an activity diagram for "Rent Video."

Figure 4.15 is the activity diagram for the "Rent Video" use case. Not surprisingly, the diagram reflects the narrative specification for the use case (Table 4.4). The processing begins when either a customer card or video medium is scanned. These two actions are considered independent of each other (shown by the use of a fork).

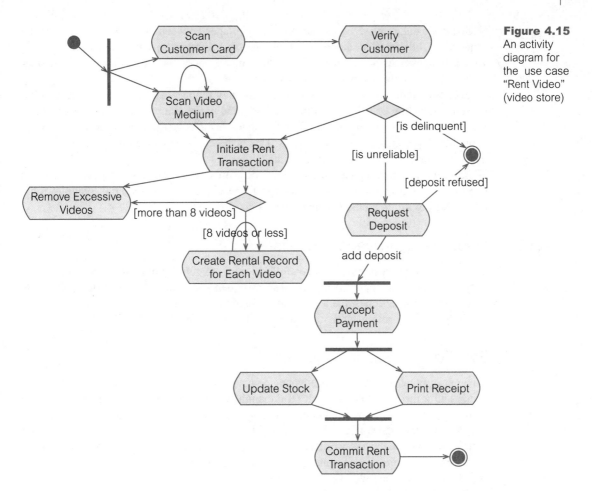

Figure 4.15
An activity diagram for the use case "Rent Video" (video store)

The action `Verify Customer` checks the customer history and the computation proceeds after evaluating the decision (branch) conditions. If a customer is delinquent, then "Rent Video" terminates. If a customer is unreliable, then we will request a deposit before concluding the transaction. If a customer has a good record, then the action `Initiate Rent Transaction` fires.

The second branch condition ensures that no more than eight videos are rented out to a single customer. After payment is accepted, another fork allows for concurrent execution of the actions `Update Stock` and `Print Receipt`. These concurrent threads are joined before the action `Commit Rent Transaction` fires and the entire processing terminates.

Modeling interactions

4.3.3

Sequence diagrams and collaboration diagrams are two kinds of interaction diagram. They show the patterns of *interactions* between objects necessary to accomplish a use case, activity, operation, or other behavioral component.

Sequence diagrams show an exchange of messages between objects arranged in a time sequence. Collaboration diagrams emphasize the relationships between objects along which the messages are exchanged. We find the sequence diagrams more useful in analysis and the collaboration diagrams in design.

Because interaction models refer to objects, they require that at least the first iteration of state modeling has been completed and that major classes of objects have been identified. Although interactions affect the states of objects, interaction diagrams do not explicitly model state changes in objects. This is the domain of state-change specifications and statechart diagrams (Sections 3.2.5 and 4.4).

Interaction diagrams can be used to determine *operations* (methods) in classes (Sections 3.2.4.3 and 4.3.4). Any message to an object in an interaction diagram must be serviced by some method in that object's class.

4.3.3.1 Discovering message sequences

The discovery of message sequences follows on from activity models. *Actions* in an activity diagram are mapped to *messages* in a sequence diagram. If the abstraction levels used in the construction of the activity model and the sequence model are similar, then the mapping between actions and messages is quite straightforward.

4.3.3.2 Specifying message sequences

When specifying messages, it is advantageous to distinguish between a message that is a signal and a message that is a call (Rumbaugh *et al.*, 1999). A *signal* denotes an asynchronous inter-object communication. The sender can continue executing immediately after sending the signal message. A *call* signifies a synchronous invocation of an operation with provision for the return of control to the sender. From the object-oriented implementation viewpoint, signals imply *event processing* and calls imply *message passing* (Maciaszek and Liong, 2004).

Methods activated by messages may or may not return some values to the caller. If no value is to be returned, then the *return type* is void. Otherwise, the return type is some primitive type (e.g. char) or non-primitive type (i.e. a class). Return types are not normally shown on sequence diagrams. If necessary, a special return line (dotted and arrowed) can be used to explicitly show the return type. Note that the return type is not the same as the return (*callback*) message.

4.3.3.3 Example for sequence specifications

Example 4.18 (university enrolment)

Refer to Examples 4.9 and 4.12 and to the use case "Enter Program of Study" in Figure 4.11. Our task is to construct a sequence diagram for this activity of the use case that is concerned with adding a student to a course offering.

We are not concerned here with the verification of the entered program of study. Another use case ("Validate Program of Study") handles the verification of prerequisites, timetable clashes, special approvals, etc. Our task is only to check whether the course on which the student wants to register is offered in the next semester and if it is still open (there are places available).

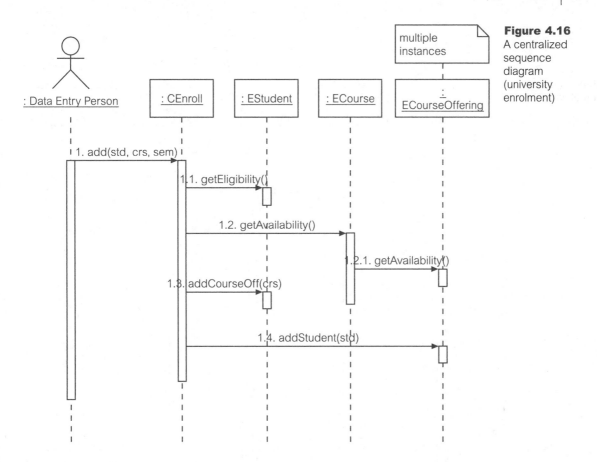

Figure 4.16
A centralized
sequence
diagram
(university
enrolment)

Figures 4.16 and 4.17 illustrate two quite contrasting solutions to the problem – centralized and distributed (Fowler, 2004). The sequence diagram in Figure 4.16 is a *centralized* solution reminiscent of procedural programming style. In this approach, one class (`CEnroll`) takes charge of doing most of the work. The sequence diagram in Figure 4.17 is a *distributed* solution, in which many objects are involved in fulfilling the service. There is no central point of control. The processing intelligence is distributed among multiple objects. Normally, the distributed approach is preferred for a good (reusable and supportable) object-oriented solution.

In both solutions, an actor (`Data Entry Person`) is introduced to initiate processing. In UML, the initiator of processing does not need to be known. The first message – called the *found message* (Fowler, 2004) – can come from an undetermined source. However, many CASE tools do not support undetermined sources.

Processing begins when the *control* object `CEnroll` receives a request to `add()` a student (identified by argument `std`) to a course (argument `crs`) in a semester (argument `sem`). In both solutions, `CEnrol` engages `EStudent` to continue processing. However, in the centralized solution (Figure 4.16), `EStudent` is only asked to return its eligibility for enrolment (e.g. if the student paid the fees). In the distributed solution (Figure 4.17), on the other hand, `EStudent` is entrusted with checking its own eligibility and proceeding to enroll itself, if eligible.

Figure 4.17
A distributed
sequence
diagram
(university
enrolment)

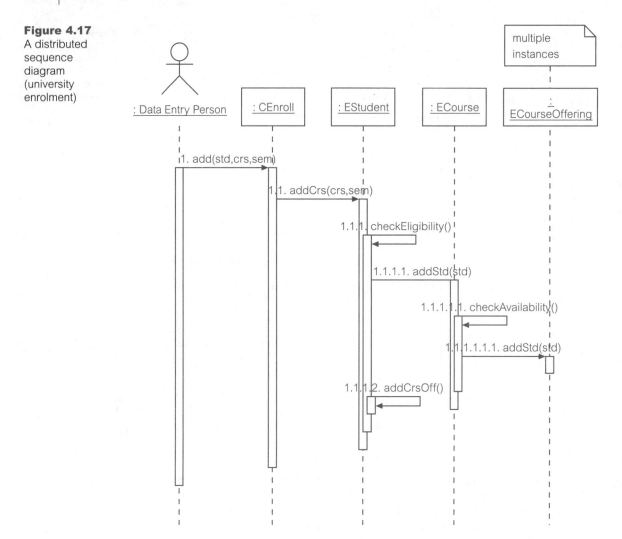

Assuming that EStudent is eligible to enroll, in the centralized approach CEnroll is again in charge (pretending to be what is sometimes called a *God class*). In the distributed approach, EStudent takes the responsibility for requesting ECourse to get enrolled. To be able to do request services of ECourse, EStudent has been passed crs and sem in the arguments of addCrs().

In reality, EStudent does not enroll in ECourse, but in ECourseOffering. This necessitates communication between ECourse and potentially multiple instances of ECourseOffering. Enrolling a student in a course offering requires establishing a bidirectional association between relevant EStudent and ECourseOffering objects. Once more, in the case of a centralized solution, CEnroll establishes such an association. In the case of a distributed solution, ECourseOffering establishes a link to EStudent and returns itself to EStudent so that EStudent can set the link to ECourseOffering.

Modeling operations 4.3.4

A *public interface* of a class is determined by the set of *operations* that the class offers as a service to other classes in the system. Such operations are declared with public visibility. It is only through the public interfaces that objects can collaborate to execute use cases and activities.

Public interfaces are first determined towards the end of the analysis phase, when the state and behavior specifications are largely defined. In analysis, we define only the *signature* of each public operation (operation name, list of formal arguments, return type). In design, we will provide a definition (e.g. some pseudo-codes) for the algorithms of *methods* that implement operations.

Discovering class operations 4.3.4.1

Class operations are best discovered from sequence diagrams. Every *message* in a sequence model must be serviced by an *operation* in the destination object (Section 3.2.4.3). If the sequence models are fully developed, the determination of public operations is an automatic task.

In practice, however, the sequence diagrams – even if developed for all use cases and activities – might not provide sufficient detail to permit discovery of all public operations. In addition, sequence diagrams might not be available for operations that cross use-case boundaries (for instance, where a business transaction spans more than one use case).

For these reasons, supplementary methods for operation discovery can be helpful. One such method comes from the observation that objects are responsible for their own destiny and, therefore, they must support four primitive operations:

1. create
2. read
3. update
4. delete.

These are known as *CRUD operations* (Section 2.5.2.1). CRUD operations allow other objects to send messages to an object to request:

- a new object instance;
- access to the state of an object;
- modification of the state of an object;
- that an object destroys itself.

Specifying class operations 4.3.4.2

At this stage of the lifecycle, a class diagram needs to be modified to include *operation signatures*. The scope of operations may also be determined. By default, *instance scope* is assumed (the operation applies to *instance objects*). *Class* (*static*) *scope* must be declared explicitly (the "$" sign in front of an operation name). Class scope states that the operation applies to the *class object* (Section 3.1.2.3).

Other properties of operations, such as concurrency, polymorphic behavior and algorithm specification, will be specified later during design.

4.3.4.3 Example for operation specifications

Example 4.19 (university enrolment)

Refer to Example 4.18 and to the sequence diagrams in Figures 4.16 and 4.17. Our task is to derive operations from the sequence diagrams and add them to the entity classes EStudent, ECourse, and ECourseOffering.

The operations specified in the class model in Figure 4.18 are obtained directly from the sequence diagram in Figure 4.16. The icons in front of attributes signify that the attributes have *private* scope. The icons in front of operations inform that they are *public*.

The class model in Figure 4.18 not only corresponds to the sequence diagram in Figure 4.16, but it supplements it by showing return types for operations. Establishing the association between EStudent and ECourseOffering is initiated by CEnroll. However, CEnroll must obtain ECourseOffering from ECourse's getAvailability() before it can establish the association.

In the distributed solution, CEnroll only initiates the enrolment process and the rest is done through collaboration between entity objects. Figure 4.19 shows the class operations resulting from the sequence diagram in Figure 4.17. The distributed approach reinforces the spirit of object orientation, which is supposed "to use a lot of little objects with a lot

Figure 4.18
Class operation specifications for centralized interaction (university enrolment)

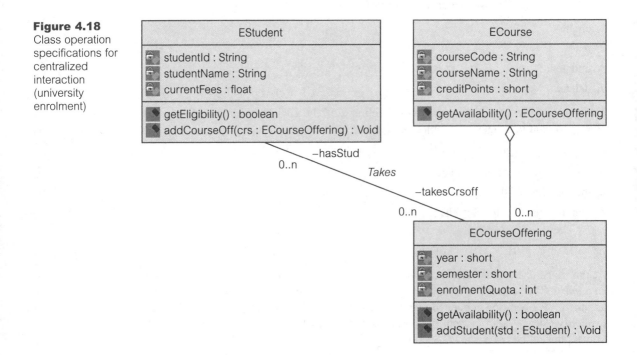

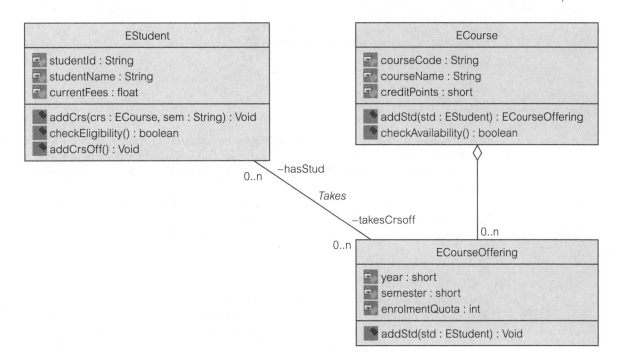

Figure 4.19 Class operation specifications for distributed interaction (university enrolment)

of little methods that give us a lot of plug points for overriding and variations" (Fowler, 2004, p.56).

State change specifications

The state of an object at a point in time is determined by the values of its attributes, including relationship attributes. State specifications define the class attributes (among other issues). Behavior specifications define the class operations, some of which have *side effects* (i.e. they alter the state of an object). However, to understand how an object can change its state over time, we need a more targeted view of the system. Such a view is provided by the statechart models.

The importance of state change specifications varies between application domains. The modeling of state changes in business applications is much less critical than in engineering and real-time applications. Many *engineering and real-time applications* are all about state changes. In modeling such systems, we have to concentrate on state changes from day one: What happens if the temperature is too high? What if the valve is not closed? What if the container is full? etc.

In this textbook, we are predominantly concerned with *business applications* where state changes are less frequent. Therefore, the modeling of state changes is typically done towards the end of the analysis (and then continued with much greater depth in the design).

Many of the state change specifications define *exceptional conditions* in the system. It is natural that exceptions to the normal behavior of the system are modeled after the normal behavior is specified.

4.4.1 Modeling object states

The modeling of object states is done with statechart diagrams (Section 3.2.5.2). A state graph (state machine) is a graph of states and transitions. State models are built for each class that exhibits interesting *dynamic behavior*. Not all classes in the class diagram will be in this category.

Statechart diagrams can also be used to describe the dynamic behavior of other modeling elements, for example use cases, collaborations, or operations. However, this is infrequent, and some CASE tools may not support such functionality.

4.4.1.1 Discovering object states

The process of discovery of object states is based on the analysis of the attribute content in a class and deciding which of these attributes are of special interest to use cases. Not all attributes determine state changes. For example, the modification of a phone number by a customer does not change the state of the `Customer` object. The customer still has the phone; the number of the phone is not relevant. But the deletion of the phone number may be a state change of interest to some use cases. The customer is not reachable by phone any more.

Similarly, a change of phone number that includes a change of area code may be an interesting state change indicating that a customer has moved to another geographical location, and this change might need to be noted and modeled in a statechart diagram.

4.4.1.2 Specifying object states

The basic UML notation for statechart specifications has been explained in Section 3.2.5.2. To use this notation successfully, an analyst must understand how different concepts interrelate, which combinations of concepts are unnatural or not allowed, and what notational shortcuts are possible. It is also likely that a CASE tool will introduce some restrictions, but perhaps also some interesting extensions.

A state transition fires when a certain event occurs *or* a certain condition is satisfied. This means, for example, that a transition line does not have to be labeled with an *event name*. A *condition* itself (written in square brackets) can fire the transition whenever an *activity* in the state is completed and the condition evaluates to true.

Some states (e.g. `Door is Closed`) are idle, doing nothing. Other states (e.g. `Door is Closing`) are more animated and are supported by an explicit *activity*. Such an activity within a state is known as a *do activity*. A do activity can be named within a state icon with the `do/` keyword (e.g. `do/close the door`).

In a typical situation, a transition is triggered by a signal event or a call event. A *signal event* establishes an explicit, asynchronous one-way communication between two objects. A *call event* establishes a synchronous communication in which the caller waits for a response. Two other kinds of event are *change event* and *time event*. In particular, time events that fire transitions based on the absolute or relative notion of time are very useful in some models.

Another consideration in statechart modeling relates to the possibility of specifying *entry actions* inside a state icon (with the entry/ keyword) or on an incoming transition. Similarly, *exit actions* can be placed inside state icons (with the exit/ keyword) or on outgoing transitions. Although the semantics are not affected, the choice of which technique to use can influence the readability of the model (Rumbaugh *et al.*, 1991).

Example for statechart specifications 4.4.1.3

Example 4.19 (video store)

Refer to the class EMovie in Example 4.10 (Figure 4.8). Our task is to specify a statechart diagram for EMovie.

The statechart for EMovie is given in Figure 4.20. The diagram demonstrates different ways in which transitions can be specified. The transitions between the states Available and Not in Stock specify parameterized event names together with action names and guarded conditions. On the other hand, the transition from the state Reserved to Not Reserved lacks an explicit trigger event. It is triggered by the completion of activity in the state Reserved, provided that the condition [no more reserved] is true.

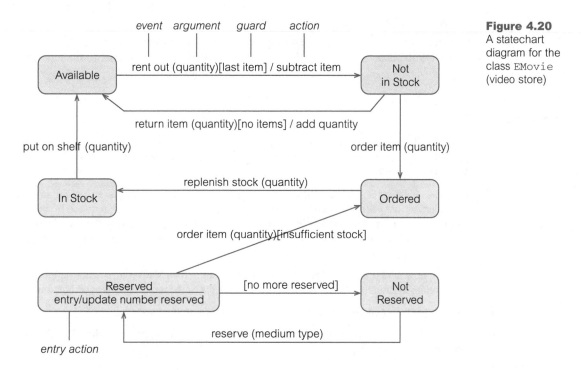

Figure 4.20
A statechart diagram for the class EMovie (video store)

Summary

This has been the nuts and bolts chapter in the textbook – it explained the critical import-ance of architecture in system development and presented UML in full action. The PCMEF architecture introduced in this chapter has been adhered to in UML modeling and will be taken more advantage of in successive chapters.

The case studies introduced in Chapter 1, and already used in Chapters 2 and 3, pro-vided the illustrative material. All frequently used UML models have been put to the task. The motto of the chapter was "there are no black or white, zero–one, true–false solutions in IS analysis models." For every problem there are many potential solutions. The trick is to arrive at a solution that will satisfy customer requirements and that will work.

■ State specifications describe the IS world from the *static* perspective of *classes*, their *attribute* content, and their *relationships*. There are many methods of *class discovery*, but none of them offers a single "cookbook recipe." A mix of methods that suits the analyst's knowledge and experience is a practical answer to class discovery. Classes are specified in UML *class diagrams*. The diagrams visualize classes and three kinds of relationship between them: *associations*, *aggregations*, and *generalizations*.

■ Behavioral specifications describe the IS world from the *operational* perspective (in order not to use the overloaded term – the *functional* perspective). The driving force for behavioral specifications, and indeed for requirements analysis and system design in general, are *use cases*. *Use-case diagrams* provide only simple visualization – the real power of use cases is in their *narrative specifications*. Other behavioral diagrams are derived from use-case models. They include *activity diagrams*, *interactions diagrams*, and the addition of *operations* to classes.

■ State change specifications describe the IS world from a *dynamic* perspective. Objects are bombarded by events, and some of these events cause changes to objects' *states*. *Statechart diagrams* allow modeling of state changes.

Questions

Q1 Consider the seven PCMEF architectural principles defined in Section 4.1.3. Two of these principles are most responsible for delivering hierarchical, rather than network, architectures. What are they? Explain.

Q2 Consider Figure 4.21, which shows classes grouped in three packages and communication dependencies between the classes. Show how these dependencies can be reduced by introduc-ing an interface in each of the three packages. Each interface would define public services available in the respective package. Communication between packages will then be channeled via interfaces.

Q3 Discuss how functional and data requirements identified in the requirements determination phase relate to state, behavior and state-change models of the requirements specification phase.

Q4 Explain the pros and cons of using CASE tools for requirements specification.

Q5 Explain the main differences in the four approaches to class discovery (other than the mixed approach).

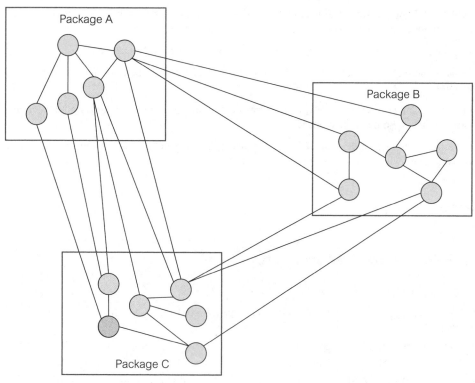

Figure 4.21
A network of intercommunicating objects
Source: Maciaszek and Liong (2004). Reprinted by permission of Pearson Education Ltd

Q6 Discuss and contrast the processes associated with the discovery and specification of class attributes and class operations. Would you model attributes and operations in parallel or separately? Why?

Q7 Auto-generation of code for Figure 4.6 (Example 4.8) will fail. Why?

Q8 Refer to the class model in Figure 4.8 (Example 4.10). Explain why `EMovie.is_in_stock` is modeled as a *derived* attribute and `EVideoMedium.percentage_excellent_ condition` as a *static* attribute.

Q9 Ternary and derived associations are not desirable in analysis models. Why? Give examples.

Q10 Refer to the class model in Figure 4.6 (Example 4.8). Consider the top part of the model defining classes and associations between `EPostalAddress`, `ECourierAddress`, `EOrganization`, and `EContact`. Think about the different ways of modeling the same requirements. Can the model be made more flexible to accommodate potential changes to the requirements? What are the pros and cons of different solutions?

Q11 Refer to the class model in Figure 4.7 (Example 4.9). How would the semantics of the model change if the class `EAcademicRecord` were modeled as an "association as a class" linked to the association `Takes`? How would the model with "association as a class" be influenced if the aggregation between `ECourse` and `ECourseOffering` were reversed (i.e. if `ECourseOffering` contained `ECourse`)?

Q12 Inheritance without polymorphism is possible but not terribly useful. Why? Give an example.

Q13 Which UML models specifically target behavior specification? Explain their individual strengths and how they interrelate to define the behavior of the system.

Q14 Explain how use cases differ from business functions or business transactions.

Q15 What is the difference between a decision (branch) and a fork in activity diagrams? Give an example.

Q16 Give an example of an «include» relationship and an «extend» relationship between use cases. What is the main difference?

Q17 Give an example of a class with few attributes. Discuss which attributes can trigger a state transition and which attributes are indifferent to state changes.

Exercises (video store)

Additional requirements (video store)

Consider the following additional requirements for video store:

1. Tapes/disks returned late induce a payment equal to an extra rental period. Each movie medium has a unique identification number.

2. Movies are ordered from suppliers who are generally able to supply tapes/disks within one week. Typically, several movies are ordered in a single order to a supplier.

3. Reservations are accepted for a movie that is on order and/or because all copies of a particular movie are rented out. Reservations are also accepted for movies that are neither in store nor on order, but a customer is then asked for a deposit of one rental period.

4. Customers can make many reservations, but a separate reservation request is prepared for each movie reserved. A reservation may be canceled due to lack of response from a customer, more precisely one week from the date the customer was contacted that the movie was available for rental. If a deposit has been paid, it is then credited to the customer's account.

5. The database stores the usual information about suppliers and customers, i.e. addresses, phone numbers, etc. Each order to a supplier identifies the ordered movies, tape/disk formats, and quantities, and also an expected delivery date, purchase price, and applicable discounts.

6. When a tape/disk is returned by a customer or is delivered from a supplier, reservations are satisfied first. This involves contacting the customer who made the reservation. In order to ensure that reservations are properly handled, both the "reserved movie has arrived" contact with the customer and the subsequent rental to the customer are related back to the reservation. These steps ensure that reservations are properly carried through.

7. A customer can borrow many tapes or disks, but each borrowed video medium constitutes a separate rental record. For each rental, the checkout, due-in, and return dates and times are recorded. The rental record is later updated to indicate that the video has been returned and that the final payment (or reimbursement) has been made. The clerk who authorizes the rental is also recorded. Details about a customer and rentals are kept for a year to enable the customer rating to be determined based on historical information. Old rental details are kept for auditing purposes for the year.

8. All transactions are made by cash, electronic money transfer, or credit card. Customers are required to pay the rental charges when tapes/disks are checked out.

9. When a tape/disk is returned late (or it cannot be returned for whatever reason), a payment is taken either from the customer's account or directly from the customer.

10. If a tape/disk is overdue by more than two days, an overdue notice is sent to the customer. Once two overdue notices on a single tape/disk have been sent, the customer is noted as delinquent, and the next rental is subject to the manager's decision to remove the delinquent rating.

E1 Refer to the additional requirements above and to Example 4.2 (Section 4.2.1.1.7). What new classes can be derived from the extended requirements?

E2 Refer to the additional requirements above, to Exercise E1, and to Example 4.10 (Section 4.2.4.3). Extend the class model of Figure 4.8 (Example 4.10) to include the extended requirements. Show classes and relationships.

E3 Refer to the additional requirements above and to Example 4.15 (Section 4.3.1.3). Study the narrative specification for the use case `Rent Video` in Table 4.4 (Example 4.15). Ignore the last paragraph in the main flow section of the table (this paragraph refers rather to the use case `Maintain Customer`). Develop a separate use-case diagram to depict *child* use cases for `Rent Video`.

Exercises (contact management)

F1 Refer to Example 4.8 (Section 4.2.2.3). Develop a statechart diagram for the class `EEvent`.

F2 Refer to Example 4.8 (Section 4.2.2.3). Consider the classes `EOrganization`, `EContact`, `EPostalAddress`, and `ECourierAddress`. As an extension to the model in Figure 4.6, allow for a hierarchical structure to organizations, i.e. an organization can consist of smaller organizations. Improve the class model by using generalization and at the same time extend it to capture the hierarchy of organizations.

Exercises (university enrolment)

Additional requirements (university enrolment)

Consider the following additional requirements for university enrolment:

■ The university is organized into divisions. The divisions divide into departments. Academics work for a single department.

■ Most degrees are managed by one division, but some are managed jointly by two or more divisions.

■ New students receive their acceptance form and enrolment instructions by mail and/or email.

■ Continuing students, who are eligible to re-enroll, receive enrolment instructions together with the notification of their examination results. All instructions and notifications are available to students via web-based access to the university system. A student may also elect to receive instructions and notifications by mail or email.

■ Enrolment instructions include the class timetable for the course offerings.

■ During the enrolment, students may consult an academic adviser in their division of registration on the formulation of a program of study.

■ Students are not restricted to studying only courses offered by their division of registration and may at any time change their division of registration (by completing a change of program form available from the Student Office).

■ To take certain courses, a student must first pass the prerequisite courses with the required grade (i.e. a straight pass may not be sufficient). A student who has not passed a course satisfactorily may attempt to do the same course again. Special approvals by the delegate of the head of the relevant division are needed to enroll in a course for the third time or when requesting waivers of prerequisites.

■ Students are classified as part-time if they are enrolled for the year in course offerings carrying a combined total of fewer than 18 credit points (most courses are worth 3 credit points).

■ Special permission needs to be obtained to enroll in a program of course offerings carrying a combined total of more than 14 credit points in a given semester.

■ Each course offering has one academic in charge of it, but additional academics may be involved as well.

G1 Refer to the additional requirements above and to Example 4.1 (Section 4.2.1.1.7). What new classes can be derived from the extended requirements?

G2 Refer to the additional requirements above, to Exercise G1, and to Example 4.9 (Section 4.2.3.3). Extend the class model of Figure 4.7 (Example 4.9) to include the extended requirements. Show classes and relationships.

G3 Refer to the additional requirements above and to Example 4.13 (Section 4.3.1.3). Extend the use-case model of Figure 4.11 (Example 4.13) to include the extended requirements.

G4 Refer to the additional requirements above and to Example 4.18 (Section 4.3.3.3). Develop a collaboration diagram (Section 3.2.4.2) that extends the sequence diagram of Figure 4.16 (Example 4.18) to include the checking of prerequisites – a student will only be added to the course if he/she has passed the prerequisite courses.

G5 Refer to Example 4.19 (Section 4.3.4.3) and to the solution of Exercise G4 above. Use the collaboration diagram to obtain a corresponding class model and add operations to classes. Show the relationships between classes, including dependency relationships. Show the complete signatures of operations (arguments and return types).

Answers to odd-numbered questions

Q1 – answer

The two principles are the NCP and the APP.

The NCP principle forbids direct object communication between non-neighboring layers. This enforces hierarchical communication sequences such that, for example, A needs to communicate with B to get to C. As a result, A talks to B and B talks to C, but A does not talk to C. In a network, A could talk to C.

The APP principle offsets the rigidity of the NCP principle. It is sometimes awkward to force and follow long chains of messages to allow communication between non-neighboring layers, in particular when the layers are far apart. Introducing a separate layer of interfaces that allows objects in non-neighboring layers to be acquainted without undesirable dependencies is a solution to the dilemma created by the APP principle.

Admittedly, the UNP principle also assists hierarchies and counteracts networks. However, the main benefit of the UNP principle is in reducing object dependencies by eliminating upward dependencies, not in neutralizing networks. For this reason, the UNP principle is not included in the answer to this question.

Q3 – answer

Functional and data requirements captured in the *requirements determination* phase are the *service statements* – they define the desired services of the system in terms of their functions and data. In the *requirements specification* phase, the requirements are formally modeled in state, behavior, and state-change *diagrams*.

The specification models provide different views of the same set of requirements. A particular requirement may be modeled in all three diagrams, each diagram giving a particular viewpoint of the requirement design.

This said, it is also fair to say that *state models* express most of the data requirements and *behavior models* capture most of the function requirements. *State change models* apply uniformly to both data and functional requirements as well as to the system constraints (non-functional requirements).

Eventually, the classes in the state model are extended with the detailed design of operations. The final state model embodies all system internal workings and represents both data and functional requirements.

Q5 – answer

The four approaches to class discovery are:

1. noun phrase approach;
2. common class patterns approach;
3. use-case driven approach;
4. CRC (class-responsibility-collaborators) approach.

The *noun phrase approach* seems to be the easiest and quickest to apply. Lexical tools can support the search for nouns in the requirements document. However, overreliance on the vocabulary in picking up classes may be deceptive and inaccurate.

The *common class patterns approach* is an attractive option when combined with another approach, but it is unlikely to produce complete results when used alone. The approach seems to be missing a system reference point, be it the list of requirements (noun phrase approach), the set of use cases (use-case driven approach), or workshops with users (CRC approach).

The *use-case driven approach* demands a prior investment in the development of use cases. The classes are discovered from the analysis of use-case models. The sets of classes from all use cases need to be integrated to arrive at the final class list. Only classes directly demanded by the use cases can be contemplated. This may be a hindrance to the future evolution of the system, because the class models will be strictly matching the system functionality represented in the current use cases.

The *CRC approach* is the most "object-oriented" of the four approaches. It identifies classes to implement discussed business scenarios. It emphasizes the class behavior (operations), and it can lead to the discovery of predominantly "behavioral" classes (as opposed to static "informational" classes). However, it also determines the attribute content of each class. In this sense, the CRC approach is at a lower level of abstraction and can be used in addition to one of the previous three approaches.

Q7 – answer

The auto-generation will fail because no unique role names are provided for associations between `EEvent` and `EEmployee`, and the CASE tool may not be able to generate differently named instance variables for associations to the same class. For example, it is not possible to have three variables named `theEEmployee` in the class `EEvent`. There is a need for variables such as `theCreatedEmp`, `theDueEmp`, and `theCompletedEmp`.

Q9 – answer

Semantic modeling must be unambiguous. Each model must have only one interpretation. *Ternary associations* lend themselves to multiple interpretations and are therefore undesirable. Consider a ternary association called `FamilyUnit` between `Man`, `Woman`, and `Residence` (Maciaszek, 1990). Suppose that the association has the multiplicity one at all its ends except that the membership of `Residence` in the association is optional (i.e. a `FamilyUnit` can exist without the `Residence` object).

Such a ternary association poses many uneasy questions. Can the same person participate in more than one `FamilyUnit` if that person has been married twice? Can the same residence house more than one couple? What if the couple splits up and one of the partners is given the residence? What if that person remarries and his/her husband/wife moves into that residence?

Abandoning the ternary association and replacing it with three binary associations – Man-Woman, Man Residence, and Woman-Residence – provides a solution to difficult questions like those above. In the presence of *generalization*, the association Person-Residence could replace the last two associations, further simplifying the model.

A good analysis model should be non-redundant. It should be minimal yet complete. A *derived association* can be removed from the model without any loss of information. A derived association is really a special kind of constraint within the model, and it does not need to be explicit in the class diagram.

Consider the following *cycle of associations*: Department-Employee (one to many), Department-ResearchProject (one to many), and ResearchProject-Employee (one to many) (Maciaszek, 1990). The study of the cycle can reveal that the association Department-ResearchProject is redundant. We can always establish research projects run by a department by finding employees of that department and then following the links to the research projects in which these employees participate.

Although the association Department-ResearchProject is not necessary in the model, the analyst may still decide to retain it. The clarity of the design justifies showing such an association. This justification extends further to performance gains related to the existence of the direct traversal path between Department and ResearchProject. Finally, the association is indispensable if a department can negotiate a research project prior to naming any employees that will participate in it.

Q11 – answer

This question is a bit devious. The semantics of the model must not change if the model is to reflect the same set of user requirements. If a new model cannot represent certain semantics, then the missing semantics should be expressed by other means, for example in a narrative attachment. By the same token, if the new model is more expressive, the added semantics must be derived from some narrative document attached to the original model.

Consider the modified model in Figure 4.22. Each instance of the association class EAcademicRecord has object references to EStudent and ECourseOffering as well as two attribute values – grade and courseCode. The identity of each instance of EAcademicRecord is provided from the object references in it (corresponding to the two roles of the association – hasStud and takesCrsoff). The attribute grade informs about the grade of the student in a particular course offering.

The presence of the attribute courseCode in EAcademicRecord is more controversial. We can argue that this attribute is not needed there, because each instance of ECourseOffering (pointed to by the object reference takesCrsoff in the EAcademicRecord object) is a component of a single instance of ECourse. We can therefore follow the "pointer" from ECourseOffering to ECourse and derive the value of the attribute courseCode.

An alternative design is shown in Figure 4.23. ECourseOffering contains ECourse. The aggregation is "by reference" because ECourse is a stand-alone class that is likely to be linked in other relationships in the complete model. The fact that the attribute courseCode is now part of ECourseOffering is also evident in EAcademicRecord (courseCode is removed from it).

The main difference between the models in Figures 4.22 and 4.23 and the model in Figure 4.7 is that the models above support the same semantics with less redundancy (duplication of attribute values). EAcademicRecord does not include the attributes year and semester, and the attribute courseCode can also be dispensed with as per the discussion above. However, the information content of EAcademicRecord has to be derived from the associated objects rather than stored as part of the EStudent object (recall that in the model in Figure 4.7 EAcademicRecord is contained "by value" in EStudent).

Q13 – answer

The UML models that are most applicable for *behavior specification* are:

■ activity diagrams
■ sequence diagrams
■ collaboration diagrams.

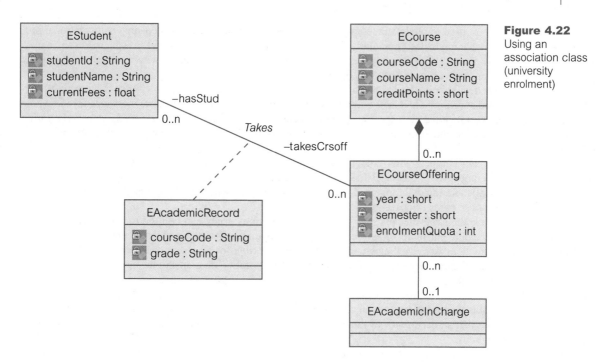

Figure 4.22
Using an association class (university enrolment)

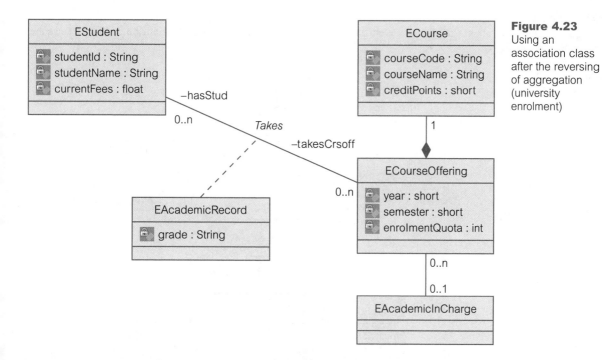

Figure 4.23
Using an association class after the reversing of aggregation (university enrolment)

Activity diagrams are best used to model computations – the sequential and concurrent steps in a computational procedure or workflow. Depending on the "granularity" of the action states in the model, an activity diagram can be used to model computations at various levels of abstraction with various levels of detail. An activity diagram can model the computations in a use case or in an operation of the class.

Sequence diagrams demonstrate the exchange of messages between objects in time sequence. Like activity diagrams, they can be used at different levels of granularity to describe the exchange of generic messages for the whole system or the exchange of detailed messages for a single operation. Sequence diagrams are used extensively during analysis. They can be used to determine operations in classes. Unlike collaboration diagrams, they do not show object relationships.

Collaboration diagrams compete with sequence diagrams in that they show the exchange of messages between objects. They can use numbering of messages to show the time dimension if necessary. Additionally, they can show object relationships. Collaboration diagrams tend to be more suitable in the design phase, where they can be used to model the realization of use cases or operations.

All three models have their role and place in behavior specifications. They can be used to show different viewpoints of the same behavior, but more often they are used to capture different behavior or the same behavior at different levels of abstraction. Activity diagrams are particularly flexible for representing models at different levels of abstraction. Sequence diagrams tend to be used in analysis, collaboration diagrams in design.

Q15 – answer

A *decision* (*branch*) splits the transition from an action state into two or more transitions, each with a separate *guard condition*. To guarantee that an occurrence of the event will trigger one of the split transitions, the guard conditions must cover every possibility.

A *fork* is a transition from an event that results in two or more concurrent action states. If the source state is active and the trigger event occurs, all the target states become active (there is no guard condition to control the activation of target states).

Figure 4.24 shows an example of a decision and a fork in a banking application that manages customer accounts.

Q17 – answer

Consider the class `ECampaign` from the telemarketing case study (ref. Figure 4.5). The attributes of that class are listed in Figure 4.25.

Figure 4.24
Decision (branch)
and fork in activity
diagrams

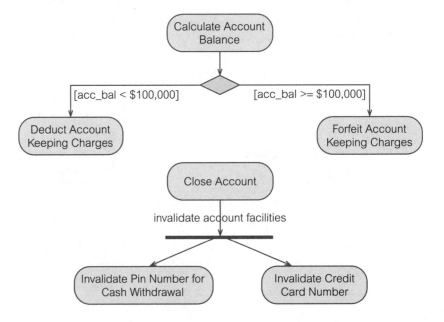

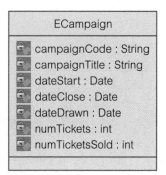

Figure 4.25
The ECampaign
class
(Telemarketing)

A class can be analyzed for *state changes* from a number of different perspectives. A separate state model can be built for each perspective. Depending on a perspective, some attributes are considered and other attributes are ignored. For example, from the perspective of telemarketing of tickets to supporters, an object of class ECampaign can be in the state of Tickets Available or Tickets Sold Out. To define these states, we are concerned only with the attributes numTickets and numTicketsSold. Other attributes are not relevant.

Similarly, from the perspective of knowing if an ECampaign is Current or Closed, we need to look at the values of attributes dateStart and dateClosed. If additionally we are interested in modeling the state Closed No More Tickets, the values of attributes numTickets and numTicketsSold will have to be considered as well.

Solutions to exercises (university enrolment)

G1 – solution

Table 4.5 contains the list of proposed classes. The classes established previously in Example 4.1 (Table 4.1) are underlined. The fuzzy class FullTimeStudent is in square brackets to signify that – although it is not mentioned directly in the extended requirements – it is included to complement the class PartTimeStudent.

Table 4.5 Additional candidate classes (university enrolment)

Relevant classes	Fuzzy classes
Course	CompulsoryCourse
Degree	ElectiveCourse
Student	StudyProgram
CourseOffering	NewStudent
Division	ContinuingStudent
Department	AcceptanceForm
Academic	EnrolmentInstructions
	ExaminationResults
	ClassTimetable
	AcademicAdviser
	RegistrationDivision
	PrerequisiteCourse
	SpecialApproval
	(SpecialPermission)
	HeadDelegate
	PartTimeStudent
	[FullTimeStudent]
	AcademicInCharge

G2 – solution

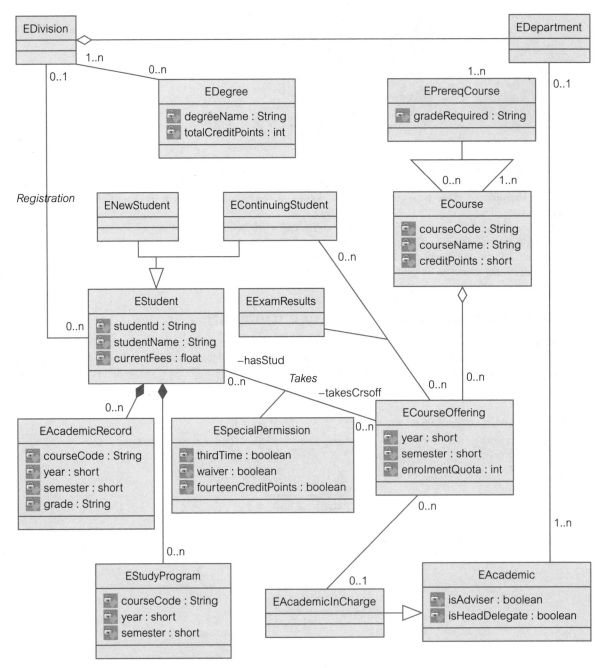

Figure 4.26 A class model (university enrolment)

G3 – solution

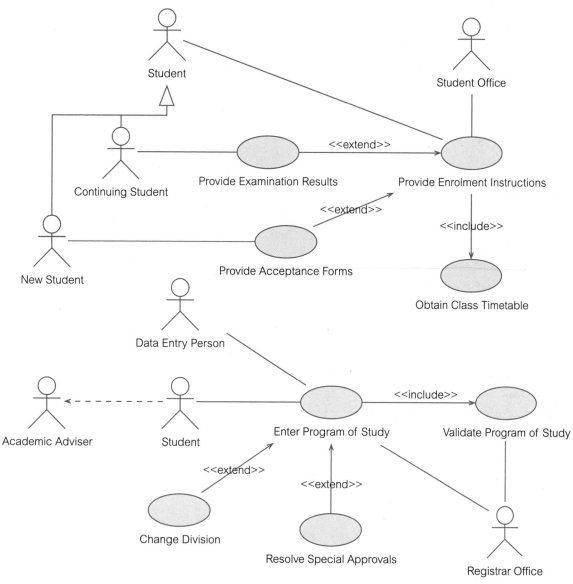

Figure 4.27 A use-case model (university enrolment)

G4 – solution

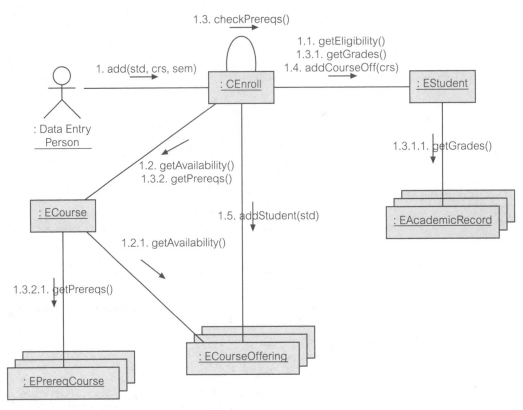

Figure 4.28 A collaboration diagram (university enrolment)

G5 – solution

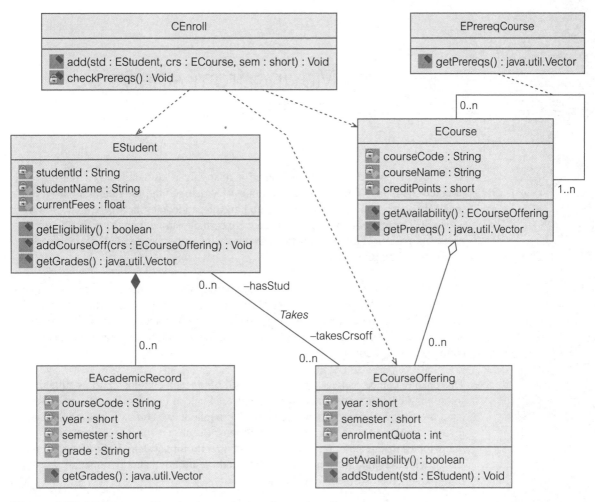

Figure 4.29 Adding operations to classes (university enrolment)

Chapter

5

Moving from Analysis to Design

The previous two chapters have painted a relatively rosy picture of visual object-oriented modeling. The examples were not very demanding, the diagrams produced in UML were attractive and useful, and the dependencies between models were apparent. The modeling techniques used were commensurate with the difficulty of the problems posed. They were sufficiently powerful to define the data structures and behavior for the problems.

The realities of software development are more complex. And there are no simple solutions to complex problems, as we observed at the very beginning of this textbook. Objects provide the current technology to construct complex contemporary systems. As such, objects need to provide the technical depth corresponding to the level of complexity they address.

This chapter can be seen as a critical appraisal of object technology and its suitability for solving complex problems. We introduce advanced concepts in class modeling, class layering, inheritance, and delegation. Throughout, we compare, pass judgments, give opinions, and suggest alternative solutions. Because of their technical character, many topics discussed in this chapter extend directly into system design. This is consistent with the ubiquitous nature of UML and the iterative and incremental process of object-oriented software development.

Advanced class modeling

The analysis modeling concepts discussed so far are sufficient to produce complete analysis models, but at a level of abstraction that does not exhaust all possible details permissible in analysis modeling (i.e. details that do not yet reveal the hardware/software solution but enrich the semantics of the model). UML includes notations for a number of additional concepts that we only alluded to in passing or that we have not addressed at all.

The additional modeling concepts include stereotypes, constraints, derived information, visibility, qualified associations, association class, and parameterized class. These concepts are optional. Many models may be acceptable without them. When used, they have to be applied with care and precision so that any future reader of the model can understand the intention of the writer without misgivings.

Extension mechanisms 5.1.1

The UML standard provides a set of modeling concepts and notations that are universally applicable in software development projects. However, this universality means that some more specific and unorthodox modeling needs may not be catered for by UML. The UML standard, like any standard, is the "lowest common denominator." It would not make sense to complicate UML by trying to provide exotic built-in modeling features that would satisfy specific application domains, software infrastructures, or programming languages.

However, there is still a need to use UML beyond its built-in capabilities. To this aim, the UML standard offers extension mechanisms. *Extension mechanisms* specify "how specific UML model elements are customized and extended with new semantics by using stereotypes, constraints, tag definitions, and tagged values. A coherent set of such extensions, defined for specific purposes, constitutes a UML *profile*" (UML, 2003, pp.2–73).

Stereotypes 5.1.1.1

A *stereotype* extends an existing UML modeling element. It varies the semantics of an existing element. It is not a new model element *per se*. It does not change the structure of UML – it enriches only the meaning of an existing notation. It allows extending and customizing the model. The possible uses of stereotypes are diverse.

Typically, stereotypes are *labeled* in the models with a name within matched guillemets (quotation symbols in French), such as «global», «PK», «include». An *iconic* presentation of stereotypes is also possible.

Some popular stereotypes are built in – they are predefined in UML. The built-in stereotypes are likely to have icons readily available in a CASE tool. Most CASE tools provide a possibility of creating new icons at the analyst's will. Figure 5.1 gives an example of a class stereotyped with an icon, with a label, and with no stereotype.

The restriction that a stereotype extends the semantics but not the structure of UML is quite insignificant. The bottom line in any object-oriented system is that *everything* in it *is an object* – a class is an object, an attribute is an object, a method is an object, etc. Hence, by stereotyping a class we can in effect create a new modeling element that introduces a new category of objects.

Because stereotypes augment the UML classification mechanisms, they can be used to create new modeling techniques and offer new modeling *profiles*. For example, UML profiles can be built for database modeling, for data warehouse design, and for the development of web-based systems. When used that way, stereotypes extend UML for a particular purpose. That purpose has frequently to do with design modeling, rather than analysis modeling. The design models conform to an implementation platform. They must, therefore, work with the modeling elements properly representing that platform.

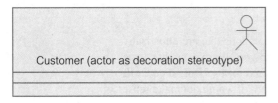
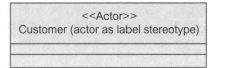

Customer (actor as icon stereotype)

Customer (actor as decoration stereotype)

<<Actor>>
Customer (actor as label stereotype)

Customer (a class with no stereotype defined)

Figure 5.1 Graphical visualizations of stereotypes

5.1.1.2 Comments and constraints

"A *comment* is a text string (including references to human-readable documents) attached directly to a model element" (UML, 2003, pp.3–26). "A *constraint* is a semantic relationship among model elements that specifies conditions and propositions that must be maintained as true; otherwise, the system described by the model is invalid" (UML, 2003, pp.3–26).

Since constraints can also be expressed as text strings, the difference between a comment and a constraint is not in the representation but in the semantic consequences. A *comment* does not have semantic force on the model. It is rather an additional explanation for modeling decisions. A *constraint* has semantic meaning to the model and (ideally) should be written in a formal constraint language. In fact, UML offers a predefined language for this purpose. The language is called OCL (Object Constraint Language) (UML, 2003).

Visually, a text string that is a *constraint* is enclosed in braces ({}). A text string that is a *comment* is not enclosed in braces. In both cases, the text can be freely written on the diagram next to the visual element to which it applies (a CASE tool should then *bind* the text to the visual element). Also in both cases, the text can be written within the UML *note* symbol. Graphically, "a *note* is a dogeared rectangle with its upper-right corner bent over" (Rumbaugh *et al.*, 1999, p.359).

Only simpler comments and constraints are shown in a model diagram. More elaborate comments and constraints (with descriptions too long to be shown on a graphical model) are stored in a CASE repository as text documents.

Certain kinds of constraint are predefined in UML. Figure 4.6 (Section 4.2.2.3) provided an example of the use of the predefined *xor-constraint*. A constraint introduced by the modeler constitutes an extension mechanism.

Stereotypes are frequently confused with constraints. Indeed, the distinction between these two concepts is blurred at times. A *stereotype* is frequently used to introduce a new *constraint* into the model – something meaningful to the modeler but not directly supported as a constraint in UML.

to be distinguished from bonus campaign

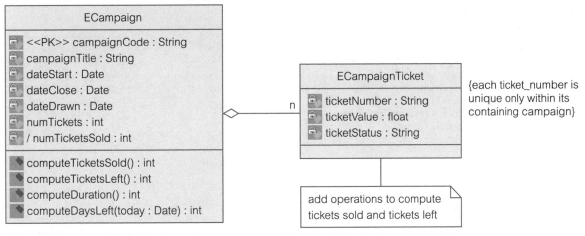

Figure 5.2 Comments (as text and within a note) and a constraint (telemarketing)

Example 5.1 (telemarketing)

Refer to Example 4.7 (Section 4.2.1.2.3). Consider the classes `ECampaign` and `ECampaignTicket` (Figure 4.5). Establish a relationship between these classes. Add operations to `ECampaign` for the computation of the number of tickets sold and still left, as well as for the computation of overall campaign duration and the number of days left before the campaign is closed.

Annotate the diagram with information that `ECampaign` is different from a bonus campaign. Also, write a reminder on the diagram that operations need to be added to `ECampaignTicket`.

Recall a part of requirement 2 in Example 4.7 stating: "All tickets are numbered. The numbers are unique across all tickets in a campaign." Make this statement into a constraint. (In the solution to Example 4.7 (Figure 4.5), we could not capture the above constraint, short of including `campaign_code` (with `ticket_number`) as a part of a composite primary key for `CampaignTicket`).

Figure 5.2 represents a simple extension to the class model to satisfy the demands of Example 5.1. The figure defines two comments and a constraint.

Example 5.2 (contact management)

Refer to Example 4.8 (Section 4.2.2.3). Assume that a new requirement has been discovered that the system does not handle the scheduling of events by employees to themselves. This means that an employee who created an event must not be the same as the employee who is due to perform that event.

Extend a relevant part of the class model (Figure 4.6), to include the new requirement.

The solution to this example (Figure 5.3) results in a constraint on association lines. This is shown as a dashed dependency arrow from the association `Created` to the association `Due`. The constraint is *bound* to the arrow.

Figure 5.3
Constraints on
association
(contact
management)

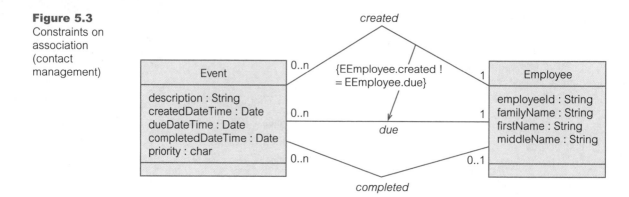

5.1.1.3 Tags

"A *tagged value* is a keyword–value pair that may be attached to any kind of model element (including diagram elements as well as semantic model elements). The keyword is called a *tag*" (UML, 2003, pp.3–29).

Like constraints, *tag values* represent arbitrary textual information in the model and are written inside curly brackets. The form is:

```
tag = value, e.g.:
{analyst = Les, status = 2nd iteration}.
```

Unlike stereotypes, tag values are not really meant to extend the UML semantics in order to create new UML profiles. It is expected that only CASE tools will provide search capabilities on tag values. However, code and report generators can read tag values in order to extend their semantic power and produce more meaningful code and reports.

Like stereotypes and constraints, few tags are predefined in UML. A typical use of tags is in providing project management information.

Example 5.3 (contact management)

Refer to Example 4.8 (Section 4.2.2.3) and to Example 5.2 above. Assume that a new requirement has been discovered: that an employee who created a task must also create – in the same transaction – the first event for that task.

Extend a relevant part of the class model (Figures 4.6 and 5.3), to include the new requirement. Use a note constraint. Also, use a tag to show on the diagram that the analyst is Les and the diagram is in its second iteration.

Figure 5.4 shows the extended model. The project information is given in a tag in the upper left corner. A note is used to express the constraint on three associations.

5.1.2 **Visibility and encapsulation**

Concepts of *visibility*, and the related notion of *encapsulation*, were introduced in Chapter 3 in relation to attribute visibility (Section 3.1.2.1.2) and operation visibility

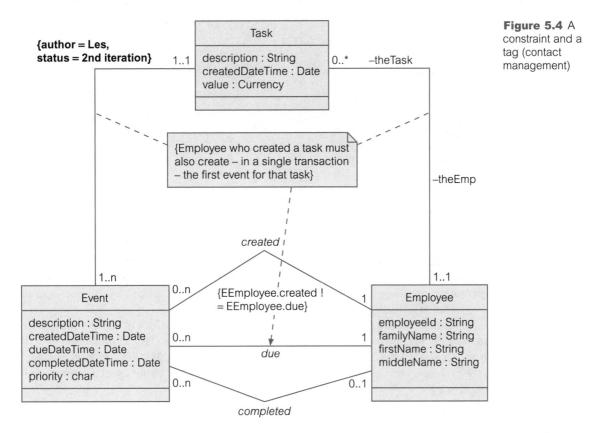

Figure 5.4 A constraint and a tag (contact management)

(Section 3.1.2.2.2). However, we have concentrated on the *public* and *private* visibility of attributes and operations. The UML standard predefines two more visibility markers – *protected* and *package* visibility. Also, the visibility can be defined for a class or interface (as opposed to the visibility of an attribute or operation).

The complete set of visibility markers for attributes and operations is:

+   for public visibility

−   for private visibility

for protected visibility

~   for package visibility.

CASE tools frequently replace this rather dull UML notation by graphically more attractive visibility markers. Figure 5.5 is an example of an alternative notation complete with corresponding Java code.

Protected visibility   5.1.2.1

Protected visibility applies in the context of *inheritance*. Having the *private properties* (attributes and operations) of a base class only accessible to objects of the base class is not

Figure 5.5
Visibility notation
in a CASE
tool and the
corresponding
Java code

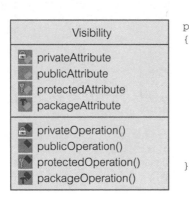

```
public class Visibility
{
    private int privateAttribute;
    public int publicAttribute;
    protected int protectedAttribute;
    int packageAttribute;

    private void privateOperation()
    public void publicOperation()
    protected void protectedOperation()
    void packageOperation()
}
```

always convenient. More often than not, the objects of a derived class (a subclass of the base class) should be allowed to access the otherwise private properties of the base class.

Consider a class hierarchy where `Person` is the (non-abstract) base class and `Employee` is a derived class. If `Joe` is an object of `Employee`, then – by definition of generalization – `Joe` must have access to (at least some) properties of `Person` (e.g. to the operation `getBirthDate()`).

In order to allow a derived class to have free access to properties of its base class, these (otherwise private) properties need to be defined in the base class as *protected*. (Recall from Section 3.1.2.1.2 that visibility applies between classes. If `Betty` is another object of `Employee`, she can access any property of `Joe`, whether public, package, protected, or private.)

Example 5.4 (telemarketing)

Refer to the problem statement for telemarketing (Section 1.5.4) and to Example 4.7 (Section 4.2.1.2.3). Problem statement 4 contains the following observation: "The schemes include special *bonus campaigns* to reward supporters for bulk buying, for attracting new contributors, etc." This observation has not yet been modeled.

Suppose that one of the bonus campaigns involves "ticket books." If a supporter buys the whole book of tickets, an extra ticket from the parent campaign is given free of charge.

Our task is to

- Update the class model to include the class `EBonusCampaign`.
- Change the visibility of attributes in `ECampaign` (Figure 5.2) so that they can be accessible to `EBonusCampaign` with the exception of `dateStart`. Make `campaignCode` and `campaignTitle` visible to other classes in the model.
- Add the following operations to the class `ECampaign`: `computeTicketsSold()`, `computeTicketsLeft()`, `computeDuration()`, `computeDaysLeft()`.
- Observe that the classes outside the inheritance hierarchy need not be interested in `computeTicketsSold()`. They need only to know `computeTicketsLeft()`. Also, `computeDuration()` is used only by the operation `ECampaign.computeDaysLeft()`.
- The class `EBonusCampaign` stores the attribute `ticketBookSize` and provides an access operation to it called `getBookSize()`.

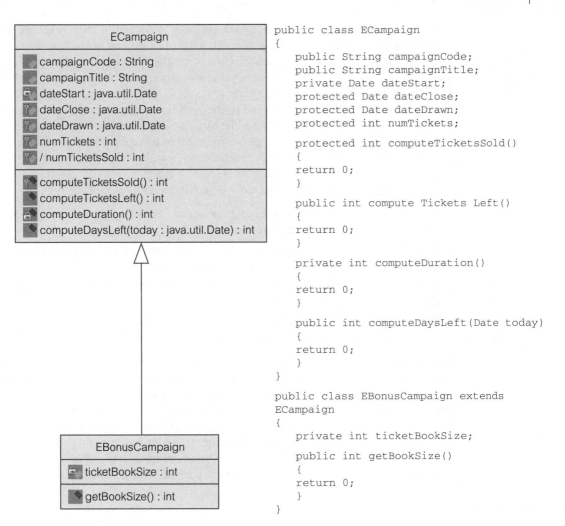

Figure 5.6 Using protected visibility (telemarketing)

Figure 5.6 shows a class model and generated Java code corresponding to the explanations above. The operation `computeDuration()` is private in `ECampaign`. The operation `computeTicketsSold()` is protected in `ECampaign`. The remaining two operations in `Campaign` are public. The operation `getBookSize()` is specific to `EBonusCampaign` and is public.

Accessibility of inherited class properties   5.1.2.2

As acknowledged by UML, *visibility* applies to objects at various levels of granularity. By usual understanding, visibility applies to *primitive objects* – attributes and operations. However, visibility can also be specified with regard to other "containers." This creates a whole tangle of overriding rules.

Consider, for example, a situation where visibility is defined in the inheritance hierarchy at the level of the base class *and* at the level of properties of the base class. Let us say, a class B is a subclass of class A. Class A contains the mixture of attributes and operations – some public, others private, yet others protected. The question is: "What is the visibility of inherited properties in class B?"

The answers to such questions depend on the visibility level given to base class A when declaring it in the derived class B. In C++, the base class could be defined as public (class B: public A), protected (class B: protected A), or private (class B: private A). In Java, however, classes (other than inner classes) can be defined with only public or package visibility (Eckel, 2003).

A typical resolution to the C++ scenario is as follows (Horton, 1997):

- The private properties (attributes and operations) of base class A are not visible to class B objects, no matter how base class A is defined in B.
- If base class A is defined as public, the visibility of inherited properties does not change in derived class B (public are still public and protected are still protected).
- If base class A is defined as protected, the visibility of inherited public properties changes in derived class B to protected.
- If base class A is defined as private, the visibility of inherited public and protected properties changes in derived class B to private.

Note that in the context of the above discussion the notion of implementation inheritance means that if a property x exists in a base class A, then it also exists in any class that inherits from A. However, inheriting a property does not necessarily mean that the property is accessible to the objects of a derived class. In particular, private properties of the base class remain private to the base and are inaccessible to objects of the derived class. This is demonstrated in Figure 5.7, which shows (accessible) properties inherited by EBonusCampaign from Figure 5.6. The private properties of ECampaign, namely dateStart and computeDuration(), are not accessible to EBonusCampaign.

5.1.2.3 Package and friendly visibility

There may be circumstances in which selected classes should be given direct access to some properties of another class, whereas for the rest of the classes in the system those properties remain private. Java supports such circumstances with *package* visibility. C++ provides a similar outcome with the definitions of *friends* – friendly operations and friendly classes.

Package visibility is the Java default. If no private, protected, or public keyword is specified for a Java attribute or operation (or for the entire class), then the obtained visibility is package, by default. Package visibility means that all other classes in the package concerned have access to such attribute, operation, or class. However, to all classes in other packages, the attribute, operation, or class appears to be private.

Protected (and public) also gives package access, but not vice versa. This means that other classes in the same package can access protected properties, but derived classes cannot access properties with package visibility if the derived and the base class are in different packages.

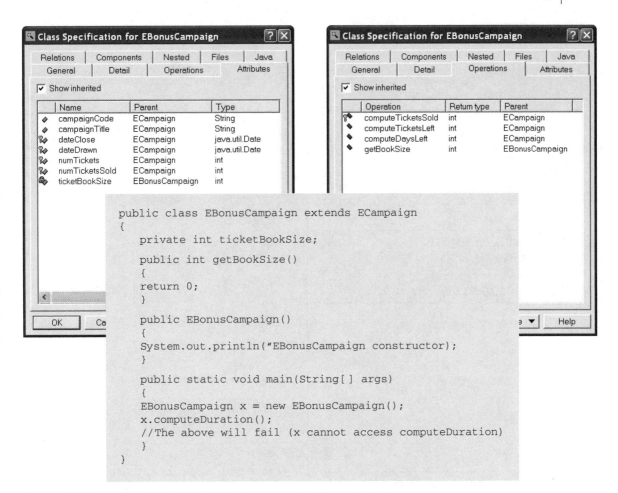

Figure 5.7 The accessibility of inherited class properties (telemarketing)

Figure 5.8 is a variation of the model in Figure 5.6 in which the private method (`computeDuration()`) and private data members (`dateStart` and `ticketBookSize`) are given package visibility. Moreover, `EBonusCampaign` as a class now has package visibility (instead of public).

As with Java package visibility, C++ *friendship* addresses situations when two or more classes are intertwined and one class needs to access the private properties of another class. A typical example may be with two classes `Book` and `BookShelf` and an operation in `Book` called `putOnBookShelf()`.

One way to solve situations like the one above is to declare the operation `putOnBookShelf()` a *friend* within the class `BookShelf` – something like:

```
friend void Book::putOnBookShelf()
```

A friend can be another class or an operation of another class. Friendship is not reciprocal. A class that makes another class a friend may not be a friend of that class.

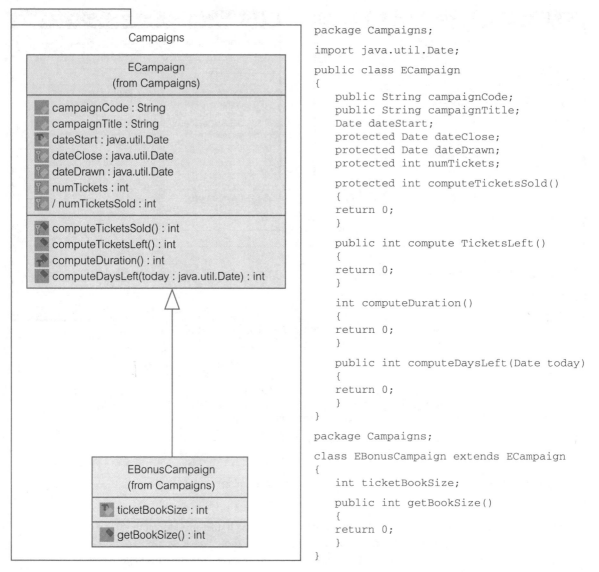

```
package Campaigns;

import java.util.Date;

public class ECampaign
{
    public String campaignCode;
    public String campaignTitle;
    Date dateStart;
    protected Date dateClose;
    protected Date dateDrawn;
    protected int numTickets;

    protected int computeTicketsSold()
    {
    return 0;
    }

    public int compute TicketsLeft()
    {
    return 0;
    }

    int computeDuration()
    {
    return 0;
    }

    public int computeDaysLeft(Date today)
    {
    return 0;
    }
}

package Campaigns;

class EBonusCampaign extends ECampaign
{
    int ticketBookSize;

    public int getBookSize()
    {
    return 0;
    }
}
```

Figure 5.8 Using package visibility (telemarketing)

A friend (operation or class) is declared *within* the class that grants the friendship. However, a friend operation is not a property of the class, so the visibility attributes do not apply. This also means that in the definition of a friend we cannot reference attributes of the class just by their names – they each have to be qualified by the class name (just as if a friend was a normal external operation).

In UML, a friendship is shown as a dashed *dependency relationship* from a friend class or operation to the class that granted the friendship. The stereotype «friend» is bound to the dependency arrow. Admittedly, the UML notation does not fully recognize and support the friend's semantics.

```
class ECampaign{
public:
    friend void ECallScheduled::getTicketsLeft();
};
```

Figure 5.9
Friend
(telemarketing)

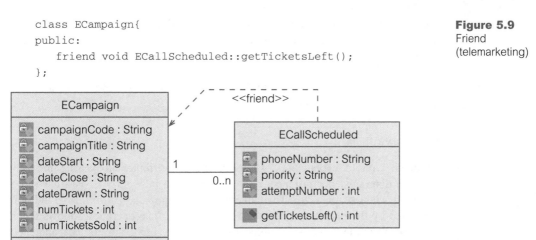

Example 5.5 (telemarketing)

Refer to Example 4.7 (Section 4.2.1.2.3). Consider the relationship between the classes ECampaign and ECallScheduled (Figure 4.5).

Objects of the class ECallScheduled are very active and need special privileges when executing their operations. In particular, they contain an operation called getTicketsLeft(), which establishes whether any tickets are left so that a supporter's order can be satisfied. It is important that this operation has direct access to the properties of ECampaign (such as numTickets and numTicketsSold).

Our task is to declare the operation getTicketsLeft() and make it a friend of ECampaign.

The UML notation in support of friendship is shown in Figure 5.9. UML recommends using a *dependency* relationship stereotyped as «friend» to indicate that ECallScheduled depends on ECampaign for friendship. This captures the fact that ECampaign grants some friendship status to ECallScheduled – getTicketsLeft() is declared a friend within ECampaign (because Campaign decides who is its friend).

Derived information   5.1.3

Derived information is a kind of *constraint* that applies (most frequently) to an attribute or an association. The derived information is computed from other model elements. Strictly speaking, the derived information is redundant in the model – it can be computed as needed.

Although derived information does not enrich the semantics of an *analysis model*, it can make the model more readable (because the fact that something can be computed is explicit in the model). The decision to show or not to show the information as derived in an analysis model is quite arbitrary, as long as it is taken consistently across the entire model.

The knowledge of what information is derived is more important in a *design model*, where optimization of access to information needs to be considered. In design models, a decision may also be taken as to whether some derived information is to be stored (after the derivation) or be dynamically computed every time it is needed. This is not a new feature – it was known in old-style network databases under the terms of *actual* (i.e. stored) and *virtual* data.

The UML notation for derived information is a solidus (/) in front of the name of the derived attribute or association.

5.1.3.1 Derived attribute

Although without explanation, we used derived attributes in passing in a couple of example diagrams. For instance, numTicketsSold in Figure 5.2 is a derived attribute within the class ECampaign. The value of the attribute numTicketsSold in Figure 5.2 is computed by the operation computeTicketsSold. The operation follows the aggregation links from the ECampaign object to the ECampaignTicket objects and checks each ticketStatus. If ticketStatus is "sold" then it is added to the count of sold tickets. When all tickets are processed, the current value of numTicketsSold has been derived.

5.1.3.2 Derived association

The derived association is a more controversial topic. In a typical scenario, a derived association happens between three classes already connected by two associations and with no third association that would close the loop. The third association is frequently needed for the model to be semantically correct (this is known as *loop commutativity*). When not explicitly modeled, the third association can be derived from the other two associations.

Example 5.6 (orders database)

Consider a simple orders database with classes Customer, Order, and Invoice. Consider further that an order is always produced by a single customer and that each invoice is generated for a single order.

Draw relationships between the three classes. Is it possible to have a derived association in the model?

Yes, it is possible to model a derived association between classes Customer and Invoice. It is called /CustInv in Figure 5.10. The association is derived due to a slightly unusual business rule that the association multiplicity between Order and Invoice is one to one.

The derived association has not introduced any new information. We could always assign a customer to an invoice by finding out a single order for each invoice, and then a single customer for each order.

5.1.4 Qualified association

The concept of a *qualified association* is a tough and controversial proposition. Some modelers like it; others hate it. Arguably, one can construct complete and sufficiently expressive class models without qualified associations. However, if qualified associations are used, they should be used consistently across the board.

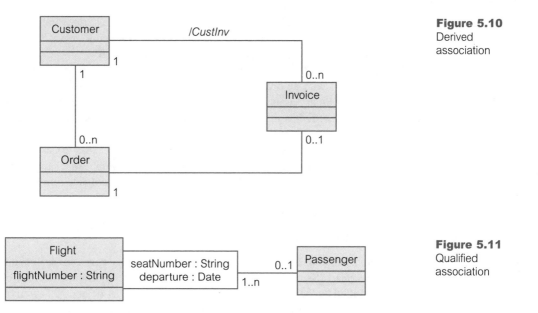

Figure 5.10
Derived
association

Figure 5.11
Qualified
association

A qualified association has an attribute compartment (a *qualifier*) on one end of a binary association (an association can be qualified on both ends, but this is rare). The compartment contains one or more attributes that can serve as an index key for traversing the association from the qualified *source class* via the qualifier to the *target class* on the opposite association end.

For example, an association between `Flight` and `Passenger` is many to many. However, when the class `Flight` is qualified by attributes `seatNumber` and `departure`, the multiplicity is reduced to one to one (Figure 5.11). The composite index key introduced by the qualifier (`flightNumber` + `seatNumber` + `departure`) can be linked to only zero or one `Passenger` object.

In the forward traversal, the association multiplicity represents a number of target objects related by the composite key (qualified object + qualifier value). In the reverse traversal, the multiplicity describes a number of objects identified by the composite key (qualified object + qualifier value) and related to each target object (Rumbaugh *et al.*, 1999).

The uniqueness introduced by a qualifier frequently provides important semantic information that cannot be captured efficiently by other means (such as constraints or an inclusion of additional attributes in the target class). In general, it is not proper or correct to duplicate a qualifier attribute in the target class.

Association class versus reified class   5.1.5

In Section 3.1.4.4 we explained and exemplified an *association class* – an association that is also a class. An association class is typically used if there is a many-to-many association between two classes and each association instance (a *link*) has its own attribute values. To be able to store these attribute values we need a class – an association class.

Simple as it seems, the concept of association class carries a tricky constraint. Consider an association class *C* between classes *A* and *B*. The constraint is that there can be only one instance of *C* for each pair of linked instances of *A* and *B*.

If such a constraint is not acceptable, then the modeler has to *reify* the association by replacing class *C* with an ordinary class *D* (Rumbaugh *et al.*, 1999). The *reified class D* would have two binary associations to *A* and *B*. Class *D* is independent of classes *A* and *B*. Each instance of *D* has its own identity, so that multiple instances of it can be created to link to the same instances of *A* and *B*, if required.

The distinction between an association class and reified class arises most frequently in the context of modeling temporal (historical) information. An example could be an employee database that maintains information about current and previous salaries of employees.

5.1.5.1 Model with association class

Objects of an *association class*, like objects of any ordinary class, are assigned their OIDs when instantiated (Section 3.1.1.3). Apart from the system-generated OIDs, objects can also be identified by their attribute values. In the case of an association class, an object takes its identity from the attributes that designate the associated classes (Section 3.1.2.1.1). Other attribute values do not contribute to the object's identification.

Example 5.7 (employee database)

Each employee in an organization is assigned a unique `empId`. The name of the employee is maintained and consists of the last name, first name, and middle initial.

Each employee is employed at a certain salary level. There is a salary range for each level, i.e. the minimum and maximum salary. The salary ranges for a level never change. If there is a need to change the minimum or maximum salary, a new salary level is created. The start and end dates for each salary level are also kept.

Previous salaries of each employee are kept, including the start date and finish date at each level. Any changes in the employee's salary within the same level are also recorded.

Draw a class model for the employee database. Use an association class.

The example statement creates a number of challenges. We know that we need to have a class to store employee details (`Employee`) and a class to store information about salary levels (`SalaryLevel`). The challenge is in modeling historical and current assignments of salaries to employees. At first it may seem natural to use an association class `SalaryHistoryAssociation`.

Figure 5.12 presents a class model with the association class `SalaryHistory-Association`. The solution is deficient. Objects of `SalaryHistoryAssociation` derive their identity from the composite key created from the references to the primary keys of classes `Employee` and `SalaryLevel` (i.e. `empId` and `levelId`).

No two `SalaryHistoryAssociation` objects can have the same composite key (the same links to `Employee` and `SalaryLevel`). This also means that the design in

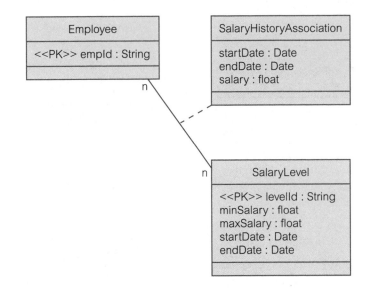

Figure 5.12
Inadequate use of
association class

Figure 5.12 will not accommodate the requirement that "any changes in the employee's salary within the same level are also recorded." The solution in Figure 5.12 cannot be sustained – a better model is needed.

Model with reified class

5.1.5.2

An association class cannot have duplicates among its object references to the associated classes. A reified class is independent of the associated classes and does not place such a restriction. The primary key of a reified class does not use attributes that designate related classes.

Example 5.8 (employee database)

Refer to Example 5.7 (Section 5.1.5.1). Draw a class model for the employee database. Use a reified class.

Figure 5.13 demonstrates a class model that uses the reified class `SalaryHistoryReified`. The class does not have an explicitly marked primary key. However, we can guess that the key will consist of `empId` and `seqNum`. The attribute `seqNum` stores the sequential number of salary changes for an employee. Every object of `SalaryHistoryReified` belongs to a single `Employee` object and is linked to a single `SalaryLevel` object. The model can now capture an employee's salary changes within the same salary level.

Note that the model in Figure 5.13 would need to be improved further. In particular, it is most likely that the assumption that "the salary ranges for a level never change" would need to be relaxed.

Figure 5.13
A better solution
with a reified class

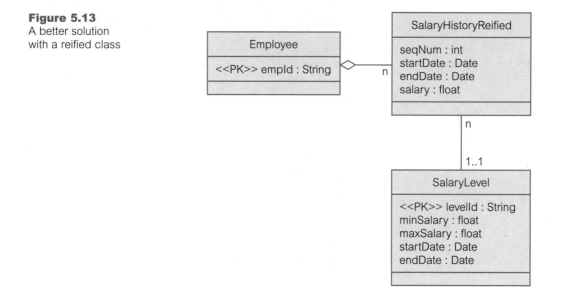

There are three main kinds of relationship between classes: association, aggregation, and generalization. The topic of generalization and inheritance has already been discussed in Section 3.1.6, but a careful reader would have noticed that we have devalued the usefulness of generalization in analysis models. *Generalization* is a useful and powerful concept, but it can also create many problems due to the intricate mechanisms of *inheritance*, in particular in large software projects.

The terms "generalization" and "inheritance" are related but not the same. It is important to know the difference. The price for imprecision is a resulting lack of understanding – frequently evident in the literature. Indeed, unless the difference is acknowledged, it is easy to engage in irrational and groundless discussions about the pros and cons of generalization and inheritance.

Generalization is a semantic relationship between classes. It states that the *interface* of the subclass must include all (public, package and protected) properties of the superclass. *Inheritance* is "the mechanism by which more specific elements incorporate structure and behavior defined by more general elements" (Rumbaugh *et al.*, 1999).

5.2.1 Generalization and substitutability

From a semantic modeling perspective, *generalization* introduces additional classes, categorizes them into generic and more specific classes, and establishes superclass–subclass relationships in the model. Although generalization introduces new classes, it can reduce the overall number of *association* and *aggregation* relationships in the model (because associations and aggregations can be made to more generic classes and still imply the existence of links to objects of more specific classes).

Based on the desired semantics, an association or aggregation from a class can link to the most generic class in the generalization hierarchy (see the class diagrams in Figures 3.36 and 4.8). Since a subclass can be *substituted* for its generic class, the objects of the subclass have all the association and aggregation relationships of the superclass. This allows the same model semantics to be captured with the smaller number of association/aggregation relationships. In a good model, the trade-off between the depth of generalization and the consequent reduction in association/aggregation relationships is properly balanced.

When used considerately, generalization improves the expressiveness, understandability, and abstraction of system models. The benefits of generalization arise from the *substitutability* principle – a subclass object can be used in place of a superclass object in any part of the code where the superclass object is accessed. However, and unfortunately, the inheritance mechanism may be used in a way that defeats the benefits of the substitutability principle.

Inheritance versus encapsulation 5.2.2

Encapsulation demands that an object's state (attribute values) be accessible only through the operations in the object's interface. If enforced, the encapsulation leads to a high level of data independence, so that future changes to encapsulated data structures do not necessitate modification of existing programs. But is this notion of encapsulation enforceable in applications?

The reality is that encapsulation is orthogonal to inheritance and query capabilities and has to be traded off against these two features. In practice, it is impossible to declare all data with *private* visibility.

Inheritance compromises encapsulation by allowing subclasses to access *protected* attributes directly. Computations spanning objects belonging to different classes may require that these different classes be *friends* of each other or have elements with *package* visibility, thus further infringing encapsulation. And one has to realize that encapsulation refers to the notion of the class, not the object – in most object programming environments (with the exception of Smalltalk) an object cannot hide anything from another object of the same class.

Finally, users accessing databases by means of SQL raise justified expectations that they want to refer directly to attributes in the queries, rather than be forced to work with some data-access methods that make query formulations more difficult and more error-prone. This requirement is particularly strong in data warehouse applications with OnLine Analytical Processing (OLAP) queries.

Applications should be designed so that they achieve the desired level of encapsulation, balanced against inheritance, database querying, and computational requirements.

Interface inheritance 5.2.3

When generalization is used with the aim of substitutability, then it may be synonymous with the notion of *interface inheritance* (*subtyping*, *type inheritance*). This is not only a "harmless" form of inheritance but in practice a very desirable form (Section 3.1.8). Apart from other advantages, interface inheritance provides a means of achieving multiple implementation inheritance in languages that do not support such inheritance (like in Java).

A subclass inherits attribute types and operation signatures (operation names plus formal arguments). A subclass is said to *support* a superclass interface. The implementation of inherited operations may be deferred until later.

There is a difference between the notions of *interface* and *abstract class* (Section 3.1.8.1). The difference is that an abstract class can provide partial implementations for some operations, whereas a pure interface defers the definition of all operations.

Figure 5.14 corresponds to Figure 3.26 (Section 3.1.8.3). The figure demonstrates an alternative visualization of the interface as a "lollipop" and includes the generated Java code.

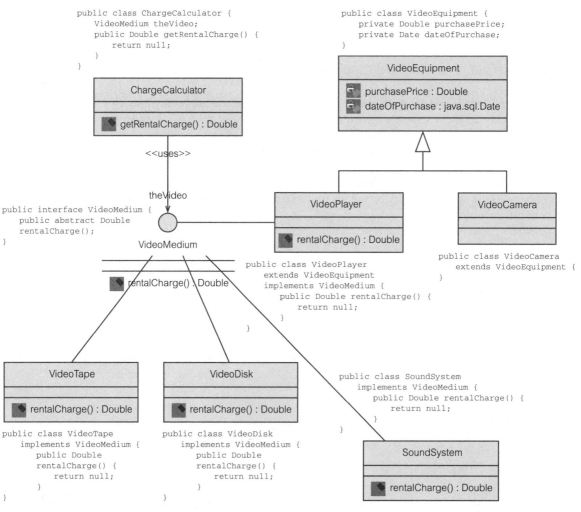

Figure 5.14 Interface and implementation inheritance

Implementation inheritance   5.2.4

As we observed in the previous section, generalization can be used to imply *substitut-ability*, and it can then be realized by an *interface inheritance*. However, generalization can also be used (deliberately or not) to imply *code reuse*, and it is then realized by an *implementation inheritance*. This is a very powerful, sometimes dangerously powerful, representation of generalization. It is also the "default" representation of generalization.

Implementation inheritance – also called *subclassing*, *code inheritance*, or *class inheritance* – combines the superclass properties in the subclasses and allows them to be *overridden* with new implementations when necessary. Overriding can mean the inclusion (call) of a superclass method in the subclass method and extending it with new functionality. It can also mean a complete replacement of the superclass method by the subclass method. Implementation inheritance allows property descriptions, *code reuse*, and *polymorphism* to be shared.

When modeling with generalization, we have to be clear which kind of inheritance is implied. Interface inheritance is safe to use as it involves only the inheritance of contract fragments – operation signatures. Implementation inheritance involves the inheritance of code – the inheritance of implementation fragments (Harmon and Watson, 1998; Szyperski, 1998). If not carefully controlled and restrained, implementation inheritance can bring more harm than good. The pros and cons of implementation inheritance are discussed next.

Proper use of implementation inheritance – extension inheritance   5.2.4.1

UML is quite specific about the alignment of inheritance with generalization and the proper use of implementation inheritance (Rumbaugh *et al.*, 1999). The only proper use of inheritance is as an incremental definition of a class. A subclass has more properties (attributes and/or methods) than its superclass. A subclass *is a kind of* superclass. This is also known as an *extension inheritance*.

The example in Figure 3.21 (repeated here for convenience as Figure 5.15, but with no constructors) represents an extension inheritance. Any `Employee` object *is a kind of* `Person` object, and a `Manager` object *is a kind of* `Employee` and `Person` object. This does not mean, though, that a `Manager` object is simultaneously the instance of three classes (see the discussion about multiple classification in Section 3.1.6.4). A `Manager` object is an instance of the class `Manager`.

The method `remainingLeave()` can be invoked on a `Manager` or an `Employee` object. It will perform differently depending on which object is called.

Note that `Person` in Figure 5.15 is not an abstract class. There will be some `Person` objects that are just that (i.e. that are not an `Employee`).

In extension inheritance, the overriding of properties should be used with care. It should be allowed only to make properties more specific (e.g. to constrain values or to make implementations of operations more efficient), not to change the meaning of the property. If overriding changed the meaning of a property, then a subclass object could no longer be substituted for the superclass object.

Figure 5.15
Extension
inheritance

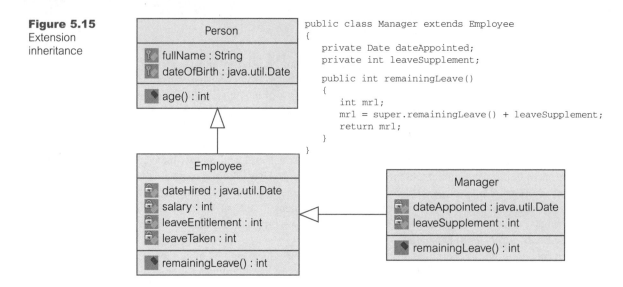

```
public class Manager extends Employee
{
    private Date dateAppointed;
    private int leaveSupplement;

    public int remainingLeave()
    {
        int mrl;
        mrl = super.remainingLeave() + leaveSupplement;
        return mrl;
    }
}
```

5.2.4.2 Problematic use of implementation inheritance – restriction inheritance

In extension inheritance, the definition of a subclass is extended with new properties. However, it is also possible to use inheritance as a restriction mechanism whereby some of the inherited properties are suppressed (overridden) in the subclass. Such inheritance is called *restriction inheritance* (Rumbaugh *et al.*, 1991).

Figure 5.16 demonstrates two examples of restriction inheritance. Because inheritance cannot be selectively stopped, the class `Circle` would inherit `minor_axis` and `major_axis` from `Ellipse` and would have to replace them with the attribute `diameter`. Similarly, `Penguin` would inherit the flying capability (the operation `fly`) from `Bird` and would have to replace it with the operation `swim` (perhaps flying under a negative altitude could make up for swimming).

Restriction inheritance is problematic. From a generalization point of view, a subclass does not include all properties of the superclass. A superclass object can still be substituted by a subclass object provided that whoever is using the object is aware of the overridden (suppressed) properties.

In restriction inheritance, the properties of one class are used (by inheritance) to implement another class. If overriding is not extensive, restriction inheritance can be of benefit. In general, however, restriction inheritance gives rise to maintenance problems. It is even possible that restriction inheritance would completely suppress the inherited methods by implementing them as empty (i.e. doing nothing).

5.2.4.3 Improper use of implementation inheritance – convenience inheritance

Inheritance that is not an extension or restriction inheritance is "bad news" in system modeling. Such an inheritance can occur when two or more classes have similar imple-

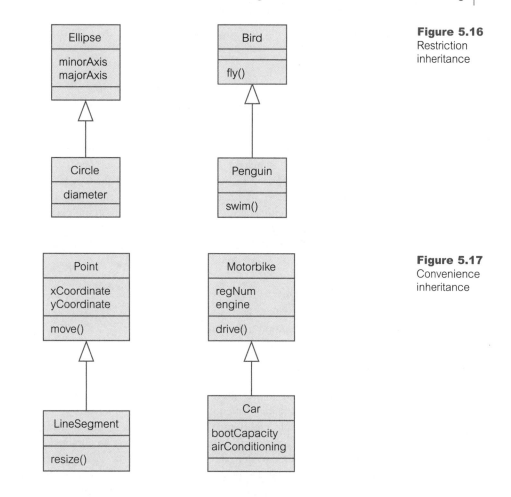

Figure 5.16
Restriction
inheritance

Figure 5.17
Convenience
inheritance

mentations, but there is no taxonomic relationship between the concepts represented by the classes. One class is selected arbitrarily as an ancestor of the others. This is called *convenience inheritance* (Rumbaugh *et al.*, 1991; Maciaszek *et al.*, 1996a).

Figure 5.17 provides two examples of convenience inheritance. The class `LineSegment` is defined as a subclass of the class `Point`. Clearly, a line segment is not a point and therefore the generalization as defined earlier does not apply. However, inheritance can be used. Indeed, for the class `Point` we can define attributes like `xCoordinate` and `yCoordinate` and an operation `move()`. The class `LineSegment` would inherit these properties and would define an additional operation `resize()`. The operation `move()` needs to be overridden. Similarly, in the second example, `Car` inherits properties of `Bike` and adds some new ones.

Convenience inheritance is improper. It is semantically incorrect. It leads to extensive overriding. The substitution principle is normally invalid because the objects are not of a similar type (`LineSegment` is not a `Point`; `Car` is not a `Motorbike`).

In practice, and regrettably, developers use convenience inheritance because many object programming environments encourage indiscriminate use of implementation inheritance. Programming languages are equipped with a myriad of tools for "power programming" with inheritance, while support for other object features (most notably aggregation) is missing.

5.2.4.4 The evils of implementation inheritance

The previous discussion does not mean that if we forbid convenience inheritance then we are fine. Implementation inheritance is a risky business by many standards. If not properly controlled and managed, inheritance can be overused and abused and can create problems that it is supposed to be solving in the first place. This is particularly true in the development of large systems with hundreds of classes and thousands of objects, with dynamically changing states of objects, and with evolving class structures (such as in enterprise information systems).

The main risk factors are related to the following troublesome concepts (Szyperski, 1998):

- fragile base class
- overriding and callbacks
- multiple implementation inheritance.

5.2.4.4.1 *Fragile base class*

The *fragile base class* (superclass) problem is about making the subclasses valid and operational while allowing the evolution of the *implementation* of their superclass (or superclasses, if multiple inheritance applies). This is a serious problem in any case, but particularly when we consider that the superclasses may be obtained from external sources outside the control of the system development team.

Consider a situation where some superclasses from which your application inherits form part of an operating system, a database system, or a GUI. If you buy an object database system for your application development, you really buy a class library to implement typical database functions, such as object persistence, transaction management, concurrency, and recovery. If your classes inherit from that class library, the impact of new versions of the object database system on your application is unpredictable (and certainly so if no precautions are taken when designing the inheritance model for the application).

The problem of the fragile base class is difficult to harness short of declaring the public interfaces immutable or, at least, short of avoiding the implementation inheritance from the superclasses outside our control. Changes to the implementation of a superclass (for which we might not even have the source code) will have a largely unpredictable effect on the subclasses in the application system. This is true even if the superclass's public interface remains unchanged. The situation can be further aggravated if the changes also affect public interfaces. Some examples are (Szyperski, 1998):

- changing the signature of a method;
- splitting the method into two or more new methods;
- joining existing methods into a larger method.

The bottom line is that to harness the fragile base class problem the developers designing a superclass should know beforehand how people are going to be reusing that superclass now and in the future. This is impossible without a crystal ball. As a bumper sticker joke says, "madness is inherited, you get it from your children" (Gray, 1994). In Section 5.3, we discuss some alternative object development methods that are not based on inheritance yet deliver the expected object functionality.

Overriding, down-calls, and up-calls   *5.2.4.4.2*

Implementation inheritance allows for selective overriding of inherited code. There are five techniques in which a subclass method can reuse code from its superclass:

1. The subclass can inherit the method implementation and introduce no changes to the implementation.
2. The subclass can inherit the code and include it (call it) in its own method with the same signature.
3. The subclass can inherit the code and then completely override it with a new implementation with the same signature.
4. The subclass can inherit code that is empty (i.e. the method declaration is empty) and then provide the implementation for the method.
5. The subclass can inherit the method interface only (i.e. the interface inheritance) and then provide the implementation for the method.

From the five reuse techniques, the first two are the most troublesome when the base class evolves. The third shows contempt for inheritance. The last two techniques are special cases: the fourth case is trivial; and the fifth does not involve implementation inheritance.

Example 5.9 (telemarketing)

Refer to the telemarketing application and to Example 5.4 (Section 5.1.2.1) in particular. Our task is to modify the class model and the generalization relationship between `Campaign` and `BonusCampaign` (Figure 5.5) to include operations that exemplify the first two reuse techniques listed above and to show down-calls and up-calls along the generalization relationship

To exemplify the first reuse technique and the down-call, consider the operation `computeTickets()` in `ECampaign`, which is inherited without modification by `EBonusCampaign`. The implementation of `computeTickets()` includes a call to `computeTicketsLeft()`. The operation `computeTicketsLeft()` exists in `ECampaign` and its overridden version in `EBonusCampaign`.

To exemplify the second reuse technique and the up-call, consider the operation `getDateClose()` in `ECampaign` and its overridden version in `EBonusCampaign`. When invoked on `ECampaign`, `getDateClose()` returns the closing date of `ECampaign`. However, when invoked in `EBonusCampaign`, it returns the larger (later) date from the comparison of the closing date of `ECampaign` and `EBonusCampaign`.

Figure 5.18 shows the model and the code constituting a possible answer to Example 5.9. The class `CActioner` invokes operations on `ECampaign` and/or `EBonusCampaign`. `CActioner` has a reference (`theECampaign`) to the subclass `EBonusCampaign`, but it

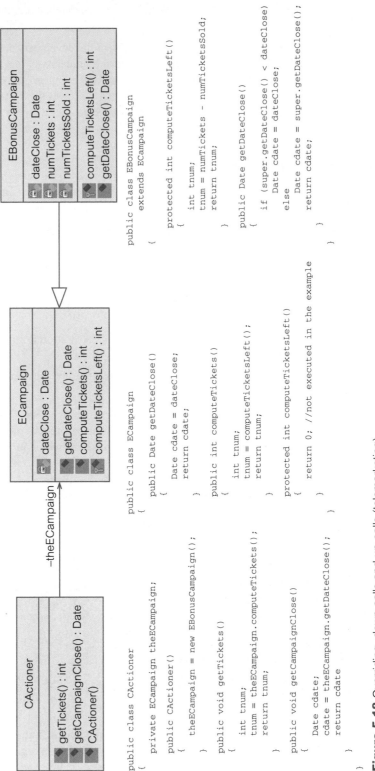

```
public class CActioner
{
    private ECampaign theECampaign;

    public CActioner()
    {
        theECampaign = new EBonusCampaign();
    }

    public void getTickets()
    {
        int tnum;
        tnum = theECampaign.computeTickets();
        return tnum;
    }

    public void getCampaignClose()
    {
        Date cdate;
        cdate = theECampaign.getDateClose();
        return cdate
    }
}
```

```
public class ECampaign
{
    public Date getDateClose()
    {
        Date cdate = dateClose;
        return cdate;
    }

    public int computeTickets()
    {
        int tnum;
        tnum = computeTicketLeft();
        return tnum;
    }

    protected int computeTicketsLeft()
    {
        return 0; //not executed in the example
    }
}
```

```
public class EBonusCampaign
    extends ECampaign
{
    protected int computeTicketsLeft()
    {
        int tnum;
        tnum = numTickets - numTicketsSold;
        return tnum;
    }

    public Date getDateClose()
    {
        if (super.getDateClose() < dateClose)
            Date cdate = dateClose;
        else
            Date cdate = super.getDateClose();
        return cdate;
    }
}
```

Figure 5.18 Overriding, down-calls and up-calls (telemarketing)

keeps that reference as the superclass ECampaign type. In reality, the assignment of an ECampaign instance to an ECampaign reference is likely to be done at run time (Maciaszek and Liong, 2004) and not as a static assignment as in Figure 5.18.

When getTickets() is called on CActioner, it executes computeTickets() on ECampaign. This uses the substitutability principle – the EBonusCampaign object held in theECampaign reference is substituted for the ECampaign object (because EBonusCampaign does not have its own, overridden, version of computeTickets()).

Next, computeTickets() calls computeTicketsLeft(). However, computeTicketsLeft() has been overridden in EBonusCampaign and therefore this overridden method is called instead. This is an example of a *down-call* from a superclass to its subclass. The result is that the number of tickets left in EBonusCampaign will be returned to CActioner.

Note that the initialization of the theECampaign reference and the successive down-call have introduced a run-time inheritance dependency from CActioner to EBonusCampaign. This dependency is not statically legitimized in the compile-time program structure. CActioner has an association to ECampaign, but not to EBonusCampaign. Such run-time dependencies are difficult to manage. They go against the EAP of the PCMEF framework (Section 4.1.3).

When getCampaignClose() is called in CActioner, it executes getDateClose() on the object referred to by the theECampaign variable. This is the EBonusCampaign object. Accordingly, getDateClose() in EBonusCampaign is called. Interestingly, getDateClose() provides an extension of the method defined in ECampaign – it contains a call to super. This is an example of an *up-call* (*callback*) from a subclass to its superclass.

Although such a call to super is understood, the combination of down-calls and up-calls introduces nasty circular dependencies on the classes involved. Additionally, these dependencies are created at run time and are, therefore, difficult to manage in view of any changes to classes.

Example 5.9 demonstrates how overriding contributes to the fragile base class problem. It also demonstrates that implementation inheritance introduces network-like communication paths, which we argued were unsustainable in large systems (Section 4.1). Message passing with implementation inheritance is all over the place. Apart from simple *down-calls* that follow the inheritance direction, *callbacks* (*up-calls*) are made.

As observed by Szyperski (1998, p.104): "In conjunction with observable state, this leads to re-entrance semantics close to that of concurrent systems. Arbitrary call graphs formed by interacting webs of objects abolish the classical layering and make re-entrance the norm."

To give justice to inheritance, callbacks are possible whenever there is a reference between objects. To quote Szyperski (1998, p.57) again: "With object reference . . . every method invocation is potentially an up-call, every method potentially a callback." Inheritance only adds to the trouble, but it does add considerably.

Multiple implementation inheritance   *5.2.4.4.3*

We introduced multiple inheritance in Section 3.1.6.3, and then in Section 3.1.8 we made the distinction between *multiple interface inheritance* (multiple supertyping) and *multiple implementation inheritance* (multiple superclassing). Multiple interface inheritance allows for merging of interface contracts. Multiple implementation inheritance permits merging of implementation fragments.

Multiple implementation inheritance does not really introduce a new "evil" of implementation inheritance. It rather exaggerates the problems caused by the fragile base class, overriding, and callbacks. Apart from the need to stop inheritance of any duplicate implementation fragments (if two or more superclasses define the same operation), it may also force the renaming of operations whenever duplicate names are coincidental (and should really mean separate operations).

In this context, it is worthwhile remembering the inherent growth of complexity due to multiple inheritance – the growth that results from the lack of support in object systems for *multiple classification* (Section 3.1.6.4). Any orthogonal inheritance branches rooted at a single superclass (Figure 3.22 in Section 3.1.6.3) have to be joined lower in the inheritance tree by specially created "join" classes.

The problems with multiple implementation inheritance have resulted in it being disallowed in some languages, most notably in Java. Java recommends using *multiple interface inheritance* (Section 3.1.8) to provide solutions that otherwise would require multiple implementation inheritance.

5.3 Advanced aggregation and delegation modeling

Aggregation is the third technique of linking classes in analysis models (Section 3.1.5). Compared with the other two techniques (conventional association and generalization), aggregation has been given the least attention. Yet aggregation is the most powerful technique we know for managing the complexity of large systems through the allocation of classes to hierarchical layers of abstraction.

Aggregation (and its stronger variation – *composition*) is a containment relationship. A *composite class* contains one or more *component classes*. The component classes are elements of their composite class (albeit elements that have their own existence). Although aggregation has been considered a fundamental modeling concept for at least as long as generalization, it has been given only marginal attention in object application development (with the exception of "perfect match" application domains, such as multimedia systems).

In programming environments (including most object databases), aggregation is implemented in the same way as conventional associations – by acquiring references between composite and component objects. Although the compile-time structure of aggregation is the same as for association, the run-time behavior is different. The semantics of aggregation are stronger, and it is (unfortunately) the programmer's responsibility to ensure that the run-time structures obey these semantics.

5.3.1 Putting more semantics into aggregation

While current programming environments ignore aggregation, object application development methods incorporate aggregation as a modeling option but give it the least emphasis.

Also (or as a consequence of the lack of support in programming environments), the object application development methods do not strive to enforce a rigorous semantic interpretation of the aggregation construct, frequently treating it as just a special form of association.

As discussed in Section 4.2.3, four possible semantics for aggregation can be distinguished (Maciaszek *et al.*, 1996b):

1. "ExclusiveOwns" aggregation;

2. "Owns" aggregation;

3. "Has" aggregation;

4. "Member" aggregation.

UML recognizes only two semantics of aggregation, namely *aggregation* (reference semantics) and *composition* (value semantics) (Section 3.1.5). We will now show how stereotypes and constraints can be used to extend the existing UML notation to represent the four different kinds of aggregation identified above.

The "ExclusiveOwns" aggregation

5.3.1.1

The *ExclusiveOwns* aggregation in UML can be represented by a *composition* stereotyped with the keyword «ExclusiveOwns» and constrained additionally with the keyword *frozen* (Fowler, 2003). The *frozen* constraint applies to a component class. It states that an object of the component class cannot be *reconnected* (over its lifetime) to another composite object. A component object can possibly be deleted altogether, but it cannot be switched to another owner.

Figure 5.19 shows two examples of the *ExclusiveOwns* aggregation. The left-hand example is modeled with the UML value semantics (a filled diamond), the right-hand with the UML reference semantics (a hollow diamond).

A Chapter object is a part of at most one CopyrightedBook. Once incorporated (by value) in a composite object, it cannot be reconnected to another CopyrightedBook object. The connection is frozen.

A BridgeCardPack contains exactly fifty-two cards. The UML reference semantics are used to model the ownership. Any BridgeCard object belongs to precisely one BridgeCardPack and cannot be reconnected to another pack of cards.

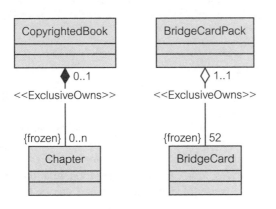

Figure 5.19 The *ExclusiveOwns* aggregation

Figure 5.20 The *Owns* aggregation

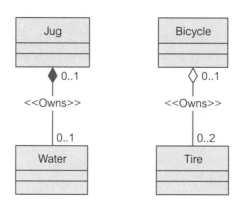

5.3.1.2 The "Owns" aggregation

Like the *ExclusiveOwns* aggregation, the *Owns* aggregation can be expressed in UML with a composition's value semantics (a filled diamond) or an aggregation's reference semantics (a hollow diamond). At any point in time a component object belongs to at most one composite object, but it can be *reconnected* to another composite object. When a composite object is deleted, its component objects are also deleted.

Figure 5.20 demonstrates two examples of the *Owns* aggregation. A `Water` object can be reconnected from one `Jug` to another. Similarly, a `Tire` object can be switched from one `Bicycle` to another. Because of the existence dependency, destruction of a `Jug` or a `Bicycle` propagates down to their component objects.

5.3.1.3 The "Has" aggregation

The *Has* aggregation would normally be modeled in UML using the aggregation's reference semantics (a hollow diamond). There is no existence dependency in a *Has* aggregation – the deletion of a composite object does not automatically propagate down to the component objects. The *Has* aggregation is characterized by only transitivity and asymmetry.

An example of a *Has* aggregation is shown in Figure 5.21. If a `Trolley` object has a number of `BeerCrate` objects and a `BeerCrate` object contains a number of `BeerBottle` objects, then the `Trolley` object has these `BeerBottle` objects (*transitivity*). If a `Trolley` has a `BeerCrate`, then a `BeerCrate` cannot have a `Trolley` (*asymmetry*).

5.3.1.4 The "Member" aggregation

The *Member* aggregation allows for *many-to-many multiplicity* of the relationship. No special assumptions are made about the existence dependency, transitivity, asymmetry, or frozen property. If needed, any of these four properties can be expressed as a UML constraint. Because of the many-to-many multiplicity, the *Member* aggregation can only be modeled in UML using the aggregation's reference semantics (a hollow diamond).

Figure 5.22 demonstrates four *Member* aggregation relationships. A `JADSession` (Section 2.2.2.3) object consists of one moderator and one or many scribes, users, and

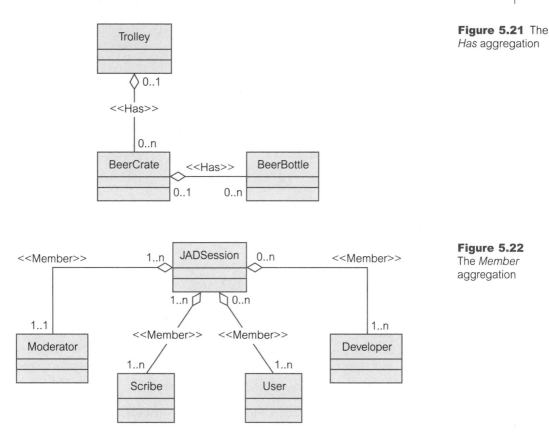

Figure 5.21 The *Has* aggregation

Figure 5.22 The *Member* aggregation

developers. Each of the component objects can participate in more than one JADSession object.

Aggregation as an alternative to generalization   5.3.2

Generalization is a superclass–subclass relationship. Aggregation is more like a superset–subset relationship. Notwithstanding this difference, a generalization can be represented as an aggregation.

Consider Figure 5.23. Customer orders that are not filled can be pending some further action. The pending order can be a back order that is to be filled once sufficient stock is available. The pending order is a future order if it is to be filled at a later date, as specified by the customer.

The left-hand model is a generalization for customer orders. The class GOrder can be a GPendingOrder. The GPendingOrder can be a GBackOrder or GFutureOrder. Inheritance ensures sharing of attributes and operations down the generalization tree.

Similar semantics can be modeled with the aggregation shown on the right-hand side in Figure 5.23. The classes ABackOrder and AFutureOrder include the attributes and operations of the class APendingOrder, which in turn incorporates the class AOrder.

Figure 5.23
Generalization
versus
aggregation

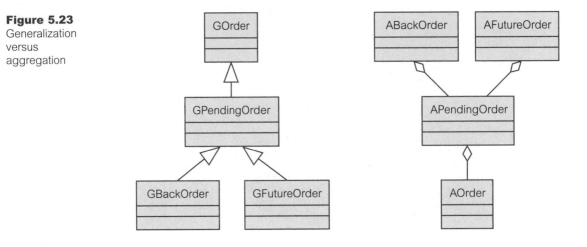

Although the two models in Figure 5.23 capture similar semantics, there are differences. The main one derives from the observation that the generalization model is based on the notion of class, whereas the aggregation model is really centered on the notion of object.

A particular GBackOrder object is also an object of GPendingOrder and GOrder. There is one *object identifier* (OID) for the GBackOrder. On the other hand, a particular ABackOrder object is built up of three separate objects, each with its own object identifier: the ABackOrder itself, the contained APendingOrder object, and the contained AOrder object.

Generalization uses *inheritance* to implement its semantics. Aggregation uses *delegation* to reuse the implementation of component objects. This is discussed next.

5.3.2.1 Delegation and prototypical systems

The computational model of inheritance is based on the notion of a class. However, it is possible to base the computational model on the notion of an object. An object-centered computational model structures objects into aggregation hierarchies. Whenever a composite object (*outer object*) cannot complete a task by itself, it can call on the methods in one of its component objects (*inner objects*) – this is called *delegation* (Section 3.1.5.3).

In delegation-based approaches, the functionality of the system is implemented by including (*cloning*) the functionality of existing objects in the newly required functionality. The existing objects are treated as *prototypes* for the creation of new objects. The idea is to search for the functionality in existing objects (*inner objects*) and then to implement the desired functionality in an *outer object*. The outer object asks for the services of inner objects as required. Systems constructed in this way, from existing prototypical objects, are called *prototypical systems*.

An object may have a *delegation relationship* to any other identifiable and visible object in the system (Lee and Tepfenhart, 1997). When an outer object receives a message and cannot complete the service by itself, it will delegate the execution of that service to an inner object. The inner object, if necessary, may forward the message to any of its own inner objects.

The inner object's interfaces may or may not be visible to objects other than the outer object. The four kinds of aggregation identified in Section 5.3.1 can be used for controlling the level of visibility of inner objects. For example, an outer object may expose the inner objects' interfaces as its own in weaker forms of aggregation (such as in a typical *Has* or *Member* aggregation). In stronger forms of aggregation, an outer object may hide its inner objects' interfaces from the outside world (thus using a stronger form of *encapsulation*).

Delegation versus inheritance

5.3.2.2

It can be shown that a delegation can model the inheritance, and vice versa. This means that the same system functionality can be delivered with inheritance or with delegation. The consensus on this issue was first reached at the conference in Orlando, Florida, in 1987 and is known as the Treaty of Orlando (Stein *et al.*, 1989).

In passing, we discussed the evils of implementation inheritance. A pressing question arises if the delegation avoids the disadvantages of implementation inheritance. The answer to this question is not straightforward (Szyperski, 1998).

From the *reuse* point of view, delegation comes very close to inheritance. An outer object reuses the implementation of the inner object. The difference is that – in the inheritance case – control is always returned to the object that receives the original message (request for service) after the service has been accomplished.

In the delegation case, once control has been passed from an outer to an inner object, it stays there. Any self-recursion has to be explicitly planned and designed into the delegation. In implementation inheritance, self-recursion always happens – it is unplanned and patched in (Szyperski, 1998). The *fragile base class* problem is but one undesired consequence of the unplanned/patched reuse.

The other potential advantage of delegation is that the sharing and reuse can be determined dynamically at run time. In inheritance-based systems, the sharing and reuse is normally determined statically when the object is created. The trade-off is between the safety and execution speed of *anticipatory sharing* of inheritance and the flexibility of *unanticipatory sharing* of delegation.

An argument in favor of delegation is that unanticipatory sharing is more natural and closer to the way people learn (Lee and Tepfenhart, 1997). Objects are naturally combined to form larger solutions and can evolve in unanticipated ways. The next section provides another viewpoint on the same issue.

Aggregation and holons – some cerebral ammunition

5.3.3

In Maciaszek *et al.* (1996a; 1996b), to restrain the complexity of object models, we proposed a new approach for describing software architectures based upon Arthur Koestler's interpretation of the structure of natural systems (Koestler, 1967; 1978). The central concept is the idea of "*holons*," which are interpreted as objects that are both parts and wholes. More precisely, they are considered as self-regulating entities that exhibit both the interdependent properties of parts and the independent properties of wholes.

Living systems are organized hierarchically. Structurally, they are *aggregations* of semi-autonomous units that display both the independent properties of wholes and the interdependent properties of parts. As Arthur Koestler would put it, they are aggregations of holons, from the Greek word *holos*, meaning *whole*, with the suffix changed to *on* to suggest a particle or part (as in proton or neutron) (Koestler, 1967).

Parts and wholes in the absolute sense do not exist in living organisms or even in social systems. Holons are hierarchically layered according to complexity, e.g. in a biological organism we can discern a hierarchy of atoms, molecules, organelles, cells, tissues, organs, and organ systems. Such hierarchies of holons are called *holocracies*.

Each holocracy layer hides its complexity from the layer above. *Looking downwards*, a holon is something complete and unique, a whole. *Looking upwards*, a holon is an elementary component, a part. Each holocracy layer contains many holons, e.g. atoms (hydrogen, carbon, oxygen, etc.), cells (nerves, muscles, blood cells, etc.).

Looking inwards, a holon provides services to other holons. *Looking outwards*, a holon requests services of other holons. Holocracies are open-ended. There is no absolute "leaf" holon or "apex" holon, except those identified as such for our interpretative convenience. Because of this characteristic, complex systems can evolve from simple systems.

Individual holons are therefore represented by four characteristics:

1. its internal charter (interactions between them can form unique patterns);
2. a self-assertive aggregation of subordinate holons;
3. an integrative tendency with regard to superior holons;
4. relationships with their peer holons.

Successful systems are arranged in holocracies that hide complexity in successively lower layers while providing greater levels of abstraction within the higher layers of their structures. This concept matches the semantics of aggregation.

Aggregation provides for the separation of concerns – it allows each class to remain encapsulated and to focus on a specific behavior (collaborations and services) of the class in a way that is unbound by the implementation of its parent classes (as it is in generalization). At the same time, aggregation allows for free movements between the stratified layers at run time.

The balance between integration and self-assertion of objects (holons) is achieved by the requirement that aggregation objects must "respect each other's interfaces" (Gamma *et al.*, 1995). Encapsulation is not broken, because objects communicate only through their interfaces. The evolution of the system is facilitated, because the object communication is not hard-coded in the implementation through mechanisms similar to inheritance.

Structurally, aggregation can model large quantities of objects by grouping them into various sets and establishing whole–part relationships between them. Functionally, aggregation allows for objects (holons) to look "upwards" and "downwards." However, aggregation is not able to model the necessary interoperability between peer holons so that they can look "inwards" and "outwards." This structural and functional gap can be filled successfully by the generalization and association relationships.

In our recommended approach, aggregation provides a "vertical" solution and generalization a "horizontal" solution to object application development. The aggregation becomes a dominant modeling concept that determines the overall framework of the system. This framework could be further formalized by providing a set of design patterns (Gamma *et al.*, 1995) specifically supporting the holon approach and utilizing the four kinds of aggregation. We hope that the above discussion provides some cerebral ammunition for the reader's own pursuits.

Summary

In this chapter, we have completed discussion of requirements analysis and bridged analysis with systems design. The object technology support for large-scale system development was scrutinized. The chapter was technically difficult in places, but it offered insights into object technology not easily found in books on systems analysis and design. Many of these insights revealed important weaknesses and downsides of object technology.

Stereotypes are the main extensibility technique of UML. In the extensibility task, they are assisted by *constraints* and *tags*. Extensibility mechanisms allow modeling beyond the predefined UML features. Because of the inventive nature of this chapter, the UML extensibility mechanisms, in particular stereotypes, were used frequently.

Public and *private* visibilities, discussed in previous chapters, give only basic support for the important notion of *encapsulation*. *Protected* visibility permits control of encapsulation within the inheritance structures. The *friend* notion and *package* visibility allow the encapsulation to be weakened to handle special situations. *Class visibility* (as opposed to the visibility of individual attributes and operations) is another important concept related to inheritance.

UML offers a number of additional modeling concepts to improve the expressiveness of class models. They include *derived attributes*, *derived associations*, and *qualified associations*. One of the most intriguing aspects of class modeling is the choice between an *association class* and a *reified class*.

The concept of *generalization and inheritance* is a double-edged sword in system modeling. On the one hand, it facilitates software reuse and improves the expressiveness, understandability, and abstraction of system models. On the other hand, it has the potential for self-destroying all these benefits if not used properly.

The concept of *aggregation and delegation* is an important modeling alternative to generalization and inheritance. *Delegation and prototypical systems* have an additional benefit of backing the hierarchical architectural structures. The *holon* abstraction provides an interesting insight into the way complex systems should be constructed.

Questions

Q1 What is a profile in UML? Search the Internet on "UML profile" and list some published profiles available to software developers.

Q2 At times, a class is allowed to instantiate only immutable objects, i.e. objects that cannot change after instantiation. How can such a requirement be modeled in UML?

Q3 Explain the difference between a constraint and a note.

Q4 Is encapsulation the same as visibility? Explain.

Q5 The visibility of inherited properties in a derived class depends on the visibility level given to the base class in the declaration of that derived class. What is this visibility if the base class is declared as private? What are the consequences for the rest of the model? Give an example.

Q6 The concept of a friend applies to a class or an operation. Explain the difference. Give an example (other than in this textbook) where the use of a friend could be desirable.

Q7 What are the modeling benefits of derived information?

Q8 When should a reified class replace an association class? Give an example (different from the one used in the book).

Q9 What is the substitutability principle? Explain.

Q10 Explain the difference between interface inheritance and implementation inheritance.

Q11 What is the fragile base class problem? What are the main reasons for fragile base classes?

Q12 Explain the difference between the *ExclusiveOwns* and *Owns* aggregation. What is the modeling advantage gained by distinguishing between these two kinds of aggregation?

Q13 Compare inheritance and delegation. What are the similarities? What are the differences?

Exercises

E1 Refer to Figure 3.14 (Section 3.1.4.2). Suppose that a teacher who manages a course offering must also teach that course offering. Modify the diagram of Figure 3.14 to capture this fact.

E2 Refer to Figures 3.20 (Section 3.1.6) and 3.21 (Section 3.1.6.1). Combine the two figures into a single class model. Design the visibility into the class model. Explain.

E3 Refer to Figure 3.16 (Section 3.1.4.4). Suppose that the system has to monitor students' assessments in multiple course offerings of the same course. This is because of the constraint that a student can fail the same course only three times (a fourth enrolment is not permitted). Extend the diagram from Figure 3.16 to model the above constraint. Use a reified class. Model and/or explain any assumptions.

E4 Refer to Example 4.10 (Section 4.2.4.3). Redraw the diagram in Figure 4.8 using aggregation in place of generalization. Explain the pros and cons of the new model.

Exercises (time logging)

Refer to the problem statement for time logging in Section 1.5.6. Consider the function in which an employee uses the stopwatch facility of the Time Logger tool to create a new time record. This function is the responsibility of a use-case subflow called "*Create Time Record – Stopwatch Entry*." The GUI window supporting this subflow is shown in Figure 5.24.

The Stopwatch Entry window is a modeless dialog box. This allows the user to access the time records in the primary window's row browser, the menus, and other features of Time Logger while the stopwatch is running. The display in Figure 5.24 shows the stopwatch in the "Running" state after it has been started from the Stopwatch menu.

The window has buttons for starting/stopping the stopwatch. When the stopwatch is running, the person can use the picklist fields and the `Description` field to fill in information about what he/she is doing. When the `Stop` button is pushed, Time Logger adds a new time record in the row browser.

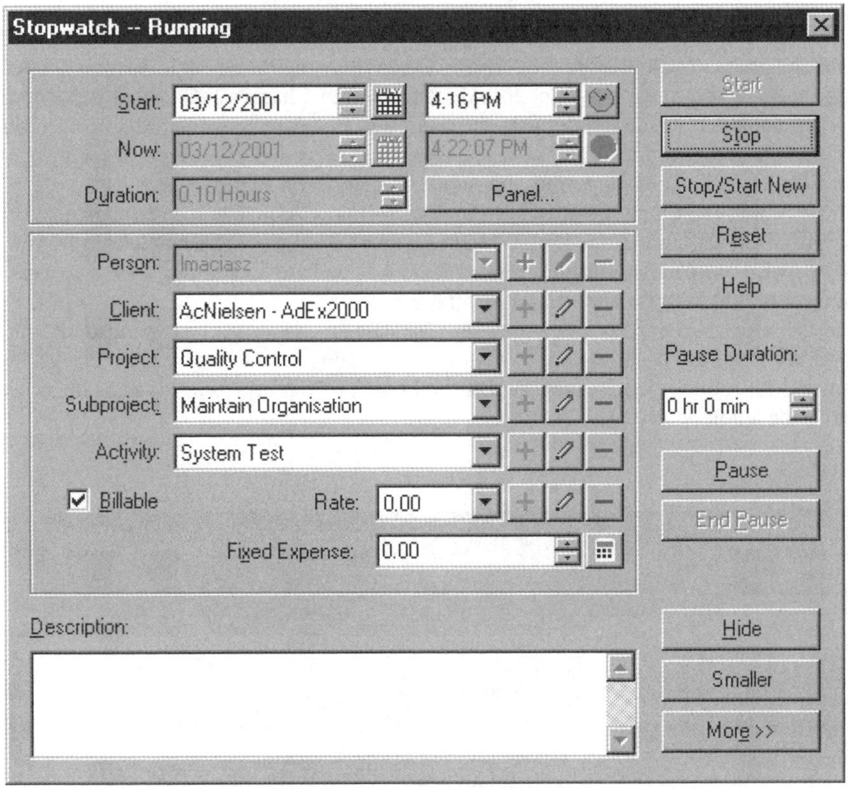

Figure 5.24
Stopwatch window
(time logging)

The `Duration` is calculated based on the contents of the `Start`, `Now`, and `Pause Duration` fields. The `Now` fields are not editable. The buttons `Pause` and `End Pause` control pause duration.

The `Reset` button cancels the stopwatch without storing a time record in the database. The `Hide` button hides the stopwatch and makes it run in the background. The hidden stopwatch can be displayed again from the Stopwatch menu.

The iconic buttons plus, pencil, and minus provide create, update, and delete functions on corresponding picklists.

F1 Design a high-level collaboration diagram for the "*Create Time Record – Stopwatch Entry*" subflow. The diagram should show only the main program classes and the flow of messages between them. The messages do not need to be numbered. There is no need to specify signatures of messages. The design should adhere to the PCMEF framework, except that there is no need for Mediator classes. Explain assumptions and potentially unclear or ambiguous messages.

F2 Based on your solution to Exercise F1, design a class diagram for the "*Create Time Record – Stopwatch Entry*" subflow. The diagram should show operations, but there is no need to show attributes. The classes need to be connected with necessary static relationships. Dependency relationships should be used between classes without static relationships, but which communicate at run time. Explain assumptions and potentially unclear or ambiguous parts of the model.

Exercises (advertising expenditure)

Refer to the problem statement for advertising expenditure measurement in Section 1.5.5. Refer also to the solutions to the exercises for AE at the end of Chapter 2. Consider the function in which an employee maintains the lists of categories and corresponding advertised products. This function is the responsibility of a use-case subflow called "*Maintain Category-Product Links*." The GUI window supporting this subflow is shown in Figure 5.25.

The "Maintain Category–Product Links" window consists of two panes, called `Categories` and `Products for [Active Category]`. (The window in Figure 5.25 contains two more panes to display related Raw Ads and Ad Links, but these two panes are not subject of this exercise and should be ignored.)

The `Categories` pane is a tree browser. The category view can be expanded or collapsed by clicking the plus or minus sign, respectively. Categories containing subcategories are identified with a folder icon. Categories at the bottom of the tree (with no subcategories) are shown using a note icon.

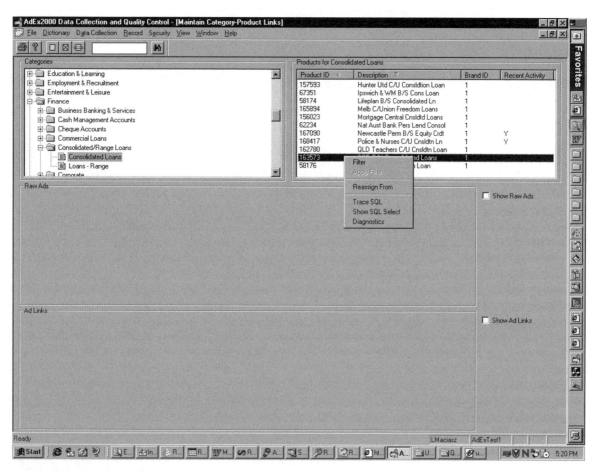

Figure 5.25 Category–Product window (advertising expenditure)
Source: Courtesy of Nielsen Media Research, Sydney, Australia

Upon selecting (highlighting) a category that does not have any subcategories, the list of products in that category is shown in a right-hand row browser's pane. Selecting a category that contains subcategories has no effect on the products' pane.

Although not part of the exercise, double clicking on any category opens an "Update Category" window. The pop-up menu contains a `Reassign From` item, which is used to reassign a product to a different category.

G1   Design a high-level collaboration diagram for the *"Maintain Category–Product Links"* subflow. The diagram should show only the main program classes and the flow of messages between them. The messages do not need to be numbered. There is no need to specify signatures of messages. The design should adhere to the PCMEF framework, except that there is no need for Mediator classes. Explain assumptions and potentially unclear or ambiguous messages.

G2   Based on your solution to Exercise G1, design a class diagram for the *"Maintain Category–Product Links"* subflow. The diagram should show operations, but there is no need to show attributes. The classes need to be connected with necessary static relationships. Dependency relationships should be used between classes without static relationships, but which communicate at run time. Explain assumptions and potentially unclear or ambiguous parts of the model.

Answers to odd-numbered questions

Q1 – answer

"A **profile** takes a part of the UML and extends it with a coherent group of stereotypes for a particular purpose, such as business modeling" (Fowler, 2003, p.63). The profile stereotypes would normally introduce new graphical icons to visually reflect domain-specific concepts. The profiles are frequently needed in *design modeling*; less so in *analysis modeling*. A good example is the profile for building web applications published by Conallen (2000).

Concerted efforts are made to introduce profiles for software development. A quick Internet search conducted at the time of this book's writing produced links to the UML profiles for (in no particular order):

- data modeling
  http://www.agiledata.org/essays/umlDataModelingProfile.html
- CORBA (Common Object Request Broker Architecture)
  http://www.omg.org/technology/documents/formal/profile_corba.htm
- Web modeling, XSD schema, business process modeling
  http://www.sparxsystems.com.au/uml_profiles.htm
- framework architectures
  http://citeseer.nj.nec.com/fontoura00uml.html
- EJB (Enterprise Java Beans)
  http://lists.w3.org/Archives/Public/www-ws/2001Jun/0000.html
- agent-oriented modeling
  http://tmitwww.tm.tue.nl/staff/gwagner/AORML/AOR-UML-Profile.pdf
- aspect-oriented modeling
  http://www.cs.ubc.ca/~kdvolder/Workshops/OOPSLA2001/submissions/26-aldawud.pdf
- requirements engineering
  http://www.cs.ucl.ac.uk/staff/A.Finkelstein/papers/umlreprofile.pdf

Q3 – answer

A *constraint* is a semantic condition or limitation placed on a UML modeling element. A constraint can be rendered graphically as a text string enclosed in curly brackets or in a note symbol. "A *note* is a dog-eared rectangle with its upper-right corner bent over" (Rumbaugh *et al.*, 1999, p.359).

Typically, more complex constraints are represented as notes. Because the note is a distinct graphical element, it can be linked visually – by relationships – to other UML modeling elements.

The note is only a graphical medium that can be used to express a constraint. The note symbol does not have a semantic clout by itself. As such, the note can be used to contain information that does not make a semantic statement. For example, the note symbol can contain a *comment*.

Q5 – answer

The implementation of *visibility* can differ significantly among object-oriented languages (ref. Page-Jones, 2000; Fowler, 2003). With regard to the question, the private properties of the base class remain private to the base class and are not accessible to objects of the derived class (independently of which kind of class inheritance is used – private, protected, or public).

If base class A is declared `private` in subclass B (`class B: private A`), then the visibility of properties inherited from A changes in B to `private`. That is, the properties that are `public` or `protected` in A become `private` properties in B. The consequence is that further specialization of B (e.g. `class C: public B`) will make it impossible for C to access any properties of A. That is, despite the fact that class C inherited properties of A, the objects of class C cannot access the private properties of A (and the private properties of B). Properties of class A have become invisible to objects of class C, although the definitions of some properties in C could have been derived from their parent properties in A.

The example in Figure 5.26 is loosely based on the C++ example in Meyers (1998). The protected attribute `tax_file_number` in Person becomes a private attribute of Student. If std is an object of Student, then an assignment like `x = std.tax_file_number` is not permitted. Similarly, the call `std.sing()` will result in error.

To C++ code corresponding to the above model:

Figure 5.26
Private class
visibility

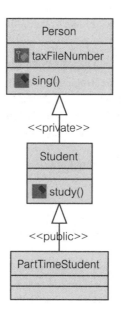

```
class Person
{
protected:
    int tax_file_number;
public:
    void sing(){};
};

class Student : private Person
{
};

void main()
{
    Student std;
    int x = std.tax_file_number;    //compiler error
    std.sing();                     //compiler error
}
```

To quote Meyers (1998): "in contrast to public inheritance, compilers will generally *not* convert a derived class (such as `Student`) into a base class object (such as `Person`) if the inheritance relationship between the classes is private."

An unhappy conclusion is that *private inheritance* is the antithesis of the "is a kind of" inheritance that we advocate in the textbook (e.g. Section 4.2.4.1). A `Student` is not a `Person` any more. "Private inheritance means is implemented in terms of. If you make a class `D` privately inherit from a class `B`, you do so because you are interested in taking advantage of some of the code that has already been written for class `B`, not because there is any conceptual relationship between objects of type `B` and objects of type `D`" (Meyers, 1998).

Private class inheritance is in many ways synonymous with *convenience inheritance*, discussed in Section 5.2.4.3 of the textbook as an improper variation of implementation inheritance. Note that UML (Rumbaugh *et al.*, 1999) recommends that private inheritance be modeled by a generalization relationship with stereotype `<<implementation>>`. Rumbaugh *et al.* (1999, p.395) state further that "Private inheritance is purely an implementation mechanism and should not be thought of as a use of generalization. Generalization requires substitutability."

Q7 – answer

Derived information does not really provide new information to a UML model, but it can enrich its semantics. It clarifies the model by bringing to light information that would otherwise be hidden from direct observation.

In an *analysis* model, derived information may be used to provide a name or definition for a noteworthy concept or user requirement. In a *design* model, derived information may be used to signify that the value of that information needs to be recomputed once the values it depends on change.

In most practical situations, derived information specifies a *constraint* on existing properties, such as some value that can be computed based on existing values. Used judiciously, derived information has the potential to simplify the model even though the information *per se* is "redundant."

Q9 – answer

The substitutability principle states that "given a declaration of a variable or parameter whose type is declared as X, any instance of an element that is a descendant of X may be used as the actual values without violating the semantics of the declaration and its use. In other words, an instance of a descendant element may be substituted for an instance of an ancestor element" (Rumbaugh *et al.*, 1999, p.458).

The "*is a kind of*" generalization relationship (Section 4.2.4.1) supports *substitutability*. Since, furthermore, the "is a kind of" relationship is implemented with *public class inheritance* (ref. Question Q5), the substitutability principle demands public inheritance. Public inheritance asserts that everything applicable to superclass objects is also applicable to subclass objects (a subclass cannot renounce or modify properties of its superclass).

Q11 – answer

The *fragile base class* problem refers to the undesirable impact that the evolution of super-classes (base classes) has on all application programs that contain subclasses that inherited from these superclasses. The impact of such changes is largely unpredictable as the designers of superclasses cannot know how subclasses are going to be reusing the superclasses' properties.

Short of demanding that a designer of a base class be a prophet, the fragile base class problem is unavoidable in object-oriented implementations. Any changes to public interfaces in the base class will necessitate adjustments in subclasses. Changes to implementation of operations inherited by subclasses may have even more dramatic consequences, albeit frequently more subtle and more difficult to recognize (this is particularly the case for default implementations that have been arbitrarily redefined in subclasses).

A special kind of the fragile base class problem arises in *multiple inheritance* (ref. Section 5.2.4.4.3). In essence, any multiple inheritance conflict is a variation of the fragile base class problem encountered by a subclass even before a superclass has been modified.

Q13 – answer

Inheritance is a *reuse* technique in generalization relationships. *Delegation* is a *reuse* technique in aggregation relationships. In most cases, the decision of whether to use inheritance (generalization) or delegation (aggregation) is straightforward – the "is a kind of" semantics demands generalization; the "has a" semantics demands aggregation.

However, as evidenced in the textbook with a contrived example (Figure 5.23 in Section 5.3.2), generalization can be implemented with aggregation. Barring such forceful modeling practices, inheritance should be used with "is a kind of" semantics and delegation with "has a" semantics.

The similarities between these two techniques amount to the fact that both are *reuse techniques*. The differences stem from the fact that inheritance is a reuse technique between *classes*, while delegation is a reuse technique between *objects*. This makes delegation more powerful than inheritance.

First, delegation can simulate inheritance, but not vice versa. Second, delegation is a run-time notion that supports the dynamic evolution of systems, whereas inheritance is a compile-time static notion. Third, a delegating (outer) object can reuse both behavior (operation implementations) and state (attribute values) of delegated (inner) objects, whereas inheritance does not inherit the state.

Solutions to odd-numbered exercises

E1 – solution

An easy solution to this question can be achieved by placing a *constraint* on the two associations (Figure 5.27). The constraint named {subset} informs that a teacher in charge must be one of the teachers teaching the course offering.

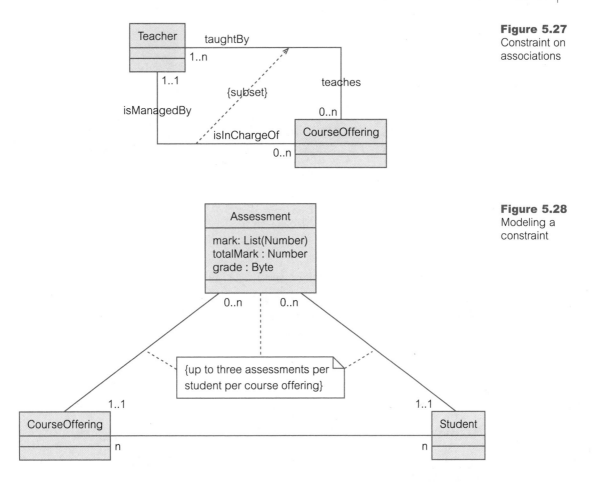

Figure 5.27
Constraint on
associations

Figure 5.28
Modeling a
constraint

E3 – solution

The solution in Figure 5.28 has been obtained by converting the association class in Figure 3.16 into an independent fully fledged class `Assessment`. The constraint note (to capture the "up to three assessments" rule) has been added and linked to `Assessment` and its associations to two other classes.

Solutions to exercises (time logging)

F1 – solution

Figure 5.29 contains a collaboration model for the stopwatch entry subflow. The subflow starts when the user activates the stopwatch from a `:CMenuItem`. The dialog box `:PStopwatch` opens up and needs to be populated with data. To this aim, it instantiates a `:CStopwatchInitializer` which takes over the responsibility to `refreshView()`.

An entity object `:ETimeRecord` is instructed to `getTimeRecord()` to be displayed in the dialog box. This action triggers a number of messages to other entity objects to `getDate()`, `getTime()`, `getPerson()`, `getClients()`, `getProjects()`, `getSubprojects()`, and `getActivities()`.

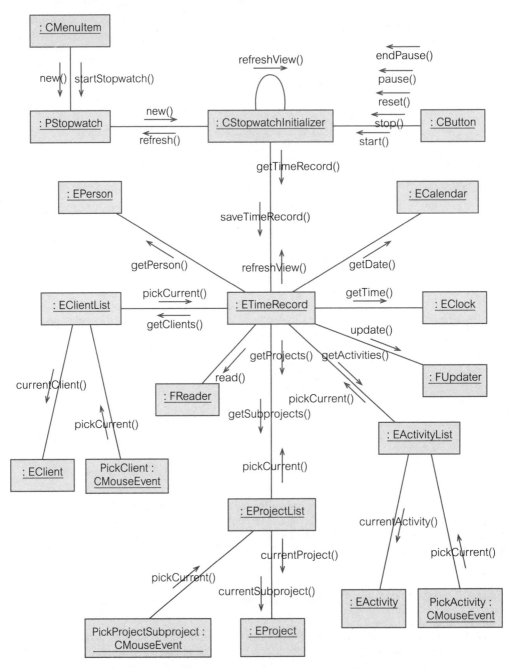

Figure 5.29 Collaboration model for stopwatch (time logging)

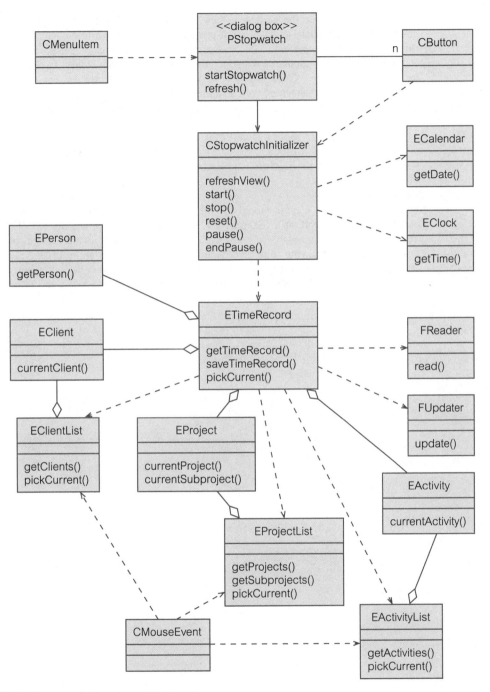

Figure 5.30 Class model for stopwatch (time logging)

The objects that are the targets of these messages will involve :FReader to access the information in the database. That is not precisely what is shown in our model. Our model is simplified and shows that only :ETimeRecord uses the services of :FReader.

Once the dialog is populated with data, the user can edit many fields. To edit picklist fields, the user involves the :CMouseEvent objects. An item selected by the mouse results in a pickCurrent() message on a corresponding container object (:EClientList, :EProjectList, or :EActivityList). As before, :FReader encapsulates access to the database.

Finally, the stop() request from :CButton to :CStopwatchInitializer results in a saveTimeRecord() message to :ETimeRecord. The task of generating the SQL update statements to modify the database is given to :FUpdater.

F2 – solution

Figure 5.30 contains a class model for the stopwatch entry subflow. The model has been obtained from the solution to Exercise F1. The diagram exemplifies the PCMEF approach. The control class CStopwatchInitializer is in the center of the design, but the main tasks of getting and saving time records are coordinated by the entity class ETimeRecord. ETimeRecord performs many of its services with the assistance of its component classes. For communication with the database, ETimeRecord depends on FReader and FUpdater.

Chapter

6

System Architecture and Program Design

This chapter is a direct continuation of the ideas and topics discussed in the last three chapters. The difference is that the subject matter is now discussed from the design perspective. Issues that were less relevant in analysis, such as the technical details of object collaborations, are now explained in depth.

Design is a low-level model of a system's architecture and its internal workings. The *design* is done in terms of the software/hardware platform on which the system is going to be implemented. In an iterative and incremental software development, the analysis models are continually "elaborated" with technical details. Once the technical details include software/hardware considerations, an analysis model becomes a design model.

The distinction between analysis and design is not clear-cut. One can talk about deeply technical issues without relating to specific software/hardware solutions. In this sense, much of the discussion in Chapter 5 could be classified as design rather than analysis.

System design encompasses two major issues: the architectural design of the system and the detailed design of the programs in the system. The *architectural design* is the description of a system in terms of its modules. It includes decisions about the solution strategies for the client and for the server components of the system. The *architectural design* involves the layered organization of classes and packages, the assignment of processes to computing facilities, reuse, and component management. Architectural design resolves the issues with regard to a *multi-tier* physical architecture as well as with regard to a *multi-layer* logical architecture.

The description of the internal workings of each module (use case) is called the *detailed design*. The detailed design develops complete algorithms and data structures for each module. These algorithms and data structures are tailored to all (reinforcing and obtrusive) constraints of the underlying implementation platform.

The *detailed design* addresses the collaboration models required for the realization of the program's demanded functionality captured in use cases. Detailed design must support the *supportability* objective of the logical architectural framework. The program must be designed to minimize *dependencies* and to make dependencies visible in the static compile-time code. Run-time object *interactions* should be carefully documented in interaction models and presented at various levels of abstraction to further facilitate the system's supportability. The program structure should adhere to recognized *design patterns*.

6.1 Distributed physical architecture

Architectural design has physical and logical aspects. Physically, architectural design is concerned with the selection of a *solution strategy* and with the *distribution* of the system workload across multiple processors. The physical architecture resolves the client and server issues as well as any middleware needed to "glue" the client and the server. It allocates processing components to computer nodes. From the UML modeling perspective, the physical architectural design uses *deployment diagrams* (Section 3.2.6.3).

Although the physical architecture resolves the client and server issues, the client and server are logical concepts (Bochenski, 1994). The *client* is a computing process that makes requests of the server process. The *server* is a computing process that services the client requests. Normally, the client and the server processes run on different computers, but it is perfectly possible to implement a client/server system on a single machine.

In a typical scenario, the *client process* is responsible for controlling the display of information on the user's screen and for handling the user's events. The *server process* is any computer node with a database of which data or processing capability may be requested by a client process.

6.1.1 Peer-to-peer architecture

The *client/server* (C/S) architecture can be extended to represent an arbitrary distributed system. Any computer node with a database can be a client in some business transactions and a server in other transactions. Connecting such nodes by a communication network gives rise to a *distributed processing* system architecture, as shown in Figure 6.1.

The distributed architecture as shown in Figure 6.1 is also known as *peer-to-peer* architecture. In this architecture, any process or node in the system may be both client and server. The need for distribution can arise from many factors, such as:

- a requirement for specialized processing on a dedicated machine;
- the need to access the system from various geographical locations;
- economic considerations when using multiple small machines may be cheaper than a large, pricey computer;
- a supportability requirement to ensure that future extensions to the system can scale up nicely.

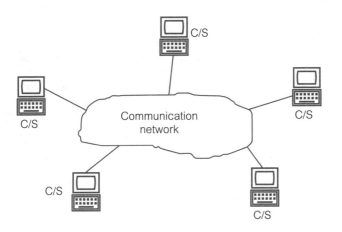

Figure 6.1
Distributed
processing
system
architecture

Clearly, offloading work to separate machines has to be assessed against the workload demanded by inter-process network communication. Minimization of network traffic while maximizing overall system throughput is a special consideration in peer-to-peer architectures. Attention has to be given to potential *deadlocks* between processes (when two or more processes are in a "deadly" embrace and cannot proceed because they hold resources on which other processes are waiting).

In a distributed processing system, the client can access any number of servers. However, the client may be allowed to access only one server at a time. This means that in a single request it may not be possible to combine data from two or more database servers. If this is possible, then the architecture supports a *distributed database* system.

Multi-tier architecture   6.1.2

One of the most important recognized practices in the development of large database-centered enterprise systems has been the necessary separation of at least three implementation concerns: GUI presentation issues, enterprise-wide business rules, and data services. This separation of concerns aligns with the *three-tier architecture* in which a separate business logic middle tier is introduced between the GUI client and the database server.

In practice, the separation of concerns may go beyond just three issues and include other services, such as web processing, network communication, or printing. A resulting *multi-tier architecture* differs from a peer-to-peer architecture in that it imposes hierarchical dependencies between the tiers of hardware and software. These hierarchical tier dependencies align well with hierarchical layers of software modules recommended by logical architectural frameworks, such as PCMEF (Section 4.1).

Figure 6.2 illustrates a possible alignment between a multi-layer logical architecture and a multi-tier physical architecture. In the figure, the presentation and control layers are shown to be potentially implemented in a web server. The remaining PCMEF layers are implemented in the application server, while engaging the database server from the foundation subsystem.

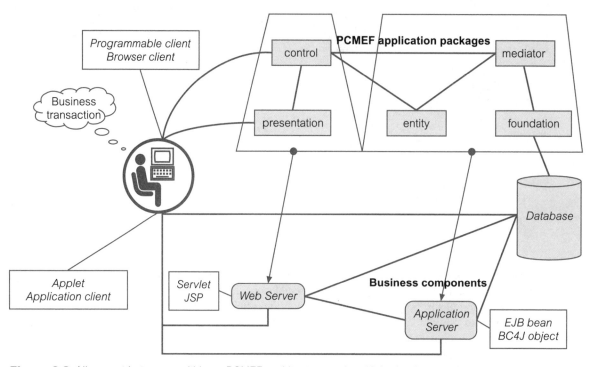

Figure 6.2 Alignment between multi-layer PCMEF architecture and multi-tier implementation architecture
Source: Maciaszek and Liong (2004). Reprinted by permission of Pearson Education Ltd.

One of the most talked-about tiers is the *application server*. This is also perhaps the least understood concept of a multi-tier architecture. The confusion relates to misunderstandings between the notions of application and business services. For the database community, these two notions are clearly different. An *application service* is what each single program executing on a database does. A *business service* is what a database enforces as business rules on all executing programs. This business rules enforcement is frequently done programmatically (by means of database triggers and stored procedures).

As a result, a three-tier architecture can be presented as consisting of application services, business services, and data services. Alas, the above distinction between an application and a business service is not always followed. It is frequent, for example, to use the name *application server* to mean a tier that handles business components and that also takes care of business rules (while still providing a separate thread of the application service to each program). At the same time, a *web server* is given the task of handling GUI presentation issues. This is how application and web servers are presented in Figure 6.2.

This said, the *application process* is a logical concept that may or may not be supported by separate hardware. The application logic can run equally well on a client or a server node, i.e. it can be compiled into the client or the server process and implemented as a dynamic link library (DLL), application programming interface (API), remote procedure calls (RPC), etc.

When the application logic is compiled into the client, then we talk about a *thick-client* architecture ("a client on steroids"). The thick client assumes workstations for user–program interaction. Normally, a thick-client architecture uses only two tiers (thick client and database server).

When the application logic is compiled into the server, then we talk about a *thin-client* architecture ("a skinny client"). The thin client assumes network computers for user–program interaction. It also assumes that the client is a web browser accessing HTML pages, Java applets, beans, servlets, etc.

Intermediate architectures, in which application logic is partly compiled into the client and partly into the server, are also possible.

Database-centered architecture 6.1.3

This book is predominantly concerned with the development of business applications and enterprise information systems. Database software plays a crucial role in such systems (Chapter 8). Accordingly, databases influence physical software architectures.

Independently of where the application logic resides, the program (client) interacts with the database (server) to obtain information for display and the user's manipulation. But modern databases can be programmed as well. We say that those modern databases are *active*.

A database program is called a *stored procedure*. A stored procedure is stored in the database itself (it is *persistent*). It can be invoked from a client program (or from another stored procedure) by a normal procedure/function call statement.

A special kind of a stored procedure – called a *trigger* – cannot be explicitly called. A trigger fires automatically on an attempt to change the content of the database. Triggers are used to implement enterprise-wide business rules, which have to be enforced in a way that is independent of the client programs (or stored procedures). Triggers enforce integrity and consistency of the database. They do not allow individual applications to break the database-imposed business rules.

We need to decide which parts of the system should be programmed into the client and which into the database. The "programmable" parts to consider include:

- user interface
- presentation logic
- application (control) function
- integrity logic
- data access

The *user interface* part of a program knows how to display information on a particular GUI, such as a web browser, Windows, or Macintosh. The *presentation logic* is responsible for handling the GUI objects (forms, menus, action buttons, etc.) as required by the application function.

The *application function* contains the main logic of the program. It captures what the application does. It is the glue that puts the client and the database together. From the perspective of the PCMEF approach (Section 4.1.1), the application function is implemented in the classes of the *control* subsystem.

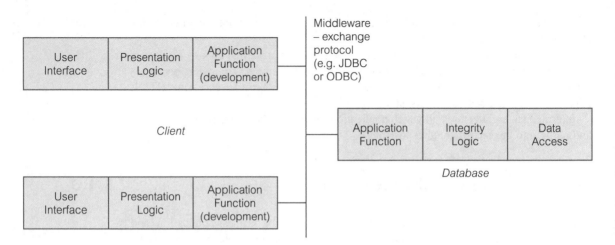

Figure 6.3 Application–database interaction

The *integrity logic* is responsible for the enterprise-wide business rules. These are the rules that apply across all application programs, i.e. all programs have to conform to them. The *data access* knows how to access persistent data on the disk.

Figure 6.3 shows a typical scenario. The user interface and presentation logic belong to the client. The data access and integrity logic (triggers) are the responsibility of the database. The application function is frequently programmed (as SQL queries) into the client during the early development phase, but it is moved to the database (as stored procedures) for the final deployment of the software product.

6.2 Multi-layer logical architecture

Software developers know that the difficulty of producing a small system cannot be compared with the difficulty of delivering a large-scale solution. A small object system is often easy to understand, implement, and deploy. A large object solution is dominated by complex *networks* of objects responding to random events that invoke a mesh of interrelated operations (methods). Without a clear architectural design and rigorous processes, large software projects are likely to fail.

A well-known cognitive psychology principle – *the 7 ± 2 rule* – states that the short-term memory of a human brain can *simultaneously* handle up to nine (7 + 2) things (graphical elements, ideas, concepts, etc.). The lower bound of five (7 − 2) indicates that fewer than five things constitute a trivial problem.

The rules of cognitive psychology do not change the fact that we have to produce large systems, and large systems are complex. Much of this complexity is human-generated, rather than essential (Section 1.1).

The main culprit is system modeling that allows for unrestricted communication between objects. Objects in such systems form *networks* – webs of cross-referenced objects. Message passing is allowed from anywhere to anywhere in the system. Down-calls and up-calls are possible. In networks, the number of communication paths between objects grows exponentially with the addition of new objects. As noted by Szyperski: "object references introduce linkage across arbitrary abstraction domains. Proper layering of system architectures thus lies somewhere between the challenging and impossible" (1998, p.57.)

Successful systems are organized in hierarchies – the network structures are restricted and carefully controlled. *Hierarchies* reduce the complexity from exponential to polynomial. They introduce layers of objects and constrain intercommunication between layers. In a typical hierarchy, only objects in adjacent layers communicate directly. The complexity is hidden and divided in separate layers.

The complexity of networks   6.2.1

To talk about the *complexity* of object systems, we need to agree on a measurement. How do we measure complexity? Complexity has different kinds and shapes. A simple, but very illustrative, measurement is the number of connections between classes. We define a *connection* as the existence of a persistent or transient link between classes (Section 3.1.1.3).

Each connection would typically allow for a bidirectional interaction between classes, i.e. from *A* to *B* and from *B* to *A*. Figure 6.4 illustrates the complexity of a network of seven classes. There are $n(n-1)/2$ possible connections between n classes. This formula, applied to seven classes, gives us 21 connections (and 42 interaction paths).

Note that we measure the complexity with regard to the number of classes, not objects. In programs, the objects – not the classes – send messages to other objects, of the same or different class. This introduces additional difficulty to the programmer responsible for delivering the application logic and managing the program's variables and other data structures. However, the main challenge is not an individual program's complexity but the complexity of the entire system of programs.

An object can send a message to another object only if there is a persistent or transient link between them. The transient (run-time) links are resolved within a single program

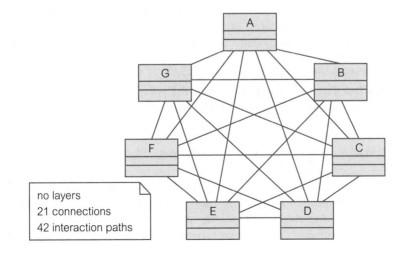

Figure 6.4
The complexity of networks

no layers
21 connections
42 interaction paths

Figure 6.5
The complexity of
hierarchies

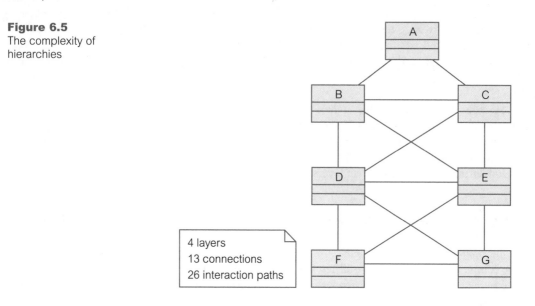

4 layers
13 connections
26 interaction paths

invocation and, therefore, they do not add to the complexity of the whole system. The persistent (compile-time) links, on the other hand, exist only if there is a connection (e.g. association) defined in the class model. The classes can be shared and reused across many programs.

6.2.2 The complexity of hierarchies

The solution to complexity control lies in reducing the network structures through grouping of classes into *class hierarchies*. In this way, classes can form naturally into layers that emphasize a hierarchical decomposition between layers while allowing for network-like interactions within the layers.

The hierarchical layering offers reductions in complexity by restricting the number of potential interaction paths between classes. The reduction is achieved by stratifying classes into layers and allowing only for direct class interactions within a layer and between adjacent layers.

Figure 6.5 shows the complexity of a seven-class hierarchy when the classes are grouped into four layers. In comparison with the network structure in Figure 6.4, the complexity is reduced from 42 to 26 interaction paths.

6.2.3 Multi-layer architectural frameworks

Architectural prerogatives for good software design have been discussed in Section 4.1. The PCMEF framework introduced there has been used in succeeding discussions in the book. The PCMEF framework enforces the demands of hierarchical organization of classes and minimization of dependencies between classes and other software elements.

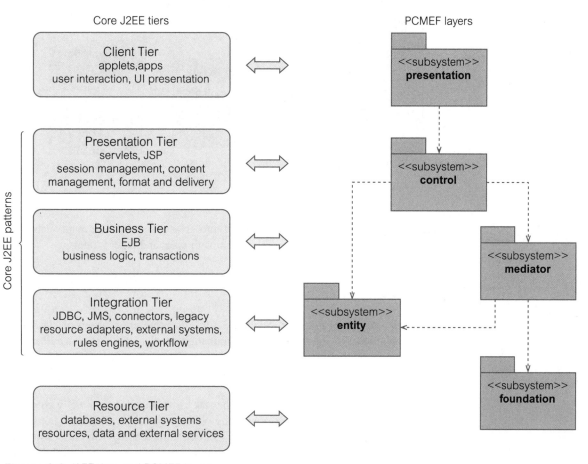

Figure 6.6 J2EE tiers and PCMEF layers
Source: modified from Maciaszek and Liong (2004)

The PCMEF framework is consistent with other known hierarchical architectures. Figure 6.6 shows the alignment between PCMEF layers and the Core J2EE tiers (Maciaszek and Liong, 2004). The J2EE tiers can be looked at as logical layers. In general, the Core J2EE tiers define best software development practices based on J2EE technologies, such as servlets, JSP (Java Server Pages), EJB (Enterprise Java Beans), web services, and XML (Alur *et al.*, 2003).

Architectural modeling

6.3

In UML, *architectural modeling* is supported by facilities for *implementation modeling* (Section 3.2.6). Implementation models are centered on such concepts as a node, component, package, and subsystem. Beyond implementation models, UML supports architectural

Figure 6.7
Packages and
classes

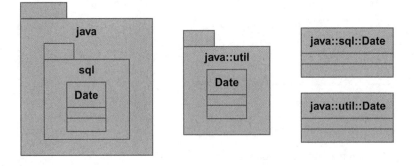

modeling through various constraints designed into class diagrams. The main such facility is the visualization of dependency relationships in class and other models.

6.3.1 Packages

UML provides a notion of *package* (Section 3.2.6.1) to represent a group of classes (or other modeling elements, e.g. use cases) (Rumbaugh *et al.*, 1999). Packages serve to partition the logical model of an application program. They are clusters of highly related classes that are themselves cohesive but are loosely coupled relative to other such clusters (Lakos, 1996).

Packages can be *nested*. An outer package has access to any classes directly contained in its nested packages. A class can be owned by only one package. This does not inhibit the class from appearing in other packages or from communicating with classes in other packages. By declaring the visibility of a class within a package, we can control the communication and dependencies between classes in different packages (Section 5.1.2.2).

A package is shown as a folder icon (Figure 6.7). A nested package is drawn inside its outer package. Each package would have its own class diagram defining all classes owned by the package. Figure 6.7 shows different ways of showing the assignment of classes to packages (Fowler, 2003) and reflects the fact that a Java programmer has the option of importing a Date class from either the java.sql or java.util library packages.

Packages can be related in two kinds of relationship: *generalization* and *dependency*. Dependency from package A to package B states that changes to B may require changes in A. Dependencies between packages are by and large due to message passing (i.e. a class in one package sending a message to a class in another package).

UML specifies a number of different categories of the dependency relationship (e.g. a *usage* dependency, *access* dependency, *visibility* dependency). We found that determining the category of dependency is not particularly helpful. The true nature of each dependency can be specified instead as a descriptive constraint in the CASE repository.

Note that a *generalization* between packages also implies a dependency. The dependency is from a subtype package to the supertype package. Changes in the supertype package affect the subtype package.

Example 6.1 (university enrolment)

A closer look at the university enrolment application reveals that the system has to be "aware" of the class timetable and of the students' grades in order to validate the enrolment of students in classes.

We do not know if "grades" and "timetable" exist as separate software modules into which our enrolment system can be plugged. If not, the enrolment system will have to include such modules.

Our task in this example is to provide a package model for university enrolment in the scope corresponding to the above observations. The model should also capture the requirement that timetable scheduling is based on the `java.sql.Date` type of the Gregorian calendar. However, the possibility of implementing timetable scheduling according to other calendars (such as Julian) also needs to be reflected in the model.

Figure 6.8 shows the packages and relationships between them for Example 6.1. `Enrolment` depends on `Grades` and `Timetable`. `Timetable` depends on `Calendar`. There can be four different calendars, shown by a generalization relationship. `Gregorian Calendar` depends on `java::sql::Date`.

Components 6.3.2

A *component* (Section 3.2.6.2) is a physical part of the system, a piece of implementation, or a software program (Lakos, 1996; Szyperski, 1998; Booch *et al.*, 1999; Rumbaugh *et al.*, 1999). Components are typically perceived as binary executable (EXE) parts of the system. But the component can also be a part of the system that is not directly executable (e.g. a source code file, data file, DLL (dynamic link library), or database stored procedure).

The characteristics of a component are (Szyperski, 1998; Rumbaugh *et al.*, 1999):

■ a unit of independent deployment (never deployed partially);

■ a unit of third-party composition (i.e. sufficiently documented and self-contained to be "plugged into" other components by a third-party);

■ that it has no persistent state (i.e. cannot be distinguished from copies of its own; in any given application, there will be at most one copy of a particular component);

■ that it is a replaceable part of a system, i.e. it can be replaced by another component that conforms to the same interface;

■ that it fulfills a clear function and is logically and physically cohesive;

■ that it may be nested in other components.

In UML 1, a component was rendered graphically as a rectangle with two smaller rectangles on its left side. UML 2 has changed this notation to reflect the fact that a component normally corresponds to a compiled class, such as a Java file obtained from a class compilation. This is shown in Figure 6.9.

A component diagram shows components and how they relate to each other. Components can be related by *dependency relationships*. A dependent component requires the services of the component pointed to by the dependency relationship. The use of dependency relationships on components has been discussed in Section 3.2.6.2.

Figure 6.8
Packages
(university
enrolment)

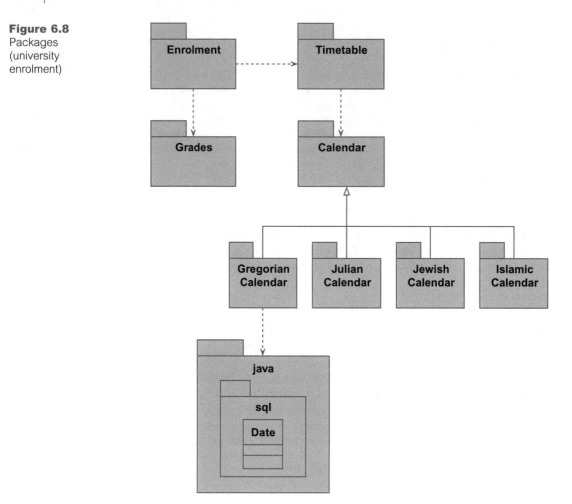

Figure 6.9
Component
notation

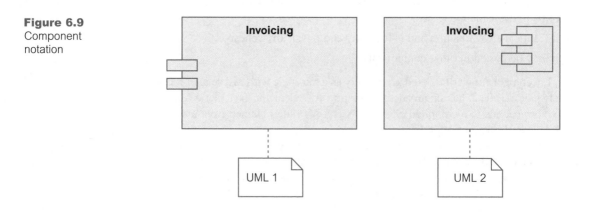

Figures 3.44 and 3.45 show examples of components (using the UML 1 notation). UML allows the modeling of component interfaces with the "lollipop" notation. If a dependency between components is negotiated through interfaces, then another component that realizes the same set of interfaces can replace a component.

Component versus package

6.3.2.1

A *package* is a grouping of modeling elements under an assigned name (Section 3.2.6.1). At the logical level, every class belongs to a single package. At the physical level, every class is implemented by at least one component, and it is possible that a component implements only one class. Abstract classes defining interfaces are frequently implemented by more than one component.

Packages are typically larger architectural units than components. They tend to group classes in a *horizontal* way – by static proximity of classes in the application domain. *Components* are *vertical* groups of classes with behavioral proximity – they may come from different domains, but they contribute to a single piece of business activity, perhaps a use case.

The above orthogonality of packages and components makes it difficult to establish dependencies between them. A frequent situation is that a logical package depends on a few physical components.

Example 6.2 (university enrolment)

Refer to the packages identified in Example 6.1 (Section 6.3.1). Consider the `Timetable` package. Assume that the package will be implemented as a C++ program that embodies the logic of allocation of university rooms to classes. The program accesses a database for room and class information. Two stored procedures will be implemented to provide that service to the program.

Draw a component diagram that demonstrates the dependencies between the package and the necessary components.

Figure 6.10 shows the component model. Three components are identified: `RoomAllocEXE`, `RoomUSP`, and `ClassUSP`. The package `Timetable` depends on these components.

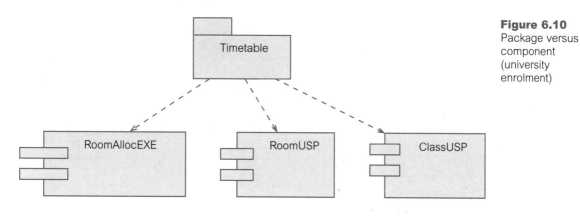

Figure 6.10
Package versus component (university enrolment)

6.3.2.2 Component versus class and interface

Like classes, components realize interfaces. The difference is twofold. First, a *component* is a physical abstraction deployed on some computer node. A *class* represents a logical thing that has to be implemented by a component to act as a physical abstraction.

Second, a component reveals only some interfaces of the classes that it contains. Many other interfaces are encapsulated by the component – they are used internally only by collaborating classes and are not visible to other components.

The interface that a component realizes may be implemented in a separate class. Such a class is called a *dominant class* (Rumbaugh *et al*., 1999). Since the dominant class represents the interface of the component, any object inside the component is reachable from the dominant class via composition links. "A dominant class subsumes the interface of the component" (Rumbaugh *et al*., 1999, p.219).

Example 6.3 (university enrolment)

Refer to the three components in Example 6.2 (Section 6.3.2.2). Assume that the component `RoomAllocEXE` initiates allocation of rooms to courses by providing the component `ClassUSP` with the class identification. To this aim, `ClassUSP` realizes the interface called `Allocate`.

The component `ClassUSP` does the rest of the job by requesting the room details from the component `RoomUSP`. To provide that service, `RoomUSP` implements the interface called `Reserve`.

Figure 6.11 demonstrates the component diagram corresponding to the requirements above.

Figure 6.11
Showing interfaces on the component diagram (university enrolment)

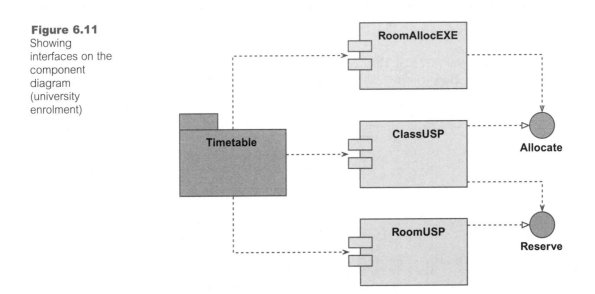

Nodes 6.3.3

In UML, a distributed physical architecture (Section 6.1) or any other architecture for the system is rendered as a *deployment diagram* (Section 3.2.6.3). A computational resource (a run-time physical object) in a deployment diagram is called a *node*. As a minimum, the node has a memory and some computing capability. The node can also be a database server, as contemporary databases are active (i.e. are programmable) servers.

In UML, a *node* is rendered graphically as a cube. The cube can be stereotyped and can contain constraints. The stereotyped cube can be an icon. Every node is given a unique name (a textual string).

A deployment diagram shows nodes and how they relate to each other. Nodes can be related by *connection relationships*. A connection relationship can be named to indicate the network protocol used (if applicable) or to characterize the connection in some other way. In general, a connection relationship is an *association* and can be modeled with typical association properties, such as the degree, multiplicity, and roles.

Figure 6.12 shows four nodes in a deployment diagram. The connection relationships indicate the form of communication between nodes.

Nodes are locations on which the components run. Nodes execute components. Components are deployed on a node. A node together with its components is sometimes called a *distribution unit* (Booch *et al.*, 1999).

Figure 6.13 shows a node called `CorporateDatabaseServer`. The node runs two stored procedures, which are represented as components `CustomerUSP` and `InvoiceUSP`.

Figure 6.14 is an alternative way of modeling the "containment" of components in a node. This notation can be extended so that the entire component diagram can be placed on a deployment diagram.

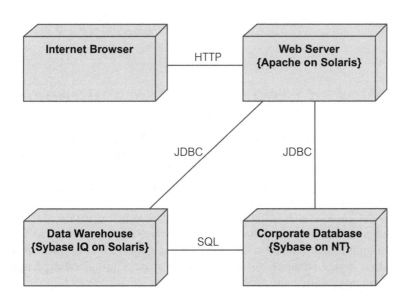

Figure 6.12
Nodes

Figure 6.13
A node with
dependencies to
components

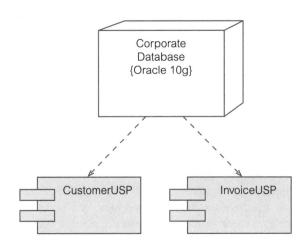

Figure 6.14
A node containing
components

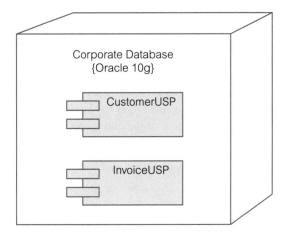

6.4 Principles of program design and reuse

Program design is an intrinsic part of overall system design. The *architectural design* (Sections 6.1–6.3) establishes the generic execution framework. The *detailed design* of the GUI and database specifies the front end and the back end of that framework. The program design fills in the gaps in this generic framework and turns it into a design document that can be handed over to a programmer for implementation.

Program design concentrates on one application program at a time. In this sense, program design is a direct extension of the *user interface design* discussed in Chapter 7. Program design is also an extension of the *database design*. It uses a portion (subschema) of the database design (Chapter 8), and it defines database procedural aspects – stored procedures and program-specific triggers.

The program's execution logic is split between the client and the server processes. The *client process* embodies most of the dynamic object collaboration in the program. A proper balance between object cohesion and coupling can harness the complexity of that collaboration. The *server process* takes care, among other things, of executing business transactions initiated by the *client process*.

Class cohesion and coupling   6.4.1

In passing, we have identified the main principles of good program design, albeit more in the context of overall system design. *Class layering* is the cornerstone of writing understandable, maintainable, and scalable programs. The proper use of *inheritance* and *delegation* is necessary to avoid delivering object-oriented programs that become legacy systems the day after deployment to the stakeholders.

A good program design ensures well-balanced *cohesion* and *coupling* of classes. The terms "cohesion" and "coupling" were coined by the structured design methods. However, the terms have a similar connotation and importance in object-oriented design (Page-Jones, 2000; Schach, 2002).

Class cohesion is the degree of inner self-determination of the class. It measures the strength of the class independence. A highly cohesive class performs one action or achieves a single goal. The stronger the cohesion the better.

Class coupling is the degree of connections between classes. It measures the class interdependence. The weaker the coupling the better (however, the classes have to be "coupled" to cooperate!).

Cohesion and coupling are at odds with each other. Better cohesion induces worse coupling, and vice versa. The task of the designer is to achieve the best balance between the two. Riel (1996) proposed a number of heuristics to address this issue:

■ Two classes should either be not dependent on one another or one class should be only dependent on the public interface of another class.

■ Attributes and the related methods should be kept in one class (this heuristic is frequently violated by classes that have many *accessor* (get, set) methods defined in their public interface).

■ A class should capture one and only one abstraction. Unrelated information, when a subset of methods operates on a proper subset of attributes, should be moved to another class.

■ The system intelligence should be distributed as uniformly as possible (so that classes share the work uniformly).

Kinds of class coupling   6.4.1.1

In order for two classes to communicate, they need to be "coupled." *Coupling* between class X and class Y exists if class X can refer *directly* to class Y. Page-Jones (2000) lists eight kinds of class coupling (which he calls direct class-reference set):

1. X inherits from Y;
2. X has an attribute of class Y;

3. X has a template attribute with a parameter of class Y;

4. X has a method with an input argument of class Y;

5. X has a method with an output argument of class Y;

6. X knows of a global variable of class Y;

7. X knows of a method containing a local variable of class Y;

8. X is a friend of Y.

6.4.1.2 The Law of Demeter

Class coupling is necessary for object communication, but it should be confined, as much as possible, to *within* the class layers (i.e. to the *intra-layer coupling*). *Inter-layer coupling* should be minimized and carefully channeled. An additional guidance for restricting the arbitrary communication between classes is offered in the Law of Demeter (Lieberherr and Holland, 1989).

The Law of Demeter specifies what targets are allowed for the messages within the class methods. It states that a target of a message can only be one of the following objects (Page-Jones, 2000):

- the method's object itself (i.e. this in C++ and Java, self and super in Smalltalk);
- an object that is an argument in the method's signature;
- an object referred to by the object's attribute (including an object referred to within a collection of attributes);
- an object created by the method;
- an object referred to by a global variable.

To restrict the coupling induced by inheritance, the third rule can be limited to the attributes defined in the class itself. An attribute inherited by the class cannot then be used to identify a target object for the message. This constraint is known as the *Strong Law of Demeter* (Page-Jones, 2000).

6.4.1.3 Accessor methods and mindless classes

As mentioned in Section 6.4.1, attributes and the related methods should be kept in one class (Riel, 1996). A class should decide its own destiny. A class can restrict other classes from accessing its own state by limiting the accessor methods in its interface. *Accessor methods* define the *observer* (get) or *mutator* (set) operations.

Accessor methods "open up" a class to internal manipulation by other classes. While coupling implies a certain amount of exploitation, an excessive availability of accessor methods may lead to a non-uniform distribution of intelligence among classes. A class with many accessor methods risks becoming *mindless* – other classes decide what is good for it.

This said, there are situations when a class has to open up to other classes. This happens whenever there is a need to implement a policy between two or more classes (Riel, 1996). Examples are abounding.

Suppose that we have two classes `Integer` and `Real` and we need to implement a "policy" for the conversion between integer and real numbers. In which of the two classes is the policy to be implemented? Do we need a `Converter` class to implement the policy? Either way, at least one of these two classes must allow accessor methods, and it will then become "mindless" with regard to that policy.

A famous quote from Page-Jones is appropriate: "On an object-oriented farm there is an object-oriented milk. Should the object-oriented cow send the object-oriented milk the uncow_yourself message, or should the object-oriented milk send the object-oriented cow the unmilk_yourself message?" (Page-Jones at OOPSLA'87.)

Example 6.4 (university enrolment)

Assume that we need to add a student to a course offering. To do so, we need to do two checks. First, we have to find out prerequisite courses for the course offering. Second, we have to check the student's academic record to establish whether the student satisfies the prerequisites. With this knowledge, we can decide whether the student can be added to the course offering.

Consider that a message `enrol()` is to be sent by a control object `:CEnroll`. Consider that three classes – `ECourseOffering`, `ECourse`, and `EStudent` – collaborate to accomplish the task. `EStudent` knows how to get the academic record, and `ECourse` knows how to find its prerequisites.

Our task is to design a range of possible interaction diagrams to solve the problem. Discuss the pros and cons of different solutions.

Figure 6.15 illustrates the first solution by means of both a sequence diagram and a collaboration diagram. The control object `CEnroll` initiates the transaction by sending the `enrol()` message to `ECourse`. `ECourse` asks `EStudent` for the academic record and checks it against its prerequisites. `ECourse` decides if `EStudent` can be enrolled and requests that `ECourseOffering` adds `EStudent` to its list of students.

The scenario in Figure 6.15 gives too much power to the class `ECourse`. `ECourse` is the policy maker. `EStudent` is mindless. The solution is unbalanced, but there is no clear way out.

We could switch the emphasis from `ECourse` to `EStudent` to obtain the solution presented in Figure 6.16. Now `CEnroll` asks `EStudent` to do the main job. `EStudent` invokes an observer method `getPrereq()` on `ECourse`. `EStudent` decides whether the enrolment is possible and instructs `ECourseOffering` to enroll the student.

Figure 6.17 illustrates a more balanced solution in which `ECourseOffering` is the policy maker. The solution is impartial with regard to `ECourse` and `EStudent`, but it makes these two objects quite idle and mindless. `ECourseOffering` acts like the "main program" (a *"God" class* in Riel's parlance (Riel, 1996)).

All solutions so far are *distributed* in nature, very much as advocated in Section 4.3.3.3. A *centralized* solution is also possible. Such a solution could rely on `CEnroll` as the policy maker. However, a better approach would be to have a separate class for the task. Such a class could be placed in the PCMEF's *mediator* layer and could be called `MEnrolmentPolicy`.

Figure 6.15
ECourse as
policy maker
(university
enrolment)

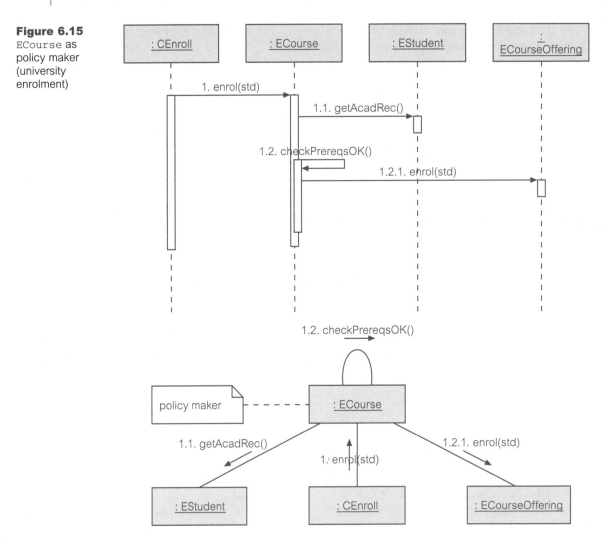

The mediator class MEnrolmentPolicy in Figure 6.18 decouples the three entity classes from the enrolment policy. This is beneficial because any changes to the enrolment policy are encapsulated in a single mediator class. However, there is a risk that the class MEnrolmentPolicy can grow into a "God" class.

6.4.1.4 Dynamic classification and mixed-instance cohesion

In Section 3.1.6.5, we raised the issue of *dynamic classification* and observed that the popular object-oriented programming environments do not support it. The price for this lack of support is frequently reflected in designing classes with *mixed-instance cohesion*.

Page-Jones (2000) states that "a class with *mixed-instance cohesion* has some features that are undefined for some objects of the class." Some methods of the class apply only to

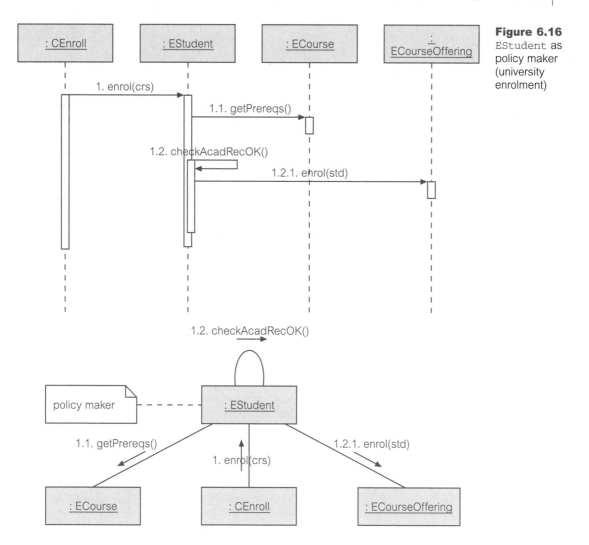

Figure 6.16
EStudent as
policy maker
(university
enrolment)

a subset of objects in that class, and some attributes make sense only for a subset of objects.

For example, the class Employee may define objects that are "ordinary" employees and managers. A manager is paid an allowance. Sending a message payAllowance to an Employee object does not make sense if that Employee object is not a manager.

To eliminate the mixed-instance cohesion, we need to extend the generalization hierarchy to identify Employee subclasses such as OrdinaryEmployee and Manager. However, an Employee object may be an OrdinaryEmployee one day and a Manager another day, or vice versa. To eliminate the mixed-instance cohesion, we need to allow objects to change classes dynamically at run time – the proverbial Catch-22 situation, if the dynamic classification is not supported.

Figure 6.17
`ECourseOffering`
as policy maker
(university
enrolment)

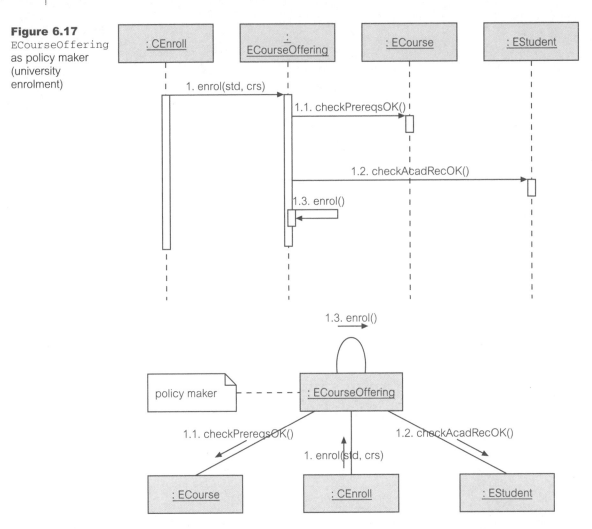

Example 6.5 (university enrolment)

Consider the following variations to Example 6.4:

■ Evening course offerings are available only to part-time students.

■ Full-time students may enroll only in daytime course offerings.

■ There is a small extra fee if a part-time student wants to enroll in an evening course offering.

■ A part-time student is automatically considered full-time when enrolled in more than six credit points (i.e. normally more than two course offerings) in a given semester (and vice versa).

Our task is to propose a highly cohesive class model with no mixed-instance cohesion. The model should then be critically appraised, and an alternative solution that avoids the problem of dynamic classification should be suggested and discussed.

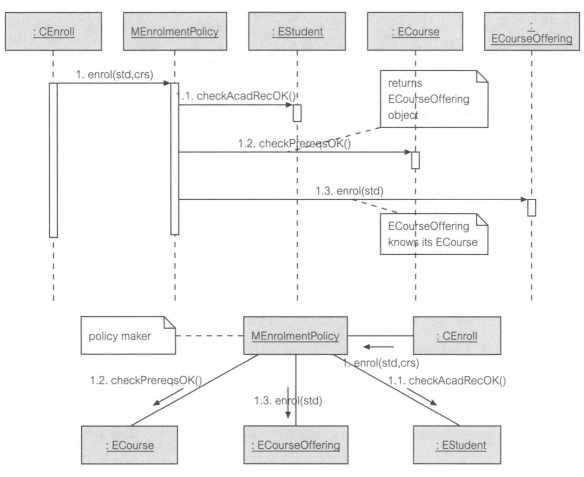

Figure 6.18 MEnrolmentPolicy as policy maker (university enrolment)

To eliminate the mixed-instance cohesion, we need to specialize Student into two subclasses PartTimeStudent and FullTimeStudent (Figure 6.19). If every student must be either part-time or full-time, then the class Student is *abstract*. The message payExtraFee(crs_off) will never be sent to an object of class FullTimeStudent, because FullTimeStudent does not have a method for it.

Granted, we still have a problem. A part-time student may have a preference for day-time course offerings (i.e. eveningPreference = 'False'), and no extra fees are then paid. In other words, we still have *mixed-instance cohesion* in PartTimeStudent. Sending a message payExtraFee(crsoff) to a PartTimeStudent will not make sense if the student takes a daytime course offering.

Figure 6.20 extends the design to eliminate this second aspect of mixed-instance cohesion. The class DayPrefPartTimeStudent does not have the method payExtraFee (crsoff). But what if a DayPrefPartTimeStudent is forced to take an evening course offering because there are no more places available in daytime course offerings?

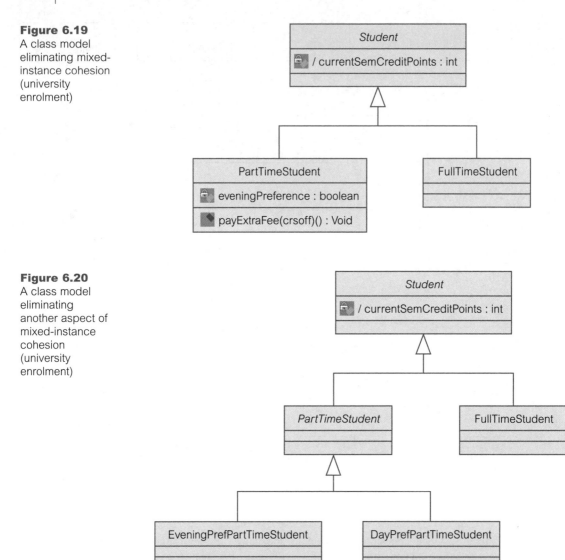

Perhaps some other fee would then apply. Should we specialize further to derive a class `UnluckyDayPrefPartTimeStudent`?

Short of getting into ridiculous situations, we may opt to abandon the idea of pushing the elimination of mixed-instance cohesion any further. And we have not even mentioned the dynamic classification yet. In reality, the current value of the attribute `currentSemCreditPoints` determines if a student is part-time or full-time.

Similarly, a student can change his/her preference for the evening or daytime course offerings at any time. In the absence of the programming environment's support for *dynamic classification*, it would be a programmer's responsibility to allow an object to change the class at run time. That's tough – very tough in the case of persistent objects with OID values containing class identifiers.

The alternative is to restrict the depth of the inheritance hierarchy, eliminate the need for dynamic classification, and reintroduce a certain amount of mixed-instance cohesion. For example, we can hang on to the class model in Figure 6.19 and resolve the problem of the evening preference by allowing an object to respond differently to the message `payExtraFee(crsoff)` depending on the value of the attribute `eveningPreference`. This can be programmed with an `if` statement as shown in the pseudo-code below:

```
method payExtraFee(crsoff) for the class PartTimeStudent
          if eveningPreference = 'False'
                  return
          else
                  do it
end method
```

Although the use of `if` statements in object-oriented code signifies an abandoning of inheritance and polymorphism, it may be unavoidable for purely pragmatic reasons. Rather than struggling with *dynamic classification*, the programmer introduces the *dynamic semantics* to a class. An object responds differently to the same message depending on its current local state. A statechart diagram would be used to design the dynamic semantics for the class. Admittedly, the *cohesion* of the class suffers in the process.

Reuse strategy 6.4.2

UML defines *reuse* as "the use of pre-existing artifacts" (Rumbaugh *et al.*, 1999). In passing, we discussed the object-oriented *techniques* for software reuse, such as inheritance and delegation (Sections 5.2 and 5.3). In this section, we address the *strategies* of software reuse. It turns out that the strategies also imply the granularity at which the reuse is done. The *granularity* can be:

- the class
- the component
- the solution idea.

Associated with granularity, there are three corresponding strategies for reuse (Coad *et al.*, 1995; Gamma *et al.*, 1995):

1. toolkits (class libraries)
2. frameworks
3. analysis and design patterns.

Toolkit reuse 6.4.2.1

A *toolkit* emphasizes *code reuse* at a class level. In this kind of reuse the programmer "fills the gaps" in the program by making calls to *concrete classes* in some library of classes. The main body of the program is not reused – it is written by the programmer.

There are two kinds (levels) of toolkit (Page-Jones, 2000):

1. foundation toolkits
2. architecture toolkits.

The *foundation classes* are widely provided by object programming environments. They include classes to implement primitive data types (such as `String`), structured data types (such as `Date`), and collections (such as `Set`, `List`, or `Index`).

The *architecture classes* are normally available as part of system software, such as an operating system, database software, or GUI software. For example, when we buy an object database system, what we really get is an architecture toolkit that implements the expected functionalities of the system, such as persistency, transactions, and concurrency.

6.4.2.2   Framework reuse

A *framework* emphasizes design reuse at a component level (Sections 3.2.6.2 and 6.3.2). As opposed to toolkit reuse, a framework provides the skeleton of the program. The programmer then "fills the gaps" in this skeleton (customizes it) by writing the code that the framework needs to call. Apart from concrete classes (for the framework itself), a framework provides a large volume of abstract classes to be implemented (customized) by the programmer.

A framework is a customizable application software. The best examples of frameworks are ERP (enterprise resource planning systems) such as SAP, PeopleSoft, Baan, or J.D. Edwards. However, the reuse in those systems is not based on pure object-oriented techniques.

Object-oriented frameworks for IS development are proposed within distributed component technologies such as CORBA, DCOM, and EJB (Section 1.1.1). They are known as "*business objects*" – "shippable" products to meet specific business or application needs. For example, a business object could be an accounting framework with customizable classes such as `Invoice` or `Customer`.

While frameworks are an attractive reuse proposition, they also have a number of drawbacks. Perhaps the most significant one is that the generic "lowest common denominator" solutions, which they deliver, are suboptimal or even obsolete. As a result, they do not give a competitive advantage to their adopters and can create a maintenance burden when chasing state-of-the-art solutions.

6.4.2.3   Pattern reuse

Patterns emphasize the reuse to the development approach. They provide ideas and examples for object interactions (Sections 3.2.4 and 4.3.3) that are known to represent good development practices leading to understandable and scalable solutions (collaborations are discussed in Section 6.5). Patterns can apply to the analysis or design phase of the development lifecycle (hence, *analysis patterns* and *design patterns*).

A pattern is a documented solution that has been shown to work well in a number of situations. These situations are identified and can be used as an index entry for the developer seeking a solution to the problem. Any known disadvantages or side effects of a pattern are listed to allow the developer to take a knowledgeable decision.

Pattern reuse is largely conceptual, though many design patterns contain sample code for the programmer's reuse. The scope of a *design pattern* (e.g. Gamma *et al.*, 1995) is that of an interaction sequence – typically larger than a class but smaller than a component. The scope of an *analysis pattern* (e.g. Fowler, 1997) depends on the level of modeling abstraction at which the pattern applies.

Behavioral and structural collaboration

The architectural design makes an impact on the detailed design in that it determines the target hardware/software platform that the detailed design must conform to. Apart from that, the detailed design is a direct continuation from the analysis. The objective is to turn the analysis models into detailed design documents from which the programmers can implement the system.

In analysis, we simplify the models by abstracting away the details that interfere with the presentation of a particular viewpoint of the system. In design, we tend to do exactly the opposite. We take one architectural part of the system at a time and add technical details to the models or create brand new design models at a low level of abstraction.

In passing, we used the term *collaboration* freely, and exchangeably with the term *interaction*, to refer to sets of objects collaborating to perform a task. In UML, the use of the term "collaboration" is terribly overloaded and changing between UML versions. The problem arises partly from the popularity of collaboration diagrams as one of the two techniques, apart from sequence diagrams, to model interactions (Section 3.2.4). Not surprisingly, UML 2 attempted to change the name of collaboration diagrams to *communication diagrams*, but acceptance of this change remains in waiting.

Short of adding to the confusion, we follow here the longstanding meaning of *collaboration* as a specification for the *realization* of use cases and operations (Booch *et al.*, 1999; Rumbaugh *et al.*, 1999). Such a specification consists of a *structural collaboration* represented by a class model and a *behavioral collaboration* represented by an interaction model (sequence or collaboration diagram).

To specify the realization of a use case (or operation), we need to have a prior detailed description of that use case (or operation). This is the purpose of a *use-case document*, discussed next.

Use-case document

As explained in Sections 3.2.1 and 4.3.1, use cases draw their strength from text descriptions of flows of events, not from the graphical visualization of use cases in diagrams. The design and implementation of programs, as well as many other lifecycle activities (such as testing), strictly follow the specifications in use-case documents.

There are many possible formats for writing a use-case document. Section 3.2.1.4 presented one such format. Irrespective of the format, a use-case document must be detailed enough to answer most, if not all, a programmer's questions. To assist in this task, use-case documents are sometimes supplemented with the sketches of GUI designs.

Example 6.6 (advertising expenditure)

Refer to exercises for advertising expenditure measurement at the end of Chapters 2 and 5. In particular, the Category–Product GUI window in Figure 5.25 can help in understanding the context of this example.

The AE system measures expenditure (costs) for advertising various products through different media. To do it properly, the AE system must maintain a coherent list of products, classify the products into categories, and recognize various brand names of products.

This example aims at writing a use-case document for maintaining product information in the AE system. Because typical maintenance activities consist of four operations – create, read, update, and delete product data – the use case is named *CRUD Product*.

The use-case document for Example 6.6 is given in Table 6.1. The document conforms to the document template previously defined and exemplified in Table 3.2 (Section 3.2.1.4) and Table 4.4 (Section 4.3.1.3).

6.5.2 Behavioral collaboration

The *behavioral part* represents the dynamics that show how the static elements collaborate. The behavioral part is modeled as *interactions* (Sections 3.2.4, 4.3.3). Apart from sequence diagrams, collaboration diagrams are frequently used for the behavioral specification of collaborations. In practice, the structural and behavioral aspects of the collaboration are likely to be developed concurrently.

Table 6.1 Use-case document for "CRUD Product" (advertising expenditure)

Use Case	CRUD Product
Brief description	This use case enables the user of the AE system to maintain information about products. It includes facilities to view (read) a list of products, create a new product, delete a product, and update the information about a product.
Actors	`Data Collection Employee`, `Data Verification Employee`, `Valorization Employee`, `Reporting Employee`.
Preconditions	The actor possesses system privileges to maintain products. Any `Employee` can view a list of products. Only `Data Collection Employees` and `Data Verification Employees` can create, update, or delete products.
Main flow	*1. Basic flow* This use case starts when an `Employee` chooses to work with `Products` by selecting the `Maintain Products` option of the AE system. The system retrieves and displays the following information for all products in a browse window. The *Read Products* subflow is performed. The `Data Collection Employee` or `Data Verification Employee` can choose to create, update, or delete a product. A corresponding dialog box window is displayed consisting of a group of fields. Non-editable fields are grayed and the cursor cannot be placed on them.

Table 6.1 (*cont'd*)

Use Case	CRUD Product

Most fields have names (prompts). The fields display the following information: `product_id`, `product_name`, `category_name`, `brand_name`, `product_status`, `created_by`, `last_modified_by`, `created_on`, `last_modified_on`, `notes`.

The dialog box window does not have an associated menu – events are activated by command buttons: `OK` and `Cancel`. The `OK` button applies the values in the window to the database and closes the window. The `Cancel` button ignores all changes, cancels the operation the user chose, and closes the window.

There are three operation modes of dialog box window: *Insert Product*, *Update Product*, and *Delete Product*.

The `Record` menu in the main menu bar is a principal way of opening a dialog box window in a particular mode. The corresponding toolbar buttons provide for accelerated opening of a dialog box window.

The dialog box window is modal – the user has to complete interaction within this window and close it before continuing with any further interaction outside the window.

Navigation between fields can be done from the keyboard by pressing `TAB` (next field) and `SHIFT+TAB` (previous field). Pressing `ENTER` navigates to the default command button – the `OK` button.

If the `Data Collection and Verification Supervisor` chooses to create a new product, the *Create Product* subflow is performed.

If the `Data Collection and Verification Supervisor` chooses to modify information about a product, the *Update Product* subflow is performed.

If the `Data Collection and Verification Supervisor` chooses to delete a product, the *Delete Product* subflow is performed.

If the `Quality Control Person` chooses to exit, the use case ends.

2. Subflows

2.1 Read products

The following information is displayed in the AE row browser window: `product_name`, `category_name`, `notes`, `created_by`, `last_modified_by`, `created_on`, `last_modified_on`.

The information is displayed in a tabular (columns and rows) view, with vertical and horizontal scroll bars, if necessary.

The display is named `Products`, and all columns are named.

The order of columns on screen can be changed (using drag and drop action).

The user can add additional columns to the browser (using right-click pop-up menu from the column bar). Optional columns that can be added are `product_id`, `category_id`, `brand_id`, `brand_name`, `product_status`.

The user can remove any column from the browser except `product_name` (using right-click pop-up menu from the column bar).

The values displayed in the rows are not editable. Double-clicking on the row opens up an *Update Product* window.

Rows can be *sorted* on two designated columns: `product_name` and `product_id`. Sort columns are distinguished visually from other columns. The current sort column is also visually distinct.

Table 6.1 (*cont'd*)

Use Case	CRUD Product

2.2 Create product

The system displays the *CreateProduct* dialog box window.

The non-editable fields are `product_id`, `created_by`, `last_modified_by`, `created_on`, `last_modified_on`. These fields have prompts but no values.

The value of the `product_id` field is automatically assigned by the database's identifier creation capability when product is inserted into the database.

The editable fields are `product_name`, `category_name`, `brand_name`, `product_status`, `notes`.

The fields that allow values to be typed in are `product_name`, `notes`.

The fields that allow a value to be selected from a database picklist (which opens by clicking at the down-arrow button) are `category_name`, `brand_name`, `product_status`.

Alternative flows: *AF1, AF2*.

2.3 Update product

The system displays the *Update Product* dialog box window and displays the product name in the title bar.

The non-editable fields are `product_id`, `created_by`, `last_modified_by`, `created_on`, `last_modified_on`. These fields have prompts and values.

The editable fields are `product_name`, `category_name`, `brand_name`, `product_status`, `notes`.

The fields that allow new values to be typed in are `product_name`, `notes`.

The fields that allow a new value to be selected from a database picklist (which opens by clicking at the down-arrow button) are `category_name`, `brand_name`, `product_status`.

Alternative flows: *AF1, AF2, AF4*.

2.4 Delete product

The system displays the *Delete Product* dialog box window and displays the product name in the title bar.

All fields are non-editable, and the system displays values in all fields.

Alternative flows: *AF3, AF4*.

Alternative flows	*AF1*	The system will not allow a product to be created/updated with a `product_name` that already exists in the database.
	AF2	The system will not allow a product to be created/updated without assigning the product to a `category_name` and `brand_name`.
	AF3	The system will not allow a product linked to adlinks to be deleted.
	AF4	The system will not allow any two update/delete dialog box windows to be opened for the same product by more than one user.

Postconditions	After a product has been successfully created/updated, the browser window highlights the row with that product information.
	After a product has been successfully deleted, the browser window is refreshed and highlights the first visible row.
	After the user exits from the use case, the `Products` window is closed.

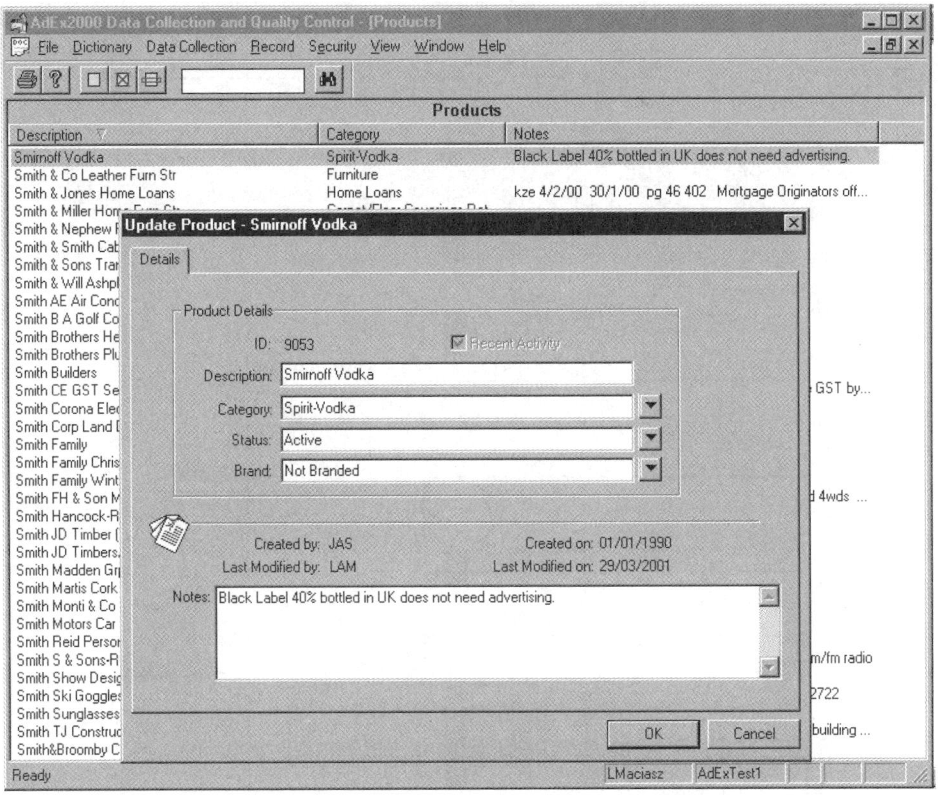

Figure 6.21
Update Product
window
(advertising
expenditure)
Source: Courtesy
of Nielsen Media
Research, Sydney,
Australia

Example 6.7 (advertising expenditure)

Refer to the exercise for advertising expenditure at the end of Chapter 5 and to Example 6.6 (Section 6.5.1). Consider the *Update Product* subflow in the use-case document in Table 6.1. Refer also to the the Update Product window in Figure 6.21.

Our task is to create a sequence and a collaboration diagram for the behavioral aspect of the *Update Product* collaboration. Restrict the design to the following actions: (1) a new Update Product window is launched from the Product Browser window (a primary window that lists the products); (2) initialize editable fields in the window (ignore non-editable fields); (3) assume that only the category_name field gets updated; and (4) the user clicks the OK button to save changes.

There is no need to introduce control classes. A presentation class is allowed to talk directly to an entity class. However, assume the existence of a mediator class, called MMapper, which has the knowledge of entity objects and can map primary keys of objects (such as category_name) to these objects (or to the OIDs of these objects).

Figure 6.22 presents a sequence diagram for Example 6.7. The model takes advantage of the UML notation to create a new object and to destroy it. The PUpdateProduct window is created with the new(prd) message. The constructor in PUpdateProduct gets the reference to the EProduct object from PProductBrowser (in the argument of new(prd)). However, as it is possible in a database system that EProduct has been

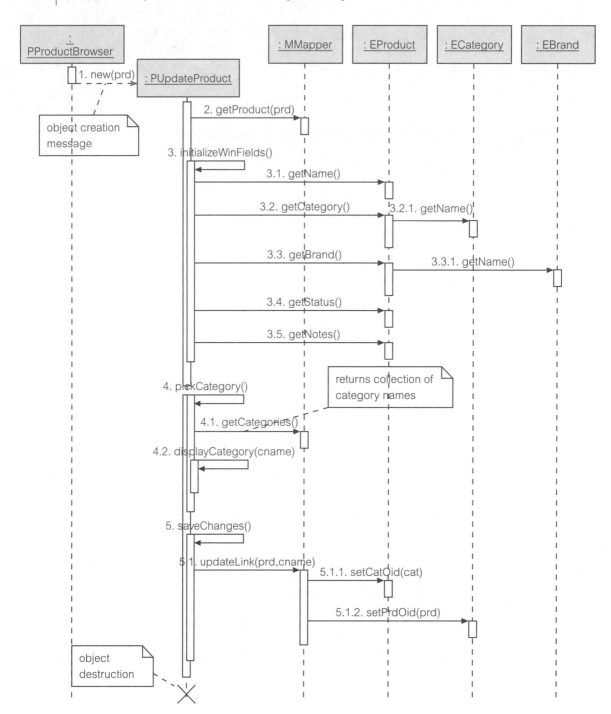

Figure 6.22 The sequence diagram for behavioral collaboration in Update Product (advertising expenditure)

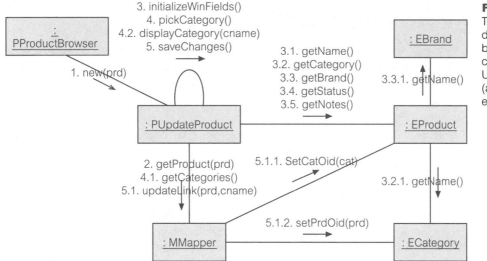

Figure 6.23
The collaboration diagram for behavioral collaboration in Update Product (advertising expenditure)

deleted/updated in the meantime by another user, PUpdateProduct immediately requests the EProduct from MMapper.

Since PUpdateProduct has the EProduct object, it can initiate a series of observer (get) messages to populate the editable fields in the window. To get category_name and brand_name values, EProduct uses its association links to ECategory and EBrand to return these values to PUpdateProduct.

Next, the sequence diagram considers a situation where the user clicks on the small picklist arrow for categories. PUdateProduct asks MMapper to get the complete list of category names. Because the mapper maps primary keys to objects, there is no need to ask all ECategory objects to return their category names. Assuming that a user picked a category from the opened picklist, PUpdateProduct displays a new category name.

Finally, the user presses the OK button to save changes. Since the only change considered is the new category name, PUpdateProduct sends an updateLink() to MMapper, passing along cname (category_name) and prd (the EProduct object). MMapper is now in position to set a new association link between EProduct and ECategory.

Figure 6.23 is a collaboration diagram corresponding to the sequence diagram in Figure 6.22. If the visual advantage (in terms of space saving) of collaboration diagrams over sequence diagrams for presenting large models has not yet been obvious, comparison of the two figures should bring this point home.

Structural collaboration 6.5.3

Collaboration has a behavioral and a structural part. The *structural part* represents the static aspect of collaboration. It is represented by a subset of class diagram corresponding to the scope of collaboration. The class diagram is *elaborated* (in comparison with its analysis version) with the implementation details. In particular, the signatures of class operations should be stated.

Example 6.8 (advertising expenditure)

Refer to Example 6.7 (Section 6.5.3). Create a class diagram for the structural aspect of the *Update Product* collaboration. There is no need to include data members in classes, just methods. However, association and dependency relationships should be defined.

Figure 6.24 is a class diagram for Example 6.8. The dependency relationships from `PUpdateProduct` to `MMapper` and `EProduct` would not be allowed by the principles of the PCEMF framework, but the example makes an exception by not introducing a control class between these classes.

A question regarding the `product_status` field may be raised with regard to Examples 6.7 and 6.8. This is a picklist field, very much like `category_name` and `brand_name`. The reason that there is no `EStatus` class can be explained by a fixed and short list of values (active, passive, etc.) that would be kept in such a class. It may, therefore, be permissible to hard-code these values in the program rather than to maintain a separate class structure for it.

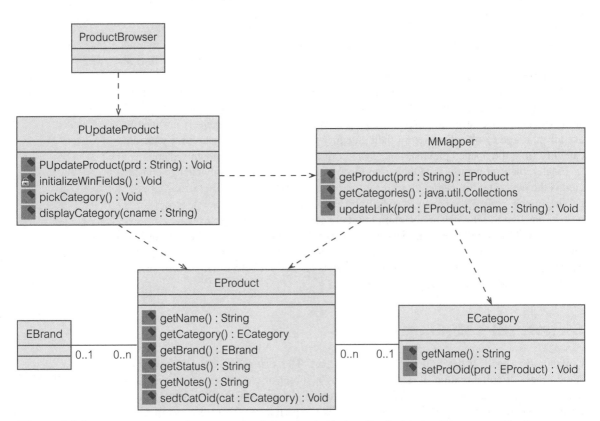

Figure 6.24 The class diagram for structural collaboration in Update Product (advertising expenditure)

Summary

If the previous chapter has moved us from analysis to design, this chapter has made it clear that design is about system implementation. The chapter addressed the two main (and distinct) aspects of design: the architectural design of the system; and the detailed design of the programs in the system.

Typical IS applications are based on the *client/server* architectural principle. Specific C/S solutions include *distributed processing systems* and *distributed database systems*. *Multi-tier systems* extend the basic C/S architecture by placing an application/business logic and the web services on separate tiers. *Database* technologies make an important contribution to modern system architectures.

Modern software systems are very complex. It is important that the modeling solutions simplify and reduce this inherent complexity as much as possible. Perhaps the most important mechanism for handling software complexity is the *hierarchical layering* of system architectures. Proper structuring of classes in *layers* (packages, subsystems), organized according to the PCMEF or similar framework, is an important architectural objective.

Architectural modeling encompasses allocation of software elements (classes, interfaces, etc.) into packages, components, and nodes. There are intricate dependencies and interactions between these concepts, mostly because of how they intersect with regard to logical and physical program and data structures.

A well-designed program maximizes *class cohesion* while minimizing *class coupling*. The coupling and cohesion principles can be achieved if the design obeys the *Law of Demeter*, which specifies the allowed object targets for the messages within the class methods. The excessive use of *accessor methods* can lead to *mindless classes*. *Mixed-instance cohesion*, albeit undesirable, may need to be allowed sporadically because the programming environment does not support *dynamic classification*.

Reuse is a major design consideration affecting architectural as well as detailed design issues. The choices are between *toolkit reuse*, *framework reuse*, and *pattern reuse*. The choices are not exclusive – a mix of reuse strategies is recommended. Reuse from external sources has to be aligned with the internal design of packages, *components*, classes, and interfaces. The computational resources are eventually represented as *deployment* diagrams.

The detailed design concentrates on *collaborations*. A collaboration specifies the realization of a use case or an operation. A collaboration models the message passing between objects. Issues to consider, and discussed in previous chapters, include overriding, overloading, iteration, templates, self-messages, asynchronous messages, and callbacks. *Structural* aspects of collaboration are modeled in class diagrams; *behavioral* aspects in sequence and/or collaboration diagrams.

Questions

Q1 Explain the difference between a distributed processing system and a distributed database system.

Q2 What is a three-tier architecture? What are its advantages and disadvantages?

Q3 What do we mean by an active database?

Q4 What is the complexity of a network of nine classes (measured as the number of possible connections between these classes)? Draw a hierarchy with four layers for these nine classes. What reduction in complexity can be achieved in a four-layer hierarchy?

Q5 Suppose that a class model for a banking application contains a class called `Interest-Calculation`. What PCMEF layer does that class belong to? Explain.

Q6 What is the purpose of the mediator layer in the PCMEF approach?

Q7 What is the purpose of the foundation layer in the PCMEF approach?

Q8 Compare toolkit and framework reuse.

Q9 How are components and packages related to each other?

Q10 How is the design affected by the principles of class cohesion and coupling?

Q11 What is a "mindless class?"

Q12 Explain the correlations between dynamic classification and mixed-instance cohesion.

Q13 How could we classify message/method types (apart from constructors and destructors)?

Q14 A sender of a message may or may not send itself (its OID) to the target object. Does this statement apply to asynchronous messages? Explain.

Q15 What is the difference between overriding and overloading?

Q16 What is collaboration? Which UML diagram is used for designing the structural aspect of collaboration? Explain its suitability for this task.

Q17 Which UML diagrams can be used for designing the behavioral aspect of collaboration? Compare their suitability for this task.

Q18 Object systems implement the many multiplicity of an association link by means of some collection (set, list, etc.) of references. In Java, the implementation would normally use the `Collection` interface from a Java library `java.util.Collection`. In C++, the implementation would normally use the notion of a parameterized type known as a class template. Discuss how the associations in class models in Figures 5.12 and 5.13 (Section 5.1.5) would be implemented in Java and in C++.

Exercises (video store)

Additional requirements (video store)

Consider the following additional requirements for video store (repeated here from the end of Chapter 4 for convenience):

1. Tapes/disks returned late induce a payment equal to an extra rental period. Each movie medium has a unique identification number.

2. Movies are ordered from suppliers who are generally able to supply tapes/disks within one week. Typically, several movies are ordered in a single order to a supplier.

3. Reservations are accepted for a movie that is on order and/or because all copies of a particular movie are rented out. Reservations are also accepted for movies that are neither in store nor on order, but a customer is then asked for a deposit of one rental period.

4. Customers can make many reservations, but a separate reservation request is prepared for each movie reserved. A reservation may be canceled due to the lack of response from a customer, more precisely one week from the date the customer was contacted that the movie was available for rental. If a deposit has been paid, it is then credited to the customer's account.

5. The database stores the usual information about suppliers and customers, i.e. addresses, phone numbers, etc. Each order to a supplier identifies the ordered movies, tape/disk formats, and quantities, and also an expected delivery date, purchase price, and applicable discounts.

6. When a tape/disk is returned by a customer or is delivered from a supplier, reservations are satisfied first. This involves contacting the customer who made the reservation. In order to ensure that reservations are properly handled, both the "reserved movie has arrived" contact with the customer and the subsequent rental to the customer are related back to the reservation. These steps ensure that reservations are properly carried through.

7. A customer can borrow many tapes or disks, but each borrowed video medium constitutes a separate rental record. For each rental, the checkout, due-in, and return dates and times are recorded. The rental record is later updated to indicate that the video has been returned and that the final payment (or reimbursement) has been made. The clerk who authorizes the rental is also recorded. Details about a customer and rentals are kept for a year to enable the customer rating to be determined based on historical information. Old rental details are kept for auditing purposes for the year.

8. All transactions are made by cash, electronic money transfer, or credit card. Customers are required to pay the rental charges when tapes/disks are checked out.

9. When a tape/disk is returned late (or it cannot be returned for whatever reason), a payment is taken either from the customer's account or directly from the customer.

10. If a tape/disk is overdue by more than two days, an overdue notice is sent to the customer. Once two overdue notices on a single tape/disk have been sent, the customer is noted as delinquent, and the next rental is subject to the manager's decision to remove the delinquent rating.

F1   Refer to the requirements above, to various examples for video store in Chapters 3 and 4, and in particular to the use-case model in Figure 4.13 (Section 4.3.1.3).

     Design a structural collaboration diagram for the realization of the "Reserve Video" use case.

F2   Refer to the requirements above, to various examples for video store in Chapters 3 and 4, and in particular to the use-case model in Figure 4.13 (Section 4.3.1.3).

     Design a behavioral collaboration diagram for the realization of the "Reserve Video" use case.

F3   Refer to the requirements above, to various examples for video store in Chapters 3 and 4, and in particular to the use-case model in Figure 4.13 (Section 4.3.1.3).

     Design a structural collaboration diagram for the realization of the "Return Video" use case.

F4   Refer to the requirements above, to various examples for video store in Chapters 3 and 4, and in particular to the use-case model in Figure 4.13 (Section 4.3.1.3).

     Design a behavioral collaboration diagram for the realization of the "Return Video" use case.

F5   Refer to the additional requirements above, to various examples for video store in Chapters 3 and 4, and in particular to the use-case model in Figure 4.13 (Section 4.3.1.3).

     Design a structural collaboration diagram for the realization of the "Order Video" use case.

> **F6** Refer to the additional requirements above, to various examples for video store in Chapters 3 and 4, and in particular to the use-case model in Figure 4.13 (Section 4.3.1.3).
>
> Design a behavioral collaboration diagram for the realization of the "Order Video" use case.

> **F7** Refer to the additional requirements above, to various examples for video store in Chapters 3 and 4, and in particular to the use-case model in Figure 4.13 (Section 4.3.1.3).
>
> Design a structural collaboration diagram for the realization of the "Maintain Customer" use case.

> **F8** Refer to the additional requirements above, to various examples for video store in Chapters 3 and 4, and in particular to the use-case model in Figure 4.13 (Section 4.3.1.3).
>
> Design a behavioral collaboration diagram for the realization of the "Maintain Customer" use case.

> **F9** Refer to Example 4.17 (Section 4.3.2.3). Consider the action `Update Stock` in Figure 4.15. Draw an activity diagram for the realization of the operation `Update Stock`.

Exercises (advertising expenditure)

For questions G2 and G3 below, consider the following additional information on the AE system.

- The AE system maintains associations between an ad, the product it advertises, the advertiser who pays for the exposure of the ad, and the agency responsible for booking that exposure. These associations are called *adlinks*. Outlets that have exposed the ad can be derived from the descriptions of ad instances of that ad.

- The AE system allows the business relationships of an adlink to be changed, i.e. to change the advertiser, agency, or product associated with an ad. This may be done as a simple update when a correction is required (i.e. when a human error occurred before). This may also be done as a business change (e.g. when a different agency starts booking the ad). In the latter case, the historical business relationships (i.e. historical adlinks) are retained.

- The use case "*Relink Ad as Correction*" enables the user to modify an adlink by changing its advertiser, agency, or product ("relinking an ad" and "modifying an adlink" are conceptually the same function). The use case starts when the user selects an adlink in the Ad Link Row Browse window (Figure 6.25), uses the mouse right click to open a pop-up menu, and activates the "Modify Adlink" menu item.

- The resulting dialog box window, called "Modify Ad Links," serves a double purpose of relinking ads as corrections and relinking ads as business changes. Only one of these two options can be activated at a time (by means of the user selecting one of two option buttons provided in the dialog box).

- The "Modify Ad Links" window shows the adlink information (copied from the selected adlink in the browser window) and allows the user to change the adlink's agency and/or advertiser and/or product. Only agencies, advertisers, and products currently stored in the database can be used for the adlink modification. Any change of agency, advertiser, or product is immediately visible in the "Modify Ad Links" window, but the changes to the database are made only after the user presses the `Save` button. The changes can be canceled at any time prior to the user activating the `Save` action.

- In most circumstances, the modification of an adlink as correction will be defining a new association of the ad to advertiser, agency, and product where the advertiser–agency link has been defined before (in an existing adlink). In cases where a new relationship between the advertiser and agency is being created, only users with the system privileges to perform this task may create the new advertiser–agency link unless the association with the agency is the first for the advertiser (i.e. it is a new advertiser that has not been linked to an agency yet).

- The "Modify Ad Links" window in Figure 6.25 is shown on the background of the Ad Link row browse window. The analysis of both windows reveals that an ad can be linked several times to the same advertiser/agency/

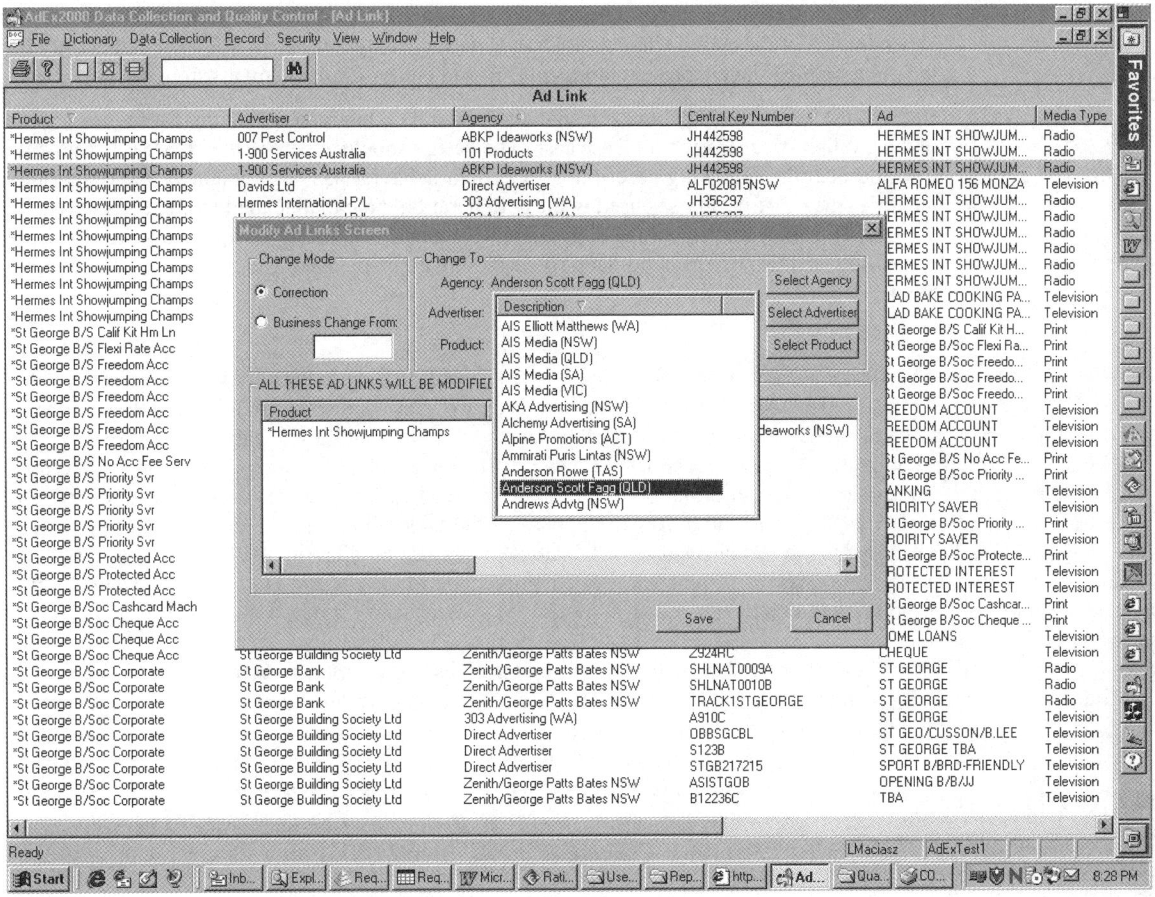

Figure 6.25 Ad Link Row Browse and Modify Ad Links windows
Source: Courtesy of Nielsen Media Research, Sydney, Australia

product. There are a few reasons why this may be the case, but this exercise does not explain these reasons (apart from the requirement that historical adlinks are to be retained in the database). Consequently, there is no expectation that a solution to the exercise will allow the possibility of an ad being linked several times to the same advertiser/agency/product.

■ When the "Modify Ad Links" screen is opened, all command buttons (except `Cancel`) and entry fields are disabled until the user selects the `Change Mode: Correction` or `Business Change` option button. The pane with adlinks contains a row with the details of the adlink to be modified. Once the mode has been selected, the user can press a command button `Select Agency`, `Select Advertiser`, or `Select Product`. Each of these command buttons pops up a picklist from which an agency, advertiser, or product can be selected into the corresponding fields.

■ Pressing `Save` modifies the ad's adlink with a new agency and/or advertiser and/or product. The dialog box is then dismissed and the primary window highlights the modified adlink and shows the corrected information. The Cancel button dismisses the dialog box without modifying the adlink.

G1 Refer to the problem statement in Section 1.5.5 and to "Solutions to exercises (advertising expenditure)" at the end of Chapter 2. Draw a package diagram for the AE system, but only for the three PCMEF layers presentation, control, and entity. Explain any assumptions.

G2 Refer to the requirements above. Design a behavioral collaboration diagram for the realization of the "Relink Ad as Correction" use case. The design should adhere to the PCMEF framework. Consider that the following description of system behavior has been obtained (the description identifies the principal classes used in the collaboration; note that no mediator classes are used). To identify events that trigger messages, show the guard conditions (in square brackets) in front of message names. There is no need to show signatures of messages and no need to number the messages.

When a :PAdlinkBrowser object receives a double-click event on an adlink row, it instantiates a :CAdlinkViewer. :CAdlinkViewer needs to refresh its state with the current information in the database. To this aim, it sends a getAdlink() message to :EAd that requests its adlinks in the get() message to :EAdlink. To refresh its state, :EAdlink instructs :FReader (by means of a refresh() message) to access the database. The refreshed adlink information is returned to :CAdlinkViewer, which instantiates a :PAdlinkModification to show the adlink row in the pane of the dialog box.

The behavioral collaboration model encapsulates all database access for reading in :FReader and access for database modification in :FUpdater. In practice, the communication between the classes in the foundation package layer and the persistent database is quite complex (Maciaszek and Liong, 2004) and is beyond this exercise.

The command buttons and entry fields in the dialog box are disabled until the user selects the Change Mode: Correction or Business Change. A setAction() message from :CMouseEvent informs :PAdlinkModification to enable buttons and fields. The selection of a command button on :CMouseEvent instantiates a :CPicklistViewer, which in turn instantiates a :PPicklist (by interrogating :EAgency, :EAdvertiser, or :EProduct and using :FReader to access the database). When the user picks an item from the picklist, a setField() message instructs :PAdlinkModification to update the relevant agency, advertiser, or product field on the screen.

When the user presses the OK button, :CMouseEvent sends a set() message to :EAdlink so that the user's corrections to the ad's adlink can be propagated down to the database. To achieve this, :EAdlink instantiates an :FUpdater. The instantiation triggers an update() self-message. Further intricacies of the update transaction are not to be shown.

G3 Refer to the solution to Exercise G2 below. Design a structural collaboration diagram for the realization of the "Relink Ad as Correction" use case. The object creation (new()) and destruction methods do not need to be shown. Instead, the instantiation relationships (dotted arrow-head lines) should show how objects are instantiated. The classes should also be connected by association/aggregation relationships (solid lines) and by dependency relationships (stereotyped with <<depends>>). There is no need to show relationship multiplicities. There is also no need to show signatures of methods.

Answers to odd-numbered questions

Q1 – answer
A distributed database system is a superset of a distributed processing system. In a *distributed processing system*, a client program can connect to multiple databases, but each database access/update statement in such a program can be addressed to only one of these databases.

A *distributed database system* relaxes the above restriction. This means that a client program can contain access statements that combine data from multiple databases and update statements that modify data in multiple databases (Date, 2000). Ideally, the access/update statements should operate "transparently" on data, i.e. the user must not be aware where the data resides. The databases may be "heterogeneous," i.e. they may be managed by different database management systems.

Distributed database systems are difficult to implement. The difficulties derive mostly from stiff requirements for transaction management and query processing.

Q3 – answer

An *active database* is capable of storing not only data but also programs. Such stored programs can be invoked by their names or can be triggered by events that attempt to update the database.

Contemporary commercial database management systems are active. They provide programmatic extensions to SQL, such as PL/SQL in Oracle or Transact SQL in Sybase/SQL server, which allows programs to be written and stored in a database dictionary. These programs can be invoked from application programs or triggered as a result of modification events on the database.

Programs in active databases are "computationally complete," but they are not "resource complete". They are able to execute any computation, but they may not be able to access external resources, such as talking to a GUI window or an Internet browser, sending an email or SMS, or monitoring an engineering device.

Q5 – answer

Such a class would naturally belong to the *control* layer. This class embodies the program logic (which is the main purpose of the control layer). The class `InterestCalculation` provides a level of isolation between user events (presentation layer) and the database content (represented at run time by classes of the entity layer). Changes to the way the interest calculation is computed (program logic) will be localized to the class `InterestCalculation` and will not affect boundary or entity classes.

Q7 – answer

The *foundation* layer encapsulates (within the application program) knowledge of the persistent database, other data sources, and any external services. It serves as an interface between the persistent database data and the representation of that data in the program's entity classes.

Objects of the foundation package are responsible for reading data from the database and writing data to the database. The foundation package also takes responsibility for connecting to and disconnecting from the database, for providing current information about the database to the program, for configuring the database parameters to suit the program, and for handling transactional requests (commits and rollbacks).

Q9 – answer

In a typical situation, components and packages represent sets of classes. However, these representations are at different levels of abstraction and are frequently orthogonal.

Package is a logical concept that does not have immediate implementation connotations, and it is not a unit of software reuse (although individual classes within a package can be designed for reuse).

Component is a physical concept, normally distributed for *reuse* as a run-time executable. A component "publishes" its external interface (its services) in a contractual manner. The internal implementation of the operations in a component's interface is not published. Components can be interconnected via their interfaces even if they are implemented in different programming languages.

Component is a compilation unit. Component can contain many classes, but only one of these classes can be *public* (i.e. can have public visibility). The name of the component's compilation unit (e.g. `Invoice.java`) must correspond to the name of its public class (`Invoice`). Some visual modeling tools (such as Rational Rose) create components automatically when the Java code is generated for public classes (one component per public class).

A *package* is an architectural grouping of classes. The grouping is obtained by static proximity of classes in the application domain. A *component* offers a set of operations to the environment in which it functions. This set of operations captures the behavioral proximity of classes and may be of use in more than one application domain.

Q11 – answer

A *well-designed class* provides services to other classes, not just reveals its attribute values. A well-designed class also takes responsibility for controlling its state space, and it does not allow other classes to set its attribute values. A class that is not well designed (as per these two observations) is *mindless*.

A class is mindless if its public interface consists mostly of accessor methods, i.e. observer (`get`) methods and mutator (`set`) methods. In practice, most classes provide some accessor methods to allow sufficient coupling between otherwise cohesive classes.

Q13 – answer

Messages can be classified in a number of ways. The principal classification can be to divide messages into (Page-Jones, 2000):

- read messages (interrogative, present-oriented messages);
- update messages (informative, past-oriented messages);
- collaborative messages (imperative, future-oriented messages).

A sender of a *read message* requests information from the receiver (target object) of the message. A method that executes as a result of a read message is sometimes called an *observer* (`get`) method.

A sender of an *update message* provides information to the receiver so that the receiver can update its state with the information provided. A method invoked by an update message is sometimes called a *mutator* (`set`) method.

Read and update messages are also known as *accessor* messages. The related observer and mutator methods are termed accessor methods.

A sender of a *collaborative message* involves a contribution of the target object in a larger task that demands the collaboration of multiple objects. A collaborative message is a message in a chain of messages. Each collaborative message can be a read or update message.

As an aside, we note that UML classifies messages into signals and calls (Rumbaugh *et al.*, 1999). A *signal* is a one-way asynchrononous communication from sender to receiver. A *call* is a two-way synchronous communication in which the sender invokes an operation on the receiver. A call can be seen as a signal message followed by a return value. The classification into read, update, and collaborative messages relates to calls.

Q15 – answer

Both overriding and overloading imply that there are several methods with the same name. The difference is that:

- *Overriding* relates to inheritance and polymorphism. A method in a superclass can be overridden by a method in a subclass. Not only has the overridden method the same name as the superclass method but also the signatures of both methods must be the same. (An abstract operation must be polymorphic, and its implementation must be provided in subclasses. This is not considered overriding, because the abstract operation does not have a method in the superclass.)
- *Overloading* relates to the existence of multiple methods with the same name in the same class. Clearly, the signatures of these methods must be different.

Q17 – answer

The design of the behavioral aspect of collaboration is concerned with capturing the dynamics of method invocations that lead to the implementation of a behavior (typically a use case or an operation). This is best modeled with *interaction diagrams*, i.e. sequence diagrams and collaboration diagrams.

In practice, *sequence diagrams* are less frequently used for modeling of the behavioral aspect of collaboration because they do not visualize the static relationship links (mostly associations) used for message passing, and they are visually less attractive for presenting large and detailed models. *Collaboration diagrams* do not have these drawbacks. In particular, the visualization of links in collaboration diagrams provides a nice connection from behavioral to structural collaboration.

Solutions to exercises (advertising expenditure)

G1 – solution

Figure 6.26 shows a package diagram for AE. The three packages nested in the `Presentation` package correspond to the screen visualizations demanded by the three major functional units in the AE "value chain." Packages within the `Entity` package correspond to main "business objects." Packages within the `Control` package contain classes responsible for the application control logic.

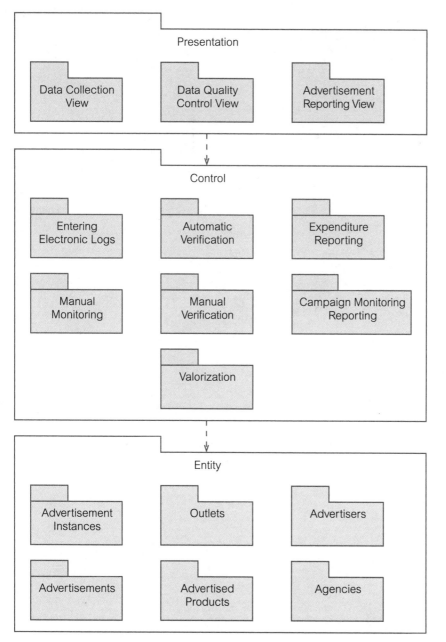

Figure 6.26
Package diagram (advertising expenditure)

G2 – solution

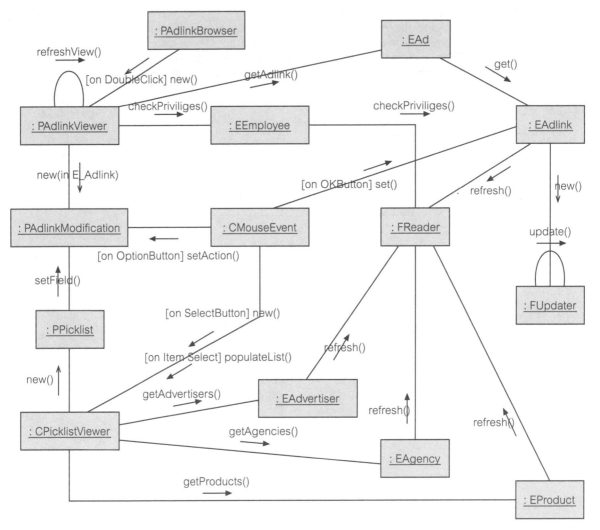

Figure 6.27 The collaboration diagram for behavioral collaboration (advertising expenditure)

G3 – solution

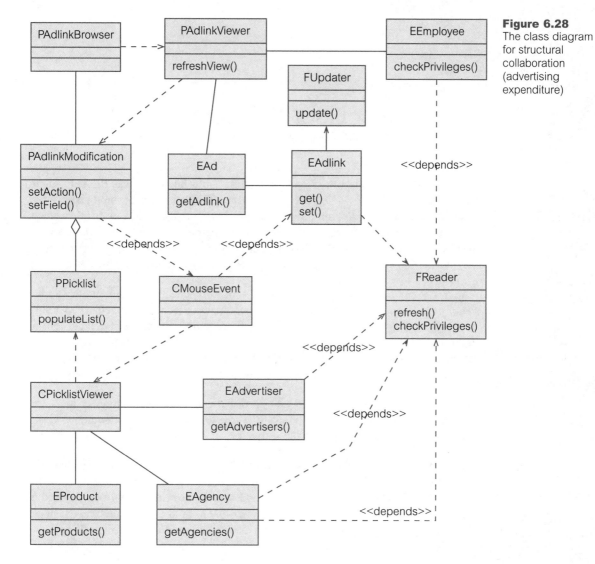

Figure 6.28
The class diagram for structural collaboration (advertising expenditure)

Chapter

7

User Interface Design

The days when screens were dumb and green and a keyboard was the only input device are gone. Today screens are intelligent (even if they get their intelligence from a server) and colorful, and the user is equipped with a mouse (not to mention voice and touch) to control the program's execution. The program can still be designed to disallow illegal or unauthorized events, but the shift of control from the algorithm to the user has changed the way that UI systems are designed and implemented.

The development of user interfaces begins with early sketches of UI windows in the requirements analysis phase. These sketches are used for requirements gathering, in storyboarding sessions with the customers, for prototyping, and for inclusion in the use-case documents. During the design, the UI windows for the application are developed to conform to the underlying UI presentation software and to the peculiarities and constraints of the chosen programming environment.

In Chapter 6 and elsewhere, we emphasized that enterprise information systems are invariably client/server (C/S) solutions. It is true to say that if server solutions *make* the software, client solutions *sell* the software.

UI clients can be divided into programmable clients and browser clients (Singh *et al.*, 2002; Maciaszek and Liong, 2004). A *programmable client* is typically a thick client (Section 6.1.2) with a program residing and executing on it and with access to the client's machine storage resources. A *browser client*, on the other hand, represents a web-based UI and needs a server to obtain its data and programs. This is a thin client. It is also called a web client.

Whatever the client, the UI design must follow some universal principles of good UI design while taking advantage of the latest technologies in human–computer interaction. The UI design is a *multidisciplinary activity*. It requires the multidisciplinary skills of a *team* – a single person is unlikely to have the knowledge demanded by the multifaceted considerations of UI design. A good UI design requires the combined skills of a graphic artist, a requirements analyst, a system designer, a programmer, a technology expert, a social and behavioral scientist, and perhaps a few other professions depending on the nature of the system.

A typical process in the UI design for IS applications begins with *use cases*. The *analyst* describing the flow of events for a use case has some visual image of the UI to support the human–computer interaction. In some cases, the analyst may choose to insert graphical depictions for user interfaces in the use-case document. Complex human–computer interactions cannot be adequately described in prose alone. Occasionally, the process of gathering and negotiating customer requirements necessitates the production of UI sketches.

The *designer* involved in specifying collaborations for realization of use cases must have a clear visual image of UI screens. If the analyst has not done this before, the designer will be the first person to produce depictions for user interfaces. The designer's depictions must conform to the underlying UI technology – windowing and widget toolkits, Internet browsers, etc. A *technology expert* may need to be consulted to exploit technological features successfully.

Before collaboration designs (Section 6.5) are passed on to programmers for implementation, a "user-friendly" prototype of UI screens needs to be constructed. This task should engage *graphic artists* and *social and behavioral scientists*. Together they can offer a UI that is attractive and usable.

The *programmer's* task is not just to blindly implement the screens but also to suggest changes motivated by the programming environment. In some cases, the changes may be improvements. In other cases, the changes may worsen the design due to programming or performance restrictions.

The above short discussion makes it clear that UI design is a very comprehensive task. Many books have been written to emphasize different aspects of UI design (e.g. Galitz, 1996; Ruble, 1997; Fowler, 1998; Olsen, 1998; Constantine and Lockwood, 1999; Windows, 2000).

In this chapter, we concentrate on what the system *designer* must know to design a successful interface collaboratively and what he/she must do to visualize *navigation paths* between windows and other elements of the UI. The latter task can benefit from a UML profile known as a *UX (use experience) storyboard*.

From UI prototype to implementation   **7.1**

The central issue in UI design is that the *user is in control* (with the proviso that the system, not the user, controls system integrity, safety, and security). A modern object-oriented program is *event-driven*. Objects respond to events (messages). Internal communication between objects is triggered by external user-activated events.

The UI look and feel sells the software product to the customer. A UI prototype can serve the double purpose of evaluating the "feel" of the UI screen and conveying its functions. The real "look" of the screen is delivered in the implementation phase.

Example 7.1 (contact management)

Refer to the problem statement for contact management (Section 1.5.3) and to the successive examples for contact management in Chapter 4. In particular, consider the design of the class `Organization` in Examples 4.6 (Section 4.2.1.2.3) and 4.8 (Section 4.2.2.3).

The purpose of this example is to demonstrate the change that a UI screen for updating information about `Organization` can undergo from an initial prototype to final implementation. We assume that the underlying UI technology is Microsoft Windows.

A UI prototype for `Organization`, developed during early requirements analysis, is presented in Figure 7.1. Its main purpose is to visualize data and control objects in the window. The feedback obtained from the users and the ideas of the UI development team will change not only the window's "look" and "feel" but perhaps also its content.

Figure 7.2 shows how the `Maintain Organization` window can potentially be presented during the system design phase. As can be seen, the designer opted for a dialog box with tabbed pages and a number of other look-and-feel changes. The changes have been

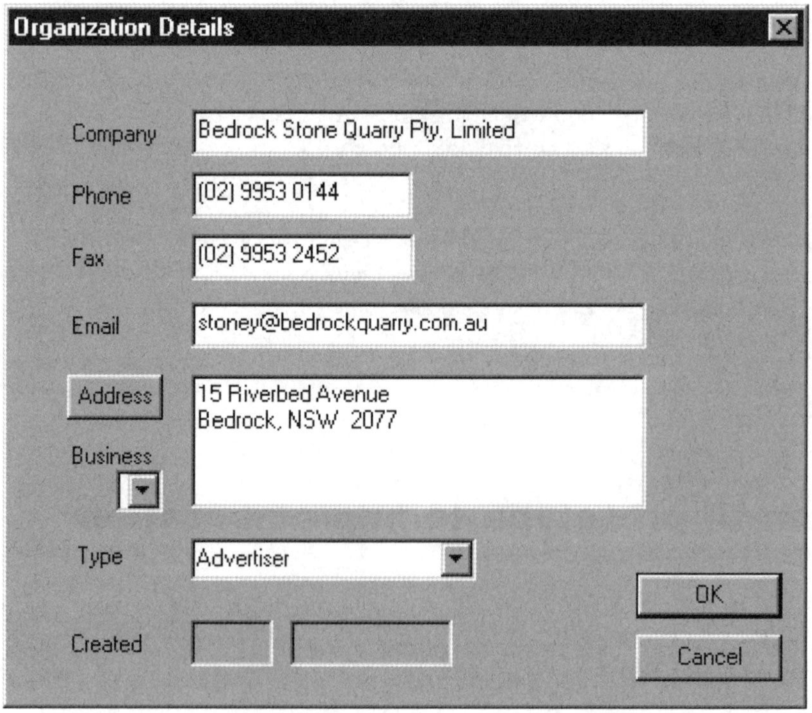

Figure 7.1
Analysis-phase window prototype (contact management) Source: Courtesy of Nielsen Media Research, Sydney, Australia

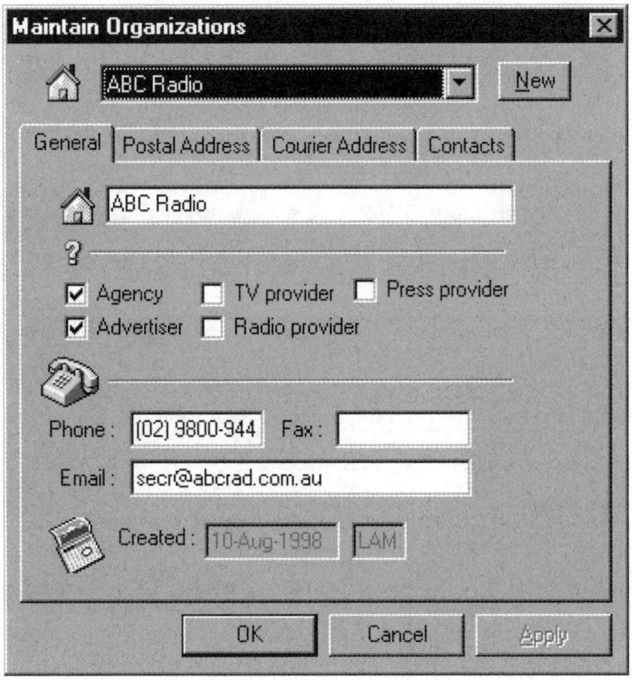

Figure 7.2
Design-phase
window prototype
(contact
management)
Source: Courtesy
of Nielsen Media
Research, Sydney,
Australia

made to conform to the Microsoft Windows GUI design principles and to accommodate functional requirements overlooked in the initial prototype.

The design in Figure 7.2 still has problems with regard to the look and feel, implementation constraints, and with satisfying functional requirements. As a result, the final implemented window is again different, as demonstrated in Figure 7.3.

The implemented window in Figure 7.3 disallows a drop-down list for selecting organization name (a dialog box is a secondary window opened to allow a particular organization to be updated). The classification possibilities of `Organization` are now disabled for editing (because an organization cannot have its classification changed by the user of this system). Other changes include larger sizes of fields, introduction of a group of fields called `History`, etc.

Guidelines for UI design

7.2

The UI design centers on the user. Associated with this observation is a range of guidelines to software developers. The guidelines are published by the manufacturers of UIs (e.g. Windows, 2000). They are also discussed in many books (e.g. Galitz, 1996; Ruble, 1997).

The *UI guidelines* constitute the foundations on which the developer builds. They should be at the back of the developer's mind in all UI design decisions. Some of the

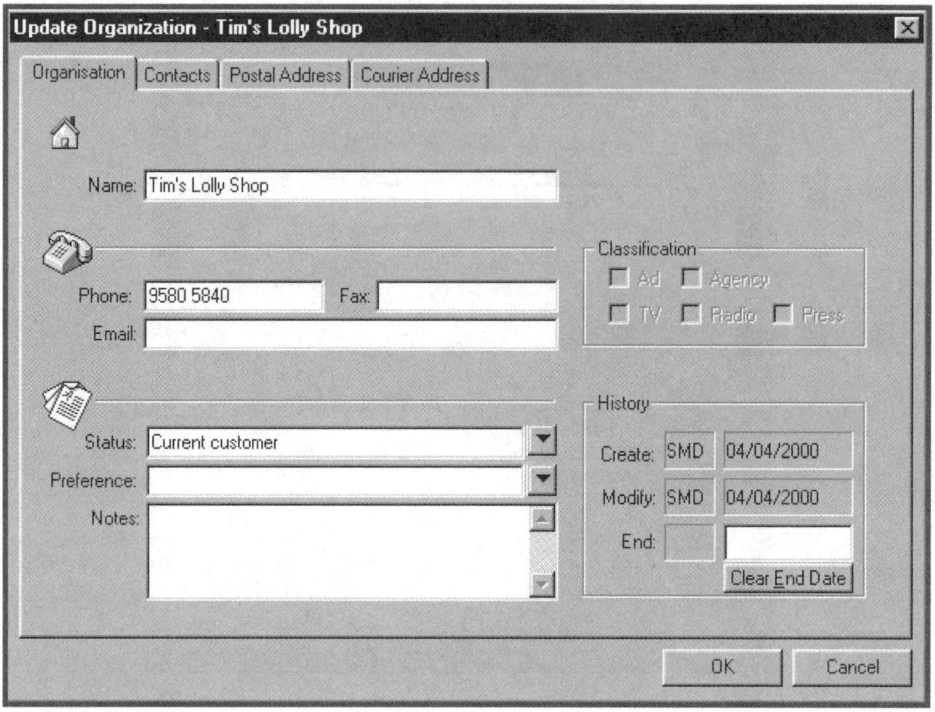

Figure 7.3
Implemented
window (contact
management)
Source: Courtesy
of Nielsen Media
Research, Sydney,
Australia

guidelines sound like aged pieces of ubiquitous wisdom; others have been motivated by modern UI technology.

7.2.1 User in control

The *user in control* is the principal UI guideline. This could be better called the *user's perception of control*. Some call it the *no mothering* principle – the program should not act like your mother and do things for you (Treisman, 1994). The underlying meaning is that the user initiates actions, and if as a result the program takes control then the user obtains a necessary *feedback* (an hourglass, wait indicator, or similar).

Figure 7.4 demonstrates a typical flow of control in a human–computer interaction. A user event (a menu action, mouse click, screen cursor movement, etc.) can open a UI window or invoke a program – typically, a 4GL-SQL program in IS applications. The program temporarily takes control from the user.

Program execution can return control back to the same or another window. Alternatively, it can call another 4GL-SQL module or can invoke an external routine. In some cases, the program can in fact do things for the user. This may happen, for example, when the program needs to do a computation that is normally associated with an explicit user event or if the program moves the cursor to another field on the screen and the event of leaving the original field has exit processing associated with it.

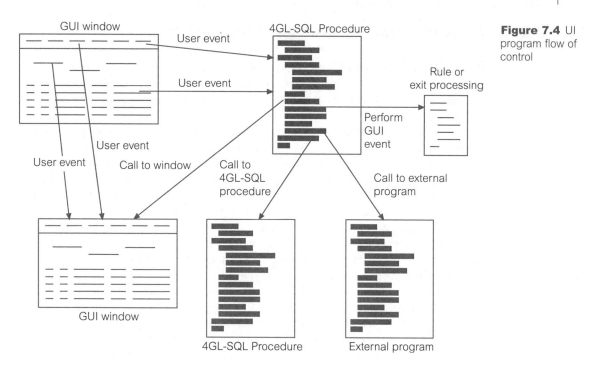

Figure 7.4 UI program flow of control

Consistency

7.2.2

Consistency is arguably the second most important guideline of good interface design. Consistency really means adherence to standards and the usual way of doing things. There are at least two dimensions to consistency:

1. conformance to the UI vendor's standards;
2. conformance to the naming, coding, and other UI-related standards developed internally by the organization.

Both dimensions are important, and the second (over which the developers have influence) must not contradict the first. If an application is developed for Windows, then the Windows look and feel must be delivered. On a Macintosh, replacing the celebrated apple menu with a kangaroo menu, as the author of this book once attempted, is not a good idea!

A UI developer must not be too creative or innovative in the interface design. Being so will erode the confidence and ability of users, who should be presented with a familiar and predictable environment. As Treisman (1994) observed, imagine what a car designer would do to the driving community if new cars were released with the accelerator and brake pedals swapped around!

Conformance to naming, coding, abbreviations, and other internal standards cannot be underestimated either. This includes the naming and coding of the menus, action buttons, and screen fields. It also includes any standards for the placement of objects on the screen and consistent use of other UI elements across all internally developed applications.

7.2.3 Personalization and customization

Personalization and *customization* (known jointly as *adaptability*) are two related guidelines. UI personalization is simply customization for personal use, whereas customization – as we understand it here – is an administrative task of tailoring the software to different groups of users.

An example of personalization is when a user reorders and resizes columns in a row browse (grid) display and saves these changes as his/her personal preference. The next time the program is activated, the personal preferences are taken into account.

An example of customization is when the program can operate differently for novice and advanced users. For instance, novice users may be offered explicit help and extra warning messages for user events perceived to be dangerous.

In many cases, the distinction between personalization and customization is blurred or negligible. Changing menu items and creating new menus are cases in point. If done for personal use, it is personalization. If done by a system administrator for the user community at large, it is customization.

An Internet-age feature related to personalization and customization is the user's *locale* information (Lethbridge and Laganiere, 2001). An application can adapt to the user's locale (such as the user's spoken language, character set, currency, and date formats) by simply querying the operating system on which the program executes.

Another important adaptability issue is for the application to adjust to people with disabilities. For example, blind people would require that the application delivers Braille or speech. Deaf people would require that sound be substituted by visual output. Other disabilities may require different measures.

7.2.4 Forgiveness

A good interface should allow users to experiment and make mistakes in a forgiving way. *Forgiveness* encourages an explorable interface, because the user is allowed to take erroneous routes but can be "rolled back" to the starting point if necessary. Forgiveness implies a multi-level *undo* operation.

This is easily said, difficult to implement. The implementation of forgiveness into the interface is a particular challenge in multi-user database applications. The user who withdrew (and spent) money from a bank account cannot possibly undo this operation! He/she can rectify the problem only by depositing the money back into the account in another transaction. Whether or not a forgiving interface should be warning the user of the consequences of cash withdrawal is a debatable issue (and one that relates to the personalization guideline).

7.2.5 Feedback

The *feedback* guideline is a spin-off of the first guideline – the user in control. To be in control implies knowledge of what is going on when the control is temporarily with the program. The developer should build into the system visual and/or audio cues for every user event.

In most cases, an hourglass or a wait indicator is sufficient feedback to show that the program is doing something. For those parts of the application that may experience occasional performance problems, a more vivid form of feedback may be necessary (such as the display of an explanatory message). Either way, the developer must never assume that the application performs so quickly that the feedback is unnecessary. Any surge in application workload will prove the developer painfully wrong.

Aesthetics and usability 7.2.6

Aesthetics are about the system's visual appeal. *Usability* is about the ease, simplicity, efficiency, reliability, and productivity in using the interface. Ultimately, both are about *user satisfaction*. This is where the UI developer needs the assistance of a graphic artist and a social and behavioral expert.

There are many golden rules for an aesthetic and usable design (Galitz, 1996; Constantine and Lockwood, 1999). Issues to consider include the fixation and movement of the human eye, the use of colors, the sense of balance and symmetry, the alignment and spacing of elements, the sense of proportion, and the grouping of related elements.

The guideline of aesthetics and usability turns the UI developer into an artist. It is good to remember in this context that "simple is beautiful." In fact, *simplicity* is frequently considered as yet another UI guideline, strongly related to the aesthetics and usability guideline. Simplicity in complex applications is best achieved by the "divide and conquer" approach – the progressive disclosure of information so that it is shown only when needed, possibly in separate windows.

UI containers and components 7.3

There are two main aspects of UI design – the design of windows and the design of windows' input and editing controls. Both depend on the underlying UI environment. In the following discussion, we concentrate on the Microsoft Windows environment (Windows, 2000; Maciaszek and Liong, 2004).

A typical Windows application consists of a single main application window, the *primary window*. The primary window is supported by a set of pop-up windows, the *secondary windows*. The secondary windows support the user's activities in the primary window. Many activities supported by secondary windows are CRUD (create, read, update, and delete) operations on the database.

From the programming perspective, windows are *UI containers*. These are rectangular areas of a UI screen that contain other containers, menus, and controls (action buttons, etc.). Containers can be primary windows, but also dialogs (secondary windows), panes, and panels.

Together, containers, menus, and controls constitute *UI components*. Java provides a UI component kit for building applications and applets, called Swing, which is a library of classes and interfaces. Swing's concrete classes are named starting with the letter J, e.g. `JDialog`, `JButton`.

7.3.1 Primary window

A *primary window* has a border (frame). The frame contains a title bar (caption bar) for the window, a menu bar, toolbars, a status bar, and the window's viewable and modifiable content. Horizontal and vertical scroll bars are used to scroll through the content, if required.

The window's viewable and modifiable content can be organized into panes. Panes permit different but related information content to be seen and manipulated. Figure 7.5 demonstrates a primary window that displayed after a successful login to an application. The pane on the left contains an application map in the Windows Explorer style (the Close button in the upper right corner of the pane informs the user that the pane can be dismissed, if so desired). The commentary explains the well-known Windows terminology.

A typical distinguishing feature of a primary window is the existence of the menu bar and toolbar. The toolbar contains action icons for the most frequently used menu items. The toolbar icons duplicate these menu items. They provide a quick way of executing frequent actions.

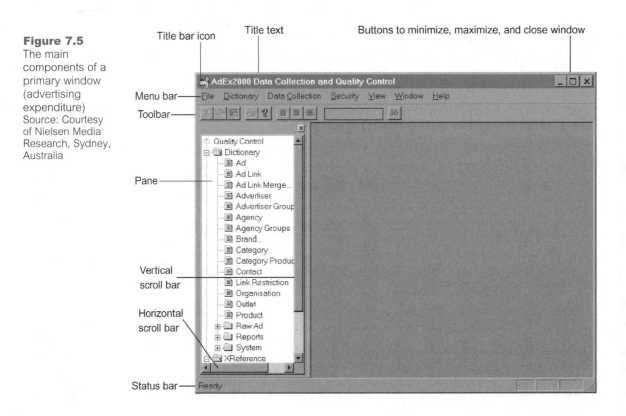

Figure 7.5
The main components of a primary window (advertising expenditure)
Source: Courtesy of Nielsen Media Research, Sydney, Australia

Example 7.2 (advertising expenditure)

Refer to the problem statement for advertising expenditure (Section 1.5.5) and to Examples 6.6–6.8 (Section 6.5). In particular, consider Figure 6.21 (Section 6.5.2) and show the design of the primary window from which the Update Product dialog box is launched. Include in the design a pane similar to the one shown on the left-hand side of Figure 7.5.

Figure 7.6 demonstrates the primary window for Example 7.2. The left-hand pane contains a tree browser (Section 7.3.1.2). The tree browser allows selection of a particular "data container" to be displayed in the right-hand pane. The right-hand pane is a row browser (Section 7.3.1.1).

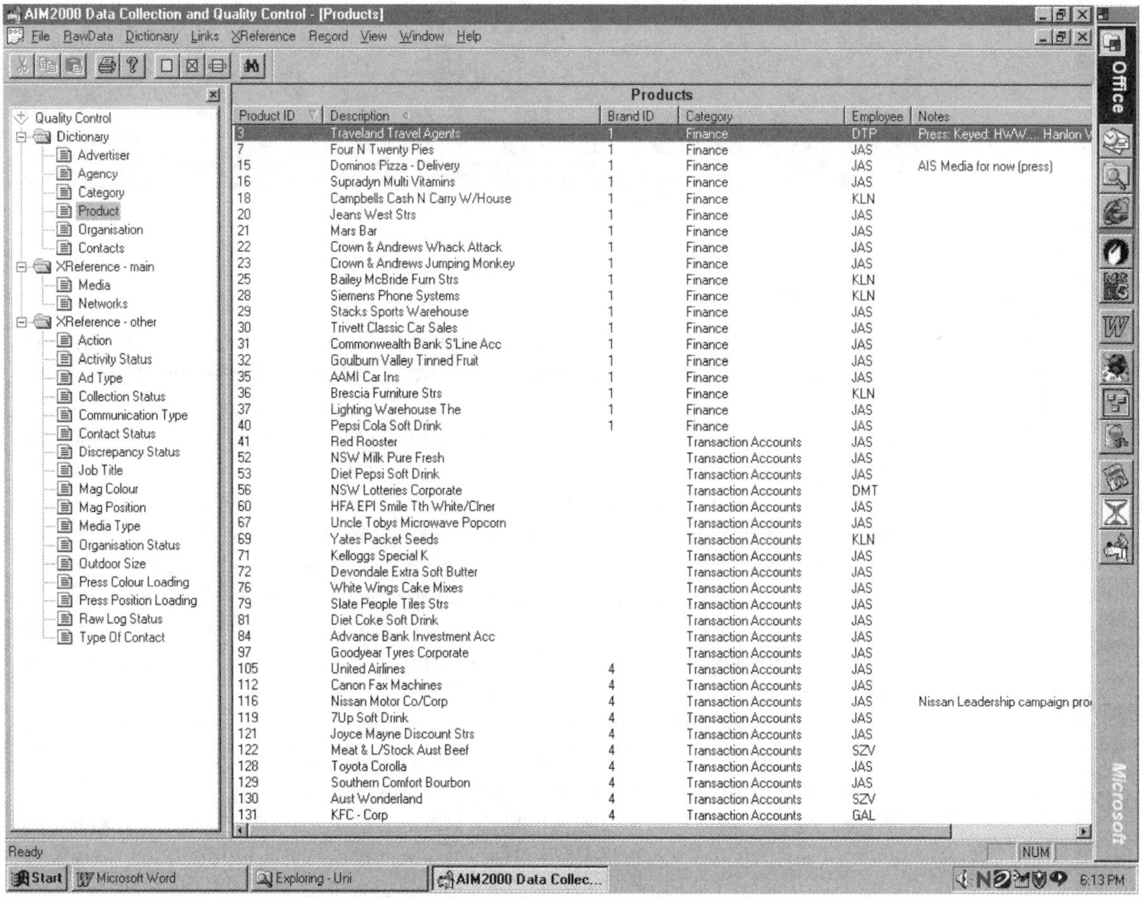

Figure 7.6 A primary window showing list of products (advertising expenditure)
Source: Courtesy of Nielsen Media Research, Sydney, Australia

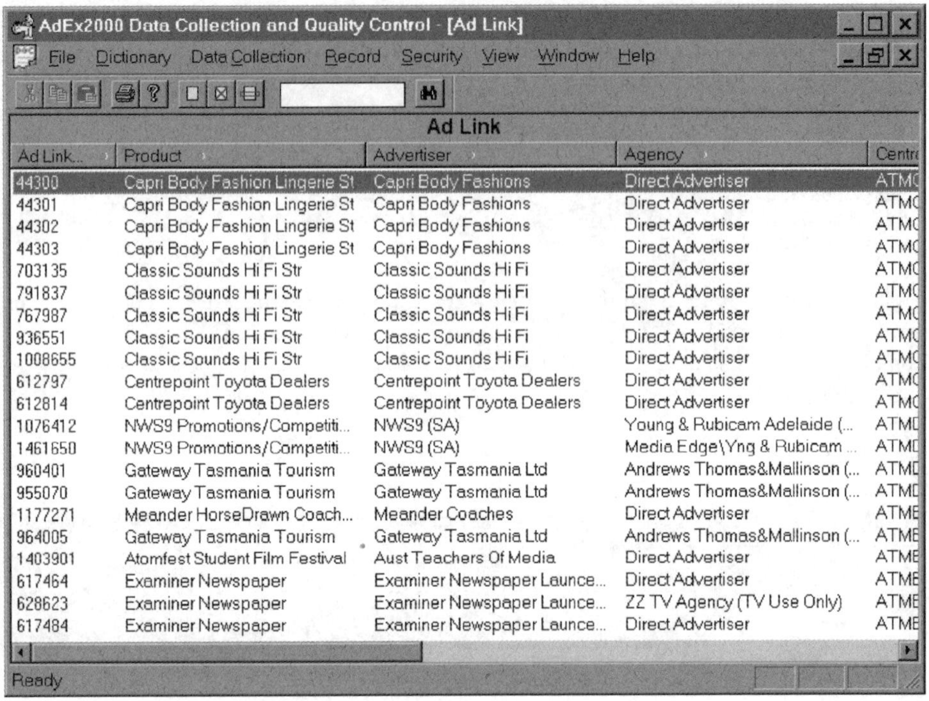

Figure 7.7
A row browse
window
(advertising
expenditure)
Source: Courtesy
of Nielsen Media
Research, Sydney,
Australia

7.3.1.1 Row browser

A frequent use of the primary window in IS applications is to provide a "row browse" display of database records, such as employee records. Such a window is sometimes called a *row browser*. The user can browse up and down through the records using the vertical scroll bar or keys on the keyboard (Page Up, Page Down, Home, End, and up and down arrows).

Figure 7.7 is an example of a row browser. The document – labeled `Ad Link` – inside the primary window is a *child window* (to be explained later). The child window has its own set of *window buttons* (Minimize, Restore, Close) placed in the right corner of the menu bar. The columns of the browser's grid are *resizable*, and their positions can be *rearranged*. The circular dents next to column names indicate that the column is *sortable* – clicking at the column will sort the records in ascending or descending order of that column's values.

At any particular time, only one row (record) is active in the browser. Double-clicking on that record would normally display an "edit window" with details of that record. The *edit window* allows the content of the record to be modified.

Panes can be used to split the window vertically or horizontally, or even both ways. Figure 7.8 demonstrates a horizontal split. As the window title informs, the three panes are used to display the products by advertiser and by agency. The middle pane shows the advertisers belonging to the advertising agency currently selected (highlighted) in the top pane. The bottom pane then shows the products advertised by a selected advertiser.

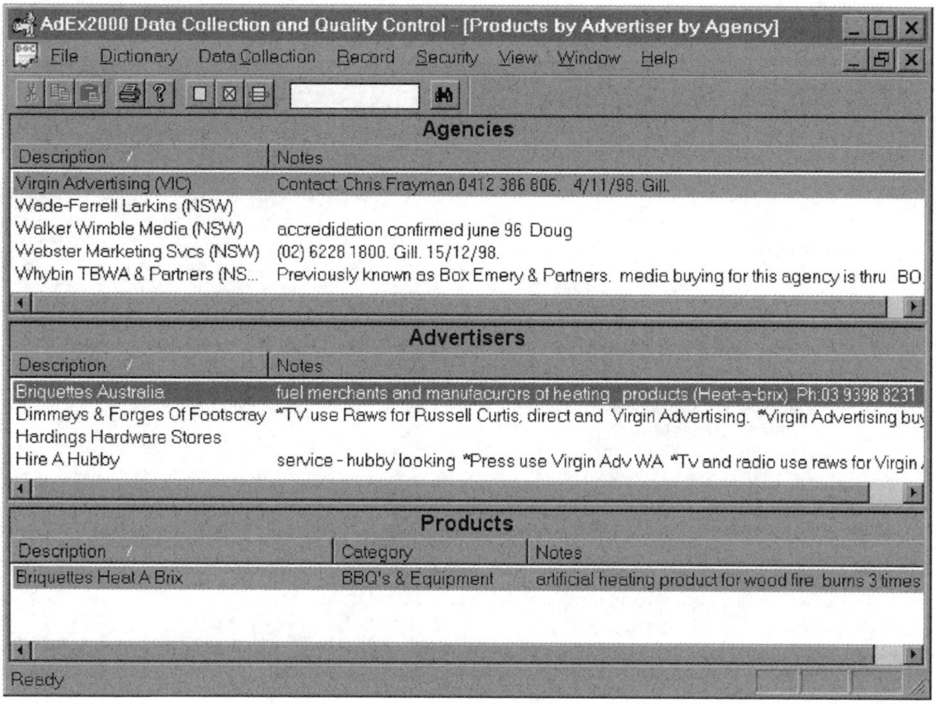

Figure 7.8
A multi-pane row
browse window
(advertising
expenditure)
Source: Courtesy
of Nielsen Media
Research, Sydney,
Australia

Tree browser

7.3.1.2

The other popular way of using the primary window is as a tree browser. A *tree browser* displays related records as an indented outline. The outline contains controls that allow the tree to be expanded or collapsed. A well-known example of a tree browser is the display of computer folders in Windows Explorer.

Unlike a row browser, a tree browser would allow in-place modifications, i.e. it would allow the content of the window to be modified without activating an edit window. Modifications in a tree browser are done through "drag and drop" operations.

Figure 7.9 demonstrates a tree browser in the left pane of the window. The right pane is a row browser. Selecting an agency group record in the tree browser displays the agencies of that agency group in the row browser.

Web page

7.3.1.3

A *web page* can also be treated as a special kind of primary window if it is used as an entry point of a web application. Unlike in conventional IS applications, the menu bar and toolbar of a web page are not used for application tasks. They are used for generic web-surfing activities. The user events in web applications are normally programmed through action buttons and active hyperlinks.

Figure 7.10 depicts a web page showing one of the pages on a book website (for one of the books of the author of this textbook). The browser's menu bar and toolbar do not apply

Figure 7.9
A window with
tree browse and
row browse panes
(advertising
expenditure)
Source: Courtesy
of Nielsen Media
Research, Sydney,
Australia

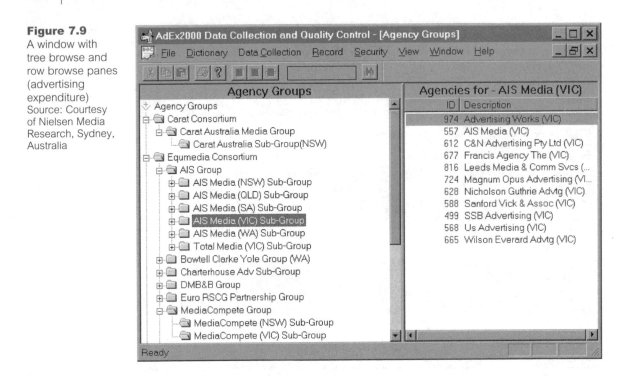

to the contents of the web page. A built-in and cascading menu in the left-hand pane of the page contains hyperlinks that allow the user to move between the website's pages.

7.3.2 Secondary window

Disregarding some trivial IS applications, a *secondary window* supplements its primary window. It extends the functionality of the primary window, in particular for operations that modify the database (i.e. the insert, delete, and update operations).

A secondary window is typically *modal* with respect to the primary window. The user must respond and close the secondary window before interacting with any other window of the application. *Modeless* secondary windows are possible but not recommended.

The *logon window* is a simple example of a secondary window. The logon screen example in Figure 7.11 demonstrates the main visual differences between the primary and secondary window. A secondary window does not have any "bars" – a menu bar, toolbar, scroll bars, or status bar. User events are achieved with *command buttons* (*action buttons*), such as OK, Cancel, Help.

Secondary windows come in various forms and shapes. A secondary window can be a

■ dialog box

■ tab folder

■ drop-down list

■ message box.

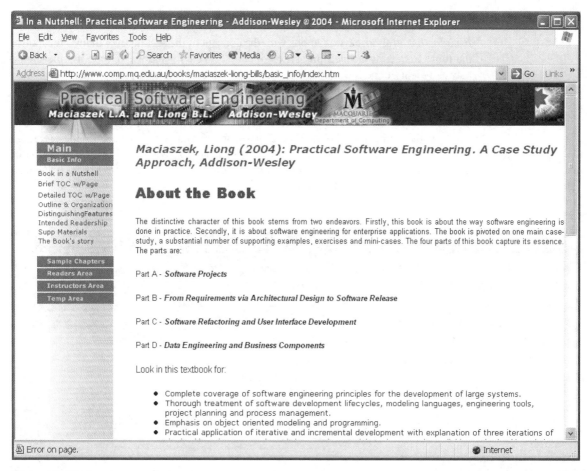

Figure 7.10 A web page window

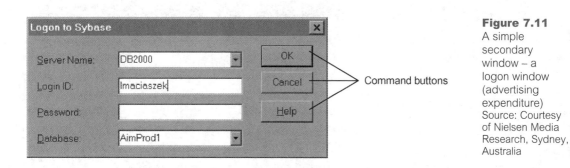

Figure 7.11
A simple
secondary
window – a
logon window
(advertising
expenditure)
Source: Courtesy
of Nielsen Media
Research, Sydney,
Australia

7.3.2.1 Dialog box

A *dialog box* is almost synonymous with the concept of the secondary window. It captures the most frequently needed properties of the secondary window. It supports the dialog between the user and the application. Dialog implies that the user enters some information to be considered by the application.

Figure 7.12 contains an example of a dialog box. It is an insert window used for inserting new TV ad instances in the database. The user can insert/modify any *editable field* value in the white field boxes. Some fields are placed within named frames (e.g. `Ad Instance Attributes` in the upper right corner). The window provides an option of inserting new values and closing the window (`Save and Close` button) or inserting new values and clearing the fields for the next insertion (`Save and Next` button).

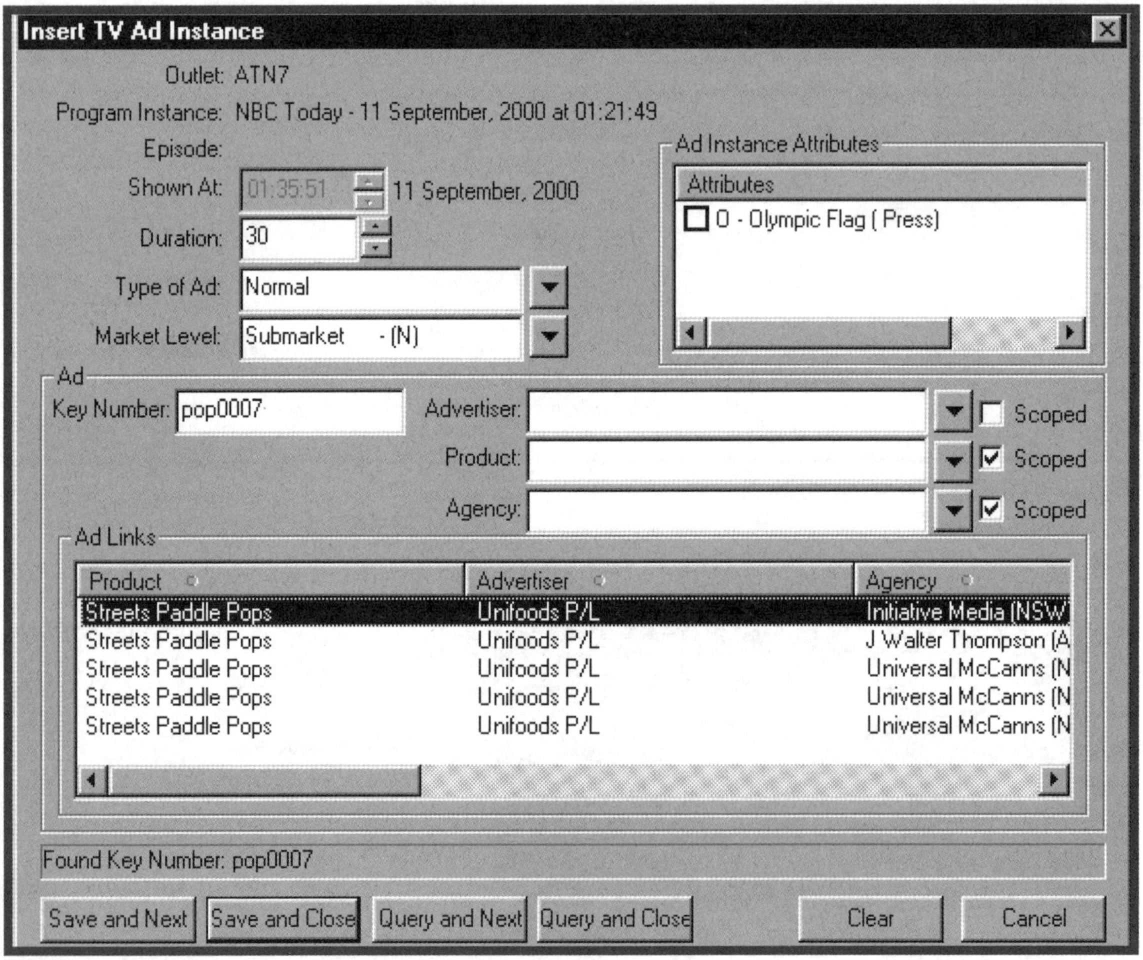

Figure 7.12 A dialog box (advertising expenditure)
Source: Courtesy of Nielsen Media Research, Sydney, Australia

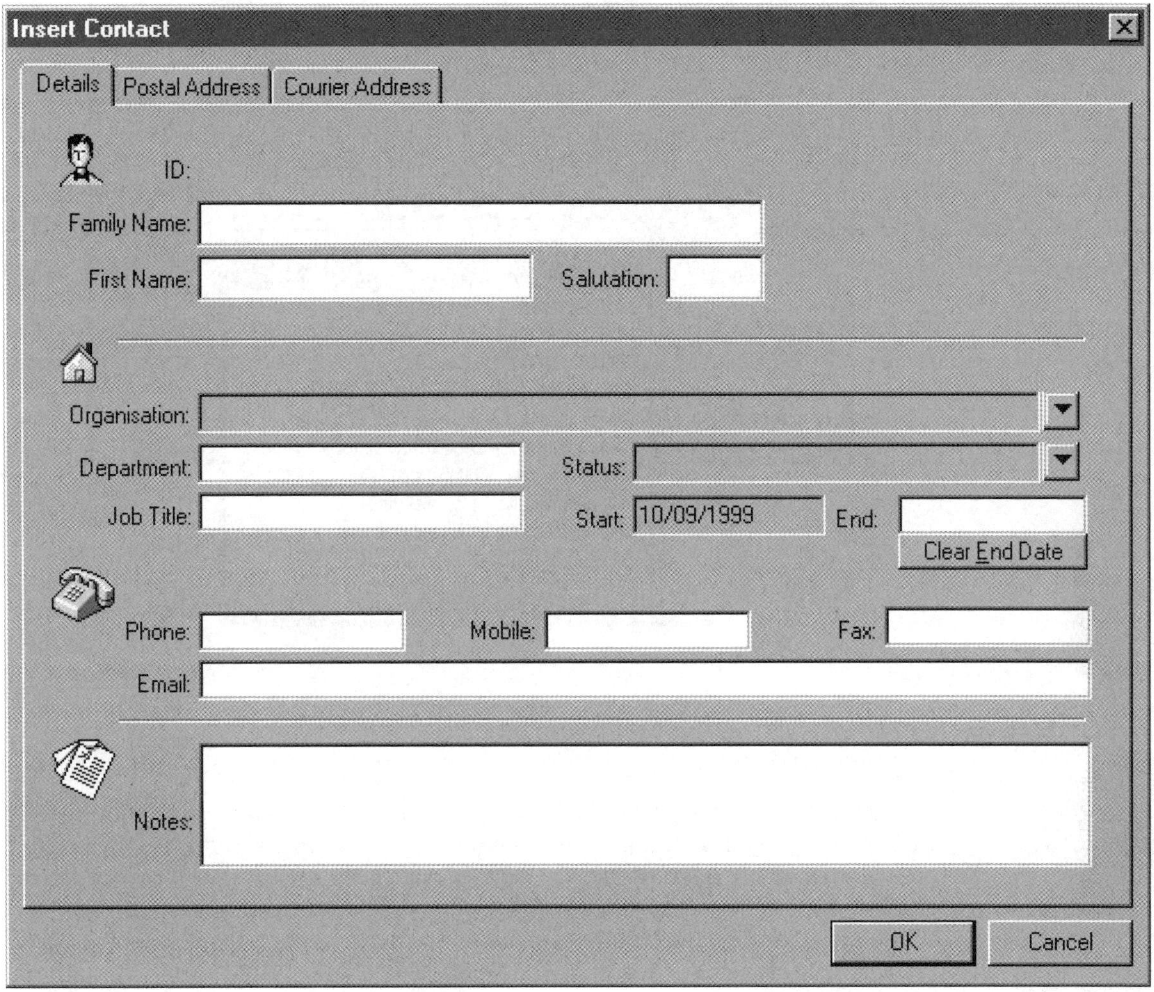

Figure 7.13 A tab folder (contact management)
Source: Courtesy of Nielsen Media Research, Sydney, Australia

Tab folder

7.3.2.2

A *tab folder* is useful when the amount of information to be displayed in a secondary window exceeds the window's "real estate" and the subject matter can be broken logically apart into information groups. At any point in time, information from one tab is visible on the top of the stack of tab sheets. (The Microsoft Windows name for a tab folder is a *tabbed property sheet*, and each tab is called a *property page*.)

Figure 7.13 demonstrates a tab folder for inserting information about a new contact person. The three tabs divide the large volume of information to be entered by the user into three groups. The command buttons at the bottom of the screen apply to the whole window, not just to the currently visible tab page.

Figure 7.14
A drop-down list
(advertising
expenditure)
Source: Courtesy
of Nielsen Media
Research, Sydney,
Australia

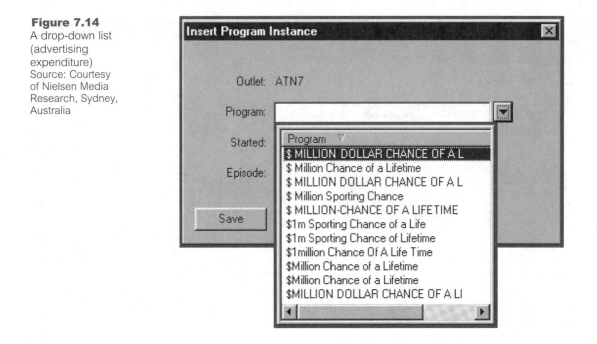

7.3.2.3 Drop-down list

In some cases, a *drop-down list* (or a set of drop-down lists) is a convenient substitute for a tab page. A drop-down list provides a *picklist* of choices from which the user can select one that applies. For insert operations, the user can type in a new value to be added to the drop-down list the next time it is opened.

In general, a drop-down list does not need to be restricted to a simple list of values as in Figure 7.14. It can be a tree browser of values.

7.3.2.4 Message box

A *message box* is a secondary window that displays a message to the user. The message can signify a warning, an explanation, an exceptional condition, etc. Command buttons in the message box offer one or more reply choices to the user.

Figure 7.15 shows a message that requires acknowledgment (the OK button) by the user.

7.3.3 Menus and toolbars

The UI components include menus and toolbars. In the Java Swing library, the names of the classes imply the provided functionality of menus: e.g. JMenuBar, JMenu, JMenuItem, JCheckBoxMenuItem, JRadioButtonMenuItem.

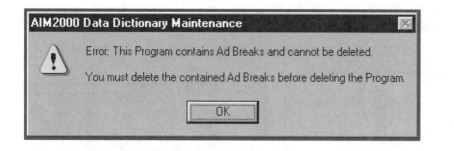

Figure 7.15
A message box
(advertising
expenditure)
Source: Courtesy
of Nielsen Media
Research, Sydney,
Australia

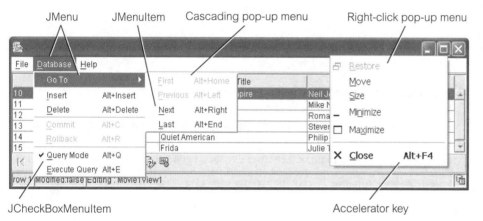

Figure 7.16
Menus
Source: Maciaszek
and Liong (2004).
Reprinted by
permission of
Pearson Education
Ltd

Menu items are grouped into lists, which can be opened by means of actions called pull-down, cascading, or pop-up (the latter is activated by pressing the right mouse button).

Menu items have the responsibility of responding to user events by firing some processing. Normally menu items are launched by a *mouse click*. More frequently used menu items may have accelerator keys implemented for them. An *accelerator key* allows the menu item to be launched from the keyboard without opening the menu list. Also, quicker access to a menu item in an open list is provided by typing the initial (underlined) letter of the item name.

Figure 7.16 demonstrates a variety of menus (Maciaszek and Liong, 2004). It also refers to some Swing classes that implement them.

Selecting from menu lists and using accelerator keys are still not the most efficient ways of activating menu actions. For the most frequently used menu items, the UI designer should provide toolbar buttons. A *toolbar* contains actions and controls that duplicate the functionality of the most useful menu items.

A toolbar can be placed in a fixed position in the window frame, or it can float, i.e. it can be undocked from a frame into a separate small window and position elsewhere on the screen's real estate (Maciaszek and Liong, 2004). Swing supports toolbars with the `JToolBar` class. Figure 7.17 shows examples of toolbars.

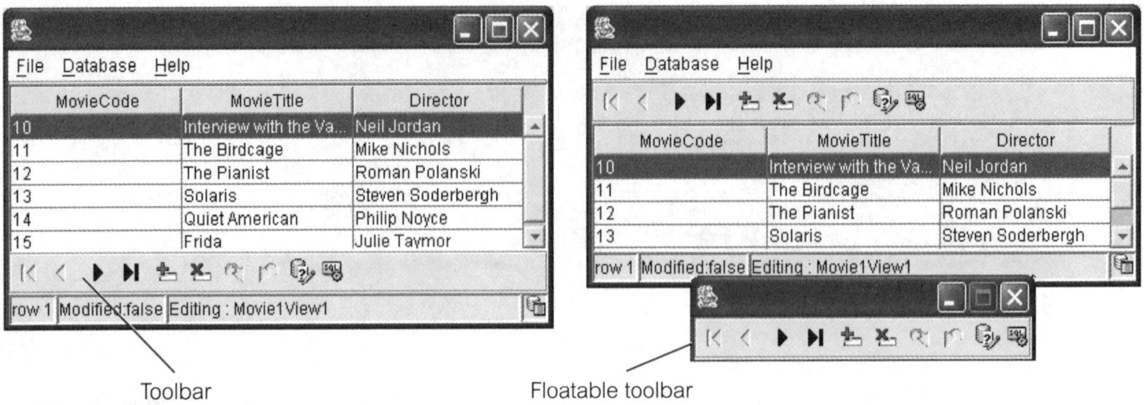

Toolbar   Floatable toolbar

Figure 7.17 Toolbars
Source: Maciaszek and Liong (2004). Reprinted by permission of Pearson Education Ltd

7.3.4 Buttons and other controls

Menus and toolbars are manifestations of *event processing* implemented in the user interface. Similar manifestation of event processing is provided by UI controls. *Controls* are designed to intercept, understand, and implement user events. In general, controls can be divided into:

■ actions buttons (inherited in Swing from an abstract class called `AbstractButton`);

■ other controls (inherited directly from a root abstract class called `JComponent`).

Figure 7.18 is a visualization of Swing controls such that the names for controls are the names of the classes used to implement them (Maciaszek and Liong, 2004).

The differences between various buttons are sometimes subtle, so some explanation may be in place. `JButton` fires an event as soon as it is pressed and pops up again (unless the event results in a new window and hides the button). By contrast, `JToggleButton` remains pushed down (after a mouse click on it) until it is pressed again.

`JRadioButton` and `JCheckBox` are two categories of `JToggleButton`. `JRadioButton` is used to implement a group of buttons such that only one of these buttons is selected at any one time. `JCheckBox` is an independent control that can be set to either true (with a checkmark) or false (without a checkmark).

`JList`, `JTree`, and `JComboBox` are controls with direct applicability to the implementation of some containers discussed earlier. `JList` is used in the implementation of a row browser (Section 7.3.1.1), `JTree` in the implementation of a tree browser (Section 7.3.1.2), and `JComboBox` in the implementation of a drop-down list (Section 7.3.2.3).

7.4 Web UI design

"A Web application is a Web system that allows its users to execute business logic with a web browser" (Conallen, 2000, p.10). The *business logic* can reside on the server and/or

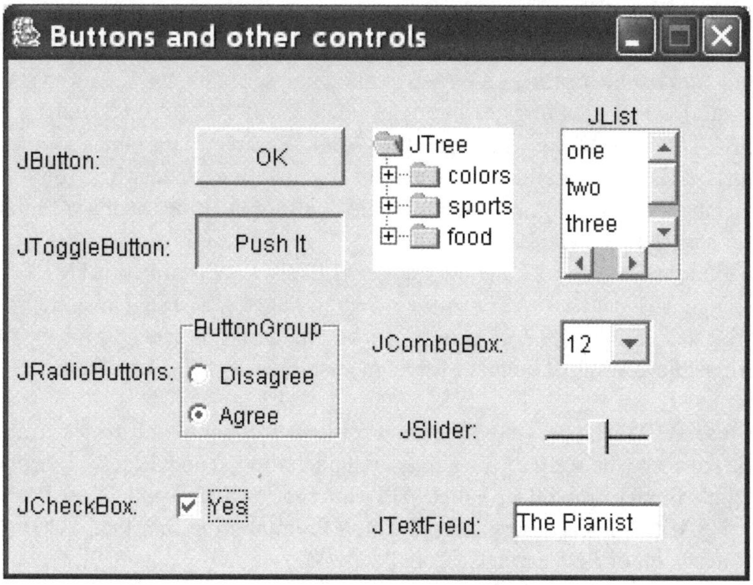

Figure 7.18
Buttons and
other controls
Source: Maciaszek
and Liong (2004).
Reprinted by
permission of
Pearson Education
Ltd

the client. A *web application* is therefore a kind of distributed C/S system (Section 6.1) with a website. In this sense, most discussion in this chapter applies directly to web applications.

An Internet client *browser* renders *web pages* on a computer screen. A *web server* delivers the web pages to the browser. Web page documents can be *static* (unmodifiable) or *dynamic*. A web page document can be a *form* that a user fills in. *Frames* can be used by the application to divide the screen's real estate so that the user can view multiple web pages at the same time.

A web application can include an *application server* (Section 6.1.2) to manage the application logic and to monitor the application state. In more active web applications, state monitoring is an important system activity to keep track of the actions of online users.

A simple technique to monitor state is to store a *cookie* in the browser – a short string of characters that represents the state of an online user. Because the number of online users to be monitored by the web or application server is arbitrarily large, a *session timeout* may be imposed on the online user's activity. If the user is not active for 15 minutes (the typical timeout), the server disconnects from the client. The cookie itself may or may not be removed from the client machine.

Scripts and applets are used to make the *client page* dynamic. A *script* (e.g. written in JavaScript) is a program interpreted by the browser. An *applet* is a compiled component that executes in the browser's context but has only limited access to other resources of the client computer (for security reasons).

A web page can also have scripts executed by the server. Such a page is called a *server page*. A server page has access to all the resources of the database server. Server pages manage client sessions, place cookies on the browser, and build client pages (i.e. build page documents from the server's business objects and send them back to the client).

Standard *data access libraries* are used to allow the scripts in the server pages to access the database. Typical enabling technologies include ODBC (Open Database Connectivity), JDBC (Java Database Connectivity), RDO (Remote Data Objects) and ActiveX Data Objects (ADO). In a situation where an organization standardizes on a particular database management system, low-level function calls to DBLib (Database Library) allow more direct access to the database.

The enabling technology for the *web server* is likely to be scripted HTML (HyperText Markup Language) pages – ASP (Active Server Pages), or JSP (Java Server Pages). The enabling technology for *web pages* can be client scripts (JavaScript or VBScript), XML (eXtensible Markup Language) documents, Java applets, JavaBeans, or ActiveX controls.

Clients use HTTP (HyperText Transfer Protocol) to obtain web pages from the web server. The page may be scripted, or it may contain compiled and directly executable DLL (dynamic link library) modules, e.g. ISAPI (Internet Server Application Programming Interface), NSAPI (Netscape Server Application Programming Interface), CGI (Common Gateway Interface), or Java servlets (Conallen, 2000).

The *cookie* serves as a primitive mechanism for maintaining connection between the client and the server in what is otherwise a *connectionless Internet* system. More sophisticated mechanisms for connecting clients and servers turn the Internet into a *distributed object system*. In a distributed object system, objects are uniquely identified with OIDs (Section 3.1.1.3), and they communicate by obtaining each other's OIDs. The principal mechanisms are CORBA, DCOM, and EJB. In these technologies, objects can communicate without using HTTP or going through a web server (Conallen, 2000).

The deployment architecture capable of supporting more sophisticated web applications includes four tiers of computing nodes (Section 6.1.2):

1. client with browser;
2. web server;
3. application server;
4. database server.

The browser of the *client node* can be used to display static or dynamic pages. Scripted pages and applets can be downloaded and run within the browser. Additional functionality can be supplied to the client's browser with objects such as ActiveX controls or JavaBeans. Running application code on the client, but outside the browser, may satisfy other UI requirements.

The *web server* handles page requests from the browser and dynamically generates pages and code for execution and display on the client. The web server also deals with customization and parameterization of the session with the user.

The *application server* is indispensable when distributed objects are involved in the implementation. It manages the business logic. The business components publish their interfaces to other nodes via component interfaces such as CORBA, DCOM, or EJB.

The business components encapsulate persistent data stored in a database, probably a relational database. They communicate with the *database server* via database connectivity protocols such as JDBC or ODBC. The database node provides for a scalable storage of data and multi-user access to it.

Window navigation

To the user, the application appears as a set of collaborating windows. It is the task of the UI designer to organize the dependencies between windows in a coherent, easy to understand, structure. The user should never feel lost among opened windows.

Ideally, the link from the primary window to the top secondary window currently opened should be a path, not even a hierarchy. This can be achieved by making a secondary window *modal* with respect to the previous window.

While the UI design should facilitate the user's exploration of the interface, a good design of the *menu* and *toolbar* structures remains the principal technique to explain the application's capabilities. The menu commands available to the user in pull-down and slide-off menus indirectly explain the dependencies between windows.

The graphical depiction of UI windows – through prototyping or other UI layout tools – does not inform how the windows can actually be *navigated* by the user. We still need to design the *window navigation model*. A window navigation model should consist of diagrams visualizing screen containers and components and showing how the user can traverse from one window to another.

When the first edition of this book was written, UML did not offer a graphical modeling technique to model window navigation. Consequently, the approach taken in the book was to stereotype UML activity diagrams to model window navigation. Luckily, between the first and the second edition of the book, UML has offered a profile, called *user experience (UX) storyboards*, to address the issue of UI design in general, and window navigation in particular (Heumann, 2003).

As an aside, the change in the modeling focus of activity diagrams between UML 1 and UML 2 makes activity diagrams less useful for window navigation modeling. The change has to do with making activity diagrams akin to Petri nets by concentrating solely on action states (ref. answer to Q17 at the end of Chapter 3).

User experience storyboards

User experience (UX) storyboards (Heumann, 2003) shift the design focus from the "guts" of the system to the UI. They supply an alternative design path for use cases. Rather than using the use-case specifications to design the state and behavior of the system, the UX approach emphasizes the expectations of the use-case actors and the demands of the PCMEF presentation layer.

In the absence of UX storyboards or similar window navigation models, the designer has no choice but to enrich the use-case specifications by including window prototypes as part of the use-case documents. This has been the approach used in this book so far whenever we have felt that the understanding of use-case descriptions lacked precision without presenting screen prototypes.

Modeling with UX storyboards consists of five steps (Heumann, 2003):

1. *Add actor characteristics to the use case* – this includes a definition of the actor's (user's) (Section 3.2.1.1) computer familiarity, domain knowledge, and frequency of accessing the system.

2. *Add usability characteristics to the use case* – usability (Sections 2.1, 7.2.6) is a non-functional requirement, normally defined as system constraints in supplementary specifications (Section 2.6.4). The usability characteristics include helpful hints (e.g. how to make the UI easier to use or easier to implement) and any rigorous requirements that must be conformed to (e.g. system response time, acceptable error rates, learning times).

3. *Identify UX elements* – this refers to the identification of UI containers and components (Section 7.3). A specially stereotyped class model is used to represent UX elements.

4. *Model the use-case flows with the UX elements* – this is UX-driven behavioral collaboration modeling (Section 7.5.2). UML sequence and collaboration diagrams are used to depict the interaction between the user and the UI presentation screens or between the presentation screens themselves.

5. *Model screen navigation links for the use case* – this is UX-driven structural collaboration modeling (Section 7.5.3). Stereotyped UML class diagrams are used to depict associations along which the navigation between UX elements takes place.

All in all, UX storyboards aim at giving justice to the UI design as an inherent part of system design. They represent the modeling aspects of UI design and are concerned with issues such as (Kozaczynski and Thario, 2003):

- user presentation screens;
- user-instigated screen events that the system must react to;
- data that the system displays to the screen;
- data that the user enters on the screen for further processing;
- the screen's decomposition to smaller areas that should be managed separately from other areas;
- transitions (navigation) between screens.

The UX storyboarding profile introduces several stereotypes for classes. The main stereotypes are <<screen>>, <<input form>>, and <<compartment>>. All these stereotypes are at a relatively high level of abstraction. A more complete list of stereotypes could consider other UX elements, perhaps classified by structural and behavioral collaboration. A possible list is:

1. Structural UX elements:
    - primary window
        - pane in primary window
    - row browser
    - tree browser
    - web page.

2. secondary window:
   - dialog box
   - message box
   - tab folder.

3. window data:
   - text box
   - combo box
   - spin box
   - column
   - row
   - group of fields.

4. Behavioral UX elements:
   - drop-down menu item
   - pop-up menu item
   - toolbar button
   - command button
   - double click
   - picklist selection
   - keyboard key
   - keyboard function key
   - keyboard accelerator key
   - scrolling button
   - window close button.

Modeling UX elements

The UML UX profile offers only a few stereotypes to serve as the primary UX modeling elements. The most encompassing is a stereotype for a *package* called <<storyboard>>. This stereotype defines a package that contains a UX storyboard.

The UML *classes* can be stereotyped as:

- <<screen>> – the screen abstraction defines a window or a web page rendered on the screen.

- <<input form>> – this stereotype represents a window's container or a web page form through which the user can interact with the system by entering data or by activating some actions. The input form is a part of a screen. This can be a class derived from Java Swing library, such as JInternalFrame, JTabbedPane, JDialog, or JApplet.

- <<compartment>> – this stereotype represents any region of a screen that can be reused by multiple screens. This can be, for example, a toolbar.

The UX class elements contain the UI dynamic content (fields on the screen) and any actions associated with screens, input forms, and compartments. The UX profile predefines some tags (Section 5.1.1.3) associated with the *fields* (Kozaczynski and Thario, 2003). Other tags can be added by the UX designers. Three most interesting tags specify if a field is:

1. *editable* – indicates if the field can be modified by the user or not;
2. *visible* – indicates if the field is displayed on the screen or hidden from the user's view (but still accessible to the program);
3. *selectable* – indicates if the field can be selected (highlighted or otherwise shown as active).

For example, a field can have tag values such as {editable = true, visibility = visible} or {editable = false, visibility = hidden}. Alternatively, the fact that a field is visible can be indicated by marking it with a public visibility icon (a plus (+) symbol in front of the name in the UML standard). For hidden visibility, a private visibility marker (a minus (–) sign) can be used.

There are two categories of *action* to be listed in the UX classes: user actions and environmental actions (Heumann, 2003). *User actions* are any UI events coming from the user. *Environmental actions* are any UI events coming from the system. Navigation to a new screen is one of the most noticeable environmental actions. The UX profile recommends that environmental actions be distinguished with a dollar sign prefixing the action's name.

Example 7.3 (advertising expenditure)

Refer to Figure 7.5 (Section 7.3.1). Our task is to identify the main UX modeling elements (class-level stereotypes) representing the content of the screen in this figure.

Figure 7.19 presents a UX class model that represents the content of the screen in Figure 7.5. The screen consists of four compartment and one input form.

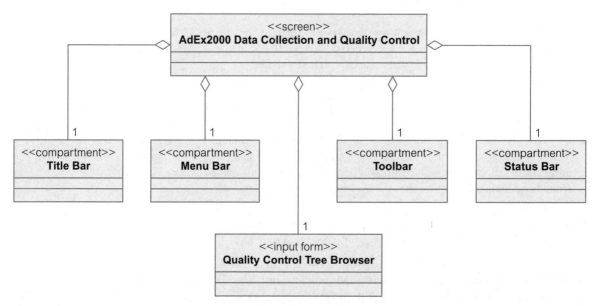

Figure 7.19 UX elements for the primary window (advertising expenditure)

Behavioral UX collaboration   7.5.3

Once the class-level UX elements are known, it is possible to start modeling the UX flows of events between these elements. The UX flows of events capture the behavioral aspect of a UX collaboration. Accordingly, the UML interaction diagrams (sequence and/or collaboration diagrams) are used to represent UX flows of events.

Example 7.4 (contact management)

Refer to Figures 7.3 (Section 7.1) and 7.6 (Section 7.3.1). Figure 7.3 is the Update Organization window. The window features a field (drop-down list) named Status. This field defines the status of the organization from the contact management perspective (e.g. that the organization is a potential, past, or current client).

The list of organization statuses is short and relatively fixed (Figure 7.20), but there is an occasional need to modify the list (insert, update, or delete a list item). The user can display the current list (possibly for updating or deleting) by double-clicking on the "Organisation Status" option in the tree browser seen on the left-hand side in Figure 7.6. However, to insert a new organization status, the user has to select (highlight) the "Organisation Status" option in the tree browser and then use an Insert action from the menu bar (the "Record" item in Figure 7.6) or from a toolbar (a small square icon in Figure 7.6).

Our task in this example is to identify the UX elements and to design a behavioral UX collaboration for the process of inserting a new organization status. Normally, modeling with UX storyboards replaces the need for window prototypes, but to assist us in this example, Figure 7.21 shows a possible Insert Organisation Status window.

The UX elements for Example 7.4 include three classes from Figure 7.19, namely `Quality Control Tree Browser`, `Menu Bar`, and `Toolbar`. The UX class model in Figure 7.22 presents the remaining classes needed for Example 7.4. These are the classes associated with the window to insert new organization status (Figure 7.21).

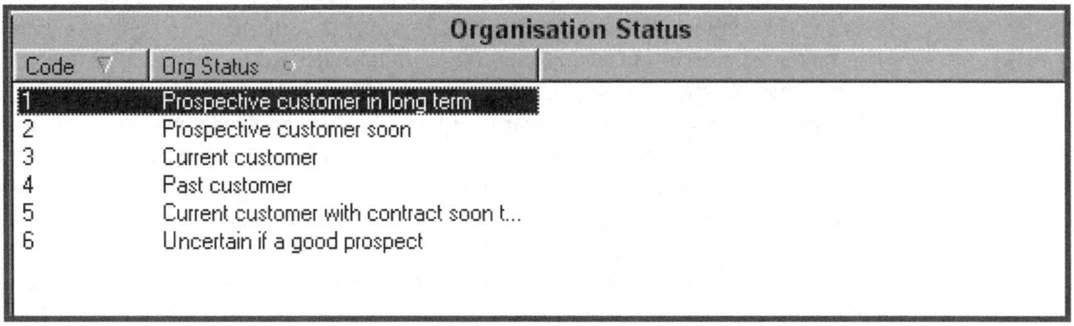

Organisation Status		
Code ▽	Org Status ○	
1	Prospective customer in long term	
2	Prospective customer soon	
3	Current customer	
4	Past customer	
5	Current customer with contract soon t...	
6	Uncertain if a good prospect	

Figure 7.20 Organization status (Contact Management)
Source: Courtesy of Nielsen Media Research, Sydney, Australia

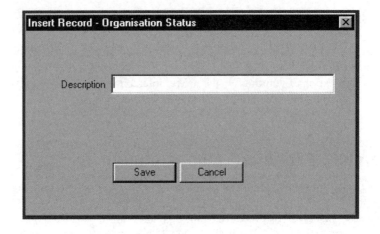

Figure 7.22
UX elements for
a dialog box
(contact
management)

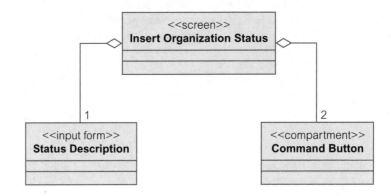

Figure 7.23 is a sequence diagram for the *UX behavioral collaboration* necessary to fulfill the requirements of Example 7.4. The model shows branching due to the conditionality of some user actions. For example, the user has an option to obtain the `Insert Organization Status` screen by using either a `Menu Bar` (event 2) or a `Toolbar` (event 3). The branched event flows can be rejoined at some point (e.g. events 4 and 5). Note that after pressing the `Save` or `Cancel` button the user is presented with the main screen containing the `Quality Control Tree Browser`.

UX collaboration models are restricted to human–computer interaction. This means, from the PCMEF perspective, that the only classes involved are from the presentation layer. Hence, for example, the model in Figure 7.23 does not show any processing involved in saving a new organization status in the database and showing this new status in the Organization Status row browser (Figure 7.20).

Similarly, the model does not make any reference to the fact that when a status description is saved, the database generates a `Code` for it (Figure 7.20). The fact that the code needs to be displayed in the Organization Status row browser is a matter for another UX collaboration model (but such a model is beyond Example 7.4).

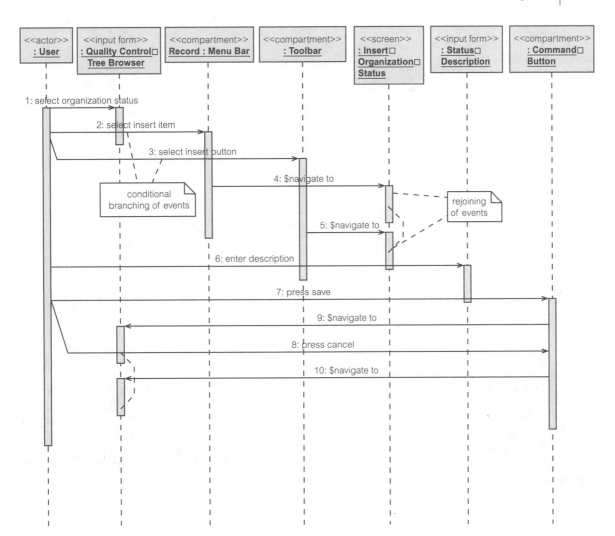

Figure 7.23 A sequence diagram for UX behavioral collaboration (contact management)

Structural UX collaboration   7.5.4

As in the case of any other UML collaboration modeling (Section 6.5), the structural aspect of UX collaboration is largely derivable from the behavioral UX collaboration. *Structural UX collaboration* produces a UX-stereotyped class diagram. The attribute box of each class presents the dynamic content for a screen, input form, or compartment. The operation box of each class presents user and environmental events.

The structural UX collaboration model serves as a *navigation diagram* for the use case that is the basis of the UX storyboard. To this aim, the structural UX model shows arrowed relationships between classes to indicate possible navigations between screens, input forms, and compartments.

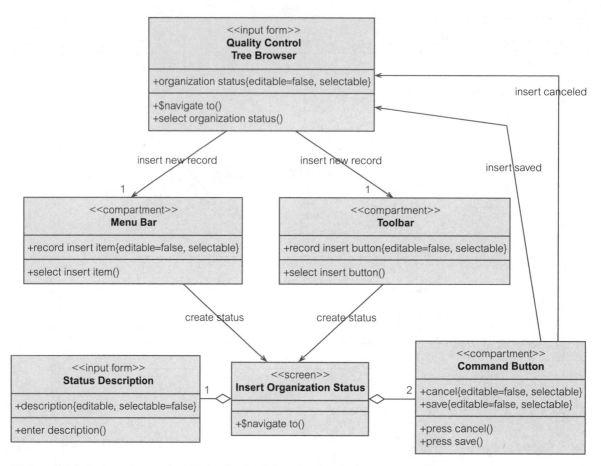

Figure 7.24 A class diagram for UX structural collaboration (contact management)

Example 7.5 (contact management)

Refer to Example 7.4 (Section 7.5.3). Our task is to produce a structural UX collaboration model corresponding to the behavioral UX collaboration model in Figure 7.23.

The model requested by Example 7.5 is demonstrated in Figure 7.24. The classes and the events within classes have been derived directly from the sequence diagram in Figure 7.23. The dynamic content for classes has been specified according to the windows shown in Figures 7.6 and 7.21 (however, we emphasize again that in most situations UX storyboards alleviate the need for developing window layouts or prototypes).

The dynamic content of the UX classes in Figure 7.24 is annotated with tag values. The tags specify the editability and selectability of fields. The visibility of fields is marked with a plus sign in front of their names (meaning that the fields are visible).

Navigation diagrams like that in Figure 7.24 should be defined for all use cases in the system. It is also possible to build navigation diagrams for activities or even actions of activity diagrams. Higher-level navigation diagrams, showing the main navigation paths between all screens in the system, may be desirable as well.

Summary

The development of the UI spans the software production lifecycle – it starts in the analysis phase and extends to the implementation. In this chapter, we have addressed the UI design for a variety of clients, including web browsers. With regard to thick clients, the Microsoft Windows environment has been emphasized. We have also introduced a UML profile, called a UX storyboard, which offers a graphical notation to depict the window design and navigation.

UI design is a *multidisciplinary activity* requiring the combined expertise of different professions. The design must adhere to the *guidelines* published by the manufacturer of a windows interface adopted in the project. The guidelines specify such issues as the user-in-control principle, consistency, personalization, customization, forgiveness, feedback, aesthetics, and usability.

The design of a UI requires familiarity with the various containers and components available for a particular client platform. The *containers* define various windows and web pages used in the application. A *primary window* can be a row browser, tree browser, or web page. A *secondary window* can be a dialog box, tab folder, drop-down list, or message box. A secondary window can be *modal* or *modeless* with regard to its primary window.

Containers are considered to be one category of UI *component*. Menus, toolbars, and controls are other kinds of component. A Java Swing library offers the whole range of interfaces and classes for working with containers and components.

Modern *web applications* place their own demands on UI design. These demands include the visualization aspects of *web pages* in the browsers. They also include programming aspects that result in *dynamic pages*. The programming aspects extend the responsibilities of web and application servers.

The visual design of individual windows is only one aspect of UI development. The second relates to *window navigation*, which captures the possible navigation paths between application windows and other UI elements. In this chapter, we introduced a UML profile (*UX storyboards*) to address this issue.

Questions

Q1　Refer to Figures 7.4 (Section 7.2.1) and 7.15 (Section 7.3.2.4). Figure 7.15 presents a message box informing that a business rule has been violated by an attempt to delete information about a `Program` ("program" refers to a TV or radio program). Figure 7.4 shows that business rule processing is invoked from a 4GL-SQL procedure, not from a GUI window. Why? Could a business rule, like in Figure 7.15, be activated directly as a GUI window event?

Q2　How is a primary window different from a secondary window?

Q3 What is a pane? How is it useful in Windows UI design?

Q4 The Java Swing library consists mostly of so-called lightweight components, but some Swing components are heavyweight. Search the literature and/or Internet to find out about these two kinds of Swing component and describe the difference.

Q5 What is a tab folder? How is it different from a dialog box?

Q6 JavaServer Faces (JSF) is a new technology that aims at defining something like a Swing library for web-based user interfaces. Search the Internet to establish the current status of JSF. Describe your findings.

Q7 This chapter introduces server pages but does not mention the related technology of servlets. Find out what is the difference between these two technologies and describe it briefly.

Q8 Explain why the UX profile recommends tags to describe the properties of the dynamic content of UX classes. Could not tags be replaced by constraints?

Exercises (contact management)

F1 Refer to the problem statement for contact management (Section 1.5.3) and to the successive examples for contact management in Chapter 4. The users require that the contact management application be modeled on the functionality of the Calendar window in Microsoft Outlook (Figure 7.25).

The primary window should display the activities scheduled for the day for the employee who is using the system. The Calendar control can display past and future activities. The events scheduled for a particular time of the day (timed events) are to be displayed as in the Microsoft

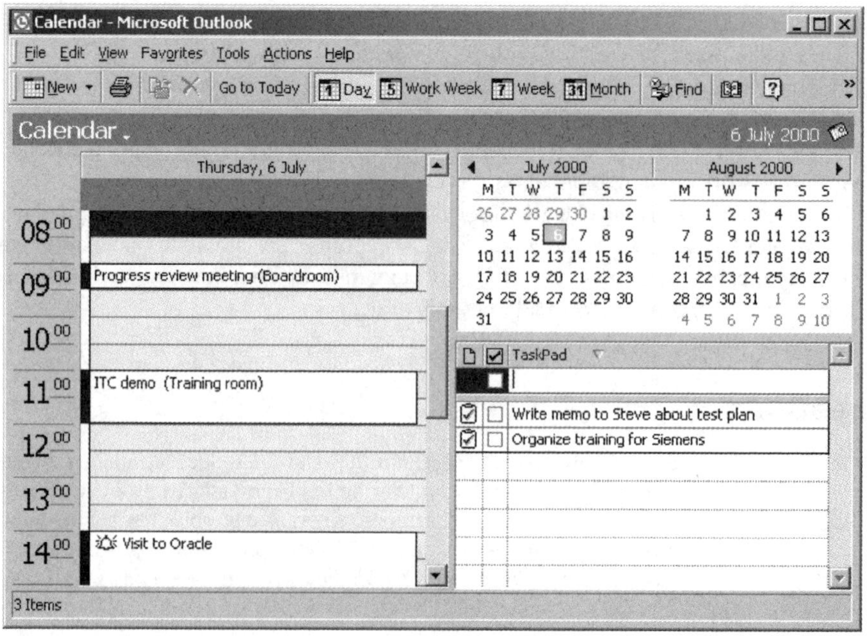

Figure 7.25
Microsoft Outlook
– Calendar
window
Source: Screen
shot reprinted by
permission from
Microsoft
Corporation

Outlook left pane. However, there is also a requirement to show and handle untimed, outstanding (due in the past), and completed events.

Design a primary window for contact management that conforms to the above requirements.

F2 Refer to the problem statement for contact management (Section 1.5.3) and to the successive examples for contact management in Chapter 4. Refer also to Exercise F1 in this chapter and to the solution provided.

Assume that the primary window for contact management does not permit certain manipulations on events. For example, entering a new event or updating an existing event must be done through a secondary window – a dialog box.

By double-clicking on an event in the primary window, a dialog box should appear showing full details for that event. The dialog box displays not just the event information but also the data about its encompassing task as well as the organization and contact to which the event relates.

The event details that can be displayed and possibly modified include the event type (called action), a longer description (called notes), the date, time, and user (employee) for an event's creation, and the scheduled, due, and completion time for the event.

Design a dialog box for event manipulation that conforms to the above requirements.

F3 Refer to the problem statement for contact management (Section 1.5.3) and to the successive examples for contact management in Chapter 4. Refer also to Exercises F1 and F2 in this chapter and to the solutions provided.

Consider the tab folder for Update Organization in Figure 7.3 (Section 7.1). One of the tabs is called Contacts. The purpose of it is to allow access and modification of contact data (`EContact` class) from this tab folder. Otherwise, the user would always have to return to the primary window and activate a separate secondary window for Contacts.

Design the content of the Contacts tab.

F4 Refer to Examples 7.3 (Section 7.5.2) and 7.4 (Section 7.5.3). As stated in Example 7.4 with reference to Figure 7.6 (Section 7.3.1), the user can display the current list of organization statuses by double-clicking on the "Organisation Status" option in the tree browser. This action will display the list of statuses (as a row browser) in the right-hand pane of the window in Figure 7.6. The list will be displayed as in Figure 7.20 (Section 7.5.3).

If the user wants to update any status, she/he has to select (highlight) the status record on the list. There are three possibilities for obtaining the "Update Status" dialog box: (1) by double-clicking on the selected record; (2) by selecting an Update action from the menu bar (the "Record" item in Figure 7.6); or (3) by clicking on a toolbar button (a square with an overlapping rectangle in Figure 7.6).

Design a behavioral UX collaboration for the process of updating organization status. Make sure that a successful update gets reflected in the list of statuses (Figure 7.20). Show only the third option (a toolbar button) for navigation to the "Update Status" window.

F5 Refer to Exercise F4 and to its provided solution (Figure 7.29). Produce a structural UX collaboration model corresponding to the behavioral UX collaboration model in Figure 7.29.

Exercises (telemarketing)

Additional requirements (telemarketing)

Consider the following additional requirements for telemarketing:

1. The `Telemarketing Control` window is the primary control interface for the Telemarketing application. The window displays to the telemarketer a list of the calls in the current queue. When the telemarketer requests a call from the queue, the system establishes the connection and the telemarketer is able to process a connected call. The `Call Summary` information displays on the screen – it shows the start time, the finish time, and the duration of the current call.

2. Once connected, the `Telemarketing Control` window displays information about the current call – who has been called, about what campaign, and what kind of call is being made. If there is more than one call scheduled for the current phone number, then the telemarketer is given the option of cycling through these calls.

3. At any stage during the conversation, the telemarketer can view the supporter's history (the `Supporter History` window) with regard to previous campaigns. Similarly, details about the campaign to which the current call is pertaining can be viewed (the `Campaign` window).

4. The GUI provides for quick recording of call outcomes. The possible outcomes are placement (i.e. tickets have been ordered), callback, unsuccessful, no answer, engaged, machine (i.e. answering machine), fax, wrong (i.e. wrong number), and disconnected.

5. The `Campaign` window displays campaign details, ticket details, and prize details for the campaign. The campaign details include the identifying number, the title, the start, the close, and the prize drawing dates. The ticket details include the number of tickets in the campaign, how many have been sold, and how many are still available. The prize details include the prize description, the prize value, and the place of the prize (the first, second, or third).

6. The `Supporter History` window shows the past call history and the past campaign history for the supporter. The call history lists the recent calls, the types of these calls, the outcomes, and the identification of the campaigns and of the telemarketers. The campaign history informs about ticket placements and prize winnings by the supporter.

7. On selecting the `Placement` action, the `Placement` window is activated. The `Placement` window allows the user to allocate tickets to the supporter and to record the payment.

8. On selecting the `No Answer` or `Engaged` action, the "no answer" or "engaged" outcome is recorded in the system for each of the current calls. The calls are then rescheduled by the system for another time tomorrow, provided that each call is below the limit for attempts determined by the type of call.

9. Upon selecting the `Machine` action, the "machine" outcome is recorded in the system. The duration of the call is set for the first of the current calls only. The calls are then rescheduled by the system for another time tomorrow, provided that each call is below the limit for attempts determined by the type of call.

10. On selecting the `Fax` or `Wrong` action, the "fax" or "wrong" outcome is recorded in the system. The duration of the call is set for the first of the current calls only. The supporter data is then updated to "bad phone" for each supporter with the current phone number.

11. Upon selecting the `Disconnected` action, the "disconnected" outcome is recorded in the system. The supporter data is then updated to "bad phone" for each supporter with the current phone number.

12. Upon selecting the `Callback` action, the "callback" outcome is recorded in the system. The duration of the call is set for the first of the current calls only. The `Call Scheduling` window is invoked to obtain the

date and time for the callback to be arranged. The calls are then rescheduled by the system (with the new priority) for the date and time obtained by the Call Scheduling window. The types of new calls are set to "callback."

13. Upon exiting the Placement window, if all of the remaining tickets in the campaign have just been allocated, then all further calls to supporters for that campaign are pointless. Any such calls must be removed from the call queue.

G1 Refer to the problem statement for telemarketing (Section 1.5.4) and to telemarketing examples in Chapters 4 and 5. Consider the class diagram in Example 4.7 (Section 4.2.1.2.3).

Modify and extend the class diagram in Figure 4.5 to support the additional requirements specified above.

G2 Refer to telemarketing requirements, including the additional requirements above. Also consider your solution to Exercise G1.

Design and sketch the primary window for telemarketing. The window should contain a row browser with the list of calls currently scheduled to telemarketers. Some calls would be explicitly scheduled to a specific telemarketer – perhaps as a result of an explicit request from the supporter. The window should provide facilities to refresh the display of the queue (by polling the database server), to request the next call from the queue, and to switch to the next campaign.

G3 Refer to telemarketing requirements, including the additional requirements above. Also consider your solutions to Exercises G1 and G2.

Design and sketch the main secondary window for telemarketing. The window, called Current Call, shows the primary set of information and actions available to the telemarketer when the phone connection to the supporter is being attempted and established by the automatic dialing capability of the system. The command buttons in the window should be grouped into three categories: (1) Call Details, (2) Call Outcome, and (3) two generic buttons (Next Call and Cancel).

G4 Refer to telemarketing requirements, including the additional requirements above. Also consider your solutions to Exercises G1, G2, and G3.

Design and sketch the Supporter History window. The window should present five groups of fields: (1) Calls in this Campaign, (2) Address/Phone, (3) History/Winnings, (4) Preferred Hours, and (5) Payment Status.

G5 Identify the main UX modeling elements (class-level stereotypes) representing the content of the primary window from your solution to Exercise G2.

G6 Identify the main UX modeling elements (class-level stereotypes) representing the content of the main secondary window from your solution to Exercise G3.

G7 Identify the main UX modeling elements (class-level stereotypes) representing the content of the secondary window from your solution to Exercise G4.

G8 Design a behavioral UX collaboration for the process defined in requirement 3 in the additional requirements above. Requirement 3 states: "At any stage during the conversation, the telemarketer can view the supporter's history (the Supporter History window) with regard to previous campaigns. Similarly, details about the campaign to which the current call is pertaining can be viewed (the Campaign window)."

G9 Design a structural UX collaboration corresponding to the behavioral UX collaboration that you have developed as your solution to exercise G8.

Answers to odd-numbered questions

Q1 – answer

Business rules are defined for the system as a whole, not for each individual window or even individual application program. An attempt to delete a `Program` may be initiated by a user from a GUI window, but it should invariably result in invocation of a 4GL-SQL procedure executing within the database environment (not within the client code). The database procedure will then attempt to delete the `Program` information from the database. At this point, the database will check the deletion against the business rules, normally implemented as *trigger* programs within the database. The message in Figure 7.15 comes from such a trigger.

Triggers cannot be explicitly called. They are "triggered" by events, such as the delete event. Technically, a delete event could come directly from a client program. This would happen if the delete event from the user were serviced by an SQL `Delete` command (from the client straight to the database), rather than by calling a 4GL-SQL procedure (a stored procedure). However, this would not be a recommended practice. Apart from other drawbacks, issuing SQL commands from the client would force the client code to service any error messages returned by the server (instead of using the stored procedure to interpret such errors for the client).

Q3 – answer

A *pane* is a "sub-window" within the primary window. It is a part of the window that allows for separate display of information. A pane may have its own scrollbars to allow its entire content to be viewed. A window may have more than one pane.

Panes are very useful in GUI design because primary windows are frequently very "busy" and demand that a variety of data be displayed. Panes allow related information to be displayed in separate viewing areas.

Q5 – answer

A *dialog box* is the main kind of secondary window that serves *editing* purposes. A *tab folder* is really a more sophisticated kind of dialog box. Each tab page in a tab folder permits editing of information. Although each tab page can have its own command buttons, the button to save changes to the database applies at the tab folder level (rather than at the tab page level).

The difference between a dialog box and a tab folder relates to the amount of information that can be handled by these windows. Whenever the "real estate" of a dialog box is too small to display and edit the data fields and values, a tab folder provides a convenient alternative solution.

Q7 – answer

A *servlet* is (Java) code that dynamically creates HTML pages. It is Java code with embedded HTML elements. A *server page* (a Java Server Page – JSP) is the opposite – an HTML page with embedded Java code (tags and scriplets) to manage the dynamic content of the page and to supply data to it (Maciaszek and Liong, 2004).

If we consider that the servlet code may be supported by Java Server Pages and that JSP is compiled to a servlet prior to running, the difference is quite insignificant. What is more important is that once a servlet is loaded in a web server, it can connect to a database and maintain the connection for more than one client. This is called *servlet chaining*. It allows one servlet to pass a client request to another servlet.

Solutions to exercises (contact management)

F1 – solution

Figure 7.26 shows the primary window for contact management. The Calendar control is designed as a detachable "floating" window to conserve space. It can be closed if so desired. For each event in the left-hand pane, the event's short description and either an organization or contact name is shown. For some events, additional information may be shown as well, e.g. the organization's or contact's phone number, a fax number, or address. Although not clearly visible in the black and white reproduction, color is used in the left pane to signify the priority assigned to the event (high in red, normal in black, and low in blue).

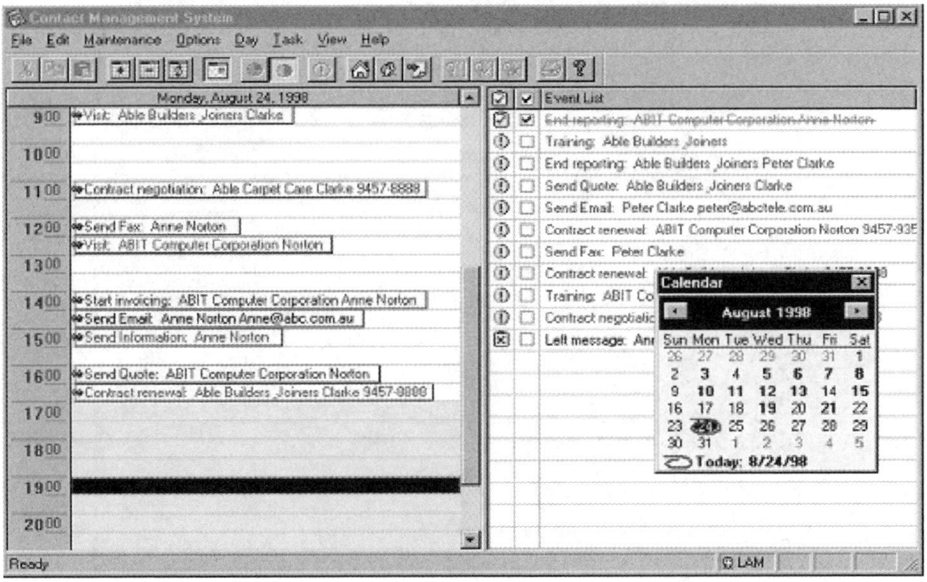

Figure 7.26
A primary window
(contact
management)
Source: Courtesy
of Nielsen Media
Research,
Sydney, Australia

The right-hand pane serves three purposes. It displays three kinds of event. *Completed* events are removed from the left-hand pane and placed at the top of the right-hand pane. The text is in blue type and crossed out. The main reason why a completed event is not removed altogether from the display is that the completed event may need to be "uncompleted" (perhaps we thought prematurely that the event was done but found out later that it was not quite done).

The *outstanding* events are listed in the right pane. They are in red. Finally, the *untimed* events are shown in black and listed at the bottom of the right pane. The left-hand side column in the pane is designed with colorblind users in mind. The icons there signify the three kinds of event possible in the right pane.

F2 – solution

Figure 7.27 is the proposed solution to the example. Note that the `Organization` and `Contact` fields are not editable, because the "target" of the event cannot be changed. Similarly, the field values next to the prompt `Created` are not editable.

The field values adjacent to the prompt `Completed` are not editable in the sense that the user cannot type in them. However, pressing the `Complete` button will automatically insert the date, time, and user values in these fields. After completing the event, the user still has the possibility of "uncompleting" it because the `Complete` button is then renamed `Uncomplete`.

The user has the possibility of saving changes to the database and returning to the primary window by clicking the `OK` button. Alternatively, the user can `Cancel` the changes and stay in the dialog box. Finally, the user can press the `New Event` button, which will save the changes (after the user's confirmation), clear all the fields in the dialog box, and allow the user to create a new event (without returning to the primary window).

F3 – solution

As shown in Figure 7.28, the `Contacts` tab displays only the names of the contacts in an organization. However, the tab has its own set of command buttons to `Add`, `Edit`, or `Delete` the currently highlighted contact. An action to `Add` or `Edit` a contact will result in a `Maintain Contacts` secondary window opening up on top of the `Maintain Organizations` window. The `Maintain Contacts` window will be modal with regard to the `Maintain Organizations` window.

Figure 7.27 — Details dialog box

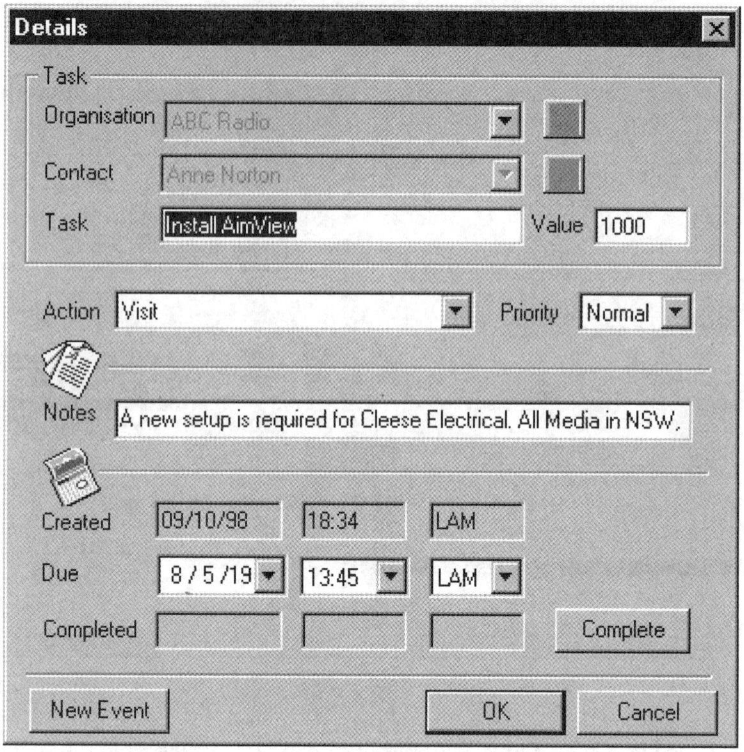

Details
Task
Organisation: ABC Radio
Contact: Anne Norton
Task: Install AimView   Value: 1000
Action: Visit   Priority: Normal
Notes: A new setup is required for Cleese Electrical. All Media in NSW,
Created: 09/10/98   18:34   LAM
Due: 8/5/19   13:45   LAM
Completed:
New Event   OK   Cancel

Figure 7.28 — Maintain Organisations tab folder

Maintain Organisations
ABC Radio   New
General	Postal Address	Courier Address	**Contacts**
Leonard Norton   Anne Norton
Elle Norton   Gloria Norton
Add   Edit   Delete
OK   Cancel   Apply

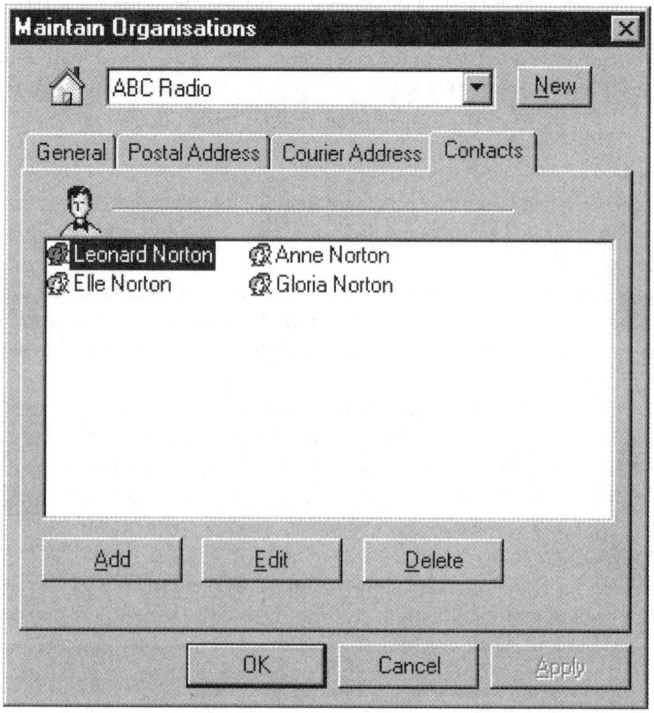

F4 – solution

Figure 7.29 presents a solution to Exercise F4. The solution should be self-explanatory.

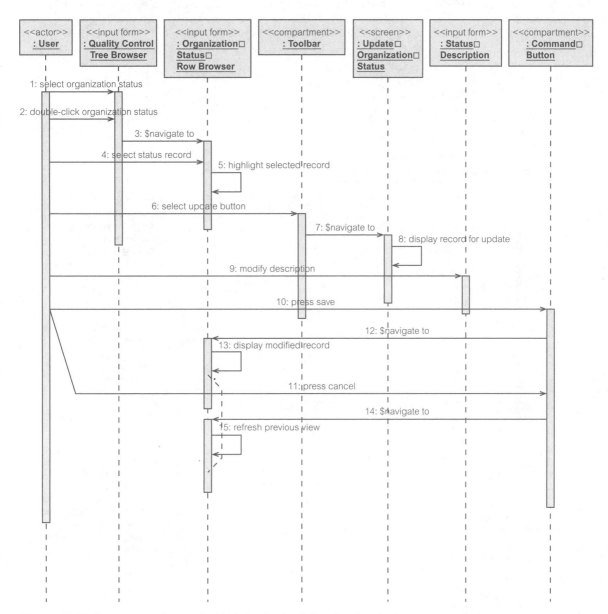

Figure 7.29 A sequence diagram for UX behavioral collaboration (contact management)

F5 – solution

Figure 7.30 presents a solution to Exercise F5. The solution should be self-explanatory, but the comparison with a UX structural collaboration for inserting a new status in Figure 7.24 may have educational value. Note, for example, that `status code` is now a dynamic content of `Update Organization Status`, while `description` is a dynamic content of `Status Description`. However, because `Status Description` is contained in `Update Organization Status`, `description` is also included in the dynamic content of `Update Organization Status`.

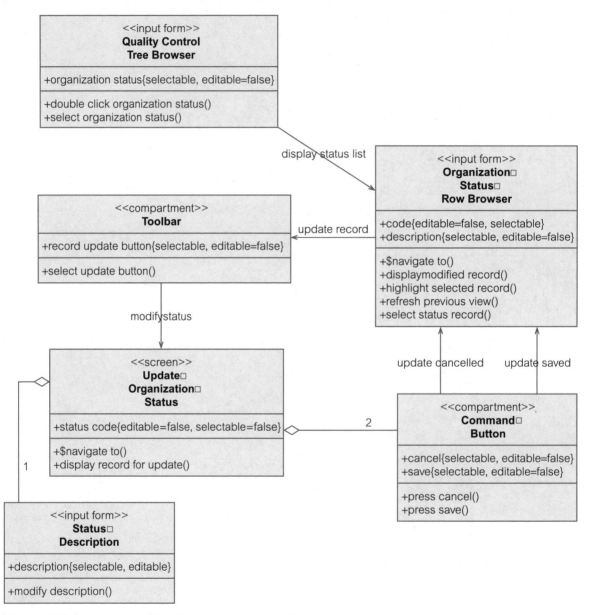

Figure 7.30 A class diagram for UX structural collaboration (contact management)

Chapter

8

Persistence and Database Design

Information systems are by definition multi-user systems. *Database management systems* (DBMSs) provide the technology to support concurrent access by large numbers of users and application programs to the same data store. Application programs depend on databases not just for data but also for database-provided functions that resolve any concurrency conflicts, ensure secure access to data, guarantee data consistency, take care of recovering from transaction failures, etc. Some of these functions are an inherent part of the DBMS software. Other functions on which application programs depend must be coded by the database programmers. The conclusion is obvious – a good database design that can accommodate and support *all* application programs is the necessary condition for an information system to deliver the intended functionality.

In UML, class diagrams define the data structures required by an application. The data structures that have persistent presence in the database are modeled as the entity classes ("business objects") and as the relationships between entity classes. The entity classes correspond to the "E" letter in the PCMEF framework (introduced in Section 4.1.1. and used throughout the book). The entity classes need to be mapped to the data structures recognized by the database. These data structures vary depending on the underlying database model, which can be object-oriented, object-relational, or relational.

Over the last twenty years, the relational database (RDB) model has conquered the database software market. It has replaced the earlier hierarchical and network database models. In the second half of the 1990s, vendors of relational database management systems (RDBMS) were put on notice by the object database (ODB) model, the Object Database Management Group (ODMG) standards, and various object database management system (ODBMS) products.

As a consequence, ORDBMS products emerged and may still be destined to play a dominant role in the future. Traditional RDBMS vendors, such as Oracle and IBM, offer the most influential of these products today, and Microsoft's push into this market has grown significantly. In the meantime, pure ODBMS products have not increased their market share – they have shifted to become object storage APIs to support interoperability between client applications and any server data sources, in particular relational databases.

Although the future may no longer belong to the RDB model, business inertia is such that a decade or more will pass before large systems migrate to ORDB or ODB technology. There will also be many new applications developed using RDB technology, simply because businesses will not need the sophisticated and difficult-to-master object solutions.

This said, the latest database standard, known as SQL:1999, calls itself an object-relational database standard (Melton, 2002), while also being the standard for traditional relational databases (Melton and Simon, 2001). SQL:1999 adds object-oriented features to the relational model while keeping the relational model conceptually intact. The object-oriented features fall short of the expectations of object-oriented software developers, but they constitute a step in the right direction.

In this chapter, we explain the connection between business objects and persistence, we review the relational database model, and we discuss the mapping of objects to databases and vice versa. We explain conversions from the entity classes, associations, aggregations, and generalizations to the data structures available in the relational database models. The scope of the textbook has not allowed us to explain the "schema integration," i.e. the integration of overlapping database structures resulting from the demands of many application programs competing for the same database resources.

8.1 Business objects and persistence

Throughout the book, we have been carefully distinguishing between the development of a client application and the design of a server database. We have emphasized that the class models and PCMEF subsystems contain the application classes, not the storage database structures.

The *entity classes* represent persistent database objects in the application. They are *not* persistent classes in the database. They are *called* persistent with the understanding that prior to the application program's termination the latest images of entity objects will be stored persistently in the database. This will allow future activation of the same or other application programs to obtain these entity objects again by loading them from the database to the program's memory. Consequently, the interaction between business objects and persistent database has to be carefully designed.

A persistent database can be a relational (e.g. Sybase, DB2, Oracle), object-relational (e.g. UniSQL, Oracle) or object database (e.g. ObjectStore, Versant). It is unlikely that the storage model for a new system can be any of the older models such as hierarchical (e.g.

IMS), network (e.g. IDMS), inverted or similar model (e.g. Total, Adabas). In some cases, but not really in modern IS applications, the persistence can be implemented in simple flat files.

The *relational model* dominates in business systems and, therefore, this is the only model discussed in detail in this chapter. Curiously enough, the first edition of this book also contained discussion of object and object-relational databases. We can only hope that these two models get more presence in enterprise information systems to warrant presenting them again in future editions of this book.

Levels of data models 8.1.1

The database community has developed its own view on the world of modeling. Databases *store data*. Historically, the database community has concentrated on *data models* (i.e. state models in the UML parlance). The current capability of databases to *store and execute programs* has extended this perspective to include *behavior models* (centered on triggers and stored procedures), but data modeling remains the "bread and butter" of database development.

A *data model* (also called a *database schema*) is an abstraction that presents the database structures in more understandable terms than as raw bits and bytes. A popular classification of data model layers recognizes three abstractions:

1. external (conceptual) data model;
2. logical data model;
3. physical data model.

The *external schema* represents a high-level *conceptual data model* required by a single application. Because a database normally supports many applications, multiple external schemas are constructed. They are then integrated into one conceptual data model.

The most popular conceptual data modeling technique uses *entity-relationship* (*ER*) *diagrams* (e.g. Maciaszek, 1990). Although ER modeling remains popular among database designers, it gives way to UML class modeling as the technique of choice for all conceptual modeling, i.e. the conceptual modeling of applications and of databases.

The *logical schema* (also sometimes called the *global conceptual schema*) provides a model that reflects the logical storage structures (tables, etc.) of the database model to be used for system implementation (typically, a relational model). The logical schema is a global integrated model to support any current and expected applications that need to access information stored in the database.

The *physical schema* is specific to a particular DBMS (such as Oracle10g). It defines how data are actually stored on persistent storage devices, typically disks. The physical schema defines such issues as the use of indexes and clustering of data for efficient processing.

The *lower-engineering CASE tools* (i.e. the CASE tools targeting system design and implementation) normally provide a data-modeling technique that targets a vast variety of specific DBMSs. In effect, they provide a capability for constructing a combined logical/physical model and immediately generating the relevant SQL code.

8.1.2 Integrating application and database modeling

Modeling of an application program and modeling of a database are disjoint activities. The former is done by application developers, the latter by database administrators or designers. The reason for this split is that a database must be developed independently of applications (but not "in spite of" the applications!). A single database must serve multiple different application programs. It must be a compromise solution that resolves any conflicts and overlaps in data access demands by applications.

An application developer is usually given a model for a database that the application needs to access. Having this, the application developer needs to design the necessary mappings between the program model and the database model.

Figure 8.1 demonstrates how UML models for an application relate to persistent database models. The arrows show the dependencies between modeling elements. The downward dependency principle (DDP) of the PCMEF architectural framework (Section 4.1.3) extends on the communication between the application and the persistent database.

The `foundation` subsystem is solely responsible for communication with the database. All SQL queries and calls to stored procedures from the application are generated by the `foundation` classes and passed to the database server. Any data and other results returned by the database server are first delivered to the `foundation` classes before they can make their way up to the `entity` subsystem.

Classes of the `entity` subsystem represent the "business objects" placed in the memory of an application program. The mapping rules between business objects and their corresponding records in database tables must be carefully defined.

The mapping rules are used by the `mediator` subsystem, which is responsible for managing the application's memory cache and for any movement of objects between the memory and the database. This means that the `mediator` subsystem is the first port of call when a `control` class needs to access a business object and it does not have a prior handle (reference) on that object. This also means that the `mediator` subsystem must manage *business transactions* within which any sequences of database access and modification are conducted.

8.1.3 Underpinnings of object-database mapping

The mapping between the application and the database may be a convoluted issue. There are two fundamental reasons for the mapping difficulty. First, the storage structures of the database may have little to do with the object-oriented paradigm. Second, the database is almost never designed for a single application.

The first reason amounts to the conversion of *non-object-oriented structures*, typically relational tables, to classes in the entity subsystem. Even if the target database is an object database, the peculiarities of the database will necessitate careful conversion.

The second reason demands an optimal database *design for all applications*, not just the one under consideration. All applications acting on the database should be prioritized for business significance so that those applications that are most important to the organization have the database structures tuned to them. Equally importantly, the database designer

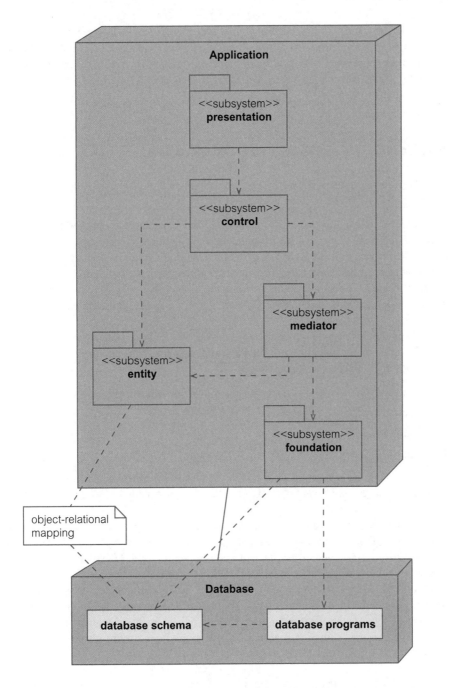

Figure 8.1
Integrating
application and
database
modeling

should always look to the future, anticipate future demands for data by forthcoming applications and design the database to accommodate these demands.

The odds are that the persistent database layer is going to be a *relational database*, because relational database technology dominates the marketplace. For large enterprise databases, the change to the *object database* technology will be evolutionary and will go through an intermediate (if not final) stage of *object-relational* technology. For now, we consider here only the *relational database* model. In terms of object–database mapping, this is semantically the most restrictive model and therefore the most difficult model to map.

8.2 Relational database model

The RDB modeling primitives are primitive indeed. The simplicity of the RDB model, which derives from the mathematical *set* concept, is both its strength and its weakness. The mathematical foundations make the model *declarative* in nature (as opposed to *procedural*). The user declares *what* is needed from the database rather than instructing the system *how* to find the information (an RDBMS knows how to find data in its own database).

But what is simple at first becomes quite complex when the problem to solve gets complicated. There are no simple solutions for complex problems. To solve a complex problem we need sophisticated machinery. To start with, we need sophisticated data-modeling primitives.

Perhaps the best way to characterize the RDB model is to state what it does not support. From the major modeling primitives available in the ODB and/or ORDB models, the RDB does not support:

■ object types and associated concepts (such as inheritance or methods)

■ structured types

■ collections

■ references.

The main modeling primitive in the RDB model is a *relational table* that consists of columns. Table *columns* can take only *atomic values* – structured values or collections of values are not permitted.

The RDB model is adamant about any user-visible *navigational links* between tables – they are explicitly *precluded*. The relationships between tables are maintained by comparing values in columns. There are no persistent links. The ORDB utility to maintain predefined relationships between tables is called the *referential integrity*.

Figure 8.2 shows RDB modeling primitives and dependencies between them. All concepts are named with singular nouns, but some dependencies apply to more than one instance of the concept. For example, a referential integrity is defined on one or more tables. The concepts shown in Figure 8.2 are discussed next in this chapter.

8.2.1 Columns, domains, and rules

Relational databases define data in tables of columns and rows. A data value stored on the intersection of any column and row must be a simple (indivisible) and a single (not repeating) value. We say that the *columns* have *atomic domains* (data types).

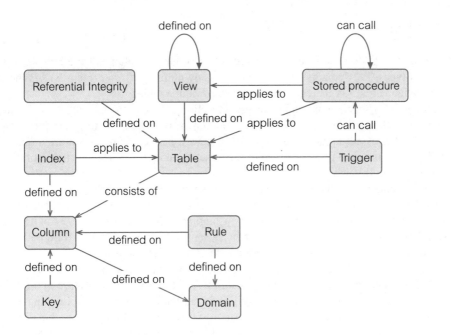

Figure 8.2
Dependencies
between database
modeling
primitives

A *domain* defines the legal set of values that a column can take. The domain can be anonymous (e.g. `gender char(1)`) or it can be named (e.g. `gender Gender`). In the latter case, the domain `Gender` has been defined earlier and used in the definition of the column. A possible syntax for the domain definition could be:

```
create domain Gender char(1);
```

A *named domain* can be used in the definition of many columns in different tables. This enforces consistency between these definitions. Changes to the domain definition are automatically reflected in column definitions. Although an attractive option at first glance, its use is impeded once the database has been *populated*, i.e. loaded with data.

Columns and domains can have *business rules* that constrain them. The business rule can define:

- *default value* (e.g. if no value is provided for `city`, assume "`Sydney`");
- *range of values* (e.g. the allowed `age` is in the range `18` to `80`);
- *list of values* (e.g. the allowed `color` is "`green`", "`yellow`," or "`red`");
- *case of value* (e.g. the value must be in upper or lower case);
- *format of value* (e.g. the value must start with the letter "`K`").

Only very simple business rules concerning single columns or domains can be defined with the *rule* facility. More complex rules spanning tables can be defined as *referential integrity* constraints. The ultimate mechanism for defining business rules is a *trigger*.

8.2.2 Tables

A *relational table* is defined by its fixed set of columns. Columns have built-in or user-defined types (i.e. domains). Tables can have any number of *rows* (records). As the table is a mathematical *set*, there are no duplicate rows in a table.

A column value in a particular row may be allowed to be NULL. The NULL value means one of two things: "the value is at present unknown" (e.g. I don't know your birth date) or "the value does not apply" (e.g. you cannot have a maiden name if you are a man). The null value is not zero or a space (empty) character value; it is a special stream of bits that denotes the null value.

A consequence of the RDB model's requirement of "no duplicate rows" is that every table has a *primary key*. A *key* is a *minimal* set of columns (possibly one) such that the values in these columns *uniquely* identify a single row in the table. A table can have many such keys. One of these keys is arbitrarily chosen as the most important for the user – this is the *primary key*. Other keys are called *candidate* or *alternate keys*.

In practice, an RDBMS table does not have to have a key. This means that a table (without a unique key) may have duplicate rows – a pretty useless feature in a relational database as two rows with the same values for all their columns are not distinguishable. This is different for ODB and ORDB systems, where the OID provides such a distinction (two objects may be equal but not identical, like two copies of this book, for example).

Although UML can be stereotyped for modeling relational databases, it is more convenient to use a specifically targeted diagramming technique for the logical modeling of relational databases. Figure 8.3 demonstrates one such notation. The target database is DB2.

The table Employee consists of nine columns. The column dept_id and the last three columns accept NULL values. The column emp_id is the primary key. The column dept_id is a foreign key (explained in the next section). The columns {family_name, date_of_birth} define a candidate (alternate) key. The column gender is defined on the domain Gender.

Because of the RDB restriction that a column can take only atomic single values, we have encountered difficulty with modeling employee names and phone numbers. In the former case, we used two columns: family_name and first_name. The columns are not grouped or otherwise related in the model. In the latter case, we opted for a solution with two columns (phone_num1, phone_num2), allowing a maximum of two phone numbers per employee.

Figure 8.3
Table definition in
an RDB

Employee			
emp_id	CHAR(7)	\<pk\>	not null
family_name	VARCHAR(30)	\<ak\>	not null
first_name	VARCHAR(20)		not null
date_of_birth	DATE	\<ak\>	not null
gender	Gender		not null
phone_num1	VARCHAR(12)		null
phone_num2	VARCHAR(12)		null
salary	DEC(8,2)		null

Figure 8.4 SQL
generated for
table definition

```
--================================================================
--  Domain: "Gender"
--================================================================
create distinct type "Gender" as CHAR(1) with comparisons;
--================================================================
--  Table: "Employee"
--================================================================
create table "Employee" (
    "emp_id"              CHAR(7)                     not null,
    "family_name"         VARCHAR(30)                 not null,
    "first_name"          VARCHAR(20)                 not null,
    "date_of_birth"       DATE                        not null,
    "gender"              "Gender"                    not null
        constraint "C_gender" check ("gender" in ('F','M','f','m')),
    "phone_num1"          VARCHAR(12),
    "phone_num2"          VARCHAR(12),
    "salary"              DEC(8,2),
primary key ("emp_id"),
unique ("date_of_birth", "family_name")
);
```

Once the table has been defined in a CASE tool, the code to create the table can be generated automatically, as shown in Figure 8.4. The generated code includes the definition of the domain Gender and the definition of the business rule defined on that domain.

Referential integrity

8.2.3

The RDB model maintains relationships between tables by means of *referential integrity* constraints. The relationships are not fixed row-to-row connections (using pointers, references, or similar navigational links). Instead, an RDB "discovers" row-to-row connections each time the user requests the system to find a relationship. This "discovering" is done by comparing the *primary key* values in one table with the *foreign key* values in the same or another table.

A *foreign key* is defined as a set of columns in one table whose values are either NULL or are required to match the values of the primary key in the same or another table. That primary-to-foreign key correspondence is called the *referential integrity*. The primary and foreign keys in a referential integrity must be defined on the same domain, but they do not have to have the same names.

Figure 8.5 shows a graphical representation for referential integrity. As the result of drawing a relationship between the tables Employee and Department, the foreign key dept_id is introduced to the table Employee. For each Employee row, the foreign key value must either be NULL or match one of the dept_id values in Department (otherwise an employee would work for a department that does not exist).

The additional description on the relationship line defines *declaratively* the behavior associated with the referential integrity. There are four possible *declarative referential integrity constraints* associated with *delete* and *update* operations. The question is what to

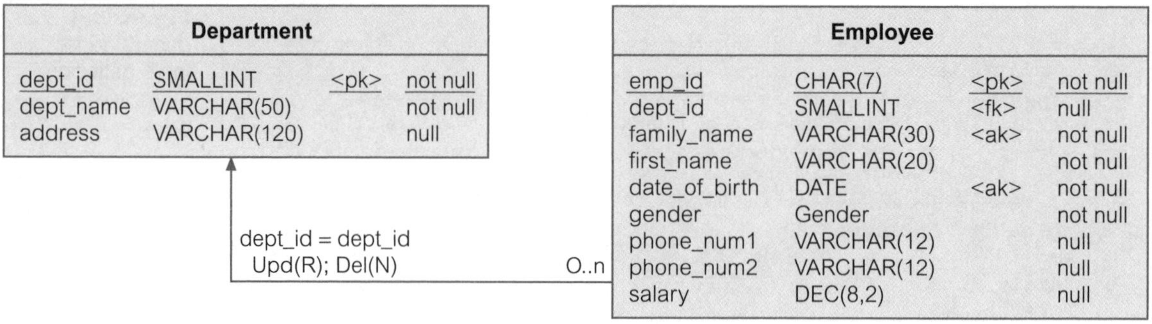

Figure 8.5 Graphical representation for referential integrity

Figure 8.6 SQL generated for referential integrity

```
alter table "Employee"
    drop foreign key "RefToDepartment";

alter table "Employee"
    add foreign key "RefToDepartment" ("dept_id")
        references "Department" ("dept_id")
        on delete set null;
```

do with `Employee` rows if a `Department` row is deleted or updated (i.e. when `dept_id` gets updated). There are four possible answers to this question:

1. `Upd(R); Del(R)` – *restrict* the update or delete operation (i.e. do not allow the operation to go ahead if there are still `Employee` rows linked to that `Department`).

2. `Upd(C); Del(C)` – *cascade* the operation (i.e. delete all linked `Employee` rows).

3. `Upd(N); Del(N)` – *set null* (i.e. update or delete the `Department` row and set `dept_id` of the linked `Employee` rows to `NULL`).

4. `Upd(D); Del(D)` – *set default* (i.e. update or delete the `Department` row and set `dept_id` of the linked `Employee` rows to the default value).

Although not shown in Figure 8.5, the *change parent allowed* (*cpa*) *constraint* could also be defined for a referential integrity. The cpa constraint states that records in a child (foreign) table can be reassigned to a different record in a parent table. For example, the cpa constraint could in fact be defined on the relationship in Figure 8.5, as it normally expected that an `Employee` can be reallocated to another `Department`. The cpa constraint is the opposite of the *frozen constraint* that is enforced by the *ExclusiveOwns* aggregation (Section 5.3.1.1).

Figure 8.6 shows the SQL statements generated automatically based on the graphical model in Figure 8.5. The foreign key in the table `Employee` is dropped in the first `alter` statement and then recreated in the second `alter` statement. Note that the referential integrity is specified for the delete operations, but not for the update. The reason is that `restrict` is the only declarative constraint allowed for the update operations, so `restrict` is implicitly assumed.

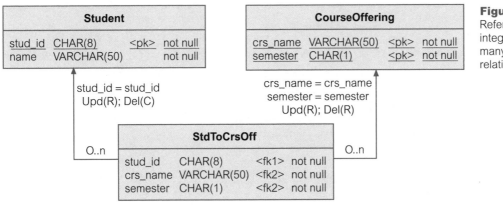

Figure 8.7
Referential
integrity for a
many to many
relationship

The modeling of referential integrity gets complicated when the relationship between tables is many to many, as between `Student` and `CourseOffering` (Figure 4.7 in Section 4.2.3.3). To be able to manage the problem under the RDB restriction that a column cannot take multiple values, we need to introduce an *intersection table*, such as `StdToCrsOff` in Figure 8.7. The only purpose of the table is to model the many-to-many relationship and specify the declarative referential integrity constraints.

Note from Figure 8.7 that because the primary key in `CourseOffering` is a composite key consisting of two columns (`crs_name` and `semester`), the corresponding foreign key in `StdToCrsOff` is also composite. Although not indicated in the model, the primary key for `StdToCrsOff` is a composite key consisting of all three columns in the table.

Triggers 8.2.4

The *rules* and *declarative referential integrity* constraints allow simple business rules to be defined on the database. They are not sufficient to define more complex rules or to define any exceptions to the rules. An RDB solution to this problem (standardized in SQL:1999) is a trigger.

A *trigger* is a small program, written in an extended SQL, that is executed automatically (triggered) as a result of a modification operation on a table on which the trigger has been defined. A modification operation can be any of the SQL modification statements: `insert`, `update`, or `delete`.

A trigger can be used to implement *business rules* that go beyond the capability of the SQL `rule` statement (Section 8.2.1). For example, the business rule that forbids changes to the `Employee` table during weekends can be programmed into a trigger. Any attempt to issue an SQL `insert`, `update`, or `delete` on the table during a weekend will result in the trigger firing and the database refusing to execute the operation.

A trigger can also be used to enforce more complex referential integrity constraints. For example, our business rule may state that on deleting a `Department` row, the `Employee` who is the manager of that department should also be deleted but all other employees should have `dept_id` values set to `NULL`. Such a business rule cannot be enforced declaratively. We need a procedural trigger to enforce it.

Figure 8.8 SQL
trigger generated
from a database
schema definition

```
create trigger keepdpt
   on Department
   for delete
   as
   if @@rowcount = 0
      return /* avoid firing trigger if no rows affected */
   if exists
      (select * from Employee, deleted
      where Employee.dept_id =
         deleted.dept_id)
      begin
         print 'Test for RESTRICT DELETE failed. No deletion'
         rollback transaction
         return
      end
      return
go
```

Once triggers are used to enforce referential integrity in the database, the declarative referential integrity constraints are normally abandoned. Mixing procedural and declarative constraints is a bad idea because of occasionally intricate interdependencies between them. Consequently, the dominant practice today in enterprise databases is to program the referential integrity in triggers alone. The issue is not as daunting as it may look, because a good CASE tool can generate much of the code automatically.

For example, the trigger code generated by a CASE tool for the Sybase RDBMS is shown in Figure 8.8. The trigger implements the `Del(r)` declarative constraint – i.e. it does not allow the `Department` row to be deleted if there are still `Employee` rows associated with it.

The `if` statement checks whether the SQL `delete` operation (which fired the trigger) is going to delete any rows at all. If not, the trigger does not proceed – no harm can be done. If `Department` rows can be deleted, then Sybase stores these (about to be deleted) rows in an internal table called `deleted`. The trigger then does an *equality join* operation on `dept_id` on the tables `Employee` and `deleted` to find out if there are any employees working for the department(s) to be deleted. If so, the trigger refuses the `delete` action, displays a message and rolls back the transaction. Otherwise, the `Department` rows are allowed to be deleted.

Triggers are a special kind of stored procedure (Section 8.2.5) that cannot be called – they trigger themselves on `insert`, `update`, or `delete` events on a table. This implies that each table can have up to three triggers. Indeed, in some systems this is the case (e.g. Sybase, SQL Server). In other systems (e.g. Oracle, DB2), additional variants of events are identified, leading to the possibility of having more than three triggers on each table. (The availability of more kinds of trigger does not provide more expressive power in trigger programs, though.)

Triggers can be programmed to enforce *any business rules* that apply to the database and cannot be violated by any client program or an interactive SQL DML statement. A user of a client program may not even be aware that the triggers "watch" what is being modified in the database. If the modifications do not violate business rules, the triggers are not visible to the programs. A trigger makes itself known to the user when a DML command cannot be allowed. The trigger will notify the user of the problem by displaying an informational message on the program's screen and refusing to perform the DML operation.

Stored procedures

8.2.5

The Sybase RDBMS first introduced *stored procedures*, and they are now part of every major commercial DBMS. Stored procedures turn a database into an active programmable system.

A *stored procedure* is written in an extended SQL that allows for such programming constructs as variables, loops, branches, and assignment statements. A stored procedure is given a name, can take input and output parameters, and it is compiled and stored in the database. A client program can call a stored procedure as if it was any internal subroutine.

Figure 8.9 illustrates the advantages of a client program calling a stored procedure rather than sending a complete query to the server. A query constructed in a client program is sent to the database server over the network. The query may contain syntax and other errors, but the client is not able to eliminate them – the database system is the only place where such verification can be done. Once verified, the DBMS checks whether the caller is authorized to run the query. If so, the query is optimized to determine the best access plan to data. Only then can it be compiled, executed, and the results returned to the client.

On the other hand, if a query (or the whole set of queries) is written as a stored procedure, then it is optimized and compiled into the server database. A client program does not need to send a (possibly large) query over the network – it instead sends a short call with the procedure name and a list of actual parameters. If lucky, the procedure may reside in the DBMS memory cache. If not, it will be brought to memory from the database.

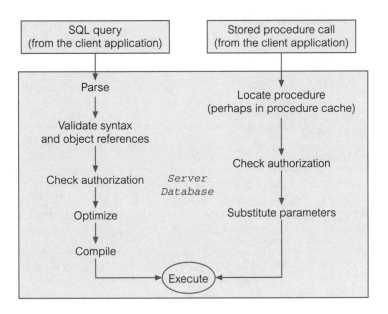

Figure 8.9
A comparison of client SQL and stored procedure invocation

The user's authorization is scrutinized as in the case of an SQL query. Any actual parameters replace formal parameters, and the stored procedure executes. The results are returned to the caller.

As can be seen in the above scenario, stored procedures provide a much more efficient ways of accessing the database from a client program. The performance advantages are due to the savings in *network traffic* and no need for *parsing and compilation* each time a client request is received. Even more importantly, a stored procedure is *maintained in a single place* and can be called from many client programs.

8.2.6 Views

A *relational view* is a stored and named SQL query. Because a result of any SQL query is a transient table, a view can be used in place of a table in other SQL operations. A view can be derived from one or more tables and/or one or more other views (Figure 8.2).

Figure 8.10 shows a graphical representation and the generated code for the view EmpNoSalary – the view displays all information from the table Employee except the salary column. The create view statement below the figure demonstrates that a view is really a named query that executes each time an SQL query or update operation is issued on the view.

Theoretically, a view is a very powerful mechanism with many uses. It can be used in support of *database security* by restricting users from seeing table data. It can present data to users in *different perspectives*. It can *isolate the application from changes* to table definitions, if the changed definition is not part of the view. It allows easier expression of *complex queries* – the query can be built in a "divide and conquer" fashion by using multiple levels of views.

Figure 8.10
A relational view and the code generated

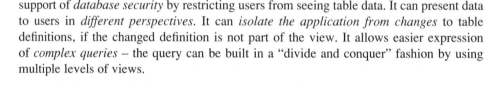

```
=================================================================
- - View: "EmpNoSalary"                                     --
=================================================================
create view "EmpNoSalary" () as
      select Employee.emp_id, Employee.dept_id,
             Employee.family_name, Employee.first_name,
             Employee.date_of_birth,Employee.gender,
             Employee.phone_num1, Employee.phone_num2
      from Employee;
```

In practice, the use of the view concept in the RDB model is severely restricted by its inability to allow view updates. A *view update* is the possibility of sending a modification operation (an SQL insert, update, or delete) to the view and changing the underlying base table(s) as a result. SQL support for view updating is very limited and takes advantage of special triggers, so called *instead of triggers*.

Normal forms   8.2.7

Arguably, one of the most important but at the same time least understood concepts in the RDB design is *normalization*. A relational table must be in a *normal form* (NF). There are six normal forms:

- 1st NF
- 2nd NF
- 3rd NF
- BCNF (Boyce–Codd NF)
- 4th NF
- 5th NF.

A table that is in a higher NF is also in all lower NFs. A table must be at least in the 1st NF. A table with no structured or multi-valued columns is in the 1st NF (and that is the fundamental requirement of the RDB model).

A table in a low NF can exhibit so-called update anomalies. An *update anomaly* is an undesirable side effect as a result of a modification operation (`insert`, `update`, `delete`) on a table. For example, if the same information is repeated many times in the same column in the table, then an update of that information must be performed in all places or the database will be left in an incorrect state. It can be shown that update anomalies are incrementally eliminated with the table reaching higher NFs.

So how do we normalize a table to a higher NF? We can bring a table to a higher NF by splitting it vertically along columns into two or more smaller tables. These smaller tables are likely to be in higher NFs, and they replace the original table in the RDB design model. However, the original table can always be reconstructed by joining the smaller tables in an SQL `join` operation.

The scope of this book does not allow us to treat normalization theory in any detail. The reader is referred to such textbooks as Date (2000), Maciaszek (1990), Silberschatz *et al.* (1997), and Ramakrishnan and Gehrke (2000). The main point that we would like to make is that a good RDB design naturally arrives at a good normalization level.

What do we mean by a good design in the normalization context? A *good design* means that we understand how the RDB is going to be used by a mix of update and retrieval operations. If the database is very dynamic, i.e. it is subjected to frequent update operations, then we will naturally create smaller tables to better localize and facilitate these updates. The tables will be in higher NFs, and the update anomalies will be reduced or eliminated.

On the other hand, if the database is relatively static, i.e. we frequently search for information but we update the database content sporadically, then a *denormalized design* will pay off. This is because a search in a single large table is going to be much more efficient than the same search on multiple tables, which need to be joined together before the search starts.

8.3 Object-relational mapping

Mapping from a UML class model to the RDB schema design has to consider the limitations of the RDB model. The issue is that of trading some *declarative semantics* of class diagrams for the *procedural solutions* in logical schema designs. In other words, it might not be possible to express some built-in declarative semantics of classes in the relational schema. Such semantics will have to be resolved procedurally in database programs, i.e. in stored procedures (Section 8.2.5).

Mapping to the RDB models has been extensively studied in the context of the ER and extended ER modeling (e.g. Maciaszek, 1990; Elmasri and Navathe, 2000). The principles are the same, and all major issues have been identified in those studies. The mapping must not simply conform to an RDB standard (SQL92 or SQL:1999) but must also relate to the target implementation RDBMS.

8.3.1 Mapping entity classes

The mapping of entity classes to relational tables must obey the 1st NF of tables. The columns must be atomic. This restriction of the relational model turns out to be no issue, because UML has a similar restriction. Attributes of UML classes are defined on *atomic data types* and, depending on the target programming language, on a few *built-in structured data types* (`Date`, `Currency`). Similar structured data types are likely to be supported by an RDBMS.

Still, doubts remain. What about simple questions like: "What if an employee has many phone numbers? How should I model this during analysis? Do I really need to have a separate class of phone numbers?" A similarly troublesome question seems to be: "Can I model an employee name as a single attribute but with the internal structure recognizing that the name consists of the family name, first name, and middle initial? Do I really need to have a separate class of employee names?"

Example 8.1 (contact management)

Refer to the class specifications for contact management in Example 4.6 and Figure 4.4 (Section 4.2.1.2.3). Consider the classes `EContact` and `EEmployee`.

`EContact` has the attributes `familyName` and `firstName` but does not have the concept of a contact name. Similarly, `EEmployee` contains `familyName`, `firstName`, and `middleName`, but we could not ask the database about an employee name because such a concept does not exist.

`EContact` has the attributes `phone`, `fax`, and `email`. The current model does not allow for a contact to have more than one `phone`, `fax`, or `email` – quite an unrealistic assumption in practice.

Map the classes `EContact` and `EEmployee` to an RDB design such that a number of alternative mapping strategies are demonstrated.

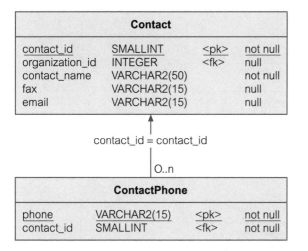

Figure 8.11 Mapping entity classes to RDB design (contact management)

A solution to this example is shown in Figure 8.11. The target RDBMS is DB2. The solution assumes the Oracle RDBMS. We modeled `contact_name` as an atomic data type in the table `Contact`. Each `Contact` is allowed only one `fax` and one `email`. However, we do allow any number of `phones`. The table `ContactPhone` serves this purpose.

In the table `Employee`, we maintain three separate attributes for `family_name`, `first_name` and `middle_initial`. However, the database does not have any knowledge of `employee_name` as a combined concept for these three attributes.

Mapping associations

8.3.2

The mapping of associations to RDB involves the use of *referential integrity* constraints between tables. Any association that is one-to-one or one-to-many can be directly expressed by inserting a *foreign key* in one table to match the primary key of the other table.

In the case of *one-to-one association*, the foreign key can be added to either table (to be decided on the basis of the association usage patterns). Also, in the case of one-to-one association, it may be desirable to combine the two entity classes in one table (depending on the desired normalization level).

For *recursive* one-to-one and one-to-many associations, the foreign key and primary key are in the same table. Each *many-to-many association* (whether recursive or not) requires an intersection table as demonstrated in Figure 8.19.

Example 8.2 (contact management)

Refer to the association specifications for contact management in Example 4.8 and Figure 4.6 (Section 4.2.2.3). Map the diagram in Figure 4.6 to an RDB model.

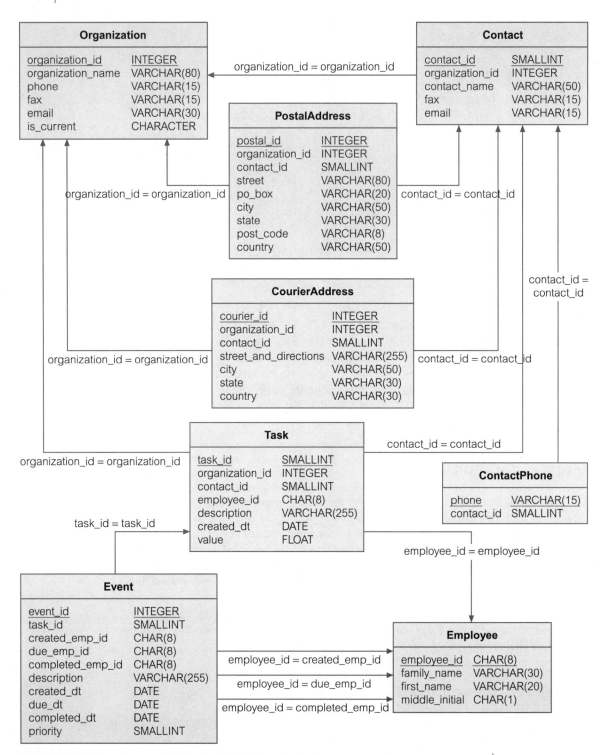

Figure 8.12 Mapping associations to RDB design (contact management)

This example proves to be quite straightforward due to the lack of many-to-many associations in the UML association specifications. The RDB diagram (for the DB2 RDBMS) is shown in Figure 8.12. Consistently with RDB principles, we created a number of new columns as primary keys. We decided to retain the model in Figure 8.11 as a partial solution to this example. To conserve space, we suppressed the display of the columns' null definitions and key indicators.

The referential integrity constraints between `PostalAddress` and `CourierAddress` on the one hand and `Organization` and `Contact` on the other hand are modeled with foreign keys in the address tables. This is slightly arbitrary, and the constraints could have been modeled in the opposite direction (i.e. with foreign keys in `Organization` and `Contact`).

Mapping aggregations   8.3.3

An RDB does not understand the difference between association and aggregation, except when implemented procedurally in triggers or stored procedures. The main principles for association mapping (Section 8.3.2) apply to the mapping of aggregations. Only when an association can be converted to a number of resultant relational solutions would the semantics of aggregation (as a special form of association) influence the decision.

In the case of the strong form of aggregation (i.e. *composition*), an attempt should be made to combine the subset and superset entity classes in a single table. This is possible for one-to-one aggregations. For *one-to-many aggregations*, the subset class (in the strong and weak forms of aggregation) must be modeled as a separate table (with a foreign key linking it to its owning table).

Example 8.3 (university enrolment)

Refer to the aggregation specifications for university enrolment in Example 4.9 and Figure 4.7 (Section 4.2.3.3). Map the diagram in Figure 4.7 to an RDB model.

This example includes two aggregation relationships – a composition from `Student` to `AcademicRecord` and a weak aggregation from `Course` to `CourseOffering`. Both are one-to-many aggregations and require separate "subset" tables.

In the UML model in Figure 4.7, we assumed (naturally enough) an indirect navigational link from `AcademicRecord` to `Course`. In an RDB design, we may want to establish a direct referential integrity between the tables `AcademicRecord` and `Course`. After all, `AcademicRecord` has the attribute course_code as part of its primary key. The same attribute can be made into a foreign key to the table `Course`. This is shown in Figure 8.13 (for the IBM Informix RDBMS).

The *many-to-many association* between the classes `Student` and `CourseOffering` leads to another interesting observation, albeit not related to the aggregation mapping. The association results in an intersection table `StdToCrsOff` with the primary key to be composed from the primary keys of the two main tables.

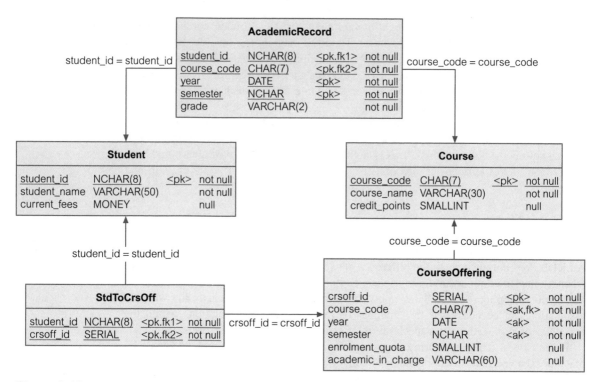

Figure 8.13 Mapping aggregations to RDB design (university enrolment)

The primary key for `CourseOffering` could be {`course_code`, `year`, `semester`}. However, such a key would result in a cumbersome primary key for `StdToCrsOff`. We opted, therefore, for a system-generated primary key in `CourseOffering`. It is called `crsoff` and its type is `SERIAL` (in Informix, the type to generate unique identifiers is called `SERIAL`; the same type may be called something else in other RDBMSs – for example, it is called `IDENTITY` in Sybase, `UNIQUEIDENTIFIER` in SQL Server, and `SEQUENCE` in Oracle).

8.3.4 Mapping generalizations

The mapping of generalization relationships to an RDB can be done in a variety of ways, but the principles are less convoluted than might be expected. However, it must be remembered that expressing a generalization in an RDB data structure ignores issues that make the generalization tick – inheritance, polymorphism, code reuse, etc.

To illustrate the generalization mapping strategies, consider the example in Figure 8.14. There are four strategies for converting a generalization hierarchy to an RDB design model (although some further variations of these strategies are possible):

1. Map each class to a table.
2. Map the entire class hierarchy to a single "superclass" table.

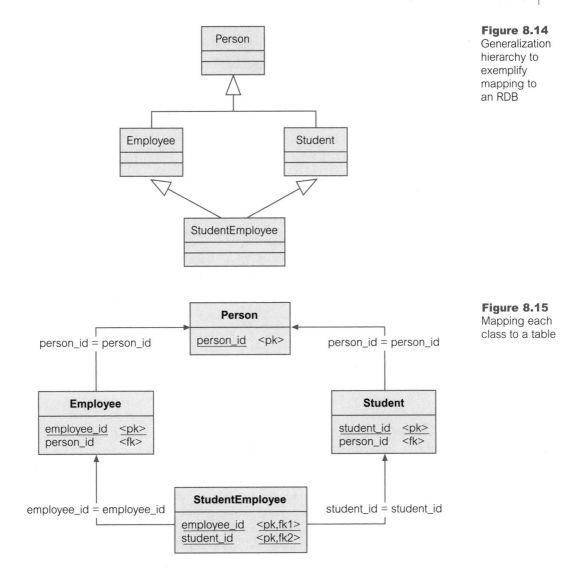

Figure 8.14
Generalization
hierarchy to
exemplify
mapping to
an RDB

Figure 8.15
Mapping each
class to a table

3. Map each concrete class to a table.

4. Map each disjoint concrete class to a table.

The first mapping strategy is illustrated in Figure 8.15. Each table has its own primary key. The solution presented does not tell us whether a "subclass" table "inherits" some of its columns from the "superclass" table. For example, is person_name stored in Person and "inherited" by Employee, Student, and StudentEmployee? "Inheriting" really means a join operation, and the performance penalty of the join may force us to have person_name duplicated in all tables of the hierarchy.

The second mapping strategy is illustrated in Figure 8.16 (in SQL Server RDBMS). The table Person would contain the combined set of attributes in all classes of the

Figure 8.16
Mapping the class
hierarchy to a
table

Figure 8.17
Mapping each
concrete class to
a table

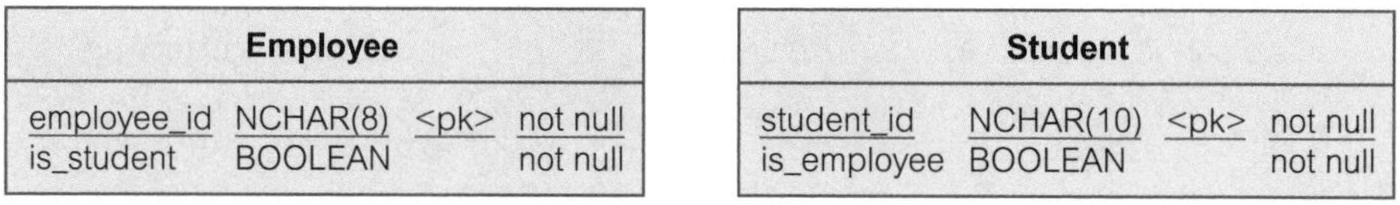

Figure 8.18
Mapping each
disjoint concrete
class to a table

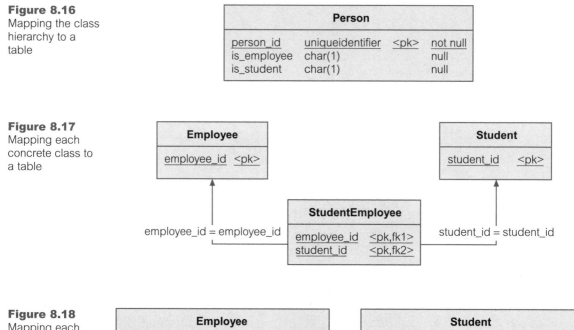

generalization hierarchy. It also contains two columns (`is_employee` and `is_student`) to record whether a person is an employee, a student, or both.

To illustrate the third mapping strategy, we assume that the class `Person` is abstract. Any attributes of the class `Person` are "inherited" by the tables corresponding to the concrete classes. The result will be similar to that shown in Figure 8.17.

Still assuming that the class `Person` is abstract, the last strategy is illustrated in Figure 8.18 (in Informix RDBMS). As opposed to the model in Figure 8.15, we assume that whether an employee is also a student, and vice versa, is always known. Hence, `not null` for the two `BOOLEAN` columns.

Example 8.4 (video store)

Refer to the generalization specifications for video store in Example 4.10 and Figure 4.8 (Section 4.2.4.3).

Our task is to map three classes from the diagram in Figure 4.8 to an RDB model. We will use the third strategy of mapping each concrete class to a table. The classes to be mapped are `EMovie`, `EVCRTape`, and `EDVD`.

We need to consider how to handle the derived attribute `isInStock` and the static attribute `percentExcellentCondition`.

The RDB design (for Sybase RDBMS) in Figure 8.19 contains a table for each of the three concrete classes (`Movie`, `VCRTape`, and `DVD`). The tables include inherited columns.

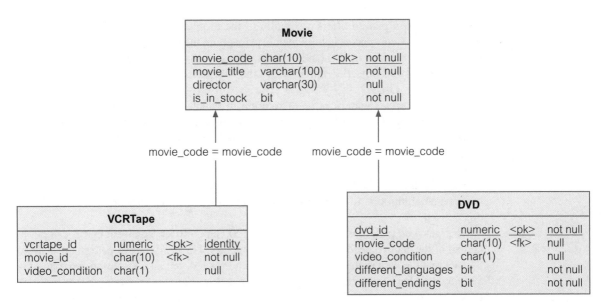

Figure 8.19 Mapping generalizations to RDB design (video store)

The columns `different_languages`, `different_endings`, and `is_in_stock` are typed as `bit`. By definition, the `bit` type does not allow null values (`bit` is either zero or one).

The column `is_in_stock` is set to true (one) if there is at least one tape or disk with a particular movie in stock. This is not terribly useful information if a customer is interested in only one of the two video media. A better solution would be to have two `bit` columns or to assume that this information is never stored, i.e. it is derived (calculated) whenever a customer requests a tape or disk.

The static attribute `percentExcellentCondition` is not stored in any table in our design. The only table where it could be sensibly stored is `Movie`. If stored, the same considerations as for the attribute `is_in_stock` would apply.

Patterns for managing persistent objects   8.4

The management of persistent objects is undoubtedly the main challenge in application programming. This is the area that particularly requires a good set of design patterns (Section 6.4.2.3). Such a set is provided by the *PEAA* (patterns of enterprise application architecture) patterns (Fowler, 2003). Maciaszek and Liong (2004) describe a few of these patterns, including:

- identity map
- data mapper
- lazy load
- unit of work.

The *identity map* pattern offers a solution to the problem of assigning object identifiers (OIDs) to persistent objects held in memory, mapping these OIDs to memory addresses of these objects, mapping other identifying attributes of objects to their OIDs, and providing a single registry of object identifiers that other objects in the program can use to access objects by their OIDs.

The *data mapper* pattern offers a solution in which the program knows at all times if a required object is in memory cache or has to be retrieved from the database. If the object is in memory, then a data mapper can find out if it is *clean* (i.e. if its state (data content) in memory is in sync with the corresponding record in a database table). If the object is *dirty* (not clean), then a data mapper initiates a new retrieval from the database. The knowledge of whether an object is clean or dirty can be kept by the data mapper, but a better solution is to keep this information in the identity map or even in the entity object itself.

The *lazy load* pattern is defined by Fowler (2003, p.200) as "an object that doesn't contain all of the data you need but knows how to get it." The need for this pattern arises from the fact that the data in the database are very interrelated, but an application can load only a limited number of objects to the memory cache. However, it is important for the program to be able, at any time, to load more data related to the objects already in memory.

The *unit of work* pattern offers a solution in which the program knows which objects in memory are embraced by a business transaction, and therefore should be handled in unison with regard to committing any changes in these objects to the database. This pattern makes the application program aware of business transactions. It "maintains a list of objects affected by a business transaction and coordinates the writing out of changes and the resolution of concurrency problems" (Fowler, 2003, p.184).

8.4.1 Searching for persistent objects

As discussed in Section 8.1.2 and elsewhere, the PCMEF architecture addresses enterprise applications and can accommodate the PEAA and similar patterns. Figure 8.20 is an activity diagram presenting typical transition flows when the application program searches for a persistent object (Maciaszek and Liong, 2004).

In a typical scenario, a user would request an entity object (e.g. invoice information) by interacting with some presentation object (e.g. a UI window). In the PCMEF framework, such a request would be forwarded to a *control object* (i.e. an object in the control subsystem). The control object would ask a *data mapper object* to get the entity object. The data mapper class is normally placed within the mediator subsystem.

A *data mapper object* would have a number of overloaded methods providing different search strategies depending on what information is passed to the mapper by the control object. Typical possibilities are (Maciaszek and Liong, 2004):

- A control object knows the OID of an object and passes it to a data mapper object.
- A control object knows some attribute values of an object and passes them to a data mapper object.
- A control object knows of another object X that holds a reference to the entity object that is the search target and passes X to a data mapper object.

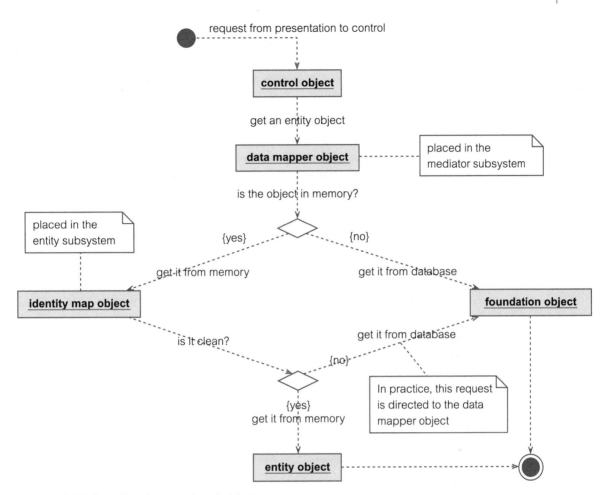

request from presentation to control

control object

get an entity object

data mapper object --------- placed in the
mediator subsystem

is the object in memory?

placed in the
entity subsystem

{yes}   {no}

get it from memory   get it from database

identity map object   **foundation object**

is it clean?   get it from database

{no}

In practice, this request
is directed to the data
mapper object

{yes}
get it from memory

entity object

Figure 8.20 Searching for a persistent object

Note that in the first case the control object may elect to enquire an identity map object directly, and circumvent the data mapper object. This is possible because the control subsystem can communicate directly with the entity subsystem (Figure 8.1).

In the second case, the data mapper uses the attribute values obtained from the control object to construct a proper message to the identity map object. The identity map object will then initiate further search based on the attribute values.

In the third case, the data mapper object cannot be of immediate help, and the request must be delegated to the identity map object. Once the object holding the reference is retrieved, the identity map can ascertain whether the reference links to an entity object held in memory. If the object is in memory, it can be returned to the control object (and further up to the presentation object). If not, a database retrieval is necessary.

As shown in Figure 8.20, it is not enough to find an entity object in memory. The object should be clean, i.e. it should contain the current data values as in the database. The information whether an object is clean is normally held in the object itself (by some kind of marker, so that each entity object is marked as clean or dirty).

In cases when an entity object is found but is dirty or when it is not found in the memory cache, a data mapper object initiates the search in the database. The note in Figure 8.20 makes it clear that the data mapper object mediates all searches to the database and, therefore, the entity subsystem does not communicate directly with the foundation subsystem (as per the PCMEF framework – Figure 8.1).

Because a data mapper object has such an important mediating role, sending messages from the control subsystem directly to the entity subsystem should be restricted to the situations where a control object is certain that a clean entity object exists in memory. Since most of the time a control object cannot have such a certainty, the communication should go through a data mapper object in the mediator subsystem.

8.4.2 Loading persistent objects

The diagram in Figure 8.20 does not explain what it takes to *load* a persistent object from a database to memory if that object does not exist in the program's memory or is there but is marked as dirty. The load operation is also known as a *check-out* operation (meaning that an object is checked out from the database to memory).

Figure 8.21 is a sequence diagram for loading an EContact object from the Contact table (ref. Example 8.1, Section 8.3.1). The model assumes that MDataMapper knows that the EContact object is not in memory and immediately proceeds to the database

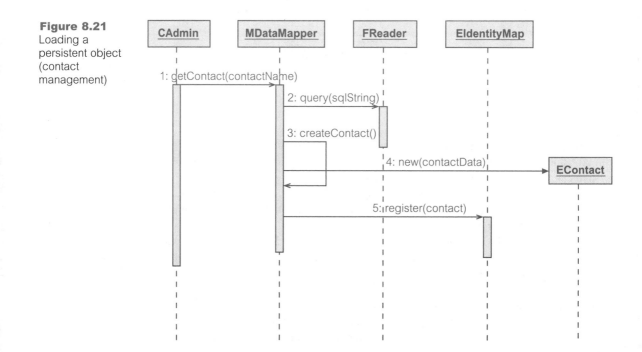

Figure 8.21
Loading a persistent object (contact management)

to get the object. To make the search possible, CAdmin passes contactName as a search condition value in argument to getContact().

In the model in Figure 8.21, MDataMapper builds an SQL search string and passes it to FReader in the query() message. FReader then handles any communication with the database and obtains the data from the Contact table. These data are then returned to MDataMapper. In general, the SQL query could be fully constructed in FReader, rather than in MDataMapper.

MDataMapper now has data to build an EContact object. This process is initiated in the createContact() method. This method is responsible for construction of a new EContact object. The message new() does this.

To conclude the loading process, MDataMapper requests that EIdentityMap register the newly created EContact object (and mark it as clean). The registration involves adding EContact's OID to various maps managed by EIdentityMap. The most obvious map is the map between EContact's OID and the EContact object itself. Another map may exist to link EContact's OID with its contactName (assuming the contactName is a unique identifier).

Unloading persistent objects 8.4.3

Unloading (also known as *check-in*) is the opposite operation to loading. There are three main circumstances when an entity object needs to be unloaded (Maciaszek and Liong, 2004):

1. The application created a new entity object, and this object needs to be persistently stored in the database.

2. The application updated an entity object, and the changes need to be persistently recorded in the database.

3. The application deleted an entity object, and the corresponding record must be deleted from a database table.

Figure 8.22 demonstrates the interaction sequence for the third situation, where an object is deleted by the application. Assuming that CAdmin knows that an EContact object needs to be deleted, it invokes the deleteContact() service on MDataMapper. MDataMapper constructs an SQL string for the delete() operation and asks FWriter to get the database to delete the pertinent record from the Contact table.

Once FWriter returns (to MDataMapper) the information that the database record has been deleted, MDataMapper sends an unregister() message to EIdentityMap. Following successful removal of any EContact information from the maps maintained by EIdentityMap, MDataMapper requests EContact to destroy() itself.

Implementing database access 8.5

Applications programs interact with databases for data. A client program must use a database language – typically SQL – to access and modify the database. As shown in

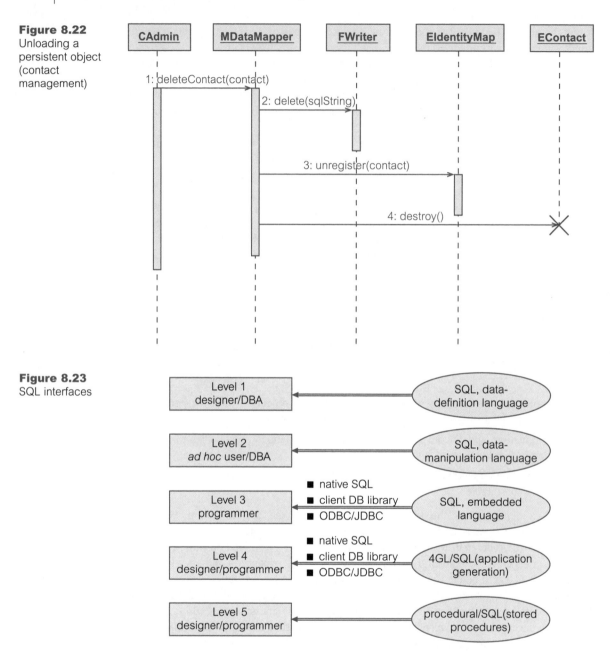

Figure 8.22
Unloading a persistent object (contact management)

Figure 8.23
SQL interfaces

Section 8.4, the `foundation` subsystem (and classes such as `FReader`, `FWriter`) is responsible for communication with the database. However, the models in Section 8.4 did not show how this communication is implemented.

To understand how a client program communicates with a database server, we need to recognize that SQL comes in different dialects and can be used at different levels of programming abstraction. Figure 8.23 distinguishes five levels of SQL interface:

1. At *level 1*, SQL is used as a data-definition language (DDL). DDL is a specification language for defining the database structures (database schema). A database designer and a database administrator (DBA) are the main users of Level 1 SQL.

2. At *level 2*, SQL is used as a data-manipulation language (DML) or as a query language. However, the term *query language* is a misnomer, because SQL at level 2 serves the purpose of not only retrieving data but also modifying it (with insert, update, and delete operations).

   A wide range of users use level 2 SQL, from "naive" *ad hoc* users to experienced DBAs. SQL at this level is *interactive*, which means that a user can formulate a query outside any application programming environment and immediately run it on a database. Level 2 SQL is an entry point to learning more elaborated SQL at the next levels.

   Application programmers use SQL at levels above level 2. At these higher levels, SQL permits *record-at-a-time processing* in addition to the *set-at-a-time processing* facility available (as the only option) at level 2. The set-at-a-time processing takes one or more tables (sets of records) as the input to a query and returns a table as the output. Although a powerful facility, it is difficult and dangerous to use with complicated queries.

   To be certain that a query returns correct results, the programmer must have the possibility of browsing one by one through the records returned by a query and deciding what to do with these records on a one-at-a-time basis. Such a record-at-a-time processing capability is called a *cursor* and is available in SQL at levels above level 2.

3. *Level 3* SQL is *embedded* in a conventional programming language, such as C or COBOL. Because a programming language compiler does not understand SQL, a precompiler (preprocessor) is needed to translate SQL statements into function calls in the DB library provided by the DBMS vendor. A programmer may elect to program using the DB library functions directly, in which case the precompiler is not needed.

   A popular way of interfacing a client program with databases is via *open database connectivity* (ODBC) or *Java database connectivity* (JDBC) standards. To program in this way, an ODBC or JDBC software driver for a particular DBMS is required. ODBC and JDBC provide a standard database language, above SQL, which is translated by the driver into the native DBMS SQL.

   ODBC/JDBC have the advantage of decoupling the program from the native DBMS SQL. If the program needs to be migrated in the future to a different target DBMS, then a straightforward replacing of the driver should do the trick. More importantly, working with ODBC/JDBC allows a single application to issue queries to more than one DBMS.

   The disadvantage of ODBC/JDBC is that it is the "lowest common denominator" for SQL. A client application cannot take advantage of any special SQL features or extensions supported by a particular DBMS vendor.

4. *Level 4* SQL uses the same strategies for embedding SQL in client programs as level 3 SQL. However, level 4 SQL provides a more powerful programming environment of an application generator or a fourth-generation language (4GL). A 4GL comes equipped with "screen painting" and UI building capabilities. Since IS applications require sophisticated GUIs, a 4GL/SQL is a frequent choice for building such applications.

5. *Level 5* SQL complements levels 3 and 4 by providing the possibility of moving some SQL statements from the client program to an active (programmable) server database. SQL is used as a programming language (e.g. PL/SQL in Oracle or Transact SQL in Sybase and SQL Server). The server programs can be called from within the client programs, as discussed in Section 8.2.5.

8.6 Designing business transactions

A *transaction* is a logical unit of work that comprises one or more SQL statements executed by a user. A transaction is a unit of *database consistency* – the state of the database is consistent after the transaction completes. To ensure that consistency, the transaction manager of a DBMS serves two purposes: *database recovery* and *concurrency control*.

According to SQL standards, a transaction begins with the first executable SQL statement (in some systems, an explicit `begin transaction` statement may be required). A transaction ends with a `commit` or `rollback` statement. The `commit` statement writes the changes persistently to the database. The `rollback` statement erases any changes made by the transaction.

The transaction is *atomic* – the results of all SQL statements in the transaction are either committed or rolled back. The user determines the duration (size) of a transaction. Depending on the business needs, application domain, and user–computer interaction style, a transaction can be as short as one SQL statement or it can involve a series of SQL statements.

8.6.1 Short transactions

Most conventional IS applications require *short transactions*. A short transaction contains one or more SQL statements that must be completed as quickly as possible so that other transactions are not held up.

Consider an airline reservation system in which many travel agents make flight bookings for travelers around the world. It is essential that each booking transaction is performed quickly by the DBMS, so that the availability of flight seats is updated, and the database gets ready to process the next transaction waiting in the queue.

8.6.1.1 Pessimistic concurrency control

Conventional DBMSs, with the notable exception of ODBMSs, have been designed with short transactions in mind. These systems work according to *pessimistic concurrency control*. *Locks* are acquired on every persistent object that a transaction processes. There are four kinds of lock on an object:

1. *Exclusive (write) lock* – other transactions must wait until the transaction holding such a lock completes and releases the lock.

2. *Update (write intent) lock* – other transactions can read the object, but the transaction holding the lock is guaranteed to be able to upgrade it to the exclusive mode as soon as it has such a need.

3. *Read (shared) lock* – other transactions can read and possibly obtain an update lock on the object.

4. *No lock* – other transactions can update an object at any time; suitable only for applications that allow "*dirty reads*" – i.e. a transaction reads data that can be modified or even deleted (by another transaction) before the transaction completes.

Levels of isolation 8.6.1.2

Associated with these four kinds of lock are the four *levels of isolation* between concurrently executing transactions. It is the responsibility of the system designer to decide which level of isolation is appropriate for the mix of transactions on the database. The four levels are (Khoshafian *et al.*, 1992):

1. *Dirty read possible* – transaction t1 modified an object, but it has not committed yet; transaction t2 reads the object; if t1 rolls back the transaction, then t2 obtained an object that in a sense never existed in the database.

2. *Non-repeatable read possible* – t1 has read an object; t2 updates the object; t1 reads the same object again, but this time it will obtain a different value for the same object.

3. *Phantom possible* – t1 has read a set of objects; t2 inserts a new object into the set; t1 repeats the read operation and will see a "phantom" object.

4. *Repeatable read* – t1 and t2 can still execute concurrently, but the interleaved execution of these two transactions will produce the same results as if the transactions executed one at a time (this is called *serializable execution*).

Typical GUI-based interactive IS applications require short transactions. However, the level of isolation may differ between different transactions in the same application. The SQL statement set transaction can be used for that purpose. The trade-off is obvious – increasing the level of isolation reduces the overall concurrency of the system.

However, one crucial design decision is independent of the above considerations. The beginning of the transaction must always be delayed to the last second. It is unacceptable to start a transaction from a client window and then make the transaction wait until it obtains some additional information from the user before it can actually complete the job.

The user may be very slow in providing that information or may even elect to shut the computer down while the transaction is running. The *transaction timeout* will eventually roll back the transaction, but the harm to the overall system throughput has been done.

Automatic recovery 8.6.1.3

Murphy's law states that if something can go wrong, it will. Programs may contain errors, running processes can hang or be aborted, the power supply can fail, a disk head can crash, etc. Fortunately, a DBMS provides *automatic recovery* for most situations. Only in the case of the physical loss of disk data is a DBA's intervention necessary to instruct the DBMS to recover from the last database *backup*.

Depending on the state of the transaction at failure point, a DBMS will automatically perform a *rollback* or *roll forward* of the transaction as soon as the cause of the problem has been eliminated. The recovery is automatic, but a DBA can control the amount of

Figure 8.24
Automatic
recovery

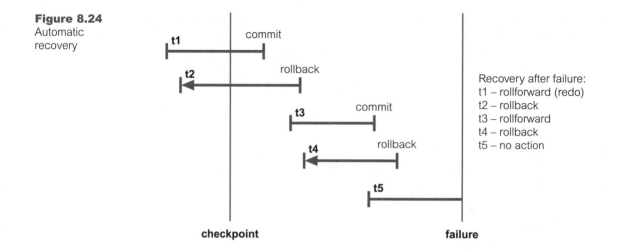

Recovery after failure:
t1 – rollforward (redo)
t2 – rollback
t3 – rollforward
t4 – rollback
t5 – no action

recovery time by setting the frequency of *checkpoints*. A checkpoint forces the DBMS to stop all transactions temporarily and write all the transactional changes (made since the previous checkpoint) to the database.

Figure 8.24 illustrates the issues involved in automatic recovery from failure (Kirkwood, 1992). Transaction t1 committed after the checkpoint but before the system failure. As a DBMS does not know if all changes after the checkpoint have been physically written to the database, it will *roll forward* (*redo*) transaction t1 after it recovers from the failure.

Transaction t2 had a rollback applied to it between the checkpoint and the failure. As in the case of transaction t1, the DBMS does not know if the rollback changes reached the disk – the DBMS will perform the *rollback* again.

Other transactions started after the checkpoint. Transaction t3 will be *rolled forward* to guarantee that its changes are effected in the database. Similarly, transaction t4 will be repeated, i.e. *rolled back*.

Transaction t5 would not require any remedial action by the DBMS, because it was executing at the time of failure. Any changes done by t5 before the failure have not been written to the database. All intermediate changes have only been written to the log file. The user is aware that the transaction was executing at the time of failure and may resend the transaction when the DBMS is up and running again.

8.6.1.4 Programmable recovery

While unexpected system failures are automatically recovered from by a DBMS, designers and programmers should control any anticipated transaction problems. A DBMS provides a range of rollback options to apply in the program so that it can recover gracefully from a problem, possibly without the user realizing that things went wrong at some point.

To start with, UI guidelines such as the user in control and forgiveness (Section 7.2) demand that a program allow the user to make mistakes and recover from them. A programmer-controlled rollback applied in the right places in the program can restore the database to the previous state (i.e. *undo* the mistake), provided that the transaction has not committed.

If the transaction has committed, then the programmer may still have the option of writing a *compensating transaction*. The user can then request the execution of the compensating transaction to undo the changes to the database. Compensating transactions are designed specifically to allow programmable recovery and should be modeled in use cases.

Savepoint

8.6.1.4.1

A *savepoint* is a statement in a program that divides a longer transaction into smaller parts. *Named savepoints* are inserted in strategic places in the program. The programmer then has the option of rolling back the work to a named savepoint rather than to the beginning of the transaction.

For example, a programmer may insert a savepoint just before an `update` operation. If the `update` fails, then the program rolls back to the savepoint and attempts to execute the update again. Alternatively, the program may take any other action to avoid aborting the transaction altogether.

In larger programs, savepoints may be inserted before each subroutine. If a subroutine fails, it may be possible to roll back to the beginning of that subroutine and re-execute it with revised parameters. If necessary, a specially designed and programmed recovery subroutine can do the mopping up so that the transaction can resume execution.

Trigger rollback

8.6.1.4.2

A *trigger rollback* is a special kind of savepoint. As explained in Section 8.2.4, a trigger can be used to program a business rule of any complexity. At times it may be undesirable to roll back the whole transaction when a trigger refuses to modify a table (due to the transaction's attempt to breach a business rule). The transaction may want to take remedial action.

For the above reason, a DBMS may provide a trigger programming possibility to roll back either the whole transaction or just the trigger. In the latter case, the program (possibly a stored procedure) can analyze the problem and decide on further action. Even if the whole transaction eventually has to be rolled back, the program may have the possibility of better interpreting the cause of the error and displaying a more intelligible message to the user.

Designing stored procedures and triggers

8.6.1.5

The *window navigation* approach presented in Section 7.5 could be extended to the application program logic related to the management of the transaction states. The resulting *program navigation* models could identify stored procedures and triggers. The purpose, definition, and detailed design of each stored procedure and trigger would then need to be provided. In particular, some pseudo-code notation ought to be employed to define the algorithms.

As an example, we present an algorithm for the stored procedure `DeleteEvent` related to the contact management application (Figure 8.25). The procedure checks whether the user (employee) attempting to delete an event is the same employee who created the event. If not, the delete operation is rejected. The procedure also checks whether the event is the only one remaining for the task. If so, the task is deleted as well.

Figure 8.25
Pseudo-code
for a stored
procedure
(contact
management)

```
BEGIN
INPUT PARAMETERS (@event_id, @user_id)
Select Event (where event_id = @event_id)
IF @user_id = Event.created_emp_id
    THEN
        delete Event (where event_id = @event_id)
        IF no more events for
            Task.task_id = Event.task_id AND
            Event.event_id = @event_id
        THEN
            delete that Task
        ENDIF
    ELSE
        raise error ('Only the creator of the event can
                    delete that event')
ENDIF
END
```

The stored procedure `DeleteEvent` contains `delete` statements to delete records from the tables `Event` and `Task`. These `delete` statements would fire delete triggers on these tables, if present. If the algorithms for these triggers go beyond the normal referential integrity checking, the designer should provide pseudo-code specifications for them as well (including the decision on rollback strategy – a trigger rollback or a transaction rollback).

8.6.2 Long transactions

Some new classes of IS application encourage cooperation between users. These applications are known as *workgroup computing* applications or *computer-supported cooperative work* (CSCW) applications. Examples include many office applications, collaborative authoring, computer-aided design, and CASE tools.

In many ways, workgroup computing applications have database requirements that are orthogonal to the traditional database model with short transactions that isolate users from each other. Workgroup computing applications require long transactions, version management, and collaborative concurrency control.

The ODB model provides a framework for workgroup computing, and many ODBMS products target this application domain. Users in a workgroup computing application share information and are made aware of the work they do on shared data. They work in their own *workspaces* using personal databases of data *checked-out* (copied) from the common workgroup database. They work in a *long transaction* that can span computer sessions (users can take breaks then continue working in the same long transaction after returning).

The dominant aspect of a long transaction is that it is not allowed to be rolled back automatically without trace by the system because of failures. To appreciate this requirement, imagine my despair if this textbook were now to be "rolled back" due to a computer failure! A rollback of a long transaction is controlled by the users by means of *savepoints* that persistently store objects in the users' private databases.

The notion of *short transaction* is not eradicated from a workgroup computing application. Short transactions are necessary to guarantee atomicity and isolation *during* the check-out and check-in operations between the group database and private databases. *Short locks* are released afterwards, and *long persistent locks* are imposed by the group database on all checked-out objects.

Related objectives of the long transaction model include (Hawryszkiewycz *et al.*, 1994; Maciaszek, 1998):

- allowing the exchange of information (even if temporarily inconsistent) between co-operating users;

- detecting data inconsistencies and mediating their resolutions;

- taking advantage of object versionability to provide controlled sharing without loss of work in case of system failures.

Summary

This chapter has reflected on the paramount importance of databases in software development. All major issues related to application–database interaction were discussed. The target database model was assumed to be the relational model.

There are three levels of data model: external, logical, and physical. In this chapter, we have concentrated on the *logical model*. The *mapping of objects to databases* has been understood as the mapping of a UML class model to a logical data model within a relational database.

Mapping to the *RDB logical model* is occasionally cumbersome because of the underlying semantic simplicity of relational databases. The RDB model does not support object types, inheritance, structured types, collections, or references. Data are stored in *tables* related by *referential integrity* constraints. *Triggers* can be used to program the semantics captured in business rules implied in UML class models. *Stored procedures* and *views* can be used to capture some modeling constraints that cannot possibly be expressed in tabular data structures. *Normalization* can further influence the mapping.

An application program needs to communicate with a database. The communication must not break the adopted *architectural framework*. The PCMEF framework integrates very well with database design. There are various design patterns for managing *persistent objects* in the application code. Models for searching, loading, and unloading persistent objects were shown.

When designing the application–database collaboration, consideration needs to be given to the five levels of *SQL interface*. *Level 5 SQL* is of particular interest because it allows the user to program the database directly. Stored procedures and triggers heavily influence the server aspect of program design.

A *transaction* is a logical unit of database work that starts in a consistent database state and ensures the next consistent state when finished. Transactions ensure *database concurrency* and *database recovery*. Conventional database applications require *short transactions*. Some new database applications work in *long transactions*.

Questions

Q1 Explain the three levels of data model.

Q2 Refer to Figure 8.1 (Section 8.1.2) and explain the meaning of the dependencies involving the foundation subsystem, database schema, and database programs.

Q3 What is referential integrity? How is it useful for mapping from a UML class model?

Q4 Explain the four declarative referential integrity constraints.

Q5 What is a trigger? How is it related to referential integrity?

Q6 Can a stored procedure call a trigger? Explain.

Q7 What is a good normalization level for a database? Explain.

Q8 Refer to Figure 8.11 (Section 8.3.1). The relationship between `Contact` and `ContactPhone` shows the multiplicity 0..n. How can this multiplicity constraint be enforced in the database?

Q9 Refer to Figure 8.22 (Section 8.4.3). Consider a situation in which an entity object needs to be unloaded to the database as a result of an update operation, instead of delete. How would the sequence diagram differ in such a case?

Q10 Describe briefly the five levels of SQL interface.

Q11 What are the advantages of a stored procedure call over an SQL query submitted from the client program to the database? Are there any circumstances that would make us use an SQL query instead of a stored procedure call?

Q12 Describe briefly the locks in pessimistic concurrency control.

Q13 Describe briefly the levels of transaction isolation.

Q14 Can the amount of database recovery time be controlled by the designer/DBA? Explain.

Q15 What is a compensating transaction? How can it be used in program design?

Q16 What is a savepoint? How can it be used in program design?

Exercises (contact management)

F1 Refer to Example 7.4 (Section 7.5.3) and to Exercise F4 in the Exercises (contact management) section at the end of Chapter 7. Consider Figure 7.29, which is the solution to this exercise in the Solutions to Exercises (contact management) section, also at the end of Chapter 7. Refer to message number 8 in Figure 7.29 (`display record for update`). Extend the sequence diagram (starting from message 8) to account for the management of persistent objects, as discussed in Section 8.4. Explain the model.

F2 Refer to Example 7.4 (Section 7.5.3) and to Exercise F4 in the Exercises (contact management) section at the end of Chapter 7. Consider Figure 7.29, which is the solution to this exercise in the Solutions to exercises (contact management) section, also at the end of Chapter 7. Refer to message number 10 in Figure 7.29 (`press save`). Extend the sequence diagram (starting from message 10) to account for the management of persistent objects, as discussed in Section 8.4. Explain the model.

F3 Refer to the problem statement for contact management (Section 1.5.3) and to the successive examples for contact management in Chapters 4, 5, 7, and 8. In particular, consider Example 5.3 (Section 5.1.1.3). Identify the database triggers for the `Event` table.

F4   Refer to the problem statement for contact management (Section 1.5.3) and to the successive examples for contact management in Chapters 4, 5, 7, and 8. Identify the database triggers for the `Task` table.

F5   Refer to the problem statement for contact management (Section 1.5.3) and to the successive examples for contact management in Chapters 4, 5, 7, and 8. Identify the stored procedures to act on the `Event` table. Also specify pseudo-code algorithms for the stored procedures identified.

Exercises (telemarketing)

G1   Refer to Exercise G1 in the Exercises (telemarketing) section at the end of Chapter 7. Consider the class diagram that you obtained as your solution to this exercise. Map the class diagram to a relational database model. Explain the mapping.

G1   Refer to Exercise G8 in the Exercises (telemarketing) section at the end of Chapter 7. Consider the sequence diagram that you obtained as your solution to this exercise. Identify any events (messages) in the diagram that will result in actions related to the management of persistent objects, as discussed in Section 8.4. Extend the diagram to include the management of persistent objects. Explain the model.

Answers to odd-numbered questions

Q1 – answer

Data modelers, i.e. people specializing in modeling database structures, distinguish three levels of data model: external, logical, and physical.

The external and logical models are *conceptual models* that do not consider the intricacies of a particular DBMS, but they normally conform to the model that is dominant today – the relational database model. This adherence to the relational model is frequently reflected in a trimmed-down expressiveness of the entity–relationship (ER) diagramming technique typically used for external and logical modeling ("trimming down" is due to the underlying semantic simplicity of the relational model).

The *external data model* is constructed for the scope of a single application system. The application is normally defined as one executable program that connects to a database. The external data model defines the database structures needed for that application.

Usually, a database supports many applications. The database requirements of these applications may overlap and conflict. It is, therefore, necessary to integrate the external models in a single *logical data model*. A well-designed logical data model is almost dissociated from individual applications and provides a database structure on which any existing and future applications can be built.

The *physical data model* is obtained by transforming the logical model into a design that corresponds to a particular DBMS and to a particular release of that DBMS. The resulting physical model enables the designer to generate code to create database schemas (including triggers and indexes) and possibly to load test data into the database tables.

Q3 – answer

Referential integrity is the principal RDB technique for ensuring that the data in the database are accurate and correct. Referential integrity states that a database must not contain foreign key values that do not match some primary key values.

Referential integrity is an RDB way of implementing associations between data structures. Consequently, associations (and aggregations) in UML class diagrams are mapped to primary-to-foreign-key relationships in RDB models.

Q5 – answer

A *trigger* is a procedural (programmatic) way of implementing the business rules on data. In fact, some business rules on relationships between data in the database cannot be implemented declaratively, and triggers then provide the only way of programming such referential integrity rules.

In effect, triggers subsume *declarative referential integrity*. The trigger code can be generated automatically to account for any declarative referential constraint. This code can then be manually extended or re-programmed to enforce more exotic business rules.

Q7 – answer

A good *normalization level* delivers a database schema that is optimal, in terms of performance and maintenance, for the ways that the database is used. Since database usage patterns consist of a mixture of retrieval and update operations, a good normalization level implies a trade-off between retrieval and update such that the most important retrieval and update operations get preferential treatment as far as the normalization of tables is concerned.

Database tables that are *dynamic* (their content is frequently updated) should be normalized to a high NF. On the other hand, tables that are relatively *static*, possibly updated by some batch processes outside peak hours, should be denormalized to a low NF. As a result, some tables in the database may be in a high NF and other tables in a low NF.

Q9 – answer

The question is slightly hypothetical as the extent of the update is not specified and the exact design of the entity classes (`EIdentityMap` and `EContact`) is not known. For example, it is possible to have only one instance of `EIdentityMap` in the program or to have a separate instance of it for each entity class. In the latter case, the status of an entity object (clean or dirty) may be maintained in `EIdentityMap`, instead of in the entity object itself.

The main difference between the delete and update scenarios is that unloading due to update does not (normally) lead to the destruction of the entity object. The object is "unloaded" to the database by executing an SQL update operation on the `Contact` table. However, the `EContact` object will be retained in the memory cache. Moreover, the `EContact` object is clean and should be marked as such. The marking will involve a `setClean()` or similar message from `MDataMapper` to either `EIdentityMap` or directly to `EContact`.

Q11 – answer

Stored procedures have important performance advantages over SQL queries submitted from the client. The advantages relate to much reduced network traffic and to the fact that stored procedures are optimized, compiled, and ready to "fire."

In large systems, stored procedures allow highly modularized code to be written that can be reused and nested in larger stored procedures as well as invoked from many different application programs.

An SQL query may still need to be used from a client program in circumstances in which the user is given an opportunity to construct (indirectly through the UI) *dynamic queries* to the database – in other words, when the client program cannot know ahead of time what processing (query criteria) will be demanded by the user.

Q13 – answer

SQL (and distributed object models such as CORBA/EJB) supports four levels of *transaction isolation*. These four levels were named differently in the chapter to facilitate readers' understanding and to follow the book's flow of logic. The four levels are (the chapter's descriptions are in parentheses):

1. read uncommitted (dirty read possible)

2. read committed (nonrepeatable read possible)

3. repeatable read (phantom possible)

4. serializable (repeatable read).

Read uncommitted means that the database does not issue read (shared) locks while reading data. Consequently another transaction can read an uncommitted transaction that might get rolled back later (hence "dirty read"). This isolation level ensures only that physically corrupt data will not be read.

Read committed means that the database will require read locks to read data. Only committed data can be read, but the data can be changed before the end of the transaction.

Repeatable read means that locks are placed on all data that are used in a transaction, and other transactions cannot update the data. However, other transactions might insert new items into the data set, and if the transaction reads from that data set again then "phantom reads" may occur.

Serializable means that locks are placed on all data that are used in a transaction, and other transactions cannot update or insert into that data set.

Note that if a database supports only *page-level locking* (there is no support for row-level locking), then the repeatable read and serializable levels are synonymous. This is because other transactions cannot insert individual rows of data before the first transaction is finished (because the entire page of data is locked).

Q15 – answer

A *compensating transaction* reverses the effect of a transaction that has already committed. Compensation is an important recovery mechanism in situations where the user must undo changes made to the database and expects that the program will provide such an undo operation (e.g. as a menu item). In some cases, it may be possible and desirable to design into the program a compensating transaction that can undo to a number of levels (i.e. one undo after another more than once).

In some *advanced transaction models* that employ savepoints, subtransactions are allowed to commit changes to the database. A recovery from the successive failure of a transaction will then require a compensating transaction so that a committed subtransaction can be undone without causing a cascading abort of (perhaps many) other transactions.

Solutions to exercises (CM)

F1 – solution

The screen `Update Organization Status` is similar to the window presented in Figure 7.21 (Section 7.5.3), except that the `statusCode` is also shown as a non-editable field. When the program navigates into this screen, there is a need to find the latest value for `statusDescription`. Accordingly, a message is sent to `CAdmin` to `getOrgStatus()` (Figure 8.26). `CAdmin` delegates this request to `MDataMapper`.

As discussed in Section 8.4.1 (Figure 8.20), `MDataMapper` attempts to obtain the `OrgStatus` object from the memory cache. If the `EOrgStatus` object exists in memory and is clean, processing will terminate (after the `EOrgStatus` object is returned and displayed in the `Update Organization Status` screen).

Otherwise, the program has to search for the `EOrgStatus` object in the database (after destroying any dirty `EOrgStatus` object, if such a dirty object is in the cache). The remaining messages follow the pattern described in Section 8.4.2 (Figure 8.21).

F2 – solution

Making a change to an organization status necessitates updating the database as well as modifying the entity object held in the memory cache. As seen in Figure 8.27, the `save()` request is forwarded by `CAdmin` to `MDataMapper`. The request passes the OID of `EOrgStatus` as well as modified `orgStatusData`. With this information, `MDataMapper` can engage `FWriter` to update the database.

Provided that the database update is successful, `MDataMapper` engages `EIdentityMap`, so that the memory-held `EOrgStatus` object gets modified with a new `statusDescription`. The model in Figure 8.27 assumes that `EOrgStatus` holds a flag indicating whether or not it is clean. The flag value is modified with the `setClean()` message.

F3 – solution

There is a need for two *triggers* on the `Event` table, namely:

1. on `insert` (`ti_event`);
2. on `update` (`tu_event`).

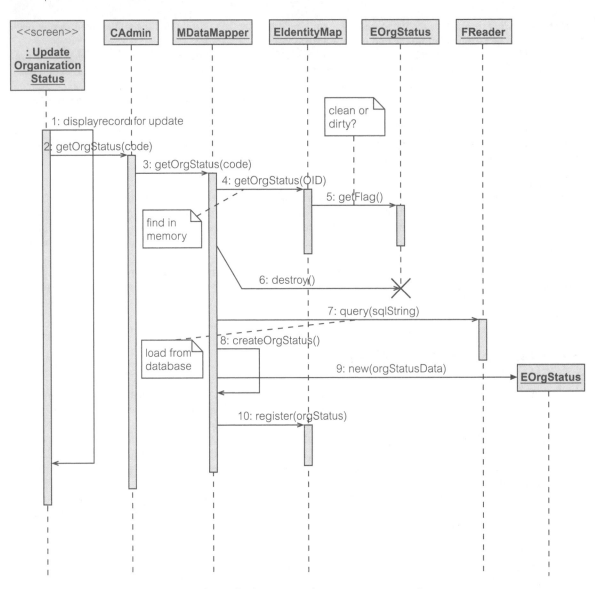

Figure 8.26 Managing persistency after a display request (contact management)

The *insert trigger* will ensure that:

■ Foreign key `Event.task_id` must correspond to an existing `Task.task_id`.

■ Foreign key `Event.created_emp_id` corresponds to an existing `Employee.emp_id`.

■ Foreign key `Event.due_emp_id` corresponds to an existing `Employee.emp_id`.

■ Foreign key `Event.completed_emp_id` corresponds to an existing `Employee.emp_id` or be `NULL`.

The *update trigger* will ensure that the same business rules as the insert trigger in case an attempt is made to update the foreign key columns:

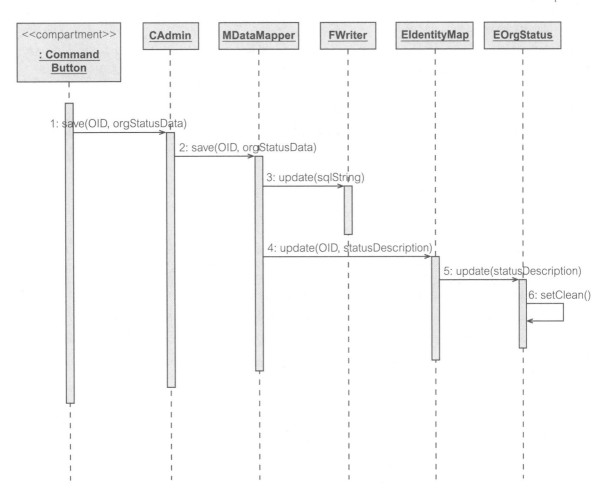

Figure 8.27 Managing persistency after an update request (contact management)

- `Event.task_id`
- `Event.created_emp_id`
- `Event.due_emp_id`
- `Event.completed_emp_id.`

F4 – solution
There is a need for three *triggers* on the `Task` table, namely:

1. on insert (`ti_task`);
2. on update (`tu_task`);
3. on delete (`td_task`).

The *insert* trigger will ensure that:

- Foreign key `Task.contact_id` corresponds to an existing `Contact.contact_id`.
- Foreign key `Task.created_emp_id` corresponds to an existing `Employee.emp_id`.

The *update trigger* will ensure that:

- Foreign key `Task.contact_id` cannot be modified to a non-existent `Contact.contact_id`.
- Foreign key `Task.created_emp_id` cannot be modified to a non-existent `Employee.emp_id`.
- Primary key `Task.task_id` cannot be modified if associated events still exist in the `Event` table.

The *delete trigger* will ensure that on delete of a task:

- All associated events in the `Event` table are also deleted (the "cascade" of delete stops at the `Event` table).

F5 – solution

Stored procedures to further support transactional integrity of the `Event` table (i.e. they modify `Event` and must cooperate with the triggers) include:

- a stored procedure to save event (`SaveTaskEvent_SP`);
- a stored procedure to delete the last event for the task (`DeleteEvent_SP`).

Stored procedures that modify the `Event` table without the risk of violating foreign key references to other tables include (note that a stored procedure that modifies a table without the risk of violating foreign key references is either not modifying any of the foreign key columns or the application program ensures that foreign key values are correct (by, for example, using database-driven picklists for value selections)):

- a stored procedure to store the fact that an event has been completed (`CompleteEvent_SP`).

Stored procedures that only retrieve information from the database and "touch" on the `Event` table include:

- a stored procedure to find daily activities of employees in the contact management subsystem (`DailyActivity_SP`).

The following *algorithm* is obeyed by the procedure `SaveTaskEvent_SP`:

```
BEGIN

INPUT PARAMETERS (all known (not null) fields corresponding to columns in tables Task and Event)

IN/OUT PARAMETERS (@task_id, @event_id)

IF @task_id is null
   AND other Task fields are not nulls
   (except @value that can be null)
   THEN
      insert into Task
   ELSE
      IF @task_id is not null
         AND at least one other Task field is not
            null
         THEN
            update Task
      ENDIF
ENDIF

IF @task_id is not null
   IF @event_id is null
      AND other required Event fields are not nulls
      THEN
         insert into Event
      ELSE
```

```
        IF @event_id is not null
            THEN
                update Event
            ENDIF
    ENDIF
ENDIF
```

Any other case not allowed by the application, but if allowed the triggers will roll back the transaction with appropriate error message

```
END
```

The *algorithm* for procedure DeleteEvent_SP:

```
BEGIN

INPUT PARAMETERS (@event_id, @user_id)

Select Event (where event_id = @event_id)

IF @user_id = Event.created_emp_id
    THEN
        delete Event (where event_id = @event_id)
        IF no more events for
            Task.task_id = Event.task_id AND
            Event.event_id = @event_id
        THEN
            delete that Task
        ENDIF
    ELSE
        raise error ("Only creator of the event can
                      delete that event")
ENDIF

END
```

The *algorithm* for procedure CompleteEvent_SP:

```
BEGIN

INPUT PARAMETERS (@event_id, @completed_dt, @completed_emp_id)

IF all parameters are not null
    THEN
        update Event (where event_id = @event_id)
    ELSE
        raise error
ENDIF

END
```

The *algorithm* for procedure DailyActivity_SP:

```
BEGIN

INPUT PARAMETERS (@date, @user_id)

OUTPUT PARAMETERS (all columns from tables Task, Event, and selected columns from
tables Contact and PostalAddress)
```

```
LOOP (until no more Events found)
Select Event (where (due_dt <= @date OR
                    completed_dt = @date) AND
                    due_emp_id = @user_id)
Select Task for that Event.task_id
Select ActionXref for that Event.action_id
Select Contact for that Task.contact_id
Select PostalAddress for that Contact.contact_id
ENDLOOP

END
```

Chapter

9

Testing and Change Management

Testing and change management are not separate phases of the lifecycle – they span the lifecycle. *Testing* is not just the debugging of programs. It is part of quality management. *Quality management* divides into quality assurance and quality control. *Quality assurance* is about proactive ways of building quality into a software system. *Quality control* is about (mostly reactive) ways of testing the quality of a software system.

Test-driven development, popularized by the agile software development methods, is a very practical way of conducting quality assurance. Test-driven development builds quality into a software system by an outright demand that test code has to be written before the application code and that the application must pass the test to be quality assured.

The development artifacts of every lifecycle phase must be tested. Similarly, *change management* does not just apply to enhancements requested by stakeholders or to defects found during testing. Change management is the fundamental aspect of overall project management – change requests must be documented, and the impact of each change on development artifacts must be tracked and retested after the change has been realized.

Traceability underlies testing and change management. Traceability captures, links, and tracks all important development artifacts, including requirements. The ultimate aim of traceability is to enable the generation of complete system documentation that is guaranteed to be correct and consistent across various documents and models – from requirements to technical and user documentation.

The traceability items can be textual statements or graphical models. Traceability establishes explicit links between the traceability items. The links can be direct or indirect. The links allow an impact analysis to be undertaken if any item on the traceability path is changed.

Earlier in the book, we distinguished between system services and system constraints. Traceability, quality, and change management are frequently associated with system services that manifest themselves in the use-case requirements. However, one must not forget that enforcement of system constraints must also be tested and managed.

9.1 Test concepts

Testing is not an unanticipated event. On the contrary, it is an important part of the overall quality management plan (Maciaszek and Liong, 2004). A *test plan* should address such issues as test schedules, budget, tasks (test cases), and resources. A test plan would also normally encroach on change management issues, such as the handling of defects and enhancements.

The test and change management *documentation* is an integral part of other system documents, including the use-case documents (Figure 9.1). The system *features* identified in the business use-case model (Section 2.5.2) can be used to write the initial test plan. The use-case model is then used to write test-case documents and determine *test requirements*. *Defects* found during testing are documented in the *defects document*. Any unimplemented *use-case requirements* are listed in the *enhancements document*.

When a CASE tool is used, the developers have the option of either:

■ producing narrative documents and then using them to create requirements (test requirements, use-case requirements, etc.) in the CASE repository; or

■ using the CASE tool to enter the requirements into the repository and then generating documentation.

Figure 9.2 shows an excerpt from a test-case document used to enter *test requirements* into the repository. Similarly to the use-case requirements, test requirements are numbered and organized hierarchically. Many test requirements correspond directly to use-case requirements. Hence, the main section in the document is called "Conformance to Use-Case Specs."

Other sections of a test-case document would identify requirements for GUI testing, database testing, and testing of generic reusable components. These kinds of test must be

Figure 9.1
Documents
relevant to testing
and change
management

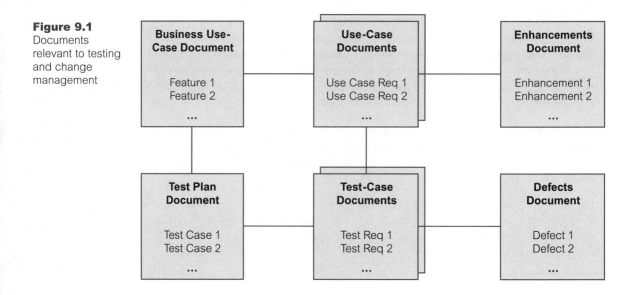

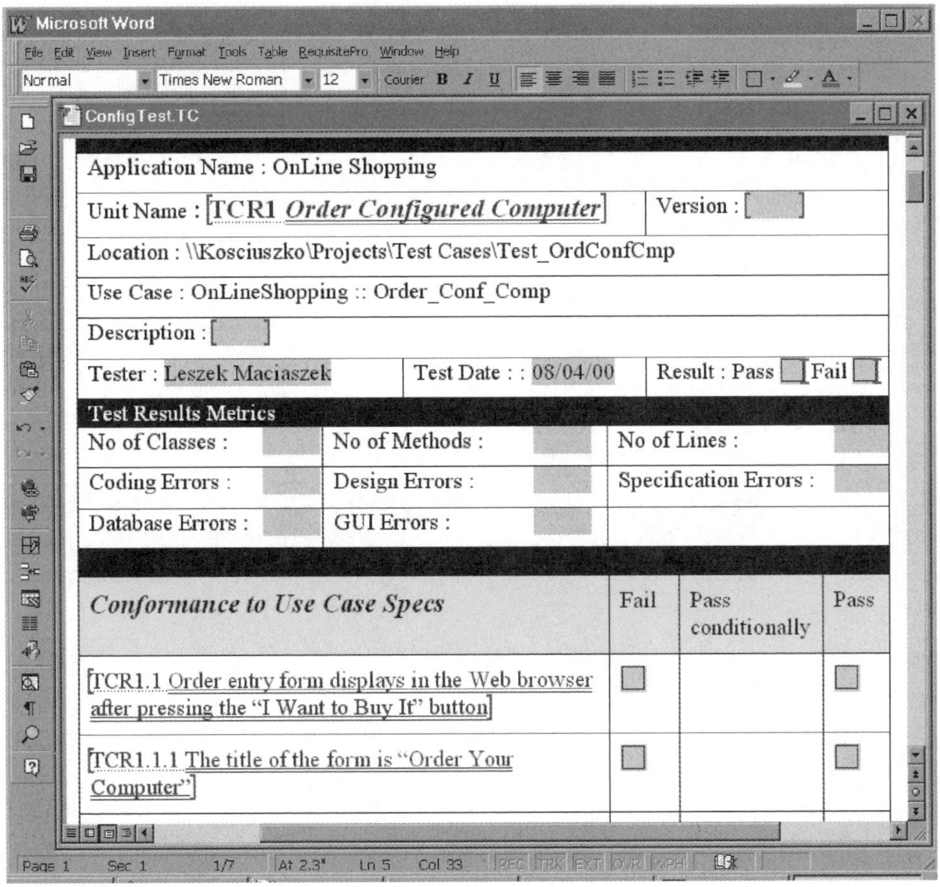

Figure 9.2
Test- case
document
Source: Screen
shot reprinted by
permission from
Microsoft
Corporation

included as part of testing of functional units for two reasons: first, to test the GUI, database, or generic components (such as those that end up in the dynamic link library) we need the functional context within which the input and output data make sense; second, the GUI, database, and generic components may show defects only in the context of some, but not all, functional tests.

The test-case documents are used to record test outcomes, hence the three columns next to each test requirement in Figure 9.2. A test requirement can fail the test, pass it conditionally (in which case an explanation is required), or pass it unconditionally.

Use-case and the resulting test requirements are used to develop *test cases*, which were identified earlier in the *test plan*. Statements in a test-case document can be (should be) traceable down to test requirements and then to use-case requirements.

For the purpose of conducting the tests, test cases are realized in *test scripts*. Test scripts identify the *steps* (that a tester has to follow) and *verification points* (questions that a tester has to find answers for) necessary to ascertain if test requirements are satisfied in the software product. Test scripts can be combined into larger *test suites*. Test suites can create a hierarchy in which larger test suites contain smaller test suites.

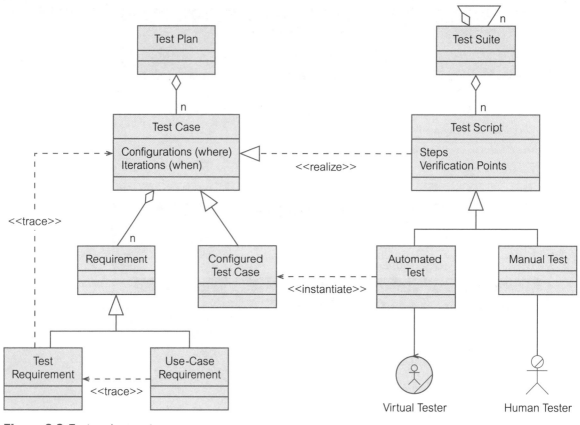

Figure 9.3 Test environment
Source: modified from Maciaszek and Liong (2004)

The interplay of test concepts discussed above is shown in Figure 9.3 as a class model (Maciaszek and Liong, 2004). The class model also shows that some test scripts can be automated and others can only be tested manually.

A *manual test* is conducted by a human tester by simply executing the unit (application program) under test and observing the execution outcome. An *automated test* is performed by a virtual tester, which is a dedicated test workstation set up to launch the unit under test and automatically perform the steps and verification points of a test script.

A virtual tester is a *capture/playback tool*. First, the tool creates a test script by capturing the GUI and other events occurring during the execution of the unit under test. Then, the tool can play back the recorded script and check over and over again whether the unit under test performs as expected (as prerecorded). Accordingly, automated testing is used extensively for regression testing. "*Regression testing* is the re-execution of relevant acceptance tests on successive code iterations. The aim of regression testing is to ensure that iterative extensions (increments) to the code have not resulted in unintended side effects and errors in the old parts of the code that were not supposed to change during the iteration" (Maciaszek and Liong, 2004, p.396).

Test techniques

The selection of *test techniques*, which can be employed for product or process testing, depends on various factors. The main factor is the nature of the product/process under test. It is clear that different test techniques are demanded by a software program, a software model, and a document. Another factor is the required coverage and scrutiny of the test. Also, different techniques need to be used for testing of system services (Section 9.2.1) and for testing of system constraints (Section 9.2.2).

Testing system services

Schach (2002) distinguishes between the informal and methodical testing of system services. Every developer performs an *informal test* while modeling or implementing a system service. By its nature, informal testing is imperfect. A person who developed a service is the least likely person to find faults in that service.

The informal testing is only of marginal significance, and it must be supplemented by methodical testing. There are two main kinds of *methodical testing* (Schach, 2002):

1. Non-execution-based (formal reviews):
   - walkthroughs
   - inspections.
2. Execution-based:
   - testing to specs
   - testing to code.

Walkthroughs

A *walkthrough* is a type of formal brainstorm review that can be conducted in any development phase. It is a friendly meeting of developers, carefully planned and with clear objectives, an agenda, duration, and membership. Many IS development teams conduct walkthroughs on a weekly basis.

A few days *prior to a walkthrough meeting*, the participants are handed the materials (models, documents, program code, etc.) that are to be reviewed at the meeting. The materials are collected and distributed to the participants by the walkthrough moderator. The participants study the materials and supply the moderator with their comments, still prior to the meeting.

The meeting is relatively short (two–three hours at most). *During the meeting*, the moderator presents the comments and opens a discussion on each item. The purpose of the meeting is to pinpoint the problem, not to harass the developer! The developer behind the problem is not important and may even be anonymous (although normally this would not be the case). The whole idea is to confirm the existence of a problem. A solution to the problem must not even be attempted.

Acknowledged problems are entered on a *walkthrough issues list* (Pressman, 2001), which is given to the developer after the meeting. The list is used by the developer to make corrections to the software product or process reviewed. Once the corrections have been made, the developer informs the moderator, who takes a decision whether a follow-up walkthrough is necessary.

There is lots of evidence that walkthroughs work very well. They introduce rigor and professionalism to the development process, contribute to productivity and to meeting deadlines, have very important informational outcomes, and improve software quality.

9.2.1.2 Inspections

Like a walkthrough, an *inspection* is a friendly meeting but done under close supervision by the project management. Its purpose is also to identify defects, validate that they are in fact defects, record them, and schedule when and by whom they have to be fixed.

Unlike the walkthroughs, inspections are conducted less frequently, may target only selected and critical issues, and are more formal and more rigorous. An inspection is organized in a number of stages. It starts with the *planning stage*, which identifies the inspection membership and the inspection target area.

Prior to the inspection session, a short *informational meeting* may be set. During the informational meeting, the developer whose product is to be inspected introduces the subject. The inspection materials are handed over to the participants during or before the informational meeting.

The *informational meeting* usually takes place one week before the inspection meeting. This gives the inspection team time to study the materials and prepare for the meeting. During the meeting, the defects are identified, recorded, and numbered. Immediately after the meeting, the moderator prepares the *defect log* – ideally recorded in a *change management tool* associated with the project.

The developer is normally requested to resolve the defects quickly and record the resolution in the change management tool. The moderator would verify the defect resolution and decide if *reinspection* is needed. Once satisfied with the resolution, the moderator – in consultation with the project manager – submits the development module to the *software quality assurance* (SQA) group in the organization (if such a group exists).

The SQA group should consist of some of the best people in the organization. The group must not be associated with the project, except in the capacity of quality assurance. The group (not the original developers!) is made responsible for the final quality of the product.

9.2.1.3 Testing to specs

Testing to specs is an execution-based test type. It applies to executable software products, not to documents or models. It is also known under a variety of different names, such as *black-box testing*, functional testing, and input/output-driven testing.

The principle of testing to specs is that the developer treats the test module as a black box that takes some input and produces some output. No attempt is made to understand the program logic or computational algorithms.

Testing to specs requires that the *test requirements* are derived from the *use-case requirements*, and then identified and documented in a separate test plan and test-case documents. These documents provide a test scenario for the tester. The scenarios can be recorded in a *capture–playback tool* and used repeatedly for *regression testing*.

Testing to specs is likely to discover defects normally difficult to catch by other means. In particular, testing to specs discovers *missing functionality* – something that (hopefully) has been documented as a use-case requirement (and therefore a test requirement) but has never been programmed. It can also discover the missing functionality that has never been documented in the use cases but is manifestly missing in the system implementation.

Testing to code 9.2.1.4

Testing to code is the second form of execution-based testing. It is also known under the names of *white-box testing*, glass-box testing, logic-driven testing, and path-oriented testing.

Testing to code starts with careful analysis of the program's algorithms. Test cases are derived to *exercise the code* – i.e. to guarantee that all possible execution paths in the program are verified. The test data are specially contrived to exercise the code.

Testing to code can be supported by the capture–playback tools and then used for regression testing. However, the nature of testing to code requires the extensive involvement of the programmer in utilizing the tools. Many of the playback scripts need to be written by the programmer rather than generated by the tool. Even if generated, they may need to be extensively modified by the programmer.

Like all other forms of execution-based testing, testing to code cannot be exhaustive, because of the combinatorial explosion in the number of possible test cases with even a modest growth in the program's complexity. Even if it were possible to test every execution path, we could not guarantee that we have detected every defect. The old testing adage holds: testing can eliminate only some errors; it cannot prove the program correct!

Testing system constraints 9.2.2

The *testing of system constraints* is predominantly *execution-based*. Its purpose is to determine that the system constraints were implemented as listed in the requirements and test documents. The testing of system constraints includes such issues as:

- user interface testing
- database testing
- authorization testing
- performance testing
- stress testing
- failover testing
- configuration testing
- installation testing.

The first two types of system constraint test – the *user interface* and *database testing* – are very closely associated with the testing of system services. They are normally conducted in parallel with tests of system services. As such, they are included in test documents produced for the testing of system services.

9.2.2.1 User interface testing

UI testing is intertwined with the overall software development process. It starts as early as in the requirements phase with activities such as storyboarding, inclusion of window drawings in use-case documents, and GUI prototyping. These early UI tests concentrate on the fulfillment of functional requirements and on usability.

Later, when the system has been implemented, methodical *post-implementation UI testing* is required. Tests are conducted first by the developers, then by the testers, and – prior to the software release – by the customers (*pilot tests*). The following is a sample list of questions in a test document designed for post-implementation UI tests (Bourne, 1997):

- Does the window name correspond to its function?
- Is the window modal or modeless? Which should it be?
- Is a visual distinction made between the required and optional fields?
- Can the window be resized, moved, closed, and restored? Should it be?
- Are any fields missing?
- Are there any spelling mistakes in titles, labels, prompt names, etc.?
- Are command buttons (`OK`, `Cancel`, `Save`, `Clear`, etc.) used consistently across all dialog boxes?
- Is it always possible to abort the current operation (including the delete operation)?
- Are all static fields protected from editing by users? If the application can change the static text, is this being done correctly?
- Are consistent font types and sizes applied to static text fields? Are they spelled correctly?
- Do the sizes of edit boxes correspond to ranges of values that they take?
- Are all edit boxes initialized with correct values when the window opens?
- Are the values entered into edit boxes validated by the client program?
- Are the values in drop-down lists populated correctly from the database?
- Are edit masks used in entry fields as specified?
- Are error messages legible and easy to act on?

9.2.2.2 Database testing

Like UI testing, database testing is inherent in many other kinds of test. Much of the black-box testing (testing to specs) is based on database input and output. However, separate methodical database testing is still necessary.

Post-implementation database testing includes extensive white-box (to code) testing. The most significant part of database testing is *transaction testing*. Some other aspects of the database can be extracted into separate tests, e.g. performance, concurrency, and authorization.

As with the UI tests, the same database tests need to be conducted repeatedly for all different application functions. The issues to be addressed in the database tests should be extracted into a generic document. This generic document should then be attached to all function (system services) tests. The following is an exemplary set of issues that the database tests should address (Bourne, 1997):

- Verify that the transaction executes as expected with correct input. Is the system's feedback to the UI correct? Is the database content correct after the transaction?

- Verify that the transaction executes as expected with incorrect input. Is the system's feedback to the UI correct? Is the database content correct after the transaction?

- Abort the transaction before it finishes. Is the system's feedback to the UI correct? Is the database content correct after the transaction?

- Run the same transaction concurrently in many processes. Deliberately make one transaction hold a lock on a data resource needed by other transactions. Are users getting understandable explanations from the system? Is the database content correct after the transactions have terminated?

- Extract every client SQL statement from the client program and execute it interactively on the database. Are the results as expected and the same as when the SQL is executed from the program?

- Perform interactive white-box testing of every more complex SQL query (from a client program or from a stored procedure) involving outer joins, union, subqueries, null values, aggregate functions, etc.

Authorization testing

9.2.2.3

Authorization testing may be treated as an inherent extension of the first two types of system constraint test. Both the client (user interface) and server (database) objects should be protected from unauthorized use. Authorization testing should verify that the security mechanisms built into the client and the server will in fact protect the system from unauthorized penetration.

Although ultimately the database bears the consequences of security breaches, protection starts at the client. The *user interface* of the program should be able to configure itself dynamically to correspond to the *authorization* level of the current user (*authenticated* by the user ID and password). Menu items, command buttons or even entire windows should be made inaccessible to users if they do not have proper authorization.

Not all security loopholes can be addressed at the client. The support for authorization is a significant component of any DBMS. *Server permissions* (*privileges*) fall into two categories. A user may be given selective permissions to:

- access individual *server objects* (tables, views, columns, stored procedures, etc.);
- execute SQL statements (select, update, insert, delete, etc.).

Permissions for a user may be assigned directly at a *user level* or at a *group level*. Groups allow the security administrator to assign permissions to a group of users in a single entry. A user may belong to none or to many groups.

To allow greater flexibility with managing authorization, most DBMSs introduce one more authorization level – the *role level*. The role allows the security administrator to grant permissions to all users who play a particular role in the organization. Roles can be nested – i.e. the permissions granted to different role names can overlap.

In larger IS applications, *authorization design* is an elaborate activity. Frequently, an *authorization database* is set up alongside the application database to store and manipulate the client and server permissions. The application program consults the database after the user's logon in order to identify the user's authorization level and configure itself to that user.

Any changes to database permissions are driven from the authorization database – i.e. nobody, even the security administrator, is allowed to change the application database permissions directly without first updating the authorization database.

9.2.2.4 Testing of other constraints

The testing of system constraints also includes:

- performance testing
- stress testing
- failover testing
- configuration testing
- installation testing.

Performance testing measures the performance constraints demanded by the customer. The constraints relate to *transaction speed and throughput*. The tests are conducted for different system workloads, including any anticipated *peak loads*. Performance testing is an important part of *system tuning*.

Stress testing is designed to break the system when abnormal demands are placed on it – low resources, an unusual contention for resources, abnormal frequency, quantity or volume. Stress testing is frequently coupled with performance testing and may require similar hardware and software *instrumentation*.

Failover testing addresses the system's response to a variety of hardware, network, or software malfunctions. This kind of testing is closely related to the *recovery* procedures supported by the DBMS.

Configuration testing verifies how the system operates on various software and hardware configurations. In most production environments, the system is expected to run successfully on various client workstations that connect to the database using a variety of network protocols. The client workstations may have different software installed (e.g. drivers) that can conflict with the expected setups.

Installation testing extends configuration testing. It verifies that the system operates properly on every platform installed. This means that the tests of system services are rerun.

9.3 Test-driven development

Agile software development methods (Section 1.4.4.4) popularized *test-driven development*. The idea is to write test cases and scripts as well as test programs before the application code (the unit under test) is developed (designed and programmed). This reversing of the "normal" sequence of activities causes the application code to be written as a response to a test code, and the test code can be used to test the application code as soon as it is available.

Test-driven development has numerous advantages, notwithstanding the fact that it allows user requirements (and the use-case specifications) to be clarified before the programmer writes the first line of the application code. The test code includes *verification points* to verify whether all user requirements are met by the application. In a way, the test code is written to challenge and to fail the application code.

Because the test code exists beforehand, the programmer can write the application code to specifically address all test verification points in order to assert the functionality demanded by the test. Consequently, test-driven development takes a very proactive role and in fact drives the software development, not just the software verification.

The popularity of test-driven development resulted in the availability of relevant patterns (Section 6.4.2.3) and frameworks (Section 6.4.2.2). These provide ideas as well as libraries of classes and interfaces in support of test-driven development. One of the most popular *testing frameworks* for Java development is an open source tool called JUnit (JUnit, 2004).

JUnit is a framework developed according to one of the best-known *design patterns*, called the *composite pattern* (Gamma *et al.*, 1995). JUnit offers a Java interface named `Test`. The interface is implemented by two classes: `TestCase` and `TestSuite`. A `TestResult` class, associated with `TestCase`, collects the test outcomes. Figure 9.4 shows the class model for JUnit. The model uses the composite pattern.

As the composite pattern, `TestSuite` is a composite class that implements the `Test` interface, but it can also contain one or more `Test` interfaces. Because `Test` is

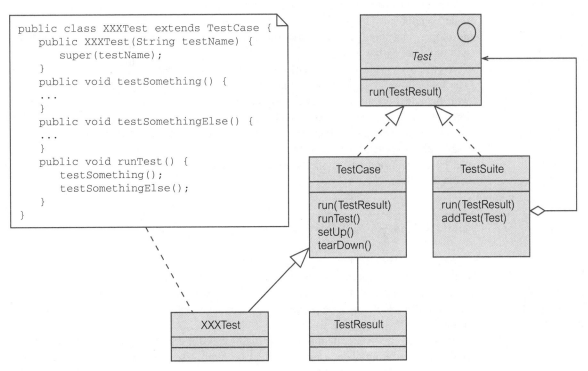

Figure 9.4 JUnit as the composite pattern
Source: Maciaszek and Liong (2004). Reprinted by permission of Pearson Education Ltd

implemented by both `TestCase` and `TestSuite`, a `TestSuite` object can contain one or more `TestCase` objects and/or one or more other `TestSuite` objects.

A *test unit*, such as `XXXTest`, is implemented as a subclass of `TestCase`, which can manipulate the concrete objects in the composition via the `Test` interface. In effect, `XXXTest` implements test cases to execute on a test unit indicated in the model by the `XXX` prefix (e.g. `XXX` may be a name of a class to be tested). As shown in the code fragment in Figure 9.4, `XXXTest` would use its `runTest()` method to run a test unit by calling the desired test cases. JUnit offers a visual interface to run tests, indicate test progress, and report test results (Maciaszek and Liong, 2004).

9.4 Managing change

Testing reveals *defects*, which need to be fixed. To be fixed, the defects must be submitted as *change requests* and allocated to developers. Some change requests may relate to *enhancements* rather than defects. Both defects and enhancements undergo status changes, may be prioritized, have owners, and need to be traced to their origins in test- and use-case documents.

Managing change is a big task in any multi-developer software project. Consider a scenario where two different defects are allocated to two different developers for fixing but it turns out that correcting these seemingly unrelated defects requires changes in the same code component. Unless the developers are made aware of the possible conflict, both developers can simultaneously work on the corrections, and eventually the more recent fix will undo the earlier fix.

To manage change properly, a *change request management tool* is necessary (Figure 9.5). The tool allows changes to be managed online, and it ensures that all developers work with the latest documents. Changes to documents introduced by one project member are immediately available to fellow developers. Potential conflicts are resolved through *locking* or *version control* mechanisms. In the former case, a locked document is temporarily unavailable to other developers. In the latter case, multiple versions of the same document can be created, and any conflicts between versions are resolved through negotiations at some later time.

9.4.1 Submitting a change request

Typically, a *change request* is either a defect or an enhancement. A change request is entered into the project repository. Once it has been entered into the repository, the developers can monitor the progress made on the change request, observe its *status*, and act on it. *Actions* that can be performed on a change request depend on the current status of the request.

Figure 9.6 shows the main tab in the dialog box for entering defects (Rational, 2000). A defect will be numbered and described in detail. The priority, severity, project, and owner information can be entered from the drop-down lists of applicable choices (the attribute values in drop-down lists and elsewhere on the form can be customized to suit the

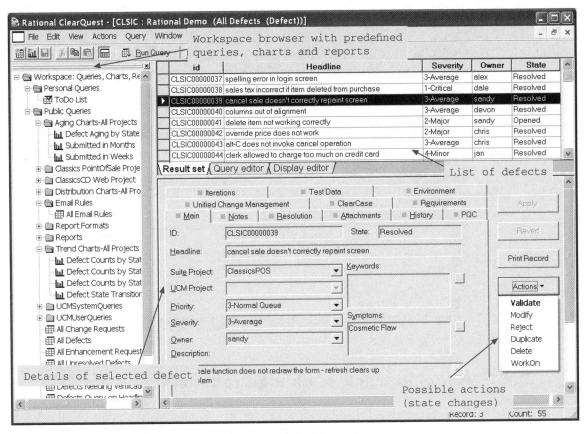

Figure 9.5 Change management with IBM Rational ClearQuest
Source: Rational Suite tutorial (Rational, 2002); Maciaszek and Liong (2004). Reprinted by permission of Pearson Education Ltd.

project's needs). Other fields allow descriptive information to be entered, including the possibility of attaching related documentation such as code fragments.

The action of *submitting* a change request can result in automatic *email notifications* to team members. The change request is then in the Submitted status. The project management can customize the tool to allow predefined actions in each status. For example, when in the Submitted status, the possible actions can be (Figure 9.7):

- Assign (to a team member);
- Modify (some details of the request);
- Close (probably as a result of fixing it);
- Duplicate (found to be reported before under a different ID);
- Postpone (don't worry about it for now);
- Delete (without fixing);
- WorkOn (we keep working on it).

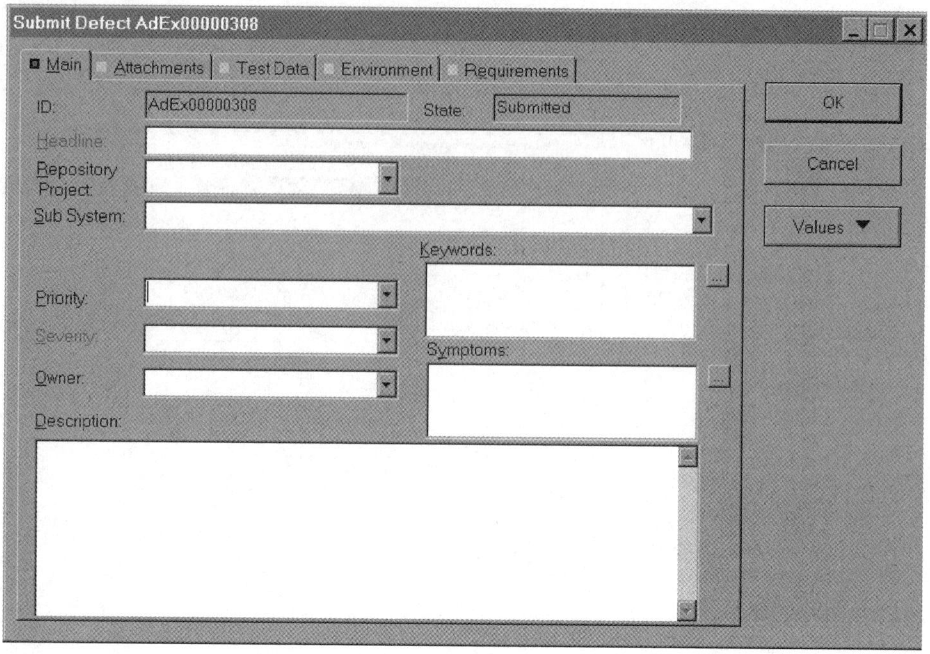

Figure 9.6
ClearQuest
interface to submit
a defect

9.4.2 Keeping track of change requests

Each change request is assigned to a team member. The team member can Open the change request. When in the Open state, no other team member can modify the state of the request.

When the change request is resolved, the developer can execute the Resolve action on it. The details of the resolution can be entered and email notification can be sent to the project managers and testers. The testers may need to perform the Verify action on the resolved change request.

At any stage, the change request management tool can track the requests and produce easy-to-understand charts and reports (*project metrics*). Charts and reports can assess the number of unassigned defects, reveal workloads of each team member, and show how many defects are still unresolved.

Figure 9.8 shows the chart for active defects by priority. Six defects are to be resolved immediately, fifty-five should be given high attention, sixty-seven are in the normal queue, and sixty-eight have low priority.

9.5 Traceability

Traceability, testing, and change management are not aims in themselves and must not be overdone. The developers should concentrate on developing, not tracing, testing, or managing change. There is a significant cost to the project associated with these issues.

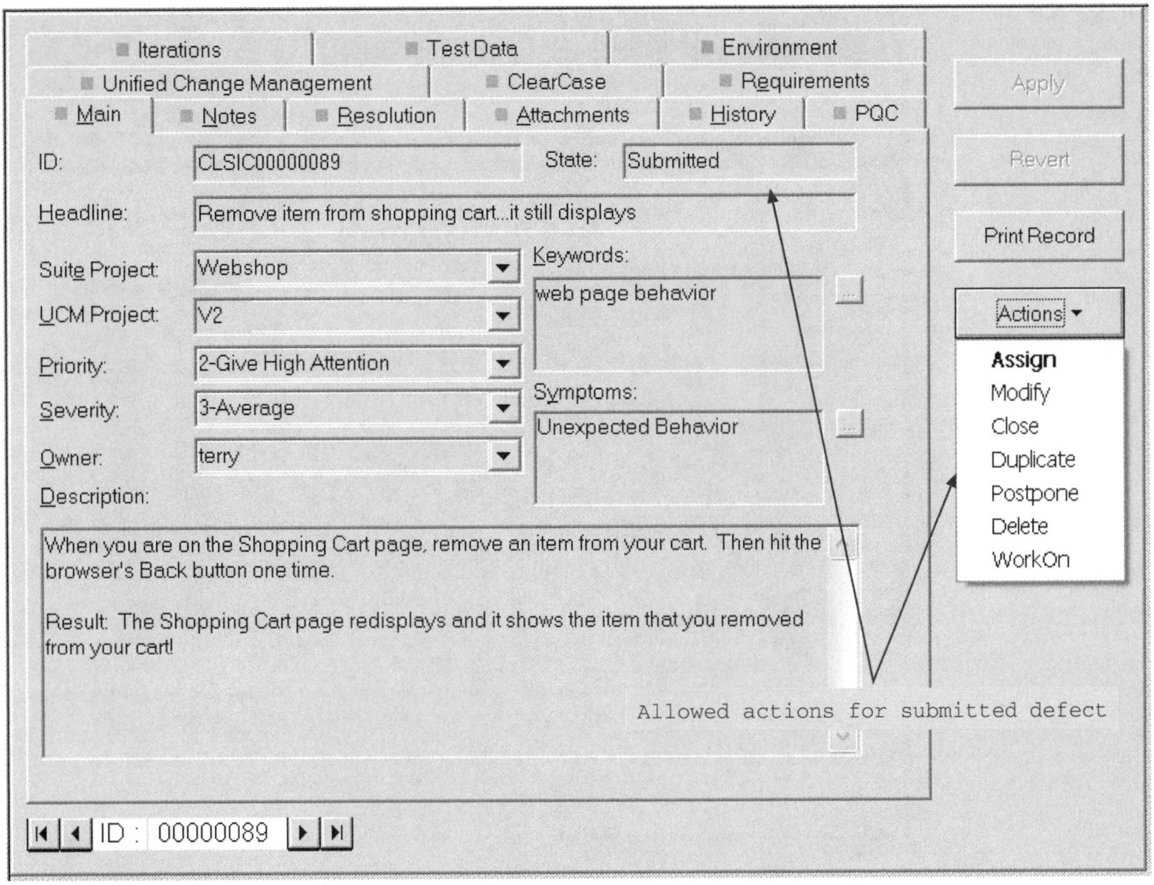

Figure 9.7 Defect management with IBM Rational ClearQuest
Source: Rational Suite tutorial (Rational, 2002); Maciaszek and Liong (2004). Reprinted by permission of Pearson Education Ltd

However, there is also a significant long-term cost to the project associated with *not* managing these issues.

Since traceability underpins testing and change management, a *cost–benefit analysis* should be used to determine the scope and depth of project traceability. As a minimum, traceability should be maintained between the use-case requirements and defects. In a more elaborated model, the test requirements could be added between the use-case requirements and defects on the traceability path. In an even more sophisticated model, the traceability agenda can include system features, test cases, enhancements, test verification points, and other software development artifacts.

In the rest of this chapter, we will consider the traceability model consistent with the links between system documents shown in Figure 9.1. The business use-case document lists *system features*. The test plan document identifies *test cases*. Features are linked to test cases and to *use-case requirements* in the use-case documents. *Test requirements* in the test-case documents can be traced back to test cases and use-case requirements. Test

Figure 9.8
Metric chart of
defects by priority

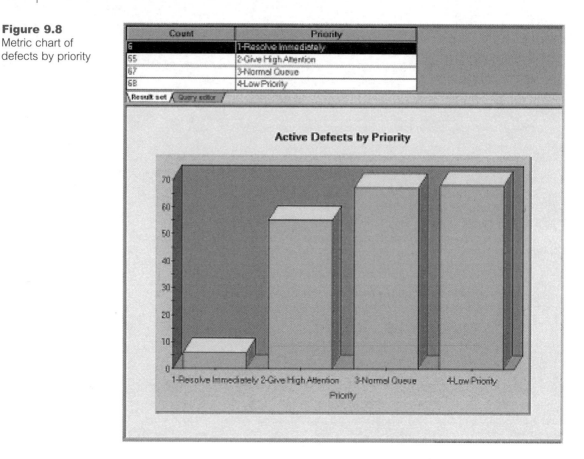

Count	Priority
6	1-Resolve Immediately
55	2-Give High Attention
67	3-Normal Queue
68	4-Low Priority

requirements are linked to *defects* and *enhancements* are traced to use-case requirements. The trace from defects to *enhancements* is not needed.

9.5.1 System features to use cases and use-case requirements

A *system feature* is a generic piece of functionality to be implemented in the system. It is a business process shown as an important benefit of the system. Normally, a system feature corresponds to a *business use case* in a business use-case model (Section 2.5.2). If a business use-case model is not formally developed, then system features are identified in a *vision document* (or similarly named strategic project document).

Each system feature is realized by a set of *use-case requirements* in one or more *use cases*. Tracing use cases back to stakeholder needs (expressed in system features) helps to validate the correctness of the use-case model. This strategy "scopes" requirements capture and facilitates completion of the requirements phase. It can also assist in incremental development and delivery of the product.

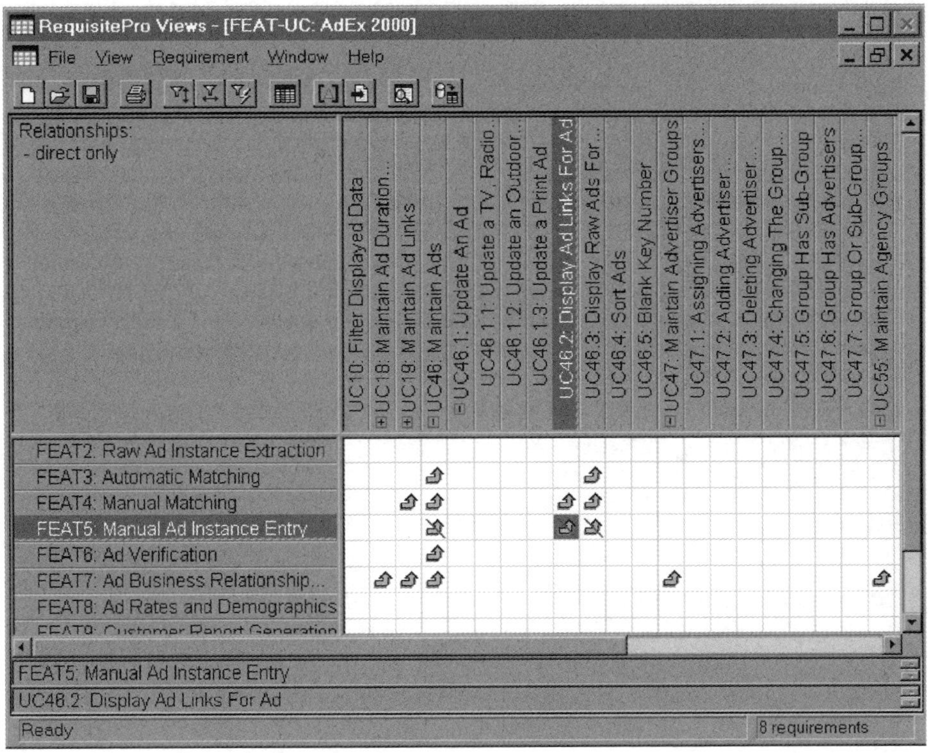

Figure 9.9
Traceability from features to use cases and use-case requirements
Source: Courtesy of Nielsen Media Research, Sydney, Australia

A problem may arise with this strategy if the use-case requirements within each use case are only indirectly linked to features. This can lead to situations where there is a trace between a feature and a use case, yet most use-case requirements have nothing to do with the feature. Deciding whether or not the trace between the feature and the use case is still valid may prove to be a daunting and unsustainable task.

To avoid the scalability and long-term problems associated with this strategy, the traceability matrix should trace the features not only to the use cases but also directly to the use-case requirements. This is possible if each use case is itself treated as the highest-level use-case requirement with a hierarchy of specific use-case requirements under it.

This is shown in Figure 9.9. The columns contain use cases and use-case requirements within use cases. The hierarchical display of use-case requirements can be expanded or collapsed. The arrows signify the traces from features to use cases and use-case requirements. Some arrows are crossed over. These are *suspect traces*. A trace becomes suspect when a *from* or *to* requirement changes. The developer needs to examine the suspect links before clearing them.

Test plans to test cases and test requirements   9.5.2

A *test plan* document is for test cases what a business use-case document is for use cases. The test plan identifies the high-level project information and the software components

Figure 9.10
Traceability from
test plan to test
case and test
requirements
Source: Courtesy
of Nielsen Media
Research, Sydney,
Australia

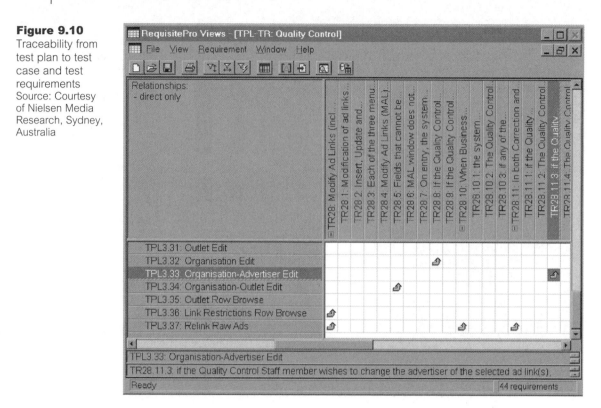

(*test cases*) that should be tested. The test plan also describes the testing strategy for the project, the required test resources, the effort, and the cost.

Each test case identified in the test plan is to be written as a test-case document. Mapping test requirements to test cases and test plans brings similar benefits to the traceability between features, use cases, and use-case requirements: the scoping of test capture, scalability, etc.

Figure 9.10 shows the traceability matrix from the test plan to test cases and test requirements within test cases. The hierarchical display of test requirements can be collapsed and expanded.

9.5.3 UML diagrams to documents and requirements

Traceability and change management do not apply just to narrative documents and textual requirements stored in the CASE repository. The repository also stores UML models. The graphical objects in UML diagrams can be hyperlinked to documents and requirements.

The traceability between UML visual artifacts and any other repository records (in particular documents and requirements) can be established for various UML *graphical icons*. Perhaps the most important of these icons are the use cases in use-case diagrams.

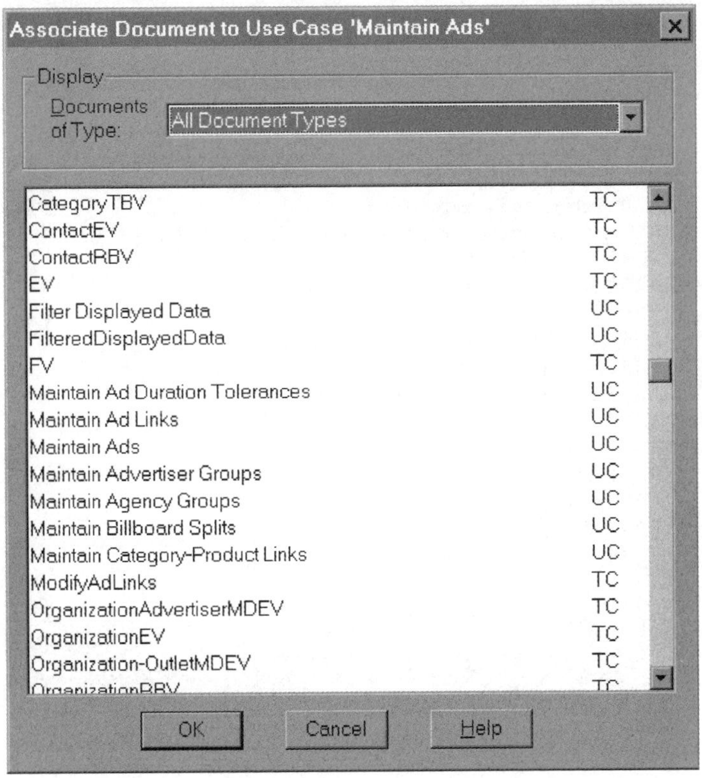

Associate Document to Use Case 'Maintain Ads'		✕
Display		
Documents of Type:	All Document Types ▾	

CategoryTBV	TC
ContactEV	TC
ContactRBV	TC
EV	TC
Filter Displayed Data	UC
FilteredDisplayedData	UC
FV	TC
Maintain Ad Duration Tolerances	UC
Maintain Ad Links	UC
Maintain Ads	UC
Maintain Advertiser Groups	UC
Maintain Agency Groups	UC
Maintain Billboard Splits	UC
Maintain Category-Product Links	UC
ModifyAdLinks	TC
OrganizationAdvertiserMDEV	TC
OrganizationEV	TC
Organization-OutletMDEV	TC
OrganizationRBV	TC

OK   Cancel   Help

Figure 9.11
Hyperlinking
document to use-
case graphical
icon
Source: Courtesy
of Nielsen Media
Research, Sydney,
Australia

Figure 9.11 shows a dialog box for hyperlinking a use-case graphical icon (`Maintain Ads`) to a document. The hyperlinking is done from within a UML use-case diagram. The linked document can be any of the documents in the repository, including those shown in Figure 9.1.

Figure 9.12 shows a dialog box for hyperlinking a use-case graphical icon (`Maintain Ads` again) to a use-case requirement. In general, it is possible to link the icon to a requirement of any type.

Use-case requirements to test requirements   9.5.4

Traceability between use-case requirements and test requirements is critical in assessing whether the application meets the business requirements established for it. The links between these two requirement types allow the user to track defects via test requirements back to use-case requirements and system features (Figure 9.1).

Figure 9.13 shows the traceability matrix with traces between the use-case requirements and test requirements. Note that both the use-case requirements and test requirements are structured hierarchically. The hierarchical levels at which the traces are defined can be predetermined.

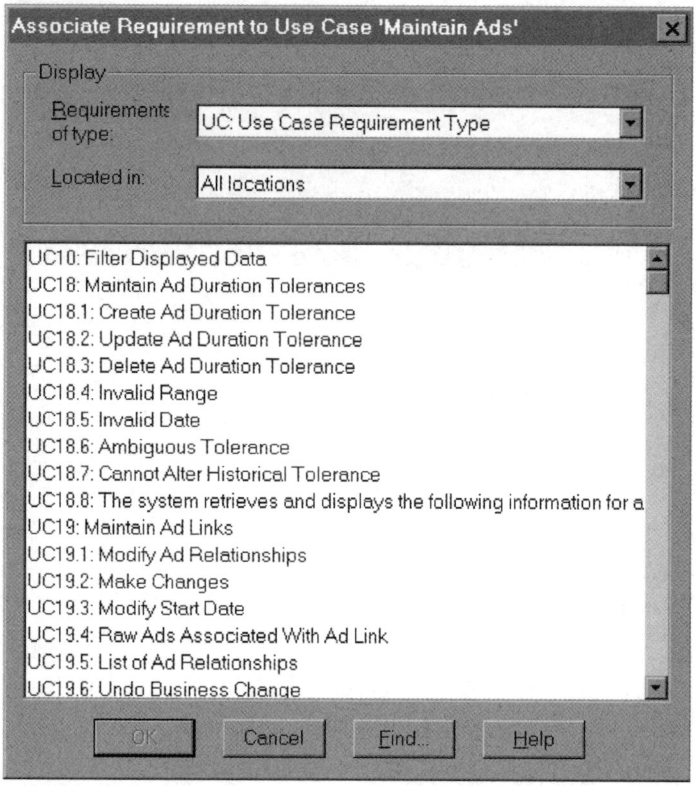
Associate Requirement to Use Case 'Maintain Ads'
Display
Requirements of type:
UC: Use Case Requirement Type
Located in:
All locations
UC10: Filter Displayed Data
UC18: Maintain Ad Duration Tolerances
UC18.1: Create Ad Duration Tolerance
UC18.2: Update Ad Duration Tolerance
UC18.3: Delete Ad Duration Tolerance
UC18.4: Invalid Range
UC18.5: Invalid Date
UC18.6: Ambiguous Tolerance
UC18.7: Cannot Alter Historical Tolerance
UC18.8: The system retrieves and displays the following information for a
UC19: Maintain Ad Links
UC19.1: Modify Ad Relationships
UC19.2: Make Changes
UC19.3: Modify Start Date
UC19.4: Raw Ads Associated With Ad Link
UC19.5: List of Ad Relationships
UC19.6: Undo Business Change
OK
Cancel
Find...
Help

Figure 9.12
Hyperlinking requirement to use-case graphical icon
Source: Courtesy of Nielsen Media Research, Sydney, Australia

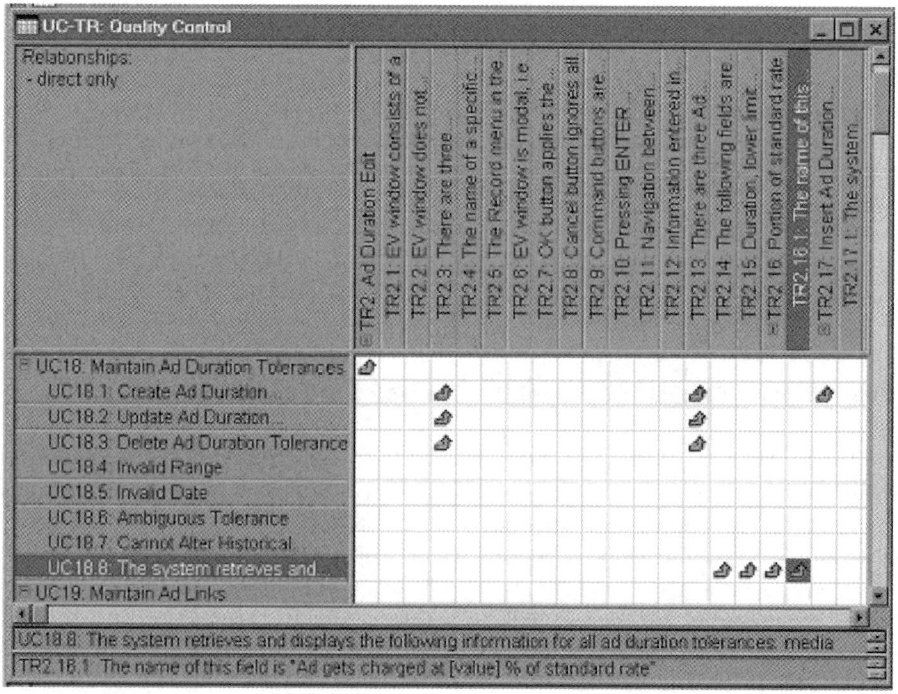
UC-TR: Quality Control
Relationships:
- direct only
TR2: Ad Duration Edit
TR2.1: EV window consists of a
TR2.2: EV window does not...
TR2.3: There are three...
TR2.4: The name of a specific...
TR2.5: The Record menu in the...
TR2.6: EV window is modal, i.e...
TR2.7: OK button applies the...
TR2.8: Cancel button ignores all
TR2.9: Command buttons are...
TR2.10: Pressing ENTER...
TR2.11: Navigation between...
TR2.12: Information entered in...
TR2.13: There are three Ad...
TR2.14: The following fields are...
TR2.15: Duration, lower limit...
TR2.16: Portion of standard rate
TR2.16.1: The name of this...
TR2.17: Insert Ad Duration...
TR2.17.1: The system...
UC18: Maintain Ad Duration Tolerances
UC18.1: Create Ad Duration...
UC18.2: Update Ad Duration...
UC18.3: Delete Ad Duration Tolerance
UC18.4: Invalid Range
UC18.5: Invalid Date
UC18.6: Ambiguous Tolerance
UC18.7: Cannot Alter Historical...
UC18.8: The system retrieves and...
UC19: Maintain Ad Links
UC18.8: The system retrieves and displays the following information for all ad duration tolerances: media
TR2.16.1: The name of this field is "Ad gets charged at [value] % of standard rate"

Figure 9.13
Traceability from use-case requirement and test requirement
Source: Courtesy of Nielsen Media Research, Sydney, Australia

Test requirements to defects

Test-case documents are written in the form of scripts containing the test requirements to be verified when testing. The scripts are used in *manual* tests, but many of these scripts can be *automated* for use in *capture-and-playback* testing tools. Test requirements in test-case documents can then be used to establish verification points in these automated tests.

A *verification point* is a requirement in the script that is used (in *regression testing*) to confirm the state of a test object across different versions (builds) of the application under test (AUT). There are various types of verification point (Rational, 2000). A verification point can be set to check that a text has not changed, that numeric values are accurate, that two files are the same, that a file exists, that menu items have not changed, that computation results are as expected, etc.

Automated testing requires working with two data files – a baseline data file and an actual data file. During *capture*, the verification point records object information in the *baseline data file*. The information is the baseline against which to compare in subsequent tests (*playbacks*). The results of these comparisons are stored in the *actual data file*. Each *failed verification point* needs to be investigated further and, if necessary, entered into the change management tool as a *defect*.

Ultimately all defects – whether discovered in automated or manual tests – must be linked to the test requirements. Figure 9.14 shows a tool that displays all defects in the row browser in the upper part of the window. A currently selected defect can be associated

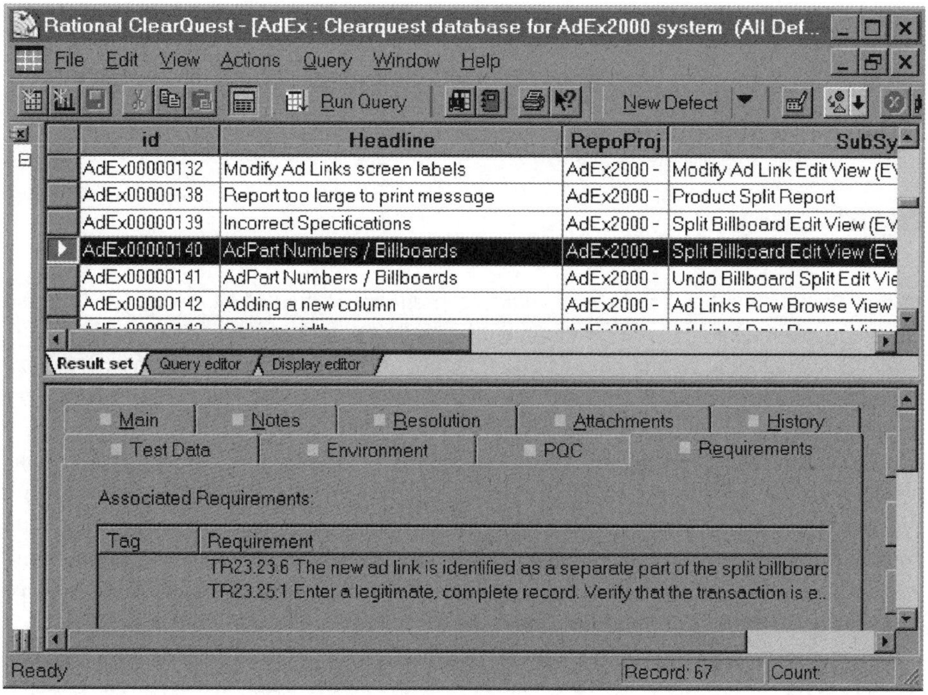

Figure 9.14
Traceability from test requirement to defect
Source: Courtesy of Nielsen Media Research, Sydney, Australia

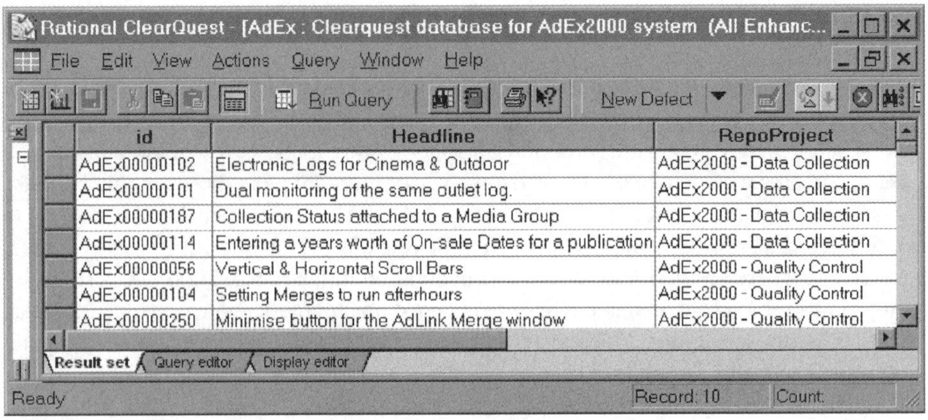

Figure 9.15
Enhancements
Source: Courtesy
of Nielsen Media
Research, Sydney,
Australia

with one or more test requirements. In the example, two test requirements are traced to the highlighted defect.

9.5.6 Use-case requirements to enhancements

Defects need to be traced directly to the test requirements. Enhancements (to be implemented in a future release of the product) must have their explanation in the use-case requirements. In rare situations when a defect has been converted to an enhancement, the traceability links between use-case requirements and test requirements would allow the user to trace the defect to the enhancement.

Figure 9.15 demonstrates that a single tool (see Figure 9.14) can be used to manage enhancements and defects, or indeed any other change requests.

Summary

In this chapter, we have addressed testing and change management issues. Testing and change management span the development lifecycle. As part of the all-embracing *quality management* agenda, testing has two, quite orthogonal, dimensions. It is a reactive (*post factum*) activity when used as a *quality control* mechanism. However, it can be a very proactive *quality assurance* activity when used within the framework of *test-driven development*. In all cases, testing and change management assume that the *traceability* links between system artifacts exist and have been properly maintained during the development.

Testing can be divided into the testing of system services and the testing of system constraints. *Testing of system services* can be non-execution-based or execution-based. *Non-execution-based testing* includes walkthroughs and inspections. *Execution-based testing* can be *testing to specs* or *testing to code*.

The *testing of system constraints* includes a large range of relatively disparate tests that relate to such issues as user interface, database, authorization, performance, stress, failover, configuration, and installation. Some system constraints tests are conducted in parallel with the system services tests; others are done independently.

Testing and change management require specialized *documentation*, such as test plans, test-case documents, and defect and enhancement documents. *Test requirements* are identified in the *test-case documents* and linked to the use-case requirements in the use-case documents.

A *change request* is normally either a *defect* or an *enhancement*. A change management tool allows a change request to be submitted and kept track of as the developers address it. A vital part of the change management tool relates to the establishment of *traceability* paths between change requests and other system artifacts, in particular test requirements and use-case requirements.

Questions

Q1 Testing and change management span the development lifecycle. What other activities span the lifecycle? Explain the aims of these activities.

Q2 Refer to Figure 9.1 (Section 9.1). Explain the interplay between enhancements and defects. Why is the enhancements document linked to the use-case documents and the defects document linked to the test-case documents? Should there not be a link between the enhancements document and the defects document?

Q3 Refer to Figure 9.3 (Section 9.1). Why does a virtual tester have to be a dedicated test workstation?

Q4 How is a walkthrough different from an inspection?

Q5 What is the role of the SQA group in an organization?

Q6 What is an authorization database? What is its role in system development and testing?

Q7 What other system constraints testing is stress testing closely related to? Explain.

Q8 What other system constraints testing is installation testing closely related to? Explain.

Q9 What actions would you allow on an enhancement in an opened state? Explain the meaning of these actions.

Q10 Visit the web page for JUnit (www.junit.org). Report briefly on the latest improvements to the JUnit framework.

Q11 What is a verification point?

Q12 What is a suspect trace? Give an example.

Q13 Explain the difference between a baseline data file and an actual data file.

Answers to odd-numbered questions

Q1 – answer
Important lifecycle-spanning activities, apart from testing and change management, are (Maciaszek and Liong, 2004):

- project planning (Section 1.4.3.1)
- metrics (Section 1.4.3.2)
- configuration management

- people management
- risk management.

Project planning (and tracking) is a lifecycle activity aiming at the estimation (and verification) of how much time, money, effort, and resources are consumed by the project. In its broader meaning, project planning also encompasses quality assurance, people management, risk analysis, and configuration management.

To be able to plan for the future, we need to measure the past. *Metrics* collection is the activity of measuring the software product and the software process. Metrics is a complex and tricky domain, as not everything of value in software development can be assigned quantitative numbers. Nevertheless, an approximate number is better than no number, and there is lots of evidence that the collection of metrics is a necessary condition for success in system development.

Configuration management goes hand in hand with change management. Configuration management adds the "teamwork" dimension to change management. The aim of configuration management is to store versions of software artifacts produced by the development team, make these versions available on demand to various members of the team, and combine the versions into configured software models and products.

An information system is a social system. It is not possible to produce a successful software product without proper attention to the people component. *People management* embraces such activities as acquiring of staff, creating and motivating teams, establishing effective communications between people, conflict resolution, and other team development issues (such as team organization, training, appraisals, performance reports, and external feedback).

Risks are "potentially adverse circumstances that may impair the development process and the quality of products" (Ghezzi *et al.*, 2003, p.416). "*Risk management* is a decision-making activity that assesses the impact of risks (uncertainties) on decisions. It weighs distributions of possible project outcomes versus the probabilities of arriving at these outcomes" (Maciaszek and Liong, 2004, pp.72–3). Clearly, risk management spans the lifecycle and monitors the project from inception to conclusion; it may in fact demand that the project be terminated at any point when risks become too high and indefensible.

Q3 – answer

A *virtual tester* is a capture/playback machine for regression testing. It replays the test scripts previously recorded and monitors whether the application code behaves as before, i.e. whether it produces the same events and outputs as written in the test script. It is, therefore, essential that the entire test environment be fixed and stable.

Only a workstation dedicated for testing and not used for any other purpose can ensure a fixed and stable testing environment. It is essential that the machine use the same version of the operating system and has a minimal (and the same) amount of additional system software installed.

In particular, the machine must not be connected to the Internet, email facilities, etc. This is because any Internet event can be intercepted by the test program running and interpreted as an (unexpected) event generated by the application under test.

Q5 – answer

The *SQA* (*software quality assurance*) group is responsible for a planned and systematic evaluation of the quality of software products and processes. The group checks that software standards and procedures exist and are followed throughout the software development lifecycle. To ensure that the role of the SQA group is fulfilled, the group – not the developers – is made responsible for the quality of the delivered product.

Software quality is evaluated through process monitoring, product evaluation, formal reviews, audits, and testing. The evaluation is undertaken at quality assurance *approval points* determined in software development and control processes. The product of SQA is an *audit report* to management containing the findings of reviews, tests, etc. and recommendations to bring the development into conformance with standards and procedures.

Q7 – answer

Stress testing executes a system for abnormal conditions – low resources, peak loads, frequencies, quantities, or volumes. Stress testing is closely related to *performance testing*, because performance degradations frequently occur when the system executes in stress conditions.

In practice, stress testing and performance testing can be performed concurrently and can use similar test scripts and similar hardware and software instrumentation.

Q9 – answer

Actions allowed on an opened enhancement request depend on the development practice adopted. The list of permitted actions is normally customizable in CASE tools to suit the software process. A possible list of actions is:

- Close (as a result of its resolution or by managerial decision)
- Modify (some details of the enhancement)
- Delete (without addressing it; perhaps recorded in error)
- WorkOn (we keep working on it)
- Postpone (we can address it at some future time).

Q11 – answer

A *verification point* is a point in a regression test script that shows whether a test requirement has been met. It is used to verify the state of a test object across different program versions. Verification points can be set to:

- test for a numeric or other value, for a number within a range, for a blank field, etc.;
- compare the contents of two files or other data sets;
- check for existence of a file, a database table, etc.;
- capture and compare the state of the GUI menu items, common controls, data windows, etc.;
- check for the existence of a GUI window or a specified software module in memory;
- capture and compare websites.

During program *capture* (recording), the verification point intercepts the test object information and stores it as the baseline of expected behavior. During *playback*, the verification point obtains the test object information and compares it with the baseline. A *regression test* is passed if the playback script confirms that the program performs as intended and verification points return correct data.

Q13 – answer

Most verification points create a *baseline data file*. If, during playback, the captured data is different from that in the stored baseline data file, the verification point fails and an *actual* (failed) *data file* is created.

If the script is played many times and fails many times, a separate actual data file is created each time (typically with the same name but with consecutively numbered file extensions). The name of the actual file is normally the same as the name of the verification point.

Chapter

10

Tutorial-style Review and Reinforcement

This is a *review and reinforcement* chapter. It exemplifies all the important models and processes of the software development lifecycle. The explanations are pivoted on a single application domain (*online shopping*) and adopt the style of a comprehensive and complete *tutorial*. The sequence of discussion and the presentation of answers and solutions follow the sequence adopted in the textbook. Indeed, it is possible (and even recommended) to refer to this chapter, to reinforce the knowledge gained, when going through previous chapters of the book

Apart from its RR (review and reinforcement) purpose, this chapter has a *value-added aspect*. It demonstrates all important software development artifacts (models, diagrams, documents, etc.) as an integrated set and shows how all these artifacts fit together. Moreover, the tutorial refers to a web-based application, and as such it challenges the developer with "bleeding-edge" technology.

Tutorial statement: online shopping (customer order processing)

A *computer manufacturer* offers the possibility of purchasing computers via the Internet. The customer can select a computer on the manufacturer's web page. The computers are classified into servers, desktops, and portables. The customer can select a standard configuration or can build a desired configuration online. The configurable components (such as memory) are presented as drop-down lists (picklists) of available options. For each new configuration, the system can calculate price.

To place an order, the customer must fill out the shipment and payment information. Acceptable payment methods are credit cards and checks. Once the order has been entered, the system sends a confirmation email message to the customer with details of the order. While waiting for the arrival of the computer, the customer can check the order status online at any time.

The back-end order processing consists of the steps needed to verify the customer's credentials and payment method, to request the ordered configuration from the warehouse, to print an invoice, and to request the warehouse to ship the computer to the customer.

Use-case modeling

Actors

Step 1 (online shopping)

Refer to the tutorial statement above and consider the following extended requirements to find *actors* in the online shopping application:

1. The customer uses the manufacturer's online shopping web page to view the standard configuration of the chosen server, desktop, or portable computer. The price is also shown.

2. The customer chooses to view the details of the configuration, perhaps with the intention of buying it as is or to build a more suitable configuration. The price for each configuration can be computed at the customer's request.

3. The customer may choose to order a computer online or may request that the salesperson contact him/her to explain order details, negotiate the price, etc. before the order is actually placed.

4. To place an order, the customer must fill out an online form with shipment and invoice address, and with payment details (credit card or check).

5. After the customer's order has been entered into the system, the salesperson sends an electronic request to the warehouse with details of the configuration ordered.

6. The details of the transaction, including an order number and a customer account number, are emailed to the customer, so that the customer can check the status of the order online.

7. The warehouse obtains the invoice from the salesperson and ships the computer to the customer.

Figure 10.1 shows the three actors that are manifestly present in the specifications. These are `Customer`, `Salesperson`, and `Warehouse`.

Use cases

Step 2 (online shopping)

Refer to step 1 of the tutorial (Section 10.1.1) and find *use cases* in the online shopping application.

Customer   Salesperson   Warehouse

Figure 10.1
Actors (online shopping)

Table 10.1 Assignment of requirements to actors and use cases (online shopping)

Req #	Requirement	Actor	Use case
1	The customer uses the manufacturer's online shopping web page to view the standard configuration of the chosen server, desktop, or portable computer. The price is also shown.	Customer	Display Standard Computer Configuration
2	The customer chooses to view the details of the configuration, perhaps with the intention of buying it as is or to build a more suitable configuration. The price for each configuration can be computed on the customer's request.	Customer	Build Computer Configuration
3	The customer may choose to order a computer online or may request that the salesperson contact him/her to explain order details, negotiate the price, etc. before the order is actually placed.	Customer Salesperson	Order Configured Computer Request Salesperson Contact
4	To place an order, the customer must fill out an online form with shipment and invoice address, and with payment details (credit card or check).	Customer	Order Configured Computer Verify and Accept Customer Payment
5	After the customer's order has been entered into the system, the salesperson sends an electronic request to the warehouse with details of the configuration ordered.	Salesperson Warehouse	Inform Warehouse About Order
6	The details of the transaction, including an order number and a customer account number, are emailed to the customer so that the customer can check the status of the order online.	Salesperson Customer	Order Configured Computer Display Order Status
7	The warehouse obtains the invoice from the salesperson and ships the computer to the customer.	Salesperson Warehouse	Print Invoice

To address this tutorial problem, we can construct a table that assigns the functional requirements to the actors and use cases. Note that some potential business functions may not be within the scope of the application – they are not to be transformed into use cases.

Table 10.1 assigns the function requirements listed in step 1 of the tutorial to the actors and the use cases. The warehouse's tasks of configuring the computer and shipping it to the customer are considered to be *out-of-scope* functions.

Figure 10.2 demonstrates the use cases for online shopping in the UML graphical notation.

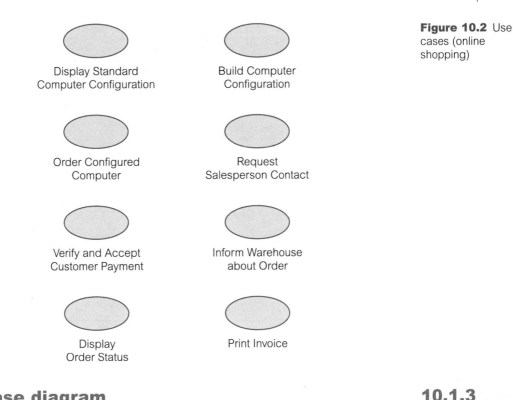

Figure 10.2 Use cases (online shopping)

Use-case diagram 10.1.3

Step 3 (online shopping)

Refer to the previous steps of the tutorial and draw a *use-case diagram* for the online shopping application.

A solution to this tutorial step can be obtained directly from the information contained in the previous steps. The only additional consideration may be the relationships between use cases. The diagram is presented in Figure 10.3. The meaning of the <<extend>> relationship is that the use case Order Configured Computer can be extended by Customer with the use case Request Salesperson Contact.

Documenting use cases 10.1.4

Step 4 (online shopping)

Refer to the previous tutorial steps and write a *use-case document* for the use case Order Configured Computer. Use your general knowledge of typical order processing tasks to derive details not stated in the requirements.

The solution to this tutorial step is presented in a tabular form (Table 10.2).

Figure 10.3
Use-case diagram
(online shopping)

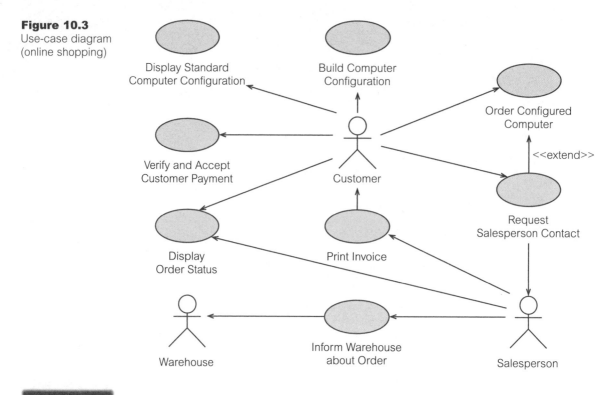

10.2 Activity modeling

10.2.1 Actions

Step 5 (online shopping)

Refer to step 4 of the tutorial. Analyze the main and alternative flows in the use-case document. Find actions for the use case `Order Configured Computer` in the online shopping application.

Table 10.3 lists the statements in the main and alternative flows of the use-case document and identifies action states. Note the system's (not actor's) viewpoint in naming activities. The actions identified in Table 10.3 are drawn in Figure 10.4.

10.2.2 Activity diagram

Step 6 (online shopping)

Refer to steps 4 (Section 10.1.4) and 5 (Section 10.2.1) of the tutorial and draw an *activity diagram* for the use case `Order Configured Computer` in the online shopping application.

Table 10.2 Narrative specification for use case "Order configured computer" (online shopping)

Use case	Order configured computer
Brief description	This use case allows a `Customer` to enter a purchase order. This includes providing a shipment and invoice address as well as payment details.
Actors	`Customer`
Preconditions	The `Customer` points an Internet browser to the computer manufacturer's order entry web page. The page displays the details of a configured computer together with its price.
Main flow	The use case begins when the `Customer` decides to order the configured computer by choosing the `Continue` (or similarly named) function when the order details are displayed on the screen.
	The system requests that the `Customer` enter the purchase details, including name of the salesperson (if known), shipment details (customer's name and address), invoice details (if different from shipment details), a payment method (credit card or check), and any comments.
	The `Customer` chooses the `Purchase` (or similarly named) function to send the order to the manufacturer.
	The system assigns a unique order number and a customer account number to the purchase order and stores the order information in the database.
	The system emails the order number and customer number to the `Customer`, together with all order details, as confirmation of the order's acceptance.
Alternative flows	The `Customer` activates the `Purchase` function before providing all mandatory information. The system displays an error message and requests that the missing information be supplied.
	The `Customer` chooses the `Reset` (or similarly named) function to revert to an empty purchase form. The system allows the `Customer` to enter the information again.
Postconditions	If the use case was successful, the purchase order is recorded in the system's database. Otherwise, the system's state is unchanged.

Figure 10.5 shows an activity diagram for step 6 of the tutorial. `Display Current Configuration` is the initial action state. When in the state `Display Purchase Form`, the `timeout` condition finishes the execution of the activity model. Alternatively, the state `Get Purchase Details` is activated. If the purchase details are incomplete, the system again enters the state `Display Purchase Form`. Otherwise, the system goes into the state `Store Order`, followed by the state `Email Order Details` (which leads to a final state).

Table 10.3 Finding actions in main and alternative flows

No.	Use-case statement	Action state
1	The use case begins when the `Customer` decides to order the configured computer by choosing the `Continue` (or similarly named) function when the order details are displayed on the screen.	`Display Current Configuration` `Get Order Request`
2	The system requests that the `Customer` enter the purchase details, including name of the salesperson (if known), shipment details (customer's name and address), invoice details (if different from shipment details), a payment method (credit card or check), and any comments.	`Display Purchase Form`
3	The `Customer` chooses the `Purchase` (or similarly named) function to send the order to the manufacturer.	`Get Purchase Details`
4	The system assigns a unique order number and a customer account number to the purchase order and stores the order information in the database.	`Store Order`
5	The system emails the order number and customer number to the `Customer`, together with all order details, as confirmation of the order's acceptance.	`Email Order Details`
6	The `Customer` activates the `Purchase` function before providing all mandatory information. The system displays an error message and requests that the missing information be supplied.	`Get Purchase Details` `Display Purchase Form`
7	The `Customer` chooses the `Reset` (or similarly named) function to revert to an empty purchase form. The system allows the `Customer` to enter the information again.	`Display Purchase Form`

Figure 10.4
Actions for the use case "Order Configured Computer" (online shopping)

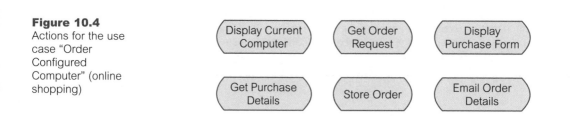

Note that only those branch conditions that (always) appear on exits from an action state are shown. The branch conditions that are internal to an action state are not explicit on the diagram. They can be inferred from the presence of multiple exit transitions, possibly with a guarded condition name in square brackets on the transition (such as `[timeout]` on exit from `Display Purchase Form`).

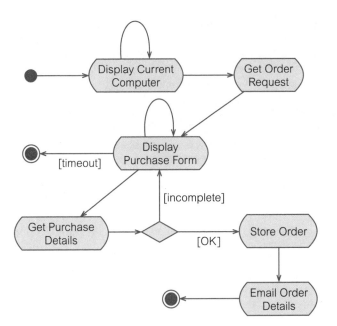

Figure 10.5
Activity diagram
for the use case
"Order Configured
Computer" (online
shopping)

Class modeling

10.3

Classes

10.3.1

Step 7 (online shopping)

Refer to the requirements defined in the tutorial statement and in step 1 of the tutorial (Section 10.1.1). Find candidate *entity classes* in the online shopping application.

Table 10.4 assigns the functional requirements in the tutorial to the entity classes. The list of classes poses many questions. For example:

- What is the difference between `ConfiguredComputer` and `Order`? After all, we are not going to store `ConfiguredComputer` unless an order for it has been placed, or are we?
- Is the meaning of `Shipment` in requirements 4 and 7 the same? Probably not. Do we need the `Shipment` class if we know that the shipment is the warehouse's responsibility and is therefore out of scope?
- Could not `ConfigurationItem` be just a set of attributes in `ConfiguredComputer`?
- Is `OrderStatus` a class or an attribute of `Order`?
- Is `Salesperson` a class or an attribute of `Order` and `Invoice`?

Answering these and similar questions is not easy and requires an in-depth knowledge of application requirements. For the purpose of this tutorial, we have chosen the list of classes as shown in Figure 10.6.

Table 10.4 Assignment of requirements to entity classes (online shopping)

Req #	Requirement	Entity class
1	The customer uses the manufacturer's online shopping web page to view the standard configuration of the chosen server, desktop, or portable computer. The price is also shown.	`Customer, Computer, (StandardConfiguration, Product)`
2	The customer chooses to view the details of a configuration, perhaps with the intention of buying it as is or to build a more suitable configuration. The price for each configuration can be computed at the customer's request.	`Customer, ConfiguredComputer, (ConfiguredProduct), ConfigurationItem`
3	The customer may choose to order a computer online or may request that the salesperson contact him/her to explain order details, negotiate the price, etc. before the order is actually placed.	`Customer, ConfiguredComputer, Order, Salesperson`
4	To place an order, the customer must fill out an online form with shipment and invoice address, and with payment details (credit card or check).	`Customer, Order, Shipment, Invoice, Payment`
5	After the customer's order has been entered into the system, the salesperson sends an electronic request to the warehouse with details of the configuration ordered.	`Customer, Order, Salesperson, ConfiguredComputer, ConfigurationItem`
6	The details of the transaction, including an order number and a customer account number, are emailed to the customer so that the customer can check the status of the order online.	`Order, Customer, (OrderStatus)`
7	The warehouse obtains the invoice from the salesperson and ships the computer to the customer.	`Invoice, (Shipment), (Salesperson), Computer, Customer`

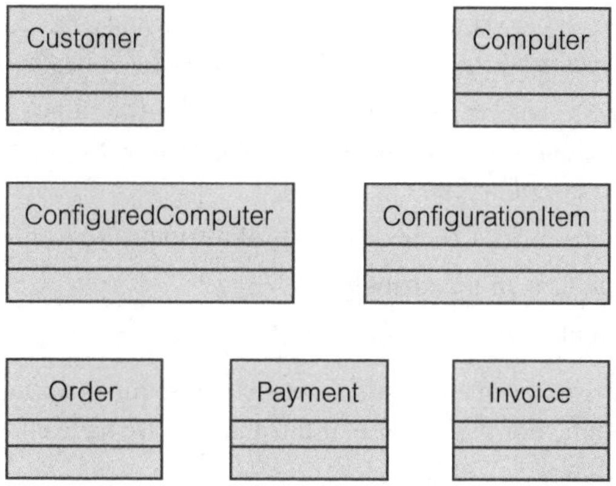

Figure 10.6
Classes (online shopping)

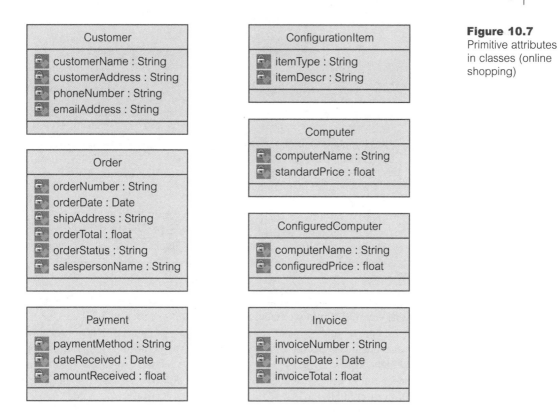

Figure 10.7
Primitive attributes
in classes (online
shopping)

Attributes   10.3.2

Step 8 (online shopping)

Refer to steps 5, 6, and 7 of the tutorial. Think about attributes for the classes in Figure 10.6. Consider only *attributes with primitive types* (Section 3.1.2.1).

Figure 10.7 shows the classes with primitive attributes. Only the most interesting attributes have been shown. The attributes of ConfigurationItem warrant brief explanation. The attribute itemType will have values such as processor, memory, screen, and hard drive. The attribute itemDescr will further describe the item type. For example, the processor in the configuration may be an Intel 2,000 MHz with 1,024 k cache.

Associations   10.3.3

Step 9 (online shopping)

Refer to the previous steps of the tutorial. Consider the classes in Figure 10.7. Think what access paths between these classes are required by the use cases. Add *associations* to the class model.

Figure 10.8
Associations
(online shopping)

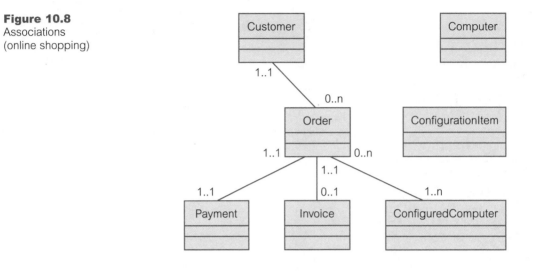

Figure 10.8 shows the most apparent associations between the classes. We made a few assumptions when determining association *multiplicities* (Section 3.1.4.2). `Order` is from a single `Customer`, but `Customer` may place many `Orders`. `Order` is not accepted unless the `Payment` has been specified (hence, one-to-one association). `Order` does not have to have an associated `Invoice`, but `Invoice` is always related to a single `Order`. An `Order` is for one or many `ConfiguredComputers`. A `ConfiguredComputer` may be ordered many times or not at all.

10.3.4 Aggregations

Step 10 (online shopping)

Refer to the previous steps of the tutorial. Consider the models in Figures 10.7 and 10.8. Add *aggregations* to the class model.

Figure 10.9 adds two aggregation relationships to the model. `Computer` has one or more `ConfigurationItems`. Likewise, `ConfiguredComputer` consists of one or many `ConfigurationItems`.

10.3.5 Generalizations

Step 11 (online shopping)

Refer to the previous steps of the tutorial. Consider the models in Figures 10.7 and 10.9. Think how you can extract any common attributes in the existing classes into a higher-level class. Add *generalizations* to the class model.

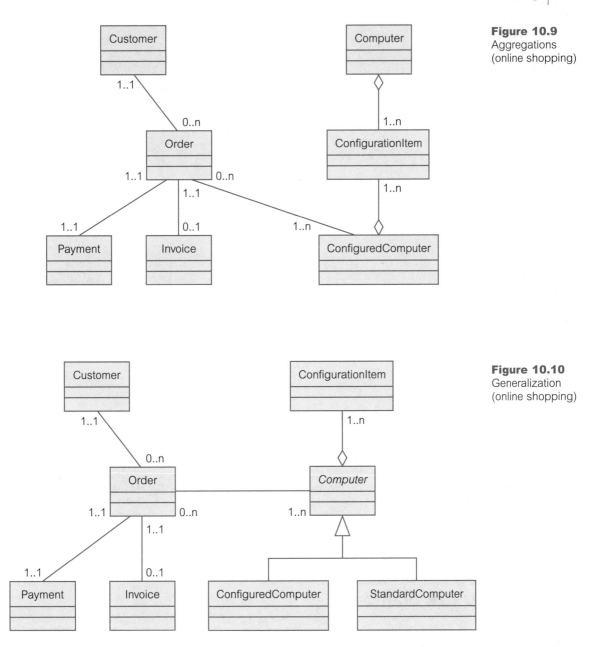

Figure 10.9
Aggregations
(online shopping)

Figure 10.10
Generalization
(online shopping)

Figure 10.10 shows a modified model with the class Computer changed to a generic *abstract* class for two *concrete* subclasses: StandardComputer and ConfiguredComputer. Order and ConfigurationItem are now linked to Computer, and Computer can be either StandardComputer or ConfiguredComputer.

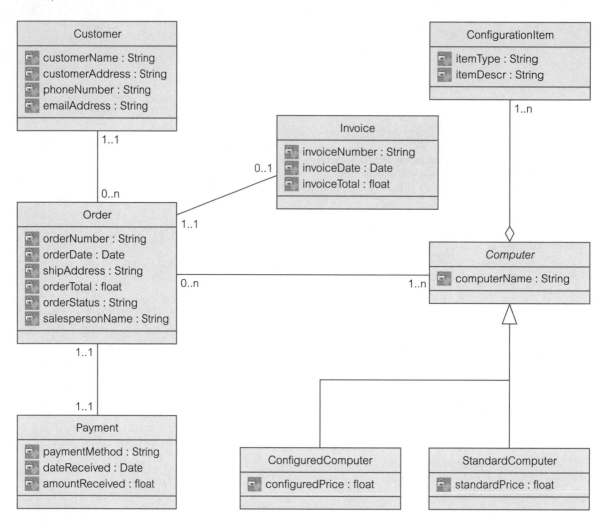

Figure 10.11 Class diagram (online shopping)

10.3.6 Class diagram

Step 12 (online shopping)

Refer to the previous steps of the tutorial. Combine the models in Figures 10.7 and 10.10 to show a complete class diagram. Modify attribute content of classes as necessitated by the introduction of the generalization hierarchy.

Figure 10.11 is a class diagram for the online shopping application. It is not a complete solution; e.g. more attributes would be required in a pragmatic solution.

Interaction modeling

Sequence diagram

Step 13 (online shopping)

Refer to the activity diagram in Figure 10.5 (Section 10.2.2). Consider the first action step in the diagram, `Display Current Computer`. Construct a sequence diagram for this action. As per the PCMEF framework, prefix the names of the classes involved with a letter indicating the PCMEF subsystem to which the class belongs. However, show only presentation and entity classes, and assume that the presentation layer can communicate directly with the entity layer.

For better understanding of the task, refer to Figures 10.12 and 10.13. Figure 10.12 (Sony, 2004) shows a possible "custom configuration" web page through which a customer can set up the required (current) configuration. Figure 10.13 (Sony, 2004) is a web page that displays summary information about the current configuration after the customer has pressed a submit button on the web page in Figure 10.12.

A sequence diagram for "display current configuration" is shown in Figure 10.14. When the outside actor (`Customer`) chooses to display the configuration of a computer, he/she presses the `Submit` button on the `PCustomConfiguration` web page. This event is serviced by a self-method `submit()`.

The `submit()` method sends a `getCurrentConf()` to `EComputer`. `EComputer` is an abstract class, so in reality the message will be sent to either `EStandardComputer` or `EConfiguredComputer` (Figure 10.11). The model assumes that `PCustomConfiguration` knows whether the actor modified the standard configuration, and it can, therefore, resolve to which concrete class the `getCurrentConf()` message should go.

Because `PCustomConfiguration` *has* an `EComputer` object, it could request all details directly. However, the model in Figure 10.14 makes `EComputer` combine all information (`computerName`, `itemDescr`, and `price`) and then return all this information (in a Java collection), to `PCustomConfiguration`. In fact, `EConfigurationItem` is itself a collection of objects, and `getItemDescr()` works on this collection. The model does not explain how exactly the `getPrice()` method works.

When equipped with all the requested information, `PCustomConfiguration` constructs a new `PConfigurationSummary` web page. The constructor receives all information in the argument of the `new()` message. As a result, the constructor of `PConfigurationSummary` contains a self-method `display()`, so that the current configuration can be displayed on the screen.

Collaboration diagram

Step 14 (online shopping)

Convert the sequence diagram in Figure 10.14 to a collaboration diagram.

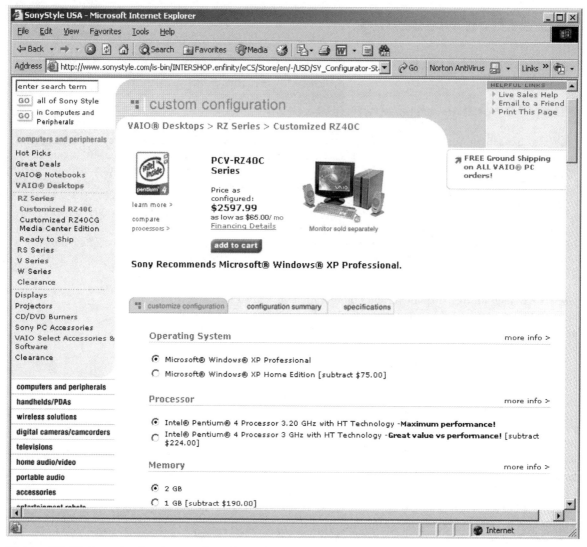

Figure 10.12 Example of custom configuration web page (online shopping)
Source: Sony (2004)

The collaboration diagram in Figure 10.15 offers an alternative view to the sequence diagram in Figure 10.14. The view is enriched by the fact that EConfigurationItem is now explicitly shown as a collection of objects.

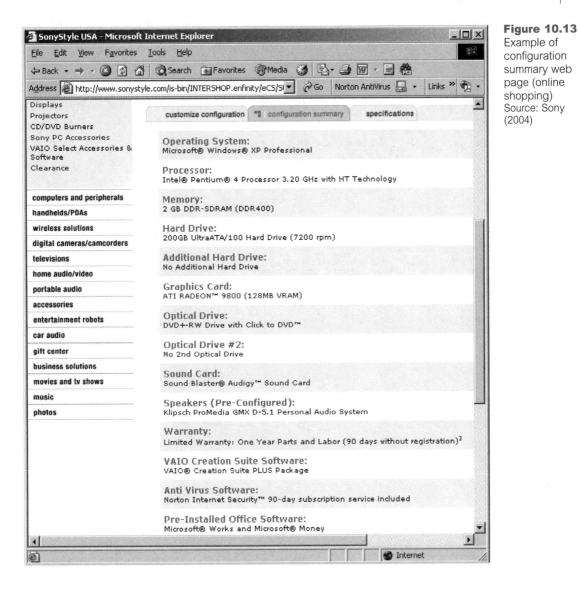

Figure 10.13
Example of
configuration
summary web
page (online
shopping)
Source: Sony
(2004)

Class methods

Step 15 (online shopping)

Refer to the class diagram in Figure 10.11 and to the collaboration diagram in Figure 10.15. For each message in the sequence diagram, add an operation to a relevant class in the class diagram. Do not redraw the whole class diagram – only show the classes extended with operations. Show dependency relationships for classes not already related by other relationships.

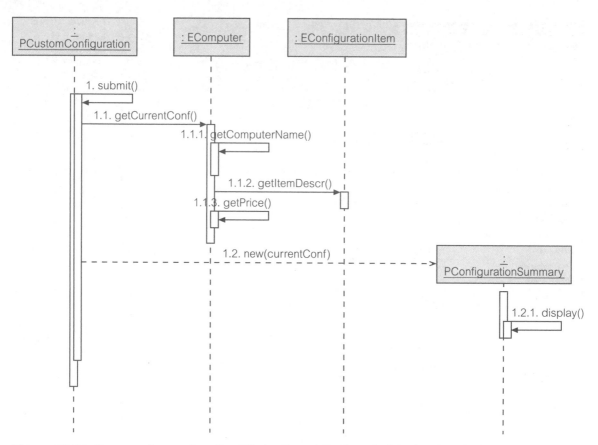

Figure 10.14 Sequence diagram for action "Display Current Configuration" (online shopping)

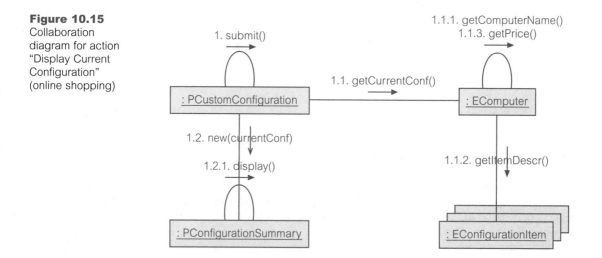

Figure 10.15
Collaboration
diagram for action
"Display Current
Configuration"
(online shopping)

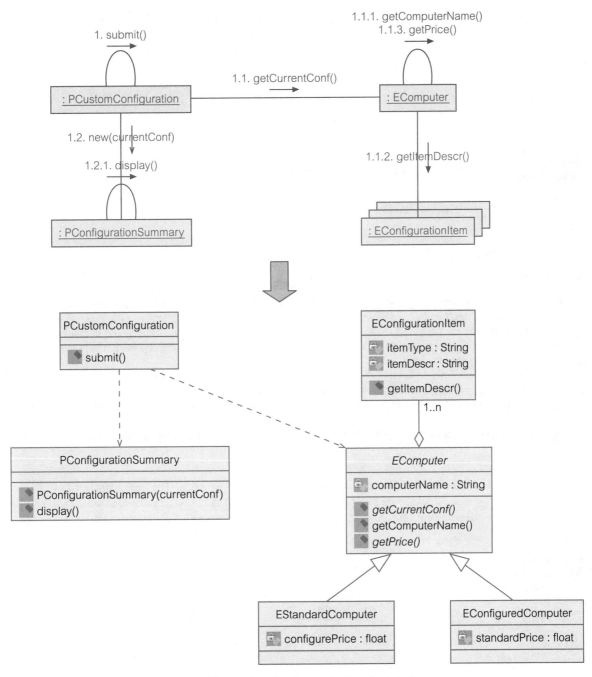

Figure 10.16 Using interactions to add operations to classes (online shopping)

The solution to this simple tutorial step is shown in Figure 10.16. Operations are added as expected. Note that the new() message results in invoking a constructor on PConfigurationSummary. PCustomConfiguration depends on EComputer and on PConfigurationSummary.

The class EComputer is an *abstract class*. getCurrentConf() and getPrice() are abstract operations inherited and implemented by the subclasses (EConfiguredComputer and EStandardComputer).

10.5 Statechart modeling

10.5.1 States and transitions

Step 16 (online shopping)

Consider the class Invoice in the online shopping application. We know from the use-case model that a customer specifies the payment method (credit card or check) for the computer when the purchase form is filled out and submitted to the vendor. This results in the generation of an order and subsequently in the preparation of an invoice. However, the use-case diagram has not clarified when the payment is actually received in relation to the invoice. We can assume, for example, that payment can be made before or after the invoice has been issued and that partial payments are allowed.

From the class model, we know that the invoice for the order is prepared by a salesperson but is eventually handed over to the warehouse. The warehouse sends the invoice to the customer together with the computer shipment. It is important that the payment status of the invoice be maintained in the system so that invoices are properly annotated.

Draw a statechart diagram that captures possible invoice states as far as payments are concerned.

Figure 10.17 is a statechart model for the class Invoice. The initial state of Invoice is Unpaid. There are two possible transitions out of the Unpaid state. On the partial payment event, the Invoice object goes into the Partly Paid state. Only one partial

Figure 10.17
States and events for the class Invoice (online shopping)

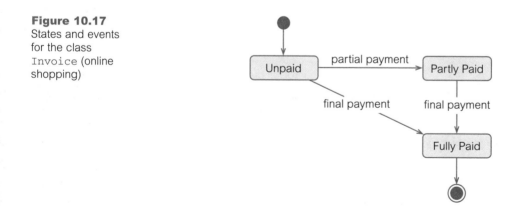

payment is allowed. The final payment event, when in an Unpaid or Partly Paid state, fires a transition to the Fully Paid state. This is the final state.

Statechart diagram   10.5.2

A statechart diagram for Order is shown in Figure 10.18. The initial state is New Order. This is one of the Pending states, the others being Back Order and Future Order. There are two possible transitions out of any of the three states nested in the Pending state.

The transition into the Canceled state is guarded by the condition [canceled]. It would be possible – without violating the statechart modeling rules – to replace the guard by the event cancel. The transition to the state Ready to Ship is labeled with a complete description containing the event, guard, and action.

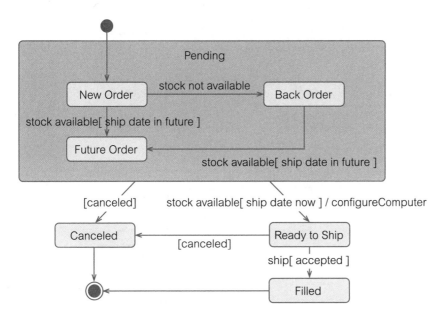

Figure 10.18
State diagram for the class Order (online shopping)

10.6 Implementation models

10.6.1 Subsystems

Step 18 (online shopping)

The layers of the PCMEF architectural framework have been modeled as subsystems. This has been consistent with an expectation (and a requirement) that the services of a subsystem are encapsulated by interfaces (ref. Section 3.2.6.1). Extend an architectural diagram for PCMEF, presented in Figure 4.1 (Section 4.1.1), such that interfaces are explicitly shown. Use the lollipop notation (ref. Figure 5.14 in Section 5.2.3).

Figure 10.19 is (hopefully) a self-explanatory answer to step 18. As an example, the `entity` subsystem implements the `Einterface` interface, which can be used by the `control` and `mediator` subsystems.

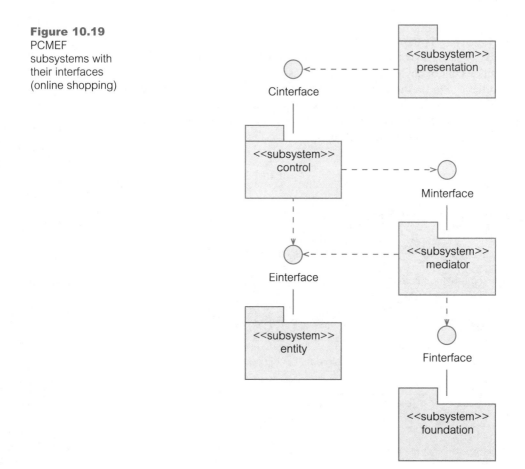

Figure 10.19
PCMEF
subsystems with
their interfaces
(online shopping)

Packages   10.6.2

Step 19 (online shopping)

Refer to the other steps of the online shopping tutorial. Naturally enough, most classes that we have defined so far represent persistent business objects. A more complete model for the system would require that other application classes be identified. This will be done successively as the design progresses. Even though we do not have application classes yet, we can speculate about packages that would group classes into coherent units according to the PCMEF approach.

Our task in this step is to think about possible packages in online shopping and the main dependencies between them. Extend the model in Figure 10.19 to include packages.

The best way to attack the example is to "impersonate the system" and imagine what needs to be done to accept a customer's order for a configured computer. The most obvious observation is that the system handles two separate functions: the computer configuration and order entry. These two functions require separate GUI windows. Hence, we can create two *presentation packages*: configuration view and order view.

On the "business side" of the class spectrum, we identified a range of classes in the class diagram (Figure 10.11). These *entity classes* can be grouped naturally into three *entity packages*: customers, computers, and orders (the latter would also include the classes Invoice and Payment). Moreover, we will require a package to be assigning OIDs to entity objects and maintaining OID maps (Section 8.4). Let us call it the identity map package.

Next we need to identify packages that glue the presentation and entity classes together, i.e. *control packages*. We need a package to configure computers and calculate configuration prices sensibly. Let us call such a package configuration provider. We also need a package responsible for entering and recording orders – an order monitor package.

Not a great deal is known about the mediator subsystem, but we know from the discussion about patterns for managing persistent objects (Section 8.4) that at least three *mediator packages* may be needed. The packages can be named after the patterns: data mapper, lazy load, and unit of work.

Finally, there is a need for one or more *foundation packages*. The main foundation package can be called crud – create–read–update–delete (Section 4.3.4.1). The crud communicates with the database tables whenever the application needs to access or modify the database content.

The crud package depends on two other foundation packages, called connection and schema. Classes in the connection package are responsible for the handling of database connections. The schema package contains the current information about the database schema objects – tables, columns, stored procedures, etc. The application can instantiate the schema objects when it starts so that it can validate that the database objects exist in the database before actually attempting to access the database (e.g. before a stored procedure is called, the application can verify, using an in-memory schema object, that the stored procedure still exists).

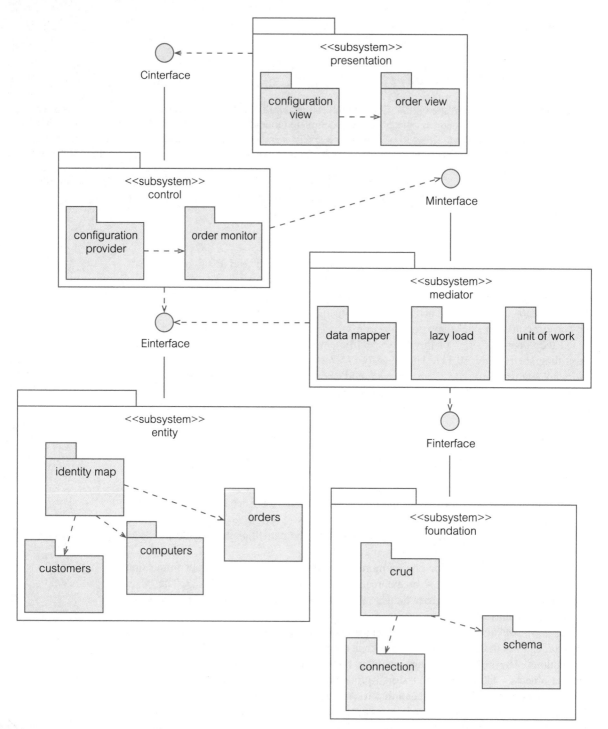

Figure 10.20 Packages (online shopping)

Figure 10.20 shows the packages as identified above. It also shows the main dependencies. The dependencies are initial and arguable. Without knowing all classes and the communication links between them, the dependencies between packages are speculative.

Components 10.6.3

Step 20 (online shopping)

Propose a component diagram for business objects in online shopping. Consider that a component is a cohesive functional unit with clear interfaces so that it becomes a replaceable part of the system. Since the implementation platform for online shopping has not been specified, the identification of smaller components (such as libraries and stored procedures) is not possible at this stage.

One way of addressing this tutorial step is to consider the typical sequence of access to web pages by an online customer wishing to purchase a computer. The guidelines can be obtained from the analysis of use cases (Section 10.1).

The first web page that an online customer would visit is the vendor's page that lists product categories (such as servers, desktops, portables), highlights the latest offers and discounts, and provides links to web pages that list the products and give short descriptions of each product. The short descriptions include prices for standard product configurations. This part of the system is concerned with advertising the products to an online shopper. It is a cohesive unit of functionality that could constitute the component called `ProductList`.

The customer's next step would be to ask for technical specifications for a chosen product. This includes a visual display of the product from different angles. This is a stand-alone web page and a good candidate for the next component called `ProductDisplay`.

Assuming that the previous web pages attracted the customer to a product, different configurations for the product may be requested to satisfy the customer's special needs and budget. This would be done through dynamic web pages where configurations can be built interactively and displayed complete with a configured price. This is another good candidate for a component. Let us call it `Configuration`.

The customer who decides to buy a product is presented with the purchase order form. The details to be entered include the name and address for shipment and invoice. The payment method is also chosen and the relevant details submitted via some secure transfer protocol. This is the fourth component – `Purchase`.

The last component that we identify in this tutorial has to do with the order fulfillment and tracking. From the customer's perspective, this provides for the possibility of viewing the status of the order on a web page (after the customer number and the order number are entered). This component can be called `OrderTracking`.

The five components identified in the above discussion are shown in Figure 10.21. The main dependencies between components are also shown. Components are physical tangible units of independent deployment – they have to be carefully designed and implemented even for small systems.

Figure 10.21
Component
diagram (online
shopping)

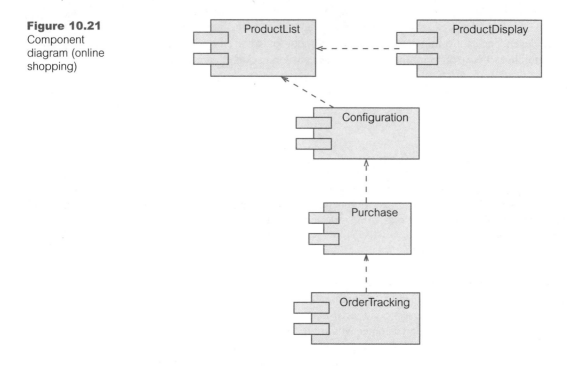

10.6.4 Nodes

Step 21 (online shopping)

Refer to the implementation models in steps 18–20 and propose a deployment diagram for online shopping. In particular, consider if there is a need in online shopping for an application server.

The connectionless nature of the Internet makes the *deployment* of a web application significantly more difficult than the deployment of a client/server database application. To start with, the web server has to be set up as the routing middleware between all client browsers and the database.

If session management cannot be solved satisfactorily with *cookie* technology, then *distributed objects* need to be engaged. Deploying distributed objects would require a separate architectural element – an application server – to be placed between the web server and the database server.

The deployment design must also address security issues. Secure transfer and encryption protocols make additional deployment demands. Careful planning is also needed with regard to network loads, Internet connections, backups, etc.

The deployment architecture capable of supporting more sophisticated web applications includes four tiers of computing nodes:

1. client with browser;
2. web server;

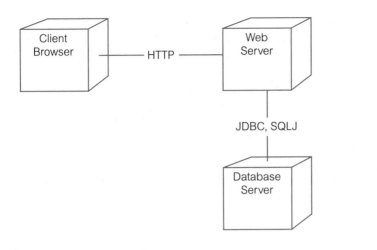

Figure 10.22
Deployment
diagram (online
shopping)

3. application server;

4. database server.

The browser of the *client node* can be used to display static or dynamic pages. Scripted pages and applets can be downloaded and run within the browser. Additional functionality can be supplied to the client's browser with objects such as ActiveX controls or JavaBeans. Running application code on the client, but outside the browser, may satisfy other UI requirements.

The *web server* handles page requests from the browser and dynamically generates pages and code for execution and display on the client. The web server also deals with the customization and parameterization of the session with the user.

The *application server* is indispensable when distributed objects are involved in the implementation. It manages the business logic. The business components publish their interfaces to other nodes via component interfaces such as CORBA, DCOM, or EJB.

The business components encapsulate persistent data stored in a database, probably a relational database. They communicate with the *database server* via database connectivity protocols such as JDBC, SQLJ, or ODBC. The database node provides for scalable storage of data and multi-user access to it.

As shown in Figure 10.22, the online shopping application can be deployed without a separate application server. The web server would execute the code in the server pages. The potential advantage of an application server is that the application components they house can be reused by other web applications to invoke the same business logic. However, online shopping is a stand-alone system, and no other web applications to take advantage of its business logic could be identified.

Object collaboration design

10.7

Collaborations define the realization of use cases and the realization of more intricate operations (simple operations do not have to be modeled as collaborations). The design of collaborations invariably leads to the *elaboration* (modifications and extensions) of existing class diagrams and to the production of new interaction diagrams (sequence and/or collaboration diagrams). Other kinds of diagram, in particular statechart diagrams, may also need to be developed or elaborated.

An important spin-off (or even a prerequisite) of collaboration design is the need to *elaborate use cases*. The use cases documented during requirements analysis are unlikely to contain sufficient level of detail for designing collaborations. The use-case specifications have to be elaborated into the design documents. New design-level use-case specifications must include the system-level demands while still maintaining the actors' perspective.

If the requirements management (Section 2.4) was laidback in analysis, there is now a last opportunity to become more formal and disciplined. The requirements should be carefully classified and numbered. To ensure proper change and traceability management, the requirements should be stored in a CASE tool repository.

Requirements need to be numbered (Section 2.4.1) and structured (Section 2.4.2). Both activities can best be accomplished with the assistance of a CASE tool. Attempts to track changes to requirements manually are destined to fail. With a CASE tool, renumbering and restructuring of requirements is easy.

Figure 10.23 shows a fragment of a use-case specification document with numbered requirements. The requirements are numbered using the Dewey decimal system with the

Figure 10.23
Excerpt from a use-case document managed by a CASE tool
Source: Screen shot reprinted by permission from Microsoft Corporation

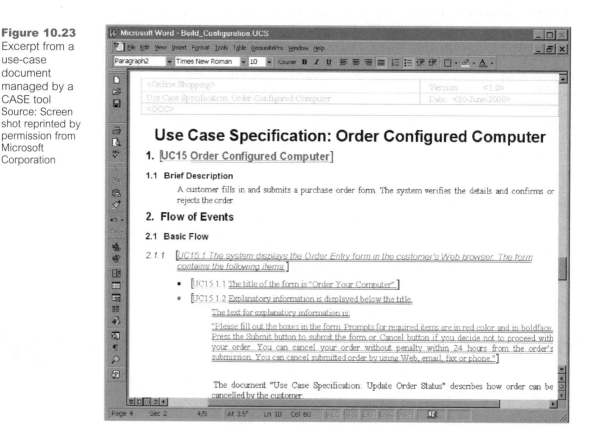

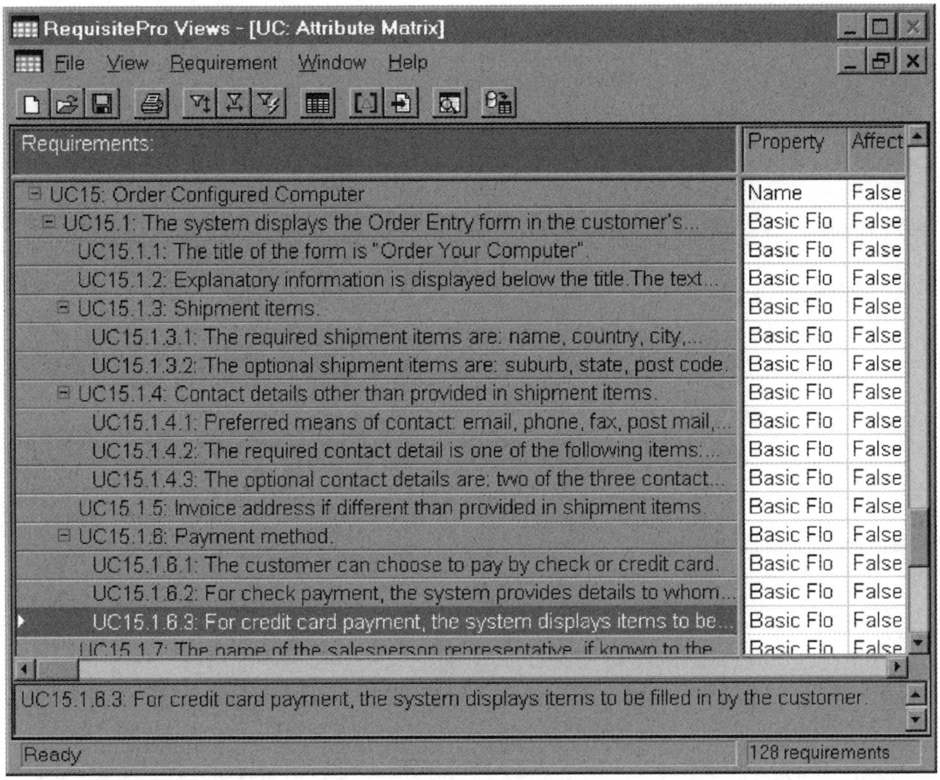

Figure 10.24
Requirements
management in a
CASE tool

prefix UC (use case). The prefix is helpful when a use-case document contains more than one type of requirement. Note that the requirements are enclosed in square brackets, underlined and displayed in green (trust us on the color issue).

Once entered into a CASE repository, the requirements can be viewed and modified by other tools supported by the CASE toolkit. Figure 10.24 demonstrates one such display in which the hierarchy of requirements is emphasized. The designer can use this display to modify any requirement or to attach various attributes to it.

Use-case design specifications

10.7.1

Step 22 (online shopping)

Refer to the use-case analysis document for online shopping in Section 10.1.4 (Table 10.2). The document is for the use case "Order Configured Computer." The document is not sufficient for designing a collaboration from it.

The purpose of this tutorial step is to elaborate the use-case document into a design-level use-case specification. The elaborated document is to be organized as in Figure 10.23. In fact, Figures 10.23 and 10.24 reveal parts of the solution to this tutorial step.

The text proper of the use-case design document is shown below. Note that the document can be printed differently to the format presented here. For example, the display and printing of use-case numbers can be suppressed.

Use-Case Specification: Order Configured Computer

1. [UC15 Order Configured Computer]

1.1 Brief Description

A customer fills out and submits a purchase order form. The system verifies the details and confirms or rejects the order.

2. Flow of Events

2.1 Basic Flow

2.1.1 [UC15.1 The system displays the order entry form in the customer's web browser. The form contains the following items.]

- [UC15.1.1 The title of the form is "Order Your Computer."]
- [UC15.1.2 The order summary information and the explanatory information are displayed below the title. The text for explanatory information is:

  "Please fill out the boxes in the form. Prompts for required items are in red color and in boldface. Press the `Submit` button to submit the form or `Cancel` button if you decide not to proceed with your order. You can cancel your order without penalty within 24 hours from the order's submission. You can cancel the submitted order by using web, email, fax or phone."]

  The document "Use-Case Specification: Update Order Status" describes how an order can be canceled by the customer.

- [UC15.1.3 Shipment items.]
  [UC15.1.3.1 The required shipment items are: name, country, city, street, courier directions.]
  [UC15.1.3.2 The optional shipment items are: suburb, state, post code.]

- [UC15.1.4 Contact details other than provided in shipment items.]
  [UC15.1.4.1 Preferred means of contact: email, phone, fax, post mail, courier mail.]
  [UC15.1.4.2 The required contact detail is one of the following items: email, phone, fax.]
  [UC15.1.4.3 The optional contact details are: two of the three contact items listed as required, postal address (if different to that provided in shipment items).]

- [UC15.1.5 Invoice address if different to that provided in shipment items.]

- [UC15.1.6 Payment method.]
  [UC15.1.6.1 The customer can choose to pay by check or credit card.]
  [UC15.1.6.2 For check payment, the system provides details to whom the check should be made out to and to what address it should be mailed. It also informs the customer that it takes three days to clear the check once received.]
  [UC15.1.6.3 For credit card payment, the system displays items to be filled out by the customer. The items are: the picklist of acceptable credit cards, credit card number, credit card expiry date.]

■ [UC15.1.7 The name of the salesperson representative, if known to the customer from previous dealings.]

■ [UC15.1.8 Two action buttons: `Submit` and `Cancel`.]

2.1.2 [UC15.2 The system prompts the customer to enter order details by placing the cursor on the first editable field (the Name item).] [UC15.3 The system allows information to be entered in any order]

■ [UC15.4 If the customer does not submit or cancel the form within 15 minutes, the alternative flow "Customer Inactive" executes.]

2.1.3 [UC15.5 If the customer presses the `Submit` button and all required information has been provided, the order form is submitted to the web server. The web server communicates with the database server to store the order in the database.] [UC15.6 The database server assigns a unique order number and a customer account number to the purchase order. The system confirms receipt of the order by displaying the assigned order number and account number.]

■ [UC15.7 If the database server is unable to create and store the order, the alternative flow "Database Exception" executes.]

■ [UC15.8 If the customer submits the order form with incomplete information, the alternative flow "Incomplete Information" executes.]

2.1.4 [UC15.9 If the customer provided an email address as the preferred means of communication, the system emails the order and customer numbers to the customer, together with all order details, as the confirmation of the order's receipt. The use case terminates.] [UC15.10 Otherwise, the order details will be mailed to the customer and the use case terminates as well.]

2.1.5 [UC15.11 If the customer presses the `Cancel` button, the alternative flow "Cancel" executes.]

2.2 Alternative Flows

2.2.1 Customer inactive

[UC15.4.1 If the customer is inactive for more than 15 minutes, the system terminates the connection with the browser. The order entry form closes. The use case terminates.]

2.2.2 Database exception

[UC15.7.1 If the database raises an exception, the system interprets it and informs the customer about the nature of the error. If the customer has disconnected, the system emails the error message to the customer and to a salesperson. The use case terminates.]

If the customer is not reachable by Internet or email, the salesperson needs to contact the customer by other means.

2.2.3 Incomplete information

[UC15.8.1 If the customer has not filled out all required items, the system invites the customer to provide the missing information. The list of missing items is displayed. The use case continues.]

2.2.4 Cancel

[UC15.11.1 If the customer presses the `Cancel` button, the form fields are cleared. The use case continues.]

3. Preconditions

3.1   The customer points the Internet browser to the system's web page. The page displays details of the configured computer together with its price. The customer presses the `Purchase` button.

3.2   The customer presses the `Purchase` button within 15 minutes from requesting the last computer configuration to be built and displayed in the browser's page.

4. Postconditions

4.1   If the customer's order submission is successful, the purchase order is recorded in the system's database. Otherwise, the system's state is unchanged.

10.7.2   User interface prototyping

Step 23 (online shopping)

In practice, the use-case design specifications at the level of detail presented in Section 10.7.1 are still insufficient to produce an object collaboration design sufficient for programming tasks. There are two main techniques to provide more information for programmers. Both are "storyboarding" techniques. The first is a storyboarding reminiscent of the film industry – sketches and prototypes for the UI screens and windows (such sketches and prototypes are then added to the use-case design documentation). The second is a storyboarding defining user experience – the UX storyboards (Sections 7.5 and 10.8)

The purpose of this tutorial step is to produce a prototype for a web page that displays the current order status to the customer.

Figure 10.25 presents a plain design for the order status page. A more complete design would also include a *client logon* page. The logon page would request that the user enters his/her account number and order number (obtained when the order was originally placed). The system would validate the user before the order status is shown.

The design in Figure 10.25 reveals (in the http address) that the order status is implemented as an *active server page* (ASP). The layout consists of five informational fields. The gray background of the fields indicates that the user cannot modify the field values (the fields are read-only). The hyperlink at the bottom of the screen enables the user to logout from the order status page.

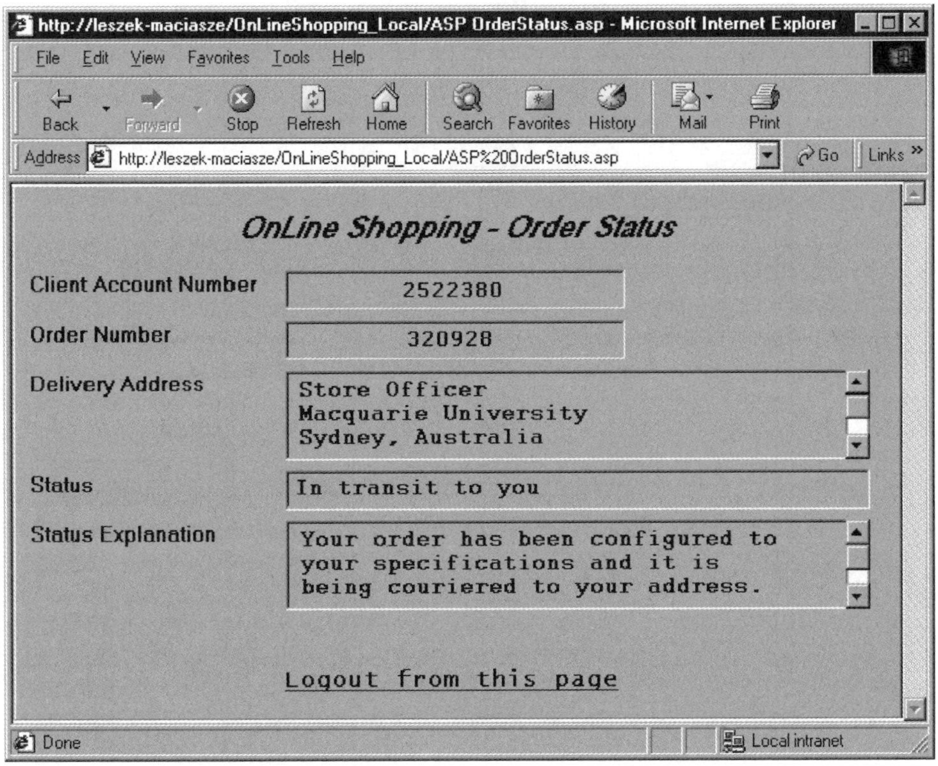

Figure 10.25
Web page for
"Display Order
Status" (online
shopping)

Behavioral collaboration   10.7.3

Step 24 (online shopping)

Refer to step 23 of the tutorial. Design a sequence diagram for behavioral collaboration in "Display Order Status."

Consider in the design the patterns for managing persistent objects (Section 8.4 and "Solutions to exercises (contact management)" at the end of Chapter 8). Make the design consistent with the class diagram in Figure 10.11 and the package diagram in Figure 10.20.

Assume that the data mapper knows that the memory cache does not contain a "clean" order status information and that a trip to the database is necessary. Once the status information has been obtained from the database, the memory cache needs to be refreshed. Assume that the refreshing means updating `EOrder` and creating a new `EOrderStatus` object.

Figure 10.26 offers a solution to step 24. Note that `MDataMapper` proceeds immediately to the database and returns the order status data to the `Order Status` screen via `CStatusMonitor` (the "screens" could have been modeled as presentation objects, e.g. `POrderStatus`, but we opted for the notation of the UX storyboards profile). The `Order Status` screen uses the `display()` message to render the data to the screen. At the same

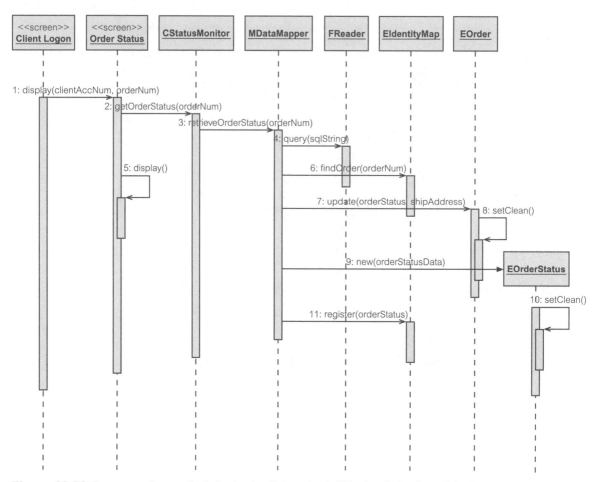

Figure 10.26 Sequence diagram for behavioral collaboration in "Display Order Status" (online shopping)

time, `MDataMapper` takes care of refreshing the entity objects in the memory cache. First, it updates `EOrder`. Next, it creates a new `EOrderStatus`. The model does not explain what should be done to link `EOrderStatus` to its `EOrder` object.

10.7.4 Structural collaboration

Step 25 (online shopping)

Refer to Step 24 of the tutorial. Design a class diagram for structural collaboration in "Display Order Status". There is no need to include data members, just methods, in all but the entity classes. Show return types of methods. Relationships, including dependency relationships, should also be defined.

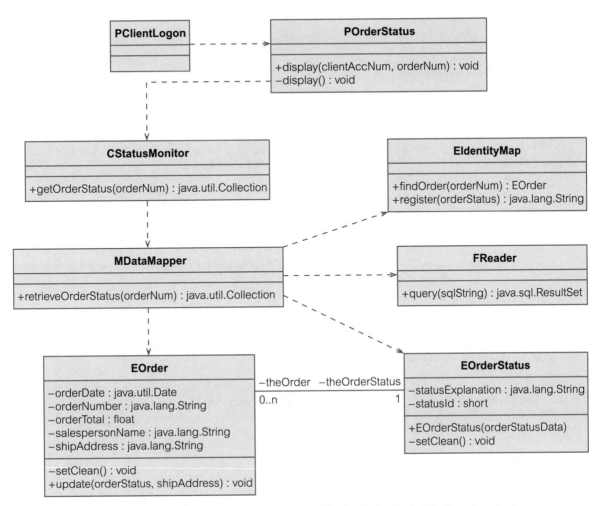

Figure 10.27 Class diagram for structural collaboration in "Display Order Status" (online shopping)

A structural collaboration model in Figure 10.27 is derived directly from the model in Figure 10.26. The main additions are the return data types for the methods and data types for attributes. The Java data types are used. The orderStatus attribute in EOrder (ref. Figure 10.11) is replaced by an association to the EOrderStatus class.

10.8 Window navigation design

10.8.1 User experience (UX) elements

Step 26 (online shopping)

Refer to step 22 of the tutorial. Study the use-case design specifications to identify the UX elements. Draw properly stereotyped UX classes for the use case "Order Configured Computer."

Figure 10.28 is a class diagram featuring the user experience (UX) elements and relationships between them. The `Computer Order` screen contains one `Order Entry` form, two `Command Button` compartments (for `Submit` and `Cancel`), and possibly one `Order Confirmation` screen. The `Incomplete Order Entry` form is a kind of `Order Entry`. `Database Exception` is modeled as a compartment to emphasize that it can be reused by multiple screens.

10.8.2 Behavioral UX collaboration

Step 27 (online shopping)

Refer to steps 22 and 26 of the tutorial. Draw a sequence diagram for behavioral UX collaboration for the use case "Order Configured Computer." Do not be unduly concerned with individual fields in the order entry form. Treat them as group entries as classified in the use-case specifications, i.e. shipment items, contact details, invoice address, payment method, and salesperson name.

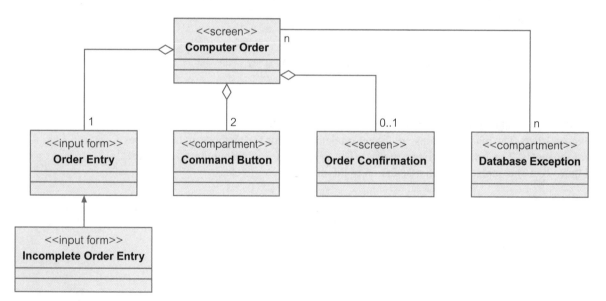

Figure 10.28 UX elements for "Order Configured Computer" (online shopping)

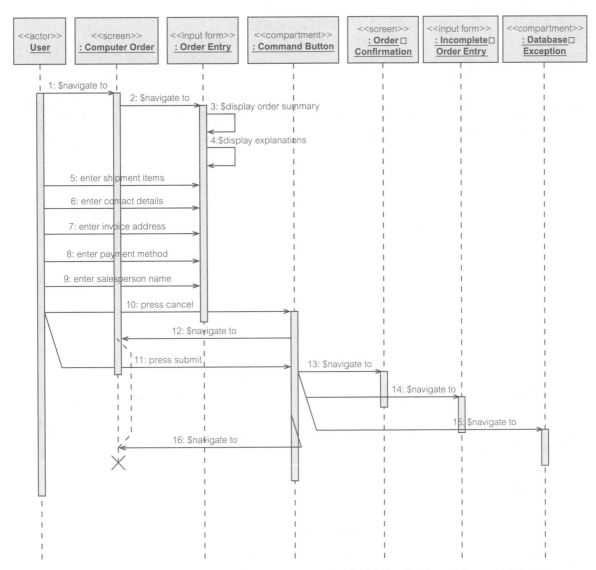

Figure 10.29 Sequence diagram for UX behavioral collaboration for "Order Configured Computer" (online shopping)

The sequence diagram in Figure 10.29 is a solution to step 27. Only a couple of points may need an explanation. Apart from the usual environmental actions of $navigate to, there are two $display actions that are also environmental. The branching of actions is quite extensive to address the alternative flows in the use case.

10.8.3 Structural UX collaboration

Step 28 (online shopping)

Refer to Steps 22, 26, and 27 of the tutorial. Develop a class diagram for structural UX collaboration for the use case "Order Configured Computer." There is no need to apply the UX tags to the dynamic content of the UX elements (i.e. to the fields in the UX classes).

Figure 10.30 presents a solution to step 28. The solution is derived from the previous models, in particular from the sequence diagram in Figure 10.29.

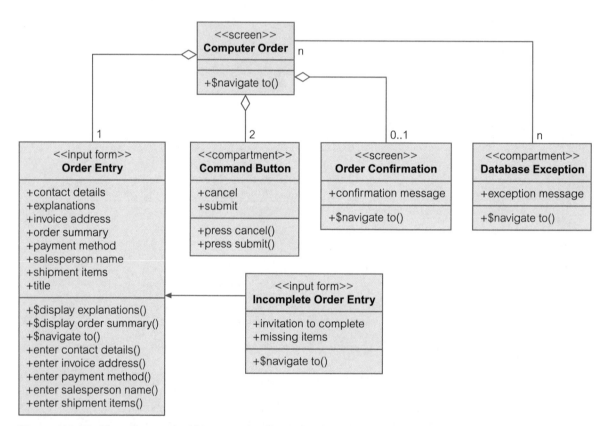

Figure 10.30 Class diagram for UX structural collaboration for "Order Configured Computer" (online shopping)

Database design

Object-relational mapping

Step 29 (online shopping)

Refer to step 12 of the tutorial. Map the class diagram in Figure 10.11 to a database schema model. Also consider the need, identified in step 25, for the order status table. Show the tables, the relationships between them, column types, and null indicators. Also show multiplicities on relationships.

The mapping in Figure 10.31 resulted in ten tables. Most mapping decisions were routine and followed the recommendations defined in Section 8.3. The generalization in Figure 10.11 was mapped using the third strategy listed in Section 8.3.4, namely to map each concrete class to a table.

In Figure 10.11, the association between Order and Computer is many to many, and such that an Order must be associated with at least one computer. The mapping in Figure 10.31 has introduced two "relationship tables" to convert a many-to-many association to two one-to-many relationships (separately for linking to StandardComputer and to ConfiguredComputer). In this mapping, the constraint that an Order must be associated with at least one computer is not maintained in the database model. The note on the diagram indicates that the constraint must be enforced procedurally (e.g. by a trigger).

Surprisingly, a very similar model was obtained for the aggregation from Computer to ConfigurationItem (Figure 10.11). The class model did not indicate that a ConfigurationItem object can be a component of more than one Computer object (it is so because a ConfigurationItem defines a type of an item, not a concrete instance of an item). Accordingly, the aggregation is really a many-to-many relationship and has to be mapped with "relationship tables" as shown in Figure 10.31.

The only other not obvious decision relates to the relationship between Order and Invoice. This relationship could be modeled by placing a foreign key in either of these two tables. The decision was taken to place the foreign key in the Order table. However, note that the foreign key (invoice_number) accepts nulls. This is caused by the 0..1 multiplicity from Order to Invoice in the class diagram (Figure 10.11).

Referential integrity design

Step 30 (online shopping)

Refer to step 29 of the tutorial and the database schema model in Figure 10.31. Consider various declarative referential integrity constraints for the delete operations (Section 8.2.3). Show which relationships in Figure 10.31 should have Del(C) or Del(N) constraints, rather than Del(R). Also show on the diagram which of the relationships allow "changing parents" (i.e. permit the cpa (change parent allowed) constraint).

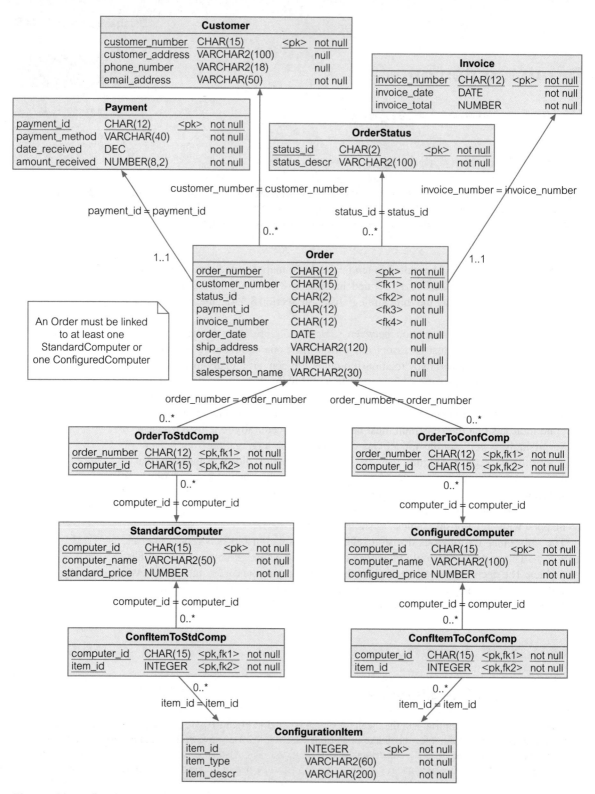

Figure 10.31 Database schema model (online shopping)

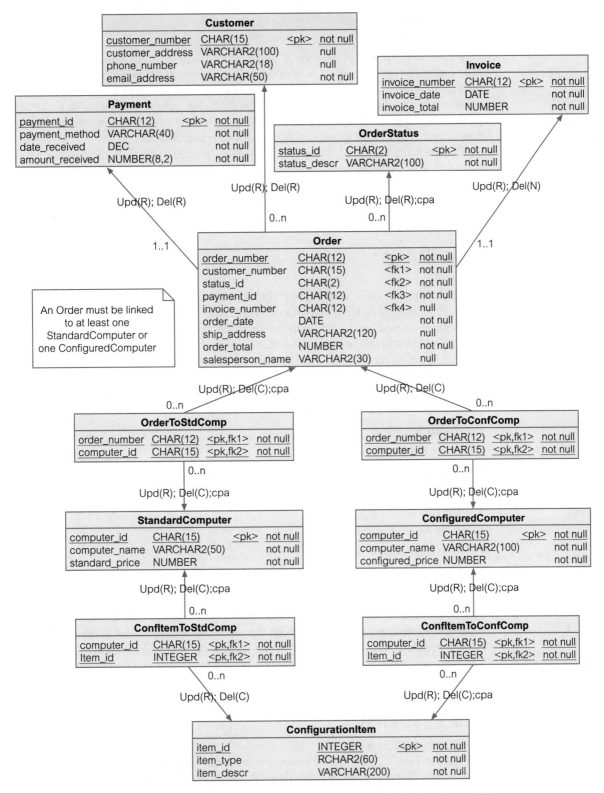

Figure 10.32 Database schema model with referential integrity constraints (online shopping)

Figure 10.32 is a modified database schema model that shows the allowed delete actions and whether the `cpa` constraint is permitted. The `cpa` constraint is permitted on the relationship between `Order` and `OrderStatus` (an `order` can change `status_id`). The `cpa` constraint is also allowed on most relationships involving "relationship tables" at the lower part of the diagram. There are two exceptions. A configured computer cannot change order, and a standard computer cannot change configuration item.

The deletion of `Invoice` will set the foreign key in `Order` to null. Records in the "relationship tables" can be freely deleted if their parent record has been deleted. This is signified by the `Del(C)` constraints on the relationships involving these tables. All other delete constraints are `Del(R)`.

Summary

This last chapter of the book has been motivated by an important (if not the most important) educational principle: to *review and reinforce* the studied material. The RR principle is embraced by most university courses – in which the last week of study is dedicated to material review and reinforcement. For such courses, this chapter will come in very handy.

The chapter applied the RR principle in a tutorial style. A single application domain – online shopping – was used to present all the important steps of requirements analysis and system design. Altogether, the material was presented in thirty interrelated software development steps. The steps were grouped into nine consecutive topics:

1. use-case modeling
2. activity modeling
3. class modeling
4. interaction modeling
5. statechart modeling
6. implementation models
7. object collaboration design
8. window navigation design
9. database design.

This chapter is in no way a substitute for the rest of the book. The chapter does not explain (with few exceptions) the theory behind the modeling decisions and solutions. Also, a tutorial contained in a single chapter cannot address all modeling and design intricacies. The exercises below address but a few other important analysis and design issues.

Exercises (online shopping)

G1 Refer to Step 2 (Section 10.1.2).

Point 6 in Table 2.1 says that the customer is to be emailed so that he/she can check the order status online. There is no use case that shows this happening. Should there be? Explain.

G2   Step 3 (Section 10.1.3) identifies `Display Order Status` as one of the use cases. The use case is to allow a customer to check the status of the computer order.

Write a use-case document for the use case `Display Order Status`. Use the document format as in step 4 (Section 10.1.4).

G3   Refer to step 9 (Section 10.3.3).

In Figure 10.8, the class `Customer` is not associated directly with the classes `Payment`, `Invoice`, and `ConfiguredComputer`. Should it be associated? If so, modify the diagram. Explain.

G4   Refer to step 11 (Section 10.3.5).

Figure 10.10 is a relatively simple example illustrating generalization. What complications might arise if differences are required between the information on invoices for `StandardComputer` sales and `ConfiguredComputer` sales? For example, there might be additional charges depending on the modifications required for `ConfiguredComputer` systems and a discount for bulk purchases of `StandardComputer` systems.

Modify the diagram to reflect such complications. Explain briefly.

G5   Refer to step 6 (Section 10.2.2).

Draw an analysis-level sequence diagram for the action `Display Purchase Form` (Figure 10.5). As a reference, consider that Figure 10.14 (step 13, Section 10.4.1) is an analysis-level sequence diagram.

G6   Refer to your solution to Exercise G5 above.

Add operations to the classes denoted by the objects in the sequence diagram. Show relationships, including dependency relationships, between the classes.

G7   Refer to step 16 (Section 10.5.1).

The statechart diagram in Figure 10.17 conforms to the restriction that only one partial payment is allowed. Suppose that this is not the case and that more partial payments are allowed. Modify the diagram accordingly.

Provide two solutions. The first solution should be for the situation in which partial payments are *a priori* designated as partial. The second solution should be for the situation in which the system has to calculate whether a payment is partial or in full.

G8   Refer to step 12 (Section 10.3.6).

Consider a part of the model with classes `Customer`, `Order`, and `Invoice`. Is it possible to introduce a derived association to the model? If so, add it to the diagram.

G9   Refer to step 12 (Section 10.3.6).

Consider a part of the model with classes `Order` and `Computer`. Change the association between `Order` and `Computer` to a qualified association to explicitly capture the constraint: "a single order item per computer on order."

G10 Refer to step 5 (Section 10.2.1).

Design a sequence diagram for behavioral collaboration in the action "Email Order Details." Take an approach similar to that of step 24 (Section 10.7.3).

G11 Refer to step 5 (Section 10.2.1).

Design a class diagram for structural collaboration in the action "Email Order Details." Take an approach similar to that of step 25 (Section 10.7.4).

G12 Refer to step 3 (Section 10.1.3).

Produce a design-level use-case specification for the use case "Verify and Accept Customer Payment." Take an approach similar to that of step 22 (Section 10.7.1).

G13 Refer to your solution to Exercise G12.

Study the use-case design specifications to identify the UX elements. Draw properly stereo-typed UX classes for the use case "Verify and Accept Customer Payment." Take an approach similar to that of step 26 (Section 10.8.1).

G14 Refer to your solutions to Exercises G12 and G13.

Draw a sequence diagram for behavioral UX collaboration for the use case "Verify and Accept Customer Payment." Take an approach similar to that of step 27 (Section 10.8.2).

G15 Refer to your solution to Exercises G12, G13, and G14.

Draw a class diagram for structural UX collaboration for the use case "Verify and Accept Customer Payment." Take an approach similar to that of step 28 (Section 10.8.3).

G16 Refer to step 29 (Section 10.9.1).

Develop an alternative database schema model to the model in Figure 10.31. Attempt to produce a model that is as different as possible while ensuring the same (or very close) declarative semantics and efficiency.

G17 Refer to Step 30 (Section 10.9.2).

Consider the relationship between `Invoice` and `Order`. Write database triggers (can be in pseudo-code) for these two tables that enforce the referential integrity between them as specified in Figure 10.32.

Bibliography

Agile (2003) http://www.agilealliance.org/home (last accessed November 2003)

Alhir, S.S. (2003) *Learning UML*, O'Reilly & Associates, 304pp.

Allen, P. and Frost, S. (1998) *Component-Based Development for Enterprise Systems. Applying the SELECT Perspective™*, Cambridge University Press, 462pp.

Alur, D., Crupi, J., and Malks, D. (2003) *Core J2EE Patterns: Best Practices and Design Strategies*, 2nd edition, Prentice Hall, 528pp.

Arthur, L.J. (1992) *Rapid Evolutionary Development. Requirements, Prototyping and Software Creation*, John Wiley & Sons, 222pp.

Aspect (2003) http://aosd.net/ (last accessed November 2003)

Bahrami, A. (1999) *Object Oriented Systems Development*, Irwin McGraw-Hill, 412pp.

Beck, K. (1999) *Extreme Programming Explained: Embrace Challenge*, Addison-Wesley, 224pp.

Bennett, S. McRobb, S. and Farmer, R. (2002) *Object-Oriented Systems Analysis and Design Using UML*, 2nd edition, McGraw-Hill, 540pp.

Benson, S. and Standing, C. (2002) *Information Systems. A Business Approach*, John Wiley & Sons Australia, 330pp.

Bloch, J. (2001) *Effective Java: Programming Language Guide*, Addison-Wesley, 272pp.

Bochenski, B. (1994) *Implementing Production-Quality Client/Server Systems*, John Wiley & Sons, 442pp.

Boehm, B.W. (1988) A spiral model of software development and enhancement, *Computer*, May, pp.61–72.

Booch, G., Rumbaugh, J., and Jacobson, I. (1999) *The Unified Modeling Language. User Guide*, Addison-Wesley, 482pp.

Bourne, K.C. (1997) *Testing Client/Server Systems*, McGraw-Hill, 572pp.

Brainstorming (2003) http://www.brainstorming.co.uk/contents.html (last accessed November 2003)

Brooks, F.P. (1987) No silver bullet: essence and accidents of software engineering, *IEEE Software*, 4, pp.10–19; reprinted in *Software Project Management. Readings and Cases* (1997), C.F. Kemerer (ed.), Irwin, pp.2–14.

CMM (1995) *The Capability Maturity Model: Guidelines for Improving the Software Process*, Addison-Wesley, 442pp.

Coad, P. with North, D. and Mayfield, M. (1995) *Object Models. Strategies, Patterns, and Applications*, Yourdon Press, 506pp.

Conallen, J. (2000) *Building Web Applications with UML*, Addison-Wesley, 300pp.

Constantine, L.L. and Lockwood, L.A.D. (1999) *Software for Use. A Practical Guide to the Models and Methods of Usage-Centered Design*, Addison-Wesley, 579pp.

Date, C.J. (2000) *An Introduction to Database Systems*, Addison-Wesley, 7th edition, 938pp.

Davenport, T.H. (1993) *Process Innovation: Reengineering Work through Information Technology*, Harvard Business School Press, 338pp.

Davenport, T.H. and Short, J. (1990) The new industrial engineering. Information technology and business process redesign. *Sloan Management Review*, Cambridge, summer, pp.11, 17.

Eckel, B. (2003): *Thinking in Java*, 3rd edition, Prentice-Hall, 1182pp. http://www.planetpdf.com/

Elmasri, R. and Navathe, S.B. (2000) *Fundamentals of Database Systems*, 3rd edition, Addison-Wesley, 956pp.

Extreme (2003) http://www.xprogramming.com/ (last accessed November 2003)

Feature (2003) http://www.featuredrivendevelopment.com/ (last accessed November 2003)

Ferm, F. (2003) The what, how, and why of a subsystem, *The Rational Edge*, June, 21p. http://www.therationaledge.com/content/jun_03/t_subsystem_ff.jsp (last accessed December 2003)

Fowler, M. (1997) *Analysis Patterns: Reusable Object Models*, Addison-Wesley, 358pp.

Fowler, M. (2003) *Patterns of Enterprise Application Architecture*, Addison-Wesley, 531pp.

Fowler, M. (2004) *UML Distilled. A Brief Guide to The Standard Object Modeling Language*, 3rd edition, Addison-Wesley, 175pp.

Fowler, S. (1998) *GUI Design Handbook*, McGraw-Hill, 318pp.

Galitz, W.O. (1996) *The Essential Guide to User Interface Design. An Introduction to GUI Design Principles and Techniques*, John Wiley & Sons, 626pp.

Gamma, E., Helm, R., Johnson, R., and Vlissides, J. (1995) *Design Patterns. Elements of Reusable Object-Oriented Software*, Addison-Wesley, 396pp.

Ghezzi, C., Jazayeri, M., and Mandrioli, D. (2003) *Fundamentals of Software Engineering*, Prentice Hall, 604pp.

Grady, R. (1992) *Practical Software Metrics for Project Management and Process Improvement*, Prentice Hall, 282pp.

Gray, N.A.B. (1994) *Programming with Class*, John Wiley & Sons, 624pp.

Hammer, M. (1990) Reengineering Work: Don't Automate, Obliterate, *Harvard Business Review*, Boston, Jul./Aug., p.104.

Hammer, M. and Champy, J. (1993a) *Reengineering the Corporation: A Manifesto for Business Revolution*, Allen & Unwin, 224pp.

Hammer, M. and Champy, J. (1993b) The Promise of Reengineering, *Fortune*, 9, p.94.

Hammer, M. and Stanton, S. (1999) How Process Enterprises Really Work, *Harvard Business Review*, Boston, Nov./Dec., pp.108–118.

Harmon, P. and Watson, M. (1998) *Understanding UML: The Developer's Guide. With a Web-Based Application in Java*, Morgan Kaufmann, 368pp.

Hawryszkiewycz, I., Karagiannis, D., Maciaszek, L., and Teufel, B. (1994) RESPONSE – Requirements Specific Object Model for Workgroup Computing, *Int. J. of Intelligent & Cooperative Information Systems*, 3, pp.293–318.

Henderson-Sellers, B. (1996) *Object-Oriented Metrics. Measures of Complexity*, Prentice Hall, 230pp.

Heumann, J. (2003) User experience storyboards: Building better UIs with RUP, UML, and use cases, *The Rational Edge*, Nov., http://www.therationaledge.com/content/nov-03/f_usability_jh.jsp, 17pp.

Hoffer, J.A., George, J.F., and Valacich, J.S. (2002) *Modern Systems Analysis and Design*, 3rd edition, Prentice Hall, 768pp.

Horton, I. (1997) *Beginning Visual C++ 5*, Wrox Press, 1054pp.

Jacobson, I. (1992) *Object-Oriented Software Engineering. A Use Case Driven Approach*, Addison-Wesley, 524pp.

Jordan, E.W. and Machesky, J.J. (1990) *Systems Development. Requirements, Evaluation, Design, and Implementation*, PWS-Kent, 648pp.

JUnit (2004) www.junit.org (last accessed February 2004)

Khoshafian, S., Chan, A., Wong, A., and Wong, H.K.T. (1992) *A Guide to Developing Client/Server SQL Applications*, Morgan Kaufmann, 634pp.

Kimball, R. (1996) *The Data Warehouse Toolkit. Practical Techniques for Building Dimensional Data Warehouses*, John Wiley & Sons, 388pp.

Kirkwood, J. (1992) *High Performance Relational Database Design*, Ellis Horwood, 266pp.

Kleppe, A., Warmer, J., and Bast, W. (2003) *MDA Explained: The Model Driven Architecture: Practice and Promise*, Addison-Wesley, 192pp.

Koestler, A. (1967) *The Ghost in the Machine*, Hutchinson, 384pp.

Koestler, A. (1978) *Janus. A Summing Up*, Hutchinson, 354pp.

Kotonya, G. and Sommerville, I. (1998) *Requirements Engineering. Processes and Techniques*, John Wiley & Sons, 282pp.

Kozaczynski, W. and Thario, J. (2003): *Transforming User Experience Model to Presentation Layer Implementations*, 11pp. http://www.cis.uab.edu/info/OOPSLA-DSVL2/Papers/Kozaczynski.pdf (last accessed January 2004)

Kruchten, P. (2003) *The Rational Unified Process: An Introduction*, 3rd edition, Addison-Wesley, 336pp.

Lakos, J. (1996) *Large-Scale C++ Software Design*, Addison-Wesley, 846pp.

Lee, R.C. and Tepfenhart, W.M. (1997) *UML and C++. A Practical Guide to Object-Oriented Development*, Prentice Hall, 446pp.

Lee, R.C. and Tepfenhart, W.M. (2002) *Practical Object-Oriented Development with UML and Java*, Pearson Education, 469pp.

Lethbridge, T.C. and Laganiere, R. (2001) *Object-Oriented Software Engineering. Practical Software Engineering Using UML and Java*, McGraw-Hill, 497pp.

Lieberherr, K.J. and Holland, I.M. (1989) Assuring Good Style for Object-Oriented Programs, *IEEE Soft.*, 9, pp.38–48.

Maciaszek, L.A. (1990) *Database Design and Implementation*, Prentice Hall, 384pp.

Maciaszek, L.A. (1998) Object oriented development of business information systems – approaches and misconceptions, *Proc. 2nd Int. Conf. on Business Information Systems BIS'98*, Poznan, Poland, pp.95–111.

Maciaszek, L.A. and Liong, B.L. (2004) *Practical Software Engineering. A Case-Study Approach*, Addison-Wesley, ~700p.

Maciaszek, L.A., De Troyer, O.M.F., Getta J.R., and Bosdriesz, J. (1996a) Generalization versus aggregation in object application development – the "ad-hoc" approach, *Proc. 7th Australasian Conf. on Information Systems ACIS'96*, Vol. 2, Hobart, Australia, pp.431–42.

Maciaszek, L.A. Getta, J.R. and Bosdriesz, J. (1996b) Restraining complexity in object system development – the "ad-hoc" approach, *Proc. 5th Int. Conf. on Information Systems Development ISD'96*, Gdansk, Poland, pp.425–35.

MDA (2003) http://www.omg.org/mda/ (last accessed November 2003).

Melton, J. (2002) *Advanced SQL:1999 – Understanding Object-Relational and Other Advanced Features*, Morgan Kaufmann, 562pp.

Melton, J. and Simon, A. (2001): *SQL:1999 – Understanding Relational Language Components*, Morgan Kaufmann, 928pp.

Meyers, S. (1998): *Effective C++: 50 Specific Ways to Improve Your Programs and Design*, 2nd edition, Addison-Wesley, 288pp.

Olsen, D.R. (1998) *Developing User Interfaces*, Morgan Kaufmann, 414pp.

OMG (2004) http://www.omg.org/uml/ (last accessed January 2004)

Page-Jones, M. (2000) *Fundamentals of Object-Oriented Design in UML*, Addison-Wesley, 458pp.

Pfleeger, S.L. (1998) *Software Engineering. Theory and Practice*, Prentice-Hall, 576pp.

Poppendieck, M. and Poppendieck, T. (2003) *Lean Software Development: An Agile Toolkit for Software Development Managers*, Addison-Wesley, 240pp.

Porter, M. (1985) *Competitive Advantage: Creating and Sustaining Superior Performance*, Free Press, 558pp.

Porter, M.E. and Millar, V.E. (1985) How Information Gives You Competitive Advantage, *Harvard Business Review*, Jul./Aug., pp.149–61.

Pressman, R.S. (2001) *Software Engineering. A Practitioner's Approach*, 5th edition, McGraw-Hill, 860pp.

Quatrani, T. (2000) *Visual Modeling with Rational Rose 2000 and UML*, Addison-Wesley, 256pp.

Ramakrishnan, R. and Gehrke, J. (2000) *Database Management Systems*, McGraw-Hill, 906pp.

Rational (2000) *Rational Solutions for Windows*, online documentation April 2000 edition, Rational Software.

Rational (2002) *Rational Suite Tutorial*, Version 2002.05.00, Rational Software, 158pp.

Responsive (2003) http://www.responsivesoftware.com/timelog.htm (last accessed December 2003)

Riel, A.J. (1996) *Object-Oriented Design Heuristics*, Addison-Wesley, 380pp.

Robertson, J. and Robertson, S. (2003) *Volere Requirements Specifications Template*, 9th edition, Atlantic Systems Guild, http://www.atlsysguild.com/GuildSite/Robs/Template.html, 62pp.

Robson, W. (1994) *Strategic Management and Information Systems. An Integrated Approach*, Pitman, 570pp.

Ruble, D.A. (1997) *Practical Analysis and Design for Client/Server and GUI Systems*, Yourdon Press, 516pp.

Rumbaugh, J. (1994) Getting started. Using use cases to capture requirements, *J. Object-Oriented Prog.*, Sept., pp.8–10, 12, 23.

Rumbaugh, J., Blaha, M., Premerlani, W., Eddy, F., and Lorensen, W. (1991) *Object-Oriented Modeling and Design*, Prentice Hall, 500pp.

Rumbaugh, J., Jacobson, I., and Booch, G. (1999) *The Unified Modeling Language Reference Manual*, Addison-Wesley, 550pp.

RUP (2003) http://www-3.ibm.com/software/awdtools/rup/ (last accessed November 2003)

Schach, S. (2002) *Classical and Object-Oriented Software Engineering*, 5th edition, McGraw-Hill, 628pp.

Schmauch, C.H. (1994) *ISO 9000 for Software Deevelopers*, ASQC Quality Press, 156pp.

Selic, B. (2003) The subsystem: a curious creature, *The Rational Edge*, July, 4pp. http://www.therationaledge.com/content/jul 03/k subsystem bs.jsp (last accessed December 2003)

Silberschatz, A., Korth, H.F., and Sudershan, S. (1997) *Database System Concepts*, 3rd edition, McGraw-Hill, 864pp.

Singh, I., Stearns, B., Johnson, M., and Enterprise Team (2002) *Designing Enterprise Applications with the J2EE Platform*, 2nd edition, Addison-Wesley, 352pp.

Smith, J.M. and Smith, D.C.P. (1977) Database abstractions: aggregation and generalization, *ACM Trans. Database Syst.*, 2, pp.105–33.

Sommerville, I. and Sawyer, P. (1997) *Requirements Engineering. A Good Practice Guide*, John Wiley & Sons, 392pp.

Sony (2004) www.sonystyle.com (last accessed February 2004)

Sowa, J.F. and Zachman, J.A. (1992) Extending and formalizing the framework for information systems architecture, *IBM Syst. J.*, 3, pp.590–616.

Standish (2003) http://www.standishgroup.com/ (last accessed November 2003)

Stein, L.A., Lieberman, H., and Ungar, D. (1989) A shared view of sharing: the Treaty of Orlando, in *Object-Oriented Concepts, Databases, and Applications*, W. Kim and F.H. Lochovsky (eds), Addison-Wesley, pp.31–48.

Stevens, P. and Pooley, R. (2000) *Using UML Software Engineering with Objects and Components*, Addison-Wesley, 256pp.

Szyperski, C. (1998) *Component Software. Beyond Object-Oriented Programming*, Addison-Wesley, 412pp.

Treisman, H. (1994) How to design a good interface design, *Software Magazine*, Australia, August, pp.32–36.

UML (2003) *OMG Unified Modeling Language Specification*, Version 1.5, OMG, 736pp.

Whitten, J.L. and Bentley, L.D. (1998) *Systems Analysis and Design Methods*, 4th edition, Irwin McGraw-Hill, 724pp.

Windows (2000) *The Windows Interface Guidelines for Software Design*, MSDN Library, CD-ROM collection, Microsoft.

Wirfs-Brock, R. and Wilkerson, B. (1989) Object-oriented design: a responsibility-driven approach, in *OOPSLA'89 Proceedings, SIGPLAN Notices*, No. 10, ACM, pp.71–5.

Wirfs-Brock, R., Wilkerson, B., and Wiener, L. (1990) *Designing Object-Oriented Software*, Prentice-Hall, 342pp.

Wood, J. and Silver, D. (1995) *Joint Application Development*, 2nd edition, John Wiley & Sons, 402pp.

Yourdon, E. (1994) *Object-Oriented Systems Design. An Integrated Approach*, Yourdon Press, 400pp.

Zachman, J.A. (1987) A framework for information systems architecture, *IBM Syst. J.*, 3, pp.276–92.

Zachman, J.A. (1999) A framework for information systems architecture, *IBM Syst. J.*, 2/3, pp.454–70.

Index

The accompanying CD

The CD accompanying this book contains:
1. Book slides
2. Book figures
3. Model files
4. Modeling tools

Modeling tools are a 'value added' benefit to the reader. There are 12 tools on the CD. Most are visual modeling tools supporting UML and code generation. Some tools emphasize related aspects of systems analysis and design, such as requirements management, database design, and visual analysis of dependencies in pre-existing code.

The included tools are *free*. Some tools are directly available for installation from this CD and other tools are available via provided Internet links. But, because nothing is free in life, 'free' means one of the following:
- The tool is a community edition (with some restrictions on the use of the software).
- The tool is available for a trial period of time (usually sufficient for a university project/assignments).
- For tools provided via Internet links, a free registration may be required (meaning that some web form needs to be filled out).
- Some tools require that a license compliance form be filled out.

Book slides are included on the CD in three formats:
- One slide per page (handy for slide shows).
- Two slides per page (suitable as handouts to students, etc.).
- Six slides per page (for compact printouts of all slides).

Book figures are provided for the benefit of those readers who would like to include and refer to the book's figures in their own presentations. The figures are viewable as PowerPoint slides and downloadable in zip files containing PowerPoint documents.

Model files contain files developed for all modeling examples and case studies in the textbook. They are available for downloading so that readers can immediately use them with a visual modeling tool. This will allow readers to experiment with examples and solutions in the book and modify/extend them as desired.

Instructions for how to use the CD

The CD consists of an integrated set of Web pages viewable in a Web browser of the reader's choice. The CD should auto-execute when inserted into the CD drive under any common Microsoft Windows operating system. Should this fail to happen, the reader can launch the CD manually from its home directory.

IMPORTANT: READ CAREFULLY
WARNING: BY OPENING THE PACKAGE YOU AGREE TO BE BOUND BY THE TERMS OF THE LICENCE AGREEMENT BELOW.

This is a legally binding agreement between You (the user or purchaser) and Pearson Education Limited. By retaining this licence, any software media or accompanying written materials or carrying out any of the permitted activities You agree to be bound by the terms of the licence agreement below.

If You do not agree to these terms then promptly return the entire publication (this licence and all software, written materials, packaging and any other components received with it) with Your sales receipt to Your supplier for a full refund.

SINGLE USER LICENCE AGREEMENT

❐ YOU ARE PERMITTED TO:

- Use (load into temporary memory or permanent storage) a single copy of the software on only one computer at a time. If this computer is linked to a network then the software may only be installed in a manner such that it is not accessible to other machines on the network.

- Make one copy of the software solely for backup purposes or copy it to a single hard disk, provided you keep the original solely for back up purposes.

- Transfer the software from one computer to another provided that you only use it on one computer at a time.

❐ YOU MAY NOT:

- Rent or lease the software or any part of the publication.

- Copy any part of the documentation, except where specifically indicated otherwise.

- Make copies of the software, other than for backup purposes.

- Reverse engineer, decompile or disassemble the software.

- Use the software on more than one computer at a time.

- Install the software on any networked computer in a way that could allow access to it from more than one machine on the network.

- Use the software in any way not specified above without the prior written consent of Pearson Education Limited.

ONE COPY ONLY
This licence is for a single user copy of the software
PEARSON EDUCATION LIMITED RESERVES THE RIGHT TO TERMINATE THIS LICENCE BY WRITTEN NOTICE AND TO TAKE ACTION TO RECOVER ANY DAMAGES SUFFERED BY PEARSON EDUCATION LIMITED IF YOU BREACH ANY PROVISION OF THIS AGREEMENT.

Pearson Education Limited owns the software You only own the disk on which the software is supplied.

LIMITED WARRANTY

Pearson Education Limited warrants that the diskette or CD rom on which the software is supplied are free from defects in materials and workmanship under normal use for ninety (90) days from the date You receive them. This warranty is limited to You and is not transferable. Pearson Education Limited does not warrant that the functions of the software meet Your requirements or that the media is compatible with any computer system on which it is used or that the operation of the software will be unlimited or error free.

You assume responsibility for selecting the software to achieve Your intended results and for the installation of, the use of and the results obtained from the software. The entire liability of Pearson Education Limited and its suppliers and your only remedy shall be replacement of the components that do not meet this warranty free of charge.

This limited warranty is void if any damage has resulted from accident, abuse, misapplication, service or modification by someone other than Pearson Education Limited. In no event shall Pearson Education Limited or its suppliers be liable for any damages whatsoever arising out of installation of the software, even if advised of the possibility of such damages. Pearson Education Limited will not be liable for any loss or damage of any nature suffered by any party as a result of reliance upon or reproduction of or any errors in the content of the publication.

Pearson Education Limited does not limit its liability for death or personal injury caused by its negligence.

This licence agreement shall be governed by and interpreted and construed in accordance with English law.